6th International Finance Conference on Financial Crisis and Governance

6th International Finance Conference on Financial Crisis and Governance

Edited by

Mondher Bellalah and Omar Masood

CAMBRIDGE
SCHOLARS
PUBLISHING

6th International Finance Conference on Financial Crisis and Governance,
Edited by Mondher Bellalah and Omar Masood

This book first published 2011

Cambridge Scholars Publishing

12 Back Chapman Street, Newcastle upon Tyne, NE6 2XX, UK

British Library Cataloguing in Publication Data
A catalogue record for this book is available from the British Library

ISBN (10): 1-4438-3308-8, ISBN (13): 978-1-4438-3308-0

With a huge sense of pride and honor, I dedicate this book to the "Yasmine Revolt" by the young people of the Tunisian Republic. This book is based upon the International Finance Conference held in Tunisia in March, 2011. Papers were submitted before the "Yasmine Revolt," and the Conference took place immediately after the revolution. This book is intended to better the understanding of the conventional finance and Islamic finance around crisis. I acknowledge the unique efforts of the Tunisian Ministry to enhance conventional and Islamic studies.

TABLE OF CONTENTS

Part 4. Debt, Crisis and Governance

Part 5. Corporate Finance

PART 1.

ON RISK, GOVERNANCE AND RISK MANAGEMENT

THE PERFORMANCE OF HYBRID MODELS IN THE ASSESSMENT OF DEFAULT RISK

SAMI ZOUARI,[1] MONDHER BELLALAH[2] AND JEAN JACQUES LEVY[3]

1. Introduction

Credit risk refers to the risk due to unpredicted changes in the credit quality of a counter party or issuer, and its quantification is one of the major frontiers in modern finance. The creditworthiness of a potential borrower affects the lending decision and the credit spread, since there is a doubt whether the firm will be able to perform its obligation. Credit risk measurement depends on the likelihood of default of a firm in meeting its required or contractual obligation, and on what will be lost if default occurs. When one considers the large number of corporations issuing fixed income securities and the relatively small number of actual defaults, one might regard defaulting as a rare event. However, all corporate issuers have positive probability of default. Models of credit risk measurement have focused on the estimation of the default probability of firms, since it is the main source of uncertainty in the lending decision. We may distinguish two large classes of credit risk models on the basis of the analysis they adopt. The first class, the set of traditional models, assume the fundamental analysis, called the non-structural model. The goal of these models, which goes back to Beaver (1966) and Altman (1968), is to distinguish which factors are more significant in assessing the credit risk of a firm. The second class, called structural models, assume the contingency claim analysis .The philosophy of these models goes back to

[1] THEMA, University of Cergy-Pontoise, 33 bd du port, 95011, Cergy, France mohsamizouari@yahoo.fr.
[2] THEMA, University of Cergy-Pontoise, 33 bd du port, 95011, Cergy, France mondher.Bellalah@u-cergy.fr.
[3] ISC PAris, France.

Black and Scholes (1973) and Merton (1974), and assumes corporate liabilities as contingent claims on the assets of the firm[4].

In this paper, we investigate the hybrid contingent claim approach with French companies listed on the Paris Stock Exchange (Euronext Paris). Our goal is to assess how the combination of continuous assessments provided by the market and the values derived from financial statements improve our ability to forecast the probability of default.

The structural model of Merton has the advantage of being flexible, since the probability of default can continually be updated with changes in the value of corporate assets. Its main drawback is that it may over- or underestimate the probability of default, since asset values are unobservable and must be extrapolated from the share prices. On the other hand, the non-structural model of Altman is more accurate because it uses the accounting data of companies, but it is less flexible. Because the frequency of information is generally annual, the probabilities of default cannot be updated during the fiscal year. The quarterly financial statements can be found, but they are not always audited by an external accounting firm.

The Bank of England estimated the hybrid model with data from British companies and found some interesting results. During a first phase, the probability of defaults are estimated using both methods separately, and subsequently, the probability of defaults of the structural model are integrated at each point in time in the non-structural model as an additional explanatory variable. The appeal of the hybrid model allows the probability of default to be continuously updated by integrating market information via the probabilities of default extracted from the structural model. In this paper, we apply the hybrid model to French companies listed on the Paris stock exchange (Euronext Paris).

This paper is organized as follows. Section 2 reviews the main models in the literature. Section 3 presents the estimated structural model and describes the data used. And finally, section 4 presents the estimation of the hybrid model and summarizes the main results.

---

[4] Another widely used category of credit risk models is the reduced form approach where the dynamics of default are given exogenously by an intensity or compensator process. For a review of these models see Jarrow and Turnbull (1995), Jarrow, Lando, and Turnbull (1997), and Duffie and Singleton (1999).

2. Review of key models for risk assessment of default

2.1 Non-structural models

Traditional non-structural models adopt fundamental analysis and try to find which factors are important in explaining the credit risk of a company. They assess the significance of these factors, mapping a reduced set of financial ratios, accounting variables and other information into a quantitative score. The latter, can be interpreted as a probability of default, and can be used as a classification system[5].

In 1966, Beaver introduced the univariate approach of discriminant analysis in the explanation of default risk of a firm. Altman in 1968 extended this to a multivariate context and developed the Z-Score model. It weights the independent variables (financial ratios and accounting variables) and generates a single composite discriminant score. In 1977 Altman, Haldeman, and Narrayman developed the ZETA model, which integrated some improvements to the original Z-Score approach. Then the binary dependent variables models, known as the logit and probit model, were used in bankruptcy prediction[6]. Ohlson (1980) used logit methodology to derive a default risk model known as O-Score. Probit (Logit) methodology weights the independent variables and allocates scores in a form of failure probability using the normal (logistic) cumulative function.

Mester (1997) recognized the prevalent use of the binary credit risk models: 70% of banks have used them in their non-listed firm lending procedure.

Several banks use this method for privately and publicly traded companies, either by buying a model, such as RiskCalc Moody's, or by programming their own estimate. One problem they often face is to build an appropriate and proper database. Very often, credit files are not computerized or do not contain historical data.

---

[5] For a review of traditional models see: Jones (1987), Cauette, Altman, and Naraynan (1998), and Saunders (2002).

[6] Jones (1987), in his review of bankruptcy literature, concludes that binary dependent variable models do not lead to notable improvements in the predictive power of fundamental analysis when compared to the earlier LDA models.

The main advantage of non-structural models is their accuracy in estimating probabilities of default. In addition, they are easy to use for financial institutions equipped with solid management systems of database and may produce very accurate default probabilities. Nonetheless, these models are not flexible, because they need information from financial statements. Thus, it is very difficult to update the probabilities of default over a year. Some financial institutions may require reporting on a quarterly basis, but they are rarely audited by accounting firms.

2.2 Structural Models

The original Merton model is based on some simplifying assumptions about the structure of the typical firm's finances. The event of default is determined by the market value of the firm's assets in combination with the liability structure of the firm. When the value of the assets falls below a certain threshold, the firm is considered to be in default. The main criticism levelled at Merton's model is that it does not account for the possibility that the firm may default before the debt matures. To improve this basic model, several extensions have been suggested in the literature.

Crosbie and Bohn (2002) summarize KMV's default probability model. KMV's default probability model is based on a modified version of the Black-Scholes-Merton framework in the sense that KMV allows default to occur at any point in time and not necessarily at the maturity of the debt. In this model multiple classes of liabilities are modelled. There are essentially three steps in the determination of the default probability. The first step is to estimate the market value and volatility of the firm's assets; the second step is calculate the distance-to-default, the number of standard deviations the firm is away from default; and the third step is to transform the distance-to-default into an expected default frequency (EDF) using an empirical default distribution.

Brockman and Turtle (2003) propose using barrier options. Thus, rather than stockholders who wait for the debt to mature before exercising a standard European call option, we have a down-and-out option on the assets, in which lenders hold a portfolio of risk-free debt and a short put option combined with a long down-and-out call option on the firm's assets. The last part gives them the right to place the company into bankruptcy when they anticipate that its financial health can only deteriorate. Wong and Choi (2004) demonstrate that estimating the parameters of the Brockman and Turtle (2003) model by maximum likelihood yields results that resemble those from the iterative estimation method used in this literature when the theoretical model is Merton's. The appeal of the maximum likelihood method is that it allows for statistical inference or, more specifically, calculating descriptive statistics for the estimated parameters, such as the value of the firm.

Tudela and Young (2003) present an application of the hybrid model. This application uses barrier options with a down-and-out call option. They estimate various models on data from non-financial English firms for the period 1990–2001. They use data on firms that did, and did not, default, for their estimates of probabilities of default in the structural model. First, they verify whether the two firm types represent different predicted probabilities of default. Second, they compare their hybrid model with other non-structural models to verify whether the additional probability of default (PD) variable is significant for explaining probabilities of default. Third, they measure the performance of their model with power curve and accuracy ratio type instruments.

3. Estimation of the probabilities of default with the structural model: Application of the Tudela and Young Model (2003) (the Bank of England model)

3.1 Model description

In this model, the authors use the theory of barrier options[7] and, more precisely, the call option down-and-out, which vanishes when the underlying asset reaches the barrier. In this model we assume that the capital structure consists exclusively of debt and equity (as Merton). The level of debt is denoted B and (T-t) represents the time remaining to maturity of the debt, the value of the firm is At, and the value at time t of the debt maturing at time T is V (A, T, t). The share value at time t is f (A, t). Therefore the total value of the firm at time t is:

$$A_t = V(A, T, t) + f(A, t) \quad (1)$$

[7] Other equity-based models of credit risk that use the concept of barrier options are Black and Cox (1976), Longstaff and Schwartz (1995), and Briys and de Varenne (1997).

To derive the probability of default using a barrier option, we suppose that the value of the firm's underlying assets follows the following stochastic process:

$$uA = A\, d_A\, dt + \sigma_A\, A\, dz \tag{2}$$

Where $dz = \varepsilon\sqrt{dt}$ and $\varepsilon \sim N\,[0, 1]$.

As to the liabilities, assume, on one hand, that the firm's liabilities L are the sum of short-term liabilities plus one-half of long-term liabilities. On the other hand, we assume that L follows a deterministic process:

$$dL = \mu_L\, L\, dt \tag{3}$$

We note the asset-liability ratio by k:

$$k = \frac{A}{L} \tag{4}$$

A default occurs when k falls below the default point called $\widetilde{k}$ at any time. To estimate the probability of default we need to model how k changes over time.

If we differentiate (4) and use (2) and (3) we get:

$$dk = (\mu_A\ - \mu_L)\, k\, dt + \sigma_A\, k\, dz \tag{5}$$

We define: $\mu_A - \mu_L = \mu_k$
And $\sigma_A = \sigma_k$

The values of μ_k and σ_k are needed to calculate the probabilities of default. Maximum likelihood techniques are used to obtain estimates of those two parameters, but to build the maximum likelihood function, we need first to derive an expression for the density function of k.

Given equation (5) we can derive the density function of $\ln\left(\frac{k_T}{k_t}\right)$. It can be shown that the defective density function is given by $\{\ln\left(\frac{k_T}{k_t}\right)\}$ by the following expression:

$$h\left(\ln\left(\frac{k_T}{k_t}\right)\right)=\frac{1}{\sqrt{2\pi\,\sigma_K^2(T-t)}}\left\{\exp\left[-\frac{\left(\ln\left(\frac{k_T}{k_t}\right)-\left(\mu_k-\frac{\sigma_k^2}{2}\right)(T-t)\right)^2}{2\sigma_k^2(T-t)}\right]\right.$$

$$\left.-\exp\left[\frac{2\ln\left(\frac{\tilde{k}}{k_t}\right)\left(\mu_k-\frac{\sigma_k^2}{2}\right)}{\sigma_k^2}-\frac{\left(\ln\left(\frac{k_T}{k_t}\right)-2\ln\left(\frac{\tilde{k}}{k_t}\right)-\left(\mu_k-\frac{\sigma_k^2}{2}\right)(T-t)\right)^2}{2\sigma_k^2(T-t)}\right]\right\} \tag{6}$$

Equation (6) represents the probability density of not crossing the barrier and being at the point $\ln\left(\frac{k_T}{k_t}\right)$ at time T. This expression is used to construct the likelihood function that we must maximize in order to obtain estimates of μ_k and σ_k. These estimates will be used to calculate the probability of default as shown below. The probability of the firm not defaulting until date T is given by the probability of $k_T > \tilde{k}$ conditionally $k_\tau > \tilde{k} \quad \forall \tau\; t \leq \tau \langle T$ =>

$$PD = 1 - \{[1 - N(u_1)] - \overline{w}\,[1 - N(u_2)]\}$$

Where:
$$u_1 = \frac{\tilde{K} - \left(\mu_k - \frac{\sigma_k^2}{2}\right)(T-t)}{\sigma_k\sqrt{T-t}}$$

$$u_2 = \frac{-\widetilde{K} - \left(\mu_k - \frac{\sigma_k^2}{2}\right)(T - t)}{\sigma_k \sqrt{T - t}}$$

$$\overline{w} = \exp\left[\frac{2\widetilde{K}\left(\mu_k - \frac{\sigma_k^2}{2}\right)}{\sigma_k^2}\right]$$

$\ln\frac{\widetilde{k}}{k_t} = \widetilde{K}$ and N is the cumulative density function of the normal distribution. In the case of a European call option, the probability of default equals N (u_1). However, for the barrier option we see that the term $\overline{w}$ [1- N (u_2)] adjusts the probability of default to take into account that the firm can default before the horizon date T.

The Bank of England set $\widetilde{k}$ = 1. We shall adopt this normalization. On the other hand we assume that the ratio, y = $\frac{X}{L}$, where X represents the market capitalization of the firm and L is its liabilities as a proxy for the ratio k = $\frac{A}{L}$ since the value of the firm's assets is unobservable.

We use Matlab to estimate μ_k and σ_k with the maximum likelihood method, then we calculate the probabilities of default. Parameters μ_k and σ_k are estimated on the basis of a 24-month window for all firms. (As starting value we take $\sigma_{k\,=\,0,4}$ and $\mu_{k\,=0,3}$). Finally, Tudela and Young find that if they add some account variables in their model, the model performance increases slightly. The final model of the Bank of England is as follows:

P D= f [probability of default (1 -2 years), profitability, Debt over assets, Cash over liabilities Sales Growth, log number of employees, GDP]

This model will be the subject of our research; the authors have applied this model to calculate the probability of default on data from non-financial English firms, and we will try to apply it to a sample of French listed companies but retain other explanatory variables for the hybrid model.

3.2 Data

In this section we present the used data and explain how we built it to calculate probabilities of default. This data is used also to estimate the hybrid model in section 4. Our initial database contains 20 companies that did not default and 14 companies that did. The study period for the probabilities of default is from January 2004 to December 2005. The methodology we use to compute the probabilities of default with the structural model requires that our data window extend 24 months prior to the estimation period for the predicted probabilities of default in order to ensure statistical reliability. Market capitalization has a monthly frequency while the values of debt are observed annually, thus the value of debt is considered during the year.

3.2.1 Companies that have defaulted

Data on companies that have defaulted are from DIANE. However, 6 companies that defaulted were removed from the database because of a lack of data (accounting and/or market) or because too large a shift between the date of publication of the last financial statement and effective date of default. Indeed many of these companies have significant gaps between these two dates. This is explained by the fact that most of the firms do not publish their financial statements during the last year prior to bankruptcy. Another explanation lies in the slow process of putting in default of certain companies. Thus we eliminated firms with a lag of more than 18 months.

3.2.2 Companies that did not default

Accounting data on companies that did not default for the year 2005 and the monthly market capitalizations are from Diane.

3.2.3 Various statistics

Financial firms are eliminated from the database because they do not generally have the same structure of financial statements as non-financial firms. Thus the final database contains a total of 23 non-financial companies; 8 of them have defaulted. The following table presents the descriptive statistics of firms retained for analysis:

Table 1: Descriptive statistics of all firms retained for analysis (in million Euro)

	NOT-DEFAULT		DEFAULT	
Statistic	**Market value**	**Liabilities**	**Market value**	**Liabilities**
Mean	130.48	44.924	38.292	23.193
Median	101.128	38.714	17.073	9.248
Maximum	386.65	156.147	190.854	120.568
Minimum	27.65	3.955	11.473	7.492
Standard deviation	94.013	36.76	61.698	39.383
Skewness	1.464	1.829	2.259	2.2591
Kurtosis	4.7749	6.7184	6.122	6.1207
Number of observations	360	30	180	16

3.3 Estimation results

Estimating probabilities of default by the structural model allows us to obtain the following results: for companies that have defaulted, the mean of probabilities of default is 33.97%, while for companies that haven't, the mean of probabilities of default is 13.54%.

The following figures show the evolution of the probabilities of default predicted for several firms. Figure 1 shows the evolution of the probabilities of default for the ones that have defaulted.

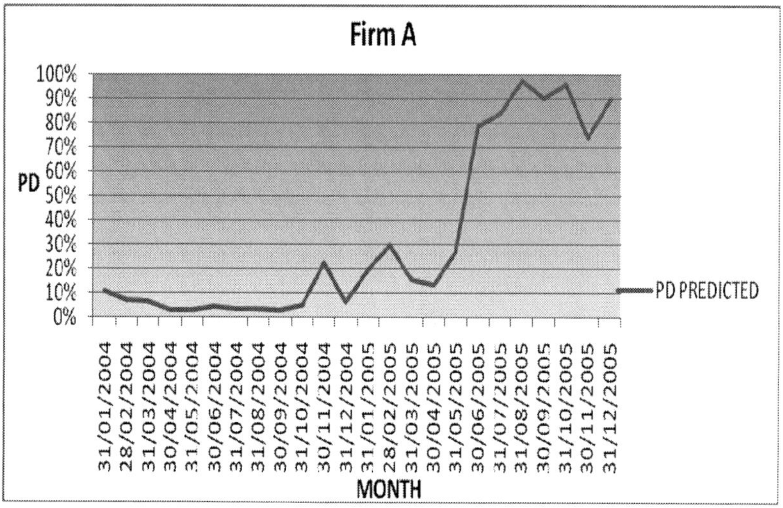

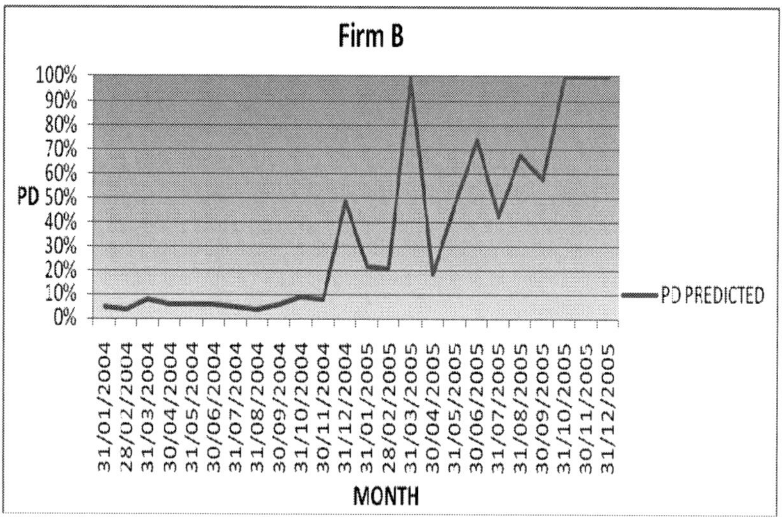

Figure 1: Monthly default probabilities (2 years) of defaulting firms

Modelling the probabilities of default of these companies seems consistent with the model, since it takes the form of probabilities of default being predicted higher when approaching the year of default. Indeed, most of the companies that did default present a similar evolution of the probabilities of default.

However, the results in Figure 2 are somewhat surprising. They represent an extreme case and show an example of the overstatement of the probabilities of default in the structural model. The model appears very sensitive to significant fluctuations in the values of this firm's stocks and provides the rationale for using the hybrid model, which contains more information for conditioning the estimates of the probabilities of default. Two smoother examples are featured in Figure 3.

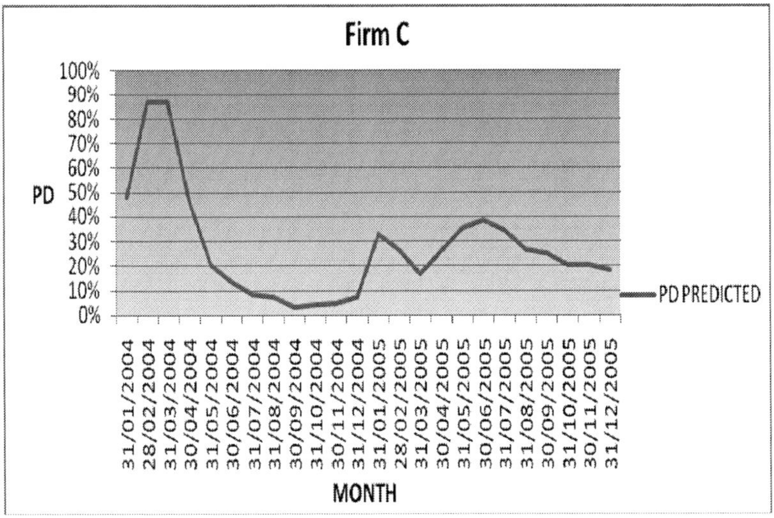

Figure 2: Monthly default probabilities (2 years) of non-defaulting firms

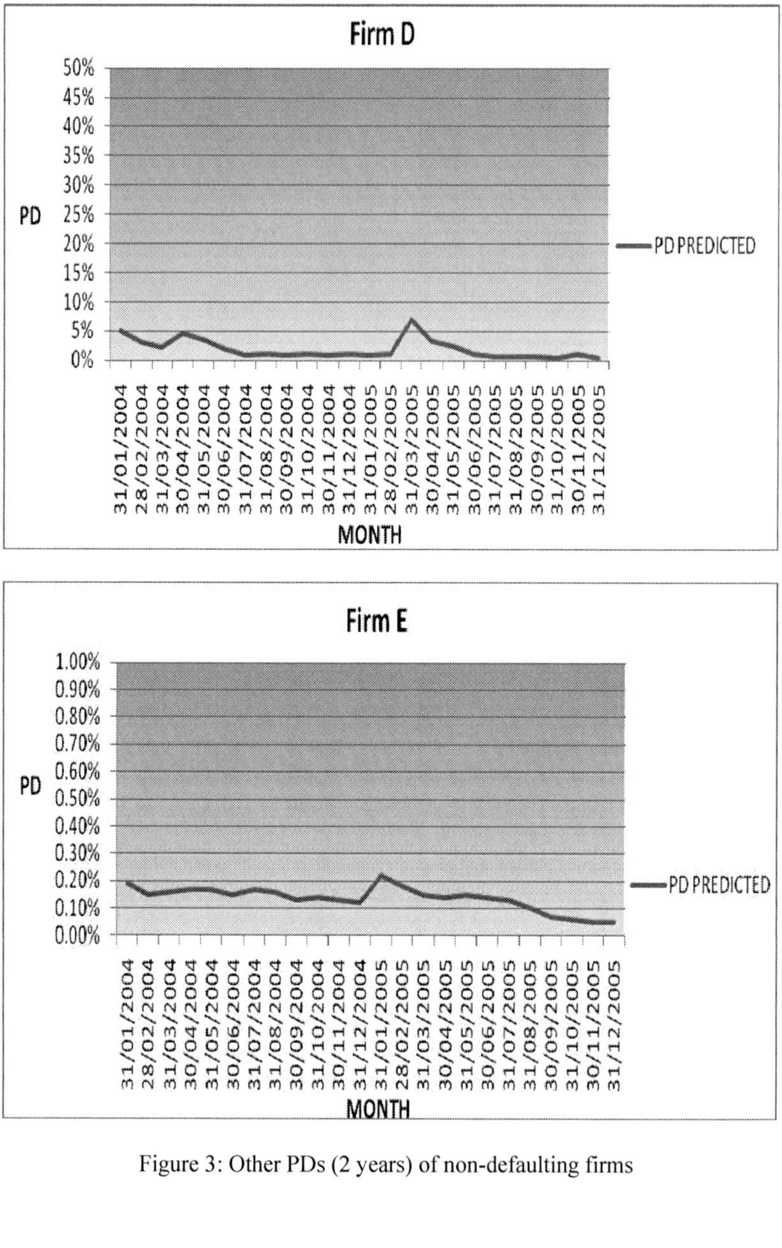

Figure 3: Other PDs (2 years) of non-defaulting firms

4. Hybrid model

4.1 Methodology

We do not estimate the model with a simple linear regression, since we know that it must reflect non-linear behaviour of the explanatory variables for defaults. In addition, it is well documented that simple linear models are inappropriate when the dependent variable is a probability. This model has the advantage of being easy to estimate but he has the disadvantage that it leads to PDs estimated to be out of the interval [0,1]. Thus, we must use other models which keep the probability of default (PD) in the considered interval; particularly the probit model. In this type of model, the dependent variable is a dichotomous variable taking the value 1 if an event occurs and 0 otherwise. In our case, the variable Y_i assumes the following values:

$Y_i = 1$ if firm I defaults, and
$Y_i = 0$ otherwise.

The vector of explanatory variables (financial ratios and accounting variables…) for firm *i* is denoted X_i, while β is the vector of weights of these variables.

The probit model assumes that there is a qualitative response variable (Y_i^*) defined by the following equation:

$$Y_i^* = \beta' X_i + \varepsilon_i. \tag{7}$$

However, in practice, Y_i^* is an unobservable latent variable. We rather observe the dichotomous variable Y_i such that:

$$Y_i = 1 \quad \text{if } Y_i^* > 0; \tag{8}$$
$$Y_i = 0 \text{ otherwise.}$$

In this formulation, $\beta' X_i$ is not $E(Y_i / X_i)$, as in the simple linear model, but rather $E(Y_i^* / X_i)$. From equations (7) and (8), we get:

$$\text{Prob}(Y_i = 1) = \text{Prob}(\varepsilon_i > -\beta' X_i) = 1 - F(\beta' X_i) \tag{9}$$

where F is the cumulative distribution function of ε_i.

The functional form of F in equation (11) depends on the retained assumptions regarding the distribution of the residual errors (ε_i) in equation (7). The probit model is based on the assumption that these errors are independently and identically distributed (i.i.d.) and follow a standard normal distribution N(0,1). The functional form can thus be written:

$$F(-\beta' X_i) = \int_{-\infty}^{-\beta' X_i} \frac{1}{(2\pi)^{\frac{1}{2}}} \exp\left[-\frac{t^2}{2}\right] dt \tag{10}$$

In this case, the observed values Y_i are simply the realizations of a binomial process whose probabilities are given by (9) and vary from one observation to the next (with X_i). The likelihood function can be defined as follows:

$$l = \prod_{Y_i=0} F(-\beta' X_i) \prod_{Y_i=1} (1 - F(-\beta' X_i)) \tag{11}$$

And the parameter estimates β are those that maximize l.

4.2 Variable selection

The main objective of this study is to verify whether combining the structural and the non-structural model into a hybrid model yields a better measure of the default risk than those obtained from structural and traditional non-structural models estimated separately. To accomplish this, our aim is to explain default deficiencies by estimating a probit model in which the explanatory variables are the estimated probabilities of default from the structural model, financial ratios, and other accounting data.

The dependent variable is binary, taking the value of 1 if the default occurs and 0 otherwise. Using the same methodology, we also estimate a model with just accounting data as explanatory variables (non-structural model) and a third probit model in which the only exogenous variable is the probability of default from the structural model (the model that contains only structural information). Thus, we examine the predictive power of the PD variable to explain corporate bankruptcy by integrating it in the non-structural model as an explanatory variable.

If we find that the estimated coefficient of the variable PD (resulting from the structural model) is statistically different from zero, the probabilities of default obtained by the structural model in this case will contain additional

information that complements that of accounting data, and we will be able to use its coefficient to update the probabilities of default when the PD from the structural model changes.
As to the choice of accounting variables and financial ratios used in the non-structural and hybrid models, we are faced with difficulties in the selection of variables given the scarcity of accounting and financial data on those French listed companies that did default. To make a sound choice, we estimated the probit model on each variable accounting separately. This enabled us to retain the most significant ones.

4.3 Estimation results

4.3.1 Estimation of the probit model with different specifications

In this section we analyse the characteristics and performance of three models: the hybrid model, the non-structural model, and the model containing only structural information. We summarize the results of these estimations in Table 2.

In Model 1, we use only the information from the structural model by considering the mean PD(2 years) from the structural model as an explanatory variable. The coefficient of PD is 0.15 per cent, and has the expected sign. It is a significant factor for predicting probabilities of default, with a p-value of less than 5 per cent and a high corrected pseudo-R^2 (52.56 per cent).

In Model 2, we estimate the non-structural model with 2 variables (the turnover and profitability ratio). The examination of Model 2 reveals that the non-structural specification largely outperforms the one using only information from the structural model (Model 1) in terms of its ability to explain corporate bankruptcy. The likelihood ratio is 17.63 for the non-structural model, versus 15.62 for the structural model with only PD as an exogenous variable (the corresponding values of R^2 are 59.34 per cent and 52.56 per cent).

Table 2: Analysis of the maximum-likelihood estimators

Parameters	Model 1	Model 2	Model 3	Model 4	Model 5
Constant	-4.2571 (0.0245)	0.6808 (0.2001)	-7.91 (0.3719)	0.7242 (0.4283)	-3.8512 (0.2486)
PD (2 years)	0.1506 (0.0226)		0.2934 (0.3252)		0.1571 (0.1886)
Profitability		-0.0405 (0.1079)	-0.0229 (0.4589)		
Turnover		-0.0161 (0.0518)	-0.0213 (0.1988)	-0.0069 (0.4615)	-0.0164 (0.3557)
Equity/Total assets				-0.0394 (0.0659)	- 0.00709 (0.8033)
Debt/Equity				0.0029 (0.8891)	0.0055 (0.8328)
Number of observations	23	23	23	23	23
Number of Defaults	8	8	8	8	8
McFadden's R squared	0.5256	0.5934	0.8277	0.6137	0.7143
Likelihood ratio	15.6209 <0.0001	17.6367 0.0001	24.6009 <0.0001	18.2408 0.0003	21.2300 0.0002
Log likelihood	-7.0496	-6.0416	-2.5596	-5.7396	-4.2450

*Into parenthesis are the p-value of estimated parameters

In Model 3, we estimate the hybrid model by adding the probabilities of default, calculated from the structural model, to the explanatory variables of Model 2. An analysis of the results reveals that the probabilities of default from the structural approach have an additional predictive power for corporate defaults than the firms' financial statements. We observe that the likelihood ratio increased from 17.63 for the non-structural model to 24.6 for the hybrid model (the corresponding values of corrected pseudo-R^2 are 59.34 per cent and 82.77 per cent). Furthermore, to acquire a better understanding of the contribution of model 3 relative to that of Model 2, we repeat this analysis in Models 4 and 5. This time, however, by changing the variables used in the non-structural model, and in Model 5 we estimate the hybrid model by adding default probabilities calculated from the structural model as an explanatory variable to Model 4.

Analysis of the results gives us the same findings, confirming the predictive power provided by incorporating the variable PD from the structural model to the non-structural model. Indeed, the likelihood ratio has increased from 18.24 for the non-structural model (model 4) to 21.23 for the hybrid model (the corresponding values of corrected pseudo-R^2 are 61.37 per cent and 71.43 per cent).

4.3.2 Various tests

In Figure 4, we reproduce the mean of the probabilities of default for companies that did default for the five models estimated so far. The mean of the probabilities of default for the model containing only the structural information is 71.41 per cent. This probability is maximized at 89.18 per cent for the hybrid model with two accounting variables (turnover and profitability ratio) (model 3). The same model but without the probabilities of default from the structural approach, comes in at 75.83 per cent. This confirms the results from the previous section.

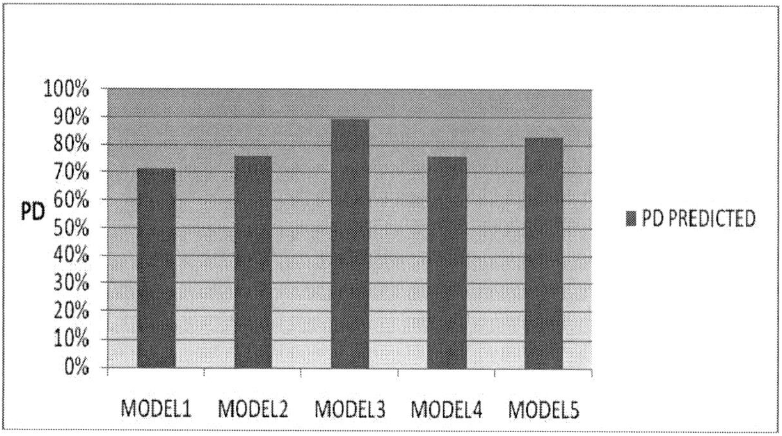

Figure 4: Probabilities of default of firms that did default

In Figure 5, we reproduce the mean of the probabilities of default for companies that did not default for the five models estimated. The mean of the probabilities of default for the model containing only the structural information is 15.73 per cent. This probability is minimized at 5.56 per cent for the hybrid model with two accounting variables (turnover and profitability ratio) (model 3). The same model but without the probabilities of default from the structural approach, has a mean of 15.3 per cent. This also confirms the results from the previous section.

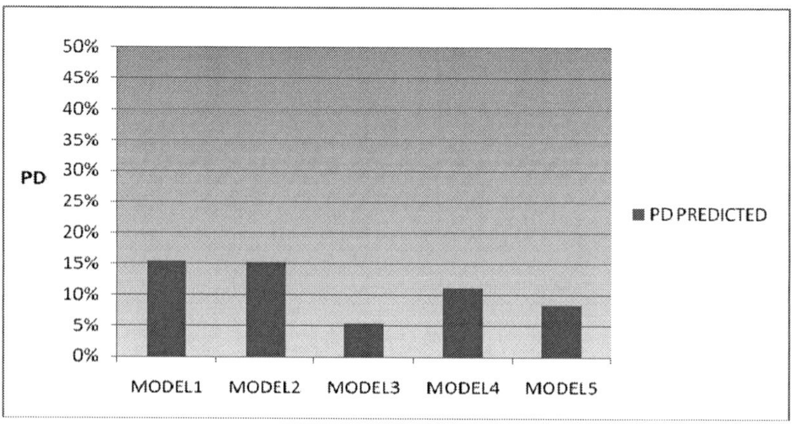

Figure 5: Probabilities of default of firms that did not default

To better visualize the performance of the hybrid models, the following figures illustrate a comparison between the predictions of the probabilities of default for two of the five models used (green curves) and the actual situation of firms (red curves). This graphs clearly show that the hybrid model dominates the others models. We again observed that the hybrid models are the best estimators of probability curves of defects.

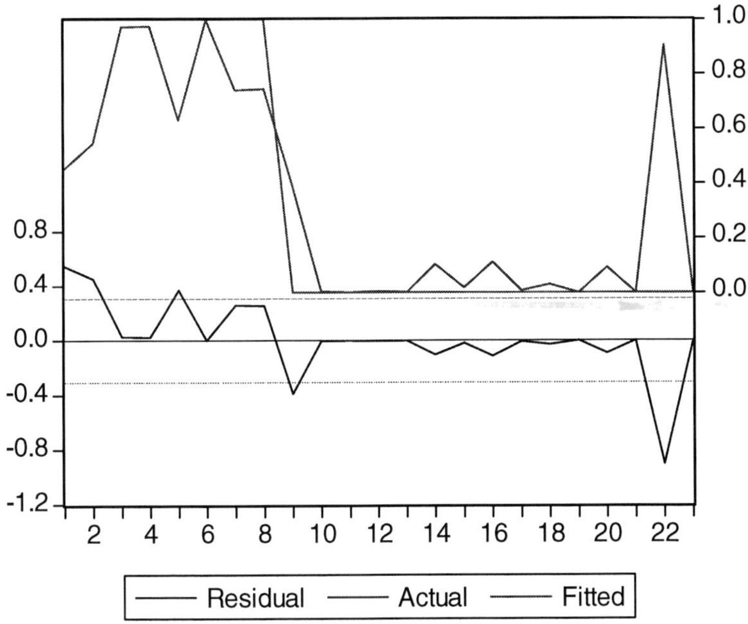

Figure 6: accuracy of score models (Model 4)

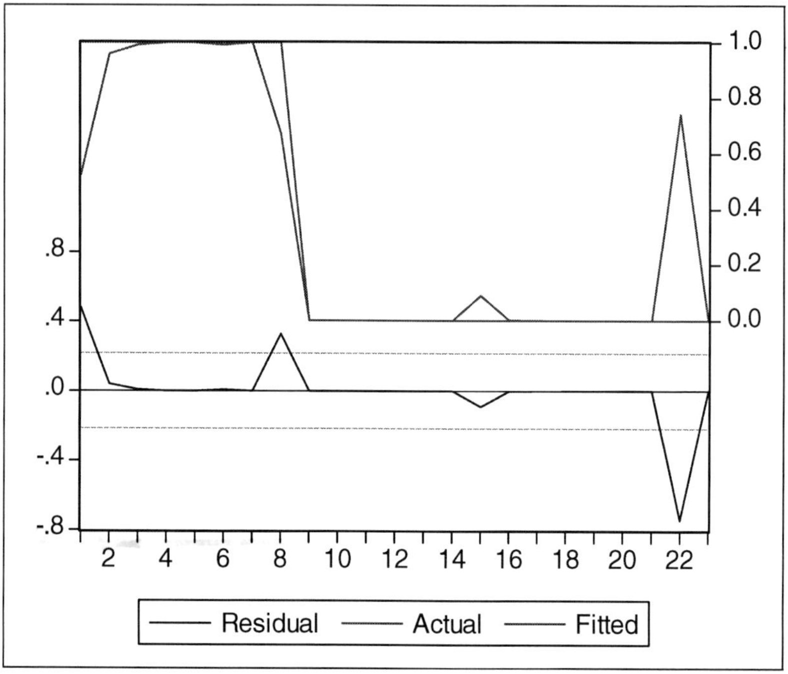

Figure 7: accuracy of hybrid models (models 3)

5. Conclusion

Credit risk measurement is an area of great and renewed interest for both academicians and practitioners. In this paper, our goal was to study a major component of credit risk, the probability of default using the methodology proposed by Tudela and Young (2003) on a sample of French companies whose shares are traded on the Stock Exchange Paris. This model has investigated the ability of hybrid models to calculate the default risk of UK companies by verifying whether combining the structural and the non-structural models into a hybrid model yields a better measure of the default risk than those obtained from structural and traditional non-structural models estimated separately.

To accomplish this, we aimed to explain default deficiencies by estimating a probit model in which the explanatory variables are the estimated probabilities of default from the structural model, financial ratios, and other accounting data.

The dependent variable is binary, taking the value of 1 if the default occurs and 0 otherwise. Using the same methodology, we have also estimated a model with only accounting data as explanatory variables (non-structural model), and a third probit model in which the only exogenous variable is the probability of default from the structural model (the model that contains only structural information).

Thus, we have examined the predictive power of the probabilities of default from the structural model to explain corporate bankruptcy by integrating it in the non-structural model as an explanatory variable.

Our results indicate that the predicted probabilities of default (PDs) contribute significantly to explaining default probabilities when they are included alongside the retained accounting variables. This confirms the results of the study of Tudela and Young (2003), and those of Dionne et al. (2005).

We note that the main limitation of our work was fixing the default barrier at any level (equal to 1 in our study). Thus, it would be interesting in future work to make the endogenous default barrier and to estimate it by the maximum likelihood method, which may increase the predictive ability model.

References

Altman, E. I. (1968), Financial Ratios, Discriminant Analysis and Prediction of Corporate Bankruptcy, *The Journal of Finance*: p 589–609.

Altman E., Haldeman R., Naranan P (1977), ZETA analysis: a new model to identify bankruptcy prediction risk of corporations, *Journal of Banking and Finance*, pp. 29-54.

Beaver (1966), Market Prices, Financial Ratios and the Prediction of Failure, *Journal of Accounting Research*, pp. 179-192.

Black, F and Cox, J (1976), Valuing corporate securities: some effects of bond indenture provisions, *Journal of Finance*, pp.351–67.

Black, F and Sholes, M (1973), On the pricing of options and corporate liabilities, *Journal of Political Economy*, pp.637-659.

Brennan, M.J. and E.S. Scwartz (1978), Corporate Income Taxes, Valuation, and the Problem of Optimal Capital Structure, *Journal of Business,* pp. 103–14.

Briys, E. and F. de Varenne (1997), Valuing Risky Fixed Rate Debt: An Extension, *Journal of Financial and Quantitative Analysis,* pp. 239–48.

Brockman, Paul ET H.J. Turtle (2003), A Barrier Option Framework for Corporate Security Valuation, *Journal of Financial Economics*, pp. 511-529.

Crosbie P., and Bohn J (2003), Modeling Default Risk, *Journal of Derivative*, pp.9-24.

Caoutte J., Altman E., Naraynan P (1998), Managing Credit Risk: The Next Great Financial Challenge, (*John Wiley & Sons*).

Dionne, Georges. Laajimi, Sadok. Mejri, Sofiane and Petrescu, Madalina (2005), Estimation of the Default Risk of Publicly Traded Companies, *working paper, Bank of Canada*, p 63.

Duan, Jin-Chuan, Gautier Geneviève and Simonato Jean-Guy (2004).On the Equivalence of the KMV and Maximum Likelihood Methods for Structural Credit Risk Models, *mimeo, HEC Montréal*, p19.

Jones (1987), Current Techniques in Bankruptcy Prediction, *Journal of Accounting Literature*, pp. 131-164.

Longstaff, F A and Schwartz, E S (1995), A simple approach to valuing risky and floating rate debt, *Journal of Finance*, pp. 789–819.

Merton, R C (1974), The pricing of corporate debt: the risk structure of interest rates, *Journal of Finance*, pp. 449–470.

Mester L (1997), What's the Point of Credit Scoring?, *Federal Reserve Bank of Philadelphia , Business Review*, pp.3-16.

Ohlson J (1980), Financial Ratios and the Probabilistic Prediction of Bankruptcy, *Journal of Accounting Research*, pp. 109-131.

Saunders, A (2002), Credit Risk Measurement: New Approaches to Value at Risk and Other Paradigms , (*John Wiley & Sons*).

Sobehart, J.R., S.C. Keenan, and R.M. Stein. (2000), Benchmarking Quantitative Default Risk Models: A Validation Methodology, Moody's Investor Service Rating Methodology.

Tudela, Merxe et Garry Young (2003), A Merton-model Approach to Assessing the Default Risk of UK Public Companies, *Bank of England, working paper* , p194- 41.

Wong, H. and T. Choi(2004),The Impact of Default Barrier on the Market Value of Firm's Asset, *Working Paper, Chinese University of Hong Kong.*

EXCESS VOLATILITY AND BEHAVIOURAL FEATURES SURROUNDING THE CRISIS PERIOD: EVIDENCE FROM THE MENA REGION

MOHAMED DERRABI[1] AND OMAR FAROOQ[2]

1. Introduction

The recent financial crisis in the West has severely affected stock markets in the Middle and North Africa (MENA) region. The crisis that erupted in the US, quickly spread across the MENA region, and resulted in the downfall of many regional stock markets. The spillover of financial crisis brought into focus many important questions, such as: How did the recent financial crisis affect stock price volatility? Did it result in a permanent shift in volatility levels? How did stock market participants react to it? What happened to risk aversion of stock market participants? The answers to these questions are important not only for policy-makers but also for market participants. Answers to these questions will help policy makers to not only recognize the main determinants of volatility, but also identify the effects of changes in volatility on real economic activity. This paper is an attempt to answer some of the above questions by documenting volatility behaviour in the MENA region during the pre-crisis, crisis, and the post-crisis periods.

Prior research on efficient market hypothesis has documented a significant impact on stock return as a result of volatility of market and macroeconomic fundamentals. The theory and previous empirical studies show that market volatility is significantly high during the periods of economic uncertainty. Many research papers and empirical studies show that market volatility cannot be explained totally by the variability of macroeconomic fundamentals (Shiller, 1981; Shiller, 1990). Substantial volatility is induced by factors and investors' overreaction behaviour

[1] ESC-Rennes, France & International University of Rabat, Morocco.
[2] Al Akhawayn University in Ifrane, Morocco.

(Henry, 1998; Koutmos, 1999). Markets have known several periods of excess volatility. Market volatility is induced by two major factors: (1) Uncertainty and variability of macroeconomic and market fundamentals; this is the "intrinsic" component of the market volatility that can be expected on the basis of expectations of market fundamentals using deterministic models. (2) Investors' psychological features considerably driving the decision making processes, especially during the periods of euphoria or market turbulence, and the speculative strategies during these periods (Dumas et al., 2009). These psychological factors induce an excess volatility or "noisy volatility" that cannot be justified by the variability of market fundamentals, and therefore is difficult to predict using fundamental analysis and is usually non-deterministic with unknown probability distribution. The noisy dimension that creates the excess volatility is explained by psychological behaviour of two kinds: (1) over-optimism and invertors' euphoria in financial markets, which encourage excitement behaviour from investors who tend to overprice traded stocks. Therefore, market prices deviate from their intrinsic values. (2) Period of market uncertainty and turbulence that exacerbates the fear and investor's risk aversion attitude. The fear to be the last to sell when stock prices are descending or expected to decrease, usually contributes to creating an excess volatility. In both cases the tendency of market prices to revert to the intrinsic value of stocks creates volatile movements around the mean that vary over time depending on the nature of the noise.

The results of this paper show significantly higher volatility during the pre-crisis period relative to the crisis period. The conditional heteroscedasticity analysis using GARCH supports the hypothesis that psychological beliefs related to over pessimism and/or over confidence contribute to excessive volatility in the MENA region. We argue that over confidence has greater influence on excess volatility during the pre-crisis period, while pessimism did not contribute as much as to excess volatility during the crisis period. The remainder of the paper is structured as follows: Section 2 discusses and summarizes the data used in this study; Section 3 presents assessment of our hypothesis; and the paper ends with Section 4 where we present conclusions.

2. Data

To verify our hypotheses, we collected weekly stock prices of 250 firms listed at various stock exchanges of the MENA region, i.e. Jordan, Kuwait, Morocco, Saudi Arabia, United Arab Emirates, Egypt, Qatar, and Bahrain.

The data was collected from the DataStream. The period of analysis was from January 2006 to March 2010. For the purpose of this paper, we classify our sample into pre-crisis, crisis, and post-crisis periods. The pre-crisis period covers the time between January 2006 and June 2007, while the crisis period and the post-crisis period spans June 2007 to December 2008, and January 2009 to February 2010, respectively.

2.1 Calculation of composite index

As a first step of our analysis, we construct a composite index (CI) using the price weighted procedure as follows. Our index is constructed from the selected markets in a way that it represents almost 60% of the whole MENA market capitalization and performance.

$$CI_t = \sum_{i=1}^{250} \frac{P_{i,t}}{D_{adj}} \qquad (1)$$

Where CI_t is the value of composite index on week t, P_{it} is the closing price of stock i on week t, and D_{adj} is the adjusted divisor on week t.

2.2 Calculation of returns

The weekly returns were calculated as the logarithmic difference of weekly composite index as follows:

$$R_{i,t} = Log\left(CI_{i,t}\right) - Log\left(CI_{i,t-1}\right) \qquad (2)$$

Where $R_{i,t}$ is the return of our sample on week t, $CI_{i,t}$ is the value of composite index on week t, and $CI_{i,t-1}$ is the value composite index on week t-1.

Table 1 presents the descriptive statistics for the weekly returns of composite index. The annualized average return and standard deviation for our sample during the period of the study are respectively 10.5% and 23%. The coefficients of kurtosis and skewness suggest the index returns are normally distributed.

Table 1: Descriptive statistics for weekly returns

Mean	0.0019
Standard Error	0.0022
Median	0.0008
Standard Deviation	0.0323
Sample Variance	0.0010
Kurtosis	1.5729
Skewness	0.0194
Range	0.2210
Maximum	-0.1060
Minimum	0.1149
Sum	0.4001
No. of observations	205

3. Methodology

3.1 Volatility clusters

Our sample contains weekly returns of 250 firms from the MENA region over the period of January 2006 to February 2010. Figure 1 shows the weekly stock returns along with a moving average return over 3 months, while Figure 2 shows a series of standard deviations calculated on a rolling window of 3 months as follows:

$$MSD(t) = \sqrt[2]{\sum_{S=t-3months}^{t} \frac{\left(CI_S - CI_{Avg}\right)}{\left(N-1\right)}} \qquad (3)$$

Where MSD is the Moving Standard Deviation using a rolling window of 3 months, CI_S is the value of composite index, and CI_{Avg} is the average of the composite index.

Figures 1 and 2 reveal evidence of the existence of excess volatility episodes before and during the crisis period. They also indicate presence of jumps in the stock price volatility in the MENA region during the period of study. The figures show that the volatility significantly decreased during the post-crisis period. The analysis of the stock price volatility shows a mean reverting process and evidence of the well-known volatility clustering effect (large return changes of either signs are followed by large changes, and small changes are followed by small changes).

Figure 1: Weekly stock returns calculated based on the composite index and moving average using a window of 3 months

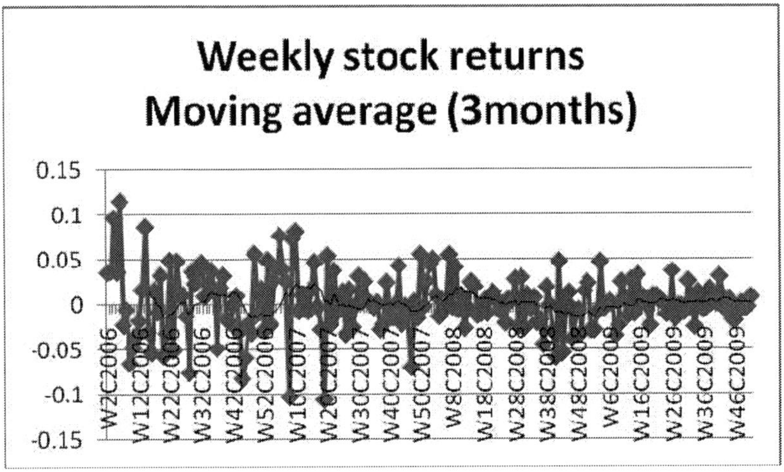

Figure 2: Standard deviation of stock market return calculated from the composite index using a rolling window of 3 months

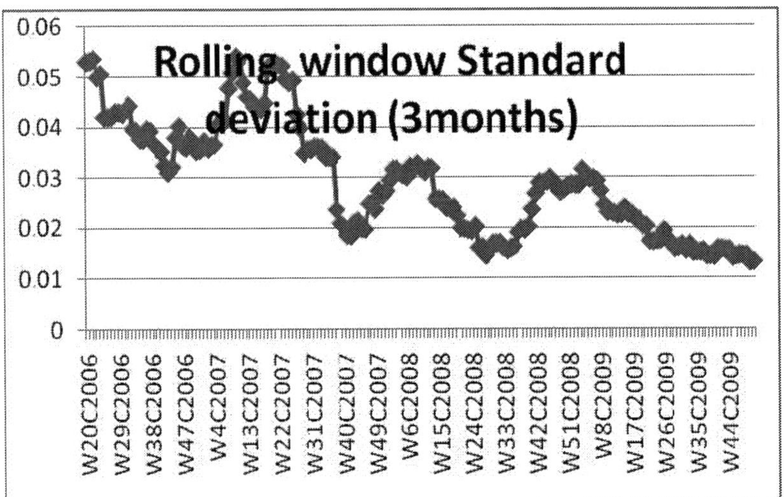

3.2 Excess volatility: Pre-crisis, crisis, and post-crisis analysis

Episodes of heightened market volatility shown in the previous figures indicate clear evidence of a lack of strong empirical relationship between stock return volatility and observable economic fundamentals. This excess volatility can be explained by the overreaction of market participants to intrinsic signals. This overreaction, irrespective of whether it is positive or negative, implies deviation of prices from their fundamental value and therefore creates sinusoidal movements around the frictionless price. The excess volatility behaviour seems to exist in individual episodes of euphoria and episodes of despair (LeRoy, 2005). In this section, we analyse the volatility behaviour in the MENA region and compare the stock return volatility during the pre-crisis, crisis, and post crisis periods. We use the F-test of equality of variances. We test the null hypothesis that crisis and post crisis periods have the same variances. The F-test results show that the variance is significantly higher during the pre-crisis and the crisis period than during the post-crisis period. The market volatility has significantly slowed down during the post-crisis period. Unexpectedly, the test also shows that the volatility during the pre-crisis period is unexpectedly and significantly higher than that of the crisis period.

Table 2: Difference in volatility across the pre-crisis, crisis, and the post-crisis periods

Panel A: Difference in volatility across the pre-crisis and crisis periods

	Pre-crisis Period		Crisis Period
Mean	0.0053		0.0004
Variance	0.0020		0.0006
No. of observations	73		73
Degrees of freedom	72		72
F-Value		6.8436	
P-value		0.0000	
Critical F-Value (One tail)		1.5279	

Panel B: Difference in volatility across the crisis and the post-crisis periods

	Crisis Period		Post-crisis Period
Mean	0.0004		0.0006
Variance	0.0006		0.0003
No. of observations	73		57
Degrees of freedom	72		56
F-Value		2.1317	
P-value		0.0018	
Critical F-Value (One tail)		1.5279	

Panel C: Difference in volatility across the pre-crisis and the post-crisis periods

	Pre-crisis Period		Post-crisis Period
Mean	0.0053		0.0006
Variance	0.0020		0.0003
No. of observations	73		57
Degrees of freedom	72		56
F-Value		2.1317	
P-value		0.0018	
Critical F-Value (One tail)		1.5279	

3.3 Investor's psychological behaviour and excess volatility

In this section, we analyse the factors explaining the excess volatility behaviour during the pre-crisis and the crisis periods in the MENA region. It is widely accepted that market volatility is driven by both macroeconomic and psychological factors (Shiller, 1990). We investigate whether the heteroscedasticity explain the high episodic excess volatility. For this purpose, we will use GARCH models introduced by Engle (1982) and Bollerslev (1986). Consistent with previous literature, we estimate the GARCH (p,q) model (where p is the order of the GARCH terms σ^2 and q is the order of the GARCH terms ε^2). The equation assumes that ε_t denotes the error terms (return residuals, w.r.t. a mean process) and it also assumes that $\varepsilon_t = \sigma_t z_t$, where $z_t \sim N(0,1)$. The series σ_t^2 are modelled as follows:

$$\sigma_t^2 = \alpha_0 + \alpha_1\varepsilon_{t-1}^2 + \ldots + \alpha_q\varepsilon_{t-q}^2 + \beta_1\varepsilon_{t-1}^2 + \ldots + \beta_q\varepsilon_{t-q}^2 = \alpha_0 + \sum_{i=1}^{q}\alpha_i\varepsilon_{t-i}^2 + \sum_{i=1}^{p}\beta_i\varepsilon_{t-i}^2 \quad \textbf{(4)}$$

Figures 3, 4, and 5 show clear evidence of volatility jumps and time varying conditional variance in our composite index. The standard error square reveals the presence of heteroscedasticity effect. The high volatility episodes ended from the year 2009.

Figure 3: Standard residuals plot of Autoregressive model AR(1)

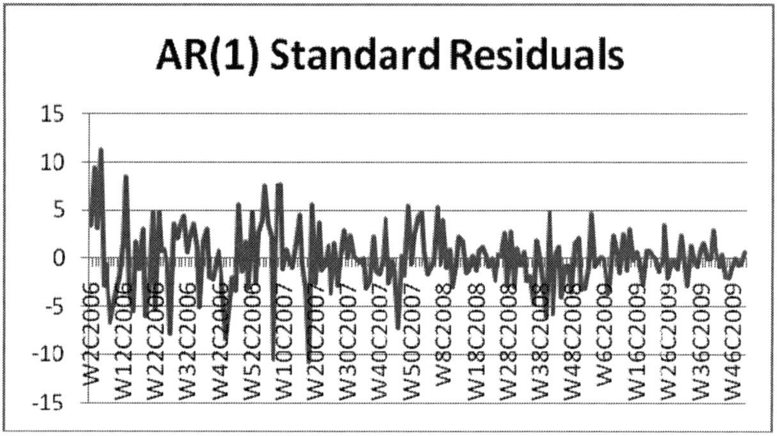

Figure 4: Detrended standard residuals of Autoregressive model AR(1) using Moving average of 3 months window

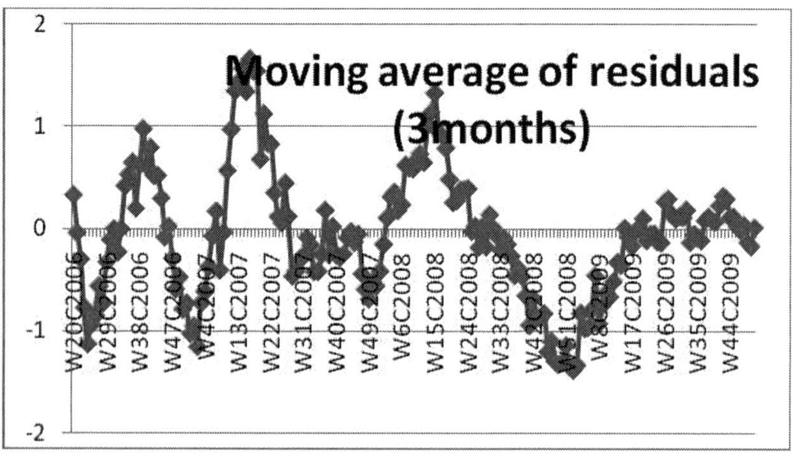

Figure 5: Square Standard residuals of Autoregressive model AR(1)

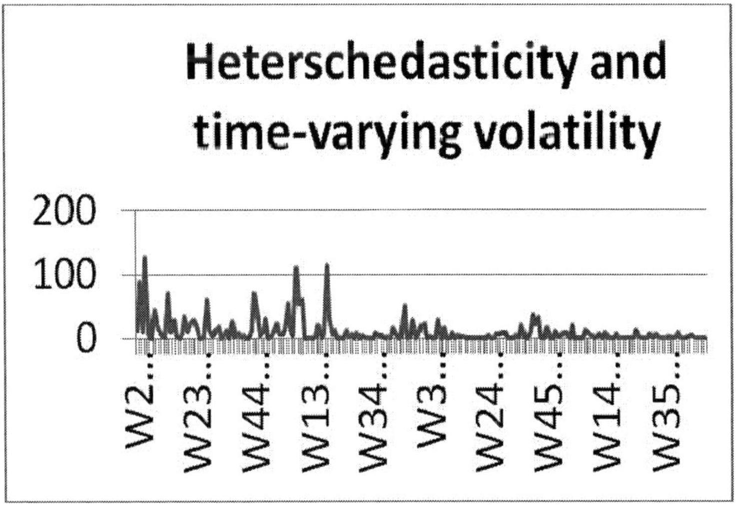

The GARCH specification confirms the results obtained by the figures. The coefficient ε^2_{t-1} is significantly different from zero and thus the assumption of homoscedastic disturbance is rejected in favour of a GARCH (1,1). The evidence of GARCH effect suggests a time varying conditional variance due to switching heteroscedasticity. The time varying conditional and mean reverting stock market volatility cannot be explained only by the variability of economic fundamentals, which represents a violation of the EMH. Psychological factors and investors' sentiments during pre-crisis (Euphoria) and crisis (turbulence) have significantly contributed to over-price reactions, and consequently to excess volatility. The emerging markets in the MENA region show little maturity. Investors tend to over react to positive and negative price expectations. The psychological beliefs exert a greater influence on the market than good economic sense arguments.

Table 3: GARCH specifications

	Coefficients	Standard Error	t-value	p-value
Intercept	6.1793	1.5445	4.0006	0.0000
SQ. Error(t-1)	0.1594	0.0643	2.4786	0.0140
SQ. Error(t-2)	-0.0009	0.0646	-0.0141	0.9887
SQ. Error(t-3)	0.1059	0.0618	1.7126	0.0883
SQ. Error(t-4)	0.0495	0.0616	0.8042	0.4222

3.4 Risk aversion attitude, overconfidence, and over price reaction

In this section, we compare the impact of two different periods on the market volatility: the pre-crisis period and the crisis period. Both periods have known high volatility episodes, as demonstrated earlier in this paper. The F-test also shows that, unexpectedly, the market volatility during the pre-crisis period, qualified as a Euphoria period, is greater than the market volatility of the crisis period, qualified as a period of uncertainty and turbulence. The F-test results are not significantly reliable in the presence of heteroscedasticity. Therefore, we use an alternate, more robust model based on GARCH and dummy variables. To examine whether the risk aversion versus overconfidence is responsible for the difference in the excess volatility, we introduce in the GARCH model a dummy variable that is equal to 0 during the pre-crisis period and during the crisis period. Our empirical model is as follows:

$$R_t = \alpha_0 + \alpha_1 R_{t-1} + \varepsilon_t \qquad (5)$$

And

$$\varepsilon^2{}_t = \lambda_0 + \lambda_1 \varepsilon^2{}_{t-1} + d\varepsilon^2{}_{t-1} dummy_{t-1} \qquad (6)$$

Our results show that Investors tend to over react to positive and negative price expectations. Investors' psychological beliefs exert a greater influence on the market than good economic sense arguments. The hypothesis of higher excess volatility due to pessimism during the crisis period cannot be accepted. On the contrary, the negative sign of the dummy variable with 10% significance level suggests that the euphoria and excitement of investors during the speculation period induced higher excess volatility than the crisis period. Contrary to major markets and the theory of risk aversion, MENA emerging markets show higher over reaction during the euphoria periods than the uncertainty periods. The overconfidence of investors during the boom period that proceeded the crisis period explains such excessive volatility. Our results are more consistent with the theory of traders' overconfidence on price movements (Bhamra and Uppal, 2009).

Table 4: Alternate GARCH specifications

	Coefficients	Standard Error	t-value	p-value
Intercept	12.1295	2.0833	5.8222	0.0000
SQ. Error	0.1546	0.0809	1.9104	0.0579
Dummy	-0.3952	0.2310	-1.7103	0.0892

* Dummy variable is equal to "0" during the pre-crisis period and equal to "1" during the crisis period. We test the null hypothesis that the dummy variable is significantly positive

4. Conclusion

In this paper, we examined the market volatility in the MENA region using a composite index constructed based on data from 250 companies listed in eight countries in the MENA region. We studied the market volatility and the excess volatility behaviour surrounding the pre-crisis, crisis, and post-crisis period. The emphasis is put on the psychological factors that contribute to this volatility behaviour. Our results reveal evidence of the existence of excess volatility episodes before and during the crisis period and that there are jumps in the stock price volatility in the MENA region during the period of study. The MENA region experienced high volatility episodes even before the crisis, and expectedly during the crisis period. The volatility has significantly decreased during the post-crisis period. The analysis of the stock price volatility shows a mean reverting process and evidence of the well-known volatility clustering effect (large return changes of either signs are followed by large changes, and small changes are followed by small changes). Our analysis shows also the presence of excess volatility during the study period before, during, and after the crisis period, which indicates a clear departure from EMH. Unexpectedly, our results show that the volatility during the pre-crisis period is significantly higher than that of the crisis period. The conditional heteroscedasticity analysis using GARCH specification supports the hypothesis that psychological beliefs related to over pessimism and/or over confidence contribute to excessive volatility in the emerging market of the MENA region. We found that over confidence behaviour during the euphoria period had a greater influence on price excess volatility than pessimism during the crisis period.

References

Bhamra, H. S. and Uppal, R., (2009). The effect of introducing a non-redundant derivative on the volatility of stock-market returns when agents differ in risk aversion. Review of Financial Economics, 22, pp. 2303-2330.

Bollerslev, T., (1986). Generalized autoregressive conditional heteroskedasticity. Journal of Econometrics, 31, pp. 307–27.

Dumas, B., Kurshev, A., and Uppal, R., (2009). Equilibrium portfolio strategies in the presence of sentiment risk and excess volatility. Journal of Finance, 64 (2), pp. 579 - 629.

Engle, R., (1982). Autoregressive conditional heteroskedasticity with estimates of the variance of U.K. inflation. Econometrica, 50, pp. 987–1008.

Henry, O., (1998). Modelling the asymmetry of stock volatility. Applied Financial Economics, 8, pp. 145–154.

Koutmos, G., (1999). Asymmetric price and volatility adjustments in Emerging Asian stock markets. Journal of Business Finance and Accounting, 26, pp. 83–102.

LeRoy, S. F., (2005). Excess Volatility. Working Paper, University of California, Santa Barbara

Shiller, R., (1981). Do stock prices move too much to be justified by subsequent changes in dividend? American Economic Review, 71, pp. 421–446.

—. (1990). Market volatility and investor behavior. American Economic Review, 80, pp. 58–62.

BASEL III: STRENGTHENING THE RESILIENCE OF THE BANKING SECTOR

MARY-FLORENCE LAMY[1]

I. Introduction

> *"One of the underlying features of the crisis was the build up of excessive on and off balance sheet leverage in the banking system". "Failure to capture major on and off balance sheet risks, as well as derivatives related exposures, was a key destabilizing factor over the past two and half a year."*
>
> —Basel Committee on Banking Supervision Consultative document-December 2009

Thus, to highlight what the incentives have been for banks to increase their leverage, develop their activity on derivatives markets on such scale, and to reduce or annihilate these incentives, is of prime importance to strengthen the resilience of the banking sector and improve the first and second pillars of the Basel II framework.

After recalling the Basel III set of recommendations in the first section, we will address this question in the second one. In the third part we will examine the enhancements of Basel III for trading book, the treatment of securitizations and credit derivatives. Then we will focus on the leverage ratio to see if it will allow regulators to identify leverage that could threaten the financial system and finally we will argue on the future improvements to the system.

[1] ESC Rouen, France.

II. BASEL III

Following a thorough analysis of the financial crisis, and two years after the Lehmann collapse, the Basel Committee has presented to the G20[2] the set of measures and improvements in the regulation framework recommended to strengthen banking system stability and resilience, called BASEL III.

They are based on the necessity to increase both capital ratio and liquidity ratio of banks, and six main axes are identified:

1) Higher quality of capital with equities and retained earnings (Tier 1) being raised to 6% of the 8% obligation. Hybrid and subordinated debts that form tier 2 are thus limited to 2% of the total obligation.

2) In addition, a capital buffer of 2.5% of equity and retained earnings should also be constituted as a countercyclical buffer to cope with procyclicality of the Basel 2 framework and to help banks cushion losses and avoid having to deleverage by selling assets in poor market conditions.

3) Minimum global liquidity standards with a short term Liquidity Coverage Ratio and a longer term Net Stable Funding Ratio.[3] They should limit adverse effects of globalization and banks' interlinkage on capital markets.

4) Internationally harmonized leverage ratio to measure banks' leverage. The objective is to implement a simple ratio taking into account all of a bank's exposures on and off-balance sheet, for which a target of 3% tier 1 on total assets is set for an observation period lasting till 2013.[4]

5) Better coverage of market risks in the trading book. The capital obligation is now the sum of the current VaR calculation, increased for default and migration risks, and of a stressed VaR calculated on the 2007-2008 crisis data or on another significant crisis period.

[2] See « BCBS Report to the G20 » October 2010

[3] BCBS « International Framework for Liquidity Risk, April 16th 2010.

[4] See annex of the Report to the G20

5) This increase of the capital required to face market risks of assets in the trading book aims at reducing the arbitrage between the trading and banking book.

6) Stronger standards for supervision, public disclosures, and risk management.

The primary role of securitization and of credit derivatives in the 2007/2008 financial crisis has been underlined in all analyses:

> "One of the underlying features of the crisis was the build- up of excessive on and off balance sheet leverage in the banking system". "Failure to capture major on and off balance sheet risks, as well as derivatives related exposures, was a key destabilizing factor over the past two and half a years."
> —Basel Committee on Banking Supervision Consultative document-December 2009

The extent and importance of off-balance sheet commitments for leading banks in the USA, as well as in Europe, was mostly unknown or not fully understood prior to the crisis: regulators and accounting boards have focused on valuation models and accounting methods to trace markets values and have underestimated the consequences of the mere size of banks' positions on derivatives for the stability of the financial system.

We will present an overview of the Basel III framework in order to understand how it addresses these failures and will allow regulators and investors to measure leverage of banks and the risks they incur in originating derivatives, trading them, and investing in them.

In the second section we will explore why banks multiplied securitizations since 2003 up till the outbreak of the crisis; in the third section we will examine the enhancements of Basel III for trading books, and the treatment of securitizations and credit derivatives; in the forth, we will focus on the leverage ratio to see if it will allow regulators to identify leverage that could threaten the financial system; and finally we will discuss the future improvements to the system.

III. Banks' Incentives for Increasing Leverage

Since Basel I, with an impressive acceleration in 2003 and 2004, banks have widely used traditional and synthetic securitizations in order to reduce their obligation in capital, to be able to renew their lending capacity, or to benefit from new lending opportunities with the highest margins.

Under the Basel I framework, a bank had to constitute 8 in capital for 100 lent to a corporate, which is said to have a risk weight of 100%, and only 1.6 for 100 lent to a bank, for which risk weight was only 20%. A SPV backed by a bank benefits from the bank's 20% risk weight.

This treatment represents a significant economy in the required capital and explains the fast development of securitization.

The introduction of internal ratings with Basel II has improved the corporate status versus the banks' status, but these last advantage stayed, and securitizations volumes exploded to represent two third of the lending activity of banks as Société Générale or RBS.

Although synthetic securitizations are technically burdensome and costly, since the originating bank pays the excess spread though the CDS premium, they stay profitable because they allow one to reduce very significantly the capital obligation by substituting a financial Risk Weight of 20% to the corporate Risk Weight of 100%, thanks to credit derivatives swaps. This was the case even if the originating bank kept the equity tranches, as in most cases, and provided a liquidity facility. The choices of exposures and of the securitizations structure were carefully done in order to optimize the final yield of the bank capital.

Michael S. Gibson (2004)[5] measured, on a 2002-2003 synthetic CDOs sample, the total loss for the equity tranche (98%) and the leverage effect versus keeping the portfolio (15 on average). Under Basel II, even if the internal rating leads to a full deduction of the equity tranche retained, its small size, 3% in this example, makes it an on-going concern. This explains the systemic use of synthetic securitizations by banks, and that:

- "Assets held in highly leveraged off-balance sheet vehicles increased dramatically

[5] Understanding the risk of CDOs, July 2004

- The leverage and risk embedded in structured products increased, making traditional measures of balance sheet leverage less meaningful"[6]

Under the Basel II framework, when a bank purchases a protection from a financial entity, either through credit derivative swaps (CDS) or a direct financial guarantee for specific exposures, the financial entity risk is substituted with the debtor's risk, so the bank benefits from 80% economy in capital obligation. This explains that it was worthwhile for European banks to invest in mezzanine tranches from US banks and to sell to them the mezzanine tranches of their own originations. This cross selling of protection has increased the linkage or interconnection between main actors and their counterparty risk, and caused the propagation of the subprime crisis to German and French banks.

> "It is fine for non-regulated institutions to invest and fund themselves via regulated institutions, if the system allows regulated institutions to invest and fund themselves in non –regulated products you have a recipe for disaster." Joseph R. Mason testimony (2010).[7]

In synthetic securitization, since 2005 the collateral was often invested in a repurchase agreement with the originating bank itself in order for it to benefit from this short-term funding, instead of being invested in highly liquid assets like sovereign notes.

This partly accounted for the liquidity shortage of 2007, since to face the cash outlays corresponding to losses, banks had to draw on their own liquidity resources instead of selling government notes that should have been laid as collateral to provide liquidity.

The second main incentive for securitization is for banks to maximize their short-term profits derived from commissions and structuring fees with this originate and distribute model which has been amplified by accounting methods allowing: "Upfront recognition of profits on structured products where some risks were retained lasting on the economic life of the transaction."[8] Of course an upfront recognition of profits generates boni of which role in the crisis is well known.

---

[6] CGFS Paper n°34 "The role of valuation and leverage in procyclicality", 2009
[7] Testimony of Joseph R. Mason before the Congress of the United States.
[8] CGFS Paper n°34 "The role of valuation and leverage in procyclicality", 2009

These incentives are still effective, and the motives of main actors for building up short term profits, whatever the consequences, are the same as before crisis, and even if the calculation of a leverage ratio adding off balance-sheet exposures to total assets is implemented, it will not fully capture risks from derivatives.

IV. Enhancing Market Risk Coverage in Trading Book

1. Counterparty risk

> "The consultative document presents proposals to strengthen the capital requirements for counterparty credit exposures arising from banks' derivatives, repo and securities financing activities." "These enhancements will strengthen the resilience of individual banking institutions and reduce the risk that shocks are transmitted from one institution to the next through the derivatives and financing channel."

Previously the counterparty risk was not directly addressed:

- for derivatives exposures, it was supposed to be included in the VaR (99%, 10days) calculation of the obligation in capital for Market Risks,
- for Repo transactions and securities financing, it was not addressed separately from the credit risk obligation on those exposures. Each bank was supposed to evaluate the counterparty risk on its activities and to manage it, since on the interbank market positions are permanently evolving and are very short-term, and there is also a great difficulty in measuring and supervising risk positions linked to securities funding. Thus banks must implement risk management tools to control this counterparty risk efficiently on a permanent basis.

In July 2009, the obligation in capital for market risks was supplemented by the amount of a stressed VaR calculated on data of a historical period of 12 months of significant financial distress. Although such a period implies counterpart defaults, the committee considers that it needs to be reinforced to actually insure banks for the counterparty risk incurred on above exposures. Consistently, the committee suggests that the capital requirement for counterparty risk should also be estimated using data from the stressed period.

2. Regulatory capital treatment for mark-to-market risk

> "Banks will be subject to a capital charge for mark-to market losses due to credit valuation adjustment (CVA risk) associated with deterioration in the credit worthiness of a counterpart. While the current Basel 2 standard covers the risk of a counterpart's default, it does not address such CVA risk, which has been a greater source of losses than those arising from outright default".

Mark-to-market losses due to Credit Valuation Adjustment (CVA) accounted for 302 billion US$ by the end of June 2008 and actual losses of only 47 billion[9]. These huge write-downs are the result of fair value. This accounting method has initiated a "liquidity-valuation destruction spiral" [10]resulting in capital destruction: when banks faced liquidity shortage they entered it; the more assets they sell, the more prices fell, the larger their losses were and the less liquidity they were given for, forcing them to sell more, and so on. These fire sale prices automatically affected the value of assets of all banks: the write-downs have caused the severe disruption of banks' wealth and massive sales of all linked assets by investors who could not see when this endless value destructive screw would finish.

Because these depreciations do not reflect actual losses or even a good predictive estimate of future losses, but only private if not partial opinions, and because they have led to a massive destruction of public savings and constitute the main cause of the financial crisis, we think that to build up capital to buffer them is not the right solution to the issue they represent.

Since valuation methods for structured product, CDS, and most derivatives are not backed by time series data observed on efficient markets and validated, we propose to simply stop the mark-to-market or mark-to-model value accounting for derivatives and to rely on historic value, with the obligation for banks to build up provisions reflecting the best bank's evaluation of a counterparty risk in terms of liquidity and depreciation when needed (due to maturity or selling prospect, and taking into account macro-hedges). A careful review by supervisors of these provisions should allow them to identify sooner actors with positions or strategies implying systemic risk issues.

---

[9] See Annex Table 1 Banks' depreciations and recapitalization.

[10] Sylvie Mathérat, "Fair Value and Financial Stability" Stability Financial Review, October 2008.

Thus the propagation of a systemic risk through herding behaviour between the few actors of these transactions would be lessened, and the liquidity factor which has contributed to price collapse on this improperly called market will not impact actors engaged in bilateral and sometimes different or longer term transactions. Moreover, fire sale prices reflecting the illiquidity of few banks will not become the benchmark to value all positions, as has been experienced in 2008[11].

The drawbacks of this accounting method are so important (incentive to risky market practices and to speculation, impressive erosion of major banks capital supported by shareholders and taxpayers, large depreciation of public savings and pension funds' portfolios) that it must no longer be maintained.

3. CDS and systemic risk

> "CDS and Financial Guarantee played a major role in the financial crisis."[12]

The concentration of CDS contracts on a small number of participants, the interconnection between them, and the fact that for derivatives major banks and financial institutions account for more than 80% of the issues, explain that the correlation on assets for financial firms is much higher than for corporate. As mentioned above, this is increased by the treatment of corporate bonds which induces banks to favour investing in CDOs or ABS rather than in bonds.

This is equally true for structured products and other securities financed with embedded derivatives.

Major issuers buy and sell protections through CDS and Equity Linked Swaps OTC and transactions concern very few firms, everyone being a counterpart of others in cross contracts; thus if one firm defaults, the whole system is impacted. This high degree of interconnectedness is the consequence of the recognition of financial guarantees and other credit risk transfer in the Basel II framework, which has led banks to a systematic recourse to credit risk transfers to levy their obligation in capital.

---

[11] See annex Table 2: Share of fair value assets and liabilities for banks.

[12] See Credit risk transfer products in Review of the differentiated nature and scope of Financial Regulation. (FSF 2010)

This concentration also accounts for the high volatility of the CDS OTC market.[13]

The notional amount of CDS totalled $45 to $62 billion in 2007 when the value of bonds from underlying corporate issuers was only $5 billion.

This discrepancy shows the magnitude of trading; the same credit risk is transferred many times. Another example shows the importance of interconnection of banks trough CDS: when it defaulted, the total CDS sold by Lehmann amounted to $72 million, but after multilateral netting, the resulting exposure was only $20 million.

The obligation to deal CDS in a CCP will diminish the counterparty risk for a bank, but not the opacity of the CDS market, nor will it provide information on banks' relative positions. Moreover, the margins call will accelerate liquidity shortage for protection sellers, even causing their destabilization, as seen with AIG and mono-lines cases.[14]

To recognize the interconnection of banks and limit the cross financial guarantees in the financial sector, a correlation factor higher than 25% is proposed. Facing this concentration risk, an evaluation of losses linked to counterparty risk can be measured with stress tests with a higher correlation ratio (40%?), or scenarios given by regulators and added to a minimum capital charge for derivatives, repos and securities financing, which is relevant and could simply be calculated as a proportion or underlying exposure for the bank.

In order to increase the incentives to use CCPs for derivatives, it is suggested that the risk-weight might be 0. We find that such a measure will again strengthen CDS propagation: as explained above, we believe that concentration and systematic risk will neither leverage nor disappear with more transparency, and that the recourse to CCPs will only reduce counterparty and operational risks on these products, but will not reduce their adverse effects on the global stability of the financial system.

---

[13] See O.W.Brown "CDS What are the risks and challenges for financial stability", 2010.

[14] See Marcus K. Brunnermeier (2009)"Deciphering the liquidity& credit crunch of 2007-2008."

4. Additional capital charge for mark-to-market counterparty risk losses for CDS

> "In addition to the capital requirements for counterparty risk based on the standardized or internal –based approaches for credit risk, a bank must calculate an additional capital charge to cover mark-to-market unexpected counterparty risk losses."[15]

This additional capital charge will be calculated for all counterparts as the market risk charge of a virtual zero-coupon bond, with notional equalling the total exposure to the counterpart and the maturity of the longest of the exposures. The spread to be used is the CDS spread and if not available, the spread of a bond from this issuer.

The market charge is calculated over a one year horizon instead of the 10 days horizon (i.e. 5 times the 10-days VaR) and includes a stressed VaR under the new July 2009 requirement.

The § 125 proposes to recognize CDS hedges in measuring the CVA loss "to provide an incentive for banks to hedge the CVA risk". We believe that it is not relevant and dangerous to further induce banks to use CDS, and especially in the case where the bank does not hold any bonds and is only exposed to valuation risk and not to actual default risk. Each movement in price or rumour could lead to soaring CDS prices without actual economic foundation, which could destabilize the underlying bonds quotation. Similarly, considering the concentration of CDS market and its high volatility, we also suggest that the spread of the bond of similar maturity of the counterparty and not the CDS spread should be directly used to calculate the IRC.

This additional charge will discourage banks from classifying derivatives and other assets in the trading book in order to avoid calculating a capital charge for credit risk, but its actual implementation will be very burdensome. For repos' exposures a simpler method might be as efficient.

5. Treatment of securitizations

In the revision of the Basel 2 framework of July 2009, the capital obligation for securitization instruments retained or held by the bank was reinforced:

---

[15] §123 to 125 Strengthening the resilience of the banking sector BCBS, 2010.

The risk weights of the non-investing tranches have been raised to 100% for BBB and 350% for BB, then deduction for poorer ratings as well as for equity. The risk weight for liquidity facilities is 50% and 20% under one year. Since we consider that liquidity crises are not foreseeable and are very sudden, the maturity of the facility is not a risk factor and the same risk weight of 50% should apply to all liquidity facilities granted by the originating bank.

"The capital obligation for re-securitization exposures (so-called square securitizations) will bear risk weights 3, 2 time higher than those required for securitization ones". However final weights stay relatively small for investment grade tranches: 20% for AAA to AA-, 50% for A+ to A- and they still represent a true incentive for banks, since the upgrading effect of securitizations on the portfolio of reference is such that they stay very interesting for banks.[16]

Moreover securitizations products cannot be treated as if they bear the same risk as a similarly rated corporate debt instrument, but deserve a specific risk evaluation in order to capture their leverage effect and illiquidity, and even operational risk at settlement, as explained by J. R. Mason.[17]

Though banks are not permitted to use their internal ratings based models for securitization, they are required to supplement capital obligation with their own estimates and we feel that the issue of an excessive reliance on external credit ratings is still to be addressed:

> The role of credit agencies in the crisis and their implication in securitizations have been fully described, as well as "*the second negative incentive, is for rating agencies to produce good ratings for exposures instead of accurate and conservative assessments.*"[18]

Considering this bias and that the models used by agencies to rate securitization tranches were revealed not to be satisfactory, we suggest that the weights in standard approach and FIRB method should be

---

[16] See BCBS Market Risk framework revision of July 2009

[17] Where did the risk go ?How misapplied bond ratings cause MBS and CDO market disruptions" Joseph R. Mason& Joshua Rosner, May 2007

[18] See "Wise men report for European Community ", 2009 & FSB" Enhancing market & institutional resilience" April 2008 & Barry Eichengreen "Ten questions about the subprime crisis", Feb 2008.

increased for investing grade tranches to favour direct financing of corporate and network. As for the risk weights of liquidity facilities, we believe that they should be taken as 50% whatever their maturity, the risk resulting more from adverse macro- economic events or market conditions rather than from their maturity.

V. Leverage Ratio

The Basel committee has announced the introduction of a leverage ratio as a supplement to the obligation in capital based on a risk based assets ratio of Basel 2.

The objective is to "*Help contain the build-up of excessive leverage in the banking system and introduce additional safeguards against attempts to game the risk-based requirements" and it will also" reinforce the risk-based requirements with a simple non risk based backstop measure based on gross exposure."* In its joint report "The role of valuation & leverage in pro-cyclicality" the FSF-CGFs working group gives a broad definition of leverage: an entity is leveraged when its exposure to risky assets is larger than its equity capital resulting from its debt funding or derivatives.

As observed for US investment banks during crisis, leverage magnifies liquidity and market risks exposure. The following table shows the increase of the gross balance sheet leverage for investment banks post-2004, and the revision of the Net Capital Rule which previously limited leverage at 15 times their capital. In order to maximize the return on capital and to generate profits and boni, they reached an impressive leverage of 30 times their capital when they failed. Relying on the magnitude of their capital, on the diversification of their exposures to various markets, and on their faith in markets to supply them with liquidity, they could not face the correlation of all assets' value collapse in 2008.

> "During the most severe part of the crisis, the banking sector was forced by the market to reduce its leverage in a manner that amplified downward pressure on asset prices, further exacerbating the feedback loop between losses, declines in bank capital, and contraction in credit availability"[19]

---

[19] Strengthening the resilience of the banking sector. §202 p60

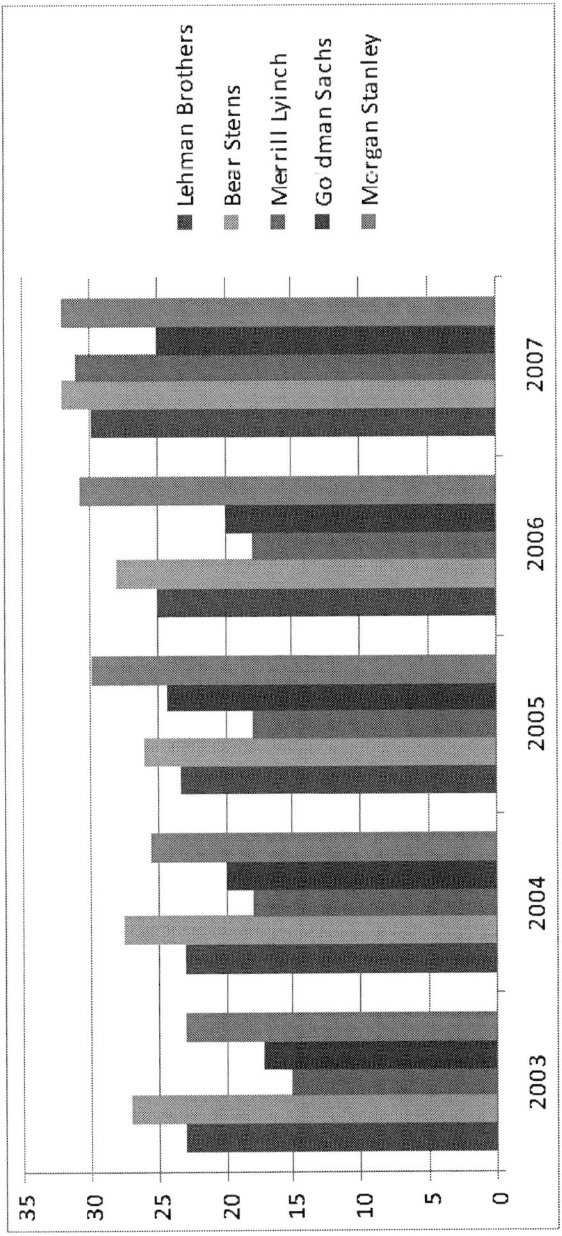
35
30
25
20
15
10
5
0
2003
2004
2005
2006
2007
Lehman Brothers
Bear Sterns
Merrill Lyinch
Goldman Sachs
Morgan Stanley

Graph 3

Bank balance sheet leverage ratio[1]

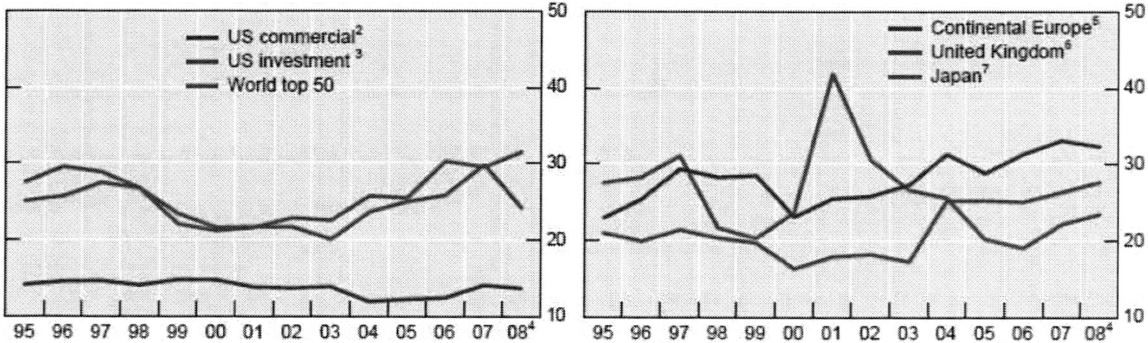

[1] Balance sheet leverage ratio (total assets divided by total equities) of individual banks weighted by asset size. [2] Bank of America, Citigroup, JPMorgan Chase, Wachovia Corporation, Washington Mutual and Wells Fargo & Company. [3] Bear Stearns, Goldman Sachs, Lehman Brothers, Merrill Lynch and Morgan Stanley. [4] Latest quarter. [5] ABN AMRO Holding, Banco Santander, BNP Paribas, Commerzbank, Crédit Agricole, Credit Suisse, Deutsche Bank, Société Générale, UBS and UniCredit SpA. [6] Barclays, HSBC, Lloyds TSB Group and Royal Bank of Scotland. [7] Mitsubishi UFJ Financial Group, Mizuho Financial Group and Sumitomo Mitsui Financial Group.

Source: Bankscope.

The gross balance sheet leverage ratio = Total assets/Equity does not capture the leverage and associated risk positions embedded in off balance sheet structures related to a bank and in the positions resulting from its activity on derivatives:

> The balance sheet leverage ratio of commercial US banks and of European banks was rather stable in the 2003/2007 period, but the leverage embedded in structure products stayed hidden[21].

The fast increase of assets held in SPV accounted for a sharp increase in leverage of sponsoring banks. Their actual exposure to these assets, resulting from retained tranches, liquidity lines, guarantees offered, and finally from the obligation to reconsolidate those SPV in their balance sheets in many cases, caused huge losses and liquidity dry-ups, which were not previously measured nor followed by regulators.

1. Proposal for a leverage ratio

The integration of off-balance sheet items is the major difficulty in establishing a meaningful leverage ratio: Positions on CDS and other written credit protections or structured credit derivatives are estimated at notional value and eventually tested. To build up the bank's total exposure as creditor on markets, the proposal[22] specifies that:

> "Physical or financial collateral, guarantee and credit mitigation purchased should not be allowed to reduce on-balance sheet exposures;
> - nettings are not allowed;
> - off-balance sheet items should be included using a flat 100% conversion factor,
> - written credit protection (e-g: credit derivatives) is included at notional value."

For measuring the exposure of other derivatives, two alternatives are proposed: on balance-sheet fair value, or the potential exposure (using Basel 2 current exposure method).

We believe that including the potential exposure is needed to fully encompass the risk taken on forward positions and written options, as it

[21] See annex Graph 4: Risk adjusted measures of leverage

[22] Strengthening the resilience §206 p61

has been demonstrated by the "Société Générale" case and other examples of non-controlled risk on derivatives or forward propositions.
We recall that on-balance sheet fair value for written options is their premia which do not measure the risk taken by selling these protections versus markets risks.

For traditional securitization with actual sale of assets (§225), as an alternative to the retained positions plus liquidity facilities and other guarantees, "the committee intends to consider the total of all underlying securitized portfolios for the bank's originated securitizations" to take into account the cases where the originator is compelled to take back assets on the balance sheet. We suggest that it could be evaluated in stress tests only, since these cases of reconsolidation stay exceptional.

The analysis of a bank's position on derivatives should help to measure its actual aggregated various exposures to market, counterparty and liquidity risks, and to allow better scaling of its leverage. "According to the treatment provided for risk mitigation (which is not recognized), synthetic securitization does not reduce the exposures amount of the underlying portfolios", thus all credit portfolios will be included in assets exposures in the leverage ratio calculation.

The consequence will be that the actual full exposure of banks to credit and market risks, including those resulting from position on derivatives, will be measured and published, which will allow comparisons between banks. This leverage ratio will reflect the objectives in capital yield and may be the ALM choices on a medium range era, which will supplement the analysis of the liquidity position of the bank given by the solvability ratios (at the end of each quarter and over a full year).

It should allow regulators to identify highly leveraged entities, which could threaten the financial system stability, and over a longer period, better measure the impact of derivatives on banks and capital markets. The comparison between large banks and the evolution of their ratio on few years will be useful to evaluate what should be a capital requirement on derivatives activity and on securities funding in order to avoid future crises of this magnitude, and to qualify the ALM performance and overall management of banks.

Conclusion

The main economic role of banks is the financing of economic activity through intermediation. It should thus be favoured in the regulatory capital requirement versus securitization, and we suggest that the Minimum Required Capital obligation should be calculated by main activities of the Bank, not to penalize the direct lending activity as it is in the Basel II framework: "Banks increasingly chose to book credit exposure in the trading book due to lower capital charge" [1]

We also suggest reviewing the treatment of lending activity and in particular the treatment of maturity, which leads to too short lending,[23] and the correlation factor in the credit risk formula, to favour financing of industry and diversification. The crisis has shown that to measure the exposure of a bank to credit risk, a review of the economics of its lending activity and of its exposures in derivatives and structured products are more meaningful that reliance on external warranties or credit enhancements or mitigation with CDS rated by agencies. The benefit obtained from buying a protection trough CDS should be greatly lowered in order to limit the advantages of CDS, and of their trading. So the drawbacks that are the transfer of risks to insurance companies, which are not allowed to be exposed to credit risk, and speculations with adverse consequences on savings portfolios and values of debts of concerned issuers, would be reduced.

In the revision of the market risk evaluation of the bank, its activity on derivatives should be measured and analysed per se to bear a relevant basic MRC for genuine risks, as well as for counterparty risk. The treatment of investments in bonds in the banking book should be reviewed in order that direct investments in corporate and government bonds would account for the major part of the portfolio of the bank (investment plus trading) and be preferred to investments in derivative CDOs, ABS and CDS for liquidity and capital markets' stability and efficiency. It is our opinion that the treatment of bonds in pillar one has led banks to replace them by CDOs and RMBS or to include them in the trading book, thus opting for mark-to-market value, and this has been specially the case for French banks.[24]

---

[23] "The treatment of Credit Risk in the Basel Accord and Financial Stability" M-F LAMY International Journal of business, 2006

[24] See CGFS Paper n°34 "The role of valuation and leverage in procyclicality" Table 1 given in exhibit 2.

Considering the liquidity management of the banks, we think that the size of the portfolio and the quality of assets held to ensure liquidity are relevant, and should be reviewed for the setting of future standards. The liquidity ratio and the leverage ratio should help to prevent cases of high leverage or ALM strategies implying a risk for interconnected banks and other financials actors.

It should also be considered that the ALM and liquidity monitoring allow banks to manage transformation and interest risks, and that under the new regulation framework they should not be induced to look for credit derivatives on markets but instead encouraged to have a capital build-up and leverage ratio objectives on a medium term horizon.

Annex

Table 1

Dépréciations et récapitulations

(en milliards de dollars ; récap. / pertes totales en %)

	Dates	Dépréciations	Pertes de crédits	Total	Récap.	Récaps/ pertes totales
2007	27-déc	74	23	97		
2008	22-janv	107	26	133		
	31	120	26	146		
	22-févr	135	26	165		
	29	154	27	181		
	07-mars	162	26	188		
	14	169	26	195		
	26	182	26	208		
	01-avr	206	26	232	136	59
	10	216	29	245	163	66
	21	248	42	290	231	80
	28	269	43	312	231	74
	09-mai	280	43	323	231	71
	19	332	47	379	266	70
	16-juin	344	47	391	310	79
	20	349	47	396	302	76

Source: Bloomberg (échantillon de plus de 70 banques internationales)

Table 2

Share of fair value assets and liabilities for banks[1]

In per cent

	2008	2007	2006	2005	2004	2003	2002
Share of FV assets[2]							
France	46.8	46.5	45.5	47.1	-	-	-
Italy	18.0	19.0	21.3	20.9	-	-	-
Japan	24.9	27.0	27.6	28.3	27.6	27.3	24.4
Netherlands	27.5	28.4	30.6	32.4	30.6	-	-
Spain	15.6	17.2	17.8	-	-	-	-
Switzerland[3]	29.6	44.8	38.7	35.5	34.8	33.4	-
United States[4]	30.4	26.9	25.0	24.8	26.0	27.2	26.3
Share of FV liabilities[5]							
France	34.1	30.1	27.9	29.0	-	-	-
Italy	9.5	9.4	9.4	9.7	-	-	-
Japan	2.2	2.9	1.9	1.8	1.4	1.5	1.8
Netherlands	19.0	15.7	14.2	15.3	13.1	-	-
Spain	5.7	6.6	6.7	-	-	-	-
Switzerland	19.5	24.1	17.5	15.1	14.1	13.3	-
United States	8.0	7.4	4.2	4.0	4.7	4.8	4.5

[1] The numbers are compiled based on information provided by members of the Working Group; figures are based on national GAAP for the United States and Japan, and IFRS for other countries. [2] Relative to total assets. [3] Credit Suisse and UBS. [4] The observations are based on numbers compiled from bank holding company (BHC) FR Y-9C reports. The BHC asset threshold for required reporting was increased from $150 million to $500 million in March 2006. Some BHCs below the threshold may also file reports in certain circumstances. [5] Relative to total liabilities.

Graph 4

Risk-adjusted measures of leverage

VaR-to-equity ratios[1]

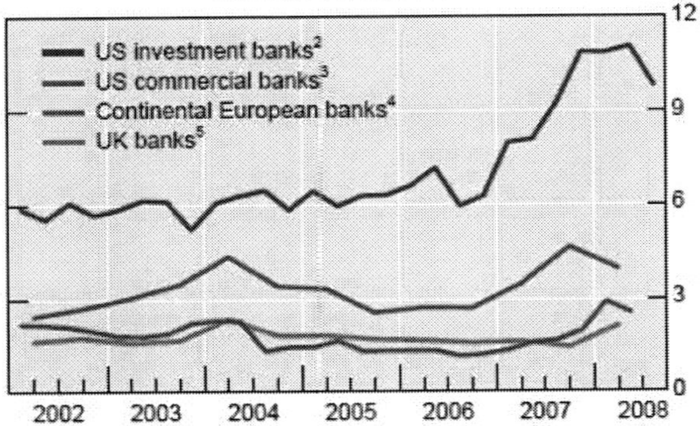

Tier 1 capital leverage[6]

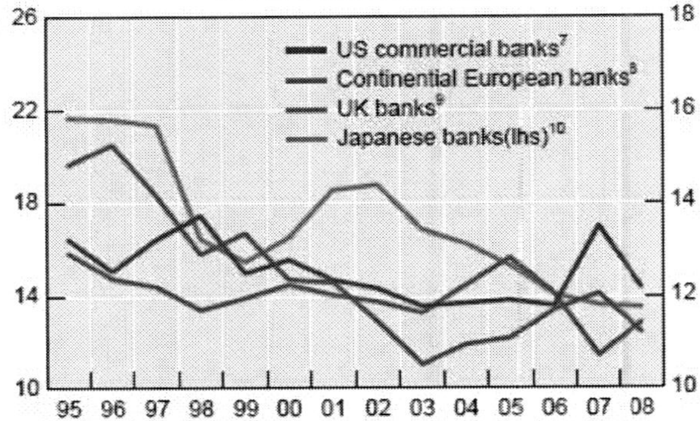

[1] Annualised trading VaR at 99% confidence divided by total equities weighted by asset size; in per cent. [2] Goldman Sachs, Lehman Brothers and Morgan Stanley. [3] Bank of America, Citigroup and JPMorgan. [4] BNP Paribas, Deutsche Bank, Société Générale and UBS. [5] Barclays, Royal Bank of Scotland and HSBC. [6] Reciprocal of Tier 1 capital ratio weighted by assets size. [7] Bank of America, Citigroup, JPMorgan, Wachcvia Corporation, Washington Mutual and Wells Fargo. [8] ABN AMRO Holding, Banco Santander, BNP Paribas, Commerzbank, Credit Suisse, Deutsche Bank, Société Générale, UBS and UniCredit SpA. [9] Barclays, HSBC and Lloyds TSB Group. [10] Mitsubishi UFJ Financial Group, Mizuho Financial Group and Sumitomo Mitsui Financial Group.

Sources: Bankscope; Bloomberg.

References

Joint FSF-CGFS working group: The role of valuation and leverage in procyclicality March 2009

Financial Stability Forum: Report on addressing the procyclicality in the financial system April 2009

Basel committee on Banking Supervision:

Credit risk transfer: developments from 2005to 2007

Review of the differentiated nature and scope of financial regulation

Enhancement to the Basel II framework (July 2009)

Report and recommendations of the cross-border bank resolution group (March 2010)

Framework for liquidity risk (December 2009)

Findings on interaction of market and credit risks. (May 2009)

Principles for sound liquidity risk management (2009)

AMF 2008 report on Credit Rating Agencies

Banzinger, Hugo. (2009). "Setting the right framework for modern financial markets." *Financial Stability Review.*

Brown, O. W. (2010). "What are the risks and challenges for financial stability." *Financial Stability Review.*

Brunnermeier, Marcus K. (2009). "Deciphering the liquidity & credit crunch of 2007-2008." *Journal of Economic Perspectives.*

Clerc, Laurent. (2008). "Valuation and fundamentals." *Financial Stability Review.*

Eichengreen, Barry. (2008). "Ten questions about the financial crisis" *Financial Stability Review.*

Jickling, Mark. (2009). "Causes of financial crisis" Federal Publications Congressional research.

Gibson, Michael. (2004). "Understanding the risk of CDOs."

Lamy, Marie-Florence. (2006). "The treatment of credit risk in the Basel accord and financial stability." *International Journal of Business.*

Mason J.R. and Rosner J. (2008). "Where did the Risk Go? How Misapplied Bond Ratings Cause Mortgage Backed Securities and Collateralized Debt Obligation Market Disruptions", Criterion Economics L.L.C

Matherat, Sylvie. (2008). "Fair value accounting and financial stability." *Financial Stability Review.*

"PSYCHOMETRIC" INDICES AND THE PREDICTION OF FINANCIAL BUBBLES: A SURVEY OF PROFESSIONAL INVESTORS

LARRY BENSIMHON[1] AND MIGUEL LIOTTIER[2]

Introduction

The financial-bubble phenomenon currently maintains an illogical relationship with the overconfidence documented in the literature. While some authors (Hirshleifer, Subrahmanyam, and Titman, 1994) see overconfidence as favouring the creation of bubbles, others (Noth and Weber, 2002) believe that it acts as a brake on such mass behaviour. This contradiction is the starting point for our study, which addresses both the reality of these forms of behaviour, and the manner in which they interact. The method employed was a questionnaire-based study conducted among institutional investors in the markets. The use of questionnaires to study behavioural finance appears to be a promising avenue of research, as this article will show. The correlation of "psychometric" data obtained directly from the answers provided by investors to questionnaires (in the form of indices of overconfidence and of the expectation of bubbles) with market data seems to be an interesting approach, particularly for understanding the development of financial crises.

The goal was to use the answers which the professional investors gave to the questionnaires to identify a number of indices, so as to identify possible linkages between these notions. The first section of this article describes the construction of the questionnaire and the conduct of the study. The second section presents its results.

[1] Assistant Professor, LIRSA, Cnam, Larry.bensimhon@cnam.fr.
[2] ISC Paris, mliottier@iscparis.com.

Section 1: Description of the questionnaire and the study

A. Questionnaire

The questionnaire needed to be a short one, given the small amount of time that these equity-market actors could make available. The questionnaire was therefore limited to about fifteen questions. An introduction comprised questions of a general nature: gender, age, and experience in the equity markets. The first part of the questionnaire then sought to determine whether the investors were affected by the markets' most common behavioural bias, namely overconfidence. In doing this we drew on the work of Lichtenstein, Fischoff, and Phillips (1982), Russo and Schoemaker (1992), Klayman, Soll, Gonzales-Vallejo, and Barlas (1999), and the studies conducted by Glaser and Weber (2007). The objective of this first part was then to use the investors' answers to identify various overconfidence scores linked to the various forms that this bias can assume. These kinds of study all employ the same methods, which in any event appear to be the only ones capable of measuring overconfidence scores. The next section describes in detail the compilation of these indices. The second and final part of the questionnaire drew on the study conducted by Shiller (2000a) on American market operators, so as to determine indices for the expectation of speculative bubbles. The explanation most often advanced for the speculative-bubble phenomenon is the existence of herd behaviour among market participants. We could then interpret these speculative-bubble indices as the operators' perceptions of herd behaviours in the equity markets. Once these indices have been developed, it then becomes possible to answer the following questions: Does overconfidence exist on the equity markets? Does one kind of overconfidence predominate over another? Are the various kinds of overconfidence correlated, and if so, how? How are the concepts of overconfidence and speculative bubbles connected?

B. The investors

The study took place between September and October 2004. The participants were selected on the basis of two criteria. The aim was to find market actors willing to respond to our questionnaire who were persons having a certain distance from the financial markets, but who would also be decision-makers.

The idea of selecting participants having a certain distance from the financial markets was important because the central issue in this study was the processing (understood as weighting) of information by the actors. This implied choosing individuals whose work included an analytical component. That excluded brokers (traders) who are in some ways financial market technicians, for whom the long-term represents little more than the next hour. The second selection criterion applied was that we had to interview decision-makers. A significant issue in our investigation of the processing of information arises from the relative weight that individuals assign to the information in their possession when they make a decision. This criterion automatically excluded financial analysts from our study, since that occupation does not involve direct participation in the markets in a decision-making capacity.

Two occupations more specifically corresponded to our criteria: sales traders and share managers.

Share managers collect information, obtain documentation on companies' histories and on movements of the stock exchange, and analyse trends in the various markets either directly via financial analysts or by using external sources: databases and trade publications. In addition, they engage in direct management, selecting the securities and the quantities to buy or sell, issuing purchase and selling orders, and monitoring the execution of such orders. Sales traders buy and sell shares but also inform and alert their clients about purchasing opportunities. These two types of occupation thus simultaneously require an analytical approach and also the making of regular decisions. It was therefore decided to target traders and share managers in the financial departments of institutional firms (mainly banks). These firms were chosen because they have the greatest influence on the markets, owing to their financial power. One final constraint: to avoid bias due to differences of environment the participants had to operate in the same market, i.e. the French equity market.

The participants were then approached in two different ways:

- By using the yearbooks of the *business schools* (mainly those of HEC and ENSAE [Paris International Business School and Paris Graduate School of Economics, Statistics, and Finance]).
- By introductions to other traders and managers via persons who had themselves taken part in the interview process. The latter method proved to be the most effective. Most of the participants quite willingly

provided a substantial number of their contacts, thereby creating a snowball effect.

The questionnaires were handled in several ways. To obtain a satisfactory rate of response, it was necessary to adjust to the preferences of the participants. Thus, of the 57 questionnaires finally collected and retained over the two-month period, 32 (about 56%) were obtained by direct contacts (meetings by appointment), 17 (about 30%) by telephone, and 8 (about 14%) electronically, via e-mail. The following section describes the participants.

57 market professionals from 18 institutional firms responded to the questionnaire. Table 2 shows the proportions of managers and sales traders who took part. Out of a total of 57 participants, 33 (about 58%) were share managers, and 24 (about 42%) were sales traders. A total of 51 men (about 90%) and 6 women (about 10%) responded to the questionnaire. The share-manager population comprises 31 men (about 94%) and 2 women (about 6%). The sales-trader population comprises 20 men (about 83%) and 4 women (about 17%). The financial market's reputation for being a highly-masculine environment is thus strongly confirmed here. We find the highest percentage of participants in the 25-35 age bracket. Out of 57 professional investors, 36 (about 63%) fall into this age bracket (versus about 3.5% under 25 years of age, 31.5% between 36 and 50, and 2% older than 50). The nature of the occupation itself may account for this distribution. The level of education is fairly high overall: these professionals are either graduates of business schools, or hold post-graduate degrees (five-years of higher education), hence the small number found in the under-25 category. In addition, these occupations are not usually ones that employees remain in throughout their careers; instead, they generally lead to management positions in banking firms - either in the trading departments themselves or in other departments, e.g. human resources. Hence the diminishing percentage of persons in the older age brackets: 31.5% in the 36-50 group and only 2% who are 51 or older.

Section 2: Results

A. Determination of the various indices

Several types of indices were identified. We first constructed "psychometric" indices, which attempt to reflect the overconfident behaviour of the participants. Next, following Shiller (2000a), we developed indices for speculative bubbles.

1. Overconfidence scores

We calculated three types of overconfidence index. Each of these types corresponds to one of the forms of overconfidence exhibited, i.e. calibration error, the "above-average" effect, and illusion of control and unrealistic optimism (Glaser and Weber (2004) as well as Biais, Hilton, Mazurier, and Pouget (2002), and Odean (1998) have listed and described these various forms of overconfidence).

➢ Calibration error (indices EC1 and EC2)

In order to obtain an index for calibration error the questionnaire asked two types of question, which led to the construction of two indices for this kind of overconfidence, which we call EC1 and EC2. The first series of questions concerned general culture. It was based on the questionnaire suggested by Russo and Schoemaker (1992), and corresponded to the first series of questions in our questionnaire. This is a widely-used method for measuring calibration error (for reviews of the literature on this subject see Lichtenstein, Fischhoff, and Phillips (1982), Yates (1990), Keren (1991), also McClelland and Bolger (1994)). The responses were processed as follows: we counted the number of answers for which the correct answer fell outside the 90% confidence interval given by the participant. This gave the percentage of errors committed by each professional investor. Note that this error percentage should be 10% for a good (well-calibrated) estimator. The results from this series of questions are summarized in Table 1. The mean error percentage is 69.79%, and the median is approximately the same (70%). These figures are sharply higher than those that might have been expected if the investors had been good estimators, i.e. 10%. This testifies to the existence of considerable overconfidence among the participants. Our results match previous studies on this subject (see the studies listed by Hilton (2001)). Russo and Schoemaker (1992) found error percentages of between 42% and 64%.

Table 1. Overconfidence indices connected to calibration error

Calibration error	**Mean error percentage**	**Median error percentage**	**Standard deviation**	**Number of observations**
Questions on general culture *(Index EC1)*	69.79%	70%	23.32%	57
Questions on equity-market predictions *(Index EC2)*	47.37%	40%	28.7%	57

The second series of questions concerned the three-month estimates of the traders and managers regarding various French stock-market indices and equities.

As above, the answers to these questions enabled the construction of a second overconfidence index, also related to the first kind of bias. For each person, we calculated the percentage of correct answers falling outside his/her suggested 90% confidence interval (Table 1 summarizes our results). The mean error percentage found was 47.4%, the median being 40%. The results are again sharply higher than the 10% result that might have been expected if the participants had been good estimators. However, note that these results, although close, are significantly lower than those from similar studies of share-price predictions, for which this percentage was located between 61% and 83% (see the study by Glaser and Weber (2007), also the article by Hilton (2001) summarizing several other studies). This slight difference may be explained by considering the period during which we conducted our study. During the months of September and October 2004 the equity markets were playing a waiting game, which may explain why, for three-month predictions, the number of errors was slightly lower than the number in comparable studies. This is confirmed when the professional investors are asked to give their opinions on equity prices in France. Of the 57 participants, 31 (54%) considered that when comparing French equity prices against measures of their underlying values, the equity prices appeared to be about right.

➢ **"Better Than Average" effect (Indices BTA1 and BTA2)**

We attempted to determine the level of the "Better Than Average" effect via two questions concerning the investors' skill and performance as compared with others:

1) ***Among the operators you know personally, what percentage possess better abilities than you for identifying shares that will have better average performances in future?***

Your answer: (give a percentage)

2) ***Among the operators you know, what percentage have obtained better results than you during the time you have occupied this position?***

Your answer: (give a percentage)

For each of the i individuals and for each of these questions, we determined overconfidence indices BTA1 and BTA2, following Glaser and Weber (2007):

- $\textbf{BTA1i} = \dfrac{50 - answer1i}{50}$
- $\textbf{BTA2i} = \dfrac{50 - answer2i}{50}$

Then: if BTAi > 0, individuals consider themselves to be above average
if BTAi < 0, individuals consider themselves to be below average
if BTAi = 0, individuals consider themselves to be average

Both indices are nil if the individuals consider themselves to be average. In contrast, if individuals consider themselves to be better than average, the value of these indices is located within the interval [0,1]. Conversely, if individuals consider themselves to be not as good as the average, the value of these indices falls within the interval [-1,0]. Our results are summarized in Table 2. The two average indices BTA1 and BTA2 are both positive, and have the values 0.39 and 0.36 respectively. Since both of these indices are also substantially greater than 0, they testify to a significant "above-average" effect among the participants. The indices are also greater than the indices measured by Glaser and Weber (2007). Those authors obtained scores of 0.12 and 0.06 for indices BTA1 and BTA2 respectively. These differences may be related to the intrinsic nature of the population investigated. Glaser and Weber (2007) were interested in private investors registered on online brokerage sites, whereas our study addressed professional investors in the equity markets. This also supports the conclusion of Griffin and Tversky (1992), according to which persons who are experts display a higher level of overconfidence than do relatively inexperienced persons.

Table 2. Overconfidence indices related to the "above-average" effect

"Above-average" effect	**Mean**	**Median**	**Standard deviation**	**Number of observations**
Question 1	30.58	30	15.24	57
Question 2	26.32	30	14.6	57
Index BTA 1	0.39	0.4	0.3	57
Index BTA 2	0.36	0.4	0.29	57

➢ **Illusion of control and unrealistic optimism (IC index)**

This concept corresponds to the third kind of overconfidence. We determined an index for this aspect of overconfidence, again following the methodology of Glaser and Weber (2007), using the following series of questions:

Assign a score between 1 (strongly agree) and 5 (strongly disagree) concerning the following four questions:

	1	*2*	*3*	*4*	*5*
I never buy shares that subsequently underperform					
I cannot identify shares that will subsequently over-perform					
Buying shares is like buying lottery tickets					
My predictions of future prices are always accurate					

The final index IC is obtained by taking the arithmetic mean of four sub-indices. The average of the IC indices is 49%, and the median is 50%. However, note that the standard deviation is relatively high (0.18) which indicates a considerable scatter of IC index values among professional investors.

2. Speculative-bubble indices

Three types of index are considered here. The first type of index to be determined is the index of expectation of positive or negative speculative bubbles (indices ABS+ and ABS-). This index was first introduced by Shiller (2000a). The index enables a contextualization of our own study by viewing it in the context of the economic situation at the time, i.e. during the last quarter of 2004. The two indices that we then determine are obtained from the preceding analysis, allowing them to be compared with the overconfidence indices calculated earlier. Our results (see table 3 and 4) show that the index of expectation of a positive speculative bubble (ABS+) (that could be seen as an estimate of the percentage of professional investors who expect a positive speculative bubble) is 25.22 in our study.

Table 3. Sub-indices for positive speculative bubbles

Toohigh&up	Updown	Riseforwhile	Seeoptimism	Up&crash	ABS+ index
0	0.123	0.24	0.6	0.298	**25.22**

The index for the expectation of a negative speculative bubble (ABS-index, see table 4), is 30.42 in our study (see Table 4).

Table 4. Sub-indices for negative speculative bubbles

Toolow&down	Downup	Fallforwhile	Seepessimism	ABS- index
0.105	0.013	0.487	0.611	**30.42**

When we compare the indices calculated above with those of Shiller (2000a), the purpose of whose article was to compare these indices over time between 1989 and 1998, we observe that they are very close to the ones he calculated in 1991. In 1991, Shiller's ABS+ index was 25.02. The one in our study, carried out in 2004, is 25.22. Similarly, the ABS- index for the same year was 29.08 for Shiller and 30.42 for 2004 in our study (Shiller's ABS+ index ranged between 14.2087 and 30.8198 during his study (going from 1989 to 1998); the ABS- index ranged between 16.3758 and 37.7014 over the same period). Shiller's study also addressed institutional investors, but on the American equity market. However, there are similarities between the economic climates of these two periods. Firstly, both are post-crash periods. In 1991, four years had passed since the 1987 crash. Similarly, in 2004, the date of this study, four years had also elapsed since the bursting of the internet bubble in 2000. These events must still have been present in the memories of the 1991 investors studied by Shiller, just as in our 2004 study. Accordingly, it is not surprising to find that these indices are not only close to Shiller's 1991 ones, but that they are also very close to each other. The ABS+ and ABS- indices are both near 30. In other words, 30% of the professional market investors questioned between September and October 2004 were expecting a positive speculative bubble, and 30% a negative one. All this testifies to the great uncertainty, even mistrust, concerning the markets that was exhibited during 2004, especially by institutional investors. We will return to this subject later on.

Since the indices for the expectation of a speculative bubble calculated by Shiller (2000a) reflect only the overall feeling of a population concerning the movement of the market, we will now calculate two other types of index connected to the concept of a bubble and derived from the preceding questions. This time the indices will be individual, and will enable a comparison with the overconfidence indices.

- **Index of the expectation of a stock-market crash (Probkrach)**

We asked the participants to indicate what, according to them, the probability was of a stock-market crash occurring in France during the next six months, while also taking into account the possibility of a crash occurring in other countries and having repercussions in France. The Probkrach index is then defined as the probability associated with the answer to this question, for each of the investors.

We immediately note a very surprising initial result which supports the preceding comments concerning investors' mistrust of the markets. We find that the index averaged 22.67% (the median being 20%). This means that the probability of the occurrence of a stock-market crash in the six months following our study was estimated by our population to be, on average, 22.67%. This index will be discussed in greater detail later on.

The next section presents the results concerning the processing of these various indices.

B. Results of the study

In view of the number of participants in our study, i.e. 57, it was decided to process the questionnaires as a single batch, without creating occupational sub-groups to separate the traders from the share managers. As mentioned earlier, our aim was to select professional investors for the investigation according to two major criteria: they should not only have a certain distance from the financial markets, but should also be decision-makers. These two aspects represent two essential functions in the occupations targeted by our study. In the following sections the results of processing the questionnaires will be presented via a series of correlation matrices, to throw light on the way in which the concepts of overconfidence and speculative bubbles, the subjects of our study, are related.

1. Correlation of overconfidence indices

We first examine the linkages that may exist between the three kinds of overconfidence. Here we compare our results with the only other study known to us (Glaser and Weber, 2007) which also attempted to understand how these various kinds of overconfidence were connected. The objective of the Glaser and Weber study was to identify the link that might exist between overconfidence and trading volume.

Table 5 shows the correlation coefficients of the five overconfidence indices, and the significance levels for each correlation.

First of all, the two calibration-error indices for the first kind of overconfidence, EC1 and EC2, are positively correlated at the 1% significance level ($p = 0.000$). Although these two indices were calculated from a series of questions of different types (the first concerning general culture and the second predictions of share prices), the fact that significant correlations were found between these two indices nevertheless confers an empirical validity on the concept of calibration error.

In just the same way, the two indices reflecting the "above-average" effect, BTA1 and BTA2, are also positively correlated at the 1% significance level ($p = 0.000$), again conferring an empirical validity on this concept. Glaser and Weber (2007) also found correlations between their two calibration-error indices, and between their two other indices, for the "Better Than Average" effect.

Table 5. Indices correlation Matrix

		EC1	EC2	ADM1	ADM2	IC	PROBKRACH
EC1	Corrélation de Pearson	1.000	.566(**)	.026	-.003	.139	.301(*)
	Valeur de p	.	.000	.857	.987	.301	.023
	Nombre d’observations	57	57	57	57	57	57
EC2	Corrélation de Pearson	.566(**)	1.000	.179	.081	.278(*)	.189
	Valeur de p	.000	.	.205	.609	.037	.160
	Nombre d’observations	57	57	57	57	57	57
ADM1	Corrélation de Pearson	.026	.179	1.000	.729(**)	.386(**)	.058
	Valeur de p	.857	.205	.	.000	.005	.685
	Nombre d’observations	57	57	57	57	57	57

ADM2	**Corrélation de Pearson**	-.003	.081	.729(**)	1.000	.253	.084
	Valeur de p	.987	.609	.000	.	.106	.595
	Nombre d'observations	57	57	57	57	57	57
IC	**Corrélation de Pearson**	.139	.278(*)	.386(**)	.253	1.000	-.137
	Valeur de p	.301	.037	.005	.106	.	.308
	Nombre d'observations	57	57	57	57	57	57
PROBKRACH	**Corrélation de Pearson**	.301(*)	.189	.058	.084	-.137	1.000
	Valeur de p	.023	.160	.685	.595	.308	.
	Nombre d'observations	57	57	57	57	57	57

* : $0.01<p<0.05$
** : $p<0.01$

The EC2 and IC indices are both positively correlated at the 5% significance level (p = 0.037). This result seems reasonable. This correlation indicates that the more persons overestimate their ability to predict share-price movements, the more they have the impression that they can predict or control the markets.

The BTA1 and IC indices are both positively correlated at the 1% significance level (p = 0.005). This also seems reasonable. A positive correlation between these two indices means that persons who consider themselves to be above average in their ability to analyse the equity market will have a greater tendency to think that the market is predictable. Glaser and Weber (2007), however, found a negative correlation between these two concepts (with a significance level of 1%, p = 0.001). Moreover, the authors were surprised by this result, and were unable to explain it.

The other correlations between overconfidence indices are not significant (a result also shared with Glaser and Weber, 2007).

2. Correlation of overconfidence indices and speculative bubbles

The EC1 and ProbKrach (see table 5) indices are positively correlated at the 5% significance level (p = 0.023). This correlation indicates that the more overconfident persons are (under the first kind of overconfidence), the more they feel that the probability of a near-term stock-market crash is high. At first sight this result may appear surprising, even absurd. It says that the more overconfident persons are, the less confidence they have in the movements of stock-market prices. However, this can be explained, specifically by the comment made a little earlier during the interpretation of Shiller's indices of expectation of a speculative bubble (Shiller, 2000a). We then emphasized the great uncertainty, even distrust or lack of confidence, regarding the markets exhibited by institutional investors, especially during 2004. Thus overconfidence, in one sense of the term, would conceal a lack of confidence (in another sense), connected in particular to the difficulty of interpreting the underlying economic models. Table 5 does not indicate any relationship connecting the two other kinds of overconfidence (the "Better Than-average" effect and the illusion of control "IC") with the Probkrach index.

Conclusion

This article describes a questionnaire-based study of 57 institutional investors in the French equity markets. The study had two objectives.

First, we wanted to determine whether issues of overconfidence, a bias widely discussed in the academic literature, were indeed a feature of the equity markets. To our knowledge, our study is the only one to have attempted to identify these biases among professional market investors. To do this we calculated a number of overconfidence indices related to the three kinds of overconfidence listed in the literature. The results show that not only are the first two kinds of overconfidence - calibration error and the "above-average" effect - indeed found among institutional investors, but also that these "psychometric" measurements are empirically reliable. During the study we also demonstrated, in particular by using an index (Probkrach) derived from our questionnaire, the existence of a lack of confidence among these institutional investors. This agrees with the results obtained by Kirchler and Maciejowsky (2002), according to which the subjects of their experiment could simultaneously have both too much and too little confidence.

The second objective of this study was to throw light on the way in which the concepts of overconfidence on the one hand, and speculative bubbles on the other hand, might be interrelated. We found no direct connection between the overconfidence index and the index for an inclination towards herd behaviour. On the other hand, we found significant positive correlations between the EC1 and Probkrach indices. Therefore not only is the first kind of overconfidence an empirically valid concept, but this kind of overconfidence is also the only kind exhibiting a connection with mass events. In this case the connection means that the more overconfident persons are, the more they think that there is a high probability of a stock-market crash in the near term. Overconfidence (in this primary sense) thus conceals a certain lack of confidence among investors, a lack connected to the difficulty of interpreting the underlying economic models. All this then testifies to the coexistence on the markets of both too much and too little confidence.

Finally, we think that use of this type of "psychometric" index, measured among the market actors themselves, could also shed new light on a number of other problems arising in the financial field. In our opinion the number of questionnaires was too small for the effective application of data-mining algorithms; however, Quinlan (1993) has suggested a solution that is suitable for small samples, from which we have obtained significant results. A return to this questionnaire four years after the collapse of Lehman Brothers would provide information on the effectiveness of this method.

References

Biais, B., D. Hilton, K. Mazurier and S. Pouget, (2002), "Psychological traits and trading strategies", *Working Paper (39)*, University of Salerno.

Glaser, M. and M. Weber (2007), "Overconfidence and trading volume", The Geneva Risk and Insurance Review, 2007 - Springer

Godechot, O. (2005), *Essai de sociologie des marchés financiers*, La découverte, June.

Griffin, D. and A. Tversky (1992), "The weighing of evidence and determinants of overconfidence", *Cognitive Psychology*, 24, 3, 411-435.

Hilton, D. (2001), "The psychology of financial decision making: Application to trading, dealing, and investment analysis", *Journal of Psychology and Financial Markets,* 2, 37-53.

Hirshleifer, D., A. Subrahmanyam, and S. Titman (1994), "Security analysis and trading patterns when some investors receive information before others », *Journal of Finance*, XLIX.

Keren, G. (1991), "Calibration and probability judgements: some critical comments and alternative perspectives", *Journal of Behavioral Decision Making*, 10, 269-278.

Kirchler, E., B., and M. Weber (2001), "Framing effects on asset markets : an experimental analysis", *Discussion Paper,* Humboldt-University of Berlin.

Klayman, J., J., Soll, C. Gonzalès-Vallejo, and S. Barlas (1999), "Overconfidence: It depends how, what, and whom you ask", *Organizational Behavior and Human Decision Processes,* 79, 216-247.

Lichtenstein, S., B. Fischoff, and Phillips, L. D. (1982), "Calibration of probabilities: The state of the art to 1980", *in Kahneman, D., Slovic, P., and Tversky, A. (eds.), Judgment under uncertainty: Heuristics and biases*, 306-334, Cambridge University Press, Cambridge, MA, 1st ed.

McClelland, A. G. R. and F. Bolger (1994), "The calibration of subjective probabilities: theories and models 1980-1993", *In G. Wright and P. Ayton (ED), Subjective probability,* 453-482. Chichester: Wiley.

Nöth, M. and M. Weber (2002), "Information Aggregation with Random Ordering: Cascades and Overconfidence", Economic Journal.

Odean, T. (1998), "Volume, Volatility, price and profit when all traders are above average. ", *Journal of finance*, 53, 6, December, 1887-1934.

Quinlan R., (1993), *C4.5: Programs for Machine Learning*, Morgan Kaufman Publishers.

Russo, J. E. and P. J. H. Schoemaker (1992), "Managing overconfidence", *Sloan Management Review*, XXXIII, 7-17.

Shiller, R. J. (2000a), "Measuring Bubble expectations and investor confidence", *Journal of Psychology and Financial Markets*, 1(1), 49–60, 2000. [CFDP 1212, CFP 1004].

Yates, J. F. (1990), *Judgement and decision making,* Englewood Cliffs, NJ: Prentice Hall.

THE GOVERNANCE OF PORTS IN THE MEDITERRANEAN: MUTATION AND CHALLENGES

LAURENT FEDI[1] AND ISABELLE PIGNATEL[2]

"The Mediterranean, the sea that is close to us." Platon.

Introduction

The major transformations in the maritime industry at the end of the 20th century dramatically changed the status of commercial ports. Revitalized by the flourishing Chinese economy (Tourret & Lacoste, 2007), the Asian ports were at the forefront of the international scene, taking the lead in containerized tonnage. The Mediterranean ports, although more modest in their performance compared to their Asian counterparts, nevertheless went through major evolutions. Faced with specialization, the increase in the size of ships (Wijnolst & Weregland, 2009), and the development of containerized traffic and its multimodal impact, the maritime ports of the Mediterranean continuously adapted in a context of increased competition destroying the advantages of their geographic situation in favour of the demands of logistical *supply chains*. The port managers had to and must still continue to develop their domain with a view to optimizing operations, the "terminalization" of the port area (Slack, 2005), as well as improving security, in particular under the instigation of the Code ISPS (2002) but also American and European regulations. Confronted *a fortiori* with the financial withdrawal of states, it has become essential to resort more to private funds for the long term development of these Mediterranean ports, notably those belonging to the MEDA countries associated with the European Union.

[1] Euromed Management, Laurent.fedi@euromed-management.com
[2] Euromed Management, Isabelle.pignatel@euromed-management.com

In the context of globalization, these States, notably those of the south bank of the Mediterranean, are currently faced with a stake which is threefold: the liberalization of their economies, the need to modernize transport infrastructures, and in particular to cope with the rapid growth of containerized traffic, which has become, following the example of all the commercial ports, the strategic core activity of their development. To meet these new challenges, the majority of Mediterranean countries have begun statutory reforms tending to transpose the exploitation methods of the "*landlord port*" from the north of Europe, in which the land and the infrastructures remain the port's property but with the operations of the equipment being operated by private companies. Therefore, their management was progressively liberalized without necessarily being totally privatized. The majority of these Mediterranean ports remain statutorily public bodies, under state authority, of a collectivity or a public organization. And yet to get these funds, ports must be attractive; namely, they must represent a long term and profitable investment.

More and more ports are becoming strategic interfaces and the question of "good governance" is being asked with growing intensity. Having been the subject of national studies (Baird, 2000) and comparisons (Debrie et al, 2007), port governance is not a new problem. In today's context, these different approaches, as pertinent as they may seem, (Comtois et al, 2003), deserve to be completed, notably in their models of analysis and in their field of application. The authors believe that they do not sufficiently focus on the Mediterranean ports and more specifically their governing boards. As their new operations' models show, the key success factors of the Mediterranean ports are no longer linked to their geographic position but to the quality of their governance and to their economic performance **(I)**. However, the governing boards, instruments for port governance, have been the subject of very few studies. The absence of research is quite surprising in a context of multiple reforms that remodel the composition and the mission of these decision-making bodies **(II)**.

I – New Operations Modalities and Port Governance in the Mediterranean

Over the past 20 years, the value of international business in the MEDA countries has increased by 250%, with a total of foreign direct investment that has multiplied by 6 in just several years (Bessamra et al, 2007). The Mediterranean, being a strategic zone for maritime transport, represents 30% of total world maritime traffic, of which 28% is hydrocarbons

(Ortolan, 2009). In view of the investments made by ship owners' and the handling operators, the strategic role of the Mediterranean ports no longer needs to be proven (Musso, 2005). The provisional flows of maritime traffic are set to double between now and 2020 with an exponential growth of captive freight and transhipment. The creation of the Union for the Mediterranean (COM, 2008) should act as an accelerator for these exchanges. And yet, the Mediterranean ports of both North and South banks, due to their inferior dimensions, their lack of reliability and competitiveness, have not always been very reassuring to investors; quite the contrary. In the Nineties, certain Southern European governments, such as Italy and Spain, began a decentralization movement along with institutional reforms in order to compensate for these shortcomings. The recent French port reform (Rézenthel, 2008), likewise the new Code of maritime ports in Tunisia, testify that this tendency is still relevant today. New port management models have been put into place **(A)**, accompanied by a new philosophy of governance **(B)**.

A – The New Port Operations' Models

The leading idea of port reforms put into place by the different states bordering the zone lies in a profound liberalization of the port sector. The objective of these reforms is clearly aimed at responding to the developments in business and international maritime transport, whose exponential growth has caused major upheavals more notably in the levels of the diverse merchandise and passenger sector. The increase in volumes handled, supported by the gigantism of the container and cruise ships, has greatly altered the dimensions of reception infrastructures. It is in this context of adaptation to new maritime industry standards that a real dynamic of liberalization and decentralization of port management has come about, encouraging new port operations' models.

Classified by the World Bank into 4 models (World Bank Port Reform Toolkit), the typology of the government of commercial ports varies, with a pointer that swings between centralized, decentralized or private management. The choice of operational model is wide, going from the *service port model,* under public control for land and commercial operations, to the *tool port service,* mainly public, but with some private operators for certain port services, to the *landlord port model,* where the plots of land belong to the port authority but whose equipment operations are carried out by private operators, to lastly the *private service port,* operated and managed by private companies for regalian as well as commercial operations. In addition to this quartet of models, where the roles of the public and private sector are clearly defined, the distribution of roles is, in practice, more complex (Balthazar and Brooks, 2001), *a fortiori* with local specificities (Brooks, 2004). Dr. Robert Rézenthel accurately demonstrated that the choice of management regime is determined by the state, who defines the status of its ports (Rézenthel, 1996). The key changes in Mediterranean port reforms lie mainly in an increased autonomy of the port authorities, a redefinition of their prerogatives and the liberalization of certain activities that historically have been monopolistic. Although administrative autonomy already exists in certain states, such as France with its *independent ports* or Italy with its *port consortium,* it was necessary to recreate or reinforce it for others, notably from a budgetary and financial point of view. In certain countries this autonomy goes hand in hand correlatively with the contractualization of relations between the state and its ports: concession contracts for the Greek port authorities (Pallis, 2007), long term contract and strategic plan for the major French maritime ports, 3 year plan for the Italian ports (Valleri et al, 2007), 5 year investment plan for the Spanish (Vaello, 2008) or Turkish ports (Oral et al, 2007). Concerning the port authorities' new missions, these consist of a clear separation between the regalian and commercial activities. Imposed *de facto* by economic constraints linked to the withdrawal of public finances and the growing need for investments, this dividing line has been formalized by the legislator. To summarize, the port managers remain public operators but concentrate on playing the role of infrastructure developer, of promoter and regulator. The financing and the commercial operations of the superstructure – equipment, terminals – is dedicated to private operators who play a significant part in the port's development. The aligning of the Mediterranean ports with those of Northern Europe is indisputable. To summarize, beyond the liberalization and the demonopolization of activities like stevedoring, port services or the relaxing of the regulations for state administered property, these new operations' models of the Mediterranean ports allow the port establishments more flexibility and entrepreneurial freedom, thus enabling them to become full-fledged economic actors. Their financial function is reinforced as they can create subsidiaries, joint-ventures (Nemouchi, 2007), purchase shares in private companies, allocate dedicated terminals (Cappocaccia, 2007; Rézenthel, 2008; Fedi and Rézenthel, 2007), etc., but their risk taking is therefore correlatively more important. The public-private partners have become *a condition sine qua non* for the future of port infrastructures (Merlin, 2009; Rézenthel, 2007). Generally speaking, the authors can claim that the perimeter of public port service (Rézenthel,

2009) of the Mediterranean ports strongly tends to be reduced to the fields of security, safety, the protection of the environment, while allowing more place for private entrepreneurship.

B – A new Philosophy for port Governance

"Governance" is defined *stricto sensu* as the *"system by which the firm is managed and controlled. The governance structure defines the allocation of rights and responsibilities amongst the different actors of the firm"* (OECD, 1999). If generally, the port in its legal form is not a private company, it functions as such and has governance structures more and more similar to the example of the board of directors and supervisory board implemented in the major maritime ports by the French port reform (Rézenthel, 2009b). *Lato sensu*, port governance is the "process of coordinating private and public actors who run the different port functions at all the levels of this port game" (Debrie and Gouvernal, 2008). The governance of a port is therefore complex as many more actors are implicated in the less corporatist interests than in the past, but which remain specific. Consequently, the governance of the port must be adapted to the needs of maritime and logistic operators who use the port space, whilst taking into consideration the demands of local and regional political bodies. Faced with these constraints, achieving a balance is not easy considering that the governance structure must be representative of these various interests in the port milieu and at the same time not be too complex. In order to make this industrial instrument competitive, priority must be given to recentralizing its governance on missions that are less wide than in the past, whilst, however, using a more systemic approach. Although the port managers concentrate on their new strategic functions – development of the port area, promotion – and regalian functions – security, safety – they are now involved in issues that go beyond just the maritime infrastructures. They participate directly in the dimensioning and the quality of the road transport and rail networks, the intermodal connections, the logistics' platforms, the dry ports (Debry and Ruby, 2009) etc., as everything that is upstream or downstream to the passage in the port has a direct incidence on the port's performance. Finally, this governance must be proactive, favouring evolutions in the transport and logistics' markets (Martin-Puerta et al, 2009). The need for reactivity is more important than in the last century due to the rapidity of the changes in these markets. Bearing in mind the perspectives for economic development in the Mediterranean zone, these sectors' needs are forever on the increase. To satisfy the demands of this new environment, which requires more anticipation in the decision process and more competitiveness in its economic performance, the composition of the governing boards plays a determining role.

II – The Governing Boards of Ports and their Impact on Performance

Firstly, the authors shall present the governing board as an essential instrument for good governance and explain the relationship between the composition of the governing board and the performance of the firm **(A)**. Secondly, they shall highlight the principle characteristics of port governance resulting from the different reforms **(B)**.

A - The Governing Board: an Essential Instrument for good Governance

Literature recognizes the different roles of the governing board (Pignatel, 2007), controlling, linking, or one of encouragement. This board plays a central role as described in the agency theory, a role of ratifying decisions and controlling their implementation (Fama and Jensen, 1983). Subsequently, it is an internal mechanism responsible for inciting the C.E.Os to be highly competitive and if the contrary were to be true, it is responsible for getting rid of them. As demonstrated by Pfeffer (1972) or Burt (1980) in their resource dependence theory, the governing board can be seen as a link, as a mechanism that allows the firm's dependence on the exterior to be managed and reduces environmental uncertainty. Lastly, it can be seen as encouragement, as a support for management as shown in the managerial hegemony theory, where the directors remain under the influence of the management and consequently the governing board has a purely ceremonial role (Mace, 1971). This key role of the governing board is also recognized in the rules of good governance, which are vigilant to the optimal functioning conditions of this decision-making body. Its composition, as well as that of the 3 committees supporting it, and more specifically the independent character of their members, is the object of careful scrutiny. The existence of rules and regulations standardizing its execution and the adoption of a self-evaluation are expected by the stakeholders, recipients of the financial communication. The governing board is the guarantor of the transparency that is necessary to obtain the trust of investors, notably on difficult points such as the C.E.O.s remuneration, the attribution of stock options or the approval of the accounts; perfectly summarized by Coulson-Thomas:

> "The governing board must be the heart and the soul of the company, the source of its ambition and its conduct. The fact that a company wins and is competitive, succeeds and remains competitive generally depends on its governing board. Without a defined objective, an alleged strategy and the desire to succeed, well-established groups can decline and die".

More so than before, the study of the doctrine on the composition of governing boards offers a wealth of lessons. Going back to the studies of Hobson and Jeidels (Fennema and Schijif, 1978), this research is not up to date and focuses initially on relations between the industry and the bank via the bodies in authority, with the researchers then trying to establish a link between the composition of the governing boards and firm performance. To be more precise, they have tried to establish the board composition which optimizes the firm's performance. These different studies have underlined certain tendencies without however being able to establish any certainties behind them. As a result, the presence of internal directors, though they may have privileged relations with the C.E.O., relations which may be harmful to their implication and autonomy, would have a positive impact on firm performance (Baker and Gompers, 2003). Inversely, the presence of external directors, particularly sought-after for their disciplinary role, paradoxically would not have an influence on performance (Pearce and Zahra, 1992). Lastly, even if independent directors are the guarantee of good governance, the independence of the board is not connected with firm performance (Bhagat and Black, 2001).

This research on the link composition/performance has been extended to all the stake-holders. Since then, the presence of women, bankers, employees, main shareholders, the C.E.O., directors' "accumulators" and even directors creating reciprocal links between boards has been thoroughly examined (Pignatel, 2007). More widely speaking, with a view to the *business case*, diversity within the governing board would seem to be a source of improved performance and constitute a differentiating factor in a sector of activity. Thus, within the same sector of activity, firms with the same recruitment policies, using the same processes, with a similar management will achieve different performances linked solely to the role of the governing board: *"To be more precise, the directors and the boards of successful companies proceed differently"* (Coulson-Thomas, 2007). If the governing board is the centrepiece of governance, and its composition a guarantee of performance, where does this leave port governance?

B – An Inventory of the Different Reforms Related to Port Governance in the Mediterranean

Port governance should be specific to this sector of activity. Here the authors are inspired by and follow on from the research carried out by Schmidt (1975), who analysed the composition of governing boards in the chemistry sector, or Coles' (2005) research on the impact of the diversification of the firm's activities on its governance, or lastly Pignatel's (2007) research on the lesser degree of openness of the governing boards in the construction, commercial, automobile reparation and domestic articles' sectors of activity. It would therefore seem that each sector of activity has its own type of governance and a governing board whose composition is often quite specific. Whereas the doctrine accurately identifies both the new issues at stake in port governance (Verhoeven, 2009) and the performance indicators inherent to this sector (Brooks and Pallis, 2008), as far as the authors know, no research has been carried out on the composition of the governing boards of ports. This can probably be explained by the lack of annual reports available or by their brevity with regards to the composition of the so called bodies of authority. The analysis of the different reforms of the Mediterranean ports does however allow us to identify several tendencies. The first being the fact that the port governing boards are more open to economic actors in the sector but also to local public authorities (municipality, territorial, regional). As can be seen in Morocco (Rézenthel, 2007), France or Spain, the objective is to create a synergy of dynamics around the port establishment and a development strategy that is shared by the local actors. Secondly, the reduction of the number of directors is also a prominent tendency; this is the case in France where there is a regulation which dictates the number of directors for each port. The alignment of the governance of port establishments with that of large firms must also be highlighted. Within the framework of the French port reform, a supervisory board and a board of directors have been systematically substituted by one governing board in order to dissociate the mission of control and that of management. These two bodies, characteristic of quoted companies recommended by the NRE and LSF laws, demonstrate the appropriation of the rules of good governance by the port sector. In addition, the administration of a large sea port is supported in its development by a *development board/counsel* which openly brings together the different stakeholders of the port area – from professional, social, associative, and territorial authority backgrounds – but whose role however remains advisory. This form of wider governance can be found in Italy, where the *Port Authority* is administered by a *Port Committee* comprised of 14 members - representatives of local authorities, trade union organizations, port users and port firms – which defines the central strategy of the port backed by an *Audit Committee* that controls the management of the port committee (Valleri et al, 2007).

It is nevertheless necessary to highlight the fact that the majority of decision making bodies of the Mediterranean ports remain, directly or indirectly, under public authority control. Firstly, the nomination of the presidents or directors of the port establishments remains the liability of the executive power. In France, this is the case of the president of the board of directors, after assent of the supervisory committee, the president of the port committee in Italy or the president of the governing board of public interest ports in Spain. The representation and public intervention within the governing bodies of the port is always high (Valleo, 2005) and often controlling. An example of this is Greece, where even though the major ports have been transformed into public companies, Pirea and Thessaloniki having been quoted on the Athens stock exchange (Vaggelas, 2007), public intervention remains high. In the same way, the directors' field of action is strictly limited, particularly when the occupation of the public port zone is at stake. Despite a reinforced autonomy of the port entities, as well as a more flexible legal framework for the concession regime applicable to port operations, the development projects require the authorization of one or several state authorities. As can be seen from the French regulations, public investments also remain closely supervised (Rézenthel, 2008). *A fortiori*, the public bodies in charge of the Maghreb ports, following the example of the *National Ports' Agency* of Morocco or Algeria, the *Office of the Merchant Navy and Ports* of Tunisia of the *Ente Pùblico Puertos del Estato* in Spain, of the *General Directorate for the Construction of Railways, Ports and Airports* in Turkey etc., clearly illustrate that the port sector remains a strategic sector of public interest requiring a certain amount of "monitoring". The qualification of the major Spanish ports as "general interest ports" reveals the influence of this strategic function. However, in order to be efficient and reactive faced with future challenges, the authors believe that these ports must be managed in a more autonomous manner without the intervention of public hierarchy in the decision making process. Just like the unique shareholding of the Algerian government in *Sogeports* – *(*Société de gestion des participations de l'État Ports - The Company for the Management of the Participations of State Ports) – or the Moroccan government in the company *Société d'operations des ports (The Port Operations Company)*, progress needs to be made in the liberalization and the transparency of port management (Rézenthel, 2008). At the same time, the fact that certain private operators are judge and jury, continuing to sit on the decision making bodies of certain ports, must not be ignored (Demangeon, 2008).

Conclusion

At one moment or another in their development, all commercial ports are confronted with the necessity to change their form of governance. The Mediterranean ports are no exception to this problem, all the more so as many ports had fallen behind the times due to their governance systems, which were centralized or falsely decentralized to the benefit of establishments whose autonomy was limited or not very efficient. The movement towards the reform of Mediterranean port governance is from now on inevitable and is reaching its phase of maturity. Having started in the Nineties and lasting through to the beginning of the 21st century, the Spanish, Italian, Greek, French, or Maghreb countries' port reforms prove that the process is often long, sometimes even empirical (Pallis, 2007), requiring several legislative interventions to bring the necessary standardizing tools for the institutional and organizational advancements. The port environment, a "stronghold" fiercely protected by certain corporate professions, remains resistant to change. However, could this also be linked to the maritime milieu which is also attached to defending its sometimes ancient customs? Following the example of the Maghreb countries, this wave of reform is very strong, whose aim is to modernize and develop infrastructures in order to offer more efficient services. These reforms must support the major port construction sites such as the deep water terminal of Tanger-Med in Morocco, Enfidha in Tunisia, in Algeria with Djen Djen the port of Alger, (Nemouchi, 2007) or again in France with Fos 2/3XL. It is important to note that although in general, the majority of these dedicated terminals in the Mediterranean ports are managed by private operators, very few are totally privatized. Taking into consideration the reforms that are underway and those in the process of finalization, it is too early to evaluate the consequences. More precisely, the efficiency of the changes in the governance of the Mediterranean ports remains to be proven. Many specialists are in agreement that this succession of reforms still does not give enough managerial and operational autonomy to port managers who are still subjected to as much bureaucratic complexity due to the structures of the state authorities as well as from political interference (Valleri, 2007). These constraints slow down the decision making process and reactivity and therefore the strategic development of the port, limited more to offering basic services to the detriment of those with value added. Criticism of this situation is particularly strong in Italy, Greece and Turkey. Moreover port competition exists on two levels; within the Mediterranean ports and also between measures implemented by the different states. The lack of coherence between the ports' individual strategies and the cannibalization of their markets has made it necessary to introduce a superior regulatory body. In this particular case, the French Inter Port Coordination Committee or the National Centre for Port Development in Greece (Pallis, 2007) serve as models. The case of the Mediterranean, with its waves of reforms, clearly demonstrates the relevance of our questioning on the search for the best possible governance of ports, which would guarantee the success of the various reforms and the improvement of the models of port governance (Musso, 2006). Nevertheless the ad-hoc governing board alone cannot be the guarantor of the success of the port; the environment will play a role, as can be seen by the integrative model by Pearce and Zahra (1989). A group of key success factors will promote the attractiveness of a port area, from the legal and financial framework, the legal security which will result from this, the richness of the hinterland, the transport services and infrastructures surrounding the port, the logistical schemas of the maritime operators, etc. Lastly, beyond governance, the authors agree with Dr. Robert Rézenthel (1996) who considers that there does not exist an *"ideal legal regime for the management of ports, otherwise we would know about it"*. However if the port regimes continue to vary from one Mediterranean state to another, it is necessary to highlight the strong tendency towards the recentralization of the port establishments' missions who no longer devote themselves (with the occasional exception) to the equipment operations, to the advantage of private operators. Although they are not perfectly transposable to all the ports, the distribution of competencies is simple: the public sector focuses on its functions of developer contractor, property and environment manager, of planning and regulating, of promoting their port space, and the private sector finances and ensures the equipment operations of the terminals. In order for this partnership to obtain good economic results, initiatives must be taken and innovation must not be neglected (Rézenthel, 2008b)!

References

Baker, M. and Gompers, P.A., 2003, "The Determinants of Board Structure at the Initial Public Offering", Journal of Law and Economics, V.46, p. 569-598.

Baird, A.J., 2000, "Port Privatisation: Objectives, Extent, Process and the UK Experience ", *International Journal of Maritime Economics* 2, 177-194

Baltazar, R. and Brooks, M.R., 2001, "The Governance of Port Devolution: a Tale of Two Countries", World Conference on Transport Research Seoul Korea.

Bessamra, S. and Saint-Laurent, B., 2007, "Investir dans la Région MEDA : pourquoi, comment ", Notes et Etudes Anima n° 22, April, p. 17.

Bhagat, S. and Black, B., 2001, "The non-correlation between board independence and long term firm performance", Journal of Corporation Law, V.27, 2001, p. 231-274.

Brooks, E., 2004, "The Governance Structure of Ports", Review of Networks Economics, vol. 3, Issue 2 – June, p. 168.

Brooks, M.R. and Pallis, A.A., 2008, "Assessing port governance models: process and performance components ", Maritime Policy and Management, Vol. 35 n° 4, p. 411-432.

Burt, R.S., 1980, "Cooptive Corporate Actor Networks: A Reconsideration of Interlocking Directorates involving American Manufacturing", Administrative Science Quarterly, n°25, p. 557.

Cappocaccia, F., 2007, "Gestion et stratégie des ports, organisation du trafic de marchandises en Méditerranée", communication Ubifrance Paris du 28 novembre 2007.

Code ISPS (2002). Amendements à l'annexe à la Convention internationale de 1974 pour la sauvegarde de la vie humaine en mer, chapitre XI-2. OMI.SOLAS/CONF.5/DC/1 12 décembre 2002. Amendements à l'annexe à la Convention internationale de 1974 pour la sauvegarde de la vie humaine en mer, chapitre XI-2, Annexe 2.

Coles, J.L. ; Naveen, D.D. and Naveen, L., 2005, "Boards : Does One Size Fit All?", Research paper, Georgia State University Research Foundation.

COM. (2008). "Communication de la Commission au Parlement européen et au Conseil : Le processus de Barcelone : Union pour la Méditerranée", document COM(2008) 319/4 du 20 mai 2008.

Comtois, C. and Slack, B., 2003, "Innover l'autorité portuaire au 21ème siècle : un nouvel agenda de gouvernance", Les cahiers scientifiques du transport, n°44, p. 11-24.

Coulson-Thomas, C., 2007, "*The directors and boards of the most successful companies do it differently*; How ''winning'' boards contribute to corporate growth", Business Strategy Series, Vol. 8 n° 5, p. 369-376.

—. 2005, "Creating a winning board: differing approaches of the boards of successful and struggling companies", Industrial and Commercial Training, Vol. 37, N°2, p. 67-72.

Debrie, J. and Ruby, C., 2009, "Approche des réformes portuaires européennes et nord-américaines (Canada) - Eléments de réflexion pour la politique portuaire française", Inrets, April, p. 9-10.

Debrie, J. ; Soppe, M. and Lavaud-Letilleul, V., 2008, "La réforme des ports italiens: éléments de réflexion pour la politique portuaire française", Revue Transport n° 447, January and February, p. 11.

Debrie, J. and Gouvernal, E., 2008, "Les ports : leur rôle, les acteurs, les trafics, la gouvernance portuaire", Inrets, p. 25.

Debrie, J., Gouvernal, E. and Slack, B., 2007, "Downloading Public Ports : challenges of governance for lower tiers of public administration", WCTR - June 24-28 - University of California, Berkeley.

Demangeon, E., 2008, "Entre réformes et privatisation", Bulletin des Transports et de la Logistique, n° 3205 du 7 janvier 2008, p. 7.

Fama, E.F. and Jensen, M.C., 1983, "Separation of Ownership and Control", Journal of Law and Economics, V.26, p. 301-325.

Fedi, L. and Rézenthel, R., 2007, "L'exploitation des terminaux portuaires face aux enjeux maritimes du 21ème siècle", DMF n° 685, October, p. 828.

Fennema, M. and Schijif, H. 1978, "Analysing Interlocking Directorates: Theory and Methods", Social Networks, V.1, p. 297-332.

Hatem, F. ; de Saint-Laurent, M. ; El Yacoubi, Y. and M'khinini, I., 2006, "Les investissements étrangers en transport dans la Région MEDA", Anima n°18, september.

J. Martín-Puerta, Rossend Bosch, B. and de Saint Laurent, B. 2009, "Investissements prioritaires pour le développement de la logistique en Méditerranée", Etude n°4, september, 60 pages.

Mace, M. 1971, "Directors: Myth and Reality", Harvard Graduate School of Business Administration.

Merlin, C., 2009, "Public-Private partnerships in the Port of Marseille", thèse MBA maritime Euromed Management, 329 pages. .

Musso, E., 2006, "La valeur socio-économique des ports", Séminaire EMAR, June, doc. Inrets p. 6.

—. 2005, “Ports and traffic in the Mediterranean arena: an overview”, Corso di Maritime and Port Economics.

Nemouchi, M., 2007, “Développement des ports algériens et opportunités de coopération”, communication Ubifrance Paris, 28th November 2007.

OECD (1999) *OECD Principles of Corporate Governance* (SG/CG(99)5), Paris: Organisation of Economic Co-operation and Development, April.

Oral, E.Z. ; Kisi,H. ; Cerit, A.G. ; Tuna, O. and Esmer, S., 2007, “Port Governance in Turkey”, Research and Transportation Economics, Volume 17, 171-184.

Ortolan, P., 2009, “Observatoire des flux en Méditerranée”, Annales IMTM, p. 147.

Pearce, J.A. II and Zahra, S.A., 1992, “Board Composition from a Strategic Contingency Perspective”, Journal of Management Studies, V.29, n°4, p. 411-438

Pearce, J.A. II. and. Zahra, S.A., 1989, “Boards of Directors and Corporate Financial Performance: A Review and Integrative Model”, V.15, N.2, 291-334.

Pfeffer; J. 1972, “Size and Composition of Corporate Boards of Directors : The Organization and its Environment”. Administrative Science Quarterly, V.17, n° 2, p. 218-229.

Pignatel, I., 2007, “Liens personnels entre les sociétés, contrôle et gouvernance”. Thèse de doctorat, sous la direction du Professeur Claude Bensoussan, Université Aix-Marseille III, 539 pages.

Rézenthel, R., 2008, “Une nouvelle stratégie pour le développement des grands ports maritimes français”, DMF n°643 et 698, p. 1060

—. 2008b, “Réforme portuaire: l’outil et le savoir-faire”, JMM du 18 juillet, p. 8.

—. 2007, “Partenariat public-privé dans les ports maritimes”, Revue du trésor, p. 252.

—. 2008, “La création des grands ports maritimes”, RFDA september-october, p. 969.

—. 2009, “L’évolution du régime des services publics portuaires”, DMF n°704, p. 530.

—. 2009b, “L’évolution de la gestion portuaire”, Les Annales de la voirie, n°133, mars 2009b, p. 7.

—. 1996, “Le droit portuaire : les sources du droit portuaire – les régimes portuaires”, Université de Lille, Tome 1.

—. 2007, “Le nouveau régime des ports marocains: une adaptation au monde contemporain”, DMF n°681, p. 456.

—. 1996, "Le droit portuaire: les sources du droit portuaire – les régimes portuaires", Université de Lille, Tome 1, p. 29. Du même auteur: "Les régimes portuaires dans le monde", DMF, p. 1163

de Saint-Laurent, B. 2007, "Développement économique et défis écologiques en Méditerranée", présentation Assises Economie de la Mer, 13-14 décember.

Schmidt, R., 1975, "The Board of Directors and Financial Interests", Academy of Management Journal, V.20.

Slack, B., 2005, "Terminalisation of ports: an academic question?", Proceedings of the international workshop on new generation of port-cities and their role in global supply chains, 12-14th décember 2005, p. 20-30

Tourret, P. and Lacoste, R. 2007, "1997 – 2007: d'un monde à l'autre", note de synthèse Isemar, décember, n°100.

Vaello, J., 2005, "Implémentation de la réforme portuaire à l'UE: l'Espagne et le port de Valencia", Training Seminar on Port Reform, Marseille, 25-26 september.

Vaggelas, G. K., 2007, "Greeks ports: Structural challenges and Forms of adjustment", Research paper, University of the Agean, Greece.

Valleri, M. A.; Lamonarca, M. and Papa, P., 2007, "Port Governance in Italy", Research in Transportation Economics, volume 17, p. 139-153.

Verhoeven, P., 2009, "European ports policy : meeting contemporary governance challenges", Maritime Policy and Management, Vol. 36 n°1, p. 79-101

Wijnolst, N. and Wergeland, T., 2009, "Shipping innovation", IOS Press BV under Auspices Euromed, 831 p.

World bank Port Reform Toolkit, www.worldbank.org/transport/ports/toolkit/

SOLVENCY AND VALUATION OF BANKS

OLIVIER LEVYNE[1]

Introduction

The Basel 3 environment, which will be the reference from 2013 onwards, is more demanding for banks from a solvency point of view. In that context, the first part of this article highlights the evolution of the regulatory rules from Basel 1 to Basel 3, and proposes, for an illustrative purpose, an example of solvency ratios calculations in Basel 2 and Basel 3 environments. The second part consists in a review of the main valuation methods of banks. This presentation, focused on analogical approaches and dividend discount model, underlines the important role of equity and the weight of the solvency constraints in such calculations. The third part is dedicated to an empirical study. Based on a large sample of European listed banks, it presents confidence intervals for the main relevant multiples; then proposes a tentative correlation analysis between the valuation multiple and the return on equity. Following from the disappointing result of such a study, an analysis of the significant difference between average relevant multiples of banks with low and high solvency ratios is conducted.

1. From Basel 1 Environment to Basel 3

After the series of US savings banks' bankruptcies at the end of the 80s, a new regulation regarding solvency was decided. From 1993 onwards, banks had to present a Cooke ratio, the minimum value of which was 8%. It was defined as the ratio between the bank's equity and its risk weighted assets (RWAs). The equity was broken down into two components: tier 1 and tier 2. Tier 1 was made of shareholders' equity (group share and minority share) and was reduced by goodwills and intangible assets. Tier 2 was made of subordinated debt. As it was relatively easy to raise

[1] PhD in Economics, Advanced PhD in Management Science, Full Professor of Finance at ISC Paris.

subordinated debt, the regulator decided to prevent the bank from financing their assets only by debt and, in that context, the eligibility of tier 2 was limited by tier 1. Assuming the possibility to raise as much subordinated debt as equity, the reference solvency ratio became a 4% tier 1 to RWAs. The risk weighted assets corresponded mainly to credit risks, and the weightings were the following: 0% for credits to States of the OECD countries (and Saudi Arabia), 20% for credits to banks of the aforementioned countries, and 100% for other credits (to corporate bodies and individuals). They also included market risks and guarantees given to clients. In the Basel 2 environment, tier 1 is broken down into core tier 1 and lower tier 1. The core tier 1 corresponds to the tier 1 of the Basel 1 environment, and the lower tier 1 includes super-subordinated debt. This environment is more demanding for various reasons. Firstly, the shareholdings in banks and other credit institutions (banks, consumer credit entities, custodians, etc.) are 50% deducted from tier 1 and 50% deducted from tier 2. Shareholdings in non-consolidated credit institutions are taken into account in the RWAs, with a 300% weight if they are listed, and 400% if they are not. Moreover, shareholdings in insurance companies, whether fully consolidated or consolidated by the equity method from an accounting point of view, are necessarily consolidated by the equity method from a solvency point of view, and are deducted from the total equity without impacting tier 1 and tier 2. The weightings used in the RWAs calculations are based on internal models, which enables having a lower contribution of a loan when the borrower's profile is less risky. The operational risk is also included in the RWAs calculation. The Basel 3 environment will be the new reference from 2013 onwards, but the solvency ratio calculation has already been defined and the brokers appreciate the banks' solvency based on this new methodology, taking the guidances given by the CEOs when they present their quarterly, halfly, and yearly results. The main feature of the Basel 3 rules is the focus on common equity, which has strong similarities with the core tier 1 in the Basel 2 environment. The main difference is that the shareholdings in financial institutions (credit institutions and insurance companies) are fully deducted from the common equity in Basel 3 instead of being deducted from tier 1 and tier 2 or from total solvency equity in Basel 2. The regulator had not given targets for core tier 1 and total tier 1 ratios in the Basel 2 environment. But, from a Basel 3 point of view, minimum levels to be reached were precised in 2010 by the Bank for International Settlements (BIS). The table hereafter presents the progressive levels to be reached from 2013 to 2019 by credit institutions.

Table 1: target core tier 1 and tier 1 ratios from 2013 to 2019

As at 01/01	2013	2014	2015	2016	2017	2018	2019
Minimum Core tier 1 ratio	3.5%	4.0%	4.5%	4.5%	4.5%	4.5%	4.5%
Capital conservation buffer				0.6%	1.3%	1.9%	2.5%
Core tier 1 including capital conservation buffer	3.5%	4.0%	4.5%	5.1%	5.8%	6.4%	7.0%
Share of deductions taken into account		20.0%	40.0%	60.0%	80.0%	100.0%	100.0%
Minimum tier 1 ratio		4.5%	6.0%	6.0%	6.0%	6.0%	6.0%
Minimum total capital ratio			8.0%	8.0%	8.0%	8.0%	8.0%

To reduce the financial constraints, 3 limitations to deductions from common equity have been defined. The significant unconsolidated investments in financial institutions (i.e. representing more than 10% of the issued rights), the mortgage servicing rights (MSRs), and the deferred tax assets (DTAs) arising from timing differences, are not deducted provided they represent less than 10% of the bank's common equity. In other terms, from a solvency point, recognition of each of these 3 assets is capped at 10% of the issued share capital. But the total recognition of the aggregate of these 3 amounts is capped at 15% of the common equity component of tier 1, which is, for that purpose, calculated prior to the deduction of these items but after all the other deductions. Moreover, the recognition of minority interests in common equity is limited so that the excess capital above the minimum solvency capital for a banking subsidiary has to be deducted in proportion to the minority interest share. The following example shows the impact of the evolution of the regulatory constraints from Basel 2 environment to Basel 3 on the core tier 1, tier 1, tier 2, and total solvency ratios. The main specificities are the following points: the core tier 1 of the banking subsidiaries are twice the minimal regulatory level, which implies a 50% decrease in minority interests; investments in banks consolidated by the equity method, the consolidated value of which is 30, are fully deducted from the core tier 1 instead of reducing tier 1 and tier 2 with a 50/50 breakdown; investments in insurance companies, the consolidated value of which is 10, reduce the core tier 1 instead of reducing only the total capital ratio; 8 of the differed tax assets have to be deducted from the core tier 1. But assuming that 5 corresponds to timing differences, this amount is recognized in equity. Moreover, MSR of 6 are also recognized. The investments in financial institutions (banks and insurance companies), the total amount of which is 40, is recognized in the core tier 1 equity only for 10% of core tier 1, before taking the impact of these various items into account. As this intermediate core tier 1 equity is 102, the maximum recognized amount is 10.2. In that context, taking MSR and DTA into account, the total amount of recognitions would be 21.2, whereas it is limited to 15% of 102, i.e. 15.3. Then a 5.9 buffer haircut has to be deducted. The detailed calculations are presented in the table below:

Table 2: solvency ratios comparison in Basel 2 and Basel 3 environments

	Basel II	Basel III
Equity group share	100,0	100,0
Minority interests	20,0	20,0
(Non eligible minority interests)		(10,0)
(Intangible assets and goodwills)	(5,0)	(5,0)
(Differed tax assets which do not arise from timing differences)		(3,0)
Core tier 1 before capped recognition		**102,0**
(Differed tax assets that arise from timing differences)		(5,0)
Buffer on differed tax assets		5,0
(Investments in financial institutions)		(40,0)
Buffer on investments in financial institutions		10,2
(Mortgage servicing rights)		(6,0)
Buffer on Mortgage servicing rights		6,0
(Buffer haircut)		(5,9)
Core tier 1	**115,0**	**66,3**
Supersubordinated debt (Lower tier 1)	10,0	10,0
(Deductions of 50% of shareholdings in credit institutions)	(15,0)	0,0
Tier 1	**110,0**	**76,3**
Subordinated debt	25,0	25,0
(Deductions of 50% of shareholdings in credit institutions)	(15,0)	0,0
Tier 2	**10,0**	**25,0**
(Deductions of shareholdings in insurance subidiaries)	(10,0)	0,0
Total solvency capital	**110,0**	**101,3**
RWAs	1 000,0	1 000,0
Core tier 1 ratio	**11,5%**	**6,6%**
Tier 1 ratio	**11,0%**	**7,6%**
Tier 2 ratio	**1,0%**	**2,5%**
Total capital ratio	**11,0%**	**10,1%**

Items which are not taken into account in the core tier 1 calculation from a Basel 2 point of view

Total differed tax assets	8
Arising from timing differences	5
Other differed tax assets	3
Investements in financial institutions	40
of which banks	30
of which insurance companies	10
MSR	6

To increase their core tier 1 ratios, banks can raise capital (hence the various rights issues and states' bail outs mainly in 2008 and 2009), or sell capital-consuming subsidiaries. Such divestments are often announced with a recapitalization to favour a financial soundness recovery more rapidly. In order to prevent the bail outs by states from being perceived as nationalizations, most of these operations consisted in hybrid capital issues. This has systematically been the case in Italy with the Tremonti Bonds issues. In France, the main retail banks (BNP, Société Générale, Crédit Agricole, BPCE) benefited from such recapitalizations in order to increase their solvency and to be therefore in a position to go on distributing loans during the economic crisis, preventing a credit crunch. Given the step up clauses of these hybrid securities (i.e. increase in the interest to be paid every year), most of them were repaid to the French State less than a year later. In Spain, a Royal Decree of March 10th 2011 has precised the target core tier 1 ratios, which have to be posted by the domestic banks in order to restore or increase confidence in the banking system. The minimum core tier 1 ratio is 8% for the listed banks and 10% for the non-listed banks, mainly savings banks. If these ratios are not reached, the banks can either go public (through an IPO) or require a capital increase from the Fund for Orderly Bank Restructuring (FROB, corresponding to the initial letters in Spanish). The following table presents the list of the Spanish banks that require such a recapitalization.

Table 3: list of Spanish banks' capital requirements

Figures in M€	Amount	Level to be met (%)	Percentage points to reach level	Adittional capital needed
Bankinter	2 144	8	1,1	333
Barclays Bank, S.A	1 005	8	2,8	552
Deutsche Bank, S.A.E	729	8	1,6	182
Bankpyme	24	8	2,0	8
SUB-TOTAL COMMERCIAL BANKS	**3 902**			**1 075**
Bankia	14 125	10	2,9	5 775
Base	6 582	10	1,8	1 447
Cívica	3 687	10	1,9	847
Mare Nostrum	3 343	10	1,6	637
Catalunyacaixa	3 148	10	3,5	1 718
Novacaixagalicia	2 851	10	4,8	2 622
Caja España de Inversiones	2 062	10	1,8	463
Unnim	1 150	10	3,3	568
SUB-TOTAL SAVING BANKS	**36 948**			**14 077**

2. Principles of a Bank's Valuation taking Solvency Constraints into Account

As with other companies, banks can be valued by different approaches, such as analogic methods, DCF, and sum of the parts. The analogic methods are based on peer groups, either listed banks or banks which have been the target of an M&A transaction. For each peer, a multiple is calculated for the relevant past and forecasted aggregates. The mean of each of the series multiples is looked upon as the sector's multiple. Two multiples are looked upon as relevant for the valuation of banks: the Price Earning Ratio (P/E) and the Price to Book Value (P/BV). The first one enables one to take the profitability of the bank into account, and the second is focused on equity that corresponds to the starting point of the core tier 1 calculation. In that context, most brokers calculate the Price to Tangible Book Value (P/TBV). For this ratio, the equity value is reduced by intangible assets and goodwills, as in the core tier 1 calculation from a Basel 2 point of view. An alternative approach is commonly conducted. It consists of studying a tentative correlation between the P/BV (or P/TBV) and the Return on Equity (RoE). If the coefficient of determination (R^2) is satisfactory (i.e. higher than 50%), a simple linear relationship such as $P/BV=a.RoE+b$ can be established based on the least squares method. The DCF approach is generally the central valuation of a company. For a corporate body, the Enterprise Value (*EV*) is the sum of the discounted free cash flows (*FCF*). In other terms,

$$EV = \sum_{t=1}^{+\infty} \frac{FCF_t}{(1+K)^t}$$

where K is the weighted average cost of capital. The *FCF* calculation is based on *EBITDA,* which is not calculated for banks. It also includes the changes in working capital requirements, which is not relevant in the banking sector. Moreover, the equity value is calculated based on *EV,* from which the net financial debt is deducted. But the balance sheet of a bank does not enable one to calculate the net financial debt. In that specific context, the DCF is replaced by the Dividend Discount Model (DDM). In this approach, the yearly cash flow corresponds to the theoretical dividend that could be paid to the shareholders taking a target core tier 1 ratio into account. From a practical point of view, assuming a 9% target core tier ratio, the yearly theoretical dividend corresponds to the difference between the effective core tier 1 and 9% of the RWAs. As in the Gordon and Shapiro formula, the discount rate of the theoretical dividends (D_t), which are calculated based on net profit after interests, is the cost of equity (k). Then the value (V) of the bank is:

$$V = \sum_{t=1}^{+\infty} \frac{D_t}{(1+k)^t}$$

The business plan of the bank being provided over a limited period (i.e. n years), the abovementioned formula can be broken down, as in a usual DCF, into 2 components:

$$V = \sum_{t=1}^{n} \frac{D_t}{(1+k)^t} + \sum_{t=n+1}^{+\infty} \frac{D_t}{(1+k)^t}$$

$$= \sum_{t=1}^{n} \frac{D_t}{(1+k)^t} + \left[\frac{D_{n+1}}{(1+k)^{n+1}} + \frac{D_{n+2}}{(1+k)^{n+2}} + ... \right]$$

Assuming a perpetuity growth rate equal to *g* beyond the nth year:

$$V = \sum_{t=1}^{n} \frac{D_t}{(1+k)^t} + \frac{D_n(1+g)}{(1+K)^n(k-g)}$$

Based on that, an alternative approach to the traditional P/BV consists of using the following formula:

$$P / BV = \frac{RoE - g}{k - g}$$

where *g* is the long term growth rate of a bank's net income, and *k* is its cost of equity. This formula enables one to take the equity requirement implied by the growth of the RWAs into account. Indeed, if the

$$\frac{RoE - g}{k - g}$$

multiple is applied to the book value of equity, then the value of the bank is

$$\frac{NI - g.Equity}{k - g}$$

where *NI* is the Net Income. Assuming a 9% target core tier 1, the level of equity is equal to 9% of the RWAs, which drives the implied formula:

$$V = \frac{NI - 9\%.g.RWA}{k - g}.$$

In other terms, V is defined as a sum of excess equities to perpetuity taking a *g* yearly growth rate of RWAs into account.

Table 4: sample of European listed banks

In M€	Country	Market Value	P/E 2010	P/E 2011e	P/BV 2010	P/BV 2011e	P/TBV 2010	P/TBV 2011e	ROE 2010	Tier 1 2011e
BARCLAYS	UK	38 359	10,0x	8,7x	0,68x	0,65x	0,82x	0,77x	6,8%	12,5%
ROYAL BK SCOT GRP	UK	27 844	n.a	13,9x	0,68x	0,64x	0,82x	0,79x	n.a	12,2%
HSBC HOLDINGS PLC	UK	130 404	13,9x	11,3x	1,29x	1,26x	1,58x	1,51x	9,3%	12,3%
STANDARD CHARTERED	UK	43 174	12,8x	12,7x	1,63x	1,59x	1,98x	1,88x	12,7%	13,2%
ERSTE GROUP BK AG	Austria	12 891	13,9x	10,7x	1,06x	0,99x	1,58x	1,47x	7,6%	10,4%
RAIFFEISEN BK INTL	Austria	7 241	8,9x	8,0x	1,06x	0,95x	1,18x	1,04x	12,2%	9,9%
DANSKE BANK A/S	Sweden	14 097	22,4x	11,8x	0,82x	0,81x	0,99x	0,97x	3,6%	15,7%
SYDBANK	Sweden	1 342	20,0x	11,1x	1,07x	0,99x	1,07x	0,99x	5,3%	14,5%
ING GROEP NV	NL	32 901	9,4x	6,0x	0,83x	0,75x	0,91x	0,87x	8,6%	11,5%
SNS REAAL GROEP NV	NL	1 115	n.a	7,3x	0,37x	0,35x	0,82x	0,86x	n.a	8,9%
KBC GROEP NV	Belgium	10 057	6,1x	5,2x	0,86x	0,82x	1,05x	1,00x	14,1%	12,1%
DEXIA	Belgium	4 496	6,7x	7,4x	0,54x	0,47x	0,69x	0,63x	8,5%	14,1%
BNP PARIBAS	France	63 856	8,3x	7,3x	0,93x	0,86x	1,16x	1,05x	11,1%	11,3%
SOC GENERALE	France	31 998	8,6x	7,2x	0,76x	0,71x	1,06x	0,94x	8,9%	10,4%
CREDIT AGRICOLE SA	France	26 062	13,2x	6,4x	0,57x	0,54x	1,03x	0,92x	4,4%	10,9%
DEUTSCHE BANK AG	Germany	39 049	11,8x	7,1x	0,84x	0,77x	1,14x	0,99x	7,1%	11,5%
COMMERZBANK AG	Germany	5 339	n.a	7,5x	0,46x	0,37x	0,62x	0,74x	11,4%	11,2%
DT POSTBANK AG	Germany	4 886	n.a	11,8x	0,97x	0,91x	1,53x	1,14x	n.a	8,9%
COMDIRECT BANK AG	Germany	1 182	19,5x	16,2x	2,30x	2,36x	n.a	n.a	11,8%	48,4%
AAREAL BANK AG	Germany	1 313	22,7x	11,5x	0,76x	0,77x	0,82x	0,78x	3,4%	12,3%
DAB BANK AG	Germany	325	20,1x	13,5x	1,97x	1,90x	2,13x	2,05x	9,8%	13,1%
UNICREDIT SPA	Italy	31 356	17,7x	10,2x	0,49x	0,48x	0,80x	0,77x	n.a	9,5%
INTESA SANPAOLO	Italy	28 415	11,0x	9,1x	0,50x	0,50x	0,97x	0,89x	4,6%	8,7%
MEDIOBANCA SPA	Italy	6 548	15,2x	11,7x	1,02x	0,97x	1,07x	1,02x	6,7%	11,5%
BCA MPS	Italy	4 960	17,8x	10,8x	0,39x	0,42x	0,71x	0,68x	n.a	9,0%
BANCO POPOLARE	Italy	3 388	9,5x	12,0x	0,16x	0,28x	0,31x	0,50x	n.a	7,6%
CREDITO EMILIANO	Italy	1 486	14,3x	10,8x	0,82x	0,78x	0,96x	0,91x	5,8%	8,9%
CREDITO BERGAMASCO	Italy	1 416	n.a	n.a	n.a	n.a	n.a	n.a	n.a	n.a.
BCA POP DI MILANO	Italy	884	15,1x	8,9x	0,29x	0,32x	0,39x	0,43x	n.a	8,0%
AZIMUT HLDG S.P.A	Italy	1 145	11,9x	10,3x	2,86x	2,43x	n.a	n.a	24,0%	n.a.
BANCA GENERALI	Italy	1 232	15,5x	13,7x	n.a	n.a	n.a	n.a	n.a	14,6%
BANCO SANTANDER	Spain	69 050	8,4x	7,8x	0,97x	0,94x	1,44x	1,38x	11,5%	10,0%
BBVA(BILB-VIZ-ARG)	Spain	37 287	7,3x	7,9x	1,04x	1,01x	1,29x	1,29x	14,2%	10,4%
BANCO POPULAR ESPA	Spain	5 558	10,8x	11,5x	0,68x	0,67x	0,78x	0,77x	6,4%	9,8%
BCO DE SABADELL	Spain	4 085	10,1x	14,2x	0,71x	0,71x	0,87x	0,88x	7,0%	10,0%
BCO ESP DE CREDITO	Spain	4 192	9,1x	9,7x	0,78x	0,74x	0,78x	0,75x	8,5%	9,6%
BANKINTER SA	Spain	2 265	15,4x	15,5x	0,94x	0,89x	1,07x	0,96x	6,1%	8,4%
BANCO PASTOR SA	Spain	864	16,0x	17,2x	0,56x	0,54x	0,58x	0,62x	3,6%	10,8%
Number of items			33	37	36	36	34	34	29	36
Mean			**13,1x**	**10,4x**	**0,91x**	**0,86x**	**1,03x**	**0,98x**	**8,8%**	**0,12x**
Standard deviation			*34,9%*	*28,6%*	59,9%	57,8%	38,5%	35,7%	48,8%	54,5%
t			*2,037*	*2,028*	*2,030*	*2,030*	*2,035*	*2,035*	*2,048*	*2,030*
Bottom of the confident interval			13,01x	10,28x	0,70x	0,67x	0,90x	0,85x	-0,10x	-0,06x
Top of of the confident interval			13,26x	10,47x	1,11x	1,06x	1,16x	1,10x	0,27x	0,30x

3. Empirical Study: Solvency Situation and Valuation

a) Description of data

The following study is focused on analysing the correlation between the profitability of banks, measured by their RoEs, and their valuation level, measured by their P/BV. For that purpose, a sample of 38 European listed banks is presented in the table below. For each bank, a P/E, a P/BV, a P/TBV, and a RoE have been extracted from Facset, which provides Reuters' data; moreover, the means and standard deviations of these aggregates have been estimated on the sample.

b) Confident intervals for multiples

It can be observed that the Z random variable, defined as

$$Z = \frac{\overline{X} - m}{\frac{S}{\sqrt{n}}}$$

has a Student distribution with *n-1* degrees of freedom, where *n* is the number of observations, $\overline{X}$ and S are the mean and standard deviation respectively, which are calculated based on the sample; *m* is the mean, of which a 95% confidence interval can be looked for. As the density of such a variable has a symmetric curve, it is possible to get *t* so that: P[-*t*<Z<*t*] = 0.95. Then P[Z<*t*] = 0.975. Hence *t* = 2.062 taking the sample with 38 banks, which implies 37 degrees of freedom; *t* is equal to 2.037 in the case of 33 observations (in the case of the 2010 P/E), 2.028 for 37 observations (2011 P/E), 2.030 for 36 observations (2010 and 2011 P/BV and P/CT1), 2.035 for 34 observations (2010 and 2011 P/TBV) and 2.048 for 29 observations (2010 RoE). If Z is replaced by its value:

$$P[-t< \frac{\overline{X} - m}{\frac{S}{\sqrt{n}}} <t] = 0{,}95, \text{ i.e.: } P[\overline{X} - \frac{tS}{\sqrt{n}} < m < \overline{X} + \frac{tS}{\sqrt{n}}] = 0{,}95.$$

Using this result, the following confidence intervals of means can be obtained for 2010:

- the average P/E has a 95% probability to be in the [13.01-13.26] range;

- the average P/BV has a 95% probability to be in the [0.70-1.11] range;
- the average P/TBV has a 95% probability to be in the [0.90-1.16] range.

c) Tentative correlation between P/BV and RoE

Based on the previous sample, an analysis of the correlation between the P/BV (explained variable on the *y* axis) and the RoE (explanatory variable on the *x* axis) is not relevant as the R^2 is equal to 47%. The graph below proposes the representation of the relationship between the P/BV and the RoE based on 2010 data. The surface area of each point is proportional to the market capitalization of the bank; the equation and the R^2 value are automatically given by Excel.

Graph 1: correlation analysis between the P/BV and the RoE

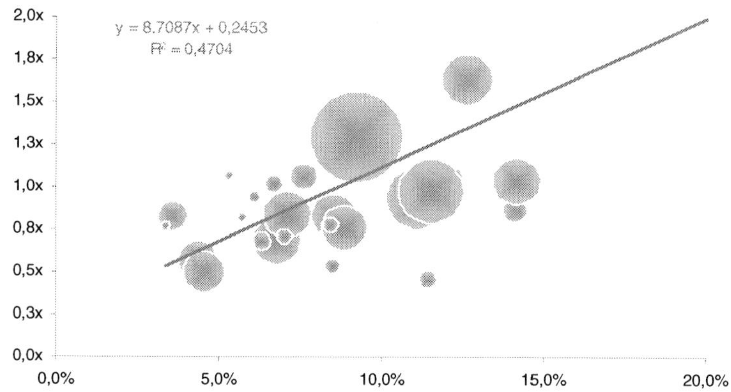

Consequently, the RoE cannot be looked upon as the main driver of a bank's P/BV.

d) Test of significance of a difference between average multiples

Given the market focus on solvency constraints, the valuation level (i.e. the P/BV) is intuitively driven by the level of capitalization. In that context, the difference between average P/BVs of high and low capitalized banks has been tested. For that purpose, 2 samples are set up: one of high capitalized banks, the 2011 estimated tier 1 of which is at least 10%; and another of low capitalized banks, the estimated tier 1 of which is lower than 10%. Both samples are extracted from the previous one, which includes 38 listed banks. Four banks with no relevant P/BV (Banca

Generali and Credito Bergamasco), one with no available Tier 1 ratio (Azimuth Holdings), and one with an abnormal tier 1 ratio (Comdirect Bank) have been excluded. The samples with a total of 34 items are presented hereafter:

Table 5: samples of listed banks with low and high tier 1 ratios

	Estimated 2011 data	P/BV Tier 1<10%	Tier 1
1	BANCO POPOLARE	0,28	7,6%
2	BCA POP DI MILANO	0,32	8,0%
3	BANKINTER SA	0,89	8,4%
4	INTESA SANPAOLO	0,50	8,7%
5	CREDITO EMILIANO	0,78	8,9%
6	SNS REAAL GROEP NV	0,35	8,9%
7	DT POSTBANK AG	0,91	8,9%
8	BCA MPS	0,42	9,0%
9	UNICREDIT SPA	0,48	9,5%
10	BCO ESP DE CREDITO	0,74	9,6%
11	BANCO POPULAR ESPA	0,67	9,8%
12	RAIFFEISEN BK INTL	0,95	9,9%

	Estimated 2011 data	P/BV Tier 1>10%	Tier 1
1	BANCO SANTANDER	0,94	10,0%
2	BCO DE SABADELL	0,71	10,0%
3	BBVA(BILB-VIZ-ARG)	1,01	10,4%
4	SOC GENERALE	0,71	10,4%
5	ERSTE GROUP BK AG	0,99	10,4%
6	BANCO PASTOR SA	0,54	10,8%
7	CREDIT AGRICOLE SA	0,54	10,9%
8	COMMERZBANK AG	0,37	11,2%
9	BNP PARIBAS	0,86	11,3%
10	ING GROEP NV	0,75	11,5%
11	DEUTSCHE BANK AG	0,77	11,5%
12	MEDIOBANCA SPA	0,97	11,5%
13	KBC GROEP NV	0,82	12,1%
14	ROYAL BK SCOT GRP	0,64	12,2%
15	HSBC HOLDINGS PLC	1,26	12,3%
16	AAREAL BANK AG	0,77	12,3%
17	BARCLAYS	0,65	12,5%
18	DAB BANK AG	1,90	13,1%
19	STANDARD CHARTERED	1,59	13,2%
20	DEXIA	0,47	14,1%
21	SYDBANK	0,99	14,5%
22	DANSKE BANK A/S	0,81	15,7%

The proposed test is a traditional Student's test, should the standard deviations of the premiums being compared be equal; otherwise, it is an Aspin-Welch test. In order to test the difference between standard deviations, the property for which the variable

$$T = \frac{S_x^2}{S_y^2} \cdot \frac{\sigma_Q^2}{\sigma_P^2}$$

obeys a Fisher-Snedecor law for parameters $n_p - 1$ and $n_Q - 1$ can be used, assuming S_X^2 is the standard variance of the P/BV for the first sample, S_Y^2 is the standard variance of the P/BV for the second sample, σ_P^2 is the variance of the P/BV for all the banks from which the first sample is issued, σ_Q^2 is the variance of the P/BV for all the banks from which the second sample is issued, n_P is the size of the first sample, and n_Q is the size of the second sample. Assuming $\sigma_P^2 = \sigma_Q^2$, $T_0 = \frac{S_X^2}{S_Y^2}$ obeys

$F(n_P\text{-}1, n_Q\text{-}1)$. The number t_0 which satisfies: $t_0 = \frac{S_X^2}{S_Y^2}$ can be determined based on the samples. The table for the Fisher-Snedecor law provides the value of the real number c, such that P[T>c] = 5%, where T obeys the law F(m,n). Thus, if t_0 > c, the assumption of equality of standard deviations must be rejected, with a 5% chance of being wrong.

Let: $T' = \dfrac{\overline{X} - \overline{Y} - (m_P - m_Q)}{\sqrt{\dfrac{(n_P-1)S_X^2 + (n_Q-1)S_Y^2}{n_P + n_Q - 2}} \cdot \sqrt{\dfrac{1}{n_P} + \dfrac{1}{n_Q}}}$.

T obeys a Student's law with n_P+n_Q-2 degrees of freedom. Thus, assuming m_P=m_Q,

$$T' = \frac{\overline{X} - \overline{Y}}{\sqrt{\dfrac{(n_P-1)S_X^2 + (n_Q-1)S_Y^2}{n_P + n_Q - 2}} \cdot \sqrt{\dfrac{1}{n_P} + \dfrac{1}{n_Q}}}$$

obeys a Student's law with n_P+n_Q-2 degrees of freedom. Using both samples, the number

$$t_0' = \frac{\overline{X} - \overline{Y}}{\sqrt{\dfrac{(n_P-1)S_X^2 + (n_Q-1)S_Y^2}{n_P + n_Q - 2}} \cdot \sqrt{\dfrac{1}{n_P} + \dfrac{1}{n_Q}}}$$

can be calculated by experimentation. It is also possible to calculate the value of the real number c such that P[-c<T<c] = $1-\alpha$, hence: c = $F^{-1}(1-\frac{\alpha}{2})$ where F is the distribution function of Student's law. Thus for a confidence level of 95%, α = 5% and c $= F^{-1}(0{,}975)$, which can be obtained directly from the Student's law table. Consequently, if $-c < t_0 < c$, then the assumption of equality of means may be accepted with a 5% chance of error. If the unknown standard deviations are different, the Aspin-Welch test can be used.

Let $T = \dfrac{\overline{X} - \overline{Y}}{\sqrt{\dfrac{S_X^2}{n_P} + \dfrac{S_Y^2}{n_Q}}}$;

T obeys a Student's law with *n* degrees of freedom, where:

$$n = \frac{\left(\dfrac{S_X^2}{n_P} + \dfrac{S_Y^2}{n_Q}\right)^2}{\left(\dfrac{S_X^2}{n_P}\right)^2 / (n_P - 1) + \left(\dfrac{S_Y^2}{n_Q}\right)^2 / (n_Q - 1)}.$$

The decision rule is the same as in the Student's test. The data to be used for the test of equality of variances are presented in the table hereunder.

Table 6: Fisher-Snedecor test for equality of variances in low and large tier 1 ratios

	Tier 1<10%	Tier 1>10%
Mean	0,61	0,87
Squared standard deviation	0,06	0,12
Observations	12	22
Degrees of freedom	11	21
t_0 stat	0,48	
T critical - one-tail	0,38	

Based on the Fisher-Snedecor law, if the variances are equal, the probability that T be higher than 0.38 is equal to 5%. Indeed, given 12 and 22 items per sample, the numbers of degrees of liberty of the Fisher-Snedecor law are 11 and 21, and the table of the law indicates that, in this case, P[T>0,38]=5%. By experimentation, based on the samples, the value of t_0 is 0.48 (i.e. 0.06/0.12), which is higher than 0.38. Therefore, there is a 95% probability that the variances are different. Then, the test of equality of means is based on the Aspin Welch methodology. The data used for this second test are presented in the table hereafter:

Table 7: Aspin Welch test for equality of means in low and large tier 1 ratios

	Tier 1<10%	Tier 1>10%
Mean	0,61	0,87
Squared standard deviation	0,06	0,12
Observations	12	22
Assumed difference between means	0	
Degrees of freedom	30	
$t_{0'}$ stat	-2,51	
T' critical - two-tail	2,04	

Based on the Student law, if the means are equal, P[-2,04<T'<2,04]=95%. By experimentation based on the samples, t_0'=-2,51, which is not included in the [-2,04-2,04] range. Thus, with a 5% probability to be wrong, it can be concluded that the average P/BV of the low and high tier 1 ratios are significantly different. In other terms, the level of the P/BV is dependent on the solvency situation of the bank.

Conclusion

The solvency of a bank is the cornerstone of its financial management. In a regulatory environment that is more and more demanding, the level of equity has become the driver of its value. On the one hand, the DDM approach is focused on the excess equity from a prudential point of view. On the other hand, in the basic approach, using listed peers, the P/BV is more reliant on the level of the tier 1 ratio than on the profitability of equity. In that context, numerous rights issues by banks, achieved since 2008 or to be achieved, for example in Spain for commercial and savings banks, are justified by the increase in solvency capital needs whereby the bank is profitable.

References

Banco de Espana's Presse Release, "*The Banco de Espana informs 12 banks they must increase their capital to comply with the Royal Decreee-Law*", 10 March 2011

Basel Committee on Banking Supervision, Bank for International Settlements, "*Annex: Main design elements*", 26 July 2010

—. Consultative Document, "*Strengthening resilience of the banking sector*", December 2009

PART 2.

INVESTMENTS AND INTERNATIONAL FINANCE

WHAT DRIVES IFDIS IN THE NIGERIAN BANKING INDUSTRY?

TONI UHOMOIBHI ABURIME[1]

I – Introduction

CBN (2001) simply defined foreign direct investment (FDI) as investments by non-residents in an economy. However, the World Bank (2007: 227) technically defined it as an investment made to acquire lasting management interest in an enterprise operating outside the economy of the investor. Thus, in order to qualify as FDI, the investment must afford some degree of management control over the enterprise. The UN defines control in this case as owning 10% or more of the ordinary shares or voting power of an incorporated firm or its equivalent for an unincorporated firm; lower ownership shares are known as indirect/portfolio investments (Moss *et al.*, 2005: 345). While inward FDI (IFDI) refers to situations in which new foreign equity capital is invested in local resources, outward FDI (Panibratov and Kalotay, 2009) refers to situations in which local capital is invested in foreign resources. Thus, every FDI has two faces, viz: IFDI to the recipient (host) country and outward FDI (OFDI) to the investing (home) country.

Moshirian (2006: 1060) is of the view that FDI in banking and other financial services relates to the movement of providers of financial services. Based on this view, IFDIs in a banking industry may result in the establishment of two different categories of foreign-owned banks, i.e. foreign bank branches and subsidiaries, in a host country. These branches and subsidiaries would have foreign banks as principal investors. However, quite a number of banks also exist in which foreign non-bank institutions and individuals hold substantial equity stake. Technically speaking, these are also foreign-owned banks. In this study, we concern ourselves with foreign-owned banks, regardless of whether their equities

[1] School of Accounting, Economics and Finance, Deakin University, Australia.

are substantially owned by foreign banks or foreign non-bank institutions and individuals or combinations of both.

The broad aim of this paper is to empirically identify significant drivers (determinants) of IFDIs in the Nigerian banking industry. To systematically achieve this aim, the remainder of the paper is organized in the following manner. The next section is a discourse of IFDIs in the Nigerian banking industry. Section 3 describes the model. Section 4 exposes the data. Section 5 presents the results. Section 6 concludes the paper.

II – IFDIs in the Nigerian Banking Industry

IFDI in the Nigerian banking industry dates back to the history of banking in the country. Indeed, the first bank to be established in colonial Nigeria, the African Banking Corporation, was a foreign bank. IFDIs continued to thrive until the 1970s when the Indigenization Decree was promulgated. The Indigenization Decree of 1972 stipulated at least 40 per cent Nigerian ownership of all enterprises operating in Nigeria; and in 1976 this was further increased to 60 per cent. The result was a drastic reduction of IFDIs in the Nigerian banking industry. For instance, between 1983 and 1984, the number of representative offices of foreign banks in Nigeria dropped from 11 to 8 (CBN, 1984: 40).

In 1986, the Federal Government of Nigeria (FGN) made efforts to encourage FDI. Perhaps the most significant effort was the introduction of the Structural Adjustment Programme (SAP) which provided the basis for the deregulation of the Nigerian economy. Under the SAP, a number of institutional, structural and market reforms were undertaken to liberalize the economy and provide an enabling environment for attracting foreign investment (CBN, 2001: 64). Several years after, numerous researchers have concluded that SAP was a colossal failure, and its impact on IFDIs in the Nigerian banking industry was never determined.

In 1988, Decree 36 established an Industrial Development Coordination Committee (IDCC). The IDCC streamlined the multiplicity of institutions responsible for the approval and registration of foreign companies in Nigeria. It had the responsibility for approving pre-investment agreements, fiscal incentives, employment permits for foreigners, foreign capital imports, and providing policy advice to the FGN (CBN, 2001: 64). In sum, its aim was to create an FDI-friendly administrative framework. Like SAP, its impact on IFDIs in the Nigerian banking industry was never determined.

In 1995, the FGN decided to relax the investment laws for foreigners, and market restrictions on non-Nigerian participation in banking services were dismantled (Aburime, 2005). The FGN accomplished this through the Nigerian Investment Promotion Commission (NIPC) Act No. 16 of 1995 and the Foreign Exchange (Monitoring & Miscellaneous Provisions) Decree 17 of the same year. Aimed at attracting FDIs, the NIPC Act allowed 100 per cent foreign ownership of firms outside the petroleum sector, although industries considered crucial to national security, such as firearms, ammunition, and military and paramilitary apparel, were reserved for domestic investors. The Act also prohibited the nationalization or expropriation of foreign enterprises except in cases of national interest. On the other hand, Decree 17 authorized any person, including non-Nigerians, to deal in, invest in, acquire or dispose of, create or transfer any interest in the securities market (CBN, 2001: 64). Thus, by removing all the existing bottlenecks to foreign investors' entry and exit, both laws aimed to encourage IFDIs in Nigeria.

The promulgation of the NIPC Act and Decree 17 ought to have marked the dawn of a new era in Nigeria that would have significantly increased the attractiveness of its banking industry to foreign investors. But, an analysis (available on request) of the existing data reveals that, although there was a nominal increase in the number of foreign banks in Nigeria (Aburime, 2005: 29), the Nigerian banking industry did not become remarkably attractive to IFDIs. The growth rate of IFDIs in the Nigerian banking industry leaped only shortly after the NIPC Act was promulgated. Thereafter, the rate continued to decline. NDIC (2002 and 2003) also reports that aggregate foreign shareholding in the Nigerian banking industry decreased from 12.53 percent in 2001 to 10.59 percent in 2002, and 9.56 percent in 2003. It was not until the 6th of July, 2004 – 31st of December, 2005 banks consolidation exercise (Aburime, 2006) that the growth rate of IFDIs in the Nigerian banking industry experienced a phenomenal increase. CBN (2005: 38) reports that the exercise attracted US$666.6 million and GBP£0.16 million worth of IFDIs in the Nigerian banking industry. When concluded, four out of twenty five banks had substantial foreign ownership, with two of them having 100 percent foreign ownership (NDIC, 2006: 25). But, after this increase, the growth rate dropped. Thus, the Nigerian banking industry did not become remarkably attractive to IFDIs.

In 2006, the FGN made some more efforts to improve IFDI in Nigeria. First, there were further removals of legal hurdles associated with the ownership of business ventures in Nigeria. Second, foreign investors were allowed to extend loans to private Nigerian entities without restrictions (CBN, 2006: 99). Third, foreign investors were guaranteed unfettered access to funds and permitted to repatriate unconditionally, dividends, profits and proceeds from foreign investment in Nigeria. Furthermore, withholding tax was reduced from 10.0 to 7.5 per cent for nationals of countries that have a double taxation agreement with Nigeria (CBN, 2006: 79). Although NDIC (2007: 82) has highlighted the fact that, by the end of 2007, sixteen out of twenty four banks had some degree of foreign ownership, out of which four had substantial foreign ownership (Standard Chartered Bank – 100 per cent foreign private ownership[2]), the FGN's efforts were not accompanied by a leap in the growth rate of IFDIs in the Nigerian banking industry. Furthermore, by 2009, ten (a reduction by six) out of the twenty four universal banks in Nigeria had some degree of foreign ownership (NDIC, 2009: 167).

Perennially, the Central Bank of Nigeria (CBN) has been in the habit of wooing foreign investors into Nigeria's financial services sector. For instance, in its bid to ensure that the consolidation of the banking industry was attained without hiccups, the CBN reached out to Chinese investors and assured them of the security of their investments in Nigeria. The CBN justified her overtures by stating that a cursory look at the banking sector in Nigeria shows that banks owned by foreign interests are doing very well (Ibe, 2004). Indeed, it is clear from Figure 1 that the relationship between foreign ownership and non-performing loans clearly becomes negative for banks in Nigeria when their degree of foreign ownership is substantial (i.e. above 40%). Thus, the substantial expansion of IFDIs in the Nigerian banking industry would most likely promote financial stability and development[3]. This evidence gives good backing to the several steps taken by the FGN since 1995 to dismantle barriers hindering the entry of foreign investments into the industry.

---

[2] Standard Chartered Bank has always been 100 per cent foreign owned since 2002.

[3] Numerous researchers (e.g. see Moshirian, 2006: 1062-1063) are of the view that foreign participation in any banking industry helps shore up bank efficiency and stability.

Figure 1 – Foreign Ownership and NPLs of Banks in Nigeria (1990 – 2009)

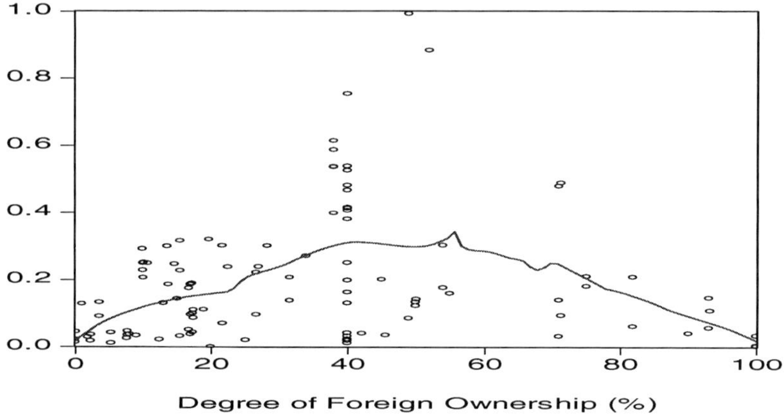

Source: Researcher's Estimations from Individual Banks' Annual Reports, Various Years
Note: The figure displays a kernel fit.

In 2009, the Governor of the CBN, accompanied by his officials and other banking industry chieftains, were in London to advertise technically insolvent banks to prospective core investors. The new investors were required to bring not just capital but management, among others (Ighomwenghian, 2009).

But, rather unfortunately, the CBN's overtures have not produced sustained results, perhaps because they were not preceded by the conduct of far-reaching studies aimed at identifying the true drivers of IFDIs in the Nigerian banking industry. Furthermore, with the growing activities, influence and significance of international funds (Thuraisamy, 2010: 182), there may be no need for the CBN to go about wooing foreign investors into Nigeria's financial services sector. Perhaps there are other more important 'pull factors' which, if appropriately factored in, could propel IFDIs into the Nigerian banking industry.

III – The Model

The following fixed effects multiple regression equation (Eq. 1) models the relationship between theoretically established IFDI drivers and actual IFDI in banks operating in the Nigerian banking industry. The fixed effects model specification is appropriate to control for firm specific differences (Hill *et al.*, 2008: 391), thus capturing unobserved idiosyncratic drivers of IFDIs into different banks. The results of a Hausman test (available on request) favour our choice of the fixed effects over the random effects approach. We constrain ourselves to modelling only 'pull' factors because we think this approach would increase the policy relevance of the study to managers of the Nigerian economy. We are compelled to adopt the natural log of VIT_{t-1} as a means to effectively linearize its exponential trend (Asteriou, 2006: 18). Also, some possible determinants of IFDI are left out of the equation to avoid the biasing effects of multicollinearity. Visual and statistical correlation tests clearly reveal that this problem does not exist in the specified function. Table 1 is a compressed exposition of all the model's remaining variables.

$$IFDI_{i,t} = \alpha_{0,i} + \delta_1 MA_{t-1} + \delta_2 \log VIT_{t-1} + \delta_3 FS_{t-1} + \delta_4 Lib_{t-2} + \delta_5 MS_{t-1} + \delta_6 ID_{t-1} + \delta_7 C_{t-1} + \varepsilon_{i,t} \quad \text{(Eq. 1)}$$

where i = bank 1,…,bank 23; t = 1996,…,2007; $IFDI_{i,t}$ is inward foreign direct investment in bank i at time t; MA_{t-1} is extent of market attractiveness at time $t-1$; VIT_{t-1} is volume of international trade at time $t-1$; FS_{t-1} is financial structure of the economy at time $t-1$; Lib_{t-2} is degree of liberalization of the banking industry at time $t-2$; MS_{t-1} is level of macroeconomic stability at time $t-1$; ID_{t-1} is level of infrastructure development at time $t-1$; C_{t-1} is level of corruption at time $t-1$; $\alpha_{0,i}$ is a bank specific constant; $\delta_{1,\ldots,7}$ are variable coefficients; and $\varepsilon_{i,t}$ is an error term.

Table 1: Variables Exposition

	VARIABLE	DEFINITION(S)	SOURCE
Regressand	$IFDI_{i,t}$	Nominal amount of paid-up share capital owned by foreign investors We assume that the factors that would cause foreign investors to purchase small portions of shares of a bank from local investors will equally cause them to purchase larger portions or even the entire stock of shares of the bank. In similar vein, we also assume that the factors that would cause foreign investors to sell small portions of shares of a bank to local investors will equally cause them to sell larger portions or even the entire stock of shares of the bank.	-
Regressors	MA_{t-1}	Average Foreign Bank Profitability (ROA) Banking Sector Development dually proxied by Total bank assets divided by GDP (1) and Total bank loans and advances divided by GDP (2)	- Aburime (2009a)
	VIT_{t-1}	Imports plus exports	Voinea and Mihaescu (2006)
	FS_{t-1}	Total stock trading volume to total bank loans and advances	Demirgüç-Kunt and Huizinga (2001)
	Lib_{t-2}	Number of foreign banks to the total number of banks Following Aburime (2009b), a bank is classified as foreign if its total paid-up share capital is at least forty percent (40%) owned by non-Nigerian individuals and/or non-Nigerian institutions. Also, Voinea and Mihaescu (2006: 23-24) uphold a 2-year lag.	Voinea and Mihaescu (2006)
	MS_{t-1}	Annual inflation rate computed by the CBN	Asiedu (2003)
	ID_{t-1} C_{t-1}	Teledensity Electricity consumption per capita (kilowatt-hours) Transparency International's Corruption Perception Index	Asiedu (2002 and 2003) Voinea and Mihaescu (2006)

IV – The Data

The data set used in this study were elicited from the World Bank's online database; the annual public financial statements of an unbalanced panel of 23 unique banks in 204 observations over the 1996 - 2007 period; and various issues of CBN annual report and statement of accounts and Nigeria Deposit Insurance Corporation (NDIC) annual reports and statements of accounts over the same period. The banks are those in which foreigners made substantial investments within the period.

V – The Results

The results of the empirical estimations are contained in Table 2. Estimated coefficients for MA_{t-1}, VIT_{t-1}, and ID_{t-1} are statistically significant, with *t*-statistic values well in excess of 2. The use of a fixed-effects estimation technique is statistically justified by the significance of all the bank-specific dummies in Eq. 1. Based on the results, each bank portends a great deal of uniqueness in its ability to attract IFDI. However, the overall regression fit, as measured by the R^2 value, does not indicate a very tight fit. The model only explains 57.81% of IFDI variation among the 23 banks included in the sample.

Table 2: Estimation Results

Variable	Coefficient	Std. Error	t-Statistic	Prob.
D23	-2.26E+11	6.92E+10	-3.269780	0.0013**
D22	-2.26E+11	6.92E+10	-3.263372	0.0013**
D21	-2.26E+11	6.92E+10	-3.261092	0.0013**
D20	-2.28E+11	6.92E+10	-3.289699	0.0012**
D19	-2.26E+11	6.92E+10	-3.269092	0.0013**
D18	-2.23E+11	6.92E+10	-3.215451	0.0016**
D17	-2.24E+11	6.93E+10	-3.239453	0.0014**
D16	-2.26E+11	6.92E+10	-3.272245	0.0013**
D15	-2.26E+11	6.92E+10	-3.269963	0.0013**
D14	-2.26E+11	6.91E+10	-3.269445	0.0013**
D13	-2.24E+11	6.92E+10	-3.229949	0.0015**
D12	-2.26E+11	6.92E+10	-3.265459	0.0013**
D11	-2.26E+11	6.92E+10	-3.270634	0.0013**
D10	-2.26E+11	6.92E+10	-3.272388	0.0013**

D9	-2.26E+11	6.92E+10	-3.269396	0.0013**
D8	-2.26E+11	6.92E+10	-3.268596	0.0013**
D7	-2.26E+11	6.92E+10	-3.269525	0.0013**
D6	-2.26E+11	6.92E+10	-3.266919	0.0013**
D5	-2.28E+11	6.92E+10	-3.295711	0.0012**
D4	-2.27E+11	6.92E+10	-3.274336	0.0013**
D3	-2.26E+11	6.92E+10	-3.270655	0.0013**
D2	-2.26E+11	6.92E+10	-3.270020	0.0013**
D1	-2.29E+11	6.92E+10	-3.302913	0.0012**
AFBP	8.48E+10	1.75E+10	4.851597	0.0000***
TBA_GDP	-3.38E+10	2.07E+10	-1.628039	0.1053
TBLA_GDP	1.63E+11	9.41E+10	1.732633	0.0850
LOG(VIT)	6.93E+09	2.21E+09	3.139999	0.0020**
LIB	2.51E+10	1.64E+10	1.527289	0.1285
INFLATION	-26397047	43155617	-0.611671	0.5416
TELEDENSITY	-2.22E+08	2.01E+08	-1.100187	0.2728
ELECTRICITY	1.87E+08	56057520	3.341131	0.0010***
CORRUPTION	1.28E+09	1.54E+09	0.829361	0.4080

R-squared	0.578100	Mean dependent var	1.15E+09
Adjusted R-squared	0.502059	S.D. dependent var	4.53E+09
S.E. of regression	3.20E+09	Akaike info criterion	46.75189
Sum squared resid	1.76E+21	Schwarz criterion	47.27238
Log likelihood	-4736.693	Hannan-Quinn criter.	46.96244
Durbin-Watson stat	1.535647		

*, ** and *** indicate significance levels of 5, 1 and .01 percent respectively.

The major conclusion that can be drawn from these results is that increased IFDI in the Nigerian banking industry in recent times could be explained by increase in the profitability of foreign banks in Nigeria, Nigeria's increasing openness to foreign trade, and increasing infrastructural development in Nigeria.

The positive and significant relationship between IFDIs in the Nigerian banking industry and Nigeria's volume of international trade could serve as a proof of the following-the-clients and defensive expansion theories of foreign banking in Nigeria.

VI – Conclusion

This paper has empirically established that foreign investors will be significantly attracted into the Nigerian banking industry when there is greater economic and infrastructural development in Nigeria. This finding underlines the need to drastically minimize disruptions to power supply and enhance the nation's productivity. Greatly improving the incentives for increased volumes of international trade is also necessary. These efforts will go a long way to minimizing the cost of doing business in Nigeria, increase the productivity of foreign investments in the country, and attracting new IFDIs in the banking industry. The FGN and the CBN must take cognizance of these facts if the Nigerian banking industry is to attract its fair share of IFDIs on a sustained basis. As it stands, the CBN needs to, for the moment, set aside its current habit of wooing foreign investors into Nigeria's financial services sector since the habit may not produce sustained results unless accompanied by far-reaching infrastructural and economic development. More investors are currently focusing on business opportunities within Africa partly because several countries within the continent have escaped the hangover from the global credit crisis (Mbaye, 2010: 9). Nigeria should seize this opportunity to implement far-reaching strategies that would make its economy more attractive to these investors.

References

Aburime, T.U. (2005) "The Future of Foreign Banking in Nigeria". *The Nigerian Banker*, April - June, 25-32.

—. (2006) "Concentration Implications of the Banks Consolidation Exercise in Nigeria". *The Nigerian Banker*, July – September, 23-30. Available at www.cibng.org/publications/Bank%20Concentration%20in%20Nigeria.pdf.

—. (2009a) "Determinants of Bank Profitability: Macroeconomic Evidence from Nigeria". *International Economics and Finance Journal*, 4 (1-2), 69-91.

—. (2009b) "Impact of Political Affiliation on Bank Profitability in Nigeria". *Journal of Global Economy*, 5 (3), 251-261. Available at http://www.rcssindia.org/.

Asiedu, E. (2002) "On the Determinants of Foreign Direct Investment to Developing Countries: Is Africa Different?". *World Development*, 30 (1), 107-119.

—. (2003) *Foreign Direct Investment to Africa: The Role of Government Policy, Governance and Political Stability*. Paper retrieved on August 7, 2003 from http://people.ku.edu/~asiedu/.

Asteriou, D. (2006) *Applied Econometrics – A Modern Approach Using EViews and Microfit*. New York: Palgrave Macmillan.

CBN (1984) *Annual Report and Statement of Accounts for the Year Ended 31st December, 1984*. Lagos: Central Bank of Nigeria.

—. (2001) *Central Bank of Nigeria Annual Report and Statement of Accounts for the Year Ended 31st December, 2001*. Abuja: Central Bank of Nigeria.

—. (2005) *Central Bank of Nigeria Annual Report and Statement of Accounts for the Year Ended 31st December, 2005*. Abuja: Central Bank of Nigeria.

—. (2006) *Central Bank of Nigeria Annual Report and Statement of Accounts for the Year Ended 31st December, 2006*. Abuja: Central Bank of Nigeria.

Demirgüç-Kunt, A. and Huizinga, H. (2001) "Financial Structure and Bank Profitability". In *Financial Structure and Economic Growth: A Cross-Country Comparison of Banks, Markets, and Development*, Cambridge, MA: MIT Press. Retrieved on March 10, 2005 from http://www.econ.worldbank.org/docs/1185.pdf.

Hill, R.C., Griffiths, W.E., and Lim, G.C. (2008) *Principles of Econometrics* (Third Edition). Hoboken, NJ: John Wiley & Sons, Inc.

Ibe, P. (2004) "N25bn Capital: CBN Woos Chinese Investors". *ThisDay News*. Retrieved on September 9, 2004 from http://www.thisdayonline.com/news/20040907news07.html.

Ighomwenghian, K. (2009) "Nigeria: When Sanusi's Tsunami Caught Nigerian Economy Unawares". *Daily Independent*, December 29.

Mbaye, S. (2010) "Africa's Single-Currency Love-in Makes No Sense". *The Age*, October 22, p. 9.

Moshirian, F. (2006) "Aspects of International Financial Services". *Journal of Banking & Finance*, 30, 1057-1064.

Moss, T.J., Ramachandran, V. and Shah, M.K. (2005) "Is Africa's Skepticism of Foreign Capital Justified? Evidence from East African Firm Survey Data". In Moran, T.H., Graham, E.M. and Blomström, M. (Eds.), *Does Foreign Direct Investment Promote Development?*, Washington, DC: Institute for International Economics, 337-366.

NDIC (2002) *Nigeria Deposit Insurance Corporation Annual Report & Statement of Accounts*. Abuja: The NDIC Research Dept.

—. (2003) *Nigeria Deposit Insurance Corporation Annual Report & Statement of Accounts*. Abuja: The NDIC Research Dept.

—. (2006) *Nigeria Deposit Insurance Corporation 2006 Annual Report & Statement of Accounts*. Abuja: The NDIC Research Dept.

—. (2007) *Nigeria Deposit Insurance Corporation 2007 Annual Report & Statement of Accounts*. Abuja: The NDIC Research Dept.

—. (2009) *Nigeria Deposit Insurance Corporation 2009 Annual Report & Statement of Accounts*. Abuja: The NDIC Research Dept.

Panibratov, A. and Kalotay, K. (2009) "Russian Outward FDI and Its Policy Context". *Vale Columbia Center on Sustainable International Investment Research Paper*, 1, October 13. Retrieved on October 16, 2009 from www.vcc.columbia.edu/documents/FDIProfile-Russia.pdf.

Thuraisamy, K. (2010) *MAF 101 Fundamentals of Finance* (3rd Edition). Sydney: Pearson Australia.

World Bank (2007) *The Little Data Book 07*. Washington, D.C.: The World Bank.

Voinea, L. and Mihaescu, F. (2006) *The Determinants of Foreign Banking Activity in South East Europe: Do FDI, Bilateral Trade and EU Policies Matter?*. Paper retrieved on September 3, 2008 from http://www.gdnet.org/pdf2/gdn_library/global_research_projects/rich_country_policies/voinea-mihaescu.pdf.

Impact of Macroeconomic Factors on Stock Exchange Prices: Evidence from USA Japan and China

Omar Masood,[1] Umie Habiba,[2] Shirley Mardonez,[3] Mondher Bellalah,[4] Georges Pariente[5] and Olivier Levyne[5]

1. Introduction

In July 2007, the global financial crisis started, USA investors lost confidence, and the subprime mortgage crisis has not only hampered the real estate stocks but also many other related sectors. This resulted in the US Federal Bank injecting a large amount of capital into the financial markets.

January 2008 was an especially volatile month in the world's stock markets, but the effects were quite different. By September of 2008, the collapse of Lehman Brothers started a new phase in the global financial crisis; stock markets around the globe crashed and became highly volatile. Therefore, investors switched their investment from risky stock markets to gold, interest rate based bonds and US Dollar or Euro currency, getting higher risk free returns.

Japan's economy declined and exports to Europe fell 3.5 percent between September of 2008 and March of 2009, its industrial production dropped by 30 percent, and GDP in the first quarter of 2009 slumped by 15.4 percent at an annualized rate.

---

[1] Royal Business School, University of East London, omar@uel.ac.uk.
[2] Islamiya College, Lahore, Pakistan, habibaumie@gmail.com
[3] Researcher, Center of Economic Studies, Externado University of Colombia, smardonez@gmail.com
[4] Universite de Cergy-Pontoise, Mondher.bellalah@eco.u-cergy.fr]
[5] Institute Superior de Commerce, ISC Paris

Despite GDP in the first quarter of 2009 falling by 5.7 percent in the United States, the net effect of international financial channels was to support its activities, as money flowed into the dollar and US assets. China was least affected by the global financial crisis, as its equity and debt markets were substantially less exposed to foreign investors than other emerging markets.

Economist James D. Hamilton has argued that the increase in oil prices in the period of 2007-2008 was also a significant cause of the recession. The crisis started in one economy and then spread out to other economies through capital markets and financial channels, and eventually affected the countries' macroeconomic indicators. It seems that there may be a causality relationship between stock market and macroeconomic indicators of a country. Hence, this study will empirically examine the long run as well as short run relationship among stock markets and macroeconomic factors in the three major economies of the world during the global financial crisis period of 2005-1 to 2010-5.

In addition the study examines whether performance of the stock market can be used as an important factor that shows the conditions of the economy of a country. Can macro-economic variables be used to predict stock market returns in above said economies?

2. Review of Literature

Stock market plays an important role in the development of the economy of a country. A number of studies have investigated the causal relationship between macroeconomic variables and stock exchange returns; as Linter (1975), Fema and Schwert (1977), Fama (1981, 1982), and Geske and Roll (1983) found out, there is a negative relationship between real stock returns and inflation in US and European stock markets. Chatrath and Ramchander (1997) and Hu and Willett (2000) provide this evidence for India, and Ahmed and Mustafa (2004) for Pakistan.

In a period of rising oil prices, transportation index declines and hence profits in that market sector. But the same price increases will be favourable to the energy sector; wind and solar enterprises can charge higher prices, but may negatively affect an emerging market economy that uses oil, but has no oil production facilities. However, Chen et al. (1986) failed to find any relationship between the stock index and the oil price in the US. Sadorsky (1990) draws attention to a negative relationship between stock returns and shocks in oil prices for US economy and his research also indicates a negative impact of shocks to real stock returns on interest rates and industrial production.

Muhammad and Rasheed (2002) show that there is no short run relationship between stock returns and rate of exchange in Bangladesh, Pakistan, India and Sri-Lanka. The study also found that there is no long run association in Pakistan and India, but for Bangladesh and Sri-Lanka evidence show a bi-directional causality.

Chin-Hong and Jayaraman (2007) show that in Fiji the stock market price index is co-integrated with real economic activities in the long run, and it adjusts rather fast from short-run deviations towards long run equilibrium level. Except for rate of interest, M2, real output and rate of exchange do granger-cause to the stock returns in the short-run.

Tursoy, Gunsel and Rjoub (2008) used OLS technique, indicating that there is no significant relation between Istanbul Stock Exchange and macroeconomic variables as it affects one industry positively but may affect other industries negatively, so each portfolio affects each different industry in a different manner and thus multifactor APT fails to explain the effect in the stock market.

Mohammad, Hussain and Ali (2009) examined the relationship between macroeconomic variables and stock prices of Karachi stock exchange. They used ARIMA model and unit root technique to make data stationary. The result indicates that there is significant relationship between interest rate, M2, exchange rate, exchange reserve and the stock prices. Few variables like industrial production index and gross fixed capital formation have negligible effects on stock prices.

Robert D. Gay (2008) used ARIMA modal in OLS technique showing that macroeconomic variables have insignificant impact on stock price for India, Brazil, China and Russia.

Mahmood, Dinniah (2009) used Error Correction Model to analyse the multivariate causality between foreign exchange rate, CPI, industrial production index and stock prices for Japan, Malaysia, Hong Kong, Thailand, Korea, and Australia. They found that there is a long run equilibrium relationship between variables only in four countries; Japan, Korea, Australia and Hong Kong, and in the short run there is no interaction in the relation between all of the above mention variables in all selected countries except between real output and stock price in Thailand and between foreign exchange rates and stock price in Hong Kong.

Andreas Humpe and Peter Macmillan (2009), within the framework of a standard discounted value model and by employing co-integration analysis, showed that US stock price is negatively related to CPI and long run interest rate, but positively related to industrial production. The results also indicate that there is a positive but insignificant relationship between US stock prices and money supply. For the Japanese data, research found two co-integrating vectors. For the first vector, the result indicated that stock prices are positively influenced by industrial production and negatively by the money supply. The results for second co-integrating vector show consumer price index and long-term interest rates are negatively influenced by the industrial production.

Ali et al, (2010) used Johansen's co-integration and Granger's Causality Test show that there is no causal relationship between macroeconomic variables and stock exchange prices in Pakistan, only co-integration found between industrial production index and stock exchange prices. Finally findings suggest that performance of macroeconomic variables cannot predict stock exchange prices and stock market prices do not reflect the macroeconomic condition of Pakistan.

G. Kutty (2010) employed the Granger causality test to investigate the relationship between stock returns and rate of exchange in Mexico and found no long run relationship between these variables.

3. Research Methodology

Variables Identification: a) Stock Exchange Price Index (SPE) using the adjusted closing stock price index of NASDAQ Composite of USA, NIKKIE 225 of Japan, and Shanghai Composite of China are employed as measurement of the countries' monthly stock market price movements; b) The interest Rate (R) use is the short run interest rate; c) Broad money supply (M3), it in addition to currency in circulation, plus sight deposits held by domestic non-banks also include time deposits and savings deposits at short-notice held by domestic non-banks; d) Industrial production index (IP), which consists of the production of mining, manufacturing, and public utilities; e) Cured oil prices (Fuel) defined as the spot oil Price FOB of the last week of the month, which is weighted by estimated export volume (Dollars per Barrel); and f) Term of Trade (TOT) established as the ratio of exports and import.

Data Collection: The model uses monthly time series data for the range 2000-1 to 2010-5 for USA, Japan, and China. The data for the TOT, R, IP, and M3 of the USA, Japan, and China were obtained from the Organization of Economic Corporation and Development (OECD), the data for oil prices (OP) and the IP of the USA were obtained from the Federal Reserve's Bank (FRB), and the data of NASDAQ, NIKKEI-225, and Shanghai were obtained from Yahoo Finance. Data of the all variables were taken in natural logarithm form for the analysis.

Econometric Techniques: The study employs Autoregressive Distributive Lag (ARDL) approach to co-integration developed by Pesaran et al. (2001), to check the existences of the long run and short run relationship between the variables. Autoregressive distributive lag (ARDL) has some merits over Johansen Juselius co-integration test (JJ Test), Vector Error Correction model (VECM), and the Enger Granger causality test, as the ARDL approach can be used irrespective of whether the variables are integrated at I(0), I(1) or mixed order, but no variable is integrated at I(2) or higher order.

The general form of the Autoregressive Distributive Lag (ARDL) model can be written as:

$$\Delta LPSE_t = \alpha_0 + \sum_{i=1}^{n} b_i \Delta LIP_{t-i} + \sum_{i=1}^{n} c_i \Delta LR_{t-i} + \sum_{i=1}^{n} d_i \Delta LM3_{t-i} + \sum_{i=1}^{n} e_i \Delta LOP_{t-i} + \sum_{i=1}^{n} g_i \Delta LBOT_{0,t-i} + \delta_1 LPSE_{t-1} + \delta_2 LIP_{t-1} + \delta_3 LR_{t-1} + \delta_4 LM3_{t-1} + \delta_5 LOP_{t-1} + \delta_6 LBOT_{t-1} \quad (1)$$

Where α, b, c, d, e, g, and δ are coefficients, Δ is used for the difference of the variables, and 'n' shows the number of lags used.

The error correction version of ARDL model is applied through a two-step procedure. **Firstly**, for checking the existence of long run relationships between variables of the model, we test the null hypothesis

H_0: $\delta_1 = \delta_2 = \delta_3 = \delta_4 = \ldots\ldots\ldots\ldots = \delta_n = 0$ (no long run relationship)

Against alternative hypothesis:

H_1: $\delta_1 \neq \delta_2 \neq \delta_3 \neq \delta_4 \neq \ldots\ldots\ldots\ldots \neq \delta_n \neq 0$ (There is long run relationship)

The ARDL bound test is based on the F-test, which has a non-standard distribution irrespective of whether the variables are integrated at I(0) or I(1). Pesaran et al. (1996) give two critical bound values. The lower bound critical values assume that all variables are of I(0) and upper bound critical values assume that all variables are of I(1). If the computed F-statistic is greater than the upper bound, reject H_0 in favour of H_1, showing co-integration. If the computed F-statistic is less than the lower bound, reject H_1 in favour of H_0, showing no co-integration. If the computed F-statistic falls between the upper bound and lower bound, the results are inconclusive. **Secondly,** after establishing the co-integration between variables, the lag order of the variables is selected by using Akaike Information Criteria (AIC). After determining the lag order of the variables, the long run parameters of the model are estimated, and then the short run co-efficient is obtained by estimating the error correction model.

This is specified as follows:

$$\Delta LPSE_t = \alpha_0 + \sum_{i=1}^{n} b_i \Delta LIP_{t-i} + \sum_{i=1}^{n} c_i \Delta LR_{t-i} + \sum_{i=1}^{n} d_i \Delta LM3_{t-i} + \sum_{i=1}^{n} e_i \Delta LOP_{t-i} + \sum_{i=1}^{n} g_i \Delta LTOT_{0,t-I} + \varphi ecm_{t-1} \quad (2)$$

Here α, b, c, d, e, and g are the short run dynamic coefficients of the model, which are convergent to the equilibrium, and φ is the speed of adjustment.

4. Empirical Result

According to the Augmented Dickey Fuller (ADF) unit root test, all variables are stationary of I(1), only the industrial production index (lip) and balance of trade (lbot) of China are stationary of I(0). The results all show that none of the variables are stationary at I(2) or a higher order. So the appropriate technique of the data analysis is the ARDL approach to co-integration.

Table No 1. Augmented Dickey Fuller Test (ADF) unit root test

COUNTRIES	VARIABLES	LEVEL	1st DIFFERENCE	DECISION
USA	Lpse	-2.142061	-5.763582***	I(1)***
	Lip	-2.470276	-5.745863***	I(1)***
	Lr	-2.339568	-6.717834***	I(1)***
	Lbot	-3.288148	-4.020912***	I(1)***
	Lfuel	-2.695400	-5.246642***	I(1)***
	Lm3	-1.172954	-3.719612**	I(1)**
JAPAN	Lpse	-2.011385	-6.061642***	I(1)***
	Lip	-2.272286	-3.968801***	I(1)***
	Lr	-2.583981	-8.613015***	I(1)***
	Lbot	-1.671331	-11.17121***	I(1)***
	Lfuel	-2.695400	-5.246642***	I(1)***
	Lm3	-1.429029	-4.423576***	I(1)***
CHINA	Lpse	-0.865322	-7.103590***	I(1)***
	Lip	-6.300622**	-------	I(0)***
	Lr	-1.631890	-3.941916**	I(1)**
	Lbot	-2.736950	-12.73121**	I(0)***
	Lfuel	-2.695400	-5.246642**	I(1)***
	Lm3	-1.227832	-3.340845*	I(1)*

*, ** and *** indicate that co-efficient is significantly different from zero at 10%, 5% and 1% probability level respectively.

Results of long run co-efficient: The computed f-statistic of the model (1) for USA is 5.124496 and for China is 7.904303, which is greater than upper bound 4.57 and significance at 5% confidence level; for Japan the f-statistic is 5.681520, which is greater than upper bound 5.23 and significant at 1% confidence level. Thus it indicates that there exists a long run co-integration among the stock exchange prices (lpse), lr, lip, lm3, lbot, and lfuel.

Given the existence of the co-integration between the variables, we estimate the ARDL model (1) to see the long run, as well as short run, dynamics of the variables of the model, by using Akaike Information Criteria (AIC) for lag selection.

The results of long run co-efficient (dynamics) shows that in USA, Japan, and China, the rate of interest is positively affected to the stock exchange prices, and highly significantly for Japan and China. This result is unlike previous research, for example, Chen et al. (1986) and Mukherjee and Naka (1995) reported negative relation between rate of interest and LPSE.

The industrial production index for the countries of study has a positive long run relation with stock exchange prices, highly significant for USA and China but insignificant for Japan. The Term of trade (TOT) has positive impact on PSE, with significant impact for Japan; it indicates that if ratio of exports and imports increases, the PSE also increases.

Consistent with the research of Mukherjee and Naka (1995), this study shows that in USA and China there is a positive relation between Money supply (M3) and LPSE; this positive relation shows that money growth is stimulating the USA economy. This study also shows that in Japan there is a negative relation between Money supply (M3) and PSE, which shows that with money growth inflation in the economy, the stock price and corporate earnings decrease.

As expected, oil prices are negatively related to the LPSE, but this result is not significant for USA, though it is significant for Japan, which indicates that increase in oil prices will lead to increase in cost of production, and consequently a fall in stock price. As China is an oil-importing country, when the price of oil increases, the cost of production increases, and consequently PSE decreases.

Table No 2. Long Run Coefficients based on Akaike Information Criterion (AIC)

	USA ARDL (2,0,3,0,1,2)			JAPAN ARDL (6,2,5,2,2,0)			CHINA ARDL (2,5,0,0,5,2)		
Regressor	**Coefficient**	**Standard Error**	**T-Ratio [Prob]**	**Coefficient**	**Standard Error**	**T-Ratio [Prob]**	**Coefficient**	**Standard Error**	**T-Ratio [Prob]**
LR	0.17265	0.1515	1.1394[.260]	0.93171***	0.18817	4.9513[.000]	4.3657***	0.97086	4.4967[.000]
LIP	2. 2795***	0.4913	4.6397[.000]	0.71774	0.45964	1.5615[.127]	0.32689	0.99572	.32829[.744]
LM3	0.35432	0.8366	.42350[.674]	-0.32825	1.1001	- 0.2983[.767]	2.7761***	0.37472	7.4086[.000]
LTOT	0.27157	0.8511	.31908[.751]	2.6703***	0.8622	3.0971[.004]	0.97878	1.3675	.71575[.478]
LFUEL	-0.0311	0.085	- .36580[.716]	-0.19551*	0.11476	- 1.7037[.097]	- 3.0039***	0.73215	- 4.1028[.000]
C	-4.333	4.6745	- .92693[.359]	7.9442	6.497	1.2228[.229]	-3.0044	5.0892	- .59035[.558]

*, ** and *** indicate that co-efficient is significantly different from zero at 10%, 5% and 1% probability level respectively.

Results of Error Correction Model: For the three countries, the results of ECM, the lagged error correction term Ecm(-1) is negative and highly significant, indicating a rapid adjustment process to equilibrium, which shows that disequilibria of the previous period shock will rapidly adjust to long run equilibrium.

The results of the short run indicate that the lag value of LPSE in USA and Japan is positive, and with significant impact for USA on stock exchange prices, showing that past stock exchange prices also influence the PSE; however for China, the lag value of LPSE has negative and insignificant impact.

For the USA, rate of interest has a positive but insignificant effect on LPSE. Lag value of industrial production index positively and highly affected the PSE. Money supply (M3) has a positive and insignificant effect on PSE. Lag value of the TOT is negatively related to PSE. Lag value of the oil prices has a positive and significant effect on LPSE.

Rate of interest significantly affects PSE in Japan, and the lag value of industrial production index negatively and highly affected the PSE. Money supply (M3) has negatively affected PSE. Lag value of TOT is negatively related with PSE. Lag value of the oil prices has a negative and significant effect on PSE.

In the case of China, the rate of interest has a positive relation with LPSE. Lag value of industrial production index positively and highly affected the LPSE. Money supply (M3) has a positive and significant effect on LPSE. Lag value of TOT is negatively related with PSE. Oil prices have highly significant relation with LPSE. In the first period, oil prices have a negative and significant effect on LPSE, but in the second period, oil prices have a positive and significant relation.

Table No 3. Error Correction Representation for the Selected ARDL Model based on Akaike Information Criterion

	ARDL (6,2,5,2,2,0) Japan Model			ARDL (2,5,0,0,5,2) China Model			ARDL (2,0,3,0,1,2) USA Model		
Regressor	Coefficient	Standard Error	T-Ratio [Prob]	Coefficient	Standard Error	T-Ratio [Prob]	Coefficient	Standard Error	T-Ratio [Prob]
dLPSE1	.31745*	0.16282	1.9497[.058]	-0.21036	0.13157	-1.5988[.117]	0.32643**	0.14589	2.2374[0.03]
dLPSE2	0.10473	0.16328	.64138[.525]						
dLPSE3	0.18327	0.14989	1.2227[.229]						
dLPSE4	0.41229*	0.15281	2.6980[.010]						
dLPSE5	-0.16364	0.13886	-1.1784 [.246]						
dLR	0.34636***	0.10912	3.1742[.003]	1.6709**	0.71623	2.3329[.024]	0.08401	0.080253	1.0468[0.3]
dLR1	-0.27924 ***	0.10729	-2.6028 [.013]	0.70895	0.63472	1.1170[.270]			
dLR2				0.54236	0.68046	.79704[.430]			
dLR3				3.2741***	0.66021	4.9592[.000]			
dLR4				1.0784	0.73616	1.4649[.150]			
dLIP	0.29462	0.498	59160[.557]	0.085616	0.26469	.32346[.748]	1.1914	0.91651	1.2999[0.2]
dLIP1	-.96185**	0.47522	-2.0240 [.050]				2.5256***	0.74754	3.3786[0.001]
dLIP2	0.4668	0.4135	1.1289[.266]				1.5499*	0.84121	1.7997[0.078]

dLIP3	-0.65697	0.41204	-1.5944 [.119]						
dLIP4	-.92555**	0.40944	-2.2605 [.029]						
dLM3	-1.6962	4.5357	-.37397 [.710]	.72710***	0.19462	3.7360[.001]	0.17241	0.41656	1.7997[0.681]
dLM31	-8.2770*	4.6861	-1.7663 [.085]						
dLTOT	-0.046672	0.24498	-.19051 [.850]	0.13457	0.18174	.74045[.463]	-0.46564	0.36148	-1.2881[0.204]
dLTOT1	-1.0326 ***	0.26348	-3.9190 [.000]	0.20734	0.39777	.52125[.605]			
dLTOT2				.76173**	0.36262	2.1007[.042]			
dLTOT3				1.0948***	0.28333	3.8640[.000]			
dLTOT4				.60826***	0.20675	2.9420[.005]			
dLFUEL	- .086356**	0.051043	-1.6918 [.098]	-.31372**	0.15631	-2.0071[.05]	0.031691	0.066016	0.48005[0.633]
LFUEL1				.37617***	0.15103	2.4906[.01]	0.14014**	0.068548	2.0444[0.046]
dC	3.5089	2.2936	1.5299[.134]	-0.7869	1.425	-.55222[.584]	-2.1085	2.4026	-0.8775 [0.384]
Ecm(-1)	-.44170 ***	0.15444	-2.8599 [.007]	- .26191***	0.086129	-3.0409[.004]	-0.4866***	0.12125	-4.0134[0]
R-Squared = 0.73452 R-Bar-Squared = 0.57228., F-stat = 5.5335[.000], DW-statistic = 2.2829				R-Squared = 0 .69156 R-Bar-Squared = 0.54505, F-stat = 5.6053[.000], DW-statistic = 1.9328			R-Squared= 0.55058 R-Bar-Squared= 0.42627, F-stat = 5.7580[.000] DW-statistic = 2.0619		

*, ** and *** indicate that co-efficient is significantly different from zero at 10%, 5% and 1% probability level respectively.

5. Conclusions

This study examines the relationships between the NASDAQ Composite of USA, NIKKIE 225 of Japan, and Shanghai Composite of China Stock exchange price Index and macroeconomic variables (term of trade, oil prices, rate of interest, money supply (M3), and index of industrial production) with particular attention on recent global financial crises.

For deep analysis, the ARDL co-integration approach and monthly data of the said variables of the period of January 2005 to May 2010 has been employed. The results show that in USA and China, in the long run (LR) as well as short run (SR), rate of interest, industrial production index, and Money supply (M3), are positively related to the stock exchange prices. The results of Japan show that rate of interest is positively and highly significantly in LR, but in SR, at first lag it has a positive relation, while at second lag it has a negative relation with stock exchange prices. For the Japan data, in LR, industrial production index has a positive and insignificant relation with stock exchange prices, and in SR, at first lag it has a positive relation, while at second lag it has a negative relation with stock exchange prices. For Japan, money supply (m3) has a positive relation in LR, but a negative and significant relation in SR, with stock exchange prices.

In all three economies, USA, Japan, and China, in the long run, term of trade (TOT) has a positive relation with stock prices. But in the USA and Japan, in the short run, TOT is negatively related with stock exchange prices. For China's data, in the short run, TOT is positively related with stock prices. In all three economies, in the long run, oil prices are negatively related to the stock exchange prices, but in the short run, in USA, oil prices have a positive relation; in Japan oil prices have a negative relation; and in China at first lag it has a positive relation, while at second lag it has a negative relation with stock exchange prices.

This study shows that the long run model can explain the USA and China stock markets, yielding consistent factor loading, but not Japan's stock market. However, the short run model cannot explain the USA, Japan and China stock markets, yielding consistent factors loading. An explanation of the difference in behaviour between the three stock markets may lie in the fact that the USA economy is most affected by financial crises, 2007, and the Japanese economy slumped after 1990, while China is least affected economy by financial crises, 2007.

The movement of stock exchange is an important indicator of economy processes. The research shows that macroeconomic variables will affect Stock Exchange Prices in USA, Japan and China, and we can use macroeconomic variables as predictors to predict stock market returns in said countries.

References

Ali, Imran, Rehman, Kashif Ur , Yilmaz, Ayse Kucuk , Khan, Muhammad Aslam , & Afzal, Hasan. (2010). Causal relationship between macroeconomic indicators and stock exchange prices in Pakistan. *African Journal of Business Management*, *4*(3), 312-319.

Canova, Fabio, Cepr, & Nicol ′O, Gianni DE (1997). Stock returns, term structure, inflation, and real activity: an international perspective.

Chatrath, Arjun and Sanjay Ramchander (1997), "Stock Prices, Inflation and Output: Evidence from India", *Applied Financial Economics*, 7, 439-445.

Chen, N. F., Roll, R. & Ross, S. 1986. Economic forces and the stock market. Journal of Business 59 (3): 83-403. Caporale, Tony and Chulho Jung (1997), "Inflation and Real Stock Prices", *Applied Financial Economics*, 7, 265-266

Fama, E. F. (1981), "Stock Returns, real Activity, Inflation, and Money", *American Economic Review*, 71, 545-564.

—. (1982), "Inflation, Output, and Money", *Journal of Business*, 55, 201-231.

Fama, E. F. and Schwert, G. W. (1977), "Asset Returns and Inflation", *Journal of Financial Economics*, 5. 115-146..

Gay, Robert D. (2008). Effect of macroeconomic variables on stock market returns for four emerging economies: Brazil, Russia, India, and china. *International Business & Economics Research Journal*, *7*(3), 1-8.

Geske, R. and Roll, R. (1983), "The Fiscal and Monetary Linkage Between Stock Returns and Inflation", *Journal of Finance*, 38, 1-33.

Hu, Xiaoqiang and Thomas D. Willett (2000), "The Variability of Inflation and Real Stock Returns", *Applied Financial Economics*, 10, 655-665

Humpe, Andreas, & Macmillan, Peter. (2009). Can Macroeconomic variables explain long-term stock market movements? A comparison of the US and Japan. *Applied Financial Economics*, *19*, 111–119.

Kutty, Goplan. (2010). The Relationship between exchange rates and stock prices: the case of Mexico. *4*(4),

Linter, John (1975), “Inflation and Security Returns”, *The Journal of Finance*, 30: 2, 259-280.

Mahmood, Wan Mansor Wan, & Dinniah, Nazihah Mohd. (2009). Stock returns and macroeconomics variables: evidence from the six Asian-Pacific countries. *International Research Journal of Finance and Economics*, *30*, 154-165.

Mohammad, Suliaman D., Hussain, Adnan, & Ali, Adnan. (2009). Impact of macroeconomics variables on stock prices: empirical evidence in. *European Journal of Scientific Research*, *38*(1), 96-103.

Mookherjee R, Yu Q (1997). Macroeconomic variables and stock prices in a small open economy: the case of Singapore. Pacific Basin Fin. J. 5(3): 377-388.

Muhammad, naeem, & Rasheed, abdul. (2002). Stock prices and exchange rates: are they related? Evidence from south Asian countries. *41*(4), 535-550.

Mukherjee T, Naka A (1995). Dynamic linkage between macroeconomic variables and Japanese stock market: an application of a Vector Error Correction Model. J. Fin. pp.461-471.

Tursoy, Turgut, Gunsel, Nil, & Rjoub, Husam. (2008). Macroeconomic factors, the APT and the Istanbul Stock Market. *International Research Journal of Finance and Economics*, (22), 49-57.

OIL PRICE FLUCTUATIONS AND EQUITY RETURNS IN NET OIL-EXPORTING COUNTRIES

MOHAMED EL HEDI AROURI,[1] MONDHER BELLALAH,[2] AMINE LAHIANI,[3] AND DUC KHUONG NGUYEN[4]

1. Introduction

In the last decade, oil price has experienced large variations. For instance, after reaching a substantial decline to less than $20 per barrel in December 2001, induced by the world economic downturns, the oil price increased to more than $130 in June 2008. As a consequence, we find in the literature several empirical investigations on the impact of oil price shocks on economic activity. These works have established that oil price shocks significantly affect economic variables in most developed and emerging countries (Cunado and Perez de Garcia, 2005; Balaz and Londarev, 2006; Gronwald, 2008; Cologni and Manera, 2008; Kilian, 2008). Moreover, some recent studies have consistently documented that oil price changes affect economic activity and stock market returns in a nonlinear fashion (Hamilton, 2003; Huang et al., 2005; Zhang, 2008; Cologni and Manera, 2009). In contrast, there has been relatively little work done on the effects of oil price shocks on stock markets. In addition, most of these works have focused on few net-oil importing developed countries. As for emerging stock markets, very few studies have been carried out.

There exist several mechanisms through which oil may affect stock prices. The most invoked rational of using oil price as a factor affecting stock prices is that in theory the value of a stock is equal to the discounted sum

[1] Professor of Finance, CRCGM, University of Auvergne & EDHEC Business School, mohamed.arouri@edhec.edu.

[2] Professor of Finance, Universite de Cergy-Pontoise.

[3] Associate Professor of Finance, LEO, University of Orléans & ESC Rennes Business School, amine.lahiani@univ-orleans.fr.

[4] Associate Professor of Finance, Dept. of Finance and Information Systems, ISC Paris School of Management, dnguyen@iscparis.com.

of expected future cash-flows. These cash-flows are affected by macroeconomic events that may be influenced by oil price changes. Therefore, oil price fluctuations may influence stock market returns. Most previous studies have investigated this relationship using low frequency (monthly or quarterly) data from net-oil importing countries. Using daily data, the present paper investigates the short-run relationships between oil price shocks and stock markets in the Gulf Cooperation Council (GCC) countries.

Investigating the links between oil prices and stock markets in GCC countries is interesting for several reasons. First, GCC countries are major suppliers of oil in world energy markets, and their stock markets are likely to be susceptible to change in oil prices. Second, the GCC markets differ from those of developed and from other emerging countries in that they are largely segmented from the international markets and are overly sensitive to regional political events. Finally, GCC markets represent very promising areas for regional and world portfolio diversification. Studying the influence of oil price shocks on GCC stock market returns is important for investors to make necessary investment decisions and for policy-makers to regulate stock markets more effectively. All these reasons highlight the interest of a study focusing on GCC countries.

The pioneering paper by Jones and Kaul (1996) tests the reaction of international stock markets (Canada, UK, Japan and US) to oil price shocks on the basis of standard cash flow dividend valuation model. They found that for the US and Canada this reaction can be accounted for entirely by the impact of the oil shocks on cash flows. The results for Japan and the UK were inconclusive. Using an unrestricted vector autoregressive (VAR), Huang et al. (1996) show a significant link between some American oil company stock returns and oil price changes. However, they find no evidence of a relationship between oil prices and market indices such as the S&P500. In contrast, Sadorsky (1999) applies an unrestricted VAR with GARCH effects to American monthly data and shows a significant relationship between oil price changes and aggregate stock returns in US. In particular, he shows that oil price shocks have asymmetric effects: positive oil shocks have a greater impact on stock returns and economy activity than do negative oil price shocks. Relying on nonlinear causality tests, Ciner (2001) provides evidence that oil shocks affect, in a non-linear manner, stock index returns in US, which is consistent with the documented influence of oil on economic activity.

Recently, some papers have tended to focus on major European, Asian and Latin American emerging markets. The results of these studies show a significant short run link between oil price changes and emerging stock markets. For instance, Papapetrou (2001) shows a significant relationship between oil price changes and stock markets in Greece. Basher and Sadorsky (2006) reach the same conclusion for other emerging stock markets using an international multifactor model. However, less attention has been given to smaller emerging markets, especially in the GCC countries where share dealings is a relatively recent phenomenon. Using VAR models and co-integration tests, Hammoudeh and Aleisa (2004) show that there is a bidirectional relationship between Saudi stock returns and oil prices changes. All the previous findings also suggest that the other GCC markets are not directly linked to oil prices and are less dependent on oil exports and are more influenced by their own domestic factors. Bashar (2006) employs VAR analysis to study the effect of oil price changes on GCC stock markets, and shows that only Saudi and Oman markets have predictive power of oil price changes.

Hammoudeh and Choi (2006) examined the long-run relationship among the GCC stock markets in the presence of the US oil market, the S&P 500 index, and the US Treasury bill rate. They found that the T-bill rate has a direct impact on these markets, while oil and S&P 500 have indirect effects. Using nonlinear co-integration tests, Maghyereh and Al-Kandari (2007) show that, in the long-run, oil price impacts the stock price indices in GCC countries in a nonlinear fashion. Finally, in a more recent study, Arouri and Jouini (2009) examine the short-run relationships between oil prices and GCC stock markets. Using a non-parametric method - a local polynomial kernel regression of order 2 with a Gaussian kernel - they show that there are some signs of nonlinearities in the link between oil and stock market returns in Qatar, Oman, and UAE. In fact, their results establish that the relationships between oil prices and stock markets in these countries are asymmetric and switching according to the oil price change values. However, the method they use does not precise the analytical form of this nonlinear link, and thus results can be hardly used in portfolio management or policy decision process. For Bahrain, Kuwait, and Saudi Arabia the authors found that oil price changes do not affect stock market returns.

As can be seen, the results of the few available works on GCC countries are too heterogeneous. These results are puzzling because most GCC countries are strongly oil exporters and are somewhat similar in their economic structure. Furthermore, the GCC economies are oil dependent and thus are sensitive to oil price changes. This article extends the understanding of the relationship between oil prices and the stock market in GCC markets by making use of recent daily data and a variety of econometric tools.

The rest of the paper is organized as follows. Section 2 presents the data. The methodology and empirical results are discussed in section 3. Summary conclusions and policy implications are provided in Section 4.

2. Data and preliminary analysis

Our goal is to examine the short and long run relationships between oil prices and stock markets in GCC countries. Unlike previous studies which use low frequency data (yearly, quarterly or monthly), we use daily data which may adequately capture interaction between oil and stock prices in the region. Our sample period runs from 7 June 2005 to 21 February 2010 for the six GCC members. Stock market indices are obtained from MSCI database. For oil, we use the daily Brent spot price obtained from the Energy Information Administration (EIA). Brent oil prices are often used as reference prices for crude oil, including oil produced by GCC countries. All prices are denominated in American dollar. Descriptive statistics are summarized in Table 1.

In Panel A, we test for the presence of unit roots in the oil price and stock market series in logarithm. To this aim, we apply the Augmented Dickey Fuller (ADF) test. The tests give the same conclusion that the price series are integrated of order (1), while the returns series are stationary.

In Panel B, we report basic statistics on returns series. On average, returns are negative over our sample period because of the 1997-2009 international financial crisis. However, oil prices have on average increased over our sample period. Skewness is negative in most cases and the Jarque-Bera test statistic (JB) strongly rejects the hypothesis of normality for all series.

Panel C reports the unconditional correlations among GCC stock market returns and oil price changes. As we can see, cross-market correlations of GCC stock returns and oil prices are not high, but are on average positive. These correlations range from 0.02 (Kuwait) to 0.37 (Qatar).

Table 1: Descriptive statistics

Panel A: Stationarity tests

	Levels	First difference
Bahrain	-2.536** (a)	-32.621***(c)
Kuwait	-1.703 (b)	-32.891***(a)
Oman	-0.323 (a)	-31.399***(a)
A. Saudi	-0.776 (a)	-33.879***(a)
UAE	-1.231 (a)	-31.186***(a)
Qatar	-0.142 (a)	-11.744***(a)
Oil	-1.916 (c)	-35.222***(a)

Panel B: Basic statistics of return series

	Bahrain	Kuwait	Oman	A. Saudi	UAE	Qatar	Oil
Mean	-0.121	-0.002	-0.015	-0.043	-0.081	-0.026	0.037
Min.	11.502	8.752	10.750	16.226	18.326	12.863	16.413
Max.	-17.983	-14.871	-17.644	-21.570	-15.497	-20.012	-12.826
Std. dev.	1.588	1.783	1.634	2.244	2.207	3.972	2.768
Skew.	-1.978	-1.249	-1.479	-1.508	-0.754	-0.563	0.104
Kurt.	27.293	14.262	24.017	18.291	14.499	6.866	7.394
JB	30519*	6704*	22692*	12238*	6776*	118*	975*

Panel C: Unconditional correlations

	Bahrain	Kuwait	Oman	A. Saudi	UAE	Qatar
Oil	0.061	0.018	0.026	0.024	0.10	0.373

Notes: In Panel A, ADF test is carried out on log-prices and returns series. (a) model without constant nor deterministic trend, (b) model with constant without deterministic trend, (c) model with constant and deterministic trend. JB refers to the empirical statistics of Jarque-Bera test for normality. *, **, and *** denote rejection of the null hypothesis at 10%, 5%, and 1%, respectively.

3. Empirical results

In this part, we examine the short-term linkages between oil prices and stock market returns in GCC countries using several econometric tools.

3.1 Structural VAR estimation

First, in order to examine the relationships between oil and GCC stock returns, we estimate a structural VAR model. The Structural VAR model has the advantage of capturing the dynamic bidirectional causality that might exist among stock returns and oil price variations in GCC countries. Results are summarized in Table 2.

Table 2: VAR estimation results

	Bahrain		Kuwait		Oman		A. Saudi		UAE		Qatar	
	Stock	Oil	Stock	Oil	Stock	Oil	Stock	Oil	Stock	Oil	Stock	Oil
μ	-0.116***	0.017	-0.005	0.033	-0.016	0.031	-0.046	0.033	-0.075	0.033	0.025	0.087
	(0.045)	(0.079)	(-0.102)	(0.425)	(0.045)	(0.402)	(0.064)	(0.079)	(0.063)	(0.079)	(0.080)	(0.070)
α	0.056	-0.136***	0.054*	-0.086*	0.096***	-0.133***	0.024	-0.023	0.098***	-0.004	0.263***	0.337***
	(0.028)	(0.050)	(0.028)	(0.044)	(0.028)	(0.048)	(0.028)	(0.035)	(0.028)	(0.036)	(0.092)	(0.081)
β	0.056***	-0.008	0.032*	-0.011	0.118***	-0.010	0.039*	-0.012	0.064***	-0.012	-0.134	0.104
	(0.016)	(0.028)	(0.018)	(0.028)	(0.016)	(0.028)	(0.023)	(0.028)	(0.022)	(0.028)	(0.294)	(0.257)
Log-Lik	-2265	-2939	-2409	-2941	-2275	-2939	-2688	-2942	-2659	-2943	-484	-461
AIC	3.754	4.870	3.993	4.873	3.772	4.870	4.455	4.876	4.408	4.876	5.562	5.298
SIC	3.767	4.883	4.006	4.886	3.784	4.883	4.468	4.889	4.421	4.889	5.616	5.352

Notes: The optimal lag order for the VAR model is selected using the SIC information criterion. For all pairs (stock market, oil), the selected lag is 1. Standard errors are given between brackets. *, **, and *** denote rejection of the null hypothesis at 10%, 5%, and 1%, respectively. μ is a constant term and α and β are the coefficients relative to the country's stock market and oil price in the VAR specification.

Several comments can be made. First previous oil price changes positively affect stock returns in all GCC countries, except Qatar. Thus, as expected, in most GCC countries, there is a positive link between oil prices and stock markets. Increases in oil prices lead to appreciations in GCC stock prices. However, the sensitivity of stock markets to oil price changes varies from one GCC country to another. Second, lagged stock market returns are significant in four out of 6 cases: Kuwait, Oman, UAE, and Qatar. This finding suggests some predictability in stock returns in GCC stock markets. Thus, these markets are not efficient. Finally, oil price changes are partly predictable based on lagged GCC stock returns and lagged oil returns.

3.2 Causality tests

Second, in order to further investigate the links between oil and stock returns in GCC countries we proceed with Granger causality tests. We implement these tests for different lags. Results are reported in Table 3.

Table 3: Granger causality test

H_0	*p*-value
Bahrain - Oil	
Bahrain does not Granger cause Oil	0.023^{**}
Oil does not Granger cause Bahrain	0.002^{***}
Kuwait - Oil	
Kuwait does not Granger cause Oil	0.316
Oil does not Granger cause Kuwait	0.071^{*}
Oman - Oil	
Oman does not Granger cause Oil	0.027^{**}
Oil does not Granger cause Oman	0.000^{***}
Saudi Arabia - Oil	
Saudi Arabia does not Granger cause Oil	0.083^{*}
Oil does not Granger cause Saudi Arabia	0.000^{***}
UAE - Oil	
UAE does not Granger cause Oil	0.035^{**}
Oil does not Granger cause UAE	0.000^{***}
Qatar - Oil	
Qatar does not Granger cause Oil	0.334
Oil does not Granger cause Qatar	0.014^{**}

Notes: *, ** and *** indicates significance at the significance levels 10%, 5%, and 1%, respectively. All causality tests are carried out at lag 2 except for Kuwait where the lag is augmented to 4 since at lag 2 there is no causality detected.

According to these results, there is bidirectional causality between oil price changes and stock market reruns in most GCC countries: Bahrain, Oman, Saudi Arabia, and UAE. The direction of short-run causality runs from oil prices to stock markets in Qatar and to some extent in Kuwait at 10%. These results are consistent with our VAR model findings: there is a strong short-run link between oil prices and stock markets in most GCC countries.

Our results are interesting at least for two reasons. First, they imply some predictability in oil and GCC stock price dynamics. Second, in contrast to several works in the extant literature, which assume the exogeneity of oil prices with respect to macroeconomic and financial variables, we document that a reverse relationship may exist, i.e. changes in some GCC stock returns do significantly affect world oil prices.

3.3 Impulse response analysis

Next, we use the estimated model to calculate a series of impulse-response functions. The Impulse response function measures the reaction of a variable to a shock in another variable. Figure 1 plots the response of each stock market return to a one-time impulse in oil price changes. The plots show a similar reaction of the GCC stock market to an oil price shock: there is a short-run impact of oil price shock on the stock markets of GCC countries since the responses are null after 4 days, except for Qatar where the impulse response reaches a peak at the two-day horizon and dies out after 6 days. However, one should mention that the intensity of the reaction of stock markets to a shock in oil prices varies considerably from one country to another, corroborating our previous findings.

Taken together, our results suggest that oil price changes affect stock market returns in GCC countries significantly in the short-run, but the importance and nature of the relationship between oil prices and stock markets differ from one GCC country to another. These findings may reflect the complexity of the transmission mechanisms of oil price shocks to stock markets in GCC countries. Indeed, oil price increases directly influence government and corporate output and earnings in GCC countries and thus may drive up stock market returns. On the other hand, since GCC countries are importers of manufactory products from developed and emerging countries, oil price increases can indirectly impact GCC markets through their influence on prices of imported products. Accordingly, increases in oil prices are often indicative of inflationary pressure in the

Figure 1. Impulse response analysis

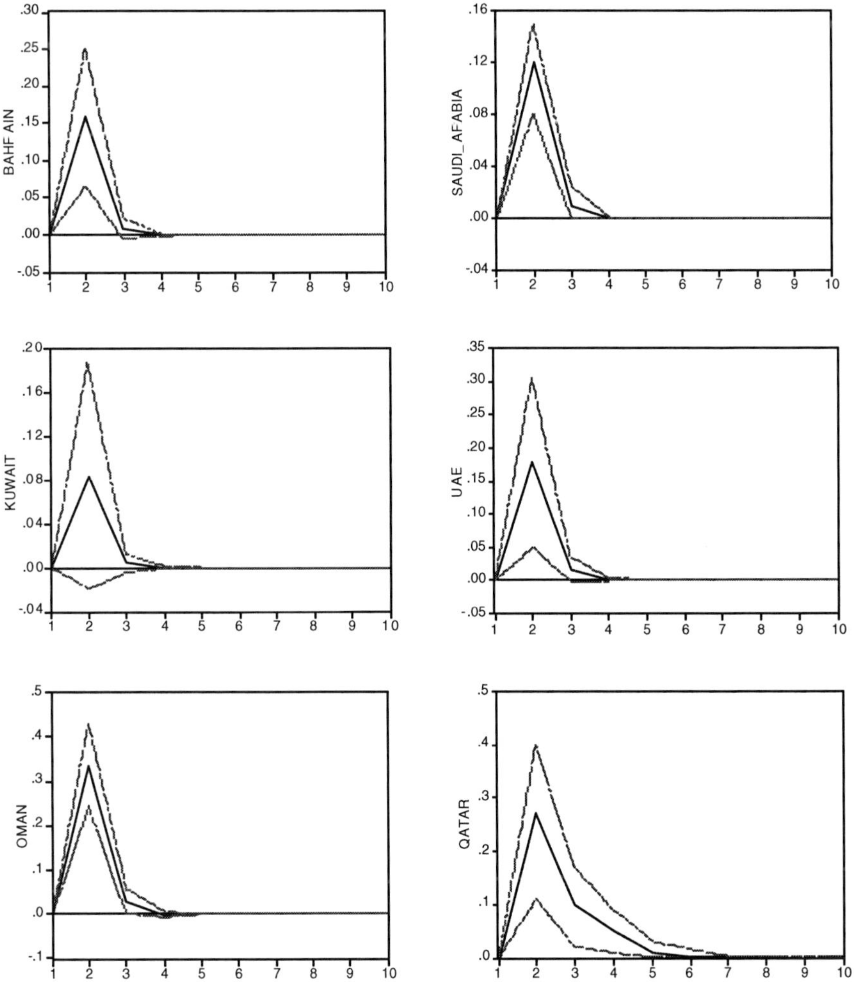

GCC economies, which in turn could indicate the future of interest rates and investment of all types. Unlike net oil-importing countries where the expected link between oil prices and stock markets is negative, the transmission mechanism of oil price shocks to stock market returns are ambiguous and the total impact of oil price shocks on stock returns depends on which of the positive and negative effects counterweigh the other. Our findings partly confirm this opinion and suggest that the effects of oil on stock markets are not the same in all GCC countries.

4. Conclusion and policy implications

This paper extends the understanding of linkages between oil prices and stock markets in GCC countries over the recent turbulent years. Since GCC countries are major world energy market players, their stock markets are likely to be susceptible to oil price shocks. Strong positive short-term relationships between oil price changes and stock markets have been found in most GCC countries. More interestingly, our findings suggest some predictability in oil and stock price dynamics in GCC countries.

The findings of the study offer several avenues for future research. First, the link between oil and stock markets in GCC countries can be expected to vary across different economic sectors. A sectoral analysis of this link would be informative. Second, evidence from international equity markets should be produced to examine the robustness of the findings. Third, the methodology applied in this article could be used to examine the effects of other energy products such as gas. Finally, further research could compare causality between oil and stock markets in GCC countries and other oil exporting countries.

References

Arouri, M., Fouquau, J., 2009. On the short-term influence of oil price changes on stock markets in GCC countries: linear and nonlinear analyses. Economics Bulletin 29(2), 806-815.

Balaz, P., Londarev, A., 2006. Oil and its position in the process of globalization of the world economy. Politicka Ekonomie 54(4), 508-528.

Bashar, Z., 2006. Wild oil prices, but brave stock markets! The case of Gulf Cooperation Council (*GCC*) stock markets. Middle East Economic Association Conference, Dubai.

Basher, S.A., Sadorsky, P., 2006. Oil price risk and emerging stock markets. Global Finance Journal 17, 224-251.

Ciner, C., 2001. Energy shock and financial market nonlinear linkages. Studies in Nonlinear Dynamics and Econometrics 5(3), 203-212.

Cologni, A., Manera, M., 2009. The asymmetric effects of oil shocks on output growth: A Markov-switching analysis for the G-7 countries. Economic Modelling, 26, 1-29.

Cologni, A., Manera, M., 2008. Oil prices, inflation and interest rates in a structural cointegrated VAR model for the G-7 countries. Energy Economics 30(3), 856-888.

Cunado, J., Perez de Garcia, F., 2005. Oil prices, economic activity and inflation: evidence for some Asian countries. Quarterly Review of Economics and Finance 45(1), 65-83.

Gronwald, M., 2008. Large oil shocks and the US economy: Infrequent incidents with large effects. Energy Journal 29, 151-71.

Hamilton, J. D. 2003. What is an Oil Shock? Journal of Econometrics, 113, 363-98.

Hammoudeh, S., Aleisa, E., 2004. Dynamic relationship among GCC stock markets and NYMEX oil futures. Contemporary Economic Policy 22 (2), 250-269.

Hammoudeh, S., Choi, K., 2006. Behavior of GCC stock markets and impacts of US oil and financial markets. Research in International Business and Finance 20 (1), 22-44.

Huang, B.N., Hwang, M.J., Peng, H.P., 2005. The asymmetry of the impact of oil price shocks on economic activities: An application of the multivariate threshold model. Energy Economics 27, 445-476.

Huang, R.D., Masulis, R.W., Stoll, H.R., 1996. Energy shocks and financial markets. Journal of Futures Markets 16 (1), 1-27.

Jones, C.M., Kaul, G., 1996. Oil and the stock markets. Journal of Finance 51(2), 463-491.

Kilian, L., 2008. Exogenous oil supply shocks: how big are they and how much do they matter for the US Economy? Review of Economics and Statistics 90, 216-40.

Maghyereh, A., Al-Kandari, A., 2007. Oil prices and stock markets in GCC countries: new evidence from nonlinear cointegration analysis. Managerial Finance 33(7), 449-460.

Papapetrou, E., 2001. Oil price shocks, stock market, economic activity and employment in Greece. Energy Economics 23(5), 511-532.

Sadorsky, P., 1999. Oil price shocks and stock market activity. Energy Economics 2, 449-469.

Zhang, D., 2008. Oil shock and economic growth in Japan: A nonlinear approach. Energy Economics 30(5), 2374-2390.

The Influence of Institutional Holdings on the Strategic Orientations of Businesses: The Case of Blue Capital in the Carrefour Group

Carole Monaco, Alain Finet and Christiane Bughin

1. Aims of the article

The opening of share capital to outside investors enables new sources of finance to be obtained and used to ensure the growth of the business. However, quotation on the Stock Exchange corresponds to the appearance of new investors, and in particular institutional holdings, in the capital structure of businesses. This then is a crucial moment in which the management style and control of the business will naturally evolve to face increasing market restrictions. These institutional holdings are often considered to be a relatively homogeneous group acting uniformly regardless of the context in which they operate. They are made up of mutual funds, insurance companies, pension funds, and hedge funds (Lavigne, 2004). The ease of access to information (B.J. Bushee, T.H. Goodman, 2007) will be a predominant criterion in their choice of acquisition of holdings (J. Golec, 2004, T.C. Chaing, E. Nelling, L. Tan, 2008, A-S Chen, B.-S. Hong, 2006). They will thus avoid businesses which have a high level of information asymmetry. According to this logic, institutional holdings will tend to favour businesses quoted on the Stock Exchange insofar as the market is more liquid, and assessment of the portfolio easier than for businesses that are not quoted (AFIC, BIPE, 2004). Given that they appear to constitute a *buffer zone* between the management team and the market (A.Finet et al, 2009), we think this type of investor merits particular attention insofar as they may constitute the *shareholding cement* of the business and as a result, have considerable influence on the strategic and financial orientations (share buybacks versus payment of dividends (R. Jain, 2007)) of businesses, their stock market valuation (S. Nagel, 2005), the business perpetuation process and, more generally, orient the configuration of a market (G. Kling, L. Gao, 2008, X. L. Wang, K. Shi, H.X. Fan, 2006). Theoretically, institutional holdings are *sought-after* - insofar as they bring capital into the business enabling it to grow - but also *demonised* due to their ability to damage the social construct of the business, by suggesting solutions that may have a harmful effect on its organisational structure. In addition, these investors are viewed with a great deal of suspicion insofar as the media highlights their influence on socially "difficult" strategic choices for businesses, also known as "stock market redundancies[1]".

In the same vein, this article aims to determine how the activism of institutional holdings operates on corporate governance and management style. To do this, we will concentrate on the way in which an institutional holding, in this case Blue Capital, influences the governance and strategic orientations adopted by Carrefour, a group within which this investor has a strong presence (it holds 15% of the group's capital). The central idea of this paper is therefore to answer the research question: "*In what way can Blue Capital's institutional activism influence the corporate governance and the management style of the Carrefour group?*"

On this basis our article will be structured as follows:

- First of all, we will theoretically define the notions of institutional holding (short or long term) and institutional activism in accordance with the long term or short term nature of the institutional holding, which is likely to have a greater or lesser involvement in the system of governance of the business;
- Secondly, and empirically, we will introduce the Carrefour group and its history.
- Thirdly, we will study Blue Capital's rise in power in order to appreciate how and to what extent this company influences the management style of the Carrefour group. We will attempt to highlight a very strong correlation between the significant nature of its presence within Carrefour and the strategic decision-making process oriented

[1] Redundancies which are not necessarily related to a difficult economic situation but which are aimed at reducing the wage bill, improving the operating income and cash flow of the business and bringing about a short term rise in the stock market valuation of the business.

towards satisfying the interests of shareholders, by using mass redundancies for example. We will also analyse the overlapping interests of the different Carrefour directors which could be a factor in understanding the strategic choices made by Carrefour and instigated by Blue Capital.

▪ Fourthly, we will conclude this article and highlight any limitations of the study and recommend further avenues of research.

2. Institutional holdings and activism: state-of-the-art

2.1 The notion of institutional activism

Depending on the size of institutional holdings, we can analyse the extent to which they use their position to influence corporate governance and management. Apart from holding large blocks of shares, they may exert considerable pressure on the management teams of businesses, a mechanism commonly known as *institutional activism* (C. Girard, 2004).

Institutional activism can thus be defined as the influence of institutional holdings on corporate performance and governance, coupled, where appropriate, with proactive efforts aimed at changing the behaviour of the firm or its rules of governance. This activism is legitimised by the size of the holding of these investors, which gives them a controlling right and a means of pressuring the directors of businesses to accept certain strategic changes (M. Bianchi, L. Enriques, 2001).

Moreover, a large number of studies have shown that the presence of shareholders holding large blocks of shares can also have negative effects on governance:

▪ Firstly, institutional holdings might try to take advantage of their position of strength to make "personal" gains to the detriment of small shareholders or other stakeholders;

▪ Secondly, the existence of institutional holdings in the capital of a business may lead smaller shareholders to avoid their liabilities and leave the larger shareholders to take all the control, thus adopting "free rider" behaviour.

▪ Thirdly, institutional holdings may pursue objectives that do not necessarily coincide with those of hands-off investors: institutional activism may harm the effectiveness of the control function devolved to the Board of Directors (Y. Altunbas *et al.* 2007).

Often thought of as partners with little engagement in the process of perpetuating the activities of the business, they appear to act according to an essentially short term logic, even if they bring about trade-offs in favour of businesses showing less volatile performances (C. Faugère, H. A. Shawky, 2003). However, this negative view of the institutional holding seems simplistic and should be supplemented by other approaches. Studies show that the way in which their activism will operate within businesses fundamentally depends on the investment time scale. From this perspective, we offer several classifications which make it possible to refine the study of institutional activism.

2.2 Classifications of institutional activism

Based on the work of M. Aglietta (2008), institutional holdings can be divided into long term investors and short term investors. The difference between these two types of investor lies in contrasting principles and aims of governance. For long term institutional holdings, the aim is to maximise the total value of the business in the long term, while short term institutional holdings maximise the share value to be taken out of the business in the short term. Several characteristics will follow:

Table 1: Comparison of long term / short term institutional holdings[2]

LT investors	ST investors
Entrepreneurship	Speculation mentality
Extra financial risks managed by the governance	Financial risks managed by diversification
Specific features of assets and irreversibility of investments	Liquidity of assets
Capital investment	Investment by financial leverage

Long term institutional holdings take shares in the medium term (10-15 years), with the aim of maximising the total value of the business in the long term. They position themselves in businesses which possess a potential for development and which do not seem to appreciate the markets: they get massively involved in corporate governance. Almost unanimously, authors show that long term institutional holdings are more

[2] Aglietta, (2008).

involved in the control and governance of businesses than short term institutional holdings.

Short term institutional holdings seek to maximise their investments and the shareholder value of the business; in the event of a disagreement with the management they prefer to sell their shares rather than get involved in corporate governance and management of the business so as to avoid monitoring costs. This selling of shares may result in a lowering of the stock market valuation of the business and therefore an increased likelihood of a takeover PO (J. Brabet, 2002). In the event of a takeover PO, the management team of the target business is often replaced by a new one, in this case, that of the initiating business; the idea being that the institutional holding estimates that another management team would be able to manage the business better than the existing one. This risk of being ousted from the decision-making process can cause directors to act in the interests of institutional holdings in order to guarantee their level of remuneration and, beyond that, to increase their managerial latitude and consolidate their position in the business.

The two criticisms generally aimed at this type of investor are, firstly, the short term view favouring short term profitability to the detriment of growth and innovation; and, secondly, *blind conformity* (even mimicry) intensifying the instability of the markets (P. - N. Giraud, 2001).
There are far fewer studies on the impact of short term institutional holdings on corporate governance. On the one hand, this may be explained by the fact that this type of investor, by definition, does not have a long term relationship with the business and therefore it is much more difficult to perceive behaviours which may be in general use. On the other hand, this is perhaps due to the fact that short term institutional holdings do not get involved in the governance of businesses in which they have shares.

3. The activism of institutional holdings: The case of Blue Capital in the Carrefour group

This qualitative study will be presented in the following way. Firstly, we will give reasons for our choice of business. Then we will introduce the Carrefour group by giving a brief outline of its history. In addition, we will try to show the development of the capital structure of the Carrefour group following the increased importance of Blue Capital and the way in which the corporate governance has undergone numerous changes in recent years under the influence of this institutional holding. We will also attempt to highlight a significant correlation between the rise in power of Blue Capital and the strategic decisions taken by the management team of the Carrefour group. Finally, we will show that the professional affinities created by the directors of Blue Capital may allow them a great deal of influence to make an impact on Carrefour's management style.

3.1 Reason for the choice of the Carrefour group

We chose the Carrefour group for several reasons. Firstly, it is a company, originally a family firm, which has been greatly influenced by the presence of the founding family. Secondly, Carrefour's capital has increased through an institutional holding, Blue Capital. Since it bought into the business in March 2007, the capital share held by this investor has continued to grow. This has enabled it to become the major shareholder in the group, supplanting Carrefour's founding family. Thirdly, the management team of the Carrefour group recently implemented a restructuring plan in Belgium, which has led to the closure of 21 shops and the loss of over 1750 jobs. We will try to show through this study that this operation implemented by the Carrefour management was instigated by the institutional holding, Blue Capital.

3.2 Presentation and history of the Carrefour group

In 1959 the Fournier and Defforey families created the Carrefour company. A year later the chain of Carrefour shops opened its first "supermarket" in France. In 1961, Promodis, a company specialising in the wholesale trade (later called Promodès), was created. This company is the result of the merger of wholesaler families managed at the time by Paul-Auguste Halley and Léonor Duval-Lemonnier. In 1963 Carrefour created the "hypermarket[3]" concept. In 1969 the supermarkets of the Promodès chain adopted the Champion brand. Carrefour then launched into international expansion and opened its first hypermarket in Belgium. In the early 70s Carrefour was floated on the Paris stock exchange. In 1972 the Promodès hypermarkets assumed the Continent brand. This brand strategy at the same time illustrates predominance in each domain (Carrefour in the hypermarket domain and Champion in the supermarket domain). During this decade the Carrefour chain continued its geographic expansion by opening shops in other parts of the world. The group thus strengthened its two-pronged strategy used, in some cases, simultaneously:

[3] Specialist trade in food and non-food products, area: 2,500m².

concentric diversification (business buybacks in the same business sector) and geographical diversification (positioning on the Spanish, Brazilian, Belgian and Argentinean markets, etc.). In 1999 Carrefour and Promodès merged to form Europe's leading group and the world's number two group, after Wal Mart. Carrefour then took control of Promodès.

With regard to the group's turnover, this is divided between types of shop: hypermarkets 62.5%; supermarkets 21.5%; and Maxi-discount 11.5%, and by geographical area: Europe 79.4%, the majority of which is in France (47.7%); America 13.7%; and Asia 7.6%. This data indicates that the strategic importance of the Carrefour group is mainly focused on the hypermarket sector in the European area.

3.3 Positioning and rise in power of Blue Capital

In the early part of 2007 the Halley family, which together with Promodès held 13.21% of Carrefour's capital, announced the dissolution of the shareholder agreement connecting them following the accidental death of Paul-Louis Halley. In March 2007 Blue Capital bought shares in Carrefour. This joint venture controlled by Bernard Arnault (LVHM) and the American institutional holding Colony Capital initially took a holding of over 9% by investing about 4 billion Euros. On 31 December 2008 its holding exceeded the 15% threshold and Blue Capital attained the rank of reference shareholder.

Table 2: Distribution of the Carrefour group's capital in %

In %	1999	2000	2001	2002	2003	2004	2005	2006	2007	2008
Family agreement	20.77	21.08	20.33	19.88	19.65	12.5	13.03	13.52	13.21	-
Employees	1.5	2.79	2.88	2.98	2.87	2.39	2.2	1.22	1.08	1.05
Holding own shares	2.05	2.25	2.43	0.6	1.02	1.21	-	-	1.55	2.74
Public	75.68	73.88	74.36	76.54	76.46	80.35	84.77	85.26	75.07	80.51
Colony Capital	-	-	-	-	-	-	-	-	9.09	14.99
Arnault Group	-	-	-	-	-	-	-	-	-	0.71

The table above shows the change in the distribution of Carrefour's capital before and after the arrival of Blue Capital. As Carrefour started out as a family firm, a relatively large part of its capital was concentrated in the hands of the Halley family until the end of 2007. However, this share tended to decline between 1999 and 2006 following in the footsteps of the capital floatation, which tended to increase, making Carrefour a business ripe for a takeover (in 2008 the floatation represented over 80%).

3.4 Blue Capital's activism on Carrefour's corporate governance and strategic orientations

The purpose of this section is to show that Blue Capital is an active institutional holding. Firstly, it seems to be a long term institutional holding insofar as its investment is in capital and is hard to reverse (given its high level of equity investment). In addition, as we will see, the extra-financial risks are managed through the lens of governance.
Secondly, and to show that Blue Capital is well and truly an active investor, we should look, firstly, at table 3 below showing the movements of Carrefour directors between 2005 and 2009, together with 2007, which is when Blue Capital bought shares in Carrefour's capital; and secondly, at the way in which this investor might be able to orient the management of the Carrefour group. We will therefore show the different reasons behind Carrefour's new capital composition which could explain some of the motivation of the major shareholders in developing the business towards a lighter model facilitating its buyout by a competitor: Wal-Mart.

- Firstly, we will analyse the way in which Blue Capital's activism has influenced the governance of Carrefour, through the lens of the Board of Directors;
- Secondly, we will analyse the way in which its activism operates on the management of Carrefour;
- Thirdly and finally, we will study the overlapping interests of the different directors of Carrefour as well as their level of influence, which could be a factor in understanding the support given to the strategic choices made by Blue Capital.

3.4.1 Changes in the structure of the Board of Directors

We now present a biography of the various directors of the business, which enables us to highlight the importance of Carrefour's family connotation until 2006. In addition we will show that the arrival of Blue

Capital corresponded to the appointment of new directors and the end of the family connotation.

For the influence of the Halley family, the ousting of Luc Vandevelde in 2006 is symptomatic. He joined Promodès in 1995 as Managing Director. Four years later he became Chairman-Managing Director of Carrefour at the time of the merger of Carrefour and Promodès. In 2004 he was appointed as director. A year later he took the position of Chairman of the Supervisory Board and was ousted in 2006 because of disagreements with the Halley family (J. Beauchet, 2010). He was then replaced by Bernard Bontoux.

Table 3: Composition of the Carrefour's Board of Directors between 2005 and 2009

2009	2008	2007	2006	2005
Robert Halley	V	V	V	V
Amaury de Seze	V	V	V	V
Jean-Martin Folz	V	V	V	
Lars Olofsson	V			
René Abate	V	V	V	V
Bernard Arnault	V			
Sébastien Bazin	V	V	V	
Nicolas Bazire	V	V	V	
Jean-Laurent Bonnafé	V			
Thierry Breton	V			
René Brillet	V	V	V	V
Charles Edelstenne	V			
Anne-Claire Taittinger	V	V	V	V
	José Luis Duran	V	V	V
		Bernard Bontoux	V	
				Luc Vandevelde

With regard to the impact of Blue Capital, several changes in the structure of Carrefour's Board of Directors have been observed since its arrival:

- Blue Capital is represented on the Carrefour Board of Directors by Nicholas Bazire, Managing Director of the Arnault group since 1999, and director of LVMH, Sébastien Bazin, Managing Director and Chairman of the Supervisory Board of Colony Capital and Bernard Arnault, major shareholder and Chairman-Managing Director of the LVMH group.
- Robert Halley, member of the founding family of Promodès was appointed Chairman of Carrefour's Supervisory Board on 7 March 2007. In 2008 (when Blue Capital bought into the business), he resigned, leaving his place to Amaury de Seze, and became Honorary Chairman of the Board of Directors.
- Amaury de Seze occupied the positions of Managing Director and Chairman-Managing Director of Volvo France from 1978. He then joined the Executive Board of the Paribas group in 1993. In 2004 he arrived at the Carrefour group and changed the system of corporate governance in 2008, a year after the arrival of Blue Capital. The *Board of Directors* formula replaced that of *Supervisory Board and Executive Board.* That is to say "*In the formula of management by an executive board and supervisory board, the distinction is between the functions of management and control of management. Management is clearly separated, unlike the formula of management by a board of directors, in which management is shared between the definition of strategic options made by the board of directors and implementation with everyday management carried out by the managing body*[4]"; this latter governance formula is considered more restrictive in terms of supervision and control. His appointment emanated from the will of the reference shareholder's representatives who were convinced that Amaury de Seze would be the appropriate person to improve the group's performance on the stock market: the stock market valuation has actually fallen by more than 40% since 2007 (the date of Blue Capital's acquisition of Carrefour shares).
- Lars Olofsson joined Carrefour's Supervisory Board in 2008 and succeeded José Luis Duran who had occupied the position of Managing Director at Carrefour since 2005. He was then relieved of his duties in 2008. The main reason stemmed from his disagreement

[4] Godard L. (1998), "Les déterminants du choix entre un Conseil d'Administration et un Conseil de Surveillance", Finance, Contrôle, Stratégie, Vol. 1, n°4, pp 39-61.

with Blue Capital concerning the group's results, particularly in France where hypermarket sales had contracted, causing a negative impact on the stock market valuation of the business. Lars Olofsson's strategy was based on repositioning the Carrefour group (as a competitive brand in terms of price) as well as refocusing the group on certain geographical areas (especially France) in order to create value for the shareholders.

3.4.2 Strategic changes brought about since Blue Capital's acquisition of shares

Blue Capital's initial aim when it bought into the business was to make its investment profitable by outsourcing Carrefour's real estate stock, estimated at between 20 and 30 billion euros. After the 2008 property crisis this plan did not see the light of day and Blue Capital experienced a loss of 30% in relation to its initial investment. Consequently, the two reference shareholders will put pressure on the management team to take decisions likely to improve the stock market valuation of Carrefour.

As well as intervening in the governance of the Carrefour group as we described above, Blue Capital also intervened in its strategy by suggesting the possible sale of its businesses in Latin America and Asia (September 2009) whose sales represent more than a fifth of its turnover. In 2009 it was also involved in a large restructuring plan in Belgium causing the loss of 1672 jobs and closure of 21 shops (14 hypermarkets and 7 supermarkets). It seems therefore that the Carrefour group wants to rapidly improve its falling performance levels. Paradoxically, the group confidently forecasts an annual growth of shareholder remuneration of 10% in future years, while the net result has shown a considerable fall in recent years.

Table 4: Future forecasts for dividends

	2009	2010	2011
Dividend	1.08	1.11	1.29
Productivity	3.09%	3.18%	3.69%

To honour these forecasts the management of the Carrefour group must take strategic measures to enable it to achieve the objective, despite a falling net result. From this perspective, redundancies enable it to improve the performance levels of the business but risk destroying its organisational balance. In practical terms, these redundancies allow it to reduce its social and operating costs. These reductions have the effect of improving the operating result and therefore improving the net result, cash-flow and level of dividends shared out. From a shareholder perspective, the redundancies may be beneficial in the short term; these are stock market redundancies (A. Finet, 2006). However, from a stakeholder perspective, they may be harmful as they risk destroying the cultural balance of the business.

The strategic choices made, correspond to a break-up of the business (even if, in this case, it only involves a single country) and constitute a break in relation to the perspective of the group's structured development, the basis of which has been, since its creation, geographical expansion and internal growth.

The plan of closures and redundancies in Belgium gives a strong signal to Blue Capital and is in line with a perspective of consolidating the expectations of the major shareholders. These restructuring measures could also affect other countries. In this respect, the group is trying to sell its businesses in Thailand, Malaysia, and Singapore. The financial press is suggesting the names Aeon (Japan's number two distributor) and Navis Capital Partners (a Malaysian firm) as buyers, so the group can focus solely on the other Asian markets in which it is positioning itself as leader. Carrefour is tending to consolidate its strong points while abandoning those activities which the business considers unlikely to grow much in the short or medium term.

While Carrefour's strategic outlook during the family management era was long term, with positioning structured on the markets which should be penetrated in accordance with a keen understanding of players' expectations, changes in the capital structure and the intrusion of Blue Capital mark a significant change in the strategic perspective adopted by the group. An obsession with improving stock market performance in the short term causes choices aimed at simplifying the business structure by leaving certain sections of the market. The objective is to rapidly improve performance indicators by simultaneously reducing managed assets and lowering the wage bill. This measure is an important step which has the final objectives, firstly, of meeting the expectations of the major shareholders and, secondly, of reducing the size of the business, which could lead to a potential buyout by a competitor business.

In conclusion, the question is why has Bernard Arnault, owner of the luxury LVMH group, become involved since 2007 in the capital of

Carrefour? Anecdotally, in 2006 the LVMH group brought a lawsuit against Carrefour, which was accused at the time of selling counterfeit Louis Vuitton bags in one of its hypermarkets in Shanghai. The world number one luxury brand won the case and Carrefour was forced to pay damages, admittedly relatively small, of 18,700 dollars. The hypothesis of resentment against the Carrefour group is perhaps "far-fetched" but, in any case, one might imagine that the alliance with Colony Capital fits in with a perspective of selling Carrefour in its entirety with an increase in value to one of its natural competitors, Wal-Mart. Accustomed to successful mergers and acquisitions, but with a small presence in Europe, Wal-Mart might want to take advantage of such strategic opportunities enabling it to extend its geographical positioning. Wal-Mart had already shown interest in some of Carrefour's businesses in Latin American and Asia. The French group had however rejected the bid, which it considered financially inadequate.

In broad outline, in future, Blue Capital's influence on Carrefour could manifest itself in the following way. It should be noted that this scenario is all the more probable as the group's stock market performance has been disappointing since Blue Capital became a shareholder in Carrefour.

This outline may however take several years and be spread over various stages:

- Increased representation of reference shareholders on Carrefour's Board of Directors;
- Simplification of Carrefour's organisational structure;
- Improvement of the group's financial structure;
- Complete sale of the business to Wal-Mart.

The scenario developed above seems all the more credible as the options desired by the representatives of the major shareholders are unlikely to be rejected by the other directors insofar as there are strong professional links with other large businesses on the Paris stock market.

The following point will be devoted to highlighting the various networks that can be detected from the Blue Capital and Carrefour sphere of influence.

3.4.3 Professional networks and affinities of Carrefour's directors

This qualitative analysis shows hotspots where people have shared interests, which enables the spheres of influence apparently circumscribed around a particular business to be significantly enlarged. In other words, the strategic ins and outs debated within Carrefour's Board of Directors certainly have a much larger influence, especially in terms of convergence of interests between the expectations of the different directors, which may lead to a zero-sum game.

The basis for our work on this section was the current list of Carrefour directors (2009). Then, for each of them, we listed the different business in which they had a seat on the Board of Directors. The results of the methodology thus consist of two levels:

- Firstly, we observed any similarities (in terms of seats on the Board of Directors) between these people. For example, Jean-Martin Folz and Jean-Laurent Bonnafé are part of the BNP Paribas supervisory body.
- Secondly, for these directors, we listed the chief shared contacts that we had selected within businesses quoted on Euronext Paris.

In the diagram below the hexagons represent Carrefour directors with their respective "primary company". The rectangles represent the shared contacts of Carrefour directors in companies in which they have a seat on the Board of Directors.

By way of illustration, Nicolas Bazire is simultaneously on the Board of Directors of Carrefour and that of LVMH. Nicolas Bazire is also a director in Atos Origin at the same time as René Abate, himself a director of Carrefour.

In concrete terms, this qualitative analysis shows the hotspots where people have shared interests, which enable the spheres of influence apparently circumscribed around a particular business to be significantly enlarged. In other words, the strategic ins and outs debated within Carrefour's Board of Directors certainly have a much larger influence, especially in terms of convergence of interests between the expectations of the different directors, which may lead to a zero-sum game.

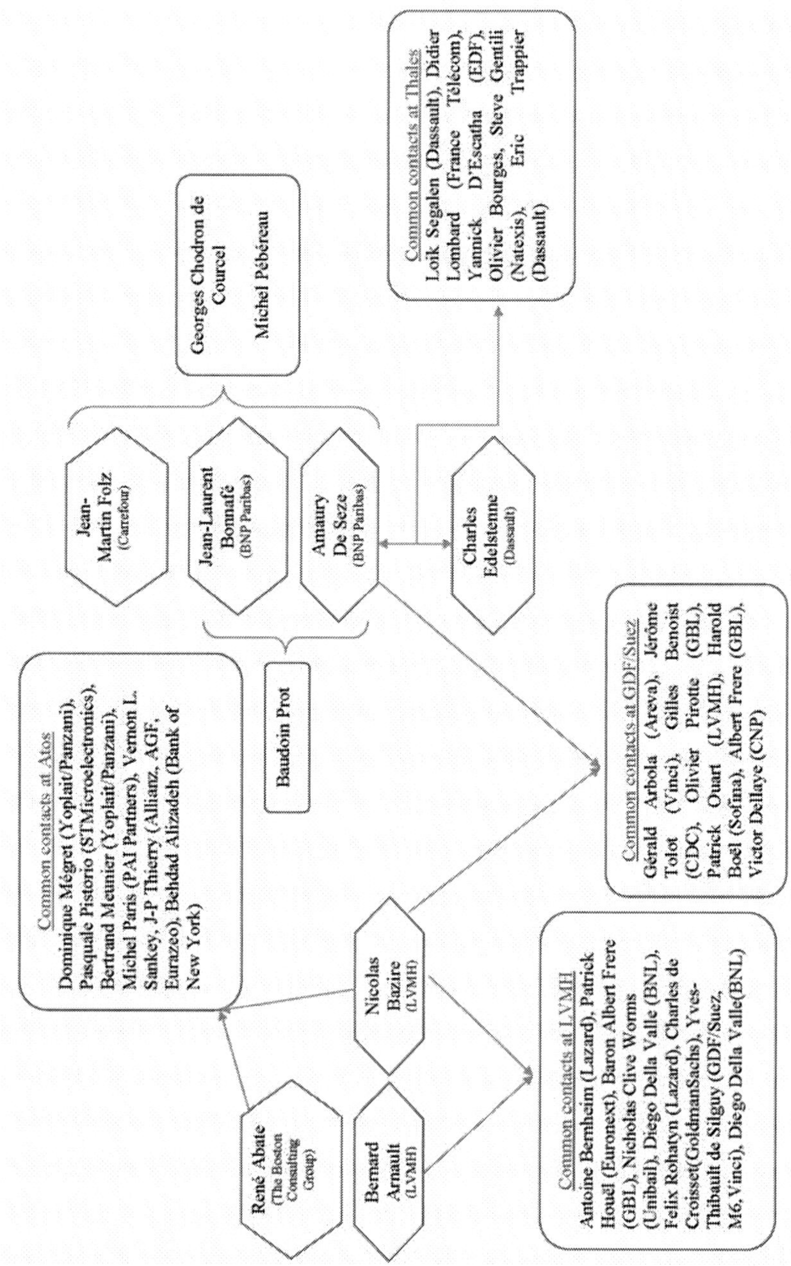
René Abate (The Boston Consulting Group)
Bernard Arnault (LVMH)
Nicolas Bazire (LVMH)
Common contacts at Atos
Dominique Mégret (Yoplait/Panzani), Pasquale Pistorio (STMicroelectronics), Bertrand Meunier (Yoplait/Panzani), Michel Paris (PAI Partners), Vernon L. Sankey, J-P Thierry (Allianz, AGF, Eurazeo), Behdad Alizadeh (Bank of New York)
Common contacts at LVMH
Antoine Bernheim (Lazard), Patrick Houël (Euronext), Baron Albert Frere (GBL), Nicholas Clive Worms (Unibail), Diego Della Valle (BNL), Felix Rohatyn (Lazard), Charles de Croisset(GoldmanSachs), Yves-Thibault de Silguy (GDF/Suez, M6,Vinci), Diego Della Valle(BNL)
Baudoin Prot
Jean-Martin Folz (Carrefour)
Jean-Laurent Bonnafé (BNP Paribas)
Amaury De Seze (BNP Paribas)
Georges Chodron de Courcel
Michel Pébéreau
Charles Edelstenne (Dassault)
Common contacts at GDF/Suez
Gérald Arbola (Areva), Jérôme Tolot (Vinci), Gilles Benoist (CDC), Olivier Pirotte (GBL), Patrick Ouart (LVMH), Harold Boël (Sofina), Albert Frere (GBL), Victor Dellaye (CNP)
Common contacts at Thales
Loïk Segalen (Dassault), Didier Lombard (France Télécom), Yannick D'Escatha (EDF), Olivier Bourges, Steve Gentili (Natexis), Eric Trappier (Dassault)

In conclusion, by using the two levels of analysis, we note an overlapping of Carrefour directors, mainly towards the financial, food processing, aeronautical, and energy sectors. These spirals could possibly explain a strong collusion of interests between these different parties. Sociologically speaking, notions of networks, or interlocking interests, become particularly important. Due to these strong capital links, and in order not to break informal agreements, the will of Carrefour directors representing Blue Capital will not be challenged by directors with whom there are significant collusions on various shared matters. By going back to two levels as we have done, a large section of the French market can be covered (in fact, nine shared businesses are listed in the CAC 40). Consequently, we think this overlapping could facilitate the possibility of strategic choices corresponding to the interests of Blue Capital, and therefore, Colony Capital, directors.

4. General conclusions

Institutional holdings are large providers of capital to ensure the growth and development of the businesses in which they invest. They are, in some cases, widely criticised due to the strategic measures they impose on directors. Theoretically, we have highlighted two types of institutional holdings according to their investment outlook: long term institutional holdings and short term institutional holdings. Naturally, their investment outlooks are significantly different and, consequently, their influence on the governance and strategic orientations of businesses will also be different. Thus, long term institutional holdings get involved in corporate governance by being represented on the Board of Directors. The influence of short term institutional holdings on the other hand is marked by market sanction, in other words, in the event of a disagreement with the management team, they sell their shares.

It should be noted that the central aim of the paper was to appreciate how the activism of Blue Capital operated. This analysis therefore enables us to answer the research question formulated. In conclusion and to give a general picture, Blue Capital's activism influences both the governance of the Carrefour group and its strategy. In fact, since the retirement of the Halley family, Blue Capital has held about 15% of Carrefour's capital. Since this acquisition of holdings, chronologically speaking, this investor was firstly represented on the Carrefour Board of Directors by three directors. Secondly, the Supervisory Board/Executive Board formula was abandoned. Thirdly, a new Chairman-Managing Director was appointed.

Since this acquisition of shares, Carrefour's stock market valuation has fallen by 40%. In addition, the group's financial and commercial ratios have also declined. To improve the performance of the business the directors pressed by the reference shareholders opted for strategic choices corresponding to giving up businesses, the general idea is that the reduction of wage and asset costs would improve the business's situation on the stock market. In a similar vein, it seems logical that organisational simplification and repositioning of the business ought to encourage a process of takeover by a competitor business. To support this hypothesis we think the shared professional interests of Carrefour's directors should facilitate the validation of this strategic orientation and process of disinvestment.

The study is limited in that it only considers a single business and a single institutional investor, in a particular context. It is therefore difficult to draw general conclusions from the results highlighted. In the same vein, we think any uniformity in the positioning strategies of individual institutional holdings with large shareholdings in businesses on the French market should be analysed.

References

L'Association Française des Investisseurs en Capital (AFIC) et BIPE, *"Les investisseurs institutionnels face au capital investissement"*, 2004, 3 pages.

Aglietta M., *"Investisseurs à long terme et gouvernance d'entreprise",* Colloque: Actes des 6èmes Journées d'Economie Financière, Hammamet, Tunisie, 2008, 15 pages.

Altunbas Y., Kara A., Van Rixtel A., *"Corporate Governance and Corporate Ownership: The Investment Behaviour of Japanese Institutional Investors"*, Documentos Ocasionales, No 0703, Banco De España, Madrid, 2007, 54 pages.

Bianchi M., Enriques L., *"Corporate Governance in Italy after the 1998 reform: What Role for the Institutional Investors?"*, Commissione Nazionale per le Società e la Borsa, Quaderni di Finanza n°43, 2001.

Beauchet J., *"Carrefour des illusions, le journal de bord d'un ex-dirigeant du groupe"*, Editions Bertrand Gobin, Rennes, 2010, 269 pages.

Brabet J., *"La main invisible des investisseurs institutionnels",* Revue Française de Gestion, vol.5, n°141, 2002, pp. 203-224.

Bughin C., Chatelin C., Depret M.-H., Finet A., Hamdouch A., Missonier-Piera F., Piot C., *"Gouvernance d'entreprise, nouveaux défis financiers et non financiers"*, Méthodes & Recherches Management, De Boeck, Bruxelles, 2009, pp. 141-164.

Bushee B. J., Goodman T. H., *"Which Institutional Investors Trade Based on Private Information about Earnings and Returns?"*, Journal of Accounting Research, n°45, 2007.

Chen X., Harford J., Li K., *"Monitoring: Which institutions matter?"*, Journal of Financial Economics, n°86, 2007, pp.279-305.

Chen A.-S., Hong B.-S., *"Institutional ownership changes and returns around analysts' earnings forecast release events: Evidence from Taiwan"*, Journal of Banking and Finance, n°30, 2006, pp.2471-2488.

Chiang T. C., Nelling E., Tan L., *"The speed of adjustment to information: Evidence from the Chinese stock Market"*, International Review of Economics and Finance, n°17, 2008, pp.216-229.

Dong M., Ozkan A., *"Insitutional investors and director pay : An empirical study of UK companies"*, Journal of Multinational Financial Management, n°18, 2008, pp.16-29.

Faugère C., Shawky H. A., *"Volatility and Institutional Investor Holdings in a Declining Market : a Study of NASDAQ during the Year 2000"*, Albany Working Paper, Working Paper Series, n°4, 2003, 26 pages.

Ferreira M. A., Matos P., *"The colors of investors' money: The role of institutional investors around the world"*, Journal of Financial Economics, n°88, 2008, pp.499-533.

Finet, A., *"Effets des annonces de licenciements sur des marchés en phase de déclin : comparaison entre le NASDAQ - OTC et le NYSE sur la période mars 2000 - mars 2002"*, Direction et Gestion, la Revue des Sciences de Gestion, n°217, 2006, pp.59-68.

Girard C., *"L'incidence de l'activisme actionnarial sur les mécanismes de gouvernance : le cas français"*, Finance Contrôle Stratégie, vol.7, n°3, 2004, pp. 91-116.

Giraud P.-N., *"La prise de pouvoir des investisseurs institutionnels: vers de nouveaux capitalismes ?"*, Economies et Sociétés, vol.35, n°5, 2001, pp.721-746.

Godard L., *"Les déterminants du choix entre un Conseil d'Administration et un Conseil de Surveillance"*, Finance, Contrôle, Stratégie, Vol. 1, n°4, 1998, pp 39-61.

Golec J., *"Are the insider trades of a large institutional investor informed ?"*, Finance Department School of Business University of Connecticut Working Paper, 2004, 44 pages.

http://www.20minutes.fr/article/549655/Economie-Carrefour-annonce-une-lourde-chute-de-ses-resultats.php

http://www.boursier.com/vals/FR/lvmh-carrefour-condamne-en-chine-pour-vente-de-faux-sacs-louis-vuitton-rumeur-2622.htm

http://www.boursier.com/vals/fr/carrefour-amaury-de-seze-prend-la-presidence-du-conseil-bernard-arnault-est-coopte-news-283878.htm

http://www.boursilex.com/directoire_et_conseil_de_surveillance.htm

http://www.boursorama.com/infos/actualites/detail_actu_societes.phtlm?num=15ad1f62d8c8b12029d897b995ed474b&org=1rPCA

http://www.challenges.fr/magazine/portrait/0140.016859/?xtmc=martin_bouygues&xtcr=34

http://www.daily-bourse.fr/carrefour-vers-une-sortie-des-pays-emergents-Feed-AOF200909281050065.php

http://www.far.be/sodia.org/vf/carfour/groupe/grcarfour2.htm

http://www.fundinguniverse.com/company-histories/GIB-Group-Company-History.html

http://www.itrnews.com/articles/83166/portrait-amaury-seze-nouvel-homme-fort-carrefour.html

http://www.jdf.com/enquete/2009/10/03/04004-20091003ARTHBD00043-l-impatience-gagne-les-deux-principaux-actionnaires-de-carrefour.php

http://www.latribune.fr/entreprises-finance/services/distribution/20100219trib000478301/les-benefices-de-carrefour-plombes-par-des-charges-exceptionnelles.html

http://www.lavenir.net/article/detail.aspx?articleid=415778

http://www.lemonde.fr/economie/article/2010/02/19/le-benefice-net-de-carrefour-en-chute-de-74-en-2009_1308284_3234.html

http://www.lexpress.fr/actualite/economie/pourquoi-carrefour-se-separe-de-jose-luis-duran_705292.html

http://www.maroc4life.com/livres/groupe%20carrefour.pdf

http://www.pubwebmaster.com/uprate/index.php/2007/03/07/513-arnault-et-colony-capital-entrent-en-force-dans-le-capital-de-carrefour

http://trends.rnews.be/fr/economie/actualite/entreprises/colruyt-detrone-carrefour-leader-historique-de-la-distribution-belge/article-1194637260447.htm

http://www.vernimmen.net/html/glossaire/definition_hedge_funds.html

Izraelewicz E., "Le capitalisme Zinzin", Editions Grasset & Fasquelle, Paris, 1999, 283 pages.

Jain R., *"Institutional and individual investor preferences for dividends and share repurchases",* Journal of Economics and Business, n°59, 2007, pp.406-429.

Kling G., Gao L., *"Chinese institutional investors' sentiment"*, International Financial Markets, Institutions and Money, n°18, 2008, pp.374-387.

Lavigne S., *"L'industrie des fonds de pension : les investisseurs institutionnels américains"*, L'Harmattan, Paris, 2004, 241pages.

Nagel S., *"Short sales, institutional investors and the cross-section of stock returns"*, Journal of Financial Economics, n°78, 2005, pp.277-309.

Ning Y., *"Large Changes in Institutional Holdings and CEO Compensation Risk", University of Houston Working Paper*, 2006, 34 pages.

Wang X. L., Shi K., Fan H. X., *"Psychological mechanisms of investors in Chinese Stock Markets"*, Journal of Economic Psychology, n°27, 2006, pp.762-780.

BACK TO ACCOUNTING BASICS: UPGRADING IFRS

GEORGES PARIENTE[1]
AND DIDIER VANOVERBERGHE[2]

1. Accounting as a support for economic growth

We are indebted to 15th-century Florentine merchants for the invention of double-entry bookkeeping. The growth of capital contributed to the development of the economy, and that double-entry bookkeeping was an integral part of it reliability, which provides the confidence for the development of commerce and business activities. So when a new system of accounting standards (the IFRS), appears at the same time as a crisis, we owe it to ourselves to examine the pertinence of the new model, beginning by studying how it differs from the old system, and the potential procyclical effects as Taylor and Goodhart (2004) did.

2. The IFRS standards, the issues, and the options in light of the facts

2.1 Some definitions for reference

Before discussing our proposal it would appear useful to distinguish certain concepts.

The market value is defined as the figure at which a transaction takes place, even if the market trades only a portion of this asset. The underlying value of an asset or liability is defined as the present value of its profits, ignoring effects due to its financing structure. The economic value is then defined as this value increased by the tax savings connected to the

[1] Dean for Research at the ISC Paris Business School.
[2] Senior Engineer of the Corps of Mines.

financing structure, and conversely reduced by the bankruptcy risks. Fair value is theoretically defined in the IFRS standards as “the amount for which an asset could be swapped, or a liability extinguished, between parties who are well informed, willing, and acting under normal competitive conditions”. This definition focuses on the value of the transaction, but in practice we accept that the real definition of fair value is what was recommended or authorized, even if the choice differs from the original definition (market value, economic value reasonably estimated in reference to models, or acquisition cost).

The acquisition cost of an asset or liability is defined as the expense incurred in acquiring it.

Finally, in what follows we will refer to the former, French-type or US GAAP standards as 'accounting standards', and the IFRS standards as 'financial standards'.

2.2 The IFRS standards: praiseworthy goals, but...

The praiseworthy intention of the creators of the IFRS, or more precisely the IASB, was to make it possible for stock-market investors to obtain a better understanding of the value of a company's assets and liabilities. The essential difference, vis-à-vis older systems, is the replacement in balance sheets of the historic acquisition cost of an asset by a "fair value" based on the discounted value of future profits. The fair value concept has also led to transferring the impacts of the gains and losses in fair value shown in the balance sheet to the new income statement (IAS 39). The fair value concept is partly linked to the following assumptions concerning the perfect market definition:

- There is no barrier to entering the market, and no participant dominates the market, and therefore cannot influence price formation.
- Information is freely available to everyone.
- There is no transaction cost, or any tax or duty.
- The securities are all perfectly divisible and perfectly tradable.
- Agents can borrow or lend without limit at risk-free rates.
- The investors are rational, and their objective is to put their wealth to work.

Harrison and Pliska (1981) proposed an interpretation of the Call formula obtained by Black and Scholes (1973) by defining the neutral-risk probability measure, linked to Absence of Arbitrage Opportunity. When there is only one risk-neutral probability, the market is said to be complete, the "game is fair" and the price of an asset fully reflects the risk carried by that asset. Lucas (1978), presenting the basic equation that links a share's market price to its expected utility, has established a consistent connection between all the models, leading to the Consumption CAPM. But that framework will occasionally not coincide with the reality and it is then enough for one of these building blocks to fail for questions of the whole structure.

2.3 … In an imperfect world

The existence of an exact fair value or market value is based on an assumption of efficient, optimal, arbitraged, complete markets. But this assumption is becoming progressively less in harmony with the reality, and in this regard we may note:

- The puzzle of risk premiums highlighted by Mehra and Prescott (1985), who questioned the unity of the structure (risk premiums that are too low in comparison to reality).
- Doubts were raised about the CAPM, in particular by Fama and French (1995), who showed the effects related to other explanatory parameters, in particular, Tobin's q effects.
- The liquidity effect and the availability of liquidity, as shown by Adrian and Shin, (2008).
- Speculative-bubble (or deflation) effects completely destroy the standard models during pre-crisis and crisis periods.
- Information-cost effects as introduced bay Merton (1987).
- Bankruptcy risks, modelled by Merton (1974) or Leland (1994).
- The Brownian geometric models and hence the normal laws are considered too simplistic to portray the reality. Moreover the forecasts of agents vary enormously and lead us to believe that only discontinuous models may be able to handle the complexity of the real world.

The installation of the IFRS's principles has quickly led to referencing the assets' market value. But firstly, although the market value of an asset theoretically corresponds to the present value of the expected profits, will the transaction in fact be carried out at a price that satisfies both the buyer and the seller, knowing also that no one can claim to know in advance what these expected flows will be? Before the crisis, the market allowed households to go into debt, using as security an over-valuation of their property. As soon as the crisis took over, the market forced over-indebted households to give up their property for a derisory sum, far from the long-term economic value. Similarly, no foresight was forthcoming from informed actors such as the banks. They sold off the assets at a price that incorporated little risk, creating the biggest bubble in recent decades. Finally, the fair price is unknown; the markets cause prices to fluctuate around - or far from - an intrinsic or basic price.

Secondly, giving up acquisitions costs we lose an economic model of the cumulative wealth creation. The wealth created is the difference between the enterprise value (V=qK) and the capitals remaining invested as defined by Vanoverberghe (2010).

In any event, the IFRS are proposing to perform evaluations without highlighting the free cash flows actually recorded.

2.4 ...but nevertheless a partially Rational world

This being so, we must however acknowledge that trades are carried out on the asset markets in a reasonable manner during certain periods, with drifts that accumulate, eventually leading to absurd prices and then to a crisis, followed by a return to the mean. They also support economic cycles of the Kondrieff type, which include a lack of knowledge of the introduction of new products, ignorance of the potential risk, with over-valuation at the beginning, under-valuation afterwards, but above all, a destruction of real value in the process.

All this leads one to think that beneath the financial values lie hidden economic ones.

3. Towards a reasonable, reasoned solution

3.1 Re-establishing the link to economic reality

Originally, accounting had the simple ambition of showing monetary flows by setting them against the reality of the physical exchanges carried. In this regard accountings that showed the costs of acquiring capital assets and cash flows provided a financial picture of a company's historical reality. Of course the accounting also included smoothed values such as provisions for depreciation. This had the immense advantage of distributing an investment over its minimum period of profitability, although this period can be criticized for not being economic. This allowed a decoupling of viewpoints. This concept was, however, judged to be inadequate, because the historical acquisition costs of an asset are different from their value as represented economically by the discounted value of the FCFs. Nevertheless, that Anglo-Saxon accounting has for many years enabled a monitoring of these real cash flows.

3.2 Accounting for both the economic reality and the financial reality

As Michel Aglietta pointed out in 2006, fair value is inadequate to encompass the irreducible disparity of realized values; imputed values (depreciation); calculated values that refer to a model as did Plantin, Sapra, and Shin (2008); and substituted values that refer to a market.

In fact, if we accept, like any merchant, that it is just as interesting to know the costs of acquisitions as to know the profits expected from those assets, we can rebuild an accounting that will be a source of pertinent information. The new standard proposed, to be called the IAFRS, would therefore require three main accounts: two derived from the old European or US GAAP standards, and one Risks and Values account linked to IFRS that would show the underlying and market values.

Figure. 1: The three main IAFRS accounts

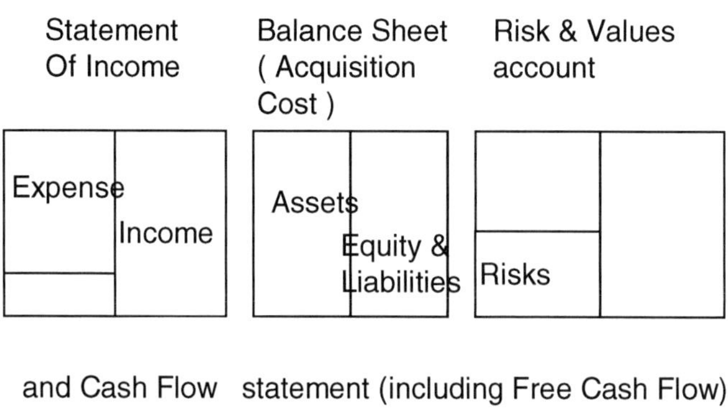

The IFRS account introduced here should display the risk versus the opportunity, in a double column: on one side, a market value split per country and business unit, on the other, an economic value supplemented by an estimate of its difference from the market's pricing. The economic value is broken down into the underlying value supplemented by the risks of bankruptcy and default. This account, would then supply a real warning light, automatically announcing discrepancies signalling an over-valuation or an under-valuation. The value of the company is, for example, the underlying value plus the effect of tax savings due to the debt, less the costs of bankruptcy as expressed by Leland.

3.3 Reintroducing economic factors

It is well known that the market value of a company at time t0 or of an asset is connected to the cost (of acquisition) of its assets by the equation due to J. Tobin:

$$\mathrm{V}_0^{\mathrm{M}} = \mathrm{q}^{\mathrm{M}} K_0 \qquad \text{Equation (1)}$$

Moreover, we can establish, as Vanoverberghe (2010) did, a microeconomic formula for the fundamental Tobin’s q (and another for the market value):

$$q^f = \frac{(ROCE - \mathrm{g_K})}{(wacc - \mathrm{g_K})} \qquad \text{Equation (2)}$$

The net rate of investment, g_K, is the net investment on capital ratio. The condition to obtain a positive Market Value Added (defined by V-K) is that ROCE must be greater than the wacc.

We thus define q by three key indicators based on real economic information.

The fact of keeping a traditional Balance-sheet account will enable recognition of the link between the economic reality (K) and the assessed financial picture (V). This can be displayed in the following way:

Figure 2 Illustration of the link between market value and capitals

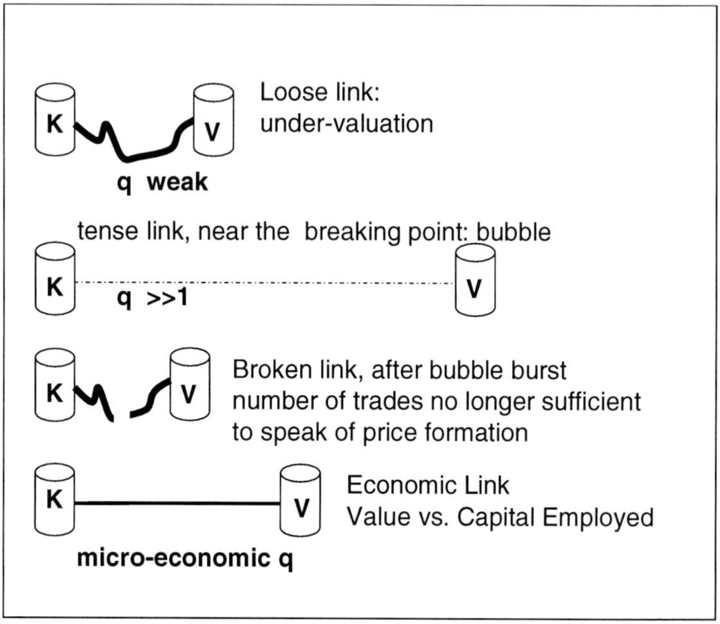

A global supervisor must be able to aggregate the risks of bankruptcy so as to limit the leverage effects by publishing the value of the associated risks. Along the same lines, the goodwill *potentially* created should not be recorded in the income statement. It may actually be related to bubbles or slumps sustained by a market without any economic rationality of capital, but either irrational problems or those connected to liquidity are expressed in the risks of bankruptcy. Knowing also, moreover, that the value of a limited number of shares traded each day does not reflect the price of the whole.

The reference used to define solvency ratios must be the underlying value, because it is the long-term value.

3.4 How does this model differ from traditional financial models?

We have shown that traditional financial models had difficulty in portraying the full reality of the markets, so it is important to show in what ways the new concept improves upon the usual models. If we consider the creation of wealth to preserve the uniqueness of price, the expected return must be equal to the cost of capital. We demonstrate easily, as Vanoverberghe (2010) did, that the real (or estimated) return on wealth μ_{W}^{d} is governed by an exact law that allows excess return expectations with two factors:

$$1+\mu_{W}^{d}=(1+\mu_{E}+\Delta\mu_{E})(1+\frac{\Delta q}{q}) \qquad \text{Equation (3)}$$

On the one hand we have the cost of capital and on the other hand an economic effect derived from a jump of microeconomic Tobin's q. This could be illustrated by the local differential form for the enterprise value:

$$\frac{dV}{V}=g_{t-,K}dt+\Delta g_{K}dt+\sigma db+\frac{\Delta q}{q}dN_{t}$$

Where N is the probability of Poisson jumps occurring for q and its components. This implies that if the return or the risk changes, the rate of investments will change. Here we give a clear explanation to the three factors model of Fama and French.

4. Conclusions

We are proposing a pragmatic approach that incorporates both the practical knowledge of our elders, starting with the Venetian merchants and Lombard bankers, and also the good intentions and gigantic efforts of the designers of the IFRS standards to use modern finance. This approach is based on strong theoretical principles that connect financial valuation to economic reality. So there is at least one way to produce standards that enable companies to be compared to avoid excessively procyclical phenomena, and to provide alerts before crises, based on both economic laws and modern finance: we have called it the IAFRS.

References

Adrian (T.) and Shin (H. S.) (2008) "Liquidity and leverage", Federal Reserve Bank of New York and Princeton University May 2008

Black (F.) and Scholes (M.) (1973) "The pricing of options and corporate liabilities", Journal of Political Economy, 81, p. 637-659

Fama E F and French K R, "Size and Book-to-Market Factors in Earnings and Returns", The Journal of Finance, Vol 50 No. 1 (Mar., 1995) pp 131-155

Harrison (Michael) and Pliska (Stanley), 1981, "Martingales and stochastic integrals in the theory of continuous trading", Stochastic Processes and Applications, vol. XI, p. 215-260.

Lucas (Robert), 1978, "Asset prices in an exchange economy", Econometrica, vol. 46, November, p.1429-1445.

Leland, H (1994), "Corporate Debt Value Bond Covenants, and Optimal Capital Structure", Journal of Finance, Vol. 4, September, pp.1213-1252.

Mehra (Rajnish) and Prescott (Edward), 1985, "The equity premium: A puzzle", Journal of Monetary Economics, vol. XV, p. 145-161.

Merton, R (1974) "On The Pricing of Corporate Debt: The Risk Structure of Interest Rates", Journal of Finance, Vol. 29, May, pp.449-470

—. (1987), "A simple Model of Capital Market Equilibrium with incomplete Information", Journal of Finance, Vol. 42, No. 3, July, pp. 483-510

Plantin (G.), Sapra (H.), and Shin (H. S.) (2008) "Marking-to-market: Panacea or Pandora's box?", Journal of Accounting Research

Taylor (A.) and Goodhart (C.) (2004), "Procyclicality and volatility in the financial system: the implementation of Basel II and IAS 39", London School of Economics, FMG

Vanoverberghe D., "Economic Wealth Added, the relevant economic measurement for profit maximization "Euro-Mediterranean Economics and Finance Review, Vol. 5, n° 4, fourth quarter 2010

FINANCIAL CRISIS? FOR AN OPTIMISTIC VIEW OF GROWTH: REVIEW OF LITERATURE AND MAIN EMPIRICAL DATA

FRÉDÉRIC TEULON[1]

Introduction

The lasting increase of quantities produced is considered beneficial as it improves the possibilities to purchase goods and services, allows populations to get out of poverty, and accounts for improving welfare.

Economic growth goes back to the origins of the industrial revolution. Before the 18th century the world was almost inactive on a productive level: from the dawn of time to the Age of Enlightenment, the average income of the world's inhabitants remained stagnant. «According to Daniel Cohen (2009), the living standard of a Roman slave does not differ significantly from that of a peasant of Languedoc *(area in the south of France)* in the 17th century. It is close to that of poor people in the modern world: around a dollar per day.»

The first industrial revolution was preceded by an agricultural revolution and the world has seen several technological breakthroughs, notably at the beginning of the 20th century with the use of electricity and the invention of the internal combustion engine. These different revolutions were the origin of long term growth.

The analysis of economic growth was the subject of a multitude of theoretical developments since Solow's (1956) neoclassical model of growth, particularly in the middle of the 1980s. At the same time, empirical studies became more commonly used, linked to debates on

[1] IPAG Business School, France.

economic convergence as well as the possible beneficial effects of an open economy: Abramovitz (1955), Denison (1961), Rogoff (2004). The idea that, under certain conditions, economic growth could involve rich countries being taken over by poor countries gave rise to numerous papers, often with contradictory results.

Five points stand out (the "stylized facts of growth"):

1. The growth of the worldwide economy is strong and stagnationist views have been refuted by facts;
2. Growth is regionally divided, but economists find it difficult to give an account of this situation. They prefer handing this question to geographers or leaving it with third world supporters;
3. There is a dissemination of growth in the world and a general improvement of living standards of populations (even in Africa). Nevertheless geographical, cultural and political restraints still exist, which can slow the process down;
4. It is necessary to break with the "prehistoric" views of growth (based on the use of always more and more labour, capital or natural resources) in favour of a view of growth potentially accessible to all, as it is founded on technological progress;
5. The depletion of natural resources and the deterioration of environmental conditions can be treated with economic tools. Current tensions are the origin of innovations which, little by little, allow suitable solutions to be found. As a result, it is possible to promote a sustainable growth.

The boom of the worldwide GDP

In the past, numerous observers appeared to be pessimistic regarding the possibilities of growth of the worldwide economy. In 1865, half a century after the famous analyses of Malthus on diminishing outputs in agriculture and the impossibility of perpetual growth ("stationary state"), the renowned neoclassical economist Stanley Jevons predicts – in a book called *The Coal Questions* – that the growth of his country is going to stop because, according to him, it is linked to coal, and the mines of the United Kingdom are about to be depleted. A century after the beginning of the industrial revolution, he considers the slowing down of economic growth to be unavoidable. With a view to compensate future generations for the excessive consumption of those resources, Jevons advises the government to reimburse the national debt!

Keynesian economists (Alvin Hansen, 1938) or Marxists (Maurice Dobb, 1946; Paul Sweezy, 1972) develop a particularly pessimistic view of future capitalism, due to either economic stagnation because of a structural saving excess, or a fall of profit rates.

For Hansen, inactivity is unavoidable due to a medium propensity to save, which is increasing with income. An additional investment at the same time increases income and production capacities. As the increase of income generates an increase of saving rates, consumption increases less than proportionally. The solution to giving markets new production capacities consists of keeping up investments. The offer has a structural tendency to exceed the demand and the long term perspective is then a stationary state.

Following the Big Depression of the 1930s, Sweezy – following the analyses of Hansen – developed the thesis of economic maturity, according to which economic development cannot continue with the same pace of the previous decades due to geographical (lack of new countries to explore), sociological (a saturation of needs), technique (a drop of the benefit rate), and demographic reasons (the decreasing population rate).

The expansion during the 1950s-1960s raised questions about the relevance of these stationary theses. Even today – and contrary to common belief – the growth rate of production on a worldwide economy level is still very high (in the order of 3% per year in volume). The situation in France (a growth trend in the order of 1 to 1.5% per year), is therefore not at all significant in the transformations that have turned the world upside down.

Growth rate of production in volume (in annual %)

	1990/2000	2001	2002	2003	2004	2005	2006	2007	2008	2009
The world	**3.1**	**2.3**	**2.9**	**3.6**	**4.9**	**4.5**	**5.1**	**5.2**	**3.0**	**-1.1**
The United States	3.4	1.4	1.7	1.9	3.2	2.6	3.0	2.7	0.6	-3.4
Japan	1.2	0.2	0.3	1.4	2.7	1.9	2.0	2.3	-0.7	-5.4
EU	2.2	2.1	1.4	1.5	2.7	2.2	3.4	3.1	1.0	-5.4
Eastern and Central Europe	2.0	0.2	4.4	4.8	7.3	6.0	6.6	5.5	3.0	-5.5
Developing countries	**3.6**	**3.8**	**4.8**	**6.2**	**7.5**	**7.1**	**7.9**	**8.3**	**6.0**	**1.7**
Developing Asia	7.4	5.8	6.9	8.2	8.6	9.0	9.8	10.6	7.6	6.2
Africa	2.4	4.9	6.5	5.4	6.7	5.7	6.1	6.3	5.2	1.7

Source: IMF, *World Economic Outlook*, on 2010

The statistics of the IMF (World Economic Outlook) show that:

- The worldwide GDP has recently reached an unparalleled level of $57,000 Bn, equalling a worldwide average income of $9000 per head;
- This growth allowed the filling of, to a great extent, the objectives of the "millennium for development" shown by the World Bank in 1990 (to reduce poverty by half for the horizon of 2015). According to the World Bank, there are 950 million people today living with less than a dollar a day compared to 1.3 thousand million twenty years ago;
- Africa, often presented as an adrift continent, experienced a growth rebound after 2000 (growth was fuelled by the demand for raw materials on the international markets);
- One of the surprising aspects of economic growth in this modern world is that countries rich in natural resources have a weaker growth rate than others (Sachs, 1995).

Fatality does not exist when it comes to development. For countries with a low standard of living, the growth recovery will depend on some initial political and economic conditions: education, opening-up to international exchange, a tax system maintained at a minimum level of GNP per head. However, once started, the country's growth recovery becomes unavoidable. Establishing new exchanges is only one aspect of an economic organisation. Countries that open up to international markets are generally those who have the best internal organisation: political and macro-economic stability, constitutional state good administration, etc. The quality of this internal organisation would be the source of growth for opened-up countries, and not the act of opening up in itself. Opening up their economy would be a natural and obvious choice to countries that are in a position to take advantage of it. The liberalisation of exchanges would be more a consequence of prosperity than one of its causes (Rodrik, 2002). According to Douglas North (1973), economists are too interested in the evolution of facts and ideas and not enough in the development of institutions. These institutions are made up of complex sets of norms, rules and behaviours, conceived for collective aims which determine the value of transaction costs as well as the efficiency of markets and the effectiveness of economic activities. Growth is possible only if societies grow wealthy by setting up institutions which create an environment conducive to exchange.

The space dimension of development

The economic analysis is usually confined to a space without dimension, in which business companies locate their plants without taking into account transport costs and sell products on markets without being concerned about shop sites (location of the consumers). Regions are considered to be isolated entities, as if their geographical locations and potential interregional links were of no importance.

This non-spatial analysis was challenged: 1) by the theories of industrial location; and 2) by third world theories regarding centre and outskirts.

In his renowned study published in 1826, Johann Heinrich von Thünen includes space into the economic analysis. Although the agents have local activities (production and consumption) which require no space dimension, exchanges are made over a certain distance, producing a cost. He studies the mechanisms of soil allocation in productive activities, to explain the distribution of a harvest around a centre (a local market town) in preindustrial Germany. He then conceives an isolated circular domain of uniform fertility, free from any obstacle with a city at its centre. Given the available production techniques, the costs of transport, relative prices of products and factors, he then deduces the optimum sites for different kinds of activities.

The model is based on halos – since von Thünen analyses the allocation of the soil in concentric rings from an endogenous perspective – the area around the centre is treated in an exogenous way (there is no explanation in regards to the location of the centre, we can assume nevertheless that it is a question of natural geographical advantages).

Following the works of Johann Heinrich von Thünen (1826), Alfred Weber (1909), and Walter Isard (1956), the theory of space in economy acquired its patent of nobility. The basic idea of geographic economy is that the forces that drive the process of outsourcing / agglomeration, and therefore influence regional development more or less unevenly, are based on variables that have geographic components to them: transport facilities, the location of populations, mobility of the factors, local competition, proximity regarding the flows of trade, the transfers of technologies, etc.

As von Thünen did for agricultural activities, Alfred Weber tries to define an explicative model for the location of industrial enterprises. His analysis is called the “location triangle”. It searches for the optimum geographical location for a firm, based on the market’s location and on the sources of raw materials (to minimise the costs of transportation). The model is used particularly for enterprises that make use of heavy materials (coastalisation of the steel industry etc.)

Where does industrial production take place? Due to the economy of scale, industrial production is concentrated on a limited number of sites. All things being equal, the favoured sites are those that have an important market of proximity, as the production on a single market minimises the costs of transportation. Other locations are served by these central location sites. This situation creates a possibility of "circular causality": industrial production has a tendency to concentrate itself in places where there are markets of significant size, but markets of significant size only exist in places where industrial production is concentrated.

Paul Krugman (1991) also contributed to a better understanding when it comes to the localisation of firms and populations. He is the first to introduce a general spatial balance model with imperfect competition and increasing returns. He shows that globalisation concentrates populations in already favoured regions and accentuates the gap between the high-tech urban centres and the underdeveloped suburbs. This concentration of activities is explained by the quest to minimise the costs of transportation, to have access to specialised services, and to get closer to consumers or to sources of raw materials. Krugman’s model also includes centrifugal forces that explain why not all activity concentrates in a single urban zone (congestion, pollution, the increase in price of lands).

Finally, the model of centre / suburbs polarisation stresses the necessity to consider underdeveloped countries as integrated into the worldwide system. In *Modern capitalism and Other Essays*, Sweezy shows Marx did not anticipate that the international division of labour would take shape as a spatial structure of development and underdevelopment dividing mankind into two opposing camps.

In the analyses of Raul Prebish (1950) or Samir Amin (1970), the worldwide capitalist system has the following features: 1) it is organised into a hierarchy and is always seeking to renew this hierarchy without fail; 2) it is functional, entirely organised from its centre, which can create conflicts; 3) its driving force is exploitation conceived as an extraction, appropriation of any economic surplus. The dependent countries would not have sector I (capital goods) and their sector II (consumer goods) would be articulated in different sector Is of developed countries.

The emerging countries and the diffusion of growth

It is necessary to pay special attention to the growth of emerging countries. Asian and Latin American countries have seen the highest growth rates over the past twenty years (industrialisation of suburbs).

In *The World Economy, a millennial perspective,* Angus Maddison (2002) announces the "big crossing": the emerging countries, which had a weight until the beginning of the 17th century, before being overtaken by occidental countries, are returning to a position of power. At the beginning of the 21st century, they were already practically playing at an equal level with the developed countries, and should widely confirm their leading role by the year 2025 (at that time, they should represent 65% of the GDPS worldwide).

Growth rate of the volume of production (in annual %)

	2007	2008	2009
developing Asia	**10.6**	**7.6**	**6.2**
China	10.1	9.6	8.7
India	7.1	7.3	5.6
ASEAN – 5	5.4	4.7	1.3
Latin America	**5.7**	**4.2**	**-2.7**
Brazil	5.7	5.1	-0.7
Argentina	8.7	6.8	-2.5
Mexico	3.3	1.3	-7.3

Source: IMF, *World Economic Outlook*, on 2010
ASEAN-5: Indonesia, Malaysia, Philippines, Thailand, Vietnam.

The growth of emerging countries is remarkable on several levels:

- It is spreading on a continental scale. In Asia it can be seen in the development of four "dragons" (Singapore, Hong Kong, Taiwan, South Korea), further spreading to the "tigers" (Malaysia, Thailand, Indonesia);
- It is accelerating. The growth of the 1990s was superior to that of the 1980s, and that of the 2000s superior to that of the 1990s;

- It is a driving element of adjustments and changing power relationships. By extrapolating current tendencies, we can see that China could become the first world power in 2030. The emerging and developing countries already represent 50% of the worldwide GDPS.

The increasing power of China and India becomes manifest in an increase in their exports of fabricated products and services, and also in an increasing number of primary product imports. This bilateral movement caused crucial changes in worldwide relative pricing. This was beneficial to raw material and agricultural product exporters, and it was also the origin of a rebound in requests from "stockholding" countries (Russia, Persian Gulf countries) with their main incomes coming from the promotion of their resources in raw materials. Even if China and India have both specialised in the textile industry, the two countries are positioned differently on the same market. China is more specialised on clothing, India on fabrics and household linen. Both sectors in which these two countries are emerging have benefited from technological advances; electronics (China) and computer services (India), have common characteristics: they are linked to new information and communication technologies (ICT), two particularly dynamic segments of international trade. In both cases these sectors are strongly internationalised and their development owes much to relocation strategies of multinational business companies.

Allocation of the worldwide GDP

United States	20%
European Union	18%
China	15%
India	6%
Japan	6%
Brazil	3.5%

Source: IMF, *World Economic Outlook*, on 2010

We can also note that the emerging countries were much less affected by the recent financial crises (crash of Nasdaq and subprime crisis) than the developed countries. Especially the Asian emerging countries were barely touched by the slowing down of worldwide economy in 2008/09.

Rogoff (2004) draws attention to the fact that no significant connection can be shown between financial globalisation and the growth of emerging countries (countries most involved in this process). He points out the problem of efficiency when it comes to the transfer of external savings and the transmission channels towards growth. More than the scale of entries of capitals, it is the indirect or collateral effects that make a difference: impact on the development of the financial sector, on the macroeconomic discipline, on the credibility of the exchange rate regime, etc. If these qualitative transformations do not take place, the consequences on capital influxes in a country can become very unpredictable.

The role of technological progress

The first economist to have questioned the near advent of a stationary state is John Stuart Mill (1848). He deems this to be attained only at a late stage, when nations would be highly developed, because he believed in the "unlimited growth of power of man over nature". Mill introduces into his reasoning what is now called technological progress and the motivations of businessmen, while considering that in the absence of technological progress growth cannot be reached: "When a country carries its production as far as it can be carried in the present state of her knowledge (…), this country reaches a stationary state, this state in which the capital cannot increase only if some refinements still survive in productive arts or an increase in power of the desire to accumulate." Within this limited horizon (the stationary state) Mill sees a mankind freed from material pressures and economic problems: humans could then dedicate themselves to tasks "of spiritual order".

Following works of Joseph Schumpeter (1912), there is a consensus within economic theory to explain contemporary growth as the result of technological progress. This consensus nevertheless leaves open questions: Is it the big innovations or the succession of technological changes which explain economic development? Is it possible to act on technological progress? Is it exogenous (Solow's model) or endogenous (Romer's model)? If the measure of investment is relatively easy, it is not the same for the technological progress which according to an expression by Moses Abramovitz remains "The measure of our ignorance".

Exogenous growth

The model of balanced growth worked out by Solow (1956) is based on the hypothesis of constant scale outputs (production increases proportionally to the measure of labour and capital factors used). In accordance with the usual neoclassical model, business companies have constant scale outputs, diminishing factorial outputs whilst remunerating the production factors in their marginal productiveness. Solow takes into account the relative pricing role of factors and the substitution of capital / labour; he uses a function of aggregated production within which the capital is considered as homogeneous.

Solow adds two traditional production factors (capital and labour) and a third factor: technological progress. The latter corresponds to the distortion of the production function (modification of all technical knowledge) which is differentiated with the elevation of the mechanisation degree (substitution of capital for labour in a context of stability and technical knowledge). It is looked at as a free good which is not included into the distribution of added value between wages and benefits; it is exogenous, i.e. it cannot be explained by economic reasoning. According to Solow, "Research fields open and close again in unpredictable ways in economy as in science and technology. It is possible to give an example to prove this by looking at the frequency with which research plans lead to something that had not been considered in the initial question. An internal logic exists – or sometimes non-logic even – in the progress of knowledge, which is widely foreign to economic logic".

In fact, Solow's model makes the long term growth rate dependant on two exogenous factors: the evolution of populations and technological progress. According to him, economic behaviours of agents (summed up in the model by the choice of saving rates) do not have an influence on growth rates (saving rates are fixed beforehand and job offers are independent of real wages). During the transition period where the economy has not yet reached its long term growth, the growth will be stronger the higher the saving rates are (saving rates determine the speed of economic convergence towards a balanced state). Once this stage is reached, growth stops depending on saving efforts (saving rates act on the level of capital per head, but not on the growth rate of the economy as a whole).

This growth presentation drives performances to converge: economies all have the same long-term growth rate, technological progress is accessible by all and the economic policy cannot change the long-term growth rate.

For Solow, all countries have access to the same technology and the technological progress rate is the same everywhere. As a result, the differences of development between countries reside in the initial levels of capital. Therefore one should see upper capital outputs in the poor countries and an influx of capital towards these countries. From the perspective of neoclassical optimism, poor countries should catch up with the countries of the temperate zone and all countries should end up growing in accordance with the rhythm of technological progress.

Endogenous growth

Romer's works (1986; 1990) confirm the fundamental idea that the accumulation of physical capital and the increase of populations are not enough to create economic growth. According to Romer, the existence of increasing scaling outputs makes it necessary to adopt a hypothesis of imperfect competition (introduction of monopolistic competition as a subjacent form of market) or assume the existence of externalities. Endogenous growth models result in a sub-optimum balance justifying some form of public intervention. They explain the unequal development of economies (absence of adjustment on behalf of the poor countries) and give new theoretical foundations to international specialisation.

Romer raised the question of why growth accelerated during the course of history. According to him, the classical approach (founded on the hypothesis of diminishing outputs) is well adapted to the extraction of raw materials: as the deposit is gradually exploited, the ore becomes more and more difficult to extract, but this type of analysis appears inappropriate to shed light on the new information economy: when a programmer develops new software or when a scientist discovers a new genetic sequence, the initial research costs are vast, but development subsequently becomes less and less costly. Software will be copied on discs, sold at a low price or it could be installed on a personal computer via the internet. For Romer the true driving element of growth is knowledge; quick transmission of ideas. There is a dynamic flow of knowledge that ensures the multiplication of discoveries and the non-stop amplification of stronger knowledge. The stake in growth is society's access to knowledge and the production of goods or services linked to ITC's.

Romer's works concern the dynamics of long-term growth, they have made him "the most influential theorist of the 1980s" (Paul Krugman). His growth model resumes the implications of the neoclassical model of Solow regarding the distribution of incomes, but he assumes the evolution of technological progress to be endogenous (i.e. explicable by economic reasoning). According to Romer, technological progress is not an external behaviour of economic agents, since it depends on the workers level of knowledge, on their capacity to invent techniques and products.

These endogenous growth theories put the positive externalities at the centre of growth. Contrary to Solow's model, on a macroeconomic level, the function of production has a growing return to scale, avoiding the reduction of marginal productiveness of production factors. The problem presented to the neoclassical theory by the hypothesis of increasing outputs (the increase in volume of factors will grow more than proportionally to the production) is that production optimisation at company level can no longer be resolved unless we assume that markets tend to strive towards a monopolistic situation.

These theoretical works try to identify the factors that are the origin of increasing outputs at a global level, even though the function of production at a company level could be in constant output. This difference leads us to think about the positive externalities non-appropriable by the business companies, which all firms benefit from. According to Romer, these externalities come from the synergy in the accumulation of physical capital *(learning by doing)* or from research and development effects. Other theoreticians of the new classical macro-economy locate them at public facilities level (Barro) or in the accumulation of human resources (Lucas).

In Romer's model, companies fix the volume of their investments according to private marginal productiveness and not according to their social marginal productiveness which is superior. As a result, the long-term growth rate resulting from a competitive balance is less than the optimum growth rate. Only economic policy measures (public expenditures, incentives to savings) can reduce this gap. The initial conditions of an economy (supply of physical and human capital) have a decisive impact on its long term trajectory.

The models of endogenous growth have led Romer to study the role of the state within the process of economic development. According to him, it is necessary to invest in education in the same way that companies need to invest in their supply of technical capital in order to increase it. Even if private research is important, we should not be mistaken about the role of the public sector in this domain. Indeed, knowledge is a "public good" to a certain extent: once conceived, a new idea is useful for all (it is added to the knowledge pool of society).

Secondly, the theory of endogenous growth stresses the fact that an increase in the rate of savings always increases (and not in a transitional way) the growth rate of the economy. So politics that corrupt the redistribution of incomes between generations has an impact on growth: financing the budget deficit or changing the retirement systems; this is also the case for fiscal policies that change the cost opportunities of savings in comparison to consumption. An increase of savings allows financing of more innovative plans and as a result speeds growth up. However, households are not aware that their savings stimulate innovation on a macroeconomic level and that it is likely to increase their future incomes (positive externalities). The social output of savings is insufficient (hence an intervention by the State is desirable).

It is important to add that the state in the models of endogenous growth is not the traditional state. So, when Romer recommends subsidising activities in case of an accumulation of growing output, it seems more efficient to him to concentrate financial efforts rather than to divide them over the whole of society. In the case of education, this interventionism can take the shape of increasing the support in favour of those who already have a high level of education. Similarly, the theorists of endogenous growth recommend refunding taxes to very skilled workers, allowing them to claim the fruit of their educational efforts. As for the rest, theorists of endogenous growth think that if we do not intervene with the forces of the market, it will only have positive effects. The market is not a purpose in itself; it is a means to let the biggest number of people partake in growth.

The negative management of externalities

One can only be taken aback by the catastrophic reports on the environment published in 1972 (Club of Rome). This cataclysmic vision is damaging. It is linked to the fact that these reports are more often of a more political nature than truly scientific.

This is the case of the Stern report (2006) financed by the British government. In this report, the experts around Stern maintain that: 1) climate change presents a real problem; 2) it is necessary to take immediate action; 3) climate policies must be guided by a cost/benefit analysis of the reduction of greenhouse gas emissions; 4) these policies must be based on market instruments such as taxes or pollution permissions. This report stresses the potentially catastrophic effects of climate change: losses equivalent to 5% of the worldwide GNPS every year, displacement of 150 to 200 million people (the climate refugees), reduction of agricultural productivity in Africa. According to this report there is a risk of an economic collapse similar to that following the World Wars or to the great depression of the 1930s.

Following pioneering works by Arthur Pigou (1920), Ronal Coase (1959), and William Nordhaus (1994), the economists created a toolkit to efficiently fight against the environmental degradation, notably against global warming, which today appears to be the main threat directly linked to gas emissions. Undesirable effects of growth on the environment can be alleviated by the use of:

- Systems based on price (taxes);
- The labelling of companies or products;
- The public subsidies to promote innovations in the field of alternative energies (solar energy, geothermal energy);
- Action on volumes (quantitative control of greenhouse gas emissions, in the style of the Kyoto protocol);

Emission trading allows companies to exchange all or part of the quotas that are allocated to them.

We can distinguish between two dimensions regarding the preservation of resources (Dasgupta, on 1979). The first dimension relates to situations where it is necessary for several states to combine their efforts (fighting against pollution, sustaining air quality or biodiversity). This is a “prisoner's dilemma” as no country can act alone, because only the participation of the biggest number of countries will have the desired impact. In fact, if emissions continue to grow elsewhere, the preservation of environmental goods is then brought about by a bigger international cooperation.

The second dimension relates to situations where states are in competition over the access to resources (exhaustion of non-renewable resources necessary for production and research of the security of supplies) which presents a source for potential conflicts.

One can trust in the inventiveness of mankind to find the necessary solutions to problems linked to the reduction of natural resources and the impossibility of sustaining ores and energy wasting forever. Despite the failure of the summit of Copenhagen (2009), we have good reasons to be optimistic. The sustainable development is within our reach, it should allow mankind to cover all needs while at the same time assuring the survival of biodiversity and ecosystems, taking into account the rightful interests of future generations.

References

Abramovitz, Moses, edited by, (1955), *Capital Formation and Economic Growth*, Princeton University Press.

Aghion, Philippe et Howitt, Peter (1997), *Endogenous Growth Theory*, MIT Press.

Amin, Samir (1970), *L'accumulation à l'échelle mondiale*, Anthropos.

Arrow, Kenneth (1962), The Economic implication of learning by doing, *Review of Economic Studies*.

Artus, Patrick (2005), *Le capitalisme est en train de s'autodétruire*, La Découverte.

Barro, Robert et Sala-I-Martin, Xavier (1991), Convergence across States and Regions, *Brookings Papers on Economic Activity*.

Barro, Robert et Sala-I-Martin, Xavier (1995), *Economic Growth*, McGraw-Hill.

Baumol, William (1986), Productivity Growth, Convergence and Welfare: what the long-run data show, *American Economic Review*.

Becker, Gary (1964), *Human capital*, Columbia University Press.

Brundtland, Gro Harlem, edited by, (1987), *Our Common future [Notre avenir à tous]*, Report of the World Commission on Environment and Development, Oxford University Press.

Coase. (1959), The Problem of Social Cost, *Journal of Law and Economics*.

Cohen, Daniel (2009), *La prospérité du vice*, Albin Michel.

Collins, Susan (1990), Lessons from Korean Economic Growth, *American Economic Review*.

Dasgupta, Partha (1979), *Economic Theory and Exhaustible Resources*, Cambridge University Press.

Denison, Edward (1961), *The sources of economic growth*, Committee for Economic Development.

Dobb, Maurice (1946), *Studies in the Development of Capitalism*, Routledge & Kegan.

Easterlin, Richard (1974), Does Economic Growth improve the Human Lot?, dans *Nations and Households in Economic Growth : Essays in Honor of Moses Abramovitz*, Academic Press Inc.

Easterly, William (2001), *The Elusive Quest for Growth: Economists' Adventures and Misadventures in the Tropics*, MIT Press.

Fogel, Robert (1964), *Railroads and American Economic Growth. Essays in Econometric History*, John Hopkins Press.

Fujita, Masahisa et Thisse, Jean-François (2002), *Economics of Agglomeration – Cities, Industrial Location and Regional Growth*, Cambridge University Press

Georgescu Roegen, Nicholas (1971), *The Entropy Law and Economic Process*, Harvard University Press.

Hansen, Alvin (1938), *Full Recovery or Stagnation?*, A. and C. Black.

Helpman, Elhanan (1995), International R&D Spillovers, *European Economic Review*.

Hoover, Edgard (1937), *Location Theory and the Shoe and Leather Industries*, Harvard university Press.

Isard, Walter (1956), *Location and Space Economy: a General Theory Relating to Industrial Location, Market Areas, Land Use, Trade, and Urban Structure*, MIT Press.

Jevons, Stanley (1865), *The Coal Question. An Inquiry Concerning the Progress of the Nation, and the Probable Exhaustion of Our Coal-Mines*, Macmillan.

Krueger, Anne (1992), *Economic Policy Reform in Developing Countries*, Blackwell.

Krugman, Paul (1991), *Geography and Trade*, MIT Press.

—. (1991), Increasing Returns and Economic Geography, *Journal of Political Economy*.

Kuznets, Simon (1959), *Six lectures on economic growth*, The Free Press.

Landes, David (1998), *The Wealth and Poverty of Nations: Why Are Some So Rich and Others So Poor?*, Norton & Company.

—. (2006), Why Europe and the West? Why not China?, *Journal of Economic Perspective*.

Latouche, Serge (2004), *Survivre au développement : De la décolonisation de l'imaginaire économique à la construction d'une société alternative*, Mille et Une Nuits.

Lucas, Robert (1988), On the Mechanics of Economic development, *Journal of Monetary Economics*.

—. (1990), Why doesn't Capital Flow from Rich to Poor Countries?, *American Economic Review*.

Maddison, Angus (1982), *Phases of capitalism development*, Oxford University Press.
—. (2002), *L'Economie mondiale, une perspective millénaire*, OCDE.
Mill,, Stuart (1848), *Principes d'économie politique.*
Nijkamp, Peter (2004), *Innovation, space and Economic Development*, Edward Elgar Publishing Ltd.
Nordhaus, William (1994), *Managing the Global Commons: The Economics of Climate Change*, MIT Press.
—. (2000), *Warming the World : Economic Models of Global Warming*, MIT Press.
North, Douglas (1973), *The Rise of the Western World*, Cambridge University Press
Pigou, Arthur (1920), *The Economics of Welfare*, Macmillan.
Prebish, Raul (1950), *The Economic Development of Latin America and its Principal Problems*, United Nations.
Rodrik, Dani (2002), Trade Policy and Economic Growth: a Skeptic guide to the Cross National Evidence, *NBER Macroeconomics Annual.*
Rogoff, Kenneth, Prasad, Eswar et Wei, Shang-Jin (2004), Effects of Financial globalization on Developping Countries: some Empirical Evidence, *IMF Occasional Paper.*
Romer, Paul (1986), Increasing Returns and Long-Run Growth, *Journal of Political Economy.*
—. (1990), Endogenous Technological Change, *Journal of Political Economy.*
Sachs, Jeffrey (2005), *The End of Poverty: Economic Possibilities for our Time*, Penguin Press.
Sachs, Jeffrey et Warner, Andrew (1995), Economic Reform and the Process of global Integration, *Brookings Papers on Economic Activity.*
Sachs, Jeffrey et Warner, Andrew (1995), Natural Resource Abundance and Economic Growth, *NBER Working Paper.*
Schultz, Theodore (1963), *The Economic value of education*, Columbia University Press.
Schumpeter, Joseph (1912), *Theorie der wirtschaftlichen Entwicklung [Théorie de l'évolution économique]*, Duncker/Humblot.
Solow, Robert (1956), A Contribution to the Theory of Economic Growth, *Quarterly Journal of Economics.*
Stern, Nicholas and al. (2006), *Report on the Economics of Climate Change.*
Sweezy, Paul (1972), *Modern Capitalism and Other Essays*, Monthly Review Press.

Thisse, Jean-François (2003), *Handbook of Regional and Urban Economics*, vol IV: *Cities and Geography*, North-Holland Publishing Company.

Thunen, Heinrich von (1826), *Der isolierte Staat in Beziehung auf Landwirtschaft und Nationalökonomie.*

Weber, Alfred (1909), *Uber der Standort der Industien.*

PART 3.

QUANTITATIVE ANALYSIS: EMPIRICAL ECONOMICS AND FINANCE ISSUES

VALUABLE DECISIONS AND INFORMATION: A QUANTITATIVE LONGITUDINAL STUDY ABOUT THE FINANCIAL AND ECONOMIC PERFORMANCE OF DOWNSIZING COMPANIES

TRISTAN BOYER[1]

Introduction

The 2008 crisis led to a decrease in the world economy. Many companies downsized their workforce in order to fit the standards they said the financial markets were awaiting. Since the 80s, the financial market has become a privileged source of "cheap" money for the quoted companies. They started to decentralize and externalize their activities, thus adopting more flexible structures, often in open networks and described as focused on their "business core".

These increasingly complex systems are responsible for the confusion felt by individuals and for the shortening of the temporal horizon over which individuals might possibly have some insight. The link that had existed until then between employer and employee was no longer seen as a long relationship likely to be based on trust; rather, it was immediately seen as a mercantile relationship. From this perspective, and if one adheres to this approach, the financial markets, accelerators of the global economy, are responsible for the weakening of the wage relation.

The waves of layoffs in companies in good financial health, *allegedly* ratified by financial markets due to a rise in the value of the share, the importance of the shareholder in managerial statements, notably through the statements about the "creation of value (for the shareholder)," management indicators such as EVA, or the constant references to the "principles of Corporate Governance," tend to support the idea of a financialization movement which would translate into management actions that go against the interests of salaried workers. Recent examples have

[1] Institut de Préparation à l'Administration et à la Gestion.

shown how much such a "dictatorship of financial markets and pension funds," which confounds and reduces the interest of the company to that of the shareholder, has been contested by the victims of layoffs as well as by society at large and the larger part of companies' shareholders.

Is layoff a valuable decision?

Stock value and layoffs

The major importance of financial markets in the managers' concern cannot be denied. But the efficiency of the decisions taken into shareholders interest - in other words: financial markets' satisfaction - does not appear as clearly as it should, especially when one considers the link between layoffs and the evolution of the company's stock price. Actually, numerous event studies (aiming at analysing abnormal returns on equity[2]) show that financial markets do not react especially well to layoffs.

The reference work in this field is that of Abowd *et al.* (1990), based on the analysis of 452 events in 1980 for 154 companies, and 195 events in 1987 for 102 companies. For each of the two years, the abnormal returns are calculated over a period around the event: -2 to +2 days in one part and -10 to -3 days on the other, so as to take into consideration a possible anticipation of the financial markets. Even if the results are not statistically significant, they show that by and large financial markets react negatively to layoff decisions. This result shatters the hypothetical link between labour cuts and increased share value.

Exploring these results further, and extending the considered abnormal returns to a 6 months period, Worrell *et al.* (1991), based their study on 194 companies during the period 1979-1987. Abnormal profits are considered within a period of -90 to +90 days around the event. The returns are of about -2% on average. It is interesting to note that the returns vary markedly depending on the context and the reasons for the layoff decision: in the case of company restructuring or reorganization, the accumulated abnormal profit during the designated period is +3.6%. In contrast, if the layoff decision arises from a need to deal with financial difficulties, the accumulated abnormal profit is -5.6%.

---

[2] An Abnormal Return is the difference between the actual return of an equity and its normal return (usually defined by the average market performance). It measures the impact of announcement.

With the same objectives, but with a restricted period of observation, Abraham & Kim (2004) look at 368 companies that announced layoffs during the 1993-1994 period in the US, focusing on the week of the announcement. On the day of the announcement, the loss of return of the share is insignificant, 0.07%; in contrast, on the day before the announcement the loss of return is 0.85%; while on the day after the announcement there is a gain of 0.15%. The loss of return during the week of the announcement amounts to 0.99%. Farber & Hallock (2009) compared the results of 14 studies about abnormal returns detected around layoff decisions ([-1 day; +1 day]) between 1970 and 1997. According to them, whatever period one takes over the last 30 years, one finds that the reaction of financial markets to layoff announcements is clearly negative. However, the reactions become less and less negative the closer we get to the most recent periods. These authors attribute this slide to a change in the nature of layoffs, which are more and more meant to improve efficiency than to respond to a shortage of demand.

By considering 118 restructuring operations announcements over the period 1988 to 1995 concerning DJIA companies[3] and the consequence one day before and one day after the announcement, Poon *et al.* (2001) find a clear negative relation between the announcement of a restructuration by the *WSJ,* especially when the restructuring appears as a charge against the firm's earnings. The abnormal excess return in that case is -0.916%.

The historical period observed by these preceding papers show a negative impact of layoff on financial return. Considering the changes in the world economy during the observed period (1970-1997), it seems important to analyse the differences between the appreciation of layoffs during the different periods of our recent economic history, from the industrial restructurations to the financialized economy. McKnight *et al.* (2002) give an interesting perspective about the evolution of investors' reactions to corporate layoffs by making a comparison between 1980-1984 (88 firms) and 1990-1995 (147 firms) in the UK. They find cumulative abnormal return (CAR) in the 5 day period of observation ([-2 days; +2 days]) to be a significant: -2.05% for the 1990s and -1.40% in the 1980s. This slide in the appreciation of layoffs is also observed when they distinguish between proactive and reactive layoffs: if proactive layoffs were granted with a CAR of +1.73% in the 80s, this premium was insignificant in the 90s

[3] 30 corporations are part of the Dow Jones Industrial Average.

(+0.3%). According to these authors, relying on Worrell *et al.*'s (1991) work, layoffs are less approved within the UK than within the US for the same period.

The importance of the strategic context of the downsizing situation leads to the sensible study of Hahn & Reyes (2004). They distinguish between layoffs due to decline or restructuring. They consider the case of 78 US firms during the period 1995-1999 announcing a reduction of their workforce larger than 1000 employees. As previous studies showed, investors' reaction to decline (low demand for the companies' product) is negative with a CAR of -1.41% in the [-1 day; +1 day] interval around the announcement and positive in the case of corporate restructuring (+1.71%).

Hillier *et al.* (2007) worked on 322 layoff announcements in 175 UK firms between 1990 and 2000. They found, as in previous literature, that depending on the cause of the layoff, the financial market reacted negatively when these layoffs were reactive in nature, (such as those responding to loss making activities and plant closures) as opposed to those proactive in nature (reorganizations, cost cutting) that cause a minimal stock price response. They also found that the larger the layoff, the worse the response from the financial markets.

Wherever and whenever these results come from, they clearly suggest that actors of the financial markets do not automatically react in a favourable way to layoff announcements. The context and the motivations for the decisions appear as decisive factors in the reactions of financial markets. In fact, if the layoff decision presents itself as an attempt to solve financial problems, financial markets do not view it as a good decision, or they view the decision as insufficient, hence the negative reaction. In contrast, if the layoff decision is due to reorganization, that is, if the reduction in workforce is but a means or a consequence of a sound or promising decision, the financial markets react favourably. In and of themselves, layoffs do not amount to a sufficiently explicit signal to occasion an increase in the share value of a company; instead, layoffs are viewed as one element of a complex decision that must be incorporated into a coherent company strategy. These studies establish the fact that, even on a short-term period around the announcement of a layoff decision, the reactions of financial markets are not unconditionally favourable.

Economic performance and layoffs

Layoffs are intended to be a means for improving the situation of a company. Considering the evidence from the literature, layoffs are not a sufficient decision to improve a company's stock price, but are they susceptible to improving the economic situation of a firm?

The study of De Meuse *et al.* (1994) confirms the absence of systematically positive effects from cuts in the workforce, even though the study does not differentiate between the contexts of the decisions. The study is developed with data from the years 1987 to 1991, and confronts the indicators of accounting return with the Tobin's Q (in the interval [-1 year; +1 year]) of 17 companies that laid off in 1989, and of 35 companies that did not layoff between 1989-1991. Whatever the index used, the lag in the performance of companies that cut their workforce only increased during the considered period.

Relying on the distinction made about the impact of layoffs on financial returns, Cascio *et al.* (1997) distinguish between the situations that led to layoffs. The study analyses the employment decisions of 537 companies during the 1981-1992 period. For all the companies, this means 5479 changes in workforce, 89% of the companies showing at least one change in the workforce for each of the years considered. On top of economic and labour variables, the authors decided to take into account the variations in assets, since layoffs accompanied by a sale of assets are not considered in the same way by financial markets. They further differentiate seven types of decisions according to the threshold of variations in employment and assets. With this data, the authors tested two hypotheses: (H1) change in the workforce has no effect on the gross profit during the current year and the two following years; (H2) change in the workforce has no effect on the stock value during the current year and the two following years.

To start, they note that the economic profit of companies that laid-off is inferior to that of companies that grew (in data corrected for sector evolution: -0.19% for the former and +2.48% for the latter), which reinforces the theory that companies that layoff are not in good economic shape. Among companies that layoff, if one distinguishes those that sell their assets from those that only downsize their workforce, one notices that the first experience an increase in total profits of 3.1% in three years, while the second experience a decrease of 2.4% over the same period. A cut in workforce is thus not sufficient to solve the problems of a company whose profits are too low, at least not over a two to three year period.

Furthermore, Cascio *et al.* (1997) noted that, by calculating the cumulative stock gains of the years 0-2, an investment in the "employment cutters" brought a 63% return while the same investment in the "employment generators" brought a 74% return. Moreover, they noticed that, among the "cutters," the best results were to be found with the ones that sold their assets. In sum, this study shows that the best performance levels are attained by the "generators," which confirms that "growth, employment, and stock performance are not incompatible".

Studying the following period, Chalos & Chen (2002) looked at the effects three years after the announcement of a cut in the workforce on the financial situation of 365 firms that made such announcements during the years 1993-1995. They differentiate the companies depending on their strategy (cost cutting, plant closure, refocusing) and found the strategic objectives partially achieved in the case of refocusing (sales per employee improved significantly, while production costs per employee did not improve). Cost cutting strategies did not prove themselves to be very effective, even if they slightly improved the situation of the company. Plant closings do not show themselves to generate any positive effects.

In 2004, De Meuse *et al.* extended their observations of their 1994 paper. They found that the positive impact of downsizing does not appear at least before three years. Depending on the size of the layoff (more or less than 10% of the workforce), they found that 8 years after the layoff(s), the first group (less than 10% layoff) did go back to a comparable situation as their competitors, avoiding bankruptcy, while the other group did not still reach a satisfying economic situation.

This set of studies confirms that the reactions of financial markets are not as simplistic as one might have believed. The financial markets' estimation of layoff announcements is not limited to a systematic decision in their favour. Quite on the contrary, the sectorial context and the motivations for the decision are at the heart of the financial markets' reaction: to cut labour simply to reduce costs does not lead to an improvement of the share value. The layoff decision occasions an improvement of the share value only if the decision is incorporated into a strategic reaction to weak performance, and only if this low performance also affects the company's entire sector of activity. It also appears that laying off can be considered a simple and unique solution, no matter the magnitude of the layoff. In fact, the bigger the layoffs, the worst the improvement. The most striking point is that neither from the financial point of view, nor from the economic one, do layoffs appear as a unique and sufficient source of improvement, unless they are part of a comprehensive and continuous strategy.

What is the valuable information?

As the previous literature showed, layoffs are not rewarded by the financial markets. Neither do they prove themselves to be a successful answer to companies' distress. Meanwhile, layoffs cannot always be avoided, and they allow companies to improve an endangered economic situation, avoiding possible bankruptcy, when they are part of a strategic and structural change.

Since managers and state representative often refer to financial markets as the main recipient of such decisions, it seemed interesting to consider how investors practically interact with those firms and what kind of information they consider. The importance of non-financial information appeared as particularly relevant when investors have to evaluate the strategic impact of a restructuring operation.

The source of non-financial information

Numerous studies show that the coherence between financial and non-financial information obtained from specific reports filed in financial reports, is the more useful for investors in making good decisions in their middle- and long-term portfolio management, especially when it comes to evaluating the strategy of a company and the risks it bears (Clinch & Magliolo (1992); Lajili & Zéghal (2005); Bryan (1997); Cole & Jones (2004)). Since a restructuration operation has to be considered as a turn in a company's strategy, and as the financial information can be easily found by investors, the arising question is to identify the source of the non-financial information and how valuable it is.

The AMAC survey has been conducted by Fortune magazine yearly since 1983. In this study, each corporation is rated relative to its competitors on eight attributes (quality of management, quality of products or services, innovativeness, ability to attract, developing and keeping talented people, long term investment value, financial soundness, use of corporate assets, and community and environmental responsibility). Zyglidopoulos (2004) studied the relation between layoffs and corporate reputation, relying on AMAC data. The respondents are senior executives and financial analysts from the ten largest companies in each of the 46 industries of the Fortune 1000 list. The data analysed covers 1988 and 1991 and is based on 527 observations. He found that downsizing generates significant losses in corporate reputation, no matter the size of the layoffs. He also found downscoping (considered as a corrective action to an over-diversification of the firm) to be damaging to corporate reputation, but in a smaller measure.

An important and particularly comprehensive study has been made by Mavrinac & Siesfeld (1998). They analyse the influence of non-financial factors in the decisions of financial market actors in order to determine the most important of these factors and their sources. The study is based on a survey of 275 American asset managers (which represents 14% of the profession) of all types of financial institutions (pension funds, insurance, banks), and on the analysis of 300 reports by independent analysts.

The sources of this information are many, and the significance of non-financial information sources is shown in this table, rated from 1 to 7:

Source	**Mean score**
Management presentations	5.54
Company filings	5.34
Sell-side analysts	4.82
Competitors	4.77
Business press	4.56
Company investor relations personnel	4.56
Customers	4.55
Buy-side analysts	4.53
Trade press	4.51
Informal networks	4.27
Independent ranking agencies	3.99
Industry trade associations	3.93
Online services	3.77

The variety of sources shows that institutional investors are ready to spend time and money for pertinent and reliable information. According to the managers questioned in this study, non-financial information sources are important indicators because they allow the managers to judge the internal functioning of the company and the real implementation of their strategies. Some of the questions posed concerned the importance investors attach to non-financial information: for 25% of investors, non-financial factors influence their decisions by more than 50%; for 60% of these, the influence of non-financial information fluctuates between 20 to 50%. On average, 35% of the investment decision is guided by non-financial factors. This figure can go up to 67% if one includes the image of the company in the non-financial factors (Greene, 1999).

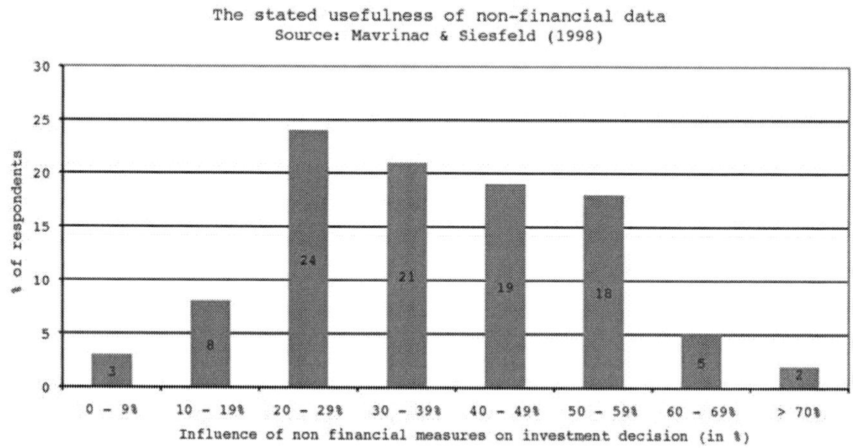

Valuable non-financial information

The important role non-financial information plays in investors' decisions raises questions concerning what information they consider relevant for their decisions. The second half of Mavrinac & Siesfeld's survey classifies this information in a hierarchy of importance. According to the study, investors clearly favour certain criteria: the implementation of the strategy; the credibility of the management; the quality of the strategy; the company's capacity for innovation in its sector; the ability to retain talented workers; the company's market share; and the management's experience.[4] These criteria depend upon a mid- to long-term estimation concerning mainly Human Resources and management factors.

The importance of non-financial measures, and especially the importance of human capital measures is tested by Lim *et al.* (2010): they compared the usefulness of human capital measures from 49 Australian senior-level executives and from 39 investors, and found that investors insist on the disclosure of such indicators more than executives do, though the latter appear to have a better knowledge of these measures. It also has been shown by Dossi & Patelli (2010) that big companies can highly benefit from this information, not only from the investors' point of view, but also from the alignment and corporate culture they favour.

An interesting consequence of such a disclosure has been shown by Orens *et al.* (2010): basing their study on the role of non-financial information within North America and Continental Europe, they provide interesting insight about the cost of capital for these firms. As investors appear to favour non-financial information disclosure, one should expect the cost of capital to be cheaper for the firms complying with this transparency policy. Surprisingly, North American firms do not clearly benefit from their involvement in non-financial disclosure, though Continental Europe companies do.

Conclusion

In this paper, we collected an extensive subset of the literature about layoffs and financial markets. We showed that, contrary to a widely held belief, financial market do not reward downsizing strategies without considering the strategy supposed to lead to such a decision. We also showed that investors have also a tendency to under-valuate the possible positive impact of layoffs.

Non-financial information has been proved to be crucial for investors, but has also been proved to be more important in Europe. Since we found the same gap between the judgement of investors (US *vs.* UK, in the first part of the paper), it appears that an interesting point to analyse in a future survey would be the differences in the representations within Europe and America. In fact, it would be interesting to analyse, especially from the

[4] Note that these criteria are aligned with those considered by Zyglidopoulos (2004).

Human Resource point of view, whether Europe and America react in the exact same way.

References

Abowd, J.M., Milkovich, G.T., & Hannon, J.M. 1990. The Effects of Human Resource Management Decisions on Shareholder Value. *Industrial and Labor Relations Review*, **43**(3), 203—236.

Abraham, S., & Kim, D.O. 2004. Layoff announcements and employment guarantee announcements: How do shareholders respond? *International Journal of Manpower*, **25**(8), 729—740.

Bryan, S. 1997. Incremental Information Content of Required Disclosures Contained in Management Discussion and Analysis. *Accounting Review*, **72**, 285—302.

Cascio, W., Young, C., & Morris, J. 1997. Financial consequences of employment-change decisions in major US corporations. *The Academy of Management Journal*, **40**(5), 1175—1189.

Chalos, P., & Chen, C. 2002. Employee downsizing strategies: market reaction and post announcement financial performance. *Journal of Business Finance & Accounting*, **29**(5-6), 847—870.

Clinch, G., & Magliolo, J. 1992. Market Perceptions of Reserve Disclosures Under SFAS No. 69. *Accounting Review*, **67**, 843—843.

Cole, C., & Jones, C. 2004. The Usefulness of MD&A Disclosures in the Retail Industry. *Journal of Accounting, Auditing and Finance*, **19**(4), 361—388.

De Meuse, K., Vanderheiden, P., & Bergmann, T. 1994. Announced layoffs: Their effect on corporate financial performance. *Human Resource Management*, **33**(4), 509—530.

De Meuse, K., Bergmann, T., Vanderheiden, P., & Roraff, C. 2004. New Evidence Regarding Organizational Downsizing and a Firm's Financial Performance: A Long-term Analysis. *Journal of Managerial Issues*, **16**(2), 155—177.

Dossi, A., & Patelli, L. 2010. You Learn From What You Measure: Financial and Non-financial Performance Measures in Multinational Companies. *Long Range Planning*, **43**(4), 498—526.

Farber, H., & Hallock, K. 2009. The changing relationship between job loss announcements and stock prices: 1970-1999. *Labour Economics*, **16**(1), 1—11.

Greene, D. 1999. Measures that matter - The path of intangible value. *In:* for Business Innovation, The Ernst & Young Center (ed), *Your Brand & the Bottom Line Conference.*

Hahn, T., & Reyes, M. 2004. On the estimation of stock-market reaction to corporate layoff announcements. *Review of financial economics*, **13**(4), 357—370.

Hillier, D., Marshall, A., McColgan, P., & Werema, S. 2007. Employee layoffs, shareholder wealth and firm performance: evidence from the UK. *Journal of Business Finance & Accounting*, **34**(3-4), 467—494.

Lajili, K., & Zéghal, D. 2005. *A Content Analysis of Risk Management Disclosures in Canadian Annual Reports*. University of Ottawa, School of management.

Lim, L., Chan, C., & Dallimore, P. 2010. Perceptions of Human Capital Measures: From Corporate Executives and Investors. *Journal of Business and Psychology*, **25**, 673—688.

Mavrinac, S., & Siesfeld, T. 1998. Measures that matter: An exploratory investigation of investors 'information needs and value priorities. *The economic impact of knowledge*, 273—294.

McKnight, P.J., Lowrie, A., & Coles, C. 2002. Investor reactions, social implications and layoff announcements in the UK: a comparison between periods. *Journal of Management and Governance*, **6**(1), 83—100.

Orens, R., Aerts, W., & Cormier, D. 2010. Web-Based Non-Financial Disclosure and Cost of Finance. *Journal of Business Finance & Accounting*, **37**(9-10), 1057—1093.

Poon, P., Newbould, G., & Durtschi, C. 2001. Market reactions to corporate restructurings. *Review of Quantitative Finance and Accounting*, **16**(3), 269—290.

Worrell, D., Davidson, W., & Sharma, V. 1991. Layoff announcements and stockholder wealth. *Academy of Management Journal*, **34**(3), 662—678.

Zyglidopoulos, S. 2004. The impact of downsizing on the corporate reputation for social performance. *Journal of Public Affairs*, **4**(1), 11—25.

TEST OF THE CUMULATIVE PROSPECTS THEORY: EXPERIMENTAL LABORATORY IN THE CONTEXT OF THE FINANCIAL INVESTMENTS IN TUNISIA

JIHÈNE JEBENIANI GOUIDER[1]
AND MOKHTAR KOUKI[2]

Introduction

The expected utility theory, proposed by Von Neumann and Morgenstern (1944) is the pioneering model of the choices analysis. However, experimentation often calls into question the behavioural standards upon which it is built, suggesting their insufficiencies and the need to extend them (Allais, 1953; Ellsberg, 1961,...) to a very broad field of research. Our work has exceeded the existing literature on the study of risk aversion by proposing an approach that combines both the techniques of experimental economy (lottery-type questions based on risky and certain assets, and questions related to attitudes) (see de Palma and Picard, 2002; 2005) and the flexibility discrete choice models (see Anderson, Palma and Thisse, 1992; McFadden, 2001; Ben-Akiva, Palma and McFadden, 2003). Our approach was consistent with both the expected utility theory and the non-expected utility theory. Under the non-expected utility theory, we used for our problematic the cumulative prospects theory (CPT) of Tversky and Kahneman (1992), the most used model in the literature (see Grandin, 2005; Broihanne, Merli and Roger, 2007).

[1] Business school of Tunis, Manouba University, Tunisia. E-mail: Jihene.Jebeniani@esct.rnu.tn
[2] School of Statistics and Information Analysis Tunis, Carthage University, Tunisia. e-mail:Mokhtar.Kouki@essait.rnu.tn

The objective of this article is to test the CPT, by resorting to laboratory experimentation that aimed to understand and model the attitudes with respect to the risk, through the standard model of decision under risk. In our experimental laboratory, we considered a deviation from the expected utility theory. It was related to loss aversion, which implies different transformation functions depending on their being profits or losses. Experiments since Kahneman and Tversky have showed that the individuals' utility functions are concave in gains and convex in losses. Moreover, the loss of utility is higher in terms of losses rather than in gains. The implications of loss aversion have not been studied more systematically in the context of financial investments. Through our econometric estimates, we tried to find these effects highlighted in the literature. This article is as follows: in the first section, we present the experimental protocol of the experimental laboratory conducted in Tunisia and the descriptive statistics of the sample. In the second section, we test experimentally the loss aversion in the CPT on the data sample. A discussion of the results is also presented. An econometric analysis of the loss aversion is given in the third section. A summary of the results of our work is presented in the conclusion.

1.Experimental laboratory

The experimental method developed by Smith (1994), which has since been adopted by a growing number of researchers in economy and psychology (Stevens and Williams, 2004; Pfiffelmann and Roger, 2005), seems to be a powerful tool for interrogating theoretical models. The originality of the experimental approach is due to the limitations of different types of production methods of behavioural data.

1.1 Definition of experimental economy

Economic experimentation consists of the economic recovery in a laboratory, a simplified economic situation for which all variables are controlled by the experimenter. The principle is to invite subjects to act as part of a game defined by the experimenter. The rules of the game take over the structure of the real rebuilt economic situation. Each decision taken by the player in the game gets a profit or a loss expressed in monetary form. The basic principle is that each player must assume financial consequences of the choices.

1.2. Experimental protocol

In the context of the experimental economy, we developed an experimental laboratory, the first in Tunisia, on the evaluation of the individual risk aversion in the context of financial investments (see Brook and Zank, 2004; Goeree, Holt and Palfrey, 2003; Holt and Laury, 2003; Luce, 2000; Roth, 1988). We conducted experiments[3] in a guided and controlled way that measured and quantified the individual reactions towards situations where the risk was on the financial investment. Respondent were encouraged to provide sincere answers with a remuneration related to their answers. Indeed, the choices of the individuals determine their earnings. The financing of our experimental sessions was assured by the French National Agency of Research (ANR). The experiments were conducted at the Business school of Tunis, in a computer room equipped with broadband Internet so as to easily get connected the site www.RiskToleranceOnLine.com. However, we adapted the questionnaire of the Web site to the Tunisian context (reference currency, adapting the invested amounts in dinars[4], Tunisian diplomas, etc.)

The experimental sessions[5] were held from February 2008 to April 2008. Given the planned treatments, 30 experimental sessions, each including between 9 and 15 subjects, were conducted. The average duration of the experiments was approximately 1 hour 30 minutes. The subjects were mainly students of second degree in economic sciences and finance, as well as teaching and administrative staff of the universities. We collected 386 respondents in this experimental laboratory. Each participant responded to 10 series of lotteries. In addition, they were informed of the number of sets of lotteries to be filled. The only modifications among the series of the lotteries game were the return laws of the lotteries and the interval where its returns vary. In the first three series (series 1 to 3) the return followed the uniform law, whereas in series 4 to 6 the return followed a symmetric binary law. These six series included negative return in order to measure the asymmetry around zero. However, in series 7 and

---

[3] Experience is a set of observation production sessions in a controlled environment.

[4] The proposed amounts were discussed here in euros. However, during the experimental sessions, we transformed the amounts into the Tunisian dinar and we calibrated the proposed sums according to the context of investments in Tunisia.

[5] The experimental session is a sequence of games within the same group of players.

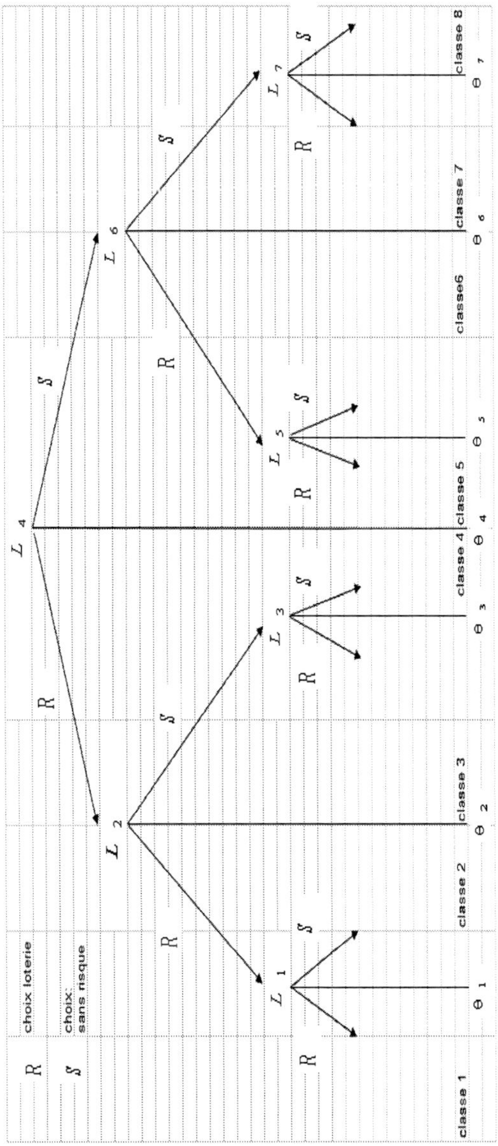

Figure 1: Representation of the decision problem: De Palma and Picard (2003, 2008)

8, the outputs had a small probability of large loss, whereas in series 9 and 10, the return had a small Jackpot probability. Figure (1) shows the decision tree of the lotteries.

The monetary incentives were varied according to the individual choice. Starting with an initial equal amount for all respondents of 30 Tunisian dinars, the final remuneration consisted of this amount multiplied by the return corresponding to the choice that was made on one of the 10 series of lotteries randomly drawn. The choice of the initial monetary values took into account several potentially contradictory constraints. We carefully selected this initial amount by resorting to excavated pilot studies (with about fifteen subjects). To be remunerated, the individual randomly drew a number between 1 and 10 that corresponded to the series determining their gain.

1.3 Descriptive statistics

According to the summaries of the statistics of the variables in the sample, we found that the sample was homogeneous in nature. Indeed, it consisted of 51.14% men. The average age was 27.341 years. Specifically, 87.33% of the population were aged less than 25 and 10.22% of the respondents were aged between 26 and 40 years. However, the most common marital status was single, with 73.33%, while the married represented only 18.92% in the sample. Moreover, 59.26% of the respondents considered themselves as novices, 29.39% rather experienced, 10.35% and 1.00% experienced and very experienced respectively. The primary objective of investment for 4.90% of respondents is to leave a legacy; 4.17% for training; 2.47% for saving for retirement; 11.10% for constructing a safety net; 17.92% to generate long-term revenue; 16.22% to generate regular income; 20.09% for buying or renovating a house; 13.20% for durable goods purchases; and 1.67% to grow their wealth. Other goals are so unlikely that they can be broadly represented as a secondary objective. Regarding the style of investors, 8.82% of respondents accept no fluctuations; 28.02% of respondents accept short term fluctuations; 53.44% of respondents accept moderate fluctuations; and 9.72% of respondents accept significant fluctuations. During a period of rise, and after loss, 26.07% of the respondents paid immediately; 54.63% waited for a turnaround; and 22.39% kept rising. However, 19.65% of respondents had already invested; 21.97% of respondents intend to reallocate some of their capital share in order to achieve their goal; 58.39% of respondents intend to gradually build capital in the coming years in order to achieve their main goal; while 0.13% did not intend to invest. After a high loss, 26.07% of respondents immediately liquidate. 54.63% of respondents expect turning. Finally, 22.39% of respondents continue. However, following a decline, 26.32% of investors immediately liquidate. 43.01% of respondents liquidate after significant loss. Similarly, 30.67% of respondents remain and accept all the changes. However, 45.00% of respondents have inheritance. Meanwhile, 24.14% of respondents did not have real estate. More than half of the sample has less than a year of investment experience. 32.97% of respondents chose a time horizon of 5 years. The average horizon reported by respondents is 10.333 years.

Each respondent made three successive choices[6]. The distribution of responses from individuals to sets of lotteries, summarized in Table (1), shows that the percentage of respondents in the category of less risk averse, "RRR," is higher than the percentage of the most risk-averse "SSS". We can say that a priori, individuals are most likely to be very sunny or very careful players.

Table 1: Recapitulation of the distributions of the choices

Range j	Choice	% sample of experimental economy
1	RRR	29.09
2	RRS	9.80
3	RSR	7.76
4	RSS	9.34
5	SRR	9.78
6	SRS	6.90
7	*SSR*	8.20
8	**SSS**	**19.14**

2. Test results of the loss aversion

Our analysis was based on the assumption that when an individual faces a risky situation, its objective function is maximizing the expected utility function. This approach is often used in the finance literature because it is robust and leads to an analytical calculation in the portfolio analysis of Machina (1982) and Machina and Pratt (1997). It is noted that since all the

[6] The three letters indicate the answers to successive questions: when the risky lottery R is selected and S for certain alternative.

results were based on the ordinal measure of risk aversion, they were checked in both the expected utility theory and the non-expected utility theory (see also Cohen, 1995). In addition, in the light of the theoretical and empirical developments of Kahneman and Tversky (1979, 1992), it is important to distinguish the positive results from the negative ones.

2.1 Modelling

To explicitly describe the influence of the attitude toward the risk of loss in investment decision makes it possible to better understand some of the reactions and provides more realism in its interpretation. As the respondents are always very suspicious of the negative return rates, there is a discontinuity and/or non-differentiability of the utility or the expected utility function around r = 0. In this perspective, a generalization of the expected utility theory is considered. In our experimental laboratory, we considered that the first six series of lotteries contain negative returns. This could be modelled in different ways. We chose the one used by Palma and Picard (2005) in transport context. If $U^V(r, M_0, \theta^V)$ is the utility in its standard formulation, the generalized utility is then:

$$GU^V(r, M_0, \theta^V) = U^V(r, M_0, \theta^V) - \gamma\, 1_{r<0} \tag{1}$$

where $1_{r<0}$ is a dummy equal to 1 if r<0 and 0 otherwise.

The generalized expected utility is thus:

$$EGU^V(L_j, M_0, \theta^V) = EU^V(L_j^k, M_0, \theta^V) - \gamma\, P(r_j < 0) \tag{2}$$

with $P(r_{j<0}) = -r_{1j}^k / r_{2j}^k - r_{1j}^k$ linear in λ_*^k or λ_+^k if $r_{1j}^k<0$ and 0 otherwise.

In our case, the reduction in the probability was much larger within the negative values of r_{1j}^k. The presence of negative outputs led to the non-differentiability of the expected utility into 0. However, if $P(r_j <0) \to 0$ if $r_{1j}^k \to 0$, there is no discontinuity in the generalized expected utility.
Alternatively, a discontinuity in the generalized expected utility could be directly modelled as such:

$$EGU^V(L_j^k, M_0, \theta^V) = EU^V(L_j^k, M_0, \theta^V) - \chi\, 1(r_{1j}^k{}_{<0}) \tag{3}$$

It is noted that the two alternative forms of the cumulative prospects theory embodied in equation (2) and (3) were not empirically equivalent. Indeed, for a given k, we considered the first j such as r_{1j}^{k} >>0. This implied that $r_{1j'}^{k}$ >>0, for all j'>j. However, equation (3) is equivalent to adding the same constant term χ to $EU^{V}(L_{j'}^{k}, M_0, \theta^{V})$ for all j'>j. Then, all the thresholds v_j^{k*}, for j' > j were affected in the same way. In contrast, equation (2) is equivalent to adding a larger term to $EU^{V}(L_j^{k}, M_0, \theta^{V})$ than that added to $EU^{V}(L_j^{k}, M_0, \theta^{V})$ when j'>j. So, v_j^{k*} were more affected for large values of j.

2.2 Experimental tests of the CPT vs. scale effects

In our non-structural approach and in the context of the lotteries series studied, the discontinuity in the generalized expected utility means that the probability of preferring a given lottery to the certain alternative is reduced when the return distribution comprises negative return r_{1j}^{k} <0. In our sample, lotteries L_1^{k} to L_3^{k} always included negative return (for all k=1, ... , 44), while lotteries L_4^{k} to L_7^{k} included positive return of some k values. We used the notation r_j^{k} >>0, which meant that L_j^{k} comprised positive return. Let us recall that if L_j^{k} only comprises positive return, then $L_{j'}^{k}$ comprises positive return for all j' > j ($r_j^{k} >> 0 \rightarrow r_{j'}^{k} >> 0$, for all j' > j). This is because, for a given value of k, our lotteries have the same expected return and the increasing variances in return. Moreover, $P(r_{j'<0}) > P(r_{j<0})$, for all j' > j.

We drew the table (2) about the fractions of the lotteries that only contain positive return and their influence on the answers. This table allowed us to test the scale effects and the CPT. The second line of the table (2) gave the proportions of the individuals, i, in the sample which $L_j^{k(i)}$ comprised only positive return ($r_j^{k(i)}$ >>0), for j = 4, ..., 7. We noted that $r_4^{k(i)}$ >>0 per 55.92% of our sample. L_5^{k} contained only positive return with 65.83% of our sample. In addition, $r_6^{k(i)}$ >>0 for 75.11% of our sample. Finally, $r_7^{k(i)}$ >> 0 for 81.26% of our sample. We have found that the more j increases, the more the percentage of having lotteries comprising only positive return increases.

In addition, the cross-tables suggested that the responses to the lotteries are significantly affected when the lotteries comprise only positive return. The third line of the table (2) showed that the answer to the first question

$L_4^{k(i)}$ changed when this lottery comprised only positive return. And this is because 57.85% of the respondents preferred $L_4^{k(i)}$ to $L_S^{k(i)}$ when $r_4^{k(i)}$ >>0 while they were only 55.68% in the whole sample. Moreover, the third line of the table (2) also showed that the fraction of the respondents who preferred $L_4^{k(i)}$ to $L_S^{k(i)}$ when $r_5^{k(i)}$ >>0 of 57.71%, is close to that of the whole sample (55.68%). Both results were in favour of the CPT because, with the pure CPT and without scale effect, the fraction of i such as $L_4^{k(i)}$ was preferred to $L_S^{k(i)}$ must be larger when $r_4^{k(i)}$ >>0 (57.71%>55.68%), but it must remain the same as the fraction in the whole sample when $r_5^{k(i)}$ >>0 (57.71% very close to 55.68%). However, when we applied the same reasoning after the third line of table (2), we found that the fraction of the respondents who preferred $L_4^{k(i)}$ to $L_S^{k(i)}$ when $r_6^{k(i)}$ >>0 is 56.14%, which is closer to that of the whole sample (55.68%) on the one hand, and lower than the fraction of the respondents who preferred $L_4^{k(i)}$ to $L_S^{k(i)}$ when $r_4^{k(i)}$ >>0 (57.85%) on the other hand. This result was in favour of the pure CPT. Similarly, the fraction of the respondents who preferred $L_4^{k(i)}$ to $L_S^{k(i)}$ when $r_7^{k(i)}$ >>0 was 55.46% which is almost the same as that in the whole sample (55.68%) and lower than the fraction of the respondents who preferred $L_4^{k(i)}$ to $L_S^{k(i)}$ when $r_4^{k(i)}$ >>0 (57.85%). We concluded that the results of the third line of table (2) were all in favour of pure CPT, while that of Palma and Picard (2002) is in favour of the scale effects. We then applied the same reasoning to the fourth line of the table (2). When the whole sample was restricted to the individuals who we asked to choose between $L_6^{k(i)}$ and $L_S^{k(i)}$ (for individuals who already preferred $L_S^{k(i)}$ to $L_4^{k(i)}$, 46.38% preferred $L_6^{k(i)}$ in the whole sample), this fraction is larger (48.60%) when the sample was restricted to $r_6^{k(i)}$ >>0, in accordance with the CPT. Similarly, the fractions of individuals when $r_4^{k(i)}$ >>0 with 44.01% or when $r_5^{k(i)}$ >>0 with 45.87% was slightly lower and stretched towards the fraction of the respondents i in the whole sample with 46.38%, which was in favour of the CPT rather than the scale effects. Moreover, when the whole sample is restricted to respondents who we asked to choose between $L_7^{k(i)}$ and $L_S^{k(i)}$ (the respondents for whom $L_S^{k(i)}$ was preferred to $L_4^{k(i)}$ and $L_S^{k(i)}$ was preferred to $L_6^{k(i)}$), in the fifth line of table (2), 40.44% preferred $L_7^{k(i)}$ in the whole sample. This fraction was larger, with 46.38% when $r_7^{k(i)}$ >>0, which was in conformity with the CPT. However, this fraction was slightly higher when $r_4^{k(i)}$ >>0, with 47.63% and $r_5^{k(i)}$ >>0, with 46.90%, which was not in favour of the CPT. However, this faction was smaller for $r_6^{k(i)}$ >>0, with 46.02%. We found that the fraction of i such as $L_7^{k(i)}$ was preferred to $L_S^{k(i)}$ was decreasing in j, when it is restricted to i such as $r_j^{k(i)}$ >>0. This result was in favour of the scale effects with the CPT. This result linked up with that of Palma and Picard

(2002), who find that the results are in favour of scale effects. Finally, the results of the last line of table (2) appeared to be inconsistent with the CPT and the scale effects when the whole sample was reduced to those respondents who were asked to choose between $L_5^{k(i)}$ and $L_S^{k(i)}$ (respondents for whom $L_S^{k(i)}$ was preferred to $L_4^{k(i)}$ and $L_6^{k(i)}$ was preferred. Indeed, 51.29% preferred $L_5^{k(i)}$ in the whole sample. However, this fraction was slightly smaller, with 49.40% when $r_5^{k(i)} >>0$, which was not in favour of the CPT. In addition, the fraction of the respondents who preferred $L_5^{k(i)}$ when $r_4^{k(i)} >>0$ was 45.90% does not tend towards the proportion of the individuals who preferred $L_5^{k(i)}$ and $L_S^{k(i)}$ in the whole sample, with 51.29%. This result was not in favour of the CPT either. Moreover, the fraction of the individuals who preferred $L_5^{k(i)}$ when $r_6^{k(i)} >>0$ was 50.96%, higher than that when $r_7^{k(i)} >>0$, with 48.94%. This result was not in favour of the scale effects because the fraction of i such as $L_5^{k(i)}$ was not decreasing in j when restricted to i such as $r_j^{k(i)} >>0$ was not in favour of the scale effects.

Table 2: Influence lotteries with entirely positive return on the answers

Lottery	$L_4^{k(i)}$	$L_5^{k(i)}$	$L_6^{k(i)}$	$L_7^{k(i)}$	Whole sample
$r_j^{k(i)} >> 0$	55.92%	65.83%	75.11%	81.26%	
$L_4^{k(i)} \succ L_S^{k(i)}$ if $r_j^{k(i)} >>0$	57.85%	57.71%	56.14%	55.46%	55.68%
$L_6^{k(i)} \succ L_S^{k(i)}$ if $r_j^{k(i)} >>0$	44.01%	45.87%	48.60%	49.78%	46.38%
$L_7^{k(i)} \succ L_S^{k(i)}$ if $r_j^{k(i)} >>0$	47.63%	46.90%	46.02%	46.38%	40.44%
$L_5^{k(i)} \succ L_S^{k(i)}$ if $r_j^{k(i)} >>0$	45.90%	49.40%	50.96%	48.94%	51.29%

2.3 Discussion of the experimental results

We noted that table (2) seemed to be in favour of the CPT more than scale effects. Indeed, we found that the fraction of the individuals i, such as $L_j^{k(i)}$ was preferred to $L_s^{k(i)}$, which should be larger when $r_j^{k(i)} >>0$, remained the same as the fraction in the whole sample when $r_{j'}^{k(i)} >>0$. While the results found in Palma and Picard (2002) were more in favour of the scale effects than the CPT, they found that the fraction of i such as $L_j^{k(i)}$ was preferred to $L_S^{k(i)}$ was decreasing in j, when it is restricted to i such as $r_j^{k(i)} >> 0$, and is significantly higher than that of the whole sample. This could be due to the nature of the data used in their sample, which was mostly hypothetical data. Let us note however that the differences in fractions were not very significant in their case because of the low sample size.

3. Econometric Analysis: CPT test

We suggest checking if these experimental results are verified during the econometric regressions. Specifically, we try to test the stability of the experimental results found previously, ceteris paribus, that are related with the ordered probit regression. The choice of the model was justified by the nature of the ordered variable related to the risk aversion, given the fact that it was estimated by the classification of the lotteries series according to the stochastic dominance of first order by making certain or risky choices, Palma and Picard (2002). As all the results were based on the ordinal measure of the risk aversion, they remained checked in the context of the non-expected utility theory and especially in the CPT.

3.1 Ordered probit model

In the ordered Probit Small (1987), $\acute{\upsilon}_i$ follows a normal distribution with variance that is equal to 1 and an average that is specific to each individual: $E(\acute{\upsilon}_i) = X_i\, \beta$, where X_i is a vector with exogenous individual characteristics and β a vector of the estimated coefficients. We assume that: $\acute{\upsilon}_i = X_i\, \beta + \nu_i$, where ν_i is an error term that follows the normal standard. The ν_j are unknown parameters to be estimated with β. The ordered probit model specifies that there is a series of thresholds ν_j^*, such as the individual i reaches the level j if and only if $\nu_{j-1}^* < \nu_i^* + X_i\, \beta \leq \nu_j^*$ if and only if $\nu_{j-1}^* - X_i\, \beta < \nu_i^* \leq \nu_j^* - X_i\, \beta$.

Let L_8^k (resp L_0^k): an artificial lottery which dominates (is dominated by) the lotteries L_1^k to L_7^k and L_S^k, the probability P_{ij}^k such that $L_{j-1}^k < L_s^k < L_j^k$ for the individual i and the series k :

$$P_{ij}^k = P(\nu_{j-1}^*(k) < \acute{\upsilon}_i \leq \nu_j^*(k)) = \Phi(\nu_j^* - X_i\, \beta) - \Phi(\nu_{j-1}^* - X_i\beta),$$
for all j=1,…,8. (5)

Let $v_0^*(k) = -\infty$, $v_8^*(k) = +\infty$ and $v_j^*(k)$, for j=1,…,7 the thresholds to be estimated the thresholds to be estimated.

3.2 Results

Firstly, we compared in our data sample the case where $r_7 >> 0$ if $r_{1,7} < 0$, with $r_{1,6} < 0$ in both cases. The lottery L_7 became more attractive since it comprised only positive return (because $r_7 >> 0$). Thus $P(L_7 > L_s > L_6)$ increased and $P(L_s > L_7)$ decreased. This corresponded to an increase in the threshold v_7^* (see tables 3 and 4). A comparative reading of the tables showed that the threshold v_7^* increased when $r_7 >> 0$ moving from 2.383 to 3.877, while it remained significant having a threshold of 1%.

Following this, we compared the case in which $r_6 >> 0$ with the case when $r_{1,\ 6} < 0$, as well as with the other unchanged conditions[7]. Likewise, a comparative reading of the tables (5, 6) showed that the threshold v_6^* increased when $r_6 >> 0$ while passing from 3.224 to 3.284 with a threshold of 1% that is significant in both cases.

[7] Knowing that the condition r_{6}>>0 implied that r_{1,5}<0 and r_{7}>>0. This is because the condition r_{j}>>0 implied r_{j^{'}}>>0 for all j^{'}>j

Table 3: CPT test: Ordered probit with $r_7^{k(i)} >> 0$ and $r^{k(i)}$ 6,1 < 0

Variables	Coefficient	Std.Err
femme	0.396***	0.122
age2	0.003	0.168
age3	-0.186	0.369
age4	1.060	0.914
Matri1	-0.561**	0.246
Matri5	0.790	0.863
Matri6	-7.543	0.212
Matri8	0.637**	0.259
Ecoclim1	0.227	0.456
Ecoclim2	-0.143	0.434
Ecoclim3	0.182	0.435
Ecocolim4	0.213	0.444
invbehave1	-0.519	0.385
invbehave2	-0.074	0.169
invbehave3	-0.098	0.122
investstyle2	1.430***	0.336
investstyle3	1.012***	0.196
investstyle4	0.877***	0.161
lossbehave2	0.055	0.164
lossbehave3	0.027	0.123
losswinsbehave2	0.451***	0.160
losswinsbehave3	0.115	0.139
addmult1	1.075	3.144
lambdaAdd	4.450	42.478
lambdaMult	13.524	14.239
thmin	0.095	0.110
obj8	0.298**	0.148
obj10	-0.034	0.136
cut1	1.449	1.138
cut2	1.901*	1.140
cut3	2.187*	1.142
cut4	2.505**	1.143
cut5	2.743**	1.143
cut6	3.284***	1.145
cut7	3.877***	1.145
Log-likelihood		**-**
$Chi^2(28)$		**838.307**
		133.884

Table 4: CPT test: Ordered probit with $r_{(7,1)}^{k(i)} < 0$ and $r_{(6,1)}^{k(i)}<0$

Variables	Coefficient	Std.Err
femme	0.228***	0.045
age2	-0.057	0.065
age3	0.770***	0.129
age4	-0.474*	0.245
Matri1	-0.037	0.095
Matri5	0.655**	0.285
Matri6	0.719**	0.323
Matri8	-0.004	0.093
Ecoclim1	0.154	0.162
Ecoclim2	0.021	0.153
Ecoclim3	0.129	0.152
Ecocolim4	0.268*	0.155
invbehave1	-0.263**	0.133
invbehave2	-0.042	0.061
invbehave3	0.105**	0.047
investstyle2	1.462***	0.113
investstyle3	0.988***	0.079
investstyle4	0.658***	0.066
lossbehave2	0.114*	0.061
lossbehave3	0.129*	0.047
losswinsbehave2	0.239***	0.062
losswinsbehave3	0.183***	0.054
addmult1	0.148*	0.088
lambdaAdd	1.128	1.893
lambdaMult	-0.101	1.919
thmin	0.039	0.043
obj8	0.120**	0.059
obj10	-0.039	0.056
cut1	0.391**	0.178
cut2	0.864***	0.179
cut3	1.132***	0.179
cut4	1.428***	0.179
cut5	1.613***	0.180
cut6	1.916***	0.180
cut7	2.338***	0.181
Log-likelihood		**-**
$Chi^2(28)$		**5609.116**
		521.456

Table 5: CPT test : Ordered probit with $r_7^{k(i)} >> 0$ and $r_{(5,1)}^{k(i)} < 0$ and $r_{(6,1)}^{k(i)} < 0$

Variables	Coefficient	Std.Err
femme	0.248***	0.084
age2	0.004	0.127
age3	-0.489***	0.253
age4	0.272	0.817
Matri1	-0.003	0.178
Matri5	-0.084	0.459
Matri6	0.862	0.569
Matri8	-0.104	0.197
Ecoclim1	-0.224	0.294
Ecoclim2	-0.279	0.272
Ecoclim3	0.065	0.273
Ecocolim4	0.029	0.279
invbehave1	-0.317	0.245
invbehave2	0.035	0.116
invbehave3	0.012	0.088
investstyle2	1.334***	0.210
investstyle3	0.864***	0.140
investstyle4	0.669***	0.121
lossbehave2	0.192	0.117
lossbehave3	0.134	0.087
losswinsbehave2	0.127	0.115
losswinsbehave3	0.139	0.098
addmult1	0.887	1.132
lambdaAdd	4.448	9.308
lambdaMult	12.838*	7.091
thmin	0.096	0.081
obj8	0.223**	0.108
obj10	-0.122	0.106
cut1	1.262	0.772
cut2	1.779**	0.772
cut3	2.040***	0.773
cut4	2.337***	0.773
cut5	2.729***	0.775
cut6	3.224***	0.776
cut7	3.585***	0.777
Log-likelihood		**- 1655.889**
$Chi^2(28)$		**160.797**

Table 6: CPT test : Ordered probit with $r_7^{k(i)}$ >> 0 and $r_{(5,1)}^{k(i)}$ <0 and $r_6^{k(i)}$ >> 0

Variables	Coefficient	Std.Err
femme	0.396***	0.122
age2	0.003	0.168
age3	-0.186	0.369
age4	1.060	0.914
Matri1	-0.561**	0.246
Matri5	0.790	0.863
Matri6	-7.543	0.569
Matri8	0.637**	0.259
Ecoclim1	0.227	0.456
Ecoclim2	-0.143	0.434
Ecoclim3	0.182	0.435
Ecocolim4	0.213	0.444
invbehave1	-0.519	0.385
invbehave2	-0.074	0.169
invbehave3	-0.098	0.122
investstyle2	1.430***	0.336
investstyle3	1.012***	0.196
investstyle4	0.877***	0.161
lossbehave2	0.055	0.164
lossbehave3	0.027	0.123
losswinsbehave2	0.451***	0.160
losswinsbehave3	0.115	0.139
addmult1	1.075	3.144
lambdaAdd	4.450	42.478
lambdaMult	13.524	14.239
thmin	0.095	0.110
obj8	0.298**	0.148
obj10	-0.034	0.136
cut1	1.449	1.138
cut2	1.901*	1.140
cut3	2.187*	1.142
cut4	2.505**	1.143
cut5	2.743**	1.143
cut6	3.284***	1.145
cut7	3.877***	1.145
Log-likelihood		**-**
$Chi^2(28)$		**838.307**
		133.884

Generally speaking, ceteris paribus $r_j>>0$ had to correspond to the increasing thresholds v_j^*. This could simply be incorporated into likelihood by introducing a dummy variable for $1_{rj>>0}$, which was equal to 1 when $r_j>>0$ and 0 otherwise. When we introduced a dummy variable $1_{rj>>0}$ for all j=1, ..., 7, as an independent variable in the ordered probit regression, we could then test the CPT as follows: Each time we introduced a dummy variable[8] $1_{rj>>0,}$ for j=1, ..., 7 in the ordered probit estimates, we noted that all the dummy of positive return had a negative coefficient which is significant with a threshold of lower than 10%. These results were in conformity with both the theoretical and experimental literature in a way that the probability of an increasing aversion will decrease in the presence of positive return. Therefore, the individual is less averse to risk with only positive return. Indeed, we noticed, following the example of Holt and Laury (2002, 2003), that the individuals are less risk averse when the profit associated with the lotteries increases. Furthermore, when we introduced a dummy $1_{rj>>0}$ in likelihood probability, we estimate a coefficient associated to δ_j such as v_j^* was replaced by $v_j^*+ \delta_j$ $1_{rj>>0}$ in probability, we noted that δ_j was positive. So, there was a threshold increase v_j^* if $r_j>>0$. Consequently, testing if δ_j is equivalent to test the CPT. Thus; a simple econometric test enabled us to test the CPT. Table (7) summarized all the thresholds without and with the condition of dummy $1_{rj>>0}$, for j=1, ..., 7, in the ordered probit regression. The fourth column gives δ_j, the difference of the values of the thresholds without and with the condition of dummy of positive return. We found that all the δ_j were positive except for δ_1. However, this result was expected because the threshold v_1^* corresponds to the indifferent individuals between the certain alternative and the alternative L_1. These individuals always chose the risky alternative even when it was comprised of a great loss, so their result was not affected if the lotteries were comprised of positive return.

[8] Seven estimates of ordered probit model are made by introducing a dummy each time 1_{r_{1}>>0}, 1_{r_{2}>>0}, 1_{r_{3}>>0}, 1_{r_{4}>>0}, 1_{r_{5}>>0}, 1_{r_{6}>>0}, 1_{r_{7}>>0}.

Table 7: Summary of the thresholds with and without dummy of positive return

Les Seuils v_j^*	Probit Ordonné sans $1_{rj>>0}$	Probit Ordonné avec $1_{rj>>0}$	δ_j
v_1^*	0.478	0.438	-0.04
v_2^*	0.891	0.908	0.017
v_3^*	1.176	1.193	0.017
v_4^*	1.443	1.468	0.025
v_5^*	1.731	1.779	0.048
v_6^*	2.033	2.089	0.056
v_7^*	2.409	2.459	0.050

3.3 Discussion of the econometric results

On the one hand, we concluded that the seven dummy $1_{rj>>0}$ for all j=1, ..., 7 were always highly significant with a negative coefficient. On the other hand, if $r_j>>0$, the corresponding thresholds v_j^* increased, thus the corresponding δ_j were positive. On the whole, we could say that there was evidence of the CPT on our sample. It should be noted that our results correspond with experimental economy literature. Indeed, the evidence of the CPT was clearer when respondents were actually able to lose money, while there was no evidence of CPT with the stated preferences on hypothetical lotteries. On the other hand, de Palma and Picard (2002) have failed to test the CPT. They find that the estimated coefficients are not significant in the ordered probit regression. This may be due to the sample size or the nature of the data, which was purely hypothetical. However, their results are in favour of the scale effects. We assume that their results have been confirmed on a larger sample and by using a more structural approach. However, such structural approaches are based on functional forms of restrictive preferences.

4. Conclusion

In this work we have had recourse to the experimental laboratory for the understanding and modelling of the attitude towards risk through the standard model of decision under risk. We have presented a study of the individuals' behaviour in the experimental laboratory conducted in Tunisia. We tested a deviation from the expected utility theory, which is the loss aversion. In fact, when individuals are faced with lotteries that only have positive return, they were less risk averse and always preferred the lottery with the certain alternative. The most significant obtained result in this work was to test the CPT in our sample econometrically via a simple econometric test. Indeed, the CPT test amounts to testing that the dummy coefficient of the positive return was significant and positive during the model estimates. This resulted in an increase in the ordinal threshold of the responding risk aversion when the corresponding lottery contained only positive return. Hence, the importance of the econometric and experimental methods, which through the development of the relatively simple econometric tests, were used to test complex models of the non-expected utility theory, and in particular the CPT in our work.

References

Allais M, 1953, "Le comportement de l'homme rationnel devant le risque, critique des postulats et axiomes de l'école américaine", Econometrica, 21, 503-546.

Anderson S, A de Palma and J-F Thisse, 1992, "Analysis of Differentiated Markets with Discrete Choice Models", MIT Press, 423p.

Ben-Akiva, M, McFadden D, de Palma A, 2003, "Hybrid Choice Models: Progress and challenges", Marketing Letters, in Press.

Broihanne, M-H, Merli M, Roger P,2007, "Finance Comportementale", Economica.

Brooks P, Zank H, 2004, "Attitudes on Gain and Loss Lotteries: A Simple Experiment", School of Economic Studies, The University of Manchester, United Kingdom.

Cohen M, 1995, "Risk-Aversion Concepts in Expected- and Non-Expected-Utility Models", The Geneva papers on Risk and Insurance, 20, 73-91.

de Palma, A and N Picard, 2002, "Measuring Risk tolerance on the web", Manuscript. University of Cergy-Pontoise, THEMA, France.

de Palma A, Picard N, 2005, "Route choice decision under travel time uncertainty, Transportation Research", 39, 295-324.

de Palma A, Ben-Akiva M, Brownstone D, Holt C, Magnac T, McFadden D, Moffatt P, Picard N, Train

Goeree JC, Holt A, Palfrey T, 2003, "Risk Averse Behavior in Generalized Matching Pennies Games", Games and Economic Behavior, 45, 97-113.

Grandin P ,2005, La finance comportementale, Banque and Marchés, 76, 81-86.

Holt C A, Susan K, 2002, "Risk Aversion and Incentive Effects", mimeo, Dept of Economics, USA, American Economic Review, 92, 1644-1655.

Holt C A, Laury SK, 2003, "Risk Aversion and Incentive Effects", American Economic Review, 92, 1644-1655.

Kahneman D, Tversky A, 1979, "Prospect theory : An analysis of decision under risk", Econometrica, 47, 263-291.

Luce DR, 2000, "Utility of Gains and Losses: Measurement-Theoretical and Experimental Approaches", Lawrence Erlbaum Publishers, London.

Machina M, 1982, "Choice under uncertainty: Problems solved and unsolved", Journal of Economic Perspectives, 1, 281-96.

Machina, MJ, Pratt JW,1997, Increasing risk: some direct construction", Journal of risk and uncertainty 14, 103-127.

Manski C, 1977, "The structure of random utility models", Theory and Decisions, 8, 229-254.

McFadden D, 2001, "Economic Choices", American Economics Review, 91, 351-378.

Pfiffelmann M, Roger P, 2005, "Les comptes d'épargne associés à des loteries : Approche comportementale et études de cas", Banque et Marchés, 78, 16-23.

Roth A,1988, "Laboratory Experimentation in Economics: A Methodological Overview", The Economic Journal, 98, 974-1031.

Schmidt U, Traub S ,2002, An Experimental Test of Loss Aversion, Journal of Risk and Uncertainty, 25, 233-249.

Smith VL, 1994, "Economics in the Laboratory", Journal of Economic Perspectives, 8, 113-131.

Stevens D, Williams A, 2004, "Inefficiency in earning forecasts: Experimental Evidence of reactions to positive vs negative information", Experimental Economics, 7, 75-92.

Tversky A, Kahneman D, 1992, "Advances in prospect theory: cumulative representation of uncertainty", Journal of Risk and Uncertainty, 5, 297-323.

Von Neumann J, Morgenstern O, 1947, "Theory of Games and Economic Behavior", Princeton University Press, Princeton.

Wakker P, Walker J, 2008, "Risk, uncertainty and discrete choice models", Marketing Letters, 19, 269-285.

A SCENARIO-BASED APPROACH TO EVALUATE SUPPLY CHAIN NETWORKS

KHALED MILI[1]

Introduction

The trade environment nowadays is characterised by two main developments. First, the deep competition in the worldwide economy has influenced companies to investigate persistently for expenditure reduction and responsiveness opportunities. Second, supply chain design has become a means of fuelling the company's competitive improvement. This implies that an important utility of a supply chain design evaluation approach is to characterise the right design. As supply chains are dynamic, different products, services, interdependencies, and processes form different scenarios. A scenario is defined by every possible sequence of environments over a given period of time. The environment is the internal and external conditions under which the supply chain network operates [3]. It is necessary then to envisage, design, and evaluate different supply chain scenarios before implementing a real one.

A number of supply chain scenarios can be designed for an organisation's supply chain. The coordination structure and performance may vary from one scenario to another. The organisation should model the complexities and evaluate the performance of the design generated from a particular scenario before implementing it. An organisation needs to understand not only the current scenarios but also how to model and evaluate future designs for the purpose of maintaining competitiveness.

Thus, the main objective of this research is to develop a new supply chain design evaluation process, which can be used to search for an optimal design. The remainder of the paper is organised as follows: Section 2 describes the Supply Chain Network (SCN) design model under

[1] E-mail: khaledmili@yahoo.fr.

uncertainty. Section 3 elaborates a supply chain design evaluation approach. The methods proposed are applied to business cases in section 4. The paper concludes in section 5.

1. Supply chain design model

The design or redesign of a supply chain network requires many strategic decisions, including the selection of suppliers, choosing the transportation means and option, location and selection of depots, etc. The total cost to serve is frequently used as the most important factor in the evaluation of supply chain network design, while enough attention in including the importance of customers' responses for the evaluation of a network is easier said than done. Subsequently, the evaluation should be based on response optimization models, where decisions are taken with adaptation to the SCN's environments. This gives rise to the multi-stage decision process through a planning horizon. As the future is unknown where some disturbances may have an effect on the SCN, the best that can be done is anticipation.

The model consists of a multi-stage supply chain network where real options can be deployed and exercised periodically, contingent on prevailing scenarios. As a result, the SCN design model under uncertainty is considered as a multi stage stochastic program with an infinite set of scenarios, a multi objective reward function, and an anticipation of adaptation-response decisions.

In this section we present a supply chain network model formulation that can be included into an evaluation model.

1.1 Deterministic program

Let us describe first a deterministic mathematical formulation for the problem considered.

The purpose of a company is to design its production distribution network by simultaneously selecting adequate logistics policies, and by allocating production capacity and locating distribution centres to support these policies, and all of these decisions are based on the anticipation of the future.

The objective of a SCN design problem is to maximize discounted expected profits, and to take the best decision design for this. Referring to [2], the following notation is used:

$t \in T$: Periods in the planning horizon
$h \in H$: Reengineering cycles in the planning horizon
$t \in T_h$: Periods in reengineering cycle h
$h(t)$: Reengineering cycle of period t
α : A discount rate, based on the weighted average costs of capital of the company.

$\mathbf{X}_t$: The level of each network's activity in period $t \in T$.
$\mathbf{F}_t$: Flow of the product in period $t \in T$.
$\mathbf{I}_t$: Level of strategic inventory of the product in period $t \in T$.
$\mathbf{U}_t$: Penalty paid to the vendor under contract if the minimum sales value specified in the contract isn't reached in period $t \in T$.
$\mathbf{Y}_h$: Binary variable equal to 1 if opening, using, or closing a platform at the beginning of planning cycle $h \in H$.
$\mathbf{W}_h$: Binary variable equal to 1 if a market-policy is selected during cycle $h \in H$.
$\mathbf{Z}_h$: Binary variable equal to 1 if a transportation capacity is selected at the beginning of cycle $h \in H$.
$\mathbf{V}_h$: Binary variable equal to 1 if a vendor is selected at the beginning of cycle $h \in H$.

A compact deterministic formulation of the supply chain network design problem is presented as follow:

$$Max\sum_{t\in T}\frac{1}{(1+\alpha)^t}\left[A_t\mathbf{F}_t - B_t\left(\mathbf{F}_t,\mathbf{X}_t,\mathbf{I}_t,\mathbf{U}_t,\mathbf{Y}_{h(t)},\mathbf{W}_{h(t)},\mathbf{Z}_{h(t)},\mathbf{V}_{h(t)}\right)\right] \quad (1)$$

$s.t$

$$C_t\left[\mathbf{W}_{h(t)},\mathbf{Y}_{h(t)}\right]\le b_t \qquad \forall t\in T \quad (2)$$

$$G_t\mathbf{F}_t + P_t[\mathbf{W}_{h(t)},\mathbf{Y}_{h(t)},\mathbf{Z}_{h(t)}]\le 0 \qquad \forall t\in T \quad (3)$$

$$M_t[\mathbf{F}_t,\mathbf{U}_t,\mathbf{X}_t,\mathbf{I}_t]+O_t[\mathbf{Y}_{h(t)},\mathbf{V}_{h(t)}]\le 0 \qquad \forall t\in T \quad (4)$$

$$L_t[\mathbf{X}_t,\mathbf{F}_t,\mathbf{I}_t]\le d_t \qquad \forall t\in T \quad (5)$$

$$\mathbf{X}_t,\mathbf{F}_t,\mathbf{I}_t,\mathbf{U}_t\ge 0 \qquad \forall t\in T \quad (6)$$

$$\mathbf{Y}_{h(t)},\mathbf{W}_{h(t)},\mathbf{Z}_{h(t)},\mathbf{V}_{h(t)}\in\{0,1\} \qquad \forall t\in T \quad (7)$$

Where $(\mathbf{X}_t,\mathbf{F}_t,\mathbf{I}_t,\mathbf{U}_t)$ are the follower variables and $(\mathbf{Y}_{h(t)},\mathbf{W}_{h(t)},\mathbf{Z}_{h(t)},\mathbf{V}_{h(t)})$ are the design variables, or the leader variables. A_t and B_t are two matrices denoting the revenues and expenditures associated with decision variables during the planning horizon. $C_t, G_t, P_t, M_t, O_t,\ L_t$ are the matrices of parameters. b_t and d_t are two left side vectors.

Equation (2) presents the constraints related to the market policy and internal location configurations via the use of platform selection variables. Equation (3) presents the goals of the company in demand and penetration level in the market, the reception and shipping capacity limits, and the network transportation capacity restrictions. Equation (4) presents limits of the supplied quantity by the vendor of each product and the benefit of the vendor's contract conditions. In addition to the constraints related to the throughput and inventory level for each platform. Equation (5) is about flow equilibrium constraints, inventory account constraints and inventory-throughput relationship constraints. Finally, non-negativity and binary constraints are given.

Relative to the resolution of uncertainty, the decision maker must determine when the decisions are made. Previous formulation of the SCN problem does not consider the timing of the decisions. In the following we present the recourse program of the SCN problem.

1.2 Multi-period two-stage stochastic program with recourse

Recourse models result when some of the decisions must be fixed before information relevant to the uncertainties is available, while some of them can be delayed until afterward.

In our problem $(\mathbf{Y}_h, \mathbf{W}_h, \mathbf{Z}_h, \mathbf{V}_h)$ corresponds to the resource levels to be acquired, and ω corresponds to a specific scenario from the whole set of scenarios denoted by Ω.

In the event that the initial decisions are taken in the beginning of the planning horizon, these decisions are denoted by $D_1 = (\mathbf{Y}_1, \mathbf{W}_1, \mathbf{Z}_1, \mathbf{V}_1)$ describing the first cycle decisions and coupled with a given scenario ω.

In order to model the first order decision variables as being dependent on the recourse variables, it is necessary to differentiate between the decisions that must be taken at the beginning of the planning horizon in the first cycle (h=1), noted as D_1 and $(\mathbf{Y}_{h(t)}, \mathbf{W}_{h(t)}, \mathbf{Z}_{h(t)}, \mathbf{V}_{h(t)})$ presenting the decisions taken in cycle *h* (*h*>1) of each period of time $t \in T$. The former decision variables are defined according to a specific scenario $\omega \in \Omega$ and they may change from one to another. These design variables are denoted by $\left(\mathbf{Y}_{h(t)}(D_1,\omega), \mathbf{W}_{h(t)}(D_1,\omega), \mathbf{Z}_{h(t)}(D_1,\omega), \mathbf{V}_{h(t)}(D_1,\omega)\right)$ showing that the design decisions during the cycle periods depend on the first ones taken at the beginning of the planning horizon under a particular scenario. D_1 does not act in response to scenario ω and it is determined before any information regarding the uncertain data has been obtained.

To take under consideration this structure of our decision problem, we may state the recourse version of the original program as follows:

$$Max \; -B_1 D_1 + E[Q(D_1,\omega)] \qquad (8)$$

$$s.t$$

$$C_1 D_1 \le b_1 \qquad (9)$$

$$D_1 \in \{0,1\} \qquad (10)$$

This sub problem determines the optimal flow, throughput, and inventory level, and the contract's penalty to perform, after the decisions related to platforms, transportation, policy, and vendor are taken.

The decision variables $\left(\mathbf{X}_t(\omega), \mathbf{F}_t(\omega), \mathbf{I}_t(\omega), \mathbf{U}_t(\omega)\right)$ are adapted to the specific combination of $\left(\mathbf{V}_{h(t)}, \mathbf{Y}_{h(t)}, \mathbf{Z}_{h(t)}, \mathbf{W}_{h(t)}\right)$ and ω obtained. In the event that the initial decisions $D_1 = (\mathbf{V}_1, \mathbf{Y}_1, \mathbf{Z}_1, \mathbf{W}_1)$ known as first stage decisions are coupled with a particular outcome, the variables $\left(\mathbf{X}_t(D_1,\omega), \mathbf{F}_t(D_1,\omega), \mathbf{I}_t(D_1,\omega), \mathbf{U}_t(D_1,\omega)\right)$ offer an opportunity to recover to the fullest extent possible.

The sub problem $Q(D_1,\omega)$ determines the optimal design decisions after the recourse decision variables are known, and it is formulated as follows:

$$Q(D_1,\omega) = Max \sum_{t\in T} \frac{1}{(1+\alpha)^t}\left[A_t(\omega)F_t(D_1,\omega)\right]$$

$$-\sum_{h>1}\sum_{t\in T_h} \frac{1}{(1+\alpha)^t} B_{h(t)}(\omega)\begin{bmatrix} F_t(D_1,\omega), X_t(D_1,\omega), I_t(D_1,\omega), U_t(D_1,\omega) \\ , Y_{h(t)}(D_1,\omega), W_{h(t)}(D_1,\omega), Z_{h(t)}(D_1,\omega), V_{h(t)}(D_1,\omega) \end{bmatrix} \quad (11)$$

s.t

$$C(\omega)\left[\mathbf{W}_{h(t)}(D_1,\omega), \mathbf{Y}_{h(t)}(D_1,\omega)\right] \le b(\omega) \qquad \forall t \in T \qquad (12)$$

$$G(\omega)\mathbf{F}_t(D_1,\omega) + P(\omega)[\mathbf{W}_{h(t)}(D_1,\omega), \mathbf{Y}_{h(t)}(D_1,\omega), \mathbf{Z}_{h(t)}(D_1,\omega)] \le 0 \qquad \forall t \in T \qquad (13)$$

$$M(\omega)[\mathbf{F}_t(D_1,\omega), \mathbf{U}_t(D_1,\omega), \mathbf{X}_t(D_1,\omega), \mathbf{I}_t(D_1,\omega)] + O(\omega)[\mathbf{Y}_{h(t)}(D_1,\omega), \mathbf{V}_{h(t)}(D_1,\omega)] \le 0 \quad \forall t \in T \qquad (14)$$

$$L(\omega)[\mathbf{X}_t(D_1,\omega), \mathbf{F}_t(D_1,\omega), \mathbf{I}_t(D_1,\omega)] \le d(\omega) \qquad \forall t \in T \qquad (15)$$

$$\mathbf{X}_t(D_1,\omega), \mathbf{F}_t(D_1,\omega), \mathbf{I}_t(D_1,\omega), \mathbf{U}_t(D_1,\omega) \ge 0 \qquad \forall t \in T \qquad (16)$$

$$\mathbf{Y}_{h(t)}(D_1,\omega), \mathbf{W}_{h(t)}(D_1,\omega), \mathbf{Z}_{h(t)}(D_1,\omega), \mathbf{V}_{h(t)}(D_1,\omega) \in \{0,1\} \qquad \forall t \in T \qquad (17)$$

It is necessary to specify that the matrixes of parameters and costs in both sides of the sub-problems depend also on the scenarios, and may change from one scenario to another.

The resulting stochastic program (8)-(17) is resolved for every generated scenario $\omega \in \Omega$.

The comparison and selection of solutions (designs) are performed by means of a number of performance measures defined in the next sections.

2. Design evaluation approach

This section presents an evaluation approach to the multi-objective design optimization that helps to identify optimum designs in presence of uncertainty during the whole planning horizon. The aim of the design evaluation phase is to select the best SCN design among those considered, including the status quo. The finite set of designs is denoted by J where $J \geq 2$.

During the planning period, anticipation is made in order to give the users or the designers the opportunity to respond to the future business environment disruptions and to adjust the structure of the SCN. Therefore the design evaluation procedure should be based on a response optimization model formulated as follows:

$$Max \sum_{t \in T} \frac{1}{(1+\alpha)^t} \left[A_t(\omega) \mathbf{F}_t(D_1^j, \omega) \right]$$

$$- \sum_{h>1} \sum_{t \in T_h} \frac{1}{(1+\alpha)^t} B_{h(t)}(\omega) \begin{bmatrix} \mathbf{F}_t(D_1^j,\omega), \mathbf{X}_t(D_1^j,\omega), \mathbf{I}_t(D_1^j,\omega), \mathbf{U}_t(D_1^j,\omega) \\ , \mathbf{Y}_{h(t)}(D_1^j,\omega), \mathbf{W}_{h(t)}(D_1^j,\omega), \mathbf{Z}_{h(t)}(D_1^j,\omega), \mathbf{V}_{h(t)}(D_1^j,\omega) \end{bmatrix} \quad (18)$$

$s.t$

$$C(\omega)\left[\mathbf{W}_{h(t)}(D_1^j,\omega), \mathbf{Y}_{h(t)}(D_1^j,\omega) \right] \leq b(\omega) \qquad \forall t \in T \quad (19)$$

$$G(\omega)\mathbf{F}_t(D_1^j,\omega) + P(\omega)[\mathbf{W}_{h(t)}(D_1^j,\omega), \mathbf{Y}_{h(t)}(D_1^j,\omega), \mathbf{Z}_{h(t)}(D_1^j,\omega)] \leq 0 \qquad \forall t \in T \quad (20)$$

$$M(\omega)[\mathbf{F}_t(D_1^j,\omega), \mathbf{U}_t(D_1^j,\omega), \mathbf{X}_t(D_1^j,\omega), \mathbf{I}_t(D_1^j,\omega)] + O(\omega)[\mathbf{Y}_{h(t)}(D_1^j,\omega), \mathbf{V}_{h(t)}(D_1^j,\omega)] \leq 0 \quad \forall t \in T \quad (21)$$

$$L(\omega)[\mathbf{X}_t(D_1^j,\omega), \mathbf{F}_t(D_1^j,\omega), \mathbf{I}_t(D_1^j,\omega)] \leq d(\omega) \qquad \forall t \in T \quad (22)$$

$$\mathbf{X}_t(D_1^j,\omega), \mathbf{F}_t(D_1^j,\omega), \mathbf{I}_t(D_1^j,\omega), \mathbf{U}_t(D_1^j,\omega) \geq 0 \qquad \forall t \in T \quad (23)$$

$$\mathbf{Y}_{h(t)}(D_1^j,\omega), \mathbf{W}_{h(t)}(D_1^j,\omega), \mathbf{Z}_{h(t)}(D_1^j,\omega), \mathbf{V}_{h(t)}(D_1^j,\omega) \in \{0,1\} \qquad \forall t \in T \quad (24)$$

2.1 Performance measures

In practice, there are two expense types which are constrained by different expenditure control mechanisms; first, the investments and expenditures which include investments in inventory, the on-going costs of operating depots to stock these inventories, the investment costs, maintenance and operating costs required to operate transportation of products. Secondly, the operative costs; these costs are related to the supply, maintenance, and recourse actions taken during the planning horizon.

Many methods are used to generate scenarios, and the most used one is the Monte Carlo procedure presented in [1]. Monte Carlo methods are a class of computational algorithms that rely on repeated random sampling to compute their results. Because of their reliance on repeated computation of random or pseudo-random numbers, these methods are most suited to calculation by a computer and tend to be used when it is unfeasible or impossible to compute an exact result with a deterministic algorithm. Due to the infinite number of plausible future scenarios, the problem is difficult to solve and some reductions of its complexity are needed. This is done by the way in which the set of generated scenarios Ω^P is replaced by representative equiprobable scenarios with probability1/M, where M is the number of independent small Monte Carlo samples.

Several plausible future scenarios are generated in independent samples of M_A acceptable-risk scenarios, M_S serious risk-scenarios, and M_U worst-case scenarios used in the filtering procedure. All these samples are generated with their respectively estimated probabilities π_A, π_S, π_U.

In order to analyse the various sources of uncertainty, the set of scenarios is portioned into two mutually exclusive and collectively exhaustive subsets [2]; Ω^P for probabilistic scenarios without deeply uncertain events, and Ω^U for others. A given scenario is defined into a set Ω^P; where $P = \{A, S\}$ and the recourses decisions $(\mathbf{X}_t, \mathbf{F}_t, \mathbf{I}_t, \mathbf{U}_t)$ adapt to the specific combination of $(\mathbf{Y}_h, \mathbf{W}_h, \mathbf{Z}_h, \mathbf{V}_h)$ and ω obtained. The set $\Omega^M = \Omega^{M_A} + \Omega^{M_S}$ is used in the evaluation stage of designs apart from the worst case scenarios Ω^U related to deep uncertainty scenarios that will be used as a decisive factor in our filtering procedure; the way in which the designs performing well in the worst case scenarios will be selected.

In order to evaluate the entire set of designs, a set of performance measures $M_i = \{M_1, M_2, \ldots, M_m\}, \quad (m \geq 2)$ is needed.

Let

$$\forall t \in T, \omega \in \Omega^M$$

$$NOP_t(D_1^j, \omega) = \left[A_t(\omega)\mathbf{F}_t(D_1^j, \omega)\right] - B_{h(t)}(\omega)\begin{bmatrix}\mathbf{F}_t(D_1^j, \omega) + \mathbf{X}_t(D_1^j, \omega) + \mathbf{I}_t(D_1^j, \omega) + \mathbf{U}_t(D_1^j, \omega) \\ +\mathbf{Y}_{h(t)}(D_1^j, \omega) + \mathbf{W}_{h(t)}(D_1^j, \omega) + \mathbf{Z}_{h(t)}(D_1^j, \omega) + \mathbf{V}_{h(t)}(D_1^j, \omega)\end{bmatrix}$$

(18)

$NOP_t(D_1^j, \omega)$ presents the net operating profits of design D_1^j in every period *t*. And let

$$NOP(D_1^j, \omega) = \sum_{t \in T} \frac{1}{(1+\alpha)^t} NOP_t(D_1^j, \omega) \quad, \forall t \in T, \omega \in \Omega^M \tag{19}$$

be the discounted net operating profits of a design D_1^j over the planning horizon T.

In our framework, we consider that the key performance indicators are the gain (design value) and the resilience of the design. These indicators are described as follows.

2.1.1. Design value

In our context, the value added by the SCN under a scenario $\omega \in \Omega^M$ is given by the net operating profits over the planning horizon.

Where

$$NOP(D_1^j, \omega) = \sum_{t \in T} \frac{1}{(1+\alpha)^t} NOP_t(D_1^j, \omega) \quad, \forall t \in T, \omega \in \Omega^M \tag{20}$$

In the case where the designs are generated by the Monte Carlo approach, the estimated probabilities are $\frac{1}{M_A}$ and $\frac{1}{M_S}$ for acceptable and serious scenarios respectively.

The first performance measure deducted from the design value indicator is its expected return value, expressed as follows:

$$E\left[NOP(D_1^j)\right] = \sum_{P=A,S} \frac{\pi_P}{M_P} \sum_{\omega \in \Omega^{M_P}} NOP(D_1^j, \omega) \quad \textbf{(M}_1\textbf{)}$$

And in order to ensure the robustness of a design during the planning horizon, the second performance measure can be its mean semi-deviation, formulated as:

$$MSD\left[NOP(D_1^j)\right] = \sum_{P=A,S} \frac{\pi_P}{M_P} MSD_P\left[NOP(D_1^j)\right]$$

(M$_2$)

$$MSD\left[NOP(D_1^j)\right] = \frac{\pi_A}{M_A} \sum_{\omega \in \Omega^{M_A}} \max\left\{\left(E[NOP(D_1^j)] - NOP(D_1^j, \omega)\right);0\right\} + \frac{\pi_S}{M_S} \sum_{\omega \in \Omega^{M_S}} \max\left\{\left(E[NOP(D_1^j)] - NOP(D_1^j, \omega)\right);0\right\}$$

In our evaluation approach we use the expected return value under the deep uncertain scenarios as a critical measure formulated by the minimum return value of the design under this type of scenario.

$$DEV\left[NOP(D_1^j)\right] = \min_{\omega \in \Omega^{M_U}} \left\{NOP(D_1^j, \omega)\right\} \quad \textbf{(M}_3\textbf{)}$$

2.1 Resilience

Due to business disruptions during the planning horizon, the SCN operations can be perturbed. The proposed stochastic programming anticipates response policies through decision variables $\left(\mathbf{X}_t(D_1,\omega), \mathbf{F}_t(D_1,\omega), \mathbf{I}_t(D_1,\omega), \mathbf{U}_t(D_1,\omega)\right)$. The costs associated with these variables must be minimized by providing better resilience strategy. We define the resilience of a generated design as the minimum distance between every demand zone location in the SCN and the second warehouse location, which is considered as an alternative in the case of damage in the first warehouse.

This performance indicator is formulated as follows:

$$RES(D_1^j) = \sum_{P=A,S} RES_P(D_1^j) + RES_U(D_1^j)$$

The performance measure extracted from this indicator can be the mean of all the resilience values of the design under every scenario. The selected design will be the one that has the minimum mean value.

$$\overline{RES}(D_1^j) = \sum_{P=A,S} \pi_P \overline{RES_P}(D_1^j) + \pi_U \overline{RES_U}(D_1^j) \qquad \textbf{(M}_4\textbf{)}$$

2.2 Filtering procedure

The decision-maker is not always a single individual. In fact, much of decision theory has evolved as a result of the need to evaluate decisions faced by groups of individuals or organizations. If the performances among different consequences are similar for all individuals in a group or organization, the group can be viewed as a single decision-making entity. If, on the other hand, the preferences of group members are disparate, the decision analysis becomes more complicated. In our problem, we assume that we have only one decision-maker and not a group of decision makers.

To filter the designs among all those generated, there are many decision making techniques; a new technique presented in [30] is defined in the following section.

The objective of this method is to determine a set of designs formed by adding mutually efficient subsets of designs, called kernels, which are obtained through a step-wise procedure; the set of these kernels is denoted by ***K***. The subset ***K*** selected at each step is globally efficient compared with designs not yet selected, and relatively homogenous in that comparison.

The idea is that an outranking relationship is used to eliminate some generated designs $X^j \quad j = 0,1,...,J$. This outranking relationship is defined by a level of concordance denoted by θ and a level of disagreement denoted by φ providing the value of each performance measure. As a result, it is only when a highest level of concordance and the lowest level are guaranteed that some designs will be excluded.

To further explain this idea, suppose that a design D_1^j dominates another design D_1^k in the whole set of performance measures. In this case, the two levels of concordance θ and disagreement φ that D_1^j dominates D_1^k is a perfect score. The difficulty is that in reality such case is very rare. For this, required levels of concordance and disagreement must be attained to conclude that a design dominates another one.

Required level of concordance:

Let $\phi_i^P(D_1^j, D_1^k)$ be a binary variable that gives the dominance relationship between every pair of designs based on the set performance measures $M_i = \{ M_1, \dots, M_m \}$ under scenarios Ω^P ; $P = A, S$.

$$\phi_i^P(D_1^j, D_1^k) = \begin{cases} 1 & \text{if } \; M_i[D_1^j, \Omega^P] \geq M_i[D_1^k, \Omega^P] \\ 0 & \text{otherwise} \end{cases} \qquad j,k \in J,\; j \neq k, \quad i = 1,\dots,m, \quad P = A,S$$

Where $M_i[D_1^j, \Omega^P]$ and $M_i[D_1^k, \Omega^P]$ are respectively the performance measure values of both designs $j,k \in J$ under scenario $\Omega^P, P = A, S$.

Let $C(D_1^j, D_1^k) = \sum_{P=A,S} \frac{1}{m} \sum_{i=1}^{m} \phi_i^P(D_1^j, D_1^k), \quad \forall j,k \in J,\; j \neq k$

$C(D_1^j, D_1^k)$ gives us comparisons between designs under both types of scenarios $\Omega^P, P = A, S$.

Based on two levels of concordance θ^A, θ^S of acceptable and serious scenarios respectively, a design D_1^j dominates D_1^k if $C\left(D_1^j, D_1^k\right) \geq (\theta^A \times \theta^S)$. Let $\theta = (\theta^A \times \theta^S)$ be the level of concordance.

Required level of disagreement:

Referring to [31, 32], and based on the idea of the ELECTRE method; this level ensures that the design selected must guarantee that its minimum value in every performance level is not less than a given level φ.

Let $\psi_i^P(D_1^j, D_1^k)$ be a binary variable that gives the dominance relationship between every pair of designs based on the set of performance measures $M_i = \{ M_1,\ldots, M_m \}$ under scenarios $\Omega^P ; P = A, S$.

$$\forall\, j,k \in J,\ j \neq k, \quad i = 1,\ldots,m, P = A, S$$

$$\psi_i^P(D_1^j, D_1^k) = \begin{cases} 1 & if \;\; Min\left(M_i[D_1^j, \Omega^P]\right) \geq Min\left(M_i[D_1^k, \Omega^P]\right) \\ 0 & otherwise \end{cases}$$

Let

$$U(D_1^j, D_1^k) = \underset{i}{Max}\left(\psi_i^A(D_1^j, D_1^k), \psi_i^S(D_1^j, D_1^k)\right) \quad \forall j,k \in J,\ j \neq k$$

Based on this, a design D_1^j dominates D_1^k if$U\left(D_1^j, D_1^k\right) \geq \varphi$.

Subsequent to these levels, the set of kernels of selected designs will result from a compromise between all the performance measures under different scenarios. This compromise is based on three properties:

1. External consistency: any design that is not included in the subset ***K*** has to be outranked by at least one of designs of ***K***. This property means that being outranked for a design is not a cause of elimination as long as the outranking does not originate from a selected design.
2. Internal consistency: the set ***K*** does not include any design that is outranked by another one in ***K*** itself. This propriety is needed in order to mitigate possible resentment between the performance measure values.

Consequently, proprieties 1, 2 are mathematically formulated in order to get the highest degrees of required concordance level θ and the required disagreement level φ.

Let $\gamma(D_1^j, D_1^k)$ be the required level of concordance where

$$\gamma(D_1^j, D_1^k) = \begin{cases} 1 & if \;\; C(D_1^j, D_1^k) \geq \theta \\ 0 & otherwise \end{cases}$$

Let $\eta(D_1^j, D_1^k)$ be the required level of disagreement where

$$\eta(D_1^j, D_1^k) = \begin{cases} 1 & \text{if } U(D_1^j, D_1^k) \geq \varphi \\ 0 & \text{otherwise} \end{cases}$$

Then a design D_1^j dominates another design D_1^k at the concordance level of $\theta = (\theta^A \times \theta^S)$ if $\gamma(D_1^j, D_1^k) = 1$ and of the disagreement level of φ. The outranking relationships between the designs can be expressed equivalently as follows:

$$\theta + \gamma(D_1^j, D_1^k) \leq C(D_1^j, D_1^k) + 1 \quad \forall j,k \;\; j \neq k$$

$$\varphi + \eta(D_1^j, D_1^k) \leq U(D_1^j, D_1^k) + 1 \quad \forall j,k \;\; j \neq k$$

Based on [30], the internal and external consistencies require that the set ***K*** must satisfy the following conditions simultaneously:

$$\sum_{k \neq j} \gamma(D_1^k, D_1^j) \times \beta(D_1^k) + \beta(D_1^j) \geq 1 \qquad \forall j$$

$$\sum_{k \neq j} \eta(D_1^k, D_1^j) \times \beta(D_1^k) + \beta(D_1^j) \geq 1 \qquad \forall j$$

$$\sum_{k \neq j} \gamma(D_1^k, D_1^j) \times \beta(D_1^k) + (n-1)\beta(D_1^j) \leq n-1, \quad \forall j$$

$$\sum_{k \neq j} \eta(D_1^k, D_1^j) \times \beta(D_1^k) + (n-1)\beta(D_1^j) \leq n-1, \quad \forall j$$

Where $\beta(D_1^k) = \begin{cases} 1 & \text{if } \;\; D_1^k \in \mathrm{K} \\ 0 & \text{otherwise} \end{cases}$

Finally the entire program to find the highest level of concordance can be expressed as follows:

$$
\begin{aligned}
& Max\left(\theta+\varphi\right) \\
& s.t \\
& \theta+\gamma(D_1^j,D_1^k)\leq C(D_1^j,D_1^k)+1 && \forall j,k \quad j\neq k \\
& \varphi+\eta(D_1^j,D_1^k)\leq U(D_1^j,D_1^k)+1 && \forall j,k \quad j\neq k \\
& \sum_{k\neq j}\gamma(D_1^k,D_1^j)\times\beta(D_1^k)+\beta(D_1^j)\geq 1 && \forall j \\
& \sum_{k\neq j}\eta(D_1^k,D_1^j)\times\beta(D_1^k)+\beta(D_1^j)\geq 1 && \forall j \\
& \sum_{k\neq j}\gamma(D_1^k,D_1^j)\times\beta(D_1^k)+(n-1)\beta(D_1^j)\leq n-1, && \forall j \\
& \sum_{k\neq j}\eta(D_1^k,D_1^j)\times\beta(D_1^k)+(n-1)\beta(D_1^j)\leq n-1, && \forall j \\
& M_i[D_1^j,\Omega^U]\times\beta(D_1^j)\geq W_i && \forall i=1,\dots,m \quad \forall j \\
& \gamma(D_1^k,D_1^j),\ \eta(D_1^k,D_1^j),\ \beta(D_1^j)\in\{0,1\} && \forall k,j \\
& \theta,\varphi\in\{0,1\}
\end{aligned}
$$

Where $P_i\ [D_1^j,\Omega^U]$ is the value of design D_1^j under worst case scenarios Ω^U and $\boldsymbol{W_i}$ is the acceptable level of this value. In other words, a design will be selected as if its performance measure values in deep uncertainty scenarios are bigger than a level $\boldsymbol{W_i}$ fixed by the decision maker for every performance measure.

References

Barber CB, Dobkin DP, Huhdanpaa HT (1996) The Quickhull Algorithm for Convex Hulls. ACM Transactions on Mathematical Software 22(4):469–483.

Didier Vila. Alain Martcl and Robert Beauregard (2007): Taking market forces into account in the design of production-distribution networks/a positioning by anticipation approach.

Hughes EJ, (2001) Evolutionary Multi-objective Ranking with K.Thiele L, Coello Coello CA, Corne D, (Eds.) Evolutionary Multi-criterion Optimization emo 2001 LNCS, vol. 1993. Springer.

Julia L. Higle (2005) A tutorial: Stochastic programming: optimization when uncertainty matters.

Klibi, W., A. Martel and A. Guitouni (2010). The Design of Robust Value-Creating Supply Chain Networks: A Critical Review, EJOR.

Klibi, W. and A. Martel (2009). The Design of Effective and Robust Supply Chain Networks, Document CIRRELT-2009-28.

Klibi, W. and A. Martel (2009). Designing Resilient Supply Networks under Disruptions, Document CIRRELT-2009-27.

Martel A. et al. (2009). Military Missions Scenario Generation for the Design of Logistics Support Networks.

Martel A. et al. (2009). Designing Global Logistics Networks for Conflict or Disaster Support: An Application to the Canadian Armed Forces.

Martel, J. M., Azondekon, S. H., & Zaras, K. (1992). Preference relations in multicriterion analysis under risk. Belgian Journal of Operations Research, Statistics and Computer Science, 31, 55–83.

Metropolis, N.; Ulam, S. (1949). "The Monte Carlo Method". Journal of the American Statistical Association (American Statistical Association) 44 (247): 335–341.

Roy, R. Y.T. Azene, D. Farrugia, C. Onisa, C. Onisa, J. Mehnen, (2009) Evolutionary multi-objective design optimization with real life uncertainty and constraints.

Samuel, B. G. and Jeffrey, L.R. (2009). Probabilistic dominance criteria for comparing uncertain alternatives: a tutorial: the international journal of management science.

Sebastien Azondekon et Komlan Sedro (1998): Approache multicritère de choix d'actifs a base de dominance stochastique.

Sten de Wit, Godfreid Augenbroe, (2002) Analysis of uncertainty in building design evaluations and its implications.

Whitmore, G.A. and Findlay, M.C. (1978). stochastic dominance: lexington books

Yao Zhang, Zhi-Ping Fan, Yan Liu (2010) A method based stochastic dominance degrees for stochastic multiple criteria decision making.

Zaras, K., & Martel, J. M. (1994). Multiattribute analysis based on stochastic dominance. In B. Munier & M. J. Machina (Eds.), Models and experiments in risk and rationality (pp. 225–248). Dordrecht: Kluwer Academic Publishers.

Zaras, K. (1999). Rough approximation of pairwise comparisons described by multiattribute stochastic dominance. Journal of Multi-Criteria Decision Analysis, 8,291–297.

Zhang, Y., et al. (2010). A method based on stochastic dominance degres for stochastic multiple criteria decision MAKING: computrs & industrial engineering.

VOLATILITY SPILLOVER AMONG ISLAMIC AND OTHERS: EMERGING STOCK MARKETS[1]

JIHED MAJDOUB[2], MOHAMED ALI HOUFI[3] AND NIZAR HARRATHI[4]

1. Introduction

This paper extends the literature on inter-regional volatility spillovers by providing empirical evidence from six emerging and Islamic stock markets using the conditional variances obtained from multivariate Generalized Autoregressive Conditional Heteroscedasticity (M-GARCH) estimations. We investigate the existence and the direction of volatility spillovers between Islamic and other emerging stock markets located in distant regions. Our findings mainly confirm the conclusions from other studies on volatility spillovers across regions. There exist volatility transmissions between the emerging markets, even though emerging countries have no strong real and financial linkages. Importantly, financial crises, cultural, and religious factors seem to change the nature of these spillover effects. In fact, volatility and return spillovers between emerging stock markets have been subject to extensive empirical research. Understanding volatility spillovers is important for portfolio diversification and hedging strategies. It is known that greater integration of international stock markets and correlated stock price volatility decreases the opportunities for international portfolio diversification (Bekaert and Harvey, 2003). Analysing the transmission of volatility between emerging and Islamic stock markets may also shed light on the nature of information flows between international markets. In the same framework, King and

---

[1] The authors are affiliate to 'Laboratory for Research on Quantitative Development Economics - University of Tunis El Manar' (LAREQUAD).

[2] Mediterranean University.

[3] University of Jendouba.

[4] University of Carthage.

Wadhwani (1990) explain the volatility spillovers by the rational attempts of agents to use imperfect information about the events relevant to stock prices.

2. Literature Review

Index return volatility is one of the most important parameters that needs to be estimated in the context of modern Portfolio choice, such as studies of Elton and Gruber (1973) and Chan et al. (1999) in the context of asset allocation, Beder (1995) and Alexander and Leigh (1997) in the context of risk management, Gibson and Boyer (1998) and Byström (2002) in the context of option pricing.

Thus, the analysis of the correlation between volatilities of the indices can give an idea of the trends in the risk between two or between several markets. Most studies focus on volatility spillovers between developed stock markets and emerging stock markets, or between emerging markets located in the same region. Lin, Engle, and Ito (1994) find that foreign returns can significantly influence the domestic returns, as in the case of Japan and the US. Within the same framework, Ng (2000) examines the magnitude and changing nature of volatility spillovers from Japan and the US and he finds that regional and world factors such as cultural and religious factors are important for market volatility and their influence tends to be greater. Following this idea, Calvo (1999) argues that developed stock markets can act as a conduit for volatility across emerging markets in different regions. In a recent study, Dungey and Martin (2007) provide empirical evidence for the role of developed markets in volatility transmission across emerging markets. In fact, empirical studies seem to support the above conjectures on volatility spillovers across regions. Using a similar methodology, Gebka and Serwa (2007) find mixed results on volatility spillovers among the emerging capital markets in Eastern Europe, East Asia, and Latin America.

3. Model Specification

In this study, we employ a multivariate generalized autoregressive conditional heteroscedasticity (MGARCH) model to capture the dynamic relationship between returns index. We first employ the BEKK model of Engle and Kroner (1995) and then in a second step, we illustrate multivariate GARCH with the constant conditional correlation of

Bollerslev (1990) and the multivariate GARCH model with the dynamic conditional correlation of Engle (2002).

3.1 Conditional volatility: the VAR (1)-MGARCH (1, 1) Model

In this study we use the vector autoregression (VAR) framework with one lag[5] to analyse interrelationship among returns index: The mean equation is given by:

$$Z_t = \Pi + \Gamma Z_{t-1} + \varepsilon_t \qquad \varepsilon_t / I_{t-1} \to N(0, H_t) \tag{1}$$

Where Z_t is a $k \times 1$ vector of daily return index at time t, Π is a $k \times 1$ matrix of constants, and Γ is a $k \times k$ matrix of parameters of lagged returns index. ε_t is a $k \times 1$ vector of random errors representing the innovation at time t with a $k \times k$ conditional variance-covariance matrix H_t. I_{t-1} represent the market information at time t-1.
Bollerslev, Engle and Wooldridge (1988) proposed a VECH-GARCH model where the conditional variance and covariance is a function of all lagged conditional variance and covariance. The model is given by:

$$vech(H_t) = A_0 + \sum_{i=1}^{q} A_i vech(\varepsilon_{t-1}\varepsilon_{t-1}^{'}) + \sum_{i=1}^{p} G_i vech(H_{t-i}) \tag{2}$$

Where 'vech' is the operator that stacks the lower triangular portion of a symmetric matrix, A_0 is a $k(k+1)/2 \times 1$ vector, and A_i and G_i are $k(k+1)/2 \times k(k+1)/2$ matrix of parameters. The problem in this formulation of multivariate GARCH model is that the number of parameters is very large. In fact, Engle and Kroner (1995) proposed a BEKK model that can be viewed as a restricted version of the VECH model. The BEKK (1,1) model has the following form:

$$H_t = C'C + A'\varepsilon_{t-1}\varepsilon_{t-1}^{'}A + G'H_{t-1}G \tag{3}$$

Where C is a $k \times k$ lower triangular matrix of constants, A and G are a $k \times k$. The diagonal parameters in matrices A and G measure the effect of the own past shocks and past volatility of market i on its conditional

[5] The AIC lag selection criterion is used.

volatility. The off-diagonal elements in matrix $A(a_{ij})$ and $G(g_{ij})$ measure respectively the cross-market effects of shock spillover and the cross effect of volatility spillover. The parameters of the BEKK model can be obtained by using maximum likelihood estimation assuming normally distribution errors. We maximized the following likelihood function:

$$L(\theta) = -T\log(2\pi) - \tfrac{1}{2}\sum_{t=1}^{T}(\log|H_t| + \varepsilon_t' H_t^{-1}\varepsilon_t) \tag{4}$$

Where T is the number of observations and θ is the vector of parameters to be estimated. We use numerical maximization techniques to maximize the non-linear likelihood function. We use both the simplex and BFGS algorithms to obtain the initial condition and the final parameter estimates of the variance-covariance matrix.

3.2 Conditional Correlation: the CCC and DCC models

Bollerslev (1990) introduced a class of multivariate GARCH models, the Constant Conditional Correlation (CCC-MGARCH), in which the conditional correlations are time-invariant and thus the conditional variances are proportional to the produce of the corresponding conditional standard deviations. This restriction greatly reduces the number of unknown parameters and thus simplifies the estimation. The conditional covariance matrix can be expressed as follows:

$$H_t = D_t R D_t = \left(\rho_{ij}\sqrt{h_{ii,t}h_{jj,t}}\right) \tag{5}$$

Where $R = \left(\rho_{ij} = E(\eta_t \eta_t')\right)$ is a symmetric $k \times k$ definite positive matrix containing the conditional correlation $\rho_{ij}\left(\rho_{ii} = 1 \ \ \forall i\right)$, $\varepsilon_t = D_t \eta_t$, η_t is an i.i.d. random vector and $D_t = diag(h_{11t}^{1/2} \ldots\ldots h_{kkt}^{1/2})$. This model assumes that the conditional variance h_{iit} follows a univariate GARCH model.

$$h_{iit} = w_i + \sum_{j=1}^{q}\alpha_{ij}\varepsilon_{i,t-j}^2 + \sum_{j=1}^{p}\beta_{ij}h_{ii,t-j}, \quad i = 1,\ldots,k \tag{6}$$

However, the assumption that the random shocks have a time-invariant conditional correlation may not be supported in many empirical studies. In order to make the conditional correlation matrix time-variant, Christodoulakis and Satchell (2002), Tse and Tsui (2002), Engle (2002), and Engle and Sheppard (2001) proposed a generalization of the CCC model[6]. Tse and Tsui (2002) introduced a varying correlation GARCH model where the conditional correlations are function of the conditional correlations of the previous period. The dynamic conditional correlation (DCC) of Tse and Tsui (2002) has the following form:

$$H_t = D_t R D_t \tag{7}$$

$$R_t = (1-\theta_1-\theta_2)R + \theta_1\psi_{t-1} + \theta_2 R_{t-1} \tag{8}$$

Where D_t is defined as in Eq.5, R is a symmetric $k \times k$ positive definite parameter matrix with unit diagonal elements, ψ_{t-1} is the $k \times k$ correlation matrix of the past P standardized residual $(\hat{\varepsilon}_{t-1} ... \hat{\varepsilon}_{t-p})$. A necessary condition to ensure the positivity of ψ_{t-1} is $P \geq k$, θ_1 and θ_2 are non-negative scalar parameters satisfying $\theta_1 + \theta_2 < 1$. Moreover, Engle (2002) proposes a different dynamic conditional correlation model. The DCC model of Engle, the covariance matrix is decomposed as follows:

$$H_t = D_t R_t D_t$$

$$R_t = diag(q_{11t}^{1/2} ...... q_{kkt}^{1/2}) Q_t diag(q_{11t}^{1/2} ...... q_{kkt}^{1/2}) \tag{9}$$

Where Q_t is a symmetric $k \times k$ positive definite matrix containing the conditional covariance of standardized residuals, given by:

$$Q_t = (1-\theta_1-\theta_2)Q_0 + \theta_1 \eta_{t-1}\eta_{t-1}^{'} + \theta_2 Q_{t-1} \tag{10}$$

Where Q_0 is the unconditional covariance matrix of η_t, η_t is defined as in Eq. 5, θ_1 and θ_2 are non-negative scalar parameters satisfying $\theta_1 + \theta_2 < 1$, θ_1 represents the impact of last shocks on a current conditional correlation, and θ_2 captures the impact of the past correlation. If θ_1 and θ_2 are statistically significant, the conditional correlations are

[6] See more details in Bauwens and al (2006)

not constant. Engle (2002) shows that the likelihood function can be written as:

$$L(\theta) = -\tfrac{1}{2}\sum_{t=1}^{T}(\log 2\pi + 2\log|D_t| + \log|R_t| \eta_t' R_t^{-1}\eta_t) \tag{11}$$

The DCC model can be estimated consistently in two stages. First, Q_t is used to calculate the dynamic conditional correlation:

$$\rho_{ij,t} = q_{ij}(q_{ii,t}q_{jj,t})^{1/2} \tag{12}$$

Second, $\rho_{ij,t}$ is used to estimate conditional covariance:

$$h_{ij,t} = \rho_{ij}(h_{ii,t}h_{jj,t})^{1/2} \tag{13}$$

Where $h_{ii,t}(h_{jj,t})$ and $h_{ij,t}$ are the conditional variance and conditional covariance generated by using univariate GARCH models.

4. Data description

For the empirical analysis, daily data are used for the six indexes, namely XU100 Index for Turkey market, JKSE Index for Indonesian market, EGX30 index for Egyptian market, IPC index for Mexican market, Shang Comp index for Chinese market, and Bovespa Index for Brazilian market. Observations are from 04/01/2005 to 27/11/2009. The data are obtained from DataStream database servers and the use of the values of indices in American dollar supposes that the international investors covered themselves against the exchange rate risk.

5. Volatility spillover

In this section, we examine the estimated result of time-varying variance-covariance by the BEKK (1, 1) model. The main results of the equation N°1 and N°3 are presented in tables 2 and 3.

The existence of any causal relation among variance and covariance included in H_t imply that the off-diagonal coefficients of $A(a_{ij})$ and $G(g_{ij})$ are statistically significant. In fact, a_{ij} and g_{ij} respectively measure the effect of their own and cross past shock and past conditional volatility of the other markets. The most important feature of the BEKK model is that it can explain causality relation among both variance and covariance. The results of estimated BEKK are shown in table 2. The forecast of the volatility of the steps became increasingly complex with the imperfections observed on the steps as well as crises and extreme moments. Volatility proves a complex function through several factors of the same market and other markets, this is shown by the transmission of the shocks enter several markets in the world. From the same point of view and after the crisis of "Subprime", the international banks lost enormous amounts of money, whereas the Islamic banks had limited losses, which pushed the theorists and the experts to consider the products of the Islamic banks. By analogy, the Islamic financial markets have a volatility moderated in front of the other emerging markets; the financial markets of the Islamic countries present a weak correlation of volatility with the other emerging markets. The results of BEKK analysis shows that the majority of the couples (Islamic Country, Emerging country) are not significant in term of shocks and in terms of volatility interpreted respectively by the coefficients A (I, J) and B (I, J). For example the couple (Egypt, China) presents a statistical value student equal to -0.207, the absolute value of which is lower than 1.96. Consequently the effect of the shock of Egypt on China is not significant, in the same way of that of China on Egypt, in more the same couple presents a B (Egypt, China) non-significant, which shows the weak correlation of volatility between these two markets. Such results justify the weak economic and social-cultural links between the two countries and make it possible to release a source of international diversification considering the weak correlation of the risk in term of correlation of volatility between the two countries. In the same way, the correlation of volatility between the index of Turkey and the volatility of the Mexican index is significant, whereas the transmission of the shock between the two markets is not significant. We can conclude that the volatility of the Islamic markets is not correlated with the remainder of the emerging markets. Such a result shows a difference in volatility between the two types of markets. Thorough analysis of the correlation between the volatility of the two types of markets can explain the advantage and utility of the Islamic markets in terms of risk diversification.

6. Constant and dynamic conditional correlation

The Analysis of the volatility between the markets through the approach of constant conditional correlation (CC) based on a model VAR (1) - MGARCH (1.1) shows that the correlation of volatility between the Islamic and emergent markets is stable during the study period. The coefficient R_{ij} is significant for the whole of the sample. This stability can be explained by the transmission of the shocks and the economic exchanges between the Islamic and emerging countries. The dynamic analysis of correlation (DCC) shows that the cross correlations of the outputs of indexes are dynamic, considering the two parameters (θ_1 and θ_2) representative of the estimate are positive and present bullish tendencies related to events of crisis. Such results were noted by Boyer et al. (1999). Other authors also announce within the same framework the persistence of memory in the correlations (Christodoulakis, 2007). However, another characteristic of the correlations observed between the Islamic markets and the remainder of the emerging markets, is asymmetry. Such results can be beneficial in terms of minimization of risk and portfolio choice. Indeed, theoretically the asymmetry of the correlation is influenced by the nature of the shock, that is, positive or negative. Martens and Poon (2001) find in this direction that the correlation answers the negative shocks more than with the positive shocks: the correlation is high in periods of strong volatility and it decreased in calm periods. The results thus confirm the variability and the instability of the cross correlations of all the markets. This is shown by an intense and very unstable correlation between the markets that started following the Subprime crisis, characterized by a strong volatility of the markets.

7. Conclusion

The analysis of the correlation of volatility between Islamic and emerging markets, through the study of the dynamic conditional correlation based on a multivariate model GARCH, shows a significance of the dynamic correlation. Consequently, the correlation between these markets is dynamic according to time and depends on the past. The study also shows that the Islamic markets, such as the Egyptian market, do not follow the same volatility as the other emerging markets and have a variation of volatility moderated compared to the others. In the same way the transmission of the shocks between this market and the remainder of the markets are not significant, such results shows the utility of the Islamic markets in terms of diversification of the risk considering the weak correlation and the absence of transmission of the shocks; Islamic markets can be a source of international diversification. This study can be extended by examining the contagion effect of Islamic banks on the stability of the volatility spillover of Islamic markets, and consequently for all over the world.

References

Alexander, C., Leigh, C. (1997). "On the covariance matrices used in Value-at-Risk models". *Journal of Derivatives*, 4, 50-62.

Alexander, G., Eun, C.S., and Janakiramanan, S., "International Listing and Stock Returns: Some Empirical Evidence", *Journal of Financial and Quantitative Analysis*, 23, June 1988, 135-152.

Bae, Kee-Hong, G. Andrew Karolyi, and Rene M. Stulz, (2002), "A New Approach to Measuring Financial Contagion", *Review of Financial Studies,* forthcoming.

Beder, T. S. (1995). "VaR: seductive but dangerous", *Financial Analyst Journal,* Sep-Oct, 12-24.

Bekaert, G., & Harvey, C.R. (1997). "Emerging equity market volatility". *Journal of Financial*

Bekaert, Geert, Campbell R. Harvey and Angela Ng, (2003), "Market Integration and Contagion", *Journal of Business,*

Bollerslev, T. (1990). "Modeling the Coherence in Short-Run Nominal Exchange Rates: A Multivariate Generalized ARCH Approach", *Review of Economics and Statistics* 72: 498-505.

Byström, H.N. (2002). "Using simulated currency rainbow options to evaluate covariance matrix forecasts". *Journal of International Financial Markets, Institutions and Money*, 12, 216-230.

Chan, L.K., Karceski, J., & Lakonishok, J. (1999). "On portfolio optimization: forecasting covariances and choosing the risk model". *Review of Financial Studies*, 12, 937-974.

Christodoulakis, G.A. and Satchell, S.E. (2002). "Correlated ARCH: modeling the time-varying correlation between financial asset returns". *European Journal of Operations Research*, volume 139, pp 351-370.

Dungey, M., R. Fry, B. González-Hermosillo and V.L. Martin (2007), "Contagion in Global Equity Markets in 1998: The Effects of the Russian and LTCMCrises", *North American Journal of Economics and Finance*, 18, 155-174.

Engle, R.F., (2002). “Dynamic conditional correlation: a simple class of multivariate generalized autoregressive conditional heteroskedasticity models”, *Journal of Business and Economic Statistics*, volume 20, pp 339-350.

Engle, R.F., and Sheppard, K. (2001). “Theoretical and Empirical Properties of Dynamic Conditional Correlation Multivariate GARCH”, *NBER Working Paper Series*, 8554.

Engle, R.F., Ito, T. and Lin, W.L. (1990). “Meteor showers or heat waves? Heteroscedastic intra daily volatility in the foreign exchange market”. *Econometrica*, volume 58, pp 525-542.

Engle, Robert and Ken Kroner, (1995). “Multivariate Simultaneous GARCH”, *Econometric Theory,* 11: 122-150.

Ewing, B. T., Forbes, S. M. and Payne, J. E. (2003). “The effects of macroeconomic shocks on sector-specific returns”. *Applied Economics*, volume 35, pp 201–207.

Ewing, B.T. (2002). “The transmission of shocks among S&P indexes”. *Applied Financial Economics*, volume 12, pp 285-290.

King, M., Wadhwani, S., 1990. “Transmission of volatility between stock markets”. *Review of Financial Studies* 3, 5–33.

Tse, YK. and Tsui, AKC. (2002). “A multivariate GARCH model with time-varying correlations”. *Journal of Business and Economic Statistics*, volume 20, pp 351-362

Appendix

Table n°1 : Descriptive Statistics of stock returns

	Turkey	Indonesia	Egypt	Mexico	China	Brazil
Mean	0.000333	0.000737	0.000684	0.000337	0.000186	0.000702
Std, Dev,	0.021	0.019	0.019	0.016	0.016	0.022
Skewness	-0.033	-0.279	-0.831	-0.557	-0.162	-0.027
Kurtosis	2.543	4.780	7.799	6.872	7.637	5.851
Jarque-Bera	344.856	1234.261	3388.938	2582.462	3113.441	1824.401
L,B $Q(10)$	15.741	32.477	46.532	29.108	6.672	12.350
ARCH-LM	18.402	40.851	8.962	27.041	96.459	98.332
ADF	-20.580	-19.856	-17.658	-20.632	-20.922	-21.190
PP	-34.036	- 31.563	- 31.638	- 31.790	-36.590	-35.258
KPSS	0.096	0.097	0.122	0.104	0.115	0.097

Notes : *,* and ***, denotes the levels of significance of 1%, 5% and 10% respectively, Ljung Box-$Q(10)$ is the statistic for serial correlation, the total number of usable observations is 1280.

Table N° 2: Estimates Results of multivariate GARCH: VAR(1)-BEKK(1,1)

Estimates Results of BEKK Model				
	Coeff	Std Error	T-Stat	Signif
a_{11}	0.050511064	0.023924635	2.11126	0.03475019
a_{12}	0.073071510	0.019389439	3.76862	0.00016415
a_{13}	0.126795508	0.020100352	6.30812	0.00000000
a_{14}	0.206162439	0.019930894	10.34386	0.00000000
a_{15}	0.014581268	0.012365015	1.17924	0.23830431
a_{16}	0.042301423	0.017441619	2.42532	0.01529510
a_{21}	0.057117625	0.025231408	2.26375	0.02358944
a_{22}	0.160012885	0.017922009	8.92829	0.00000000
a_{23}	0.092536063	0.021711575	4.26206	0.00002025
a_{24}	0.178554695	0.020901560	8.54265	0.00000000
a_{25}	0.037820157	0.011713169	3.22886	0.00124286
a_{26}	0.046412268	0.016107456	2.88142	0.00395894
a_{31}	0.072262891	0.025140717	2.87434	0.00404877
a_{32}	-0.000791763	0.016278633	-0.04864	0.96120765
a_{33}	0.202484953	0.019793345	10.22995	0.00000000
a_{34}	0.017239171	0.023427265	0.73586	0.46181632
a_{35}	0.027151881	0.009614849	2.82395	0.00474354
a_{36}	0.026320280	0.013900014	1.89354	0.05828564
a_{41}	0.121090317	0.025321701	4.78208	0.00000173
a_{42}	-0.059803771	0.020241696	-2.95448	0.00313192

a43	-0.043835901	0.022573640	-1.94191	0.05214841
a_{44}	-0.269557776	0.027308443	-9.87086	0.00000000
a_{45}	-0.002564274	0.013881557	-0.18473	0.85344453
a46	0.005331659	0.019160245	0.27827	0.78080761
a51	-0.052238381	0.046171063	-1.13141	0.25788276
a_{52}	-0.242126213	0.028680954	-8.44206	0.00000000
a_{53}	-0.087128311	0.034122214	-2.55342	0.01066711
a_{54}	-0.016883283	0.032052818	-0.52673	0.59837889
a_{55}	0.106736417	0.021421577	4.98266	0.00000063
a_{56}	-0.074629293	0.030875042	-2.41714	0.01564301
a61	0.080879203	0.031703279	2.55113	0.01073741
a_{62}	0.152049254	0.022116513	6.87492	0.00000000
a_{63}	0.036670277	0.025848572	1.41866	0.15599882
a_{64}	0.247311203	0.026936167	9.18138	0.00000000
a_{65}	0.128055921	0.015614991	8.20083	0.00000000
a_{66}	0.274444019	0.019022345	14.42745	0.00000000
g_{11}	-0.701344052	0.021279485	- 32.95870	0.00000000
g_{12}	-0.277193706	0.023377473	- 11.85730	0.00000000
g_{13}	-0.722214459	0.022416722	-32.21767	0.00000000
g_{14}	-0.151847547	0.021307689	-7.12642	0.00000000
g_{15}	-0.213038178	0.015324881	-13.90146	0.00000000
g_{16}	-0.320602115	0.020763076	-15.44097	0.00000000
g_{21}	0.240827003	0.049350907	4.87989	0.00000106
g_{22}	0.967468661	0.012478816	77.52888	0.00000000

g_{23}	0.112927039	0.019501213	5.79077	0.00000001
g_{24}	0.136315804	0.018683103	7.29621	0.00000000
g_{25}	-0.048917956	0.015834165	-3.08939	0.00200566
g_{26}	-0.030852561	0.021743396	-1.41894	0.15591669
g_{31}	-0.764824917	0.035475603	-21.55918	0.00000000
g_{32}	-0.135020632	0.019763935	-6.83167	0.00000000
g_{33}	0.623362570	0.025771536	24.18803	0.00000000
g_{34}	-0.163234140	0.020259016	-8.05736	0.00000000
g_{35}	-0.117902961	0.011424583	-10.32011	0.00000000
g_{36}	-0.181729638	0.016000850	-11.35750	0.00000000
g_{41}	-0.030048053	0.042011546	-0.71523	0.47446495
g_{42}	-0.061418820	0.029866781	-2.05643	0.03974149
g43	-0.256619197	0.027021694	-9.49678	0.00000000
g_{44}	0.243577650	0.036347925	6.70128	0.00000000
g_{45}	0.041821685	0.019008981	2.20010	0.02779970
g_{46}	-0.064077271	0.026631564	-2.40605	0.01612540
g_{51}	0.367185324	0.054823637	6.69757	0.00000000
g_{52}	0.666937046	0.041361492	16.12459	0.00000000
g_{53}	0.314105630	0.036608195	8.58020	0.00000000
g_{54}	0.280815106	0.041110958	6.83066	0.00000000
g_{55}	1.433811858	0.012614184	113.66664	0.00000000
g_{56}	0.906211744	0.020301022	44.63872	0.00000000
g61	0.133790794	0.047970371	2.78903	0.00528662
g_{62}	-0.302080524	0.025976957	-11.62879	0.00000000
g_{63}	0.004941114	0.027409499	0.18027	0.85694049

g_{64}	-0.084422072	0.024825465	-3.40062	0.00067232
g_{65}	-0.358088684	0.012407687	-28.86023	0.00000000
g_{66}	0.485833467	0.016836617	28.85577	0.00000000
LLR	22153.40432			
AIC	-34.48695			

1	2	3	4	5	6
"Turkey" (XU100)	"Indonesia" (JKSE)	"Egypt" (EGX30)	"Mexico"(IPC)	"China" (Schang Comp)	"Brazil(BOVESPA)

THE MULTIPLE STRADDLE CARRIER ROUTING PROBLEM

KHALED MILI[1] AND KHALED MELLOULI[2]

1. Introduction

Within a container terminal, different types of material handling equipment are used to tranship containers from ships to storage yard, trucks and trains, and vice versa. Over the past decades, ships have strongly increased in size, up to 8000 TEU (Twenty feet equivalent unit container). In order to use these big ships efficiently, the docking time at the port must be as small as possible. This means that large amounts of containers have to be loaded, unloaded and transhipped in a short time span, with a minimum use of expensive equipment.

A handling system for the retrieval and transport of containers are straddle carriers (SCs). SCs are used for the retrieval of containers from the stack and for transport to the quay cranes. This paper gives a plan to efficiently route the SCs inside a container terminal for loading operations.

One of the success factors of a terminal is related to the time in port for container vessels and the transhipment rates the ship operators have to pay. We focus on the process of container transport by SCs between the container ship and the storage yard. The primary objective is the reduction of the time in port for the vessels by maximizing the productivity of the Quay cranes, or in other words, minimizing the delay times of container transports that causes the Quay cranes to stop. We investigate dispatching strategy for SCs to containers and show the potential of genetic algorithm to develop the solution.

---

[1] Institute of the High Commercial Studies, department of Quantitative Methods IHEC Carthage presidency. khaledmili@yahoo.fr tel: 0021698503848

[2] Institute of the High Commercial Studies, department of Quantitative Methods IHEC Carthage presidency.

The remainder of the paper is organized as follows: section 2 is devoted to related works that solve the multiple straddle carriers routing problem (MSCRP). The next sections will be reserved to detail our methodology; and our contribution, the problem formulation. Finally our paper will be finished with an illustrative example in order to prove the efficiency of our method. Some concluding remarks and perspectives to extend this work are finally discussed.

2. Related Works

Container terminals are very specific from a material handling point of view, because of the special characteristics of both the containers and the handling equipment.

Terminals have become increasingly important and more and more scientific literature is devoted to them. This is even truer for the automated terminals which are being established to manage the increase in costs. The additional increase in ship sizes makes productivity perfection in container handling more important and therefore more research is to be expected. In this paper, we discuss the related routing problems within container handling.

Operations Research has made important contributions for container terminals. The techniques employed vary from Mixed Integer Programming formulations, to queuing models, and simulation approaches.

In 1993, Dirk Steenken et al. [11] adopted two models to solve the MSCRP. In the first model they reduce the problem to a simple TSP with assumptions that one Straddle Carrier (SC) is engaged. They use the balance and connect heuristic, applied to solve the sequencing insertions in printed circuit board assemblies; referencing Ball and Magazine (1988), various heuristics were investigated to solve this problem, like the nearest neighbour heuristic (NN), the successive or cheapest insertion (SUC), and a 2-optimal exchange method (2OP). The best results were found using the SUC method.

The expansion of this problem to a multiple one is achieved by introducing fictitious vehicle depots and by using an assumption that two jobs should not succeed each other within the same tour if there is a great difference in their due dates. They also reported that they have added another procedure to their initial solution and a new term not explained.

The second model is developed using an analogy to machine scheduling (MAS) mentioned by Maas and Vob (1991). This model is based on some dispatching rules to select insertion positions.

In 2003, V. Franqueira [7] presents a discussion about the multiple straddle carrier routing problem. Two constraints of this routing problem are discussed: the conflicts between SCs must be resolved; and container stock in the storage yard must be shared between all SCs.

The first constraint is divided into two types: a travel conflict exists when SC tries to cross another SC, and a space conflict exists when a SC tries to move to the same location where another SC is already placed.

The resolution of these types of conflict between SCs is presented by Ki Young Kim in 1998 [4] for the travel conflict of two SCs. He proposes two strategies: the waiting strategy, and the exchanging roles between SCs strategy. For the space conflict he uses a waiting strategy and a substitutive one.

The routing problem of multiple SCs (more than two) was also presented by K. Y. Kim, considering that containers are located in one or multiple blocks according to the assumptions that a pseudo work schedule would be constructed by appending the work schedules of all SCs, and there is no interference between equipments. Therefore the multiple routing is reduced to a single routing one. Solving the single SC problem for the pseudo work schedule would theoretically solve the overall problem.

However, V. Franqueira suggests that these assumptions turn the problem completely artificial, since each SC route will have to be selected manually from the output and each SC routing will have to occur in sequence, and never in parallel.

V. Franqueira presents a solution to some multiple routing problems, using the single SC routing procedure, by providing (through manual work) the container distribution table for each SC separately. However, this procedure seems inappropriate since the potential parallelism of multiple SCs is ignored.

The paper by L.N. Spasovic et al. in 1999 presents results of a research designed to evaluate the potential for improving productivity and the quality of service for a straddle carrier operation. A methodology was developed to quantify possible savings from redesigning the straddle operation. The main effort was to develop and evaluate a series of algorithms for straddle assignment and control. The algorithms differ in a manner in which the straddles are given assignments to move containers. Their research focused only on trucks. The productivity of the whole group of straddles is not analysed. This should include the straddles servicing on-dock rail, the cranes during ship loading and unloading, as well as re-warehousing of containers in the yard.

E. Nishimura et al. in 2005 [9] present in their paper a Genetic Algorithm heuristic to solve the trailer routing problem using a dynamic routing assignment method. They focus on the tours related to one cycle operation of the quay cranes. Experimental results demonstrate that the dynamic assignment is better than a static one. The drawback to their solution procedure is the complexity of the trailer routing, which may increase the possibility of human error. Trailer drivers may find it difficult to follow the complicated itineraries assigned to them, resulting in mistakes in driving.

In this paper we analysed the routing problem of SCs to support tasks between quay cranes and yard areas. Since inbound containers are usually unloaded into a designated open space, the Straddle Carriers do not have to travel much during the unloading operation. However, the time for loading depends on the loading sequence of containers, as well as the number of loaded containers. In this paper we focus on minimizing the travel time of the Straddle Carriers for loading outbound (export) containers.

In this paper, we formulate a nonlinear integer programming model for multiple SCs working with one quay crane. Based on certain operational concepts, a heuristic genetic algorithm is designed to solve this problem. We exploited the algorithm to analyse some real cases. Our study can provide companies with not only the routing plan of SCs and the estimated period of tasks finished, but also the required number of deployed SCs.

3. Problem Formulation

In previous work, (i.e. [3, 4, 5, 7]), the time distance between yard-bays is considered the main source of inefficiency in the routing scheme of the SC. The time spent by the SC inside a visited yard-bay is considered as constant. This paper differs from previous work by considering the time spent by the SC inside a yard-bay as variable. Therefore, the time spent by the SC once performing a job is divided into two parts, the first is the time spent between yard-bays, and second is the time spent inside each yard-bay.

The following notations are used to formulate the SCRP:

ts_j : thc time spent by the SC inside the yard-bay j.

y_{ij}^t : 1 if a SC moves from yard-bay i to yard-bay j in subtour t, 0 otherwise.

z_{ij}^t : 1 if a SC moves from yard-bay i to yard-bay j during partial-tour t, 0 otherwise.

n : the number of yard-bays.

l : the number of container groups.

B : the set of indices of yard-bays, $B = \{1, 2, \ldots, n\}$.

$b(h)$: the set of the yard-bay numbers where containers of group h exist.

r_t the number of containers which should be picked up during subtour t.

G : the set of indices of container groups, $G = \{1, 2, \ldots l\}$

g_t the container group number of containers which should be picked up during subtour t.

c_{hj} : the initial number of containers of group h stacked at yard-bay j.

d_{ij} : the travel distance between yard-bay i and j.

x_j^t : the number of containers picked up at yard-bay j in subtour t (a decision variable).

T: the travel time per unit travel distance.

t : subtour number, $t = 0, 1, \ldots, m, m+1$, where $t = 0$ and $m+1$ are initial and final location of the SC.

Let V present the set of locations of the SC and A the set of pathways between these locations. Let $A(V) = \{(i, j) | i, j \in V\}$.

The problem can be formulated as follows:

$$Min \sum_{t=0}^{m-1} \sum_{(i,j)\in A(B)} (Td_{ij} + ts_j) y_{ij}^t + \sum_{t=1}^{m} \sum_{(i,j)\in A(B)} (Td_{ij} + ts_j) z_{ij}^t \quad (1)$$

Subject to

$$\sum_{j\in B} (y_{ji}^{t-1} + z_{ki}^t) - \sum_{j\in B} (y_{ij}^t + z_{ik}^t) = 0 \qquad i \in B, \quad t = 1,2,...,m, \quad (2)$$

$$\sum_{(i,j)\in A(w)} Z_{ij}^t = |W| - 1 \quad \text{for all } W \subseteq B, \quad t = 1,2,...,m, \quad (3)$$

$$x_j^1 \leq M(\sum_{i\in B} z_{kj}^1 + \sum_{i\in B} y_{ij}^{t-1}), \qquad j \in b(g_1), \quad t = 1,2,...,m, \quad (4)$$

$$\sum_{j\in b(h)} x_j^t = r_t \quad (5)$$

$$\sum_{t=1}^{m} x_j^t = c_{hj} \qquad j \in b(h), \quad h = 1,2,...,l \quad (6)$$

$$y_{ij}^t \in \{0,1\} \qquad i, j \in B \qquad t = 1,2,..., m, \quad (7)$$

$$z_{ij}^t \in \{0,1\} \quad i, j \in B, \quad t = 1,2,..., m, \quad (8)$$

$$x_j^t \geq 0 \qquad j \in B, \quad t = 1,2,...,m, \quad (9)$$

M is a sufficiently large number and $|W|$ denotes the cardinality of set W.

The objective function (1) is to minimize the total travel time of the SC. Constraint (2) represents the route conservation. Constraint (3) is to prevent the looping of subtours. Constraint (4) comes from the definition of variables. Constraint (5) implies that the number of containers picked up during a subtour should be equal to the number of containers requested by the work schedule. Constraint (6) means that the total number of containers picked up during the whole tour should be equal to the initial number of containers at each yard-bay for each specific container group.

4. Genetic algorithm procedure solution

4.1 Motivations

The reasons for choosing genetic algorithm (GA) as a solution approach to the SCRP are:

- In this problem, most of the model's constraints are of equality form; therefore, obtaining feasible solutions is a hard task, and the probability of reaching infeasible solutions is greater than for the feasible ones, and therefore we need a population-based approach to better explore the routing solution. GA works on a population of the solutions simultaneously; it combines the concept of survival of the fittest with structured, yet randomized, information exchange to form robust exploration and exploitation of the solution routing.
- GA is a well-known meta-heuristic and its efficiency is verified for many problems in the literature.
- There is a tendency in the maritime transportation field to solve maritime problems using a genetic algorithm. M. Bazzazi et al, in 2008, present an efficient method to solve the storage space allocation problem. They declared that in real world cases, there are different types and sizes of containers, such as regular, empty, or refrigerated containers. The type of container may be have an effect on making a decision on the allocation of containers to the storage blocks. So the extended problem is solved by efficient GA for real sized instances. Imai et al. (2006) solve a multi-objective simultaneous stowage and load planning problem by GA. Imai, et al. (2007) solve the berth allocation problem at indented berths for mega-containerships by using GA. Lee et al. (2008) use GA to solve the quay crane scheduling problem.

4.2 Chromosome representation and decoding

We have ***(n)*** available required containers, and among them ($\boldsymbol{r}_t$) containers will be transported by ***(V)*** Straddle Carriers.

A chromosome is a set of containers that can be transported by SCs to perform the QC work schedule.

Each gene represents a required container placed at yard bay ***i***, stack ***s***, level ***l*** and transported by SC number ***v***. ***(i, s, l)*** are fixed and ***v*** varies between {***1 ... V***}.

Let $C_{l,v}^{i,s}$ design the container inside yard bay *i* in stack ***s*** at level *l* and transported by straddle carrier *v*. See figure 1.

$C_{2,1}^{1,3}$	$C_{1,10}^{8,4}$	$C_{1,5}^{6,1}$	$C_{3,8}^{2,5}$	$C_{2,3}^{10,5}$

Fig.1. A chromosome

We generate a set of chromosomes having ($\boldsymbol{r_t}$) genes which are selected from the set of (***n*** x ***V***) containers. Genetic operators are applied, and the cost of the resulting chromosome is calculated.

Each chromosome in the generation is divided into sub-chromosomes (***SH***), each one represents the list of containers transported by a particular SC.

The cost of each ***SH*** is the sum of the costs of containers picked up by the designed SC via the objective function of the problem.

Many SCs can work at the same yard map simultaneously. So in a subtour ***t***, we can find ***V*** SCs working, each one is transporting a different container. Therefore in each ***SH***, the cost of any container depends on all containers of the complete chromosome (all sub-chromosomes). This is done by updating the yard map after each handling job, and empty slots in the yard map are usually altered.

The cost of the complete chromosome is the maximum value of costs of its sub chromosomes.
The selected solution will be the chromosome of minimum cost.

4.2 Evolutionary strategy

After creating a generation, GA operators are applied.

4.2.1 Fitness function

A fitness function is applied to extract the fittest value of the generation. Given that the SCRP is a minimization problem, then the smaller the objective function is, the higher the fitness value must be [8]. As a result of many tests, E. Nishimura et al. [8] suggest the following fitness function:

$$f(y) = 1/1 + \exp(z(y)/10.000))$$

z(y) denotes the objective function value.

$$0 \leq f(y) \leq 0.5$$

4.2.2 Crossover operator

The GA selects the fittest chromosomes and applies a crossover operator to give rise to a better solution. The crossover scheme should be capable of creating a new feasible solution (child) by combining good characteristics of both parents [8].

There are many crossover operators, such as one-point, two-point, uniform, etc. For the reason of its performance, as proved in the literature, a 2-point crossover is used in our proposed algorithm.

In this crossover, two cut points are randomly chosen on the parent chromosomes. In order to create an offspring, the string between these two cut points in the first parent is first copied to the offspring, then the remaining position are filled by considering the sequence of activities in the second parent (starting after the second cut point). When the end of the chromosome is reached, the sequence continues at position 1.

Referring to E. Nishimura et al. [8] a more formal description of the procedure is as follows: let k denotes the cell number (k = 1,…,LK) in the exchanged string, and d(k) is a digit in cell k.

Crossover processing method
Step 1. Let $k = 1$.
Step 2. If $k > LK$, then go to Step 3, otherwise go to Step 4.
Step 3. Chromosomes A' and B' are feasible, then STOP. Otherwise, treat chromosomes A' as B' and B' as A' in the following steps, and let $k = 1$.

Step 4. If another cell in A' has the value of $d(k)$, let $k' = k$ and go to Step 5. Otherwise, go to Step 6.
Step 5. If there are two cells in B' having the value of $d(k')$, store the value to the cell of A' not in the interchanged string and go to Step 6. Otherwise, find a cell in A' having the value of $d(k')$ of B', let k' be the cell number, and go to Step 5.
Step 6. Let $k = k+1$ and go to Step 2.

4.2.3 Mutation operator

The mutation operator introduces random changes to the resulting chromosomes to create a new generation. This is done by varying the value of a gene with a mutation rate of probability [8].

This genetic operator introduces random changes to the chromosomes by altering the value of a gene with a user-specified probability called mutation rate.

Two genetic operators are applied to all the individuals with preset probabilities along the evolution. These two operators are a recombination operator and a mutation operator. The first is used to build offspring (children) by preserving edges (borders) from both parents. The second one is used to apply operators (insertion, swap, or inversion) to each gene with equal probabilities. In all three mutation operators, changes might occur in an intra- or inter-route way.

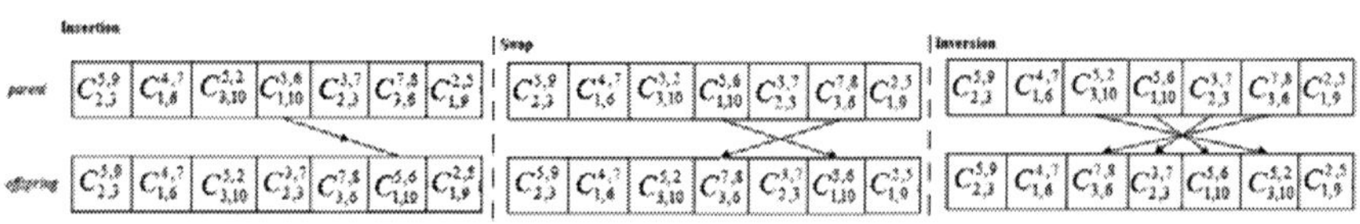

Fig.2. the three different mutations

The multiple straddle genetic procedure is presented as follows:

1. We generate $(\boldsymbol{n} \times \boldsymbol{V})$ genes, each one represents a container characterized by its position (yard bay, stack and level) and the ID of the SC that will transport it.
2. Repeat until termination:
   ▪ Reproduce set of chromosomes
   Each one is composed of $(\boldsymbol{r_t})$ genes selected arbitrarily from the set of $(\boldsymbol{n} \times \boldsymbol{V})$ containers.

Every generated chromosome has a number of straddles carriers used to transport the presented containers. This number is (***SH***) where $SH \leq V$, $SH \leq r_t$ and $SH > 0$.

- Verify the feasibility of the chromosome (container must not be transported twice or with different SCs in the same chromosome).
- Calculate fitness value of each chromosome and select best-ranking individuals having higher value for the next generation.
- Breed new generation through genetic operators applied on selected chromosomes to give birth to offspring.
- For each resulting offspring, reorganize the set of genes ordered by the number of SCs used to perform the work schedule.
- For each sub-chromosome, evaluate it by adding the costs of each container presented in it.
- To determine the cost of the entire chromosome, select the highest cost of all sub-chromosomes forming it.

3. From all resulting chromosomes generated in step 3, select the one that has minimum cost. This represents the best route.

5. Descriptive example

We have

- 5 yard-bays
- 3 SCs
- 10 stacks of 3 levels in each yard bay
- 9 containers type h_1 exist in the storage yard where **7** should be transported to the Quay Crane

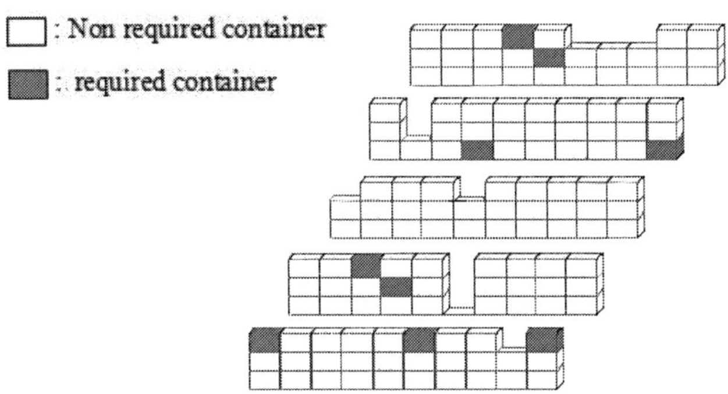

Fig.3: yard map

$\boldsymbol{n} = 9$
$V = 3$
The set of the entire required container is presented as follows:

$C_1^{1,1}$	$C_1^{1,6}$	$C_1^{1,10}$	$C_1^{2,3}$	$C_2^{2,4}$	$C_3^{4,4}$	$C_3^{4,10}$	$C_1^{5,4}$	$C_2^{5,5}$

Fig.4: the set of required containers

For each container three different genes are generated. For example for the first container $C_1^{1,1}$, the three generated genes are $C_{1,1}^{1,1}$ | $C_{1,2}^{1,1}$ | $C_{1,3}^{1,1}$, each gene represents, in addition to the required container, the SC that transports this container.

So, in general we have (9 x 3) genes, among them 7 genes must be selected.

The initial generation is formed by a set of chromosomes. Each one has 7 from the 27 available genes. After, genetic operators are applied.

The cost of each resulting chromosome is calculated and the best solution is selected.

Let Ch_1 be the resulting chromosome. See figure 5.

Ch_1 :	$C_{1,1}^{1,1}$	$C_{1,2}^{1,6}$	$C_{1,3}^{1,10}$	$C_{1,2}^{5,4}$	$C_{2,2}^{5,5}$	$C_{3,1}^{4,4}$	$C_{3,3}^{4,10}$
	↓	↓	↓	↓	↓	↓	↓
	Cost1	Cost2	Cost3	Cost4	Cost5	Cost6	Cost7

Fig.5: a resulting chromosome

In this example, there are containers that can be picked up by SC_1, SC_2 or SC_3. So we find three Sub-chromosomes ($\boldsymbol{SH} = 3$); see figures 6, 7, and 8.

$C_{1,1}^{1,1}$	$C_{3,1}^{4,4}$

Fig.6: SH_1: containers transported by SC_1

$C_{1,2}^{1,6}$	$C_{1,2}^{5,4}$	$C_{2,2}^{5,5}$

Fig.7: SH_2: containers transported by SC_2

$C_{1,3}^{1,10}$	$C_{3,3}^{4,10}$

Fig.8: SH_3: containers transported by SC_3

The cost of each gene representing a particular required container is evaluated and the cost of the whole chromosome is equal to the maximum cost between all the sub-chromosomes; see figure 9.

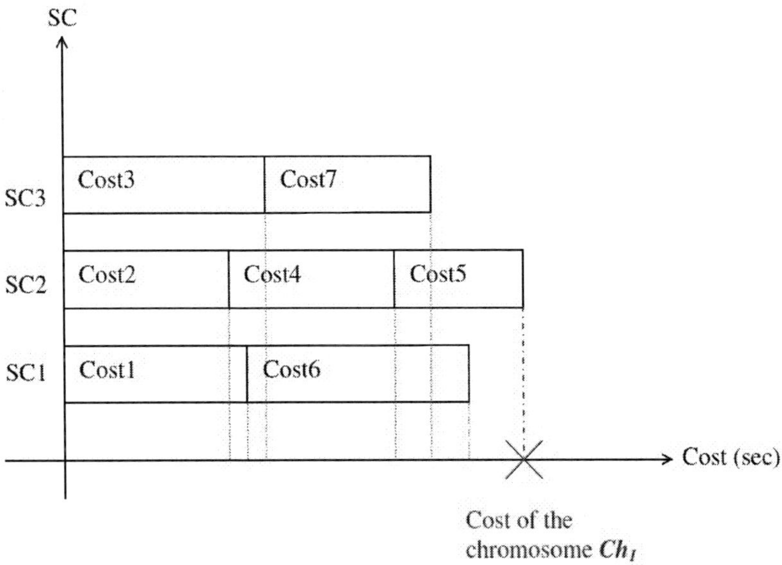

Fig 9: Cost of a selected chromosome

We calculate the cost of the work schedule for each Straddle carrier

$$\text{Cost}\ (SC_1) = \text{cost3} + \text{cost7}$$
$$\text{Cost}\ (SC_2) = \text{cost2} + \text{cost4} + \text{cost5}$$
$$\text{Cost}\ (SC_3) = \text{cost1} + \text{cost6}$$

So the cost of the whole chromosome is the highest value of costs of all its sub-chromosomes.

$$\text{Cost}\ (\boldsymbol{Ch_1}) = \text{MAX}\left\{\text{cost}\ (SC_1),\ \text{cost}\ (SC_2),\ \text{cost}\ (SC_3)\right\}$$

The same procedure is applied on all the generated chromosomes; the chromosome having minimum cost represents the best route.

6. Conclusion and future work

In this study we addressed the routing problem of Straddle carriers at a container terminal. We aim to increase the productivity of the terminal. The problem can be defined by two formulations: one for a single Straddle carrier, the other for more Straddle carriers. Although the former is a particular case of the latter, it can be treated separately.

The GA procedure that is employed for solving the problem of more than one SC is a heuristic and does not necessarily provide an optimal solution.

This paper's contribution to the literature is the development of a new, efficient routing principle of SC at a maritime container terminal, which saves yard operation time and costs.

As this SC routing has practical applications, port operators may look into ways of implementing it. The routing plan principle is useful to the container terminal management for both tactical and operational decisions.

References

Cho, D. W. *Development of a methodology for containership load planning*. Ph.D. thesis, Oregon State University, 1982.

Chung, Y. G., SU. Randhawa, ED. McDowell, *A simulation analysis for a transtainer-based container handling facility*, Computers Ind Eng 14(2) (1988) 113±25.

Kim, K.H., K. Y. Kim, *Routing straddle carriers for the loading operation of containers using a beam search algorithm,* Computers & Industrial Engineering 36 (1999) 109-136.

Kim, K.H., K. Y. Kim, *A routing algorithm for a single straddle carrier to load export containers onto a containership*, Int. J. Production Economics 59 (1999) 425- 433.

Kim, K.H., K. Y. Kim, *A routing algorithm for a single transfer crane to load export containers onto a containership , Computers & Industrial Engineering* 33 (1997) 673- 676.

M. Van Hee, K. M., R.J. Wijbrands, *Decision support system for container terminal planning*, European Journal of Operational Research 34 (1988) 262–272.

Nunes Leal Franqueira, V. *Single Vehicle Routing in Port Container Terminals,* Master thesis, Universidade Federal do Espirito Santo, Brazil. August 2003.

Nishimura, E., A. Imai, S. Papadimitriou, *Berth allocation in the public berth system by genetic algorithms*, European Journal of Operational Research 131 (2001) 282– 292.

Nishimura, E., A. Imai, S. Papadimitriou, *Yard trailer routing at a maritime container terminal*, Transportation Research Part E: Logistics and Transportation Review, Volume 41, Issue 1, (2005) 53-76.

Soriguera, F., D. Espinet and F.Robuste, *A simulation model for straddle carrier operational assessment in a marine container terminal*, Journal of Maritime Research 2006.

Steenken, D., A. Henning, S. Freigang, S. Vo, Routing of straddle carriers at a container terminal with the special aspect of internal moves OR Spectrum (1993)

Zhang, C., J. Liu, Y.-W. Wan, K.G. Murty, R.J. Linn, *Storage space allocation in container terminals*, Transportation Research. Part B: Methodological 37 (2003) 883– 903.

PART 4.

DEBT, CRISIS AND GOVERNANCE

SOVEREIGN DEBT CRISIS AND CREDIT DEFAULT SWAPS: THE CASE OF GREECE AND OTHER PIIGS

NIZAR ATRISSI[1] AND FRANÇOIS MEZHER[2]

1. Introduction

Sovereign debt and Credit Default Swap (CDS) spread levels are, in general, two main indicators of the economic behaviour in a country. The first being the determinant, and at the same time the outcome, of how excessive the spending is over the GDP of a country; whereas the latter, which is directly interconnected with the first, indicates the default risk zone of that country and how much investors are willing to pay in order to be insured against this risk.

It is obvious that Greece is one of the most indebted countries in Europe, with public debt level reaching around 113% of the nation's GDP in 2010[3]. As a direct consequence of their hefty debt service, Greece has been suffering from a severe public deficit that ranged from around 12% of GDP in 2006 to almost 14% of GDP in 2010[1]. The country's account deficit is also approximated at around 12% of GDP[1]. These figures exceed by far any European standard and are even extremely high when compared with similar macroeconomic statistics for a number of developing countries.

However, the case of Greece is not an isolated one in Europe. Many other European countries are facing similar inconveniences with their debt, deficit, and banking characteristics; countries commonly referred to as

---

[1] Université Saint-Joseph (Beyrouth), Campus des Sciences Sociales, Rue Huvelin B.P. 17-5208 - Mar Mikhaël, Beirut 1104 2020, Lebanon - nizar.atrissi@usj.edu.lb
[2] Université Saint-Joseph (Beyrouth) Campus des Sciences Sociales, Rue Huvelin B.P. 17-5208 - Mar Mikhaël, Beirut 1104 2020, Lebanon.
[3] IMF and CIA.

'PIIGS' that include Portugal, Italy, Ireland, and Spain in addition to Greece.

How can one of the European Union's most growth promising countries find itself at the forefront of a public default? Is Greece's case affecting other European countries or simply these ones have their own structural problems? Are Credit Default Swaps contributing to this problem or are they simply its consequence?

In this paper we aim at shedding some light on the European sovereign debt crisis and its interaction with the CDS markets. By examining Greece's and other European countries' economic and debt policies we will try to determine the mechanisms that have contributed to creating and maintaining the sovereign debt problems, with a special focus on CDS agreements. After diagnosing the relevant causes of Greece's economic situation, we will then establish whether these causes are intrinsic to the country's economy itself, or were they instead exogenous and thus susceptible to affect other countries in the E.U.

2. Economic and Financial Overview

The Greek economy was one of the fastest growing in the euro zone during the last decade, as it witnessed an average growth level of around 5%. A strong economy in conjunction with a low bond yields helped the country maintain a large structural deficit without notable incidents. But after the 2008 financial crisis, the Greek economy took a turn for the worse. Greece's two primary growth engines, namely tourism and shipping, were suffering from declining returns. In 2009, Greece had the second lowest IEF (Index of Economic Freedom) which made it rank 81st in the world[4] and suffers from a high level of corruption in its governmental system. By the end of 2009 and as a result of the international financial crisis, Greece faced a severe crash in its economy, leading to a rise in its unemployment rate.

[4] The Heritage Foundation (Index of Economic Freedom).

Table 1: Financing Needs for the Greek Government in 2010

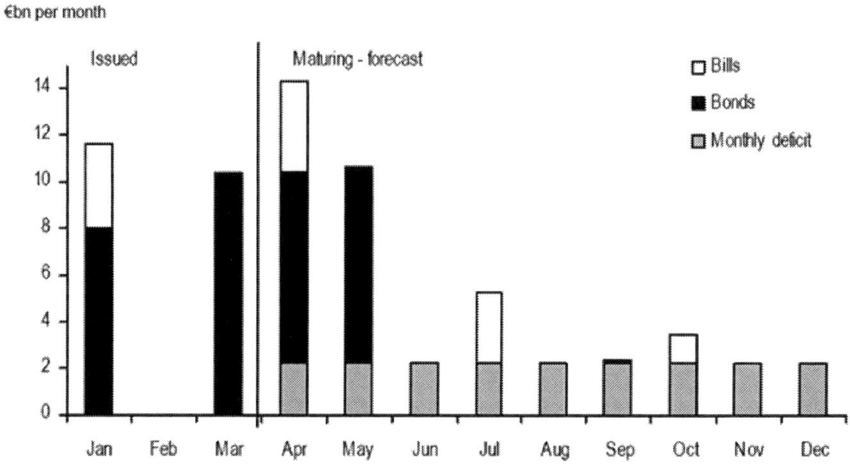

Source: Credit Suisse

Early in 2010 concerns were expressed over the excessively high sovereign indebtedness to other foreign countries. To remain within the monetary union guidelines, some EU country governments were accused of intentionally misreporting their official statistics to mask their public debts and deficits. By early 2010, it was found that Greece had paid many investment banks hundreds of millions of dollars in fees since 2001 for arranging fake transactions that hid the country's actual borrowing levels. In this context, a currency swap between Greece and Goldman Sachs had been a polemic matter which was assumed to have helped Greece hide a big portion of its sovereign debt through complex derivative schemes.

The government has been living and spending beyond its potential of debt coverage and is crucially in need of cutting its spending and importations to control its deficit.

The Forecasted Bills and Bonds that are about to mature, as well as the monthly deficits, which are described in Table 1, are adding a cumulative massive volume over Greece's overall sovereign debt pressure.

Graph 1: Europe's Web of Debt

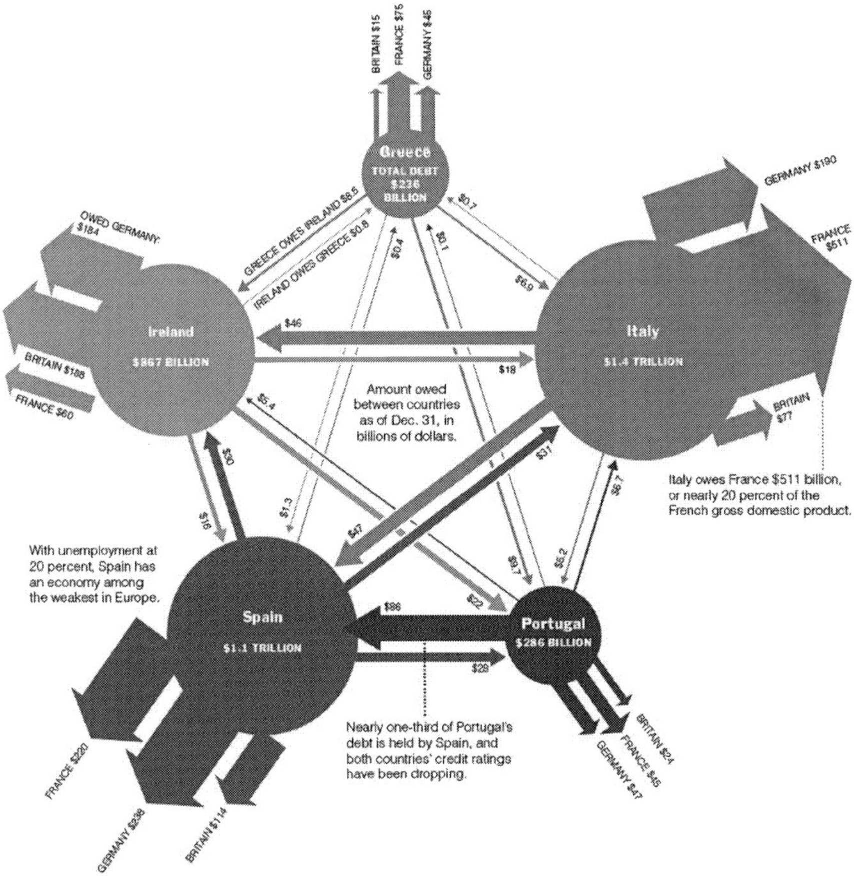

Source: Bank for International Settlements, The New York Times

However, this situation is not an exception in the European context, other peripheral countries are facing similar challenges and risks as Greece with massive debt levels and high downgrade and default risk pressures.

The amount that is owed between the PIIGS as well as their debt towards other economically stronger European countries (France and Germany in particular) is stated and detailed in Graph 1.

Greece has a sovereign debt of over USD 236 Billion with over half of it owed to France and Germany, while Portugal and Ireland have USD 286 Billion and USD 867 Billion respectively. Italy and Spain exceeded the USD 1 Trillion barrier. However, these debt levels have to be put in the context of their capacity of covering those deficits and relative to their respective Gross Domestic Product (GDP).

Table 2 presents the Public Debt, the Gross Domestic Product, and the Debt-to-GDP ratio for each of the 7 European countries. This table shows excessive indebtedness in Greece and Italy, who face serious difficulties to cover their deficits.

Table 2: Public Debts and Gross Domestic Product

	GDP (in USD Billion)	Public Debt (in USD Billion)	Public Debt (% of GDP)
France	2,666	2,125	79%
Germany	3,273	2,526	77%
Greece	342	388	113%
Portugal	222	167	75%
Italy	2,114	2,435	115%
Ireland	229	146	64%
Spain	1,466	733	50%

Source: CIA (https://www.cia.gov/library/publications/the-world-factbook/)

Many countries have crossed the 60% barrier implied by the Maastricht agreement for that particular ratio (Debt-to-GDP) that puts them in different terms with the conditions imposed by the European Union. The Maastricht agreement states a limitation on the budget deficit that should be lower than 3% of GDP and overall debt below 60% of GDP.

What makes Portugal, Ireland, and Spain as weak as the others is their high ratio of debt belonging to the same countries (Portugal and Spain for example owe around 20% of their Public Debt to France) and their high unemployment level (a rate of over 20% in Spain).

On the other hand, France and Germany remained stable, with CDS spreads at relatively low levels, as we will explore below, despite the fact that both of them are at the origin of all the loans given to these five countries (PIIGS), which puts them at high counterparty risk exposure.

3. Debt Levels, Yields and CDS Indicators

One of the indicators that display how close a country is to default is its CDS spread, which may be expressed over a less risky and safer country. In the European context, it is widely accepted and common to use Germany as a benchmark, as it has the strongest and biggest economy in the region. Graph 2 shows the CDS spreads of the PIIGS as well as Germany and France over the period from February till April 2010.

It is interesting to observe on this graph (2) the curve of the CDS spreads of these 7 European countries. Greece saw its CDS spreads more than doubling during this period. Portugal and Ireland also experienced similar spread evolution. Up until April, the rates were more or less stable and not very volatile until the market began to increasingly worry about sovereign debts. We can notice that these economies reached a peak of their spreads by the end of April when a European Union coordinated action contributed to stabilising the situation and calming the markets until further notice. This graph shows clearly how these markets are correlated with Greece, followed by Portugal, having the highest volatilities.

In order to capture the sovereign debts and CDS trends, we constructed a CDS index for the studied countries for the six month period starting on the 6th of November and which takes the value of 100 on that date. We then calculated the daily returns on these indexes. The returns that are very high on certain dates during this period, inform us about the variability of the European CDS indexes. In particular, we can notice that on the 27th and 28th of January, the CDS over the Greek market jumped to over 28% in two days, as well as from 22nd to 27th of April when it went up to about 60% of its initial value. In parallel, Portugal experienced a similar situation, where its CDS spreads were in a very volatile way over the last four months, increasing about 16% for some days. In the last few days, its spread has widened even more (27% on the 4th of May and 21% on the 5th of May) thus displaying how volatile and unexpected this index is on such a market.

Graph 2: PIIGS's CDS Spreads vs. Germany, France and UK

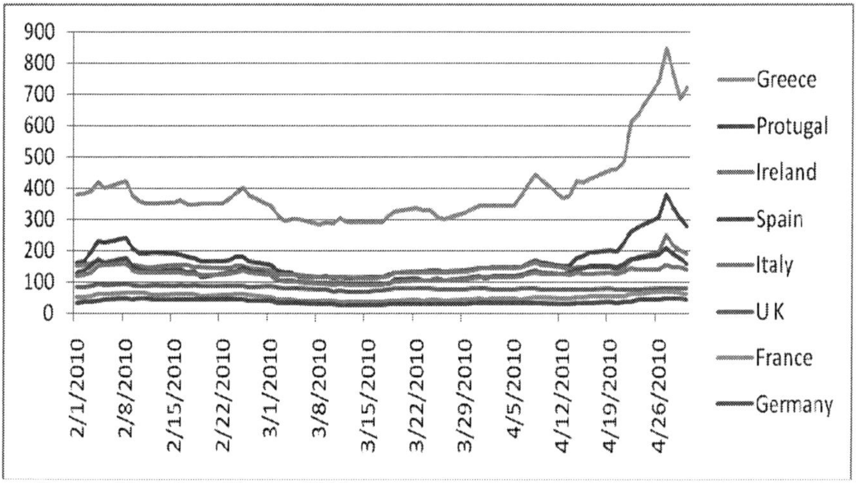

Source: Bloomberg Finance 2010

The higher the index, the more it indicates that either investors are protecting their portfolios, for fear of exposure to default at maturity of the payments, or are simply speculating on any default probability. Indeed, the indexes are so volatile to a certain point that those investors are aggressively buying these instruments in order to speculate on these countries' defaults and without having bonds to cover.

We can notice that over the observed period, the CDS indexes have been multiplied by up to 6 times their original values in some countries, such as Greece and Portugal, and by 2.5 to 3 times in Spain, Italy, France and Germany.

This action is interesting, as the higher the CDS, the more investors are asking for higher yields over the Treasury bonds issued by these governments. This behaviour is deteriorating the situation for the Greek government even more, as proven by its yield performance that in turn affects the CDS spreads.

Thus a vicious circle is created for this country, since it requires more funding to cover its new overdue debt that forces it to offer higher interest rates (yields) to seduce new investors to buy its papers.

Graph 3: Yields on Greece's Zero Coupon Bonds

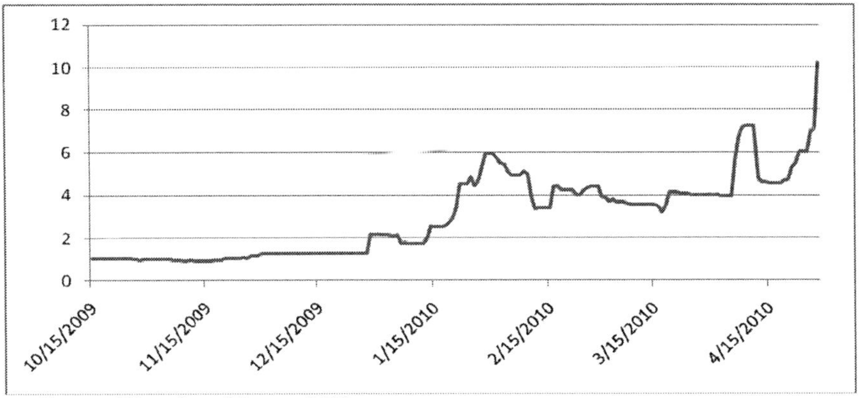

Source: Bloomberg Finance 2010

As we can see in graph 3, the yield line on the zero coupon Treasury bonds went from the area of 1% in November 2009 to 6% by the end of May 2010, with an average of 3.356% over the 7 month period: around 6 times bigger in a relatively short period of time. It is worth noting that this evolution replicates that of the CDS spreads as noted above.

We can notice that 4 out of the 7 countries presented above in Table 3 are averaging more than 1% daily change of their CDS spreads, which reflects a highly volatile fluctuation due to deficiency risks on their overdue debts. Although the average is a good indicator of the current situation, the standard deviation offers a better measure of the volatilities examined over the 7 economies.

If volatilities are to be taken into consideration (standard deviations of the CDS spreads presented in Table 3), Greece, Portugal and Spain are the countries experiencing the most serious uncertainties. On the other hand, Germany and France, although their CDS levels are relatively low, present high volatility due to their exposure to these countries.

Table 3: CDS Spreads Statistics

	Min.	Max.	Average	Standard Deviation	Average Daily Return
Greece	125.74	718.23	285.08	118.71	1.57%
Portugal	46.84	331.38	109.80	55.15	1.76%
Ireland	117.04	198.55	122.46	16.92	0.49%
Spain	54.71	171.92	89.59	22.66	1.04%
Italy	59.87	153.16	90.83	17.42	0.84%
France	20.32	68.82	39.76	13.01	1.03%
Germany	19.66	50.67	29.74	7.83	0.89%

Table 4: CDS Correlation Matrix

	Greece	Portugal	Ireland	Spain	Italy	France	Germany
Greece	1.00	0.97	0.60	0.94	0.88	0.85	0.81
Portugal	0.97	1.00	0.58	0.95	0.91	0.92	0.90
Ireland	0.60	0.58	1.00	0.62	0.55	0.34	0.42
Spain	0.94	0.95	0.62	1.00	0.96	0.90	0.88
Italy	0.88	0.91	0.55	0.96	1.00	0.92	0.90
France	0.85	0.92	0.34	0.90	0.92	1.00	0.97
Germany	0.81	0.90	0.42	0.88	0.90	0.97	1.00

The correlation between those countries is also evidenced by our calculations in Table 4. Portugal for example is correlated up to 97% with Greece. Germany and France, on the other hand, also have the same level of correlation between their CDS spreads.

Ireland may seem an exception to that analysis due to its relatively low correlation with the other 6 countries. The reason behind that may be explained by the fact that a high portion of its sovereign debt is rather held by the UK as shown in Graph 1.

It is clearly evidenced by the data that these countries are influencing one another on a daily basis. Somehow the performance of their market is correlated due to their economic, trade, financial and banking interconnections. These extremely high correlations can be partially explained by the high linkages of these economies, yet they should be more specifically regarded as not necessary fundamentally driven and being the result of higher risk aversion, panic behaviour, or even investors' speculation.

4. Conclusion

This paper aimed to analyse the 2010 sovereign debt crisis and its interactions with the CDS market in Europe. Greece and other peripheral countries, named PIIGS, are facing massive debt levels and high default risk pressures, consequently resulting in high CDS spreads.

The spreads of these instruments, that can either be used to protect the underlying asset risks or by opportunistic speculators, were extremely volatile during our period of observation.

It is clearly evidenced by our data that these countries' CDS were influencing one another, as confirmed by the very high correlations. These correlations can be explained by the economic linkages between these countries, or a result of high speculative attacks.

The more the CDS spread widened, the more the investors were asking for higher yields over the Treasury bonds issued by these governments. This investor behaviour further compounded matters for the Greek and other governments in need of new funding; as proven by their yield performance which in turn affects the CDS spreads in a vicious circle over and over again.

In this context, an open question remains: to what extent are these instruments capable of capturing the real risks of the underlying assets, which is a sovereign one in this case, especially in a crisis environment? In a recent paper, Atrissi and Mezher (2009) argued that short selling these instruments could be dangerous and value destructive, in periods of illiquidity in particular. In this context, it is worth noting that Germany, in the midst of the crisis and in a unilateral move, has put restrictions on CDS trading on its market, recognizing that its irrational usage is affecting its economy and yields.

Another emphasis can also be put in that respect on the role and market impact of the rating agencies - that appears to be intact even after the 2008 crisis - and their impartiality while putting downgrade pressure on corporate, but also sovereign, issuers.

The questions raised above gain even more legitimacy when we compare the shape of the studied countries (Public Debt, Deficit, etc.) with other industrialized countries, and namely the U.S., Japan, or U.K., that do not necessarily present better figures, whereas their CDS are at relative levels that are not reflecting these facts.

Hence, one can arguably question the role of speculation without considering the role of politics. Indeed, it is more than ever that politics matter, especially in countries facing high unemployment and imminent budgetary pressures.

References

Adler, Michael and Song, Jeong, 2010, The Behavior of Emerging Market Sovereigns' Credit Default Swap Premiums and Bond Yield Spreads, *International Journal of Finance and Economics*, Vol. 15, pp. 31-58.

Andritzky, Jochen R. and Singh, Manmohan, 2006, The Pricing of Credit Default Swaps During Distress, *IMF Working Papers*, November, pp. 1-23.

Atrissi, Nizar and Mezher, François, 2009, Marché des *Credit Default Swaps (CDS)* et Crise Financière: Bilan et Perspectives, *Proche Orient, Etudes en Management* No. 21.

Baur, Dirk G. and Joossens, Elisabeth, 2006, The Effect of Credit Risk Transfer on Financial Stability, *EUR Working Paper No. 21521 EN*, January.

Bouveret, Antoine, 2009, The Credit Default Swap (CDS) Market, *Tresor Economics*, No. 52, February.

Bryson, Jay H., 2010, Is Greece the tip of the Iceberg, *Wells Fargo Securities*, February.

Duffie, Darrell, 2008, Innovations in Credit Risk Transfer: Implications for Financial Stability, *BIS Working Paper No. 255; Rock Center for Corporate Governance Working Paper No. 6*.

Jorion, Philippe and Zhang, Gaiyan, 2008, Credit Contagion from Counterparty Risk, *Journal of Finance*, Forthcoming. Available at SSRN: http://ssrn.com/abstract=1321670

Longstaff, Francis A., Pan, Jun, Pedersen, Lasse Heje and Singleton, Kenneth J., 2007, How Sovereign is Sovereign Credit Risk?, *NBER Working Paper* No. W13658.

Monthe, Paul, 2010, The Currency Swaps to hide Greek debt?, *Next Finance*, February.

Rossi, Vanessa and Delgado Aguilera, Rodrigo, 2010, No Painless Solution to Greece's debt Crisis, *International Economics, Chatham House*, February.

Shadab, Houman B., 2010, Guilty by Association? Regulating Credit Default Swaps, *Entrepreneurial Business Law Journal*, Vol. 4, No. 2, pp. 407-466.

BOND SENSITIVITIES AND INTEREST RATE RISKS

SOUAD LAJILI JARJIR[1]
AND YVES RAKOTONDRATSMIBA[2]

1. Introduction

It is common in financial practice and theory (see for instance Hull (2003)[5]) to measure bond price changes, under a parallel shift of the interest rate curve, by means of sensitivities tools as the duration and convexity[3]. These tools (whose precise definitions will be recalled below in Section I) are consequently used by people to immunize a portfolio of assets and liabilities.

For instance the price relative change of a bond position is seen as given approximately by the sum of two terms. The first term is the opposite of duration times the small parallel shift value of the interest rates. The second term is the convexity times the square of this shift value. Such a key approximation (see identity (10) below), using the duration and convexity, is always mentioned in finance text books to be applied for small change values of interest rates. However there is no available references which precise the exact meaning of the term *small* change. Accuracy of the given approximation also remains unclear. Such a

---

[1] Souad LAJILI JARJIR: Institut de Recherche en Gestion, Université Paris – Est Créteil, Address: Institut d'Administration des Entreprises, Place de la Porte des Champs, 4 route de Choisy, 94010 Créteil Cedex(France); E-mail: souad.lajili-jarjir@u-pec.fr

[2] Yves RAKOTONDRATSIMBA, lab. Etudes Numériques des Risques et Systèmes Financiers, ECE group, 53 rue Grenelle 75007 Paris and ESLSCA group, 1 rue Bougainville 75007 Paris(France); E-mail: w_yrakoto@yahoo.com

[3] For Duration and convexity, see Macaulay 1938 [8], Samuelson 1945 [9], Weil 1973 [11], Boquist et al. 1975 [1], Livingston 1978 [7], Lanstem and Sharpe 1978 [6], Skelton et al. 1978 [10], Hawawini 1982 [4], Brown 2000 [2], Crack and Nawalkha 2001 [3], Zheng 2007 [12].

situation is little frustrating, since such accuracy is determining a bond portfolio hedging quality. Indeed using a rough approximation approach may lead to an economic loss, which goes in the opposite direction of the initial hedge intention.

Our purpose in this chapter is to revisit the *duration-convexity approximation* in order to obtain useful accuracies, which are not well developed in the finance literature as we have mentioned above. For instance, in Corollary 3 below, we will see that roughly speaking the approximation order of the bond price relative value (by using just the duration and convexity) is, at most, the cube of the bond maturity times the parallel shift value of the interest rates.

The standard approximation (using the duration and convexity) described above does not include the passage of time. Example 2 below leads us to observe that the bond relative price change approximation becomes erroneous when the elapsed time is not taken into consideration. We will consequently propose in Theorem 6 the right approximation of the bond relative price change, which will take into account both the interest rate changes and the passage of time. A new fact which appears here is that, instead of the current time duration and convexity, the suitable tools to consider are rather variant forms of them encompassing the passage of time.

Next we will observe, by considering a bond with 15 years maturity and face value of 10 million, that the approximation of the bond price absolute change is more subtle than for the price relative change. Indeed, the remainder term for this former depends on the bond face value and may be in general of a large size. This means that we need to make use of sensibilities of high orders. A statement related to this fact is given in Theorem 10.

Among the new contribution brought by our present work is the possibility to get a pointwise hedging error control of a bonds portfolio. Indeed the available results about hedging errors in literature are very often given in terms of quadratic norm estimates. The pointwise estimates appear to have an obvious economic sense in contrast with quadratic ones. However due to the length taken by the duration-convexity approximation analysis, we will develop the bond portfolio hedging error in a forthcoming paper.

As is commonly considered in most of the finance literature development, our results, described above, rely on the hypothesis that the zero interest rates curve has had a parallel shift movement.

In Section I, we investigate the approximation problem about the bond relative change value. Study of the absolute change value is performed in Section II. Further numerical examples are displayed in Section III. Finally, we will conclude.

2. Price relative change due to a parallel shift of the zero interest rates curve

2.1 Fixed income value and their sensibilities

In this chapter, we will focus on fixed income products of any kind, assuming that all future cash flows of the respective investments are known and not subject to default risk. For doing this, let us introduce the cash flow payment dates

$$t_k,\ k \in \{1,\ldots,n\},\quad 0 \le t \le t_1 < t_2 < \ldots < t_k < \ldots < t_n = T$$

such that

$$\tau_1(t) = t_1 - t < \tau_2(t) = t_2 - t < \ldots < \tau_k(t) = t_k - t < \ldots < \tau_n(t) = T - t.$$

Here t is the current time and $\tau_k(t)$, with $k \in \{1,\ldots,n\}$, represents the time elapsed until the respective k -th cash flow C_k is due.

Standard par-bond products are given by the particular cash flows

$$C_1 = \ldots = C_{n-1} = 100cN$$

and

$$C_n = 100(1+c)N$$

where $100N$ is the principal (or face value) and c is the coupon rate.

No-arbitrage considerations lead us to define the price P_t of the stream of positive cash flows $C_1,\ldots,C_k,\ldots,C_n$ by

$$P_t = \sum_{k=1}^{n} C_k D(t, t_k) \tag{1}$$

where $D(t, t_k)$ is a zero discount factor, which can be seen as the current price of a notional amount 1 due at time t_k.

As is usual in finance theory, we will work with the continuous compounding setting for which the discount factor $D(t, t+\tau)$, with $0 < \tau$, is given by

$$D(t, t+\tau) = \exp[-r_{t,\tau}\tau] \tag{2}$$

where $0 \leq r_{t,\tau}$. Very often people are used to thinking in term of discrete compounding method, such that

$$D(t, t+\tau) = (1 + \frac{1}{p}\tilde{r}_{t,\tau})^{-p\tau}.$$

Semi-annual compounding is regarded as the market standard in the US, which corresponds to the case $p = 2$. In Europe, market participants use yearly coupon payments, for which $p = 1$. Quarterly compounding is obtained by taking $p = 4$. Working with continuous discount factors, as with (2), is enough for us due to the obvious links

$$r_{t,\tau} = p\ln[1 + \frac{1}{p}\tilde{r}_{t,\tau}] \qquad \text{and} \qquad \tilde{r}_{t,\tau} = p[\exp(\frac{1}{p}r_{t,\tau}) - 1]. \tag{3}$$

With (1) and (2), it appears that the current price P_t depends both on the tenor: $t, t_1, \ldots, t_k, \ldots, t_n$ or exactly

$$\tau_1(t) = t_1 - t, \ldots, \tau_k(t) = t_k - t, \ldots, \tau_n(t) = t_n - t$$

and on the term structure of zero interest rates

$$r_{t,\tau_1(t)}, \ldots, r_{t,\tau_k(t)}, \ldots, r_{t,\tau_n(t)}$$

at this time t, which is given by the interest rates curve

$$u \in [0, \infty[\mapsto r_{t,u}.$$

Changes of this interest rates term structure over time have an effect on the fixed income securities prices. Investors who do not plan to hold the security to its maturity $T = t_n$ have to take care of the price changes which may represent a significant investment return.

Usually, people try to grasp the consequence of a parallel shift of the current zero interest rates by considering the expression

$$\sum_{k=1}^{n} C_k \exp[-(r_{t,\tau_k(t)} + \varepsilon)\tau_k(t)] \equiv P_{t,0;\varepsilon} \tag{4}$$

where $\tau_k(t) = t_k - t$, for all $k \in \{1,\ldots,n\}$. The task is then to analyse the difference $P_{t,0;\varepsilon} - P_t$ or the corresponding relative change $\frac{P_{t,0;\varepsilon} - P_t}{P_t}$. This last expression has a meaning, since we just consider positive cash flows (i.e. $P_t > 0$).

Pricing of the fixed income product, as in (1) relies on the mixture of various spot rates

$$r_{t,\tau_1(t)}, \ldots, r_{t,\tau_k(t)}, \ldots, r_{t,\tau_n(t)}.$$

Market participants care a great deal about a single yield measure in order to describe the return of an investment with multiple cash flows. For doing so, they introduce the yield-to-maturity measure y_t which is defined as the unique discount rate for all maturities that generate the currently observed price P_t

$$\sum_{k=1}^{n} C_k \exp[-y_t \tau_k(t)] = P_t. \tag{5}$$

Therefore the interest rate change effect may be grasped by means of considering the quantity

$$\sum_{k=1}^{n} C_k \exp[-(y_t + \varepsilon)\tau_k(t)].$$

The results we will obtain below in the context of zero interest rates structure can be applied in this last situation by taking $r_{t,\tau_1(t)} = \dots\dots\dots = r_{t,\tau_n(t)} = y_t$. We prefer to focus our study with the general zero rate structure approach. The concept of yield-to-maturity has several shortcomings that are particularly linked to its economic sense.

The common approximation approach of $\frac{P_{t,0;\varepsilon} - P_t}{P_t}$ is to make use of the concept of duration and convexity. The (Macaulay) duration of any fixed income product whose the price is as considered in (1) and (2) is defined by

$$\mathrm{D}ur(t) = \frac{1}{P_t}\sum_{k=1}^{n} \tau_k(t) C_k \exp[-r_{t,\tau_k(t)}\tau_k(t)]. \tag{6}$$

Note that such a duration depends also on the tenor $t, t_1, \dots, t_k, \dots, t_n$ and the time-t zero interest rates structure $r_{t,\tau_1(t)}, \dots, r_{t,\tau_k(t)}, \dots, r_{t,\tau_n(t)}$. For shortness we just denote the duration by $\mathrm{D}ur(t)$ instead of indicating all these implicit structures on which it depends (as for instance $\mathrm{D}ur_{t_1,\dots,t_n;r_{t,\tau_1(t)},\dots,r_{t,\tau_n(t)}}(t)$). Since

$$\mathrm{D}ur(t) = \sum_{k=1}^{n} \tau_k(t)\omega_k(t) \quad \text{with} \; 0 \le \omega_k(t) = \frac{1}{P_t} C_k \exp[-r_{t,\tau_k(t)}\tau_k(t)] \le 1 \; \text{and} \quad \sum_{k=1}^{n} \omega_k(t) = 1$$

the duration can be interpreted as a weighted arithmetic average of the future cash flow terms, using the discounted cash flows as the weighting scheme for these futures dates. It is crucial in further estimates to observe that

$$\mathrm{D}ur(t) \le (T - t). \tag{7}$$

As usual to take into account the convexity phenomenon, we need also to introduce the convexity

$$Conv(t) = \frac{1}{2P_t}\sum_{k=1}^{n}\tau_k^2(t)C_k \exp[-r_{t,\tau_k(t)}\tau_k(t)]. \tag{8}$$

Similarly to (7) it can be easily seen that

$$Conv(t) \le \frac{1}{2}(T-t)^2. \tag{9}$$

2.2 The classical duration-convexity approximation

From the finance literature (see for instance Hull 2003), the following approximation:

$$\frac{P_{t,0;\varepsilon} - P_t}{P_t} \approx -\mathrm{D}ur(t)\times\varepsilon + Conv(t)\times\varepsilon^2 \tag{10}$$

is well-known and used. It expresses the relationship between parallel spot rate curve shift and relative price changes of the fixed income security.

Though (10) is largely used by people, it remains nevertheless not precise. Text books apply it for $\varepsilon = \pm 0.1\%$ or $\varepsilon = \pm 1\%$. It is often stated that approximation (10) can be used for small values of ε, but there is no clear available references indicating the size of ε for which it remains reasonable to make use of (10). Actually (10) is a result of the Taylor expansion for which derivatives of order more than 3 are ignored (see for instance the proof of Proposition 1 below), so that some accuracy is consequently lost. Among our purposes in this Section is to clarify the quality of such approximation (10) with respect to the size of ε.

Given a value of ε, it may be questionable as to why to make use of the approximation (10), if instead we can just compute directly the price $P_{t,0;\varepsilon}$ as defined in (4) and consequently get the value $\frac{P_{t,0;\varepsilon} - P_t}{P_t}$.

A well-known argument in practice justifying the use of (10) is about quickly getting a value of this relative variation $\frac{P_{t,0;\varepsilon} - P_t}{P_t}$.

Actually the strength of (10) relies on the information about this relative variation when the value of ε is uncertain. Indeed if there is uncertainty about the value of ε, then $\frac{P_{t,0;\varepsilon} - P_t}{P_t}$ remains also uncertain. However in most of the cases, the investor may have more or less of an idea about the extreme value of ε. For instance she/he may suspect a parallel shift of the rate curve by ε, with $0 < \varepsilon < \varepsilon_0$ for some given ε_0. Therefore if the size of the remainder term related to approximation (10) is available from the size ε (as we obtain in our results stated below), then we may assert that

$$\frac{P_{t,0;\varepsilon} - P_t}{P_t} \approx -\mathrm{D}ur(t) \times \varepsilon_1 + \mathrm{C}onv(t) \times \varepsilon_1^2$$

for any suitable ε_1 (though the value of ε is not known). The fact that ε_1 or other values are taken has little importance, since in any case the real value of ε at the future time cannot be determined at the present time t. It just gives the investor the magnitude order of things. The main point here is rather on the error size knowledge of such an approximation. It becomes a valuable tool informing the investors on the possible economic consequences of her/his anticipation in spite of the interest rates uncertainty change.

We first state the exact value of $\frac{P_{t,0;\varepsilon} - P_t}{P_t}$ when the Taylor formula is used.

Proposition 1

Let ε be any real number. Then there is some real ρ such that

$$\frac{P_{t,0;\varepsilon} - P_t}{P_t} = -\mathrm{D}ur(t) \times \varepsilon + Conv(t) \times \varepsilon^2 - \frac{1}{6P_t}\left(\sum_{k=1}^{n} \tau_k^3(t) C_k \exp[-(r_{t,\tau_k(t)} + \rho)\tau_k(t)]\right)\varepsilon^3. \tag{11}$$

Explicit value of ρ is not known here, but the only information available we have is that $0 < \rho < \varepsilon$ or $\varepsilon < \rho < 0$ depending on the sign of ε.

In accordance with the financial practice, we just limit our analysis on the second order approximation in this Section. Though (11) may be acceptable for the approximation of $\frac{P_{t,0;\varepsilon}-P_t}{P_t}$ for small values of ε, it should be very insufficient when considering the difference $P_{t,0;\varepsilon}-P_t$. As we will see in a forthcoming paper, this last expression is crucial in the hedging and risk management point of view. For instance if the precision of the relative value $\frac{P_{t,0;\varepsilon}-P_t}{P_t}$ is about 10^{-3} and P_t has a magnitude of order 10^7 (as in the case of some bonds with time maturity of 30 years and face value of 10 million) then the approximation of $P_{t,0;\varepsilon}-P_t$ by $\{-\mathrm{D}ur(t)\times\varepsilon+Conv(t)\times\varepsilon^2\}P_t$ may suffer of an error of order 10^4. This simple observation urges us to push more on the study of a better approximation of $P_{t,0;\varepsilon}-P_t$ by high order terms. We will carry this task in the next Section. Here our study is just limited to the second order expansion.

Therefore among our purposes in this Section is to get an explicit upper bound of the remainder term $\frac{1}{6P_t}\sum_{k=1}^{n}\tau_k^3 C_k \exp[-(r_{t,\tau_k(t)}+\rho)\tau_k(t)]$.

Proposition 2

Let $\varepsilon>0$. Then we have

$$\left|\frac{P_{t,0;\varepsilon}-P_t}{P_t}-\{-\mathrm{D}ur(t)\times\varepsilon+Conv(t)\times\varepsilon^2\}\right|\leq\frac{1}{6P_t}\left(\sum_{k=1}^{n}\tau_k^3(t)C_k\exp[-r_{t,\tau_k(t)}\tau_k(t)]\right)\varepsilon^3. \tag{12}$$

$\varepsilon>0$ then $P_{t,0;\varepsilon}<P_t$. It means that the price decreases as ε increases. As in (7) and (9), it is clear that

$$\frac{1}{P_t}\left(\sum_{k=1}^{n}\tau_k^3(t)C_k\exp[-r_{t,\tau_k(t)}\tau_k(t)]\right)\leq(T-t)^3. \tag{13}$$

This last inequality with the second member of (12) leads to

$$\left| \frac{P_{t,0;\varepsilon} - P_t}{P_t} - \{-\mathrm{D}ur(t) \times \varepsilon + \mathrm{C}onv(t) \times \varepsilon^2\} \right| \leq \frac{1}{6}(T-t)^3 \varepsilon^3. \tag{14}$$

This estimate yields a practical quality control of the approximation of $\frac{P_{t,0;\varepsilon} - P_t}{P_t}$ by $-\mathrm{D}ur(t) \times \varepsilon + Conv(t) \times \varepsilon^2$. In other terms, our result (14) says the following.

Corollary 3

When the spot rate curve moves in a parallel shift of size ε, *with* $0 < \varepsilon$, *then the error in using the classical approximation (10) does not exceed* $\frac{1}{6}(T-t)^3 \varepsilon^3$

It may be noted that this maximal size error does not depend on the bond face value, and it becomes useful to have a precise idea about the magnitude of the remainder term $\frac{1}{6}(T-t)^3 \varepsilon^3$. For this purpose we consider some examples in Table 1.

Table 1: Value of the term $\frac{1}{6}(T-t)^3 \varepsilon^3$ for some values of ε and $\tau = T - t$.

ε	$\tau = 5$	$\tau = 10$	$\tau = 15$	$\tau = 30$
0.01%	2.08×10^{-11}	1.67×10^{-10}	5.63×10^{-10}	4.5×10^{-9}
0.1%	2.08×10^{-11}	1.67×10^{-10}	5.63×10^{-7}	0.0000045
0.5%	2.60×10^{-11}	2.08×10^{-5}	7.03×10^{-5}	0.0005625
0.75%	8.78×10^{-6}	7.03×10^{-5}	0.0002373	0.0018984
1%	2.08×10^{-5}	0.0001667	0.0005625	0.0045000
1.5%	2.08×10^{-5}	0.0005625	0.0018984	0.0151875
2%	2.08×10^{-5}	0.0013333	0.0045000	0.0360000

For many cases where the approximation (10) is mentioned and used in finance text books, the term $\frac{1}{6}(T-t)^3 \varepsilon^3$ remains small. It appears here that

for fixed income products whose the maturity is five years, then approximation (10) can be used up to $\varepsilon \le 2\%$. For a ten years maturity, it seems that the approximation is fully significant for $\varepsilon \le 0.75\%$. The good validity for products with 30 years maturity is limited to $\varepsilon \le 0.1\%$.
The case $0 < \varepsilon$, which corresponds to a loss, deserves particular attention for the risk management point of view. For $\varepsilon < 0$, the price appreciates, since $P_t < P_{t,\varepsilon}$ and leads to some profit in holding the position. We would like to be able to get a similar estimate as (12) when the size of ε is not too big. Observe that the problem has only a sense when

$$|\varepsilon| = -\varepsilon < \min\{r_{t,\tau_k} \mid \quad \text{for all k with } k \in \{1,\ldots,n\}\}. \qquad (15)$$

This ensures that $0 < (r_{t,\tau_k} + \varepsilon)$ for all $k \in \{1,\ldots,n\}$. Condition (15) is coherent with the fact that if the interest rate depreciates, then it cannot reach the zero level.

Precise statement for the analogous of Proposition 2 is as follows.

For all $k \in \{1,\ldots,n\}$ let us choose nonnegative numbers η_k satisfying

$$\eta_k < r_{t,\tau_k} \quad \text{where } \tau_k = t_k - t. \qquad (16)$$

Then for all $\varepsilon < 0$ such that

$$|\varepsilon| = -\varepsilon < \min\{\eta_k \mid \quad \text{for all k with } k \in \{1,\ldots,n\}\} \qquad (17)$$

we have the estimates

$$\left|\frac{P_{t,0;\varepsilon} - P_t}{P_t} - \{-Dur(t) \times \varepsilon + Conv(t) \times \varepsilon^2\}\right| \le \frac{1}{6P_t}\left(\sum_{k=1}^{n} \tau_k^3(t) C_k \exp[-(r_{t,\tau_k(t)} - \eta_k)\tau_k(t)]\right)|\varepsilon|^3 . \qquad (18)$$

In contrast with Proposition 2, devoted to the case $\varepsilon > 0$, here the estimate accuracy is only stated under condition (17). Having such a condition remains justified by (15), but the uniform estimates for all interest rate maturities, as in (17), seem to be restrictive. In order to get a practical and simple bound for the approximation size error as in Corollary 3, we also need similar estimates to (13). To this end, let us define $\eta = \max\{\eta_k \mid$ for all k with $k\{1,...,n\}\}$. Then we have:

$$\frac{1}{P_t}\left(\sum_{k=1}^{n}\tau_k^3(t)C_k \exp\left[-(r_{t,\tau_k(t)} - \eta_k)\tau_k(t)\right]\right) \le \exp[\eta](T-t)^3. \tag{19}$$

This last inequality with the second member of (18) leads to

$$\left|\frac{P_{t,0;\varepsilon} - P_t}{P_t} - \{-\mathrm{D}ur(t)\times\varepsilon + \mathrm{C}onv(t)\times\varepsilon^2\}\right| \le \frac{1}{6}\exp[\eta](T-t)^3 \mid\varepsilon\mid^3. \tag{20}$$

This estimates yields a practical quality control of the approximation of $\frac{P_{t,0;\varepsilon} - P_t}{P_t}$ by $-\mathrm{D}ur(t)\times\varepsilon + \mathrm{C}onv(t)\times\varepsilon^2$, when $\varepsilon < 0$. In other terms, our result (20) tells us that:

Corollary 5

When the spot rate curve moves in a parallel shift of size ε, *with* $\varepsilon < 0$ *satisfying assumptions (16) and (17), then the error in using the classical approximation (10) does not exceed* $\frac{1}{6}\exp[\eta](T-t)^3 \mid\varepsilon\mid^3$. For $\eta = 10\%$ then $\exp[\eta] \approx 1.1051\ldots \le 1.5$. Since in general $0 < \eta < 1$, then one can assert that at most $\exp[\eta] \le 2.7182\ldots \le 3$.

Therefore the accuracy of approximation (10) can be quickly seen from the smallness of $\frac{1}{6}\exp[\eta](T-t)^3 \mid\varepsilon\mid^3$ when $\varepsilon < 0$, or $\frac{1}{6}(T-t)^3\varepsilon^3$ when $0 < \varepsilon$, and by using data as in Table (1).

2.3 Effect of the time passage

Let us consider again a fixed-income instrument whose value P_t at the current time t is defined by (1) and (2). For clearness, we make a small change in our notations. Therefore the value P_t may be considered as given by some function P such that

$$P_t = P(\tau_1(t),\ldots\ldots,\tau_n(t); r(t,\tau_1(t)),\ldots\ldots,r(t,\tau_n(t))) \tag{21}$$

where

$$\tau_1(t) = t_1 - t, \ldots\ldots, \tau_n(t) = t_n - t;$$

and

$$r(t, \tau_1(t)) = r_{t,\tau_1(t)}, \ldots\ldots, r(t, \tau_n(t)) = r_{t,\tau_n(t)}.$$

It is clear here that we do not make use of the full zero interest rates curve $u \mapsto r(t,u)$, for all $u \geq 0$. Actually only values on points $u_i = \tau_i(t)$, for all $i \in \{1, \ldots, n\}$, are needed.

For the future time $t + s$, with $0 < s$, the interest rates curve evolves to $u \mapsto r(t + s, u)$. At the current time t, the value of $r(t + s, u)$ is unknown and can be viewed as given by some random variable. Usually people talk about a parallel shift of the zero interest rates curve, whenever for some real number ε

$$r(t + s, u) = r(t, u) + \varepsilon \qquad \text{for all maturities } u \geq 0 \qquad (22)$$

This relation means that at time $t + s$, the zero interest rate for the maturity u is the zero interest rate for the same maturity applied at time t but shifted by ε.

To simplify, for the moment, we assume that the elapsed time s is not too large in the sense that $t < t + s \leq t_1 < \ldots\ldots < t_n$.

At time t, the investor is willing to grasp the fixed-income future value P_{t+s} which is the random variable given by:

$$P_{t+s} = P(\tau_1(t+s), \ldots\ldots, \tau_n(t+s); r(t+s, \tau_1(t+s)), \ldots\ldots, r(t+s, \tau_n(t+s))).$$

Assuming a parallel shift of the interest rates curve as in (22) and using the fact that

$$\tau_i(t + s) = \tau_i(t) - s \qquad \text{for all } i \in \{1, \ldots, n\},$$

then in this case, the value P_{t+s} takes the form

$$P(\tau_1(t)-s,\ldots\ldots,\tau_n(t)-s;r(t,\tau_1(t)-s)+\varepsilon,\ldots\ldots,r(t,\tau_n(t)-s)+\varepsilon)\equiv P_{t,s;\varepsilon}. \tag{23}$$

It may be emphasized that $P_{t,s;\varepsilon}$ represents the fixed-income value at the future time $t+s$ when the time t zero interest rates curve is shifted by ε.

It should appear here the reason why we have introduced above the notation $P_{t,0;\varepsilon}$ given by

$$P_{t,0;\varepsilon} = P(\tau_1(t),\ldots\ldots,\tau_n(t);r(t,\tau_1(t))+\varepsilon,\ldots\ldots,r(t,\tau_n(t))+\varepsilon).$$

Let us recall that the investors' main concern is to get an accurate idea (preferably at the current time t) of the difference $P_{t+s}-P_t$ or the corresponding relative change $\frac{P_{t+s}-P_t}{P_t}$. For the practice point of view, it is more convenient to assume a parallel shift as in (22) rather than to deal with a general curve movement. Therefore the main issue remains now to control difference

$$P_{t,s;\varepsilon}-P_t$$

or the relative change

$$\frac{P_{t,s;\varepsilon}-P_t}{P_t}$$

whenever $s>0$.

The classical approach, as we have analysed in the previous subsection, is just focused on $P_{t,0;\varepsilon}-P_t$ and $\frac{P_{t,0;\varepsilon}-P_t}{P_t}$, i.e. just for the case $s=0$. This means that just the effect of the zero interest rate curve movement is taken into consideration. In any case, here there is no consideration of the time passage.

Such an approach seems obviously insufficient since the investor would like to grasp the fixed-income instrument value at a future time (for a given movement of the zero interest rates curve). To consider the interest rate change at the current time may appeared to be nonsense in the anticipation point of view.

Therefore in this chapter, we would like to clarify whether the time passage is very essential when willing to derive an approximation (using duration and convexity tools) of the price change at some future date.

To shed light on the general situation, we begin by introducing a numerical example. For this purpose, let us consider a zero interest rates curve (see Table II).

Table 2: Term structure at time $t = 0$ of the zero interest rates and the corresponding discount factors for 5 years maturities.

In the first column the maturities $\tau_k(t) = \tau_k = t_k - t$, for all $k \in \{1,\ldots,5\}$, are displayed. The zero interest rates $r_{t,\tau_k} = r(t,\tau_k(t))$ are given in the second column. The last column yields the corresponding discount factors $D(t,t_k) = \exp[-r_{t,\tau_k}\tau_k]$.

Maturity	Zero interest rates	Discount factors
1	1.980%	0.980392
2	2.274%	0.955539
3	2.664%	0.923185
4	3.101%	0.883330
5	3.585%	0.835898

Using the term structure in Table II, we would like to compute price and sensibilities of bonds of five year maturity. For this purpose let us introduce the time t i-th moment for $i \in \{0,1,2,3\}$:

$$M^{(i)}(t) = \sum_{k=1}^{5} \tau_k^i C_k D(t,t_k)$$

and the corresponding i-th sensitivity:

$$Sens^{(i)}(t) = \frac{1}{i!P_t} M^{(i)}(t).$$

Table 3: Price and sensitivities of a par-bond with: face value 100, annual coupon 4% and maturity 5 years. The pricing is done at time $t = 0$ where the term structure of zero interest rates is given by the previous table II.

Maturity	0 th moment	1 st moment	2 nd moment	3 rd moment
1	3.9216	3.9216	3.9216	3.9216
2	3.8222	7.6443	15.2886	30.5773
3	3.6927	11.0782	33.2347	99.7040
4	3.5333	14.1333	56.5331	226.1335
5	86.9334	434.6670	2173.3357	11227.0139
	101.9032	471.4445	2282.3137	11227.0139
Moments →	101.90	471.44	2282.31	11227.01
Moments upper bounds →		509.52	2547.58	12737.90
Sensitivities →		4.63	11.20	18.36
Sensitivities upper bounds →		5	12.5	20.83

Example 1

Computation results stored in table III yield the following results:

$P_t = M^{(0)}(t) \approx 101.90, \quad M^{(1)}(t) \approx 471.44, \quad M^{(2)}(t) \approx 2282.31, \quad M^{(3)}(t) \approx 11227.01,$

$Sens^{(1)}(t) \approx 4.63, \quad Sens^{(2)}(t) \approx 11.20$ and $Sens^{(3)}(t) \approx 18.36.$

For comparison, also displayed in this table are quick estimates like

$M^{(i)}(t) \le (T-t)^i P_t$ and $Sens^{(i)}(t) \le \frac{1}{i!}(T-t)^i$ as we have stated in (7) and (9). Therefore, here we can read that:

$$M^{(1)}(t) \le 509.52, \quad M^{(2)}(t) \le 2547.58, \quad M^{(3)}(t) \le 12737.90$$

$$Sens^{(1)}(t) \leq 5 \quad Sens^{(2)}(t) \leq 12.5 \quad \text{and} \quad Sens^{(3)}(t) \leq 20.83.$$

For $\varepsilon = 1\%$, a direct computation yields:

$$P_{t,0;\varepsilon} = 97.3010 \qquad \text{such that} \qquad \frac{P_{t,0;\varepsilon} - P_t}{P_t} \approx -4.516\%.$$

However, using the classical duration and convexity approximation, we find that:

$$-\operatorname{D}ur(t) \times \varepsilon + \operatorname{C}onv(t) \times \varepsilon^2 \approx -4.518\%.$$

As we have presented above, the common approach about the consequence of a parallel shift movement of the spot rate curve is handled by considering the relative value $\frac{P_{t,0;\varepsilon} - P_t}{P_t}$. However, this is not strictly the right way to analyse the effect of interest changes, since the elapsed time may have a non-negligible impact.

To justify our claim, we assume for instance that the term structure of zero interest rates remains the same at the future date $t+s$ with $t < t+s < t_1$. So here, we are in the case $\varepsilon = 0$ and the bond value at this time $t+s$ is given by:

$$P_{t,s;0} = \sum_{k=1}^{n} C_k \exp[-r_{t,\tau_k - s}(\tau_k(t) - s)]$$

and consequently

$$P_{t,s;0} - P_t = \sum_{k=1}^{n} C_k \{\exp[-r_{t,\tau_k - s}(\tau_k(t) - s)] - \exp[-r_{t,\tau_k(t)}\tau_k(t)]\}.$$

Even for the very particular case $r_{t,\tau_k(t)} = r = \text{fixed non negative constant, for all}$ $\mathrm{k}\{1,\ldots,\mathrm{n}\}$, the value relative change $\frac{P_{t,s;0} - P_t}{P_t}$ (for $s \neq 0$) is not zero, though the interest rate curve remains unchanged. The difference $P_{t,s;0} - P_t$ corresponds to the effect of passage of time.

To see that this observation also holds for cases other than $r_{t,\tau_k(t)} = r = \text{fixed non negative constant}$, let us introduce a term structure of zero interest rates given by the model

$$r_{t,\tau} = a + b\tau + c\tau^2 + d\tau^3 \tag{24}$$

where

$a = 0.018431140$, $b = 0.002964843$, $c = 0.000240882$ and $d = -0.0000311906$.

Here (24) was previously calibrated from market prices.

Table 4: Term structure at time $t = 0$ of the zero interest rates of maturities τ and the corresponding discount factors for 15 cash flows payment dates. The same data when the maturities are reduced of $s = 45$ days are also displayed here.

τ	$r_{t,\tau}$	$D(t,t+\tau)$	$\widetilde{\tau} = \tau - s$	$r_{t,\widetilde{\tau}}$	$D(t,t+\widetilde{\tau})$
1	2.16%	0.978626	0.875	2.12%	0.981630
2	2.51%	0.951087	1.875	2.46%	0.954866
3	2.87%	0.917636	2.875	2.82%	0.922111
4	3.21%	0.879331	3.875	3.17%	0.884332
5	3.54%	0.837869	4.875	3.50%	0.843155
6	3.82%	0.795385	5.875	3.78%	0.800672
7	4.03%	0.754252	6.875	4.01%	0.759235
8	4.16%	0.716932	7.875	4.15%	0.721304
9	4.19%	0.685592	8.875	4.19%	0.689365
10	4.10%	0.663801	9.875	4.12%	0.665986
11	3.87%	0.653481	10.875	3.90%	0.654012
12	3.48%	0.658634	11.875	3.54%	0.656986
13	2.92%	0.684514	12.875	3.00%	0.679903
14	2.16%	0.739407	13.875	2.26%	0.730556
15	1.18%	0.837353	14.875	1.32%	0.822047

Example 2

Let us consider a par-bond with a maturity of 10 years, a coupon rate value 8.5%. The current time $t=0$ characteristics of this bond can be computed from this zero interest rates curve, such that the price, duration, convexity and sensibility of third order are respectively given by:

$$P_t = P_{t,0;0} = \sum_{k=1}^{10} C_k \exp[-r_{t,\tau_k}\tau_k] \approx 135.9173,$$

$$D(t) = \frac{1}{P_t}\sum_{k=1}^{10} \tau_k C_k \exp[-r_{t,\tau_k}\tau_k] \approx 7.5066,$$

$$C(t) = \frac{1}{2P_t}\sum_{k=1}^{10} \tau_k^2 C_k \exp[-r_{t,\tau_k}\tau_k] \approx 33.2207,$$

and

$$\mathrm{Sens}^{(3)}(t) = \frac{1}{6P_t}\sum_{k=1}^{10} \tau_k^3 C_k \exp[-r_{t,\tau_k}\tau_k] \approx 103.8676.$$

Considering again the same bond and assuming the interest curve rate remains unchanged 45 days after the current time t (i.e. $s=45$), then all of these characteristics become:

$$P_{t,s;0} = \sum_{k=1}^{10} C_k \exp[-r_{t,\tau_k(t)-s}(\tau_k(t)-s)] \approx 136.4912,$$

$$D(t,s) = \frac{1}{P_{t,s;0}}\sum_{k=1}^{10} (\tau_k(t)-s) C_k \exp[-r_{t,\tau_k(t)-s}(\tau_k(t)-s)] \approx 7.3801,$$

$$C(t,s) = \frac{1}{2P_{t,s;0}}\sum_{k=1}^{10} (\tau_k(t)-s)^2 C_k \exp[-r_{t,\tau_k(t)-s}(\tau_k(t)-s)] \approx 32.2769,$$

and

$$\frac{1}{6P_{t,s;0}}\sum_{k=1}^{10} (\tau_k(t)-s)^3 C_k \exp[-r_{t,\tau_k(t)-s}(\tau_k(t)-s)] \approx 99.7183.$$

Observe that here $\frac{1}{P_t}(P_{t,s;0} - P_t) \approx 0.4222\%$.

For $\varepsilon = 0.1\%$ then:

$$-D(t)\varepsilon + C(t)\varepsilon^2 \approx -0.7473\%$$

$$(\frac{P_{t,s;0}}{P_t})\{-D(t,s)\varepsilon + C(t,s)\varepsilon^2\} \approx -0.7504\%$$

and consequently:

$$\frac{1}{P_t}(P_{t,s;0} - P_t) + (\frac{P_{t,s;0}}{P_t})\{-D(t,s)\varepsilon + C(t,s)\varepsilon^2\} \approx -0.3288\%.$$

On the other hand, a direct computation shows that the value $P_{t,s;\varepsilon}$ at time $t+s$, under a shift of ε of the zero interest rates, is given by $P_{t,s;\varepsilon} \approx 135.4882$, such that $\frac{P_{t,s;\varepsilon} - P_t}{P_t} \approx -0.3157\%$. It appears here that the approximation of $\frac{P_{t,0,\varepsilon} - P_t}{P_t}$ just by using the duration and convexity at the present time t and not taking into consideration the passage of the time, leads to the very rough number -0.7473%. The difference between the real value $\frac{P_{t,s;\varepsilon} - P_t}{P_t}$ and its approximation value by the term $\frac{1}{P_t}(P_{t,s;0} - P_t) + \frac{P_{t,s;0}}{P_t}\{-D(t,s)\varepsilon + C(t,s)\varepsilon^2\}$ is about $1.38\times10^{-4} = 1.38$ bp.

This example shows that to include both a parallel shift movement of the spot rate curve and the passage of time, the correct quantity to consider is the ratio $\frac{P_{t,s;\varepsilon} - P_t}{P_t}$ where

$$0 \le t < t+s \le t_n = T.$$

We first consider the case

$$0 \le t < t+s \le t_1 < t_2 < \ldots < t_i < \ldots < t_n = T. \tag{25}$$

Recall that t denotes the current time. With (25), we are studying the behaviour of the fixed-income future value at time $t+s$, a date which may be seen as not too far from the current time, since no cash flow is paid between the two times. Under assumption (25), the future price is:

$$P_{t+s} = \sum_{k=1}^{n} C_k \exp[-r_{t+s,\tau_k(t+s)}\tau_k(t+s)] \tag{26}$$

where

$$\tau_k(t+s) = t_k - (t+s) = \tau_k(t) - s \qquad \text{for all } k \in \{1,\ldots,n\}$$

and

$r_{t+s,\tau_k(t+s)}$ is the zero interest rate at time $t+s$ and for the time maturity $\tau_k(t)-s$. At the current time t, where the zero interest rates curve $u \in [0,\infty[\mapsto r_{t,u}$ is completely defined, the value of r_{t+s,u_k} for $u_k = \tau_k(t)-s$ is unknown and can be considered as a random variable. As is commonly done in practice, we assume that at the future time $t+s$, the initial zero interest rates curve has done a parallel shift of ε as recalled in (22), i.e.

$$r_{t+s,u} = r_{t,u} + \varepsilon \qquad \text{for all } u \geq 0. \tag{27}$$

The value of ε is not known, at the current time t, however we may more or less have an idea about the extreme size it can take, as for instance:

$$|\varepsilon| \leq \varepsilon_0$$

for some fixed ε_0 with $0 < \varepsilon_0$. Therefore from now, instead of any general future value P_{t+s} as in (26), we will deal with the special form:

$$P_{t,s;\varepsilon} = \sum_{k=1}^{n} C_k \exp\left[-(r_{t,\tau_k(t)-s} + \varepsilon)(\tau_k(t) - s)\right]$$

associated with a parallel shift of ε of the zero interest rates curve.

Variants of the duration and convexity introduced in (6) and (8), which take into account the passage of time, are defined by the following

$$\mathrm{D}ur(t,s) = \frac{1}{P_{t,s;0}} \sum_{k=1}^{n} (\tau_k(t) - s) C_k \exp[-r_{t,\tau_k(t)-s}(\tau_k(t) - s)] \tag{28}$$

$$\mathrm{Conv}(t,s)=\frac{1}{2P_{t,s;0}}\sum_{k=1}^{n}(\tau_k(t)-s)^2C_k\exp[-r_{t,\tau_k(t)-s}(\tau_k(t)-s)] \tag{29}$$

where

$$P_{t,s;0}=\sum_{j=1}^{n}C_j\exp[-r_{t,\tau_j(t)-s}(\tau_j(t)-s)]. \tag{30}$$

Observe that $P_{t,s;0}=P_t$ whenever s is allowed to be equal to 0. As mentioned in (7), (9) we also have:

$$\mathrm{Dur}(t,s)\le(T-(t+s)) \qquad \text{and} \qquad \mathrm{Conv}(t,s)\le\frac{1}{2}(T-(t+s))^2.$$

We can now state our result about the estimate of the ratio $\dfrac{P_{t,s;\varepsilon}-P_t}{P_t}$ under a parallel shift of the curve of interest rates as described in (27).

Theorem 6

Let s, with $0<s\le t_1-t$, such that (25) holds. Assume that for the future time $t+s$, the term structure of the interest rates has done a parallel shift of ε, as described in (27), with $\varepsilon>0$. Then we have the approximation

$$\frac{P_{t,s;\varepsilon}-P_t}{P_t}\approx\frac{1}{P_t}\{\sum_{k=1}^{n}C_k(\exp[-r_{t,\tau_k(t)-s}(\tau_k(t)-s)]-\exp[-r_{t,\tau_k(t)}\tau_k(t)])\}$$
$$+(\frac{P_{t,s;0}}{P_t})\{-\mathrm{Dur}(t,s)\times\varepsilon+\mathrm{Conv}(t,s)\times\varepsilon^2\}. \tag{31}$$

The size of the remainder term is governed by the following estimates

$$|\frac{P_{t,s;\varepsilon}-P_t}{P_t}$$
$$-\frac{1}{P_t}\{\sum_{k=1}^{n}C_k(\exp[-r_{t,\tau_k(t)-s}(\tau_k(t)-s)]-\exp[-r_{t,\tau_k(t)}\tau_k(t)])\}$$

$$-(\frac{P_{t,s;0}}{P_t})\{-Dur(t,s)\times\varepsilon+Conv(t,s)\times\varepsilon^2\}|$$
$$\leq\frac{1}{6P_t}(\sum_{k=1}^{n}(\tau_k(t)-s)^3C_k\exp[-r_{t,\tau_k(t)-s}(\tau_k(t)-s)])\varepsilon^3 \tag{32}$$

Now it is clear, from our above Example 2 and this result, that neither the expression $-Dur(t)\times\varepsilon+Conv(t)\times\varepsilon^2$ nor $-Dur(t,s)\times\varepsilon+Conv(t,s)\times\varepsilon^2$ is the right approximated value of the relative change $\frac{P_{t,s;\varepsilon}-P_t}{P_t}$ when the elapsed time is taken into account. There is also the residual term $\frac{1}{P_t}\{\sum_{k=1}^{n}C_k(\exp[-r_{t,\tau_k(t)-s}(\tau_k(t)-s)]-\exp[-r_{t,\tau_k(t)}\tau_k(t)])\}=(\frac{P_{t,s;0}}{P_t})-1$ which should be considered to reflect the time passage. This term is certain and already known at the current time t once the future date $t+s$ is fixed, since it depends only on the time t zero interest rates curve $u\mapsto r_{t,u}$.

In Example 2, we have seen that this residual term is nonnegative and equal to 0.4222%. This fact may be explained by the 10 year interest rates curve which is essentially an increasing curve. When considering the 15 year interest rates curve, the situation may be completely different as can be seen through the following example.

Example 3

The interest rates curve, as in Table (4), is used again. The par-bond is assumed to have a maturity of 15 years, but always with the same coupon rate value 8.5%. The characteristics of this bond, at the current time $t=0$, can be computed using this zero interest rates curve such that the price, duration, convexity and sensibility of third order are respectively given by:

$$P_t=P_{t,0;0}=\sum_{k=1}^{15}C_k\exp[-r_{t,\tau_k}\tau_k]\approx 183.6462,$$
$$D(t)=\frac{1}{P_t}\sum_{k=1}^{15}\tau_kC_k\exp[-r_{t,\tau_k}\tau_k]\approx 10.9514,$$

$$C(t)=\frac{1}{2P_t}\sum_{k=1}^{15}\tau_k^2 C_k \exp[-r_{t,\tau_k}\tau_k]\approx 72.2253$$

and

$$\text{Sens}^{(3)}(t)=\frac{1}{6P_t}\sum_{k=1}^{15}\tau_k^3 C_k \exp[-r_{t,\tau_k}\tau_k]\approx 337.6496.$$

If the interest rates curve remains unchanged, 45 days after the current time t (i.e. $s=45$), then all of these characteristics become:

$$P_{t,s;0}=\sum_{k=1}^{15}C_k \exp[-r_{t,\tau_k(t)-s}(\tau_k(t)-s)]\approx 182.217\,0,$$

$$D(t,s)=\frac{1}{P_{t,s;0}}\sum_{k=1}^{15}(\tau_k(t)-s)C_k \exp[-r_{t,\tau_k(t)-s}(\tau_k(t)-s)]\approx 10.7768,$$

$$C(t,s)=\frac{1}{2P_{t,s;0}}\sum_{k=1}^{15}(\tau_k(t)-s)^2 C_k \exp[-r_{t,\tau_k(t)-s}(\tau_k(t)-s)]\approx 70.3835$$

and

$$\text{Sens}^{(3)}(t,s)=\frac{1}{6P_{t,s;0}}\sum_{k=1}^{15}(\tau_k(t)-s)^3 C_k \exp[-r_{t,\tau_k(t)-s}(\tau_k(t)-s)]\approx 326.0895.$$

Here we observe that $\frac{1}{P_t}(P_{t,s;0}-P_t)=(\frac{P_{t,s;0}}{P_t})-1\approx -0.7782\%$.

Now we come back to the estimates (32) stated in our Theorem 6. As in (13) we also get

$$\frac{1}{P_t}(\sum_{k=1}^{n}(\tau_k(t)-s)^3 C_k \exp[-r_{t,\tau_k(t)-s}(\tau_k(t)-s)])\leq(\frac{P_{t,s;0}}{P_t})(T-(t+s))^3 \tag{33}$$

which, combined with (32), leads to the more practical error estimates

$$|\frac{P_{t,s;\varepsilon}-P_t}{P_t}$$

$$-\frac{1}{P_t}\{\sum_{k=1}^{n} C_k(\exp[-r_{t,\tau_k(t)-s}(\tau_k(t)-s)]-\exp[-r_{t,\tau_k(t)}\tau_k(t)])\}$$
$$-(\frac{P_{t,s;0}}{P_t})\{-Dur(t,s)\times\varepsilon+Conv(t,s)\times\varepsilon^2\}|$$
$$\leq\frac{1}{6}(\frac{P_{t,s;0}}{P_t})(T-(t+s))^3\varepsilon^3 \quad (34)$$

Our result in Theorem 6 deals with the upward shift of the zero interest rates curve. For the downward movement we get the following statement.

Theorem 7

Let s*, with* $0<s\leq t_1-t$*, such that (25) holds. Assume that for the future time* $t+s$*, the term structure of the zero interest rates has done a parallel downward shift of* ε*, as described in (27) with* $\varepsilon<0$*. As in Proposition 4, for all* $k\in\{1,\ldots,n\}$ *let us choose* $\widetilde{\eta}_k>0$ *such that*

$$\widetilde{\eta}_k<r_{t,\tau_k(t)-s}. \quad (35)$$

For all $\varepsilon<0$ such that

$$|\varepsilon|=-\varepsilon<\min\{\widetilde{\eta}_k \mid \text{for all k with } k\in\{1,\ldots,n\}\} \quad (36)$$

then the approximation (31) remains true. The size of the remainder term is governed by the following estimates

$$|\frac{P_{t,s;\varepsilon}-P_t}{P_t}$$
$$-\frac{1}{P_t}\{\sum_{k=1}^{n} C_k(\exp[-r_{t,\tau_k(t)-s}(\tau_k(t)-s)]-\exp[-r_{t,\tau_k(t)}\tau_k(t)])\}$$
$$-(\frac{P_{t,s;0}}{P_t})\{-Dur(t,s)\times\varepsilon+Conv(t,s)\times\varepsilon^2\}|$$
$$\leq\frac{1}{6P_t}(\sum_{k=1}^{n}(\tau_k(t)-s)^3 C_k\exp[-r_{t,\tau_k(t)-s}(\tau_k(t)-s-\widetilde{\eta}_k)])|\varepsilon|^3. \quad (37)$$

By considering

$\widetilde{\eta} = \max\{\widetilde{\eta}_k \mid \quad \widetilde{\eta}_k \text{ satisfying (35) for all k with} k \in \{1,\ldots,n\}\}$

then we have

$$| \frac{P_{t,s;\varepsilon} - P_t}{P_t} - \frac{1}{P_t}\{\sum_{k=1}^{n} C_k(\exp[-r_{t,\tau_k(t)-s}(\tau_k(t)-s)] - \exp[-r_{t,\tau_k(t)}\tau_k(t)])\} - (\frac{P_{t,s;0}}{P_t})\{-\mathrm{Dur}(t,s)\times\varepsilon + Conv(t,s)\times\varepsilon^2\} | \leq \frac{1}{6}(\frac{P_{t,s;0}}{P_t})\exp[\widetilde{\eta}](T-(t+s))^3 |\varepsilon|^3 . \quad (38)$$

In Theorems 6 and 7, the future date $t+s$ precedes the time t_1, where the first cash flow C_1 takes place.

Now we deal with the case where this future date is supposed to be sufficiently far from the current time t in the sense that

$$0 \leq t < t_1 < \ldots < t_{m-1} < t+s \leq t_m < \ldots < t_n = T. \quad (39)$$

Let us now analyse the fixed-income value at the future time $t+s$. At this moment the investor should be assumed to have received the cash flows $C_1,\ldots,C_{m-1}$. Assume for instance an annual compounding and $t_k - t_{k-1} = 1$ (year). By closing her/his position at time $t+s$, the investor expects to get an amount of $Q_{t+s} + C_m[(t+s) - t_{m-1}]$ where Q_{t+s} denotes the market value of the remaining cash flows $C_m,\ldots,C_n$ as it can be viewed at time $t+s$. The accrual payment $C_m(t+s-t_{m-1})$ corresponds to the interest payment during the time interval $]t_{m-1}, t+s]$.

It is not very appropriate to study directly the difference $Q_{t+s} - P_t$, since P_t is the time t value of the whole of the cash flows $C_1,\ldots,C_{m-1},C_m,\ldots,C_n$, but in contrast Q_{t+s} corresponds to the time $t+s$ value of the remaining cash flows part $C_m,\ldots,C_n$.

The time t value of the cash flows $C_m,\ldots,C_n$ is defined by:

$$Q_{t|t_m} = \sum_{k=m}^{n} C_k \exp[-r_{t,\tau_k(t)}\tau_k(t)] \qquad \text{where as above } \tau_k(t) = t_k - t. \quad (40)$$

It is also suitable to introduce the time $t+s$ value of the same cash flows $C_m,\ldots,C_n$, under a shift movement ε of the zero interest rates curve $u \mapsto r_{t,u}$ as:

$$Q_{t,s;\varepsilon|t_m} = \sum_{k=m}^{n} C_k \exp[-(r_{t,\tau_k(t)-s} + \varepsilon)(\tau_k(t) - s)]. \quad (41)$$

Duration and convexity, as introduced in (6) and (8), encompassing the elapsed time and suitable for the present setting are defined by

$$\mathrm{D}ur_{t_m}(t,s) = \frac{1}{Q_{t,s;0|t_m}} \sum_{k=m}^{n} (\tau_k(t) - s) C_k \exp[-r_{t,\tau_k(t)-s}(\tau_k(t) - s)] \quad (42)$$

$$\mathrm{C}onv_{t_m}(t,s) = \frac{1}{2Q_{t,s;0|t_m}} \sum_{k=m}^{n} (\tau_k(t) - s)^2 C_k \exp[-r_{t,\tau_k(t)-s}(\tau_k(t) - s)] \quad (43)$$

where

$$Q_{t,s;0|t_m} = \sum_{k=m}^{n} C_k \exp[-r_{t,\tau_k(t)-s}(\tau_k(t) - s)]. \quad (44)$$

We can now state our result about the estimate of the relative change $\dfrac{Q_{t,s;\varepsilon|t_m} - Q_{t|t_m}}{Q_{t|t_m}}$.

Theorem 8

Let s, with $t_{m-1} - t < s \le t_m - t$, such that (39) holds. Assume that for the future time $t+s$, the term structure of the interest rates has done a parallel shift of ε, as described in (27), with $\varepsilon > 0$. Then we have the approximation

$$\frac{Q_{t,s;\varepsilon|t_m} - Q_{t|t_m}}{Q_{t|t_m}} \approx \frac{1}{Q_{t|t_m}}\{\sum_{k=m}^{n} C_k(\exp[-r_{t,(\tau_k(t)-s)}(\tau_k(t)-s)] - \exp[-r_{t,\tau_k(t)}\tau_k(t)])\}$$
$$+(\frac{Q_{t,s;0|t_m}}{Q_{t|t_m}})\{-\mathrm{Dur}_{t_m}(t,s)\times\varepsilon + \mathrm{Conv}_{t_m}(t,s)\times\varepsilon^2\}. \quad (45)$$

The size of the remainder term is governed by the following estimates

$$\left|\frac{Q_{t,s;\varepsilon|t_m} - Q_{t|t_m}}{Q_{t|t_m}}\right.$$
$$-\frac{1}{Q_t}\{\sum_{k=m}^{n} C_k(\exp[-r_{t,(\tau_k(t)-s)}(\tau_k(t)-s)] - \exp[-r_{t,\tau_k(t)}\tau_k(t)])\}$$
$$\left.-(\frac{Q_{t,s;0|t_m}}{Q_{t|t_m}})\{-\mathrm{Dur}_{t_m}(t,s)\times\varepsilon + \mathrm{Conv}_{t_m}(t,s)\times\varepsilon^2\}\right|$$
$$\le \frac{1}{Q_{t|t_m}}(\sum_{k=m}^{n}(\tau_k(t)-s)^3 C_k \exp[-r_{t,\tau_k(t)-s}(\tau_k(t)-s)])\varepsilon^3. \quad (46)$$

This result deals with the upward shift of the interest rates curve. For the downward movement we get the following statement.

Theorem 9

Let s, with $t_{m-1} < t \le t_m - t$, such that (39) holds. Assume that for the future time $t+s$, the term structure of the interest rates has done a parallel downward shift of ε, as described in (27) with $\varepsilon < 0$. As in Proposition 4, for all $k \in \{m,\ldots,n\}$ let us choose $\widetilde{\eta}_k > 0$ such that

$$\widetilde{\eta}_k < r_{t,\tau_k(t)-s}. \quad (47)$$

For all $\varepsilon < 0$ such that

$$|\varepsilon| = -\varepsilon < \min\{\widetilde{\eta}_k \mid \quad \text{for all k with k} \in \{\text{m},\ldots,\text{n}\}\} \quad (48)$$

the approximation (45) remains true. The size of the remainder term is governed by the following estimates

$$
\begin{aligned}
&\left|\frac{Q_{t,s;\varepsilon|t_m}-Q_{t|t_m}}{Q_{t|t_m}}\right. \\
&-\frac{1}{Q_t}\{\sum_{k=m}^{n}C_k(\exp[-r_{t,(\tau_k(t)-s)}(\tau_k(t)-s)]-\exp[-r_{t,\tau_k(t)}\tau_k(t)])\} \\
&\left.-(\frac{Q_{t,s;0|t_m}}{Q_{t|t_m}})\{-\mathrm{Dur}_{t_m}(t,s)\times\varepsilon+Conv_{t_m}(t,s)\times\varepsilon^2\}\right| \\
&\le\frac{1}{6Q_{t|t_m}}(\sum_{k=m}^{n}(\tau_k(t)-s)^3C_k\exp[-r_{t,\tau_k(t)-s-\tilde{\eta}_k}(\tau_k(t)-s)])|\varepsilon|^3. \quad (49)
\end{aligned}
$$

As in (34), for $0<\varepsilon$, we can also state the following practical error estimates:

$$
\begin{aligned}
&\left|\frac{Q_{t,s;\varepsilon|t_m}-Q_{t|t_m}}{Q_{t|t_m}}\right. \\
&-\frac{1}{Q_t}\{\sum_{k=m}^{n}C_k(\exp[-r_{t,(\tau_k(t)-s)}(\tau_k(t)-s)]-\exp[-r_{t,\tau_k(t)}\tau_k(t)])\} \\
&\left.-(\frac{Q_{t,s;0|t_m}}{Q_{t|t_m}})\{-\mathrm{Dur}_{t_m}(t,s)\times\varepsilon+Conv_{t_m}(t,s)\times\varepsilon^2\}\right| \\
&\le\frac{1}{6}(\frac{Q_{t,s;0|t_m}}{Q_{t|t_m}})(T-(t+s))^3\varepsilon^3. \quad (50)
\end{aligned}
$$

As in (38), by considering:

$\tilde{\eta}=\max\{\tilde{\eta}_k \mid \tilde{\eta}_k \text{ satisfying (47) for all k with } k\in\{m,\ldots,n\}\}$ then for $\varepsilon<0$ satisfying (48) we have:

$$
\left|\frac{Q_{t,s;\varepsilon|t_m}-Q_{t|t_m}}{Q_{t|t_m}}\right.
$$

$$-\frac{1}{Q_t}\{\sum_{k=m}^{n} C_k(\exp[-r_{t,(\tau_k(t)-s)}(\tau_k(t)-s)]-\exp[-r_{t,\tau_k(t)}\tau_k(t)])\}$$

$$-(\frac{Q_{t,s;0|t_m}}{Q_{t|t_m}})\{-\mathrm{D}ur_{t_m}(t,s)\times\varepsilon+\mathrm{C}onv_{t_m}(t,s)\times\varepsilon^2\}|$$

$$\leq\frac{1}{6}(\frac{Q_{t,s;0|t_m}}{Q_{t|t_m}})\exp[\widetilde{\eta}](T-(t+s))^3|\varepsilon|^3. \tag{51}$$

3. Price absolute change due to a parallel shift of the zero interest rates curve

In the previous Section, we have studied the approximation problem for $\frac{P_{t,s;\varepsilon}-P_t}{P_t}$ just by using terms up to the second order. As we mentioned after Proposition 1, such an approximation may be insufficient for the absolute change $P_{t,s;\varepsilon}-P_t$ when the price P_t is larger than the remainder term involved in the relative change $\frac{P_{t,s;\varepsilon}-P_t}{P_t}$ seen in (32) and (37). For instance, when $0<\varepsilon$, then the estimate (32), can be written as:

$$|(P_{t,s;\varepsilon}-P_t)$$

$$-\{\sum_{k=1}^{n} C_k(\exp[-r_{t,\tau_k(t)-s}(\tau_k(t)-s)]-\exp[-r_{t,\tau_k(t)}\tau_k(t)])\}$$

$$-\{-\mathrm{D}ur(t,s)\times\varepsilon+\mathrm{C}onv(t,s)\times\varepsilon^2\}P_{t,s;0}|$$

$$\leq\frac{1}{6}(\sum_{k=1}^{n}(\tau_k(t)-s)^3 C_k\exp[-r_{t,\tau_k(t)-s}(\tau_k(t)-s)])\varepsilon^3 \tag{52}$$

The quality of the approximation

$$(P_{t,s;\varepsilon}-P_t)\approx\{\sum_{k=1}^{n} C_k(\exp[-r_{t,\tau_k(t)-s}(\tau_k(t)-s)]-\exp[-r_{t,\tau_k(t)}\tau_k(t)])\}$$

$$+\{\mathrm{D}ur(t,s)\times\varepsilon+\mathrm{C}onv(t,s)\times\varepsilon^2\}P_{t,s;0} \tag{53}$$

may be controlled by

$$(\sum_{k=1}^{n}(\tau_k(t)-s)^3 C_k \exp[-r_{t,\tau_k(t)-s}(\tau_k(t)-s)])\varepsilon^3.$$

Particularly the error approximation of $\left(P_{t,s;\varepsilon}-P_t\right)$ is bounded by

$$\frac{1}{6}(T-(t+s))^3\varepsilon^3 P_{t,s;0}\ .$$

For the case $T-t=15$, $\varepsilon=1\%=10^{-2}$, then, as is seen in Table(1), we have $\frac{1}{6}(T-t)^3\varepsilon^3\approx 56.25\times 10^{-5}$. As in Example 3 above, we can for instance cope with 15 year bonds with the price $P_{t,s;0}=182.217\times 10^5$ (with initial face value of 10 million). Then we are in the case of $\frac{1}{6}(T-t)^3\varepsilon^3 P_{t,s;0}\approx 10249.70$, which corresponds to the maximum loss resulting from the approximation.

Therefore, the quality of approximation (53) may be questionable if, for the investor's point of view, a size of loss of $(\sum_{k=1}^{n}(\tau_k(t)-s)^3 C_k \exp[-r_{t,\tau_k(t)-s}(\tau_k(t)-s)])\varepsilon^3$ is not acceptable. In this case, further sensitivities than the duration and convexity need to be introduced in order to obtain a better approximation. For us the better approximation means that the economical maximal loss due to neglecting the remainder term is acceptable by the investor.

Our target in this section is to perform an accurate analysis of the approximation of the (absolute) variation $Q_{t,s;\varepsilon|t_m}-Q_t$. Actually, for shortness, we deal directly with the case $t_{m-1}-t<s\leq t_m-t$ as given in (39), where m is an integer with $2\leq m$.

Let us consider the time t price Q_t of the cash flows $C_m,\ldots,C_n$ as in (40), and $Q_{t,s,\varepsilon|t_m}$ the time $t+s$ price of the same stream of cash flows and defined in (41), assuming the time t zero interest rates curve has done a parallel shift ε. To get an accurate approximation value for $Q_{t,s;\varepsilon|t_m} - Q_t$, we need to introduce suitable sensitivities of high orders as

$$\text{Sens}_{t_m}^{(i)}(t,s) = \frac{1}{i!Q_{t,s;0|t_m}} \sum_{k=m}^{n} (-(\tau_k(t)-s))^i C_k \exp[-r_{t,(\tau_k(t)-s)}(\tau_k(t)-s)] \tag{54}$$

where i is a nonnegative integer and $i! = i\times(i-1)\times(i-2)\ldots\times 2\times 1$ and $Q_{t,s;0|t_m}$ is defined as in (44). Observe that

$$\text{Sens}_{t_m}^{(1)}(t,s) = -\text{Dur}_{t_m}(t,s) \quad \text{and} \quad \text{Sens}_{t_m}^{(2)}(t,s) = \text{Conv}_{t_m}(t,s).$$

We can now state our result about the absolute change $Q_{t,s;\varepsilon|t_m} - Q_t$ under a parallel shift of the curve of interest rates as described in (27).

Theorem 10

Let s, with $t_{m-1} - t < s \le t_m - t$, such that (39) holds. Assume that for the future time $t+s$, the term structure of the interest rates has done a parallel shift of ε, as described in (27), with $\varepsilon > 0$. Then for each nonnegative integer I we have the approximation

$$(Q_{t,s;\varepsilon|t_m} - Q_t) \approx \{\sum_{k=m}^{n} C_k(\exp[-r_{t,\tau_k(t)-s}(\tau_k(t)-s)] - \exp[-r_{t,\tau_k(t)}\tau_k(t)])\}$$
$$+\{\sum_{i=1}^{I} \text{Sens}_{t_m}^{(i)}(t,s)\varepsilon^i\}Q_{t,s;0|t_m}. \tag{55}$$

The size of the remainder term is governed by the following estimates

$$|(Q_{t,s;\varepsilon|t_m} - Q_t)$$

$$-\{\sum_{k=m}^{n} C_k(\exp[-r_{t,\tau_k(t)-s}(\tau_k(t)-s)]-\exp[-r_{t,\tau_k(t)}\tau_k(t)])\}$$

$$-\{\sum_{i=1}^{I} Sens_{t_m}^{(i)}(t,s)\varepsilon^i\}Q_{t,s;0|t_m} \mid$$

$$\leq \frac{1}{(I+1)!}(\sum_{k=m}^{n}(\tau_k(t)-s)^{I+1}C_k \exp[-r_{t,\tau_k(t)-s}(\tau_k(t)-s)])\varepsilon^{I+1}. \quad (56)$$

In the practical case, instead of (56), it may be easy to use the following substitute

$$\mid (Q_{t,s;\varepsilon|t_m} - Q_t)$$

$$-\{\sum_{k=m}^{n} C_k(\exp[-r_{t,\tau_k(t)-s}(\tau_k(t)-s)]-\exp[-r_{t,\tau_k(t)}\tau_k(t)])\}$$

$$-\{\sum_{i=1}^{I} Sens_{t_m}^{(i)}(t,s)\varepsilon^i\}Q_{t,s;0|t_m} \mid$$

$$\leq \frac{1}{(I+1)!}(T-(t+s))^{(I+1)}\varepsilon^{I+1}Q_{t,s;0|t_m}. \quad (57)$$

At this stage, the main question is now about the size of a remainder term $\frac{1}{N!}(T-t)^N$. In this direction, we have data in table 5.

Table 5: Value of the term $\frac{1}{N!}(T-t)^N$ for $T-t=\tau=5$, 10, 15 and 30 years.

N	$\tau=5$ years	$\tau=10$ years	$\tau=15$ years	$\tau=30$ years
3	20.83	166.67	562.50	4500.00
5	26.04	833.33	6328.12	20250
10	2.69	2755.73	158909.38	6723214
20	3.91×10^{-5}	41.10	136678	1.43×10^{11}
40	1.11×10^{-20}	1.22×10^{-8}	0.14	1.49×10^{11}
50			2.10×10^{-6}	2360412270
78				1.45
88				5.23×10^{-5}

Table 5 is just about $\frac{1}{N!}(T-t)^N$, but the real problem is about the full remainder of $\frac{1}{N!}(T-t)^N \varepsilon^N \widetilde{Q}_t$. The choice of the integer order N should depend on the size of ε and the magnitude of $Q_{t,s;0|t_m}$.

Theorem 10 deals with the upward shift of the curve of interest rates. For the downward movement we have the following statement.

Theorem 11

Let s, with $t_{m-1}-t<s\leq t_m-t$, such that (39) holds. Assume that for the future time $t+s$, the term structure of the interest rates has done a parallel downward shift of ε, as described in (27) with $\varepsilon<0$. As in Theorem 7, let us choose $\eta_k>0$, for all $k\in\{1,\ldots,n\}$, as in (47). Then for all $\varepsilon<0$ satisfying (48) and for all nonnegativee integers I the approximation (55) remains true.

The size of the remainder term is governed by the following estimates

$$
\begin{aligned}
&|(Q_{t,s;\varepsilon|t_m}-Q_t)\\
&-\{\sum_{k=m}^{n}C_k(\exp[-r_{t,\tau_k(t)-s}(\tau_k(t)-s)]-\exp[-r_{t,\tau_k(t)}\tau_k(t)])\}\\
&-\{\sum_{i=1}^{I}Sens_{t_m}^{(i)}(t,s)\varepsilon^i\}Q_{t,s;0|t_m}|\\
&\leq\frac{1}{(I+1)!}(\sum_{k=m}^{n}(\tau_k(t)-s)^{I+1}C_k\exp[-(r_{t,\tau_k(t)-s}-\eta_k)(\tau_k(t)-s)])\varepsilon^{I+1}. \qquad (58)
\end{aligned}
$$

4. Practical implications

Now the findings of our results are illustrated through numerical examples. For this purpose, let us consider again the term structure of zero interest rates given by the model $r_{t,\tau}=a+b\tau+c\tau^2+d\tau^3$ as we have introduced in 24 with:

$a=0.018431140$, $b=0.002964843$, $c=0.000240882$ and $d=-0.0000311906$

(calibrated from market prices).

Let us consider a par-bond given by the particular cash flows $C_1 = \ldots = C_{n-1} = 100cN$ and $C_n = 100(1+c)N$ where $100N$ is the principal (or face value) and c is the coupon rate.

As in 1, the price P_t of the stream of positive cash flows $C_1, \ldots, C_k, \ldots, C_n$ is given by $P_t = \sum_{k=1}^{n} C_k D(t, t_k)$ where $D(t, t_k)$ is a zero discount factor defined (in continuous compounding setting) by $D(t, t+\tau) = \exp[-r_{t,\tau}\tau]$.

From now, we refer to *classical approach,* the usual duration-convexity approximation of $(P_{t,0;\varepsilon} - P_t)$ which does not take into consideration the passage of time. Our approach with $(P_{t,s;\varepsilon} - P_t)$, taking into consideration the passage of time s, is referred to as the *new approach*.

Table 6 recapitulates the realized profit and loss under the two approaches in absolute and relative values when the interest rate curve is shifted by ε.

We consider the case of 1,000,000 bonds, i.e. $N = 1000000$. The coupon interest rate c is about 5%. The remaining maturity n is 5 years. We assume that the time to first coupon $\tau_1(t) = t_1 - t$ is 360 days (one year).

The unit price of such a bond is 106.61 euros, such that the present time-t initial value of this bond position is $P_t = 106609701.06$ euros (no shift of interest rate curve and without time passage). Moreover, we deal with the situation where the time passage s is fixed to 45 days.

Table 6: The bond price change and realized P&L after a shift of the interest rate curve

We consider the case of 1,000,000 bonds ($100N = 100 * 1000000$ euros is the face value). The interest rate c is about 5%. The remaining maturity n is 5 years. Time to first coupon $\tau_1 = t_1 - t$ is 360 days and time passage s is about 45 days.

Shift of Interest Rate Curve ε (%)	*Classical Approach (Without Time Passage)*			*New Approach (With Time Passage)*			*Results Comparison*	
	Future Bond Value $P_{t,0;\varepsilon}$	Profit & Loss $P_{t,0;\varepsilon} - P_t$	Return (%) $\frac{P_{t,0;\varepsilon} - P_t}{P_t}$	Future Bond Value $P_{t,s;\varepsilon}$	Profit & Loss $P_{t,s;\varepsilon} - P_t$	Return (%) $\frac{P_{t,s;\varepsilon} - P_t}{P_t}$	Value Difference $P_{t,0;\varepsilon} - P_{t,s;\varepsilon}$	Relative Value Difference (%) $\frac{P_{t,0;\varepsilon} - P_{t,s;\varepsilon}}{P_t}$
-0.5	109 067 311.32	2 457 610.26	2.305	109 650 186.41	3 040 485.35	2.852	-582 875.09	-0.547
0	106 609 701.06	0	0	107 245 971.27	636 270.21	0.597	-636 270.21	-0.597
0.01	106 561 149.07	-48 551.99	-0.046	107 198 459.84	588 758.78	*0.552*	*-637 310.78*	*-0.598*
0.5	104 210 467.81	-2 399 233.25	-2.250	104 897 484.98	-1 712 216.08	-1.606	-687 017.17	-0.644
1	101 868 198.37	-4 741 502.69	-4.448	102 603 411.06	-4 006 290.00	-3.758	-735 212.69	-0.690
1.5	99 581 514.03	-7 028 187.03	-6.592	100 362 464.40	-6 247 236.66	-5.860	-780 950.37	-0.733

The main observations of the results of table 6 can be summarized as follows:

- In all cases (with an increase or a decrease of interest rates), the realized profit and losses (in absolute or relative values) given by our new approach are higher than those given by the classical one (negative numbers in the last two columns of table 6). An explanation of this first result is obvious. The present value of the stream of positive cash flows $C_1,\ldots,C_k,\ldots,C_n$ is higher tomorrow than today. So even if the interest rate curve does not change, i.e. $\varepsilon = 0$, the future bond value may rise due to the time passage affect. In our example, the investor realizes a positive return of about 0.59% after 45 days with the same interest rate curve as today. However with the common view, which does not take into consideration the elapsed time, we have $(P_{t,0;0} - P_t) = 0$.
- In the case of a decrease of interest rates (negative ε), the classical approach underestimates the profit realized by the investor because it neglects the passage of time. A decrease of interest rates by 0.5% has a positive effect on the bond value. However this positive effect is about 2.852% (3040485.35 euros) with the new approach and it is only about 2.305% (2457610.26 euros) with the classical approach.
- In the case of an increase of interest rates (positive ε), the classical approach overestimates the loss realized by the investor. An increase of interest rates by 0.5% has a negative effect on the bond value. However this negative effect is about -1.606% (-1712216.08 euros) with the new approach and it is about -2.250% (-2399233.25 euros) with the classical approach. The higher the ε is, the higher the overestimation of loss is.
- Finally, for low increase of interest rates, the results of the two methods can be contradictory. Indeed, the profit realized by the passage of time can cover the loss induced by the increase of interest rates. In our example, for an increase of about 0.01%, the classical approach gives a negative return of -0.046% (-48551.99 euros); however the new approach gives a positive return of 0.552% (588758.78 euros).

Table 7 recapitulates again the realized profit and losses of the classical and new approaches after the interest rate curve is shifted. As in the previous case, we also consider the case with 1,000,000 bonds, an interest rate coupon of $c = 5\%$, a remaining maturity $n = 5$ years, and a time to first coupon of $\tau_1 = t_1 - t = 360$ days. The difference with the situation in Table 6 is that the interest rates curve shift is fixed to $\varepsilon = 0.01\%$, but the time passage s varies from zero to 120 days. Under the classical point of view, the investor will realize a loss of about -48551.9 euros (-0.046%). Observations of results in table 7 may be summarized as follows:

- With no time passage (i.e. s equals to zero), the two approaches lead to the same result. The investor loses 48551.99 euros after a parallel shift of 0.01% of the interest rate curve. The return on her investment is about -0.046% (-48551.99/106609701.06). This first observation confirms our previous results. The classical and new approaches are identical if $s = 0$.
- For all s, with $0 < s$, the realized profit and loss from the new approach are higher than the those obtained from the classical approach. All relative value differences are negative (see last two columns of table 7). This second observation confirms also the results of table 6. With the new approach, the loss induced by the increase of interest rates is covered by the time passage effect.
- For low number of days (low s), the profit from the time passage does not cover the loss induced by the increase of interest rates, so the final realized return with the new approach is negative.
- However, the situation becomes interesting when the number of days increases (exceeding a week in our example). The investor realizes a positive return because the loss induced by the increase of interest rates is completely covered by the profit from the time passage affect. The higher the time passage is, the higher the difference between results of the new approach and the classical approach.

Now we will focus only on the new approach, as we have demonstrated earlier (see table 6 and table 7) that the classical approach gives incorrect results due to omitting the time passage effect.

Table 8 illustrates the main result given by theorem 6. Our objective is to calculate the approximation of $(\frac{P_{t,s;\varepsilon} - P_t}{P_t})$. We consider again a numerical example and compute the main finding of the new approach. Here we deal with the case of 1,000,000 bonds with a coupon interest rate $c = 8{,}5\%$ and a remaining maturity $n = 7$ years. Moreover the time to first coupon is $\tau_1 = t_1 - t = 90$ days and the time passage is $s = 7$ days.

Table 7: The bond price change and realized P&L after a shift of the interest rate curve

We consider the case of 1,000,000 bonds ($100N = 100*1000000$ euros is the face value). The interest rate c is about 5%. The remaining maturity n is 5 years. Time to first coupon $\tau_1 = t_1 - t$ is 360 days and shift of the interest rate curve (ε) is about 0.01%. In these conditions, the classical approach gives as results: Future Bond Value 106 561 149.07 ($P_{t,0;\varepsilon}$), Profit and Loss -48 551.99 euros $(P_{t,0;\varepsilon} - P_t)$ and Return -0.046% $(\frac{P_{t,0;\varepsilon} - P_t}{P_t})$. These results are compared with these of the new approach in the last two columns.

Time passage s (days)	*New Approach (With Time Passage)* Future Bond Value $P_{t,s;\varepsilon}$	Profit & Loss $P_{t,s;\varepsilon} - P_t$	Return (%) $\frac{P_{t,s;\varepsilon} - P_t}{P_t}$	*Results Comparison* Value Difference $P_{t,0;\varepsilon} - P_{t,s;\varepsilon}$	Relative Value Difference (%) $\frac{P_{t,0;\varepsilon} - P_{t,s;\varepsilon}}{P_t}$
0	106 561 149.07	-48 551.99	-0.046	0	0
1	106 575 349.04	-34 352.02	-0.032	-14 199.97	-0.013
2	106 589 547.39	-20 153.67	-0.019	-28 398.32	-0.027
10	106 703 075.00	93 373.93	0.088	-141 925.93	-0.133
30	106 986 418.63	376 717.57	0.353	-425 269.56	-0.399
120	108 251 991.01	1 642 289.95	1.540	-1 690 841.94	-1.586

In table 8, we present results for positive values of ε (an increase in interest rates) because in practice, investors are rather worried about loss incurred in their bond position. Approximation of the relative price change after a shift of interest rate curve $(\frac{P_{t,s;\varepsilon} - P_t}{P_t})$ is given by 31. The Real Error is calculated as the absolute value of the difference between the Future Relative Change and the Approximation. The Bound error is given by 32 and the Rough Bound error is given by 34.

Table 8: The approximation of relative bond price change after a shift of the interest rate curve

We consider the case of 1,000,000 bonds ($100N = 100*1000000$ euros is the face value). The interest rate C is about 8,5%. The remaining maturity n is 7 years. Time to first coupon
$\frac{1}{P_t}\{\sum_{k=1}^{n} C_k(\exp[-r_{t,\tau_k(t)-s}(\tau_k(t)-s)]-\exp[-r_{t,\tau_k(t)}\tau_k(t)])\}+(\frac{P_{t,s;0}}{P_t})\{-Dur(t,s)\times\varepsilon+C$
$\tau_1 = t_1 - t$ is 90 days and time passage S is about 7 days. The approximation is given by. The Real Error is calculated as the absolute value of the difference between the Future Relative Change and the Approximation. The Bound error is given by $\frac{1}{6P_t}(\sum_{k=1}^{n}(\tau_k(t)-s)^3 C_k \exp[-r_{t,\tau_k(t)-s}(\tau_k(t)-s)])\varepsilon^3$. The Rough Bound error is given by $\frac{1}{6}(\frac{P_{t,s;0}}{P_t})(T-(t+s))^3\varepsilon^3$.

Shift of Interest Rate Curve ε (%)	Future Relative Change (%) $(\frac{P_{t,s;\varepsilon}-P_t}{P_t})$	Approximation (%)	Real Error (bp)	Bound error (bp)	Rough Bound error (bp)
0.01	0.04	0.04	0.00	0.00	0.00
0.50	- 2.35	- 2.35	0.03	0.04	0.07
1.00	- 4.72	- 4.72	0.28	0.28	0.57
1.50	- 7.02	- 7.01	0.94	0.96	1.92

With Table 8, we can make the following observations:

- First of all, our results confirm our theoretical development because in all cases the absolute value of Real Error is lower than the Bound Error

$$\frac{1}{6P_t}(\sum_{k=1}^{n}(\tau_k(t)-s)^3 C_k \exp[-r_{t,\tau_k(t)-s}(\tau_k(t)-s)])\varepsilon^3$$

and the Rough Bound error

$$\frac{1}{6}(\frac{P_{t,s;0}}{P_t})(T-(t+s))^3\varepsilon^3$$

Moreover, the Bound Error is lower than the Rough Bound error.

- Then, the higher the shift of the interest rate curve (high positive or negative ε) is, the higher the error. However, this observation does not matter because in practice the shift of interest rates is not so high.
- Finally, for a low shift of the interest rate curve (which is closer to the real world), approximation 31 given by the new approach is very close to the relative bond price change. This is the most important result. To value their bond position, including the time passage effect, investors are invited to make use of approximation 31. In this case, they are sure that the difference between approximation 31 and the real value of $(\frac{P_{t,s;\varepsilon}-P_t}{P_t})$ does not exceed $\frac{1}{6}(\frac{P_{t,s;0}}{P_t})(T-(t+s))^3\varepsilon^3$.

5. Conclusion

In this chapter, we have demonstrated that the classical *duration-convexity approximation* of bond price changes, under a parallel shift of the interest rate curve, is wrong because of omitting the passage of time. We propose in Theorem 6 the right approximation of the bond relative price change which will take into account both the interest rate changes and the passage of time. This result is very important for academics and practitioners. One possible extension of this work is to deal with portfolio hedging errors using this approximation.

6. Proofs of Results

6.1 Proof of Proposition 1

We introduce a bit of a more general setting than Proposition 1 which is useful in the sequel. To this end, let us define the function

$$f(\varepsilon)=\sum_{k=1}^{n}C_k\exp[-(\widetilde{r}_k+\varepsilon)\widetilde{\tau}_k] \qquad (59)$$

where $0\le C_k$ and $0<\widetilde{r}_k<\widetilde{t}au_k$. For each nonnegative integer i and each real ε, this function f admits a i-th order derivative given by

$$f^{(i)}(\varepsilon)=\sum_{k=1}^{n}(-\widetilde{\tau}_k)^i C_k \exp[-(\widetilde{r}_k+\varepsilon)\widetilde{\tau}_k]. \tag{60}$$

By the classical Taylor formula, for each nonnegative integer I, we have

$$f(\varepsilon)-f(0)=\sum_{i=1}^{I}\frac{1}{i!}f^{(i)}(0)\varepsilon^i+\frac{1}{(I+1)!}f^{(I+1)}(\rho)\varepsilon^{I+1} \tag{61}$$

for some real ρ such that $0<\rho<\varepsilon$ if $0<\varepsilon$ or $\varepsilon<\rho<\varepsilon$ if $\varepsilon<0$. The conclusion in Proposition 1 is just obtained by using (59), (60), and (61). Indeed, by taking $I=2$, $\widetilde{\tau}_k=\tau_k(t)$, $\widetilde{r}_k=r_{t,\tau_k(t)}$ we have

$$f(\varepsilon)=\sum_{k=1}^{n}C_k \exp[-(r_{t,\tau_k(t)}+\varepsilon)\tau_k(t)]=P_{t,0;\varepsilon}$$

$$f(0)=\sum_{k=1}^{n}C_k \exp[-r_{t,\tau_k(t)}\tau_k(t)]=P_t$$

$$f^{(1)}(0)=-\sum_{k=1}^{n}\tau_k(t)C_k \exp[-r_{t,\tau_k(t)}\tau_k(t)]=-P_t\mathrm{D}ur(t)$$

$$f^{(2)}(0)=\sum_{k=1}^{n}\tau_k^2(t)C_k \exp[-r_{t,\tau_k(t)}\tau_k(t)]=2P_t Conv(t)$$

and

$$f^{(3)}(\rho)=-\sum_{k=1}^{n}\tau_k^3(t)C_k \exp[-(r_{t,\tau_k(t)}+\rho)\tau_k(t)].$$

Then applying (61) we get

$$P_{t,0;\varepsilon}-P_t=P_t\{-\mathrm{D}ur(t)\times\varepsilon+Conv(t)\times\varepsilon^2-\frac{1}{6P_t}(\sum_{k=1}^{n}\tau_k^3(t)C_k \exp[-(r_{t,\tau_k(t)}+\rho)\tau_k(t)])\varepsilon^3\}$$

which yields (11) in Proposition 1.

6.2 Proofs of Propositions 2 and 4

Observe that for $0<\rho$

$$\exp[-(r_{t,\tau_k(t)}+\rho)\tau_k(t)]<\exp[-r_{t,\tau_k(t)}\tau_k(t)]$$

which implies

$$|P_{t,0,\varepsilon}-P_t-\{-\mathrm{D}ur(t)\times\varepsilon+Conv(t)\times\varepsilon^2\}P_t|\le\frac{1}{6}(\sum_{k=1}^{n}\tau_k^3(t)C_k\exp[-r_{t,\tau_k(t)}\tau_k(t)])\varepsilon^3$$

and consequently inequality (12) in Proposition 2 is satisfied.

In the case $\varepsilon<0$ we have $\varepsilon<\rho<0$. Because of assumptions (16) and (17), we have $-\varepsilon<\eta_k<r_{t,\tau_k(t)}$, such that

$$0<(r_{t,\tau_k(t)}-\eta_k)<(r_{t,\tau_k(t)}+\varepsilon)<(r_{t,\tau_k(t)}+\rho).$$

Therefore

$$\exp[-(r_{t,\tau_k(t)}+\rho)\tau_k(t)]<\exp[-(r_{t,\tau_k(t)}-\eta_k)\tau_k(t)]$$

which implies

$$|P_{t,\varepsilon}-P_t-\{-\mathrm{D}ur(t)\times\varepsilon+Conv(t)\times\varepsilon^2\}P_t|\le\frac{1}{6}(\sum_{k=1}^{n}\tau_k^3(t)C_k\exp[-(r_{t,\tau_k(t)}-\eta_k)\tau_k(t)])|\varepsilon|^3$$

and consequently inequality (18) in Proposition 4 is satisfied.

6.3 Proofs of Theorems 6 and 7

We first note that

$$P_{t,s;\varepsilon}-P_t=\{\sum_{k=1}^{n}C_k(\exp[-r_{t,\tau_k(t)-s}(\tau_k(t)-s)]-\exp[-r_{t,\tau_k(t)}\tau_k(t)])\}$$
$$+\{f(\varepsilon)-f(0)\} \quad (62)$$

where $f(\varepsilon)$ is defined as in (59) with

$$\widetilde{\tau}_k=\tau_k(t)-s=t_k-(t+s)$$

and

$$\widetilde{r}_k = r_{t,(\tau_k(t)-s)}.$$

This identity (62) is true since

$$\begin{aligned}
P_{t,s;\varepsilon} - P_t &= \sum_{k=1}^{n} C_k \exp[-(r_{t,\widetilde{\tau}_k} + \varepsilon)\widetilde{\tau}_k] - \sum_{k=1}^{n} C_k \exp[-r_{t,\tau_k}\tau_k] \\
&= \{\sum_{k=1}^{n} C_k (\exp[-r_{t,\widetilde{\tau}_k}\widetilde{\tau}_k] - \exp[-r_{t,\tau_k}\tau_k])\} \\
&\quad + \{\sum_{k=1}^{n} C_k \exp[-(r_{t,\widetilde{\tau}_k} + \varepsilon)\widetilde{\tau}_k] - \sum_{k=1}^{n} C_k \exp[-r_{t,\widetilde{\tau}_k}\widetilde{\tau}_k]\} \\
&= \{\sum_{k=1}^{n} C_k (\exp[-r_{t,\widetilde{\tau}_k}\widetilde{\tau}_k] - \exp[-r_{t,\tau_k}\tau_k])\} + \{f(\varepsilon) - f(0)\}.
\end{aligned}$$

The function f, defined in (62), is such that

$$f(0) = \sum_{j=1}^{n} C_j \exp[-r_{t,(\tau_j(t)-s)}(\tau_j(t)-s)] = P_{t,s;0}$$

$$f^{(1)}(0) = -\sum_{j=1}^{n} (\tau_j(t)-s) C_j \exp[-r_{t,(\tau_j(t)-s)}(\tau_j(t)-s)] = -P_{t,s;0}\mathrm{D}ur(t,s)$$

$$f^{(2)}(0) = \sum_{j=1}^{n} (\tau_j(t)-s)^2 C_j \exp[-r_{t,(\tau_j(t)-s)}(\tau_j(t)-s)] = 2P_{t,s;0}\mathrm{C}onv(t,s)$$

and

$$f^{(3)}(\rho) = -\sum_{j=1}^{n} (\tau_j(t)-s)^3 C_j \exp[-r_{t,(\tau_j(t)-s)}(\tau_j(t)-s)].$$

Then applying (61) we get

$$\begin{aligned}
f(\varepsilon) - f(0) &= \{-\mathrm{D}ur(t,s)\times\varepsilon + \mathrm{C}onv(t,s)\times\varepsilon^2\}P_{t,s;0} \\
&\quad -\frac{1}{6}(\sum_{k=1}^{n}(\tau_k(t)-s)^3 C_k \exp[-(r_{t,(\tau_k(t)-s)} + \rho)(\tau_k(t)-s)])\varepsilon^3. \qquad (63)
\end{aligned}$$

If $0 < \varepsilon$ then, as in the proof of Proposition 2, we have

$$|-\frac{1}{6}(\sum_{k=1}^{n}(\tau_k(t)-s)^3 C_k \exp[-(r_{t,(\tau_k(t)-s)}+\rho)(\tau_k(t)-s)])\varepsilon^3| \leq \frac{1}{6}(\sum_{k=1}^{n}(\tau_k(t)-s)^3 C_k \exp[-r_{t,(\tau_k(t)-s)}(\tau_k(t)-s)])\varepsilon^3 \quad (64)$$

and if $\varepsilon < 0$, using assumptions (35) and (36), then as in the proof of Proposition 4, we get

$$|-\frac{1}{6}(\sum_{k=1}^{n}(\tau_k(t)-s)^3 C_k \exp[-(r_{t,(\tau_k(t)-s)}+\rho)(\tau_k(t)-s)])\varepsilon^3| \leq \frac{1}{6}(\sum_{k=1}^{n}(\tau_k(t)-s)^3 C_k \exp[-(r_{t,(\tau_k(t)-s)}-\eta_k)(\tau_k(t)-s)])\,|\,\varepsilon\,|^3 . (65)$$

The main ingredients which lead to the conclusions in Theorem 6 and 7 rely on (62), (63), (64) and (65). For instance estimate (32) in Theorem 6 is satisfied since

$$\begin{aligned}&|(P_{t,s;\varepsilon}-P_t)-\{\sum_{k=1}^{n}C_k(\exp[-r_{t,\tau_k(t)-s}(\tau_k(t)-s)]-\exp[-r_{t,\tau_k(t)}\tau_k(t)])\}\\&\qquad-\{-Dur(t,s)\times\varepsilon+Conv(t,s)\times\varepsilon^2\}P_{t,s;0}\,|\\&=|-\frac{1}{6}(\sum_{k=1}^{n}(\tau_k(t)-s)^3 C_k \exp[-(r_{t,(\tau_k(t)-s)}+\rho)(\tau_k(t)-s)])\varepsilon^3|\\&\leq\frac{1}{6}(\sum_{k=1}^{n}(\tau_k(t)-s)^3 C_k \exp[-r_{t,(\tau_k(t)-s)}(\tau_k(t)-s)])\varepsilon^3 .\end{aligned}$$

6.4 Proofs of Theorems 8 and 9

The ideas are similar to those used for Theorems 6 and 7. We first observe that

$$Q_{t,s;\varepsilon|t_m}-Q_{t|t_m}=\{\sum_{k=m}^{n}C_k(\exp[-r_{t,\tau_k(t)-s}(\tau_k(t)-s)]-\exp[-r_{t,\tau_k(t)}\tau_k(t)])\} +\{g(\varepsilon)-g(0)\} \quad (66)$$

where $g(\varepsilon)$ is defined by

$$g(\varepsilon)=\sum_{j=m}^{n}C_j\exp[-(r_{t,\tilde{\tau}_j}+\varepsilon)\tilde{\tau}_j] \tag{67}$$

with

$$\tilde{\tau}_j=\tau_j(t)-s=t_j-(t+s)$$

and

$$\tilde{r}_j=r_{t,(\tau_j(t)-s)}.$$

Indeed identity (66) is true since

$$\begin{aligned}Q_{t,s;\varepsilon|t_m}-Q_{t|t_m}&=\sum_{k=m}^{n}C_k\exp[-(r_{t,\tilde{\tau}_k}+\varepsilon)\tilde{\tau}_k]-\sum_{k=m}^{n}C_k\exp[-r_{t,\tau_k}\tau_k]\\&=\{\sum_{k=m}^{n}C_k(\exp[-r_{t,\tilde{\tau}_k}\tilde{\tau}_k]-\exp[-r_{t,\tau_k}\tau_k])\}\\&+\{\sum_{k=m}^{n}C_k\exp[-(r_{t,\tilde{\tau}_k}+\varepsilon)\tilde{\tau}_k]-\sum_{k=m}^{n}C_k\exp[-r_{t,\tilde{\tau}_k}\tilde{\tau}_k]\}\\&=\{\sum_{k=m}^{n}C_k(\exp[-r_{t,\tilde{\tau}_k}\tilde{\tau}_k]-\exp[-r_{t,\tau_k}\tau_k])\}+\{g(\varepsilon)-g(0)\}.\end{aligned}$$

The function g, is such that

$$g(0)=\sum_{j=m}^{n}C_j\exp[-r_{t,(\tau_j(t)-s)}(\tau_j(t)-s)]=Q_{t,s;0|t_m}$$

$$g^{(1)}(0)=-\sum_{j=m}^{n}(\tau_j(t)-s)C_j\exp[-r_{t,(\tau_j(t)-s)}(\tau_j(t)-s)]=-Q_{t,s;0|t_m}\mathrm{Dur}_{t_m}(t,s)$$

$$g^{(2)}(0)=\sum_{j=m}^{n}(\tau_j(t)-s)^2C_j\exp[-r_{t,(\tau_j(t)-s)}(\tau_j(t)-s)]=2Q_{t,s;0|t_m}Conv_{t_m}(t,s)$$

and

$$g^{(3)}(\rho) = -\sum_{j=m}^{n}(\tau_j(t)-s)^3 C_j \exp[-r_{t,(\tau_j(t)-s)}(\tau_j(t)-s)].$$

Then applying (61) we get

$$g(\varepsilon)-g(0) = \{-\mathrm{D}ur_{t_m}(t,s)\times\varepsilon + \mathrm{C}onv_{t_m}(t,s)\times\varepsilon^2\}Q_{t,s;0|t_m}$$
$$-\frac{1}{6}(\sum_{k=1}^{n}(\tau_k(t)-s)^3 C_k \exp[-(r_{t,(\tau_k(t)-s)}+\rho)(\tau_k(t)-s)])\varepsilon^3. \qquad (68)$$

If $0<\varepsilon$ then, as in the proof of Proposition 2, we have

$$|-\frac{1}{6}(\sum_{k=m}^{n}(\tau_k(t)-s)^3 C_k \exp[-(r_{t,(\tau_k(t)-s)}+\rho)(\tau_k(t)-s)])\varepsilon^3| \leq$$
$$\frac{1}{6}(\sum_{k=m}^{n}(\tau_k(t)-s)^3 C_k \exp[-r_{t,(\tau_k(t)-s)}(\tau_k(t)-s)])\varepsilon^3 \qquad (69)$$

and if $\varepsilon<0$, using assumptions (35) and (36), then as in the proof of Proposition 4, we get

$$|-\frac{1}{6}(\sum_{k=m}^{n}(\tau_k(t)-s)^3 C_k \exp[-(r_{t,(\tau_k(t)-s)}+\rho)(\tau_k(t)-s)])\varepsilon^3| \leq$$
$$\frac{1}{6}(\sum_{k=m}^{n}(\tau_k(t)-s)^3 C_k \exp[-(r_{t,(\tau_k(t)-s)}-\eta_k)(\tau_k(t)-s)])|\varepsilon|^3. \qquad (70)$$

The main ingredients which lead to the conclusions in Theorem 7 and 8 rely on (66), (68), (69) and (70). The remaining details, similar those used in proofs of Theorems 6 and 7, are left to the readers.

6.5 Proofs of Theorems 10 and 11

The ideas are similar to those used for Theorems 8 and 9. Some elements we have introduced above will be useful here. It is the case of the function g defined in (67), whose the derivative of high order i, for any nonnegative integers, is given by

$$g^{(i)}(\varepsilon) = \sum_{j=m}^{n}(-(\tau_j(t)-s))^i C_j \exp[-(r_{t,(\tau_j(t)-s)}+\varepsilon)(\tau_j(t)-s)]$$

such that

$$g^{(i)}(0)=\sum_{j=m}^{n}(-(\tau_j(t)-s))^i C_j \exp[-r_{t,(\tau_j(t)-s)}(\tau_j(t)-s)]=i!\mathrm{Sens}_{t_m}^{(i)}(t,s)Q_{t,s;0|t_m}.$$

Then applying the Taylor formula as in (61) we get

$$g(\varepsilon)-g(0)=\{\sum_{i=1}^{I}\mathrm{Sens}_{t_m}^{(i)}(t,s)\varepsilon^i\}Q_{t,s;0|t_m}$$

$$+\frac{1}{(I+1)!}(\sum_{k=m}^{n}(-(\tau_k(t)-s))^{I+1}C_k \exp[-(r_{t,(\tau_k(t)-s)}+\rho)(\tau_k(t)-s)])\varepsilon^{I+1}. \quad (71)$$

If $0<\varepsilon$ then, as in the proof of Proposition 2,

$$\exp[-(r_{t,(\tau_k(t)-s)}+\rho)(\tau_k(t)-s)]<\exp[-r_{t,(\tau_k(t)-s)}(\tau_k(t)-s)] \quad (72)$$

and if $\varepsilon<0$, using assumptions (35) and (36), then as in the proof of Proposition 4

$$\exp[-(r_{t,(\tau_k(t)-s)}+\rho)(\tau_k(t)-s)]<\exp[-(r_{t,(\tau_k(t)-s)}-\eta_k)(\tau_k(t)-s)]. \quad (73)$$

The main ingredients which lead to the conclusions in Theorem 10 and 11 rely on (66), (71), (72) and (73). For instance with $0<\varepsilon$, the estimate (56), in Theorem 10 is satisfied since

$$|(Q_{t,s;\varepsilon|t_m}-Q_t)$$

$$-\{\sum_{k=m}^{n}C_k(\exp[-r_{t,\tau_k(t)-s}(\tau_k(t)-s)]-\exp[-r_{t,\tau_k(t)}\tau_k(t)])\}$$

$$-\{\sum_{i=1}^{I}\mathrm{Sens}_{t_m}^{(i)}(t,s)\varepsilon^i\}Q_{t,s;0|t_m}|$$

$$|\frac{1}{(I+1)!}(\sum_{k=m}^{n}(-(\tau_k(t)-s))^{I+1}C_k \exp[-r_{t,\tau_k(t)-s}(\tau_k(t)-s)])\varepsilon^{I+1}|$$

$$\leq\frac{1}{(I+1)!}(\sum_{k=m}^{n}(\tau_k(t)-s)^{I+1}C_k \exp[-r_{t,\tau_k(t)-s}(\tau_k(t)-s)])\varepsilon^{I+1}.$$

References

Boquist J.A., G.A. Racette, and G.G. Schlarbaum, Duration and risk assessment for bonds and common stocks, Journal of Finance (1975), no. 30, 1360-5.

Brown G.R., Duration and risk, JRER (2000), no. 3, 337-56.

Crack T.F. and S.K. Nawalkha, Common misunderstandings concerning duration and convexity, Journal of Applied Finance (2001), 82-92.

Hawawini G., Bond duration and immunization: Early developments and recent contributions, New York Garland Publishing (1982).

Hull J.C., Options, futures, & other derivatives, Prentice Hall, Pearson Education International (2009).

Lanstem R. and W.F. Sharpe, Duration and security risk, Journal of Financial and Quantitative Analysis (1978), 653-68.

Livingston M., Duration and risk assessment for bonds and common stocks: A note, Journal of Finance (1978), no. 33, 293-95.

Macaulay F., The movements of interest rates: bond yields and stock prices in the United States since 1856, New York National Bureau of Economic Research (1938).

Samuelson P.A., The effect of interest rate increases on the banking system, The American Economic Review 35 (1945), no. 1, 16-27.

Skelton J., J. Ingersoll and R. Weil, Duration forty years later, Journal of Financial and Quantitative Analysis (1978), 621-50.

Weil R.L., Macaulay's duration: An appreciation, The Journal of Business 46 (1973), no. 4, 589-92.

Zheng H., Macaulay durations for nonparallel shifts, Annals of Operations Research (2007), 179-91.

CREDIT CRISIS AND THE COLLAPSE OF ARS MARKET

DEV GANDHI[1], PRAN MANGA[1] AND SAMIR SAADI[2]

1. Introduction

Auction-rate securities are long-term instruments with interest rates that are reset at periodic intervals through Dutch auctions. Marketed as safe and cash-equivalent investments, auction-rate securities attracted both investors and borrowers. Retail and institutional investors were attracted to ARS because they represented high-grade short-term paper with a higher yield than Treasury bills. Long-term borrowers, such as municipalities, hospitals and student loan authorities, were also attracted to the ARS market because, for a time, auction rate securities allowed them to issue long-term debt at rates much lower than on comparable long-term fixed-rate securities. The auction-rate securities market grew rapidly from 2001-2002 until 2006. It then experienced a wave of failures in 2007 and 2008. Both growth and decline were stimulated by an interaction of factors.

The auction rate securities market came into being in 1884 but grew rapidly after the decline in technology stock prices in 2001-2002. The U.S. federal funds rate had been as low as 1 percent by late 2002, and because of the historically low yields on high quality short-term bonds, investors were seeking higher-rate investment opportunities. At the same time, long-term interest rates remained considerably higher, and long-term borrowers were seeking to reduce the interest rates they were paying. Investment bankers were seeking to profit from serving both types of client, and proposed auction rate securities as a means of achieving their goals.

[1] Telfer School of Management, University of Ottawa.
[2] Queen's School of Business, Queen's University.

During the heyday of the scheme, investors were attracted to auction rate securities because they represented high-grade short-term paper with a higher yield than Treasury bills. Long-term borrowers (municipalities, hospitals, utilities, port authorities, housing finance agencies, student loan authorities and universities) - were attracted to the market because, for a time, auction rate securities allowed them to issue 20-year term debt at rates much lower than 20-year fixed rates.

The key to the market's success involved issuing bonds with long maturities, but with coupons that reset frequently, say every four or five weeks through a Dutch auction. The basic difficulty with the scheme was that borrowers were using the short end of the market to finance long term assets, and were therefore vulnerable to interest rate increases. However, borrowers could offset interest rate risk by using instruments like interest rate caps, and initially this type of insurance was not costly. At the same time, borrowers might be vulnerable to reduced credit ratings stemming from any cash flow problems that interest rate increases could bring. But this risk could be covered by default insurance, also not costly in the earlier stages of the market's development.

The ARS market worked relatively smoothly until late-2007, when defaults on subprime mortgages soared and started spreading into the mortgage securitization market. When the subprime market eventually collapsed in February 2008, additional attempts to raise funds using auction rate securities failed. The resultant collapse of the ARS market trigged a severe backlash against a number of major banks and investment firms, with both government agencies and investors accusing the former of fraudulent misconduct and of misrepresenting the nature of auction rate securities and their risks.

This paper analyses the ARS market with particular emphasis on its origins and on the factors that caused its collapse. First, we provide a general background on the ARS market in Section 2. Section 3 describes the evolution of the ARS market. Section 4 discusses the reasons behind the collapse. Section 5 provides an update on investors' attempts to recoup their losses; and Section 6 has the conclusions.

2. Defining Auction-Rate Securities

Essentially, auction rate securities represented long-term floating rate securities. They are issued in the form of municipal bonds, corporate bonds, and preferred stocks with interest rates or dividend yields that are reset periodically through Dutch auctions that establish the lowest rate capable of clearing the market. The auctions, run by the underwriters, were typically held every 7, 14, 28, 35, 49 days, or six months. Since they were first created in 1984, auction-rate securities were regarded as an attractive investment for investors. Thanks to the auction process and given that ARS were traded and callable at par, the market allowed investors to sell their securities and hence recover the face value of their investment. ARS underwriters marketed auction-rate securities as safe and liquid cash alternatives that provided higher returns than several other comparable investments such as certificates of deposit, money market funds, and Variable Rate Demand Obligations (VRDO). These features of ARSs help explain the growth of the market over the last two decades to a total of some $330 billion in early 2008. At the same time, the auction-rate securities market would not have grown so large if it were not also an attractive source of funding. Indeed, auction-rate securities allow issuers to obtain long-term financing at short-term rates. Auction-rate securities are generally more attractive than similar long-term financing alternatives, such as the VRDO for which interest rate is also reset periodically.

There are two types of ARS: bonds with long-term maturities and perpetual preferred equity with a cash dividend. Auction-rate bonds represent the major portion of the auction-rate market. The approximately $165 billion in bonds outstanding at the end of 2007 was nearly 76% of the market. These bonds, often tax-exempt, are issued by municipalities (hence the name "munis"), student-loan authorities, states and state agencies, cities, museums, and many others. Sometimes, several small borrowers get together to make a large issue. By far the most dominant groups of issuers are municipalities (roughly 50% of the market) and student-loan authorities (nearly 34% of the market).

Unlike auction rate bonds, perpetual preferred equities are not issued by government-related issuers, rather by closed-end funds. Closed-end funds' shares are typically traded on a stock exchange. The assets of a closed-end fund may be invested in stocks, bonds, or a combination of both. As of the end of 2007, the total value of auction preferred stocks issued by closed-end funds is estimated at about $63 billion, with nearly 48% of it being tax-exempt. It is noteworthy that unlike auction rate bonds, preferred stocks are not insured and generally have higher default risk. Over the past decades the leading underwriters of auction-rate securities have been Goldman Sachs, Morgan Stanley, UBS, Lehman Brothers, JPMorgan,

Citigroup, and Bank of America. The usual issue size of auction-rate securities is $25 million.

3. Evolution of the ARS Market

In the early 1980s, when financial institutions were striving to engineer new financial products that would lower their borrowing cost caused by high inflation, an investment banker at Lehman Brothers, Ronald Gallatin, invented auction-rate securities. According to Carow, Erwin, and McConnell (1999), during that period, financial institutions in the U.S. invented about 26 new financial instruments. With the exception of a few, including the ARS, most of these new and complex instruments were short-lived. The ARS main objective was to allow financing long-term debt at short-term interest rates that are reset weekly or monthly through an auction process. In 1984, American Express issued the first auction-rate securities: A $350 million issue of money-market preferred shares with a minimum purchase of $500,000. The dividends rate was reset at auction every 49 days. Following American Express, other banks, such as Citicorp (currently Citigoup) and MCorp, started selling ARS. Although the first ARS were auction-rate preferred shares, the concept soon spread to auction-rate bonds, with the first being issued on 1985 by Warrick Country to finance the Southern Indiana Gas and Eclectic Company (McConnell and Saretto, 2008).

A year after the emergence of the auction-rate securities, US Steel issued the first insured ARS. The insurance company provides coverage to ARS holders against default risk associated with the issue. In case of default, the insurance company pays principal and interest to holders of the defaulted ARS. While ARS insurance boosted both issuers' credit rating as well as investors' confidence, it did not however avert auction failure. Indeed, in 1987 the auction of the MCorp's $62.5 million preferred stock issue failed when not enough investors showed interest, marking the first auction failure in ARS market. As a result, the dividend rate on MCorp's ARS soared to a penalty rate of 13%. Subsequent auction failures in the 1990s led several large ARS issuers, such as Citigroup and JPMorgan Chase & Co, to retire their ARS as their borrowing costs surpassed 14%. These failures made investors realize that neither an AAA bond rating nor the insurance company can prevent an auction failure. In 1995, investors' confidence in ARS market wobbled again due to the SEC accusation against Lehman of manipulating 13 American Express auctions. The company agreed to pay an $850,000 fine, but without admitting or denying any misconduct.

The market took off after 2000, as the public sector started using ARS as a major source of funding. In fact, the annual sales of municipal auction-rate bonds grew from $9.56 billion to more than $40 billion in 2003 and 2004. The percentage of insured ARS has also increased, fuelling ARS market growth. In 2006, however, the annual sales of auction-rate municipal bond shrunk to about $30 billion following an SEC investigation on how ARS auctions are conducted. The critics complain that brokers/dealers controlled all information and influenced the bids, which of course violated the basic rules of auction process. Moreover, given that brokers/dealers were not required to guarantee against an auction failure, investors may have been oblivious of the true liquidity risk associated with the ARS. Brokers/dealers argued that they were trying to prevent auction failure, which would potentially impair all market participants (i.e. investors, issuers, underwriters). The SEC investigation however uncovered serious "violative practices" that go beyond the aforementioned practice and which resulted in 15 brokers/dealers being fined a total of $13.8 million for market manipulation (for more details on this issue see Neave and Saadi, 2010). Despite all of these events, the ARS market as a whole continued to expand until February 2008, at which time it froze and collapsed, as described in the following section.

4. The Collapse of the ARS Market

Although the ARS market had experienced some downturns between 1984 (when the first ASR was issued) and the end of 2006, the collapse of the market in 2008 was completely unexpected. While only 13 auction failures were recorded during the 1984-2006 period, over 1,000 occurred in the first week of February 2008 alone. Indeed, the market broke down during the week of February 13, 2008, when ARS brokers/dealers simultaneously withdrew their support for the auctions, leaving thousands of investors stranded, unable to sell, collect on, or otherwise convert their securities.

While there are different views on what caused the collapse of the ARS market, there is a consensus that the recent credit crisis was the main stimulus, as ARS market conditions have changed dramatically since the middle of 2007.

In what follows, we present the different factors that have been proposed to explain the collapse of the ARS markets. We believe, however, that the simultaneous rising of these factors (due to credit crisis) has led to the formation of a "perfect storm" that caused the market to fail. In other words, the ARS collapse should not be attributed to one factor or another, but to the accumulation of different factors.

Trouble with Monoline Insurers: As default on subprime mortgages soared and start spreading into the mortgage securitization market by late 2007, investors became wary about the ability of insurers to cover losses associated with the auction rate bonds. Despite the fact that credit ratings of ARS issuers remained high; investors were concerned about the potential credit downgrading of monoline insurers. Indeed, the demand for ARS started to decline sharply because of the concerns of credit downgrading of the two largest insurers in the auction-rate market (MBIA Inc. and Ambac Financial Group Inc.), which at that time had AAA ratings.

Brokers/Dealers Liquidity Problem: Prior to the credit crisis, brokers/dealers often bid themselves in ARS auctions to avert auction failure, although they are not obligated to do so. However, after losing hundreds of billions of dollars on subprime mortgages, broker/dealers stopped bidding at auctions for their own accounts. This led to more auction failure and a rise of the borrowing cost for ARS issuers as ARS rates jumped to the maximum level.

Increase in Demand and Decrease in Supply: As the word of the auction failure spread, ARS were as perceived as risky and illiquid investment, leading to further decline in demand for ARS. Moreover, the supply of ARS increased as holders raced to sell their ARS, creating even greater pressure to find buyers to make the auctions succeed.

Deceptive Practice by Brokers/Dealers: Selling pressure from ARS holders was trigged not only by the fear of getting stuck with an illiquid security, but also by the fear that brokers/dealers would engage in deceptive practices. Although 2006 SEC investigation uncovered some serious "violative practices", it did not lead to implementation of a legal framework that would regulate the ARS market and in particular the auction process.

5. Investors Looking for Way Out

When the ARS market collapsed in February 2008, thousands of retail and institutional investors found their funds frozen. This has trigged a panoply of lawsuits filed against brokers and underwriters of auction-rate securities for claiming that the securities were safe and liquid investments. The lawsuits aimed to push brokers and underwriters to repurchase ARS from eligible investors who bought the securities before the collapse of the market. Several brokerage firms stressed, however, that lawsuits should target ARS underwriters only, claiming that they were also misled by underwriters who had withdrawn support and stopped bidding at the auctions. However, this argument was not enough to prevent brokers from purchasing billions of dollars worth of ARS from eligible investors. For instance, Stifel Nicolaus & Co, a regional brokerage and financial services firm based in St. Louis, reached an agreement on December 2009 through which the firm will return about $180 million to its 1,200 nationwide clients by the end of 2011.

Besides the purchase of ARS, several settlements also require banks and investment firms to hire an outside-consultant to review and provide recommendations about employee training, marketing and selling of non-conventional financial products. Such agreement aims to enhance transparency and help in protecting investors from purchasing financial products without a good understanding of their potential risks.

6. Conclusion

We examined the auction rate securities (ARS) market, with a particular emphasis on its origins and on the factors that caused its recent collapse. ARS were initially regarded as an attractive source of funding for both public and private sector organizations. The ARS market expanded significantly from its origins in 1984, reaching about $330 billion of outstanding securities at the beginning of 2008. However, by mid-February 2008, the ARS market had collapsed. Different explanations of the ARS market's collapse have been put forward, including the inability of insurers to meet their obligations and the failure of broker-dealers to support the auctions due to liquidity problems. We argue, however, that the interaction of these factors (due to credit crisis) led to the formation of a "perfect storm" that created the ARS market crisis.

With the persistence of credit crisis, along with investors' and issuers' lack of confidence, the future of the ARS market is uncertain. Meanwhile, thousands of investors have been struggling to find a solution to their auction rate security (ARS) woes by filing lawsuits against brokers and underwriters of ARS. Some of these lawsuits were successful at forcing the latter to buy ARS from investors. In fact, as of December 2009, more than 20 firms, including Citigroup, Morgan Stanley, UBS, Goldman Sachs, Bank of America, and Fidelity Investments, have agreed to repurchase $61 billion of the instruments from some customers.

References

Carow, K., Gayle E. and J. McConnell. (1999) "A Survey of U.S. Corporate Financing Innovation: 1970-1997." Journal of Applied Corporate Finance 12 (1): 55-69.

McConnell, J. and Saretto, A. (2008) "Auction Failures and the Market for Auction Rate Securities." Working Paper, BSI Gamma Foundation.

Neave, E. And S. Saadi (2010). "Auction Rate Securities: Another Victim of the Credit Crisis?" Handbook of Banking Crises, Chapman-Hall/Taylor and Francis Group. Edited by Greg Gregoriou, 2010.

Skarr, D. (2005) "Auction rate securities: a primer for finance officers." Government Finance Review 21 (4): 25-28.

BEYOND THE EMU CRISIS: THE FINANCIAL AND POLITICS ISSUES

FRÉDÉRIC TEULON[1]

Introduction

The debate on the comparative advantages of fixed and floating exchanges constitutes a vast body of literature, where it has been thoroughly examined by many leading economists: Milton Friedman [1963], Harry Johnson [1973], Jeffrey Frankel [1993] etc. An important line of thought concerns the theory of optimum currency areas, originally associated with the names of Robert Mundell [1961], Ronald McKinnon [1963], and Peter Kenen [1969]. Under this approach, two highly useful stabilization instruments are an independent monetary policy and currency, especially if other such stabilization instruments are not available.

Since the 1970s, European countries have been willing to stabilize their exchange rates. The euro area is the direct heir of the European Monetary System (EMS) — established in 1979 — and of the European Monetary Union, which has steered, since 1999, the replacement of national currencies with a single currency. This area now comprises 17 countries: 11 founding countries – Germany, Austria, Belgium, Spain, Finland, France, Ireland, Italy, Luxembourg, Netherlands, and Portugal — joined by Greece in 2001, Slovenia in 2007, Cyprus and Malta in 2008, Slovakia in 2009, and Estonia in 2011.

A major event concerning monetary policy was the adoption of a statute guaranteeing the complete independence of the European Central Bank vis-à-vis European governments. Overall, several central banks became independent in the years 1980-1990 due to four factors [Cukierman and Lippi, 1999]: 1. the pursuit for price stability, after the stagflation

[1] IPAG Business School, France, f.teulon@ipag.fr.

experience in the 1970s; 2. the dismantling of exchange controls, the liberalization of capital flows, and the demands of international investors; 3. the consensus that expansionary monetary policies are unable to permanently stimulate production; 4. the pressure exerted by Germany on its European partners for their adoption of its model of monetary stability.

Today, the euro area is experiencing an unprecedented grave crisis, which is the result of the superimposition of two crises:

1. since the early 1990s, a results crisis (tending to a recession);
2. since 2009, a sovereign debt crisis (coupled with an institutional crisis). This crisis first hit Greece before spreading to other countries.

Modelling the Intertemporal Solvency of European States

Kenneth Rogoff and Carmen Reinhart [2008] have shown that a debt representing over 90 percent of a country's GDP reduces its growth by one point. The spectre of insolvency or bankruptcy of any State cannot be ruled out. In order to avoid such a debacle, current debts must be urgently transformed into "sustainable" ones, that is, they must be prevented from continuing to increase as a percentage of GDP.

Intertemporal sustainability of a State is given by the budget constraint that reflects the debt dynamics:

$$d_t = [(1+r_t)/(1+g_t)]\ d_{t-1} - s_t$$

d_t is the value of debt in period t as a percentage of GDP, r_t is the nominal interest rate, g_t the nominal growth rate, s_t the primary budget surplus (excluding debt interest payments).

The intertemporal budgetary constraint is obtained by the summation of the instantaneous constraints:

$$d_t = \sum_{j=1}^{N} [(k_{t+j}/q_{t+j}).\ S_{t+j}] + \lim_{N\to\infty} [(k_{t+N}/q_{t+N}).\ b_{t+N}]$$

$$\text{with } k_{t+j} = \prod_{i=1}^{j} (1+g_{t+i})$$

$$\text{and } q_{t+i} = \prod_{i=1}^{j} (1+r_{t+i})$$

Creditors stop offering long-term loans if they are only to receive interest on past debt, given that principal is not reimbursed (the absence of a Ponzi scheme). This requires that the pace of debt growth be lower than the interest rates.

Thus we have:

$$\lim_{N\to\infty} [(k_{t+N} / q_{t+N}).\, b_{t+N}] = 0$$

and

$$d_t = \sum_{j=1}^{+\infty} [(k_{t+i} / q_{t+i}).\, S_{t+i}]$$

The long-term stabilization of the debt to GDP ratio requires a primary surplus level *s*, such that:

$$s_t = [\,(r-g)/(1+g)]\, d_t \qquad (1)$$

If the growth rate of the GDP is higher than the interest rate ($g > r$), a country can stabilize its debt as a percentage of GDP, all the while running a primary deficit (and a fortiori, budget deficits).

Based on this model, it can be said that the Stability and Growth Pact is ill-adapted to address the problem of debt sustainability.

We note that inclusion in a currency area reduces the uncertainty associated with this relationship. Considering that in fact the debt is currency-denominated, then the relationship (1) becomes:

$$s_t = [\,[(r-g - e(1+g)/(1+g)(1+e)]]\, d_t$$

with *e* being the variation in the nominal exchange rate.

While the Euro Area was Established to Create Greater Stability, Today it is Endangered by a Crisis of Greater Magnitude

The euro area was conceived as an anti-crisis remedy. Its objectives were to eliminate currency crises and to sustain a strong euro. With this goal in mind, the Maastricht Treaty gave the European Central Bank a status guaranteeing its full independence. With these conditions, it is possible to fight more effectively against inflation: empirically, there is a decreasing (and significant) relationship between the degree of independence of a Central Bank and the inflation rate trend in a country [Cukierman and Lippi, 1999]. The euro was promoted as a requirement for opening markets among member countries, which was embodied in the slogan, "A single market, a single currency." A triple wager was made:

1. The political construction of Europe was within reach, it would necessarily follow the monetary unification;
2. According to the analyses by Kydland and Prescott [1977], the European Central Bank's independence and the rules governing budgetary policy would allow credibility to be gained vis-à-vis financial markets;
3. The euro area was necessary because there was a high level of exchange between member countries [McKinnon, 1963]. It was potentially optimal and the optimality criteria were endogenous [Frankel and Rose, 1998]. The euro area would lead to greater economic integration and the convergence of various financial situations [Pagano and von Thadden, 2004].

By extending Robert Mundell's analyses, McKinnon wondered about the conditions of optimality of currency areas by considering that the more the partnering economies are open, the more the "fixed exchange rates" solution becomes an advantage. McKinnon believes that the viability of a currency area is based less on the mobility of production factors (Mundell) than on the magnitude of trade. In an open economy, a depreciation of the exchange rate stimulates the inflation rate (because of higher import prices) and destabilizes trade with third-party countries. McKinnon concludes that countries open to each other have an interest in constituting a currency area in order to avoid being hampered by destabilizing fluctuations in exchange rates.

Frankel and Rose believe optimal currency area criteria are endogenous: countries which move to a system of fixed exchange rates or which adopt the same currency see an increase in their trade volume and their business cycles converge, which justifies ex-post monetary integration. A monetary union would create conditions for its optimality ex-post. For their part, Pagano and von Thadden [2004] show how European bond markets have become much more integrated, as a result of the Economic and Monetary Union. This development leads to greater competition among securities issuers, to greater liquidity of secondary markets, and to a convergence of interest rates.

***

The current euro area crisis should be re-examined from a broader perspective, that of a global financial crisis which developed a new dimension, one which is both cyclical and structural. The cyclical downturn began in 2007 in the United States, being both a liquidity and a banking crisis (notably marked by Lehman Brothers' bankruptcy in September 2008). This liquidity crisis is now over. Even if it may resume in the future, at present it has stalled. However this liquidity crisis was only part of a larger crisis. The structural aspect of the crisis refers to three issues:

- The first problem was the irresponsible behaviour of banks (loans to non-creditworthy households) and the relative or absolute impoverishment - depending on the country – of the middle-class and the poor, that is, approximately the working-class and lower-middle-class bracket. This situation led to a rise in household debt. This was the case in the United States, England, Spain, and Ireland. This deterioration in the financial situation of households was responsible for generating the "subprime" crisis in the U.S.;
- The second factor in this crisis was a change in international economic relations, with a displacement of the centre of gravity of today's economy from the Atlantic region (U.S. and Europe) to the Far East. This unfair competition was induced as a result of the fact that countries whose wage levels are extremely low are catching up with developed countries concerning productivity;
- The third dimension of this economic crisis refers to the currency crisis.

The dollar crisis is accompanied by a crisis in the euro area. There is no solution to this crisis: in a way, the dollar and the euro have managed to survive, but in extremely precarious conditions.

Moreover, the crisis in the euro area is also a distinct European crisis. The second act of this crisis (after the crisis of "high finance" capitalism) refers to the European sovereign debt crisis. In their presentation of the history of financial crises, Reinhart and Rogoff [2009] show that international banking crises almost always lead to sovereign debt crises. The places where these crises pick up again are the weak links in the global economy.

We have seen since 2009 a growing mistrust of investors towards the magnitude of public deficits in Europe. This distrust was first manifested vis-à-vis Greece, then Portugal, Ireland, and then finally Spain.

The situation of European countries is very worrisome, given that their macroeconomic performances have severely deteriorated. In the 1980s and 1990s, Europe chose price stability at the expense of employment, in order to implement its convergence towards a single currency, and because it wagered that eventually the benefits of the euro would solve its mass unemployment problem. Twelve years after the launch of the euro, and there are still millions of unemployed individuals in Europe. France experienced its worst decade since 1945: almost zero growth, a more critical trade deficit than ever before, its public debt out of control, all accompanied by nearly 3 million unemployed people (16 million in all of the euro area).

The euro has contributed to the misfortune of countries like Greece, Portugal, and Spain, allowing them to enjoy the benefits of artificially low interest rates. This is what Hyman Minsky called the paradox of tranquillity: when States have easy access to cheap loans, they tend to go too far. Greece and Portugal have used the euro as a shelter, being allowed to borrow at very low rates, which had been determined in connection with the average inflation rate in the area, while their own inflation rate was higher.

Yet another issue is that The Stability and Growth Pact is no longer respected. Most countries exceed the stipulated limits of 3 percent of the budget deficit and 60 percent of the public debt. The monitoring system for budgetary policies which had been implemented since the creation of the euro has not worked. During the years 2008-2010, there has been an additional escalation of deficits and debts caused in part by the bailout of banks. Europe has failed to promote budgetary sustainability. The situation in Greece is untenable: due to the 4 percent decrease of its GDP in 2010, the debt burden has reached 140 percent of GDP, which means that interest on the debt accounts for the extravagant sum of 7 percent of GDP! In 2015, despite a harsh budgetary adjustment of 10 percentage points of GDP, the debt will reach 165 percent of GDP, an unmanageable amount unless it is restructured starting today.

For countries experiencing a crisis, long-term interest rates have increased and diverged sharply. Sovereign spreads began to rise towards the end of 2008. In early 2011, while France and Germany borrowed at 3 percent, Greece was forced to issue securities with a nominal yield above 10 percent.

The 10-year sp read with Germany (in basis points)

	January 2008	January 2009	January 2010	February 2011
Greece	40	170	200	800
Ireland	25	80	125	550

The rise in nominal rates in the "peripheral countries" requires a higher primary budget surplus (s_t):

$$s_t = [\ (r_2 - g)/(1+g)]\ d_t \quad > \quad s_t = [\ (r_1 - g)/(1+g)]\ d_t \text{ lorsque } r_2 > r_1$$

Key macroeconomic indicators in several countries in the euro area (2010)

	Greece	Ireland	Spain	Portugal	Italy	France	Germany	Euro area*
P in 2010, base 100 in 1997	148.5	141.9	141.2	136.7	132.1	123.4	121.1	127.9
Private debt as percentage of GDP	79 %	191 %	173 %	160 %	86 %	92 %	98 %	97 %
Public deficit as percentage of GDP	15.4 %	14.4 %	11.6 %	9.3 %	5 %	8 %	5 %	6.3 %
Public debt as percentage of GDP	140 %	67 %	72 %	77 %	118 %	80 %	73 %	79 %
Unemployment rate	10. 2%	13.2 %	19.7%	10.8 %	9.1 %	10.1 %	7 .4 %	10.1 %

*16 countries.

Source: OCDE and Eurostat.

P: index of consumer prices

The European Crisis has revealed how Fragile the Construction of Monetary Europe Is

The crisis can be traced back to the foundations of the construction of Europe and the establishment of its monetary union, when the necessary political conditions did not yet exist.

The euro area institutions were conceived based on an incorrect or ineffectual analysis of the situation in European countries. According to Mundell's analysis, the euro area is facing asymmetric shocks. Greece has a budget problem, Ireland, a banking problem. Portugal has a private debt problem, and Spain, a combination of all three. Yet, although the specific problems differ, the implications are the same: all these countries must now endure spending cuts.

Europe must also deal with structural asymmetries that make it very difficult to manage a single monetary policy. Furthermore, these asymmetries were underestimated. They concern the functioning of labour markets, productive specializations, the nature of mortgages, the initial level of income, and, therefore, the whole convergence process. Given these asymmetries, there should be freedom to use other policies, especially budgetary policy. Yet this has been prohibited (the Stability and Growth Pact) based on the assumption that the externalities associated with public deficits are negative.

For some — especially Kenen [1969] — we must abandon the assumption of regional monoproduction (used by Mundell), which gives considerable importance to asymmetric demand shocks. Thus Kenen bases his reasoning on regions with a varied production. For such economies, a demand shock affects only a small share of exports, thus limiting the impact on growth and employment. Therefore, highly diversified regions will be less inclined to use the exchange rate as a policy tool and thus they will be more suited to forming a currency zone.

For others [Krugman, 1991], there is a profound misunderstanding of the fact that monetary union increases the heterogeneity of the whole through the inevitable process of region specialization.

In the absence of federalism, the countries which specialize in non-exportable services are necessarily in crisis: Thus institutions should be designed based on a more serious analysis of the structural economic situation.

***

As theorized by Mundell, Europe is not an optimum currency area, given that production structures are overly different and the probability of an asymmetric shock is excessively great. A currency area can only be viable if it can absorb asymmetric shocks, and if through the mobility of the workforce, the flexibility of prices and wages, or through budgetary solidarity, it offsets the loss of interest and exchange rates as an adjustment variable. There is no federal budget mechanism to compensate the losers and labour is not sufficiently mobile. Additionally, there is no real European economic government. The Euro Group (the monthly meeting of finance ministers of the euro area) is in reality a ghost of intergovernmental coordination, the EU budget is very small, and the Pact of Stability and Growth is no longer respected.

Feldstein [1997] has engaged in the debate concerning the single European currency that has divided American economists. He affirms that the euro should lead to an exacerbation of opposition within Europe, primarily within Europe and subsequently between Europe and the rest of the world. Feldstein elaborated a list comprising all the conflicts that the single currency could generate: opposition against the objectives and methods of the European Central Bank concerning monetary policy; other opposed stances due to changes in the economic cycle that some countries experience before others; further deterioration in their economic situation, and an increase in unemployment. All these disagreements would contribute to a growing distrust from the public and their leaders against the euro and Europe, and to an endless proliferation of conflicts on how power should be shared. The recent exacerbation of tensions within the euro area seems to confirm Feldstein's predictions. Let us recall that, in 2010, German Chancellor Angela Merkel proposed the exclusion of Greece from the euro area, the enforcement of automatic disciplinary action against the defaulting countries, and also to deprive them of voting rights.

Economic governance in the EU

PILLARS OF GOVERNANCE		MAIN OBJECTIVE	SECONDARY OBJECTIVES	INSTRUMENTS
Domestic market	The Brussels Commission Member States	Free circulation of goods, capital, and people	Making the EU attractive	Compliance with treaty directives
Monetary policy	ECB	Inflation < 2 percent	Growth and employment Exchange rate (strong euro)	Key interest rates
Budgetary policy	Member States	Deficit < 3 percent GDP Debt < 60 percent GDP	Medium-term budgetary balance	Multilateral surveillance Stability and Growth Pact
EU budget	The Brussels Commission Parliament	Financing for EU policies	Cohesion	Structural funds
Lisbon Strategy	The Brussels Commission Member States	Competitiveness, innovation, knowledge economy	Employment	Increased resources devoted to R&D

Germany has rejected the principle of solidarity, despite benefitting from an inflation rate that is lower than those in the Southern European countries, while simultaneously promoting its exports to these countries and trying to reduce its imports from Spain or Greece. Given that there is one single monetary policy stipulated for all countries, "Southerners" cannot restore their competitiveness through devaluations. Thus, they have no other way to support their lagging activities than by increasing demand through public deficits.

In pursuing a policy of wage restraint while hoping that the euro could be used as a weapon against inflation (the theme of the strong euro), Germany has exhibited a non-cooperative behaviour. Germany's growth strategy is based on export growth and not on domestic demand. They refuse to implement measures of financial solidarity vis-à-vis other European countries which on the other hand are the victims of policies deliberately pursued by Germany!

***

For some Keynesian economists [Atkinson et al. 1993; Blanchard and Fitoussi, 1998; Fitoussi, 2002] or for some heterodox economists [Allais, 1992; Rosa, 1998], certain neoliberal and ideological policy choices have put Europe at risk:

- Free-trade. According to Allais [1992], free trade is only viable among countries with a comparable level of development, having also a common policy framework combined with appropriate institutions. The European Union is sufficiently large to have internal competition, without member countries having to suffer the adverse impact of imports from less developed countries. The blind application of the free-trade doctrine is the cause of massive under-employment in Europe.
- Exchange policy (strong currency). Rosa [1998] estimated that in the 1990s, European economies were hampered by a policy of overvalued exchange rates, stubbornly pursued in order to launch a European currency as strong as the German mark. Consequently, we can argue in favour of adopting a realistic exchange rate [Fitoussi, 2002].
- A monetary policy heavily influenced by monetarism as well as the fight against inflation, which leads to deflationary choices.

Rosa [1998] has dismantled the European mechanism that drives the formation of a single European State. According to this author, the European monetary policy cannot be left solely to the Central Bank in Frankfurt, acting on simple technical criteria. A single policy will benefit some States at the expense of others. It therefore calls for political arbitrages, which should only be carried out by elected officials, and not mere technicians following rigid rules completely disassociated from the real economic situation of various countries.

He denounces the continuation of an anti-inflationary policy, while inflation itself has disappeared. Rosa believes that the European Central Bank should set for itself a target of battling against deflation, that is to say, to set an inflation target consistent with a level of activity needed to reduce unemployment (similar to the U.S. Federal Reserve). If one considers that there is an optimal level of inflation (around 4 to 6 percent), which allows reducing unemployment to its structural level, a slightly higher level of inflation can be accepted in order to:
— facilitate real adjustments;
— avoid zero, or even negative, inflation, which would make monetary policy ineffective in reviving overall business activity.

Does a single market truly require a single currency? No. We certainly do not need a single currency or a fixed exchange rate for business to thrive. From their trade, the U.S. generates more than 2,000 billion dollars annually, despite a fluctuating exchange rate which has experienced sharp variations in recent decades. The Free-Trade Agreement (NAFTA) has spurred the growth of trade between Canada, Mexico, and the United States, while all these countries have floating exchange rates. The exchange rates of Japan, South Korea, and other Asian trading powers fluctuate wildly. Moreover, let us not forget that only 17 of the 27 countries within the free trade zone that constitutes the European Union use the euro.

What are the Solutions?

Given the emergency situation, the "no bail-out" clause [Eichengreen and von Haggen, 1996] – the ban to help nations struggling with their budget – was lifted and support measures were adopted. The ECB has purchased securities issued by the European countries in crisis to limit soaring rates (and we must also note that in order to do this, the ECB was forced to increase its capital). The ECB resorted to a monetization of the debt for countries experiencing difficulties waiting for the permanent relief mechanism to be defined, which will be set up in 2013. These procedures were performed on the secondary bond market. Their objective was to avoid contradicting the commitment made by the ECB to not directly finance the deficit of various States. However, these actions have placed the indebted States in a situation of "moral hazard." In any case, they represent a circumvention of the Maastricht Treaty, which prohibits States from being refinanced by the ECB and also, consequently, they prohibit interventions in the debt's primary market. Thus the ECB found itself, against its will, in a position of "buyer of last resort."

As a consequence, a European Financial Stability Fund (EFSF) was established, having been endowed with €750 billion (cofinanced by the IMF). The Fund will start functioning in 2013 and it is the concrete expression of Europe's will to have a permanent procedure to support its Member States. Countries in the euro area have decided to provide their guarantee for an amount up to €440 billion, complemented by €60 billion in loans from the European Commission, and €250 billion provided by the IMF.

Proposal 1

The creation and perpetuation of the EFSF is an adequate solution for resolving financial crisis problems within the euro area.

Objection. The EFSF endowment is not sufficient to cope with future crises, when it will be necessary to think in terms of trillions of euros.

Countries experiencing difficulties have been forced to adopt deflationary measures (7 percent reduction in public expenditure for Greece in 2010). These rigorous plans have been implemented at the risk of worsening the situation in terms of growth and unemployment. We must ask if the euro should be saved at any cost, regardless of the price paid by the people of the Member States. Proponents of federalism are well aware that an end to the euro would compromise for several decades the model of a supranational Europe. The European Union and the ECB became the allies of financial markets, which demand a drastic reduction in standards of living and social spending.

Budgetary restrictions announced in the euro area (in percentage of GDP)

Year of reference	**2010**	**2011**	**2012**	**2013**
Greece	7.0	4.0	2.0	2.0
Ireland	3.0	2.0	1.5	1.0
Spain	2.5	2.9	2.0	2.0
Portugal	2.5	3.1	1.5	1.5
Italy	0.5	0.8	0.4	0.4
Finland	-1.0	0.2	0.0	0 .0
France	0.0	0.6	0.6	0.6
Germany	-1.5	0.4	0.2	0.2
Euro area	**0.2**	**1.0**	**0.7**	**0.7**

Source: Barclays Capital / BENASSY-QUERE Agnès and BOONE Laurence [2010]. Based on data on implemented stabilization programs and government announcements.

The standard way to cushion the effects of austerity policies is to add a currency devaluation measure to domestic cuts. Devaluation makes exports more competitive by substituting external demand for a squeezed domestic demand. However, since these countries no longer have a national currency, they must replace internal deflation (decrease in wages and costs) with external devaluation.

The imbalances in Portugal have persisted for several years [Blanchard, 2007]. The adjustment plan for 2010/2011 to reduce public expenditure includes measures to lower civil service and state-owned company wages (a decrease of 3.5 percent to 10 percent for those earning more than €1,500 per month), a rationalization of health expenditures, a ceiling on benefits, and an increase of two points of the VAT.

Proposal 2

The actions for emerging from a crisis and for debt sustainability must be framed through generalized policies of deflation and budget cuts. Restoring sustainable competitiveness necessarily requires lower nominal wages, reduced social spending, and lower prices of nontradable goods.

Objection. Deflation requires all contract prices to drop together and proportionately, including those of debt contracts, something which seems impossible to implement [Blanchard, 2007]. The tight fiscal policies implemented in Member States will probably preclude any economic recovery, undermining in particular the public finances and entailing new employee revenue transfers towards the banks and the holders of public debt securities. The solution would rather lie in a policy which is favourable to growth in European countries not subject to a sovereign debt crisis, in order to create a "cyclical gap" favouring peripheral countries. Europe risks committing the same mistakes of the "Gold Block[2]," composed between 1933 and 1936, after the devaluation of the pound sterling in September 1931 vis-à-vis the franc. It risks being caught in a vicious cycle of recession, deflation, and the increase of the real value of its debts.

The reduction in growth rates in the euro area requires a larger primary balance surplus of the budget (st):

$$s_t = [\,(r-g_2)/(1+g_2)]\, d_t \quad > \quad s_t = [\,(r-g_1)/(1+g_1)]\, d_t \;,\ \text{when } g_2 < g_1$$

***

A number of solutions have been discarded. The sovereign debt crisis has not caused a radical change in economic policy and governance.

A European paradox arises from the fact that treaties have laid the foundations for a federalism that dares not say its name, while the peoples and governments that represent them are unwilling to go further in this direction, because there is no agreement on who shall pay its cost and, additionally, because this federalism clashes with a reality: the existence of the European nation-states.

European countries have also refused to issue bonds guaranteed by the Union (Eurobonds). Another solution could have been to transform the Greek and Portuguese bonds into bonds guaranteed by a European Fund; however this type of measure was rejected. Each State is then responsible for its debts.

---

[2] The Bloc comprised France, Italy, Belgium, Switzerland, Poland, and the Netherlands.

Proposal 3

Issuing common bonds presents various advantages. A "European Debt Agency" [Boone and Solomon, 2010] would issue "Eurobonds" for the entire euro area and allow Member States to consolidate some of their outstanding bonds. Concerning the remaining part of the debt — a purely national debt — the spreads would be maintained, reflecting differences in various macroeconomic situations, which would encourage countries to keep their debt levels under control. A larger market, with increased liquidity, would be created in which debt could be issued at a lower cost than that currently paid in these more fragmented markets. The aim would be to pool part of the existing debt (the Juncker/Tremonti proposal) in return for which an independent agency would be authorized, on behalf of the euro area, to audit the accounts of each country.

Objection. The common rate would probably be higher than the rate used by Germany and the other exemplary countries in the euro area for their own financing. Moreover, the issuance of "Eurobonds" would not solve the problem of budgetary divergence, nor the low level of budgetary solidarity between member states.

A monetary union cannot function without a budget coordination mechanism. In the case of Europe, the demands imposed by Germany included having this mechanism overridden, and also replacing the need for solidarity by a uniform rule of budgetary solidarity (the Stability Pact, which is arbitrary and insensitive to economic contexts). However, this rule was shattered due to the expenses incurred to rescue banks.

The abandonment of national monetary policies, which had previously allowed a fine-tuned response to specific economic environments, makes the differentiation of fiscal and budgetary policies even more necessary, in order to compensate for the inadequacies of the single budgetary policy in relation to each country's particular macroeconomic developments. The increase in short-term cyclical disparities in the euro area will only be bearable if it is accompanied by large transfers of resources from the growing economies to economies in recession.

The exchange rate of the euro against the dollar (€1 = $1.30) is at an acceptable level for the strongest countries, but at an unbearable level for the weakest countries (the level of purchasing power parity can be estimated for the entire euro area at €1 = $1.15). Given that there are no more possible adjustments for the euro area by changing the value of currencies, the only option left is making adjustments by financial transfers.

Moving towards greater federalism means:

Proposal 4

To transfer much larger amounts to the budget managed by the Commission in Brussels.

Objection. There is no agreement on who shall pay the cost. Every member country is against an increase of their contribution. A "soft" consensus was reached to maintain the European budget at its current level, or 1.2 percent of EU GDP. Europe, therefore, finds itself at an impasse concerning this matter.

Proposal 5

To change the way the Commission functions in order to make the decision-making process more democratic.

Objection. Europe was built on a denial of democratic principles and practices. It is not willing to pay the price of democracy, which entails diversity and respect for all nations. The Commission is the "spokesperson" of the financial markets, who want a federal model similar to the one in the U.S., whereas European nations, attached to their sovereignty, oppose it. The discord is therefore absolute.

Proposal 6

To establish a genuine political union that would function as a counterpart to the ECB, and in one way or another, make the ECB accountable to this political entity.

Objection. Germany has clearly expressed its opposition to a change in the status of the ECB.

Mechanisms for rescheduling and restructuring the debt have not been implemented. However, governments could offer new bonds worth a fraction of the value of existing bonds. The bondholders would then be forced to choose between securities at par, with a face value equal to the existing bonds but with a longer maturity and lower interest rates, and securities below par with a shorter maturity and a higher interest rate, but with a face value that is a fraction of existing bonds.

It is indeed difficult to imagine how the peripheral countries of the euro area could escape restructuring their sovereign debts. On this point, Kenneth Rogoff is hardly optimistic. In a recent note, the former chief economist of the International Monetary Fund said that "ultimately, a significant restructuring of the private and/or public debt will probably be necessary for all euro-area countries which are encumbered by debts [...] Already facing the prospect of sluggish growth even before the introduction of budget austerity measures, they [Greece, Portugal, Ireland and Spain] risk plunging into a lost decade similar to that experienced by Latin America in the 1980s. The revival and growth dynamics of modern Latin America did not really take effect until the Brady Plan orchestrated massive debt reductions throughout the region as of 1987. A similar restructuring is probably the most likely scenario in Europe."

Nevertheless, in the case of restructuring, the banking system would be permanently affected. At the end of 2010, consolidated claims of European banks against the four most vulnerable members of the area amounted to 14 percent of EU GDP. Thus any serious action to restructure sovereign debts would inevitably provoke massive disengagement from creditors and, in the worst case scenario, start a new chapter in the international financial crisis. Public capital would then need to be re-injected into the banks, which would inevitably worsen even more the magnitude of budget deficits and destroy respective efforts to make public debts sustainable.

Will it be necessary to go further? In the beginning of 2011, Hans-Werner Sinn – President of the Ifo Institute – and Ottmar Issing – former chief economist of the European Central Bank – presented a report calling for the establishment of an "orderly" bankruptcy procedure for States in default. According to them, this is an essential instrument for long-term stabilization of the euro area. Thus no Member State would be able to count on automatic support from its partners to save it from bankruptcy, a procedure which would push investors in taking a State's default risk seriously. Moreover, even limited discounts on the sovereign debt of some countries could jeopardize the banking system of the euro area.

A Breakup Scenario is Possible

Noting the loss of market share for exports, weak productivity growth, persistent budget deficits, Patrick Artus [2005] warned: "It can thus be expected in 5 years, in 10 years, that France and Italy will be in a very difficult situation: enormous accumulated market share losses, very weak trend growth, and an unbearable public debt rate." He added: "The situation in France and Italy is even more critically exacerbated by the economic strategy followed by Germany. The latter has a non-cooperative policy of reduction of unit labour costs, in order to regain market share, especially vis-à-vis other countries in the area who do not follow the same strategy."

In fact, it is not Italy or France who are the weakest links in the euro area, but Artus' analysis remains valid even if we do not draw the same conclusions. Nevertheless, the question of the breakup of the euro area is no longer taboo, and many authors clearly address the topic: Artus [2005], Eichengreen [2007], Teulon [2009], Cotta [2010], Roubini [2010] etc.

Proposal 7

The breakup is not only possible, but very likely:

- An exit scenario, led by Germany, would be justified by its wish to relinquish its responsibility for the policy of its Southern neighbours;
- An exit scenario with the departure of countries experiencing difficulties would be justified by their need to find room to manoeuvre.

Objection. There are alternative scenarios based on a successful rescue of the euro area in the medium term:

- The aid provided by the European Financial Stability Facility would be adequate to solve problems and calm markets. Germany would commit to a cooperative scenario for an enlarged euro area for fear that if the euro disappeared in favour of the reintroduction of national currencies, the mark would then need to be reevaluated by 20 to 30 percent;
- European countries would engage in tax and budget integration;
- The restructuring of sovereign debt of countries experiencing difficulty would occur in an orderly manner.

Proposal 8

The technical and legal difficulties related to the reintroduction of a national currency are high, but they are not insurmountable.

Objection. A dismantling of the euro area would put peripheral countries in a difficult situation (capital flight, a sharp drop in the exchange rate etc.). The risk for a weakened country is to have its domestic currency collapse while its debt remains denominated in euros. The debt dynamics would be revived because of the depreciation of the nominal exchange rate in price notation (*e*).

$s_t = [\ [(r\text{-}g - e_2\ (1+g)/(1+g)(1+\ e_2)]]\ d_t \quad > \quad s_t = [\ [(r\text{-}g - e_1\ (1+g)/(1+g)(1+\ e_1)]]\ d_t$

when $e_2 < e_1$

Eichengreen [2007] insists that we cannot exclude the possibility that a member of the euro area might want to pull out of this area in order to recover its domestic currency and to re-establish a monetary policy better adapted to its situation. In the event of violent asymmetric shocks in a euro-area country, real depreciation of its currency in relation to the euro would be the only possible solution, which tends to show — once again — that Europe is not an optimum currency area.

The most obvious reason to leave the Union would be the wish to escape the identical monetary policy imposed on all countries by the single currency. Countries whose economy would experience a crisis in the coming years and which fear that it would become chronic might be tempted to leave the EMU in order to ease monetary conditions and to devalue their currencies. Even if from an economic point of view this decision would be difficult to implement, the possibility that countries facing a severe economic downturn could decide to follow this course of action cannot be ruled out.

The current crisis has renewed the debate about the need to establish a fiscal authority for the European Union. Whatever the logic of this proposal, it would pave the way for a much larger redistribution of income — this reason in itself is enough for high-income countries to want to leave the Union.

In addition, it is important to emphasize the dangers of a split into two blocks. The hypothesis purporting the establishment of a "euro-franc" or "euro-South" currency area makes little sense. It precisely neglects both theoretical teachings as well as those derived from our present experience. The economic characteristics of France, Spain, Portugal, Greece, and Italy are different enough to exclude the adoption of a single currency between these countries. They would soon find themselves in the midst of a "euro-franc" or "*euro-South*" crisis, senselessly reproducing current difficulties. We do not see what rationale could possibly exist for a monetary union between weak countries. If some peripheral countries left the euro area, they would have every incentive to revert to their local currency in order to devalue it, to boost their trade and increase their competitiveness.

A currency area where Germany would gather around itself some of its neighbours, such as Austria, Denmark or the Netherlands, might be possible because their particular economic environments are not too different (in fact, before the euro, a "mark zone" already existed). This question, however, deserves to be examined more closely before the same mistakes are repeated once again. The former president of Germany's top industry organisation, Hans-Olaf Henkel, has suggested in his book "*Save our money, Germany has been sold off*," a bestseller outside his native country, that Germany should exit the euro area and create a new union with the Netherlands, Belgium, Austria, and Finland.

Concluding Remarks

The euro area crisis extends beyond its monetary framework. Furthermore, the adopted measures to contain it seem inadequate. A breakup of the euro zone is no longer simply a possibility; nevertheless there is little chance of our witnessing a total disintegration.

The existence of a single currency for 17 highly disparate countries could only lead to a crisis. With the changeover to the euro, member States have lost control of their monetary policies and interest rates, which they can no longer adjust according to their economic situation; likewise, they can no longer react to productivity differences and to changes in aggregate demand by adjusting the respective exchange rate. It is clear that some countries would benefit from leaving the euro area; on the other hand, they would have to bear significant political and economic costs.

As per our analysis [Teulon, 2009], going back to full employment will not be possible as long as we remain in a free trade system as well as in a rigidly managed exchange system. The promise of stability made at the time of the creation of the monetary union can no longer be held and the euro could become the symbol of European disintegration. There is a harmful and dangerous premise in believing that price stability is an objective of the highest priority and that it is possible to impose this stability by means of a few budgetary rules for economies moving at different speeds.

It is clear that only monetary unions based on a prior political union (the Swiss Confederation in 1848, the Italian unification in 1861, and the German Reich in 1871) have succeeded, while those which corresponded solely to coalitions or cartels of Independent States (the Latin Monetary Union[3] established in 1865, the Scandinavian Monetary Union[4] established in 1873) did not survive the vagaries and diverse impacts of international economic and political developments. We agree with Rosa [1998] that: "The Treaty of Maastricht, which established a new fixed exchange rate system in Europe, will appear in history books as the mistake or, worse, the grave blunder of 1992, exactly as the deflationary policies of the 1930s, and in particular of the gold block."

The crisis has placed monetary Europe face to face with its contradictions. It is unclear how Europe could force the hand of destiny and compel its Member States and peoples to institutional compromises. The question to be asked is how long the euro will still survive.

References

Alesina, Alberto, Perotti, Roberto and Spolaore, Enrico (1995), "Together or Separately? Issues on the Costs and Benefits of Political and Fiscal Unions", *European Economic Review*, 39, pp 751-758.

Alesina, Alberto and Perotti, Roberto (1995), "Economic Risk and Political Risk in Fiscal Unions", *NBER Working Paper*, 4992.

Alesina, Alberto and Spolaore,Enrico (1997), "On the Number and Size of Nations", *Quarterly Journal of Economics*, November 1997, pp 1027-56.

[3] This Union comprised France, Belgium, Italy, Switzerland, Luxembourg, and Greece.

[4] This Union comprised Sweden, Denmark and Norway.

Allais, Maurice (1992), *Erreurs et impasses de la construction européenne*, ed. Clément Juglar.

Argyrou, Michael and Kontonikas, Alexandros (2010), "The EMU Sovereign-Debt Crisis: Fundamentals, Expectations and Contagion." Cardiff Business School Working Paper E, 2010/9.

Artur Patrick (2005), "La France et surtout l'Italie devront-elles sortir de la zone euro?", note de recherche de Natixis.

Atkinson, Anthony, Blanchard, Olivier, Flemmng, John, Fitoussi, Jean-Paul and al. (1993), *Competitive Disinflation and Economic Policy in Europe*, Oxford.

BAaldwin,Richard and Wyplosz, Charles (2009), *The Economics of European Integration*, McGraw-Hill.

Bayoumi, Tamim and Eichengreen, Barry (1993), "Shocking Aspects of European Monetary Integration", in: Torres Francisco and Giavazzi Francesco eds., *Adjustment and Growth in the European Monetary Union*, Cambridge University Press.

Benassy-Quere, Agnès and Boone, Laurence (2010), "Crise de l'eurozone: dettes, institutions et croissance", *La lettre du CEPII*, n°300.

Blanchard, Olivier and Fitoussi, Jean-Paul (1998), *Croissance et chômage*, rapport du CAE, La Documentation française.

Bolton, Patric and Roland, Gérard (1997), "The Break up of Nations : a Political Economy Analysis", *Quarterly Journal of Economics*, pp 1057-90.

Boone, Laurence and Salomon, Raoul (2010), "Les eurobonds sont-ils la bonne solution ?", *Le Monde*, 18 décembre.

Canzoneri, M.B. and Rogers, C.A. (1990), "Is the European Community an Optimal Currency Area?" *American Economic Review* 80 (3), pp 419-433.

Cohen, Benjamin (1993), "Beyond EMU: The Problem of Sustainability", *Economics and Politics* 5 (2), pp 187-203.

Cotta, Alain (2010), *Sortie de l'euro ou mourir à petit feu*, Plon.

Cukierman, Alex (1995), "How Can the European Central Bank Become Credible?"mimeo., paper prepared for a CEPR conference on "What Monetary Policy for the European Central Bank", Frankfurt, Germany.

—. (1996), "The Credibility Problem, EMU and Swedish Monetary Policy," Backround paper for the Swedish Government Commission on EMU, mimeo.

Cukierman, Alex and Lippi, Francisco (1999), "Central Bank Independence, Centralization of Wage Bargaining, Inflation and Unemployment - Theory and Some Evidence", *European Economic Review.*

De Grauwe, Paul (1994), "The Economics of Monetary Integration," Oxford University Press, second edition, Oxford, New York.

De Grauwe, Paul and Moesen, Wim (2009), "Gains for All: a Proposal for a Common Euro Bond." Centre for European Policy Studies. http://www.ceps.eu/book/gains-allproposal-common-eurobond.

Danthine, Jean-Pierre, Giavazzi, Francesco and Thadden, Ernst-Ludwig (2001), "The Effect of EMU on Financial Markets. A first Assessment." In C. Wyplosz (ed.), *The Impact of EMU on Europe and the Developping countries*, Oxford Universirty Press.

Eichengreen, Barry and Von Hagen, Jürgen (1996), "Fiscal Policy and Monetary Union: Federalism, Fiscal Restrictions and the No-Bailout Rule," in Horst Siebert ed., *Monetary Policy in an Integrated World Economy*, Tübingen, pp 211-231.

Eichengreen, Barry and Von Hagen, Jürgen (1996), "Federalism, Fiscal Restraints, and European Monetary Union", *American Economic Review* 86 (2), pp 135-138.

Eichengreen, Barry (2005), "Europe, the euro and the ECB: Monetary success, fiscal failure", *Journal of Policy Modeling*, 27(4), pp 427-439.

—. (2007), "The Breakup of Euro Area", *NBER working paper*.

Feldstein, Martin (1997), "The Political Economy of the European Economic and Monetary Union: Political Sources of an Economic Liability", *Journal of Economic Perspectives* 11(4), pp 3-22.

Fitoussi, Jean-Paul (1995), *Le débat interdit: Monnaie, Europe, Pauvreté*, Le Seuil.

—. (2002), *La règle et le choix. De la souveraineté économique en Europe*, Le Seuil.

Frankel, Jeffrey and Rose, Andrew (1996), "Economic Structure and the Decision to Adopt a Common Currency," Backround paper for the Swedish Government Commission on EMU, mimeo.

Frankel, Jeffrey and Rose, Andrew (1998), "The Endogeneity of the Optimum Currency Area Criteria", *Economic Journal*, vol. 108, pp 1009-25.

Friednman, Milton (1953), "The Case for Flexible Exchange Rates", *Essays in Positive Economics*, Chicago.

Goodhart, Charles (1995), "The Political Economy of Monetary Union", in Kenen ed., *Understanding Interdependence: the Macroeconomics of the Open Economy*, pp 448-505.

Gros, Daniel and Mayer, Thomas (2010), "How to deal with Sovereign Default in Europe: create the European Monetary Fund", CEPS Policy brief, n°202.

Johnson, Harry G. (1973), *Further Essays in Monetary Economics*, Harvard University Press.

Kenen, Peter B. (1969), "The Theory of Optimum Currency Areas. An Eclectic View," in Mundell and Swoboda, eds., *Monetary Problems of the International Economy*, University of Chicago Press.

—. (1995), *Understanding Interdependence. The Macroeconomics of the Open Economy*, Princeton University Press, Princeton, New Jersey.

—. (1997), "Preferences, Domains, and Sustainability", *American Economic Review*, May, Papers and Proceedings, pp 211-213.

Kydland, Finn and Prescott, Edward (1977), "Rule rather than discretion", *Journal of Political Economy*, vol 85, n°3, pp 473-492.

Machlup, Fritz (1977), *A History of Thought on Economic Integration*, Columbia University Press.

Marsh, David (2009), *The Euro: the politics of the new global currency*, New Haven: Yale UP.

McKinnon, Ronald (1963), "Optimum Currency Areas", *American Economic Review*, 53, pp 717-725.

McKinnon, Ronald and Nechyba, Thomas (1997), "Competition in Federal Systems: The Role of Political and Financial Constraints", in *The New Federalism: Can the States be Trusted?* John Ferejohn and Barry Weingast, eds. Stanford: Hoover Institution Press, pp 3–61.

Mundell, Robert A. (1961), "A Theory of Optimum Currency Areas", *American Economic Review,* 51, pp 657-665.

Ooates, Wallace E. (1999), "An Essay on Fiscal Federalism", *Journal of economic Literature*, 37(3), pp 1120-1149.

Pagano, Marco and Thadden, Ernst-Ludwig (2004), "The European Bond Markets under EMU", *Oxford Review of Economic Policy*, vol. 20, n°4, pp 531-554.

Piasni-Ferry, Jean and Posen, Adam S. (2009) (eds.), *The Euro at Ten: The Next Global Currency?*, Washington D.C., Peterson Institute for International Economics.

Reinhart, Carmen M. and Rogoff, Kenneth S. (2008), "This time is different: a Panoramic View on Eight Centuries of Financial Crises", *NBER Working Paper*, n° 13882.

Reinhart, Carmen M. and Rogoff, Kenneth S. (2009), "The Aftermath of Financial Crises." *American Economic Review Papers and Proceedings*, 99, pp 466-472.

Reinhart, Carmen M. and Rogoff, Kenneth S. (2010), "Growth in a Time of Debt", *American Economic Review Papers and Proceedings*, 100, pp 573-578.

Rosa, Jean-Jacques (1998), *L'erreur européenne*, Grasset.

Rose, Andrew (2000), "One Money, One Market: Estimating the Effect of Common Currencies on Trade", *Economic Policy*, 30, pp 7-45.

Roubini, Nouriel and Mihn, Stephen (2010), *Crisis Economics. A Crash Course in the Future of Finance*, Hardcover.

Scitovsky, Tibor (1958), *Economic Theory and Western European Integration*, Stanford.

Stiglitz, Joseph and Weiss, Andrew (1981), "Credit Rationing in Markets with Imperfect Information", *American Economic Review*, Vol. 71, pp 393-410.

Teulon, Frédéric (2009), *La Nouvelle Economie mondiale*, 7th ed., Presses Universitaires de France.

THE IMPACT OF THE QUALITATIVE FACTORS ON ETHICS JUDGMENTS OF MATERIALITY IN AUDIT

RIADH MANITA[1], HASSAN LAHBARI[2] AND NAJOUA ELLOMAL[3]

Introduction

The objective of an audit, such as defined by the IFAC standards (international Federation of the accountants), is to allow the expression of an opinion on the reliability of the images provided by the financial documents. To achieve this objective, the auditor uses a methodology which complies with audit standards. According to these standards, the auditor is brought to estimate the company's audit risks, to design its audit strategy, and to define the means and tools that he will use to best estimate these risks. In this context, materiality represents one of the principal tools set by the standards and which determines audit quality.

The materiality allows the auditor to determine the extent of the audit works, to evaluate the accounting errors materially identified by auditors, and finally to express an opinion on the reliability and the sincerity of the accounting documents. The materiality is determined by quantitative criteria, but also qualitative criteria defined by professional standards. While the professional standards (NEP 320, ISA 320, HER 107) are precise in relation to the quantitative criteria (easy to apply by the auditor, Manuel of audit of "Big4"), these standards are not precise enough about the qualitative criteria, which remain ambiguous and are subject to a big interpretation margin and auditor evaluation (Mc Kee and Elifsen, 2000). To deal with this situation, the auditors are brought systematically to apply

[1] Associate professor – Rouen Business School.
[2] Doctorant – Enseignant- Ecôle de Management de Strasbourg.
[3] Associate professor – Ecôle de Management de Lionard Devinci (EMLV).

the quantitative criteria (active net), total result, etc., while neglecting the qualitative criteria.

However, according to the S.E.C, the exclusive application of the quantitative materiality (such as 5% of the profit) is groundless in the accounting or legal literature. Quantified in terms of percentage, the estimation is only the beginning of the analysis of the materiality; it cannot be correctly used as a substitute in a complete analysis that takes into account all the relevant considerations. These criticisms led to the emission of explicit orientations in USA, such as the SAB.99 accounting bulletin (1999) and the CIFIR's report (2008) published by the SEC, and the audit standard SAS 107 (AICPA, 2006). They made the international audit normalizer (IAASB) revise the standard ISA 320 and emit the new standard ISA 450. These latter standards underline more the importance of the qualitative aspects in the determination of materiality by proposing 11 material qualitative factors (QFM). In France, the standard regarding the significant abnormality and materiality (NEP320, 2006) adapted to the international standards (ISA) by redefining in particular the materiality with regard to the users' expectations.

During the last decade, the academic literature was interested in the quantitative factors to explain the materiality judgments (Holstrum and Messier, 1982; Iskandar and Iselin, 1999; Messier et al., 2005). After the publication of the SAB 99, the academic researchers began to study explicitly the qualitative factors (Wright and Wright, 1997; Braun, 2001; Shafer, 2005; Ng and Tan, 2007; Del Corte et al., 2010). Most of these studies recognize the influence of qualitative factors on materiality judgments (Nelson et al., 2005; Braun, 2001; Ng and Tan, 2007; etc.).

In audit, the consideration of the QFMs is a matter of professional ethical judgment. This judgment does not depend only on individual factors linked to the personal and auditor's intrinsic characteristics (Rest, 1979, Kohlberg, 1969) but also on the situation's context (specific factors, inherent pressures) and on decision consequences, (Jones, 1991, Trevino and Weaver, 2003, Bel Haj, 2010) defined by Jones (1991) as "moral intensity". According to Jones (1991), the moral intensity is a multidimensional construction containing several characteristics (the scale of the consequences, the probability of the effect). He argues that the individuals identify more easily the ethical problems of strong ethical intensity. In this context, every QFM presents for the auditor a situation with a low or strong moral intensity, unless there is a consensus about the ethical nature of a given situation (Shafer, 2005).

Taking as a basis Jones' (1991) ethical judgment model, we might suggest studying the influence of the qualitative factors on the ethical judgments of materiality. This model provides an ideal frame for discussion of the QFMs' ethical perception because he allows the study of individuals' judgments when confronted with ethical problems.

In terms of contribution to theory, this work adopts a theoretical frame developed outside of the sciences of management (ethical psychology) to explain materiality judgments in audit. The methodological interest resides in the construction of real scenarios combining three qualitative factors of SAB.99 standard and a quantitative factor. The results of this study are supposed to contribute in the understanding of the materiality judgment process in the French context.

Three real scenarios implying three qualitative factors were the object of an experimental study carried out with a sample of 44 experienced auditors. The study results confirmed the influence of the qualitative factors on materiality's ethics judgments. In addition to that, our results showed that the magnitude of consequences and the social consensus are two main criteria on which ethical materiality judgments are focused. The proximity of the auditor to his client weakly influenced the ethical materiality judgments.

Firstly, we begin with a literature review concerning materiality and ethical judgment in audit. Secondly, we develop the research methodology adopted in this study. Finally, we present and discuss the results.

1-Materiality and the ethical judgment: literature review

1-1. The concept of materiality: evolution of the concept in the audit standards

Since materiality became an integral part of audit methodology, the definition and the interpretation of this concept were the subject of many discussions and were the object of several audit standards. The first standards did not provide precise orientations determining materiality. In order to resolve the information deficiency in the determination of materiality, these standards referred to the auditor's professional judgment (Thompson and al., 1990). Many Anglo-Saxon researchers have debated on the excessive practice of materiality (Levitt, 1998-2000; Chong, 1994; Carpenter and Dirsmith, 1992; Carpenter et al., 1994). The international and national professional authorities (IASB, FASB, SEC, GAO, CNCC) made considerable efforts to clarify the materiality concept and to better guide the auditors in their practice (FASB N°2, 1980; SAS N°47; SEC 1995; ISAC, 1989). However these improvements were focused on the determination of materiality quantitative criteria and ignored qualitative criteria. To avoid this problem, the American and international standards introduced important modifications to take into account materiality qualitative criteria, and published new standards (SAB 99 in the USA, and ISA 450, which comes to replace ISA 320 on an international scale). These standards include explicitly a list of 11 materiality qualitative factors (QFM) (table 2), from which auditors have to correctly evaluate anomalies of materiality that are below the quantitative thresholds (IAASB, on 2008).

1-2. The ethical judgment of materiality

The absence of a precise audit standard of materiality justified the existence of a large quantity of research dealing with various aspects of the materiality judgment process (Holstrum and Messier, 1982; Iskandar and Iselin, 1999; Messier et al., 2005; García et al., Martínez, 2007). The first works which were interested in identifying the factors implied in materiality judgment process, demonstrated the dominance of quantitative factors. Previous studies (Pattillo and Siebel, 1974; Messier, 1982; Krogsted, 1984) distinguished between the financial factors (result tendency, the total asset, total of stocks) and the non-financial factors (experience, company size). After the publication of the SAB 99, the qualitative materiality was studied by several researchers (Libby and Kinney, 2000; Braun, 200; DeZoort et al., 2003; Shafer, 2004; Nelson et al., 2005; Ng and Tan, 2007). However, these studies were only interested in materiality in a context of results management (Shafer, 2005). Merchant and Rockness (1994) found that the differences of ethical judgments for big and small tampering were rather insignificant and that the resulting intentional management on the ethical judgments remains an object of debate. Shafer et al. (1999) and Ketchand et al. (1999) studied the errors' effects, as well as certain qualitative variables (such as the probability received from the damage caused by the users of financial documents) on the auditors' materiality judgments. Both studies revealed that auditors tend to give up the anomaly correction if these anomalies are associated with a subjective judgment or with a quantitatively unimportant error (Wright and Wright, 1997; Braun, 2001; Nelson, 2003; Nelson et al., 2005). In this context, Libby and Kinney (2000) demonstrated that auditors might require the correction of the quantitatively unimportant errors if these errors generate profits inferior to the objectives set by the financial analysts. However several other qualitative factors defined by the recent audit standards (SAB 99 and ISA 450) were not studied by researchers[4].

Several explanatory models borrowed from cognitive psychology can be used to understand the decision process concerning materiality judgment (Chang, 1998; Jones, 1991; Jones and Ryan, 1997; Stead, Worrell, and Garner Stead, 1990; Trevino, 1986; Trevino and Youngblood, 1990). Certain models of ethical judgment are based on factors related to the personal characteristics of the auditor's decision and on the context of an object judgment. Generally these models appeal to three explanatory dimensions: The recognition of an ethical problem, the ethical judgment, and the creation of intention which results in an ethical behaviour. In this context, Jones's model (1991) constitutes a model which was the object of a consensus on behalf of the researchers. His model takes into consideration the individual dimension of the decision-maker and the dimension related to the situation as an object of study, but also the consequences of the decision (Jones, 1991; Trevino and Weaver, 2003; Bel Haj, 2010). These various dimensions were defined by Jones (1991) as "moral intensity".

In audit, it is obvious that the ethical judgment depends on the auditor's individual characteristics (experience, personality), on the situation as the object of judgment, but especially on the consequences of this judgment on the audited company and on the decision-maker himself (auditor reputation and independence). Therefore, Jones's (1991) theory of moral intensity constitutes a theoretical frame adaptable to study the effects of qualitative factors on auditors' materiality ethical judgments.

According to Jones's theory (1991) an individual has to go through four psychological stages to adopt an ethical behaviour.

---

[4] In this case we mean inaccuracies which are insignificant but intentional, the practice of errors compensation and certain circumstances in which the low number of inaccuracies becomes significant. This is the case for example when an inaccuracy masks a result change or tendency change.

- Firstly, he has to interpret a given situation as an ethical problem (ethical sensibility). This stage includes the identification of possible options and their consequences.
- Secondly, the individual has to decide which option is correct from the moral point of view.
- Thirdly, he has to behave in an ethical way, even if his own interest imposes an opposite attitude.
- Finally, the individual should be strong-willed enough to behave in compliance with his ethical intention (ethical behaviour).

According to Jones (1991), all the process stages of ethical decision-making are influenced by the extent of the problem related to ethical imperatives in a given situation. Jones (1991) argues that the moral intensity of a given question is influenced by six characteristics: the magnitude of the consequences, the social consensus, the probability of the effect, the immediate character on the temporal plan, the proximity, and the concentration of the effects. However, literature considers that some characteristics are more influential and dominant than others. There are two characteristics which are more influential: magnitude of consequences and the social consensus (Morris and MacDonald, 1995).

2. Methodology

Various methodologies were used to study the auditors' ethical judgments. These methodologies are made up of a questionnaire, experimental studies, and an analysis of archive data (audit manuals, auditors' working documents, published financial statements, and audit reports).

The archival research is limited by the difficulties of audit firms allowing consultation by researchers with regard to the secrets of their audit files. They explain their refusal in terms of professional secret (Acito, Bruks, and Johnson, 2009). The experimental studies are supposed to be adapted to better understand the complex character of the process driving judgment of materiality. Many researchers who analysed cognitive aspects of judgment have come to the conclusion that an experimental frame (in opposition to an investigation or archival methodology) would be better suited to achieve this objective.

Therefore a methodology based on experimentation has been chosen for this research. This methodology consists of two stages and is based on real scenarios developed with auditors.

2-1. Exploratory Study

In order to explore practices used by auditors to determine materiality in France, an internship was carried out in a big audit firm. During this internship, several audit files were studied in order to understand the practice of materiality in different domains.

In order to verify if French auditors recognize the influence of the qualitative factors defined by SAB.99 about ethical judgments of materiality, a questionnaire was prepared. This questionnaire was based on qualitative factors determined by this standard. It was submitted for evaluation to 44 experienced auditors. Every participant had to attribute to every qualitative factor determined by the standard, a note from 1 to 10 on a Likert scale of 10 points. These qualitative factors could be influenced by his judgment about materiality. If the participant agreed that every qualitative factor influenced his judgment about materiality he was attributed a note superior or equal to 5 points. 1 = Strong disagreement, 10 = Strong agreement.

This stage allowed the identification of various difficulties related to determination of materiality, to test the sensibility of auditors to qualitative factors, and to design real scenarios implying certain qualitative factors.

2-2. The experimental protocol

This stage aims at testing empirically how French auditors take environmental circumstances into account in their professional judgment about materiality according to the results of the exploratory study.

In fact, qualitative factors that obtained scores superior to 5, were classified according to their average scores. Real scenarios were elaborated for 3 factors that obtained the first ranks. These factors are related to: tendency changes, bonus granted to management, and the compensation of errors. These scenarios were elaborated with the partners of the audit firm where the internship was carried out. These scenarios were submitted to two other auditors and two researchers in audit to improve understanding of these real scenarios and to validate their contents. These scenarios constitute an ethical dilemma as far as the auditor has to choose between a strict application of the law and standards, and his personal ethical principles.

It has been establish that every scenario contains an inaccuracy, the extent of which is inferior to materiality (5% of net result). These inaccuracies could be explained by various reasons related either to bad interpretation and application of accounting standards, or to controversial subjective evaluation.

This study demonstrated that motivation and intention of the management were known (bonus, tendency change, illegal behaviour, etc.) in certain scenarios and not known in others (errors compensation, etc.).

The correction of these errors might influence tendency results (profit, loss) or may discover illegal acts. Therefore, in order to test the judgments of auditors according to Jones's (1991) model, the data related to three (from six) characteristics of moral intensity were integrated in every scenario: magnitude of consequences, social consensus, and the proximity to the client. Once the materiality of error and anomalies integrated into various scenarios were judged by auditors, the participants were asked to explain the factors that influenced their decisions (Appendix 2).

As the judgment of an auditor does not depend only on factors related to the situation, but also to individual factors, a sample was selected allowing us to avoid the maximum of statistical bias related to the three chosen factors. Two homogeneous groups of auditors were selected (according to age, experience, status in firm) according to their connection to a big or small audit firm. An experimental protocol was prepared and tested with two groups of auditors. The first sample was composed of 20 managers of Big four. The second consisted of 24 managers working for small firms.

These auditors had an average experience in the post of 2 years for the first group and 5 years for the second. The average age of participants was 30 years for the first group and 42 years for the second. Considering the impossibility of gathering the partners in the same place, several groups made up of 2 to 3 managers working in the same audit firm were interviewed.

The experimental protocol consisted of 6 stages and can be summarized as follows:

Stage 1: welcome of the participants
Stage 2: explanation of the instructions and distribution of scenarios
Stage 3: reading of the scenarios and
Stage 4: Q&A

Stage 5: quasi-experience

- Every participant answers the questions according to the provided instructions
- Ban on exchange between the subjects
- Ban on going out before all the present subjects were finished

Stage 6: Collection of participants' answers

All documents used in the experimental study were anonymous and contained an identification code sent by e-mail a few days earlier. This procedure allowed integration of the experimental data with the data collected previously.

Files were used to keep pages of documents in the predefined order. They were distributed after establishing the subjects. An oral procedure of welcome and presentation was used systematically, in the same way for various groups to assure a uniformity of the instructions. At the end of session, the files were handed in. The research objectives were explained to participants. During this explanation, participants were reassured about the anonymity of answers and the possibility for every auditor to contact the experimenter if they wished to modify or remove their answers, according to the current legal rules (CNIL) and to the business ethics of the researcher in social sciences (Myers et al., 2007: 42-66). The answers were recorded on the calculation sheet to be treated.

3- Results and discussions

3-1. The materiality of the qualitative factors of materiality

Taking as a basis the list of statutory auditors registered on the site of the CNCC, a list of auditors belonging to the big four and small audit firms was established. They were contacted by e-mail or telephone and asked to participate in our study.

A large number of auditors contacted did not wish to take part in our study. Some auditors did not answer our request in spite of being contacted again. The percentage of answers returned by auditors was relatively low. Despite our persistence, this percentage was approximately 13%.

The majority of participants strongly agreed with the SAB.99 and considered eight of nine qualitative factors as relevant for materiality judgment. For every factor the average score was above 7, except for one factor, the average score of which was inferior or equal to 5 points.

3-2. Influence of qualitative factors on the ethical judgment of materiality

For three tested scenarios, the results show that the majority of auditors questioned consider that they may influence their ethical judgment of materiality. The results also show that there are no significant differences of judgment between the auditors of the big four and those belonging to the small audit firms. In fact, the minimal frequencies of auditors having considered these three factors as significant and deserving to be included in audit reports are 66, 67% for auditors of the big four and 69% for auditors from small firms. The following table presents the frequencies of answers of the auditors for three tested factors.

For the three scenarios tested, the results demonstrate that the majority of auditors questioned consider that criteria of moral intensity might influence their ethical judgment of materiality. According to these results, there are no significant differences of judgment between the auditors of the big four and those belonging to small firms concerning the justification of their evaluation of materiality. However, the average scores of notes obtained are slightly superior for the auditors of the big four compared to those belonging to the small firms. It seems that sensitiveness of the auditors from the big four is stronger concerning criteria of moral intensity.

The results show that for these three scenarios, the magnitude of consequences was the main criteria to be considered for judgments of materiality. The strong scores of the auditors from the big four (9.1) (7.9) can be explained by the sensitiveness of auditors to the economic consequences of intentional qualitative anomalies. This result is confirmed by the new orientation of professional authorities aiming at protecting all stakeholders of the company. The auditor must certify financial statements, taking into account the expectations of users (bankers, clients, shareholders, etc.).

Table 1: the impact of the qualitative factors on the materiality judgments

	Auditors	
	Big four	**Non Big four**
1. The motivation of the inaccuracies or the omissions, quantitatively not significant (deliberate manipulation, a discord of opinion, involuntary error.)	8.53	8.12
2. If the irregularity or the omission, quantitatively unimportant, reveal a change of earnings tendency (sales, results)	8.76*	8.33*
3. If the irregularity or the omission, quantitatively unimportant, mask an incapacity to meet the expectations of financial analysts.	8.12	7.21
4. If the irregularity or the omission, quantitatively unimportant, modifies the losses into result.	8,23	7,33
5. If the irregularity or the omission, quantitatively unimportant, belongs to a division of the company which was identified as particularly important for the success of the company.	7.55	7.12
6. If the irregularity or the omission, quantitatively unimportant, allows the executives to have an incentive payment (bonus)	9.13*	8.25*

7. If the false revelation or the omission, quantitatively unimportant, consists in the dissimulation of an illegal act.	9.25*	9.11*
8. If the inaccuracy quantitatively not significant will be translated by a significant reaction in the stock market	8.43	8.21
9. If the inaccuracy or the known omission is compensated with another inaccuracy having an opposite consequences on the result.	9.33*	8.43*

*Factor having obtained the high scores and been retained within this research

Table 2 – Results of the real scenarios

	Qualitative Factor	The ethical judgment of materiality (big four auditors)		The ethical judgment of materiality (non big four auditors)	
		significant	Not significant	significant	Not significant
scenario 1	Tendency Change	66.67%	33.33%	78%	22%
scenario 2	Bonus	85%	15%	69%	21%
scenario 3	Illegal behaviour	80%	20%	83%	17%

Table 3 : averages scores of auditors

	Qualitative Factors	Criteria of ethical decision	The ethical judgment of materiality (big four auditors)	The ethical judgment of materiality (non big four auditors)
	Tendency Change	Magnitude of consequences	9.1	8.2
		social Consensus	7.2	5.5
scenario 1		Proximity	2.1	6.4
	Bonus	Magnitude of consequences	8.9	7.9
		Consensus social	7.5	5.3
scenario 2		Proximity	3.2	5.4
	Illegal behaviour	Magnitude of consequences	4.1	3.2
		Consensus social	3.12	1.5
scenario 3		Proximity	2.5	6.4

Also, the social consensus was very significant for both categories of auditors, with a higher score for the auditors from the big four. Contrary to the assumption about social consensus concerning immateriality of quantitatively unimportant errors, our study suggests that social consensus is not any more a general practice among auditors. In fact, the scenarios (1.2) show that the judgments of materiality were centred on a new social consensus with which all auditors considered that deliberate errors (tendency change, bonus) were inferior quantitative materiality (5%), and they were ethically significant with average scores superior to 5 on a scale of 10 points.

As for the criterion of proximity, the scores are higher for auditors from small firms than for the auditors belonging to the big four. It seems that auditors from small firms are more sensitive to the loss of a client and to economic consequences of their judgment than the auditors of the big four. These auditors from the big four might be worried about their reputation on the market and about their eventual loss of a client in the event of an error committed in one audit case.

Conclusion

Audit firms widely abused the strict application of the quantitative definition of materiality. Given the new regulations, the auditors are brought to better estimate the expectations of their clients and the significant character a piece of information might represent. They have to better evaluate the qualitative factors capable of dissimulating a financial situation for their clients independently of their threshold. The publication of SAB 99 gave a lot of importance to the quality approach, which became fundamental in the audit process.

Our results show that the judgments of materiality reflect considerations which are quantitative and qualitative (SAB.99). The result of our study shows the incoherence of the classic approach, according to which the net result is the dominating reference criterion to explain the decisions of correction of the anomalies. Our study shows that the qualitative factors of materiality influence the judgment of auditors about the evaluation of materiality. Our results reveal that the criteria of magnitude of consequences and the social consensus of Jones (1991) justify and motivate the judgment of auditors more than other criteria.

Our research allows enrichment of the works of the professional authorities by contributing to the understanding of the processes of judgments of materiality in France. The theoretical originality of this work resides in the borrowing of a theoretical frame from ethical psychology to explain judgments of materiality. The methodological interest consists in the construction of real scenarios combining three qualitative factors of SAB.99 adapted from the model of Jones (1991). However, our study presents certain limits related to the data collection and to the methods of analysis. However, our study is mainly limited by potential statistical bias produced by distortion of the answers of participants, who, despite all of our precautions, might have tended to follow the expectations of researchers.

Appendix 1: Real Scenarios

Scenario 1: change of tendency

The company "XLM" announced to their shareholders and their partners that the sales have increased compared to previous years. You note at the end of your audit that the invoices, which are given during the following exercise, were registered among the sales. The impact is inferior to materiality which you determined at the beginning of the task. However the correction of these anomalies would have incidence of decreasing the sales registered which reached a lower level than previous exercises. You have been designated auditor of this firm for 8 years.

Faced with this situation, what would be your judgment of the materiality of these anomalies?

1. If an important financing is subordinated to the objective expectation of sales?
2. If operations (financing) were planned?
3. If a potential buyer reserved his judgment according to realized sales?
4. In the absence of particular consequences?

Taking as a basis a Likert scale of 10 points, what is the probability of integration of these anomalies in audit reports?

1	2	3	4	5	6	7	8	9	10

Scenario 2: bonus

A company "MFC" announced to their shareholders and partners that the sales have increased compared to the previous exercises. You note at the end of your audit that the invoices, which are given during the following exercise, were registered on sales of this exercise. However the correction of these anomalies would have incidence of decreasing the sales registered which reached a lower level than previous exercises. You note that managers will perceive a bonus if sales increased compared to the previous exercise. An incentive contract was concluded with managers. Your Audit firm has certified this company for 10 years.

Considering these elements, what would be your judgment of the materiality of these anomalies?

Taking as a basis a Likert scale of 10 points, what is the probability of integration of these anomalies in audit reports?

1	2	3	4	5	6	7	8	9	10

Scenario 3: dissimilation of an illegal act
During your test about the respect of the cut-off accounting principle of the company TFO, you note that the accountant is incapable of producing an evidence of delivery. After investigation, you discover that the company accepted registering a forged invoice to allow a supplier to discount a bill and to obtain finance. The company was realize the same operation with her client and registered a forget invoice for the same amount. This operation does not have an impact on the accounting result. Your Audit firm has certified this company for 6 years.

Faced with this situation, what is your judgment of the materiality of this anomaly?

Taking as the basis a scale of 10 points, what is the probability of integration of these anomalies in audit reports?

1	2	3	4	5	6	7	8	9	10

Appendix 2: Ethical judgment factors of Jones (1991)

In the case where you judged the error or the significant abnormality, we ask you to indicate, among the following factors, which influenced your decision most.
Note on a scale of 10 points the importance of these factors (mailmen) in making your decision?

	Scenario 1	**Scenario 2**	**Scenario 3**
-Consequences of your judgment on the reputation of audit firm, its responsibility, and on the renewal of mandate			
-Incidence of your judgment (sentence) on the interest of your customer (Inequitable incidence with regard to the gravity of the malpractice).			
-Consideration of the perception (collection) of your colleagues and\or partners within the cabinet (office)			

References

American Institute of Certified Public Accountants (AICPA) (2006): Statement on Auditing Standards 107: Audit risk and materiality in conducting an audit, ASB, March.

Big Five Audit Materiality Task Force. (1998) "Report of the Big Five Audit Materiality Task Force".

Braun, K. W (2001)" The disposition of audit-detected misstatements: An examination of risk and reward factors and aggregation effects" Contemporary Accounting Research 18 (1): 71-99.

Bel Haj .S. (2010) "les facteurs explicatifs du jugement éthique en audit: état d'art" Comptabilité, le contrôle et l'audit entre changement et stabilité, France 2010

Carpenter, B. W. y Dirsmith, M. W. (1992): "Early debt extinguishment transactions and auditor materiality judgments: A bounded rationality perspective", Accounting, Organizations and Society, Vol. 17, N.º 8, pp. 709-739.

Carpenter, B. W., Dirsmith, M. W. y Gupta, P. P. (1994): "Materiality judgments and audit firm culture: Social-behavioral and political perspectives", Accounting, Organizations and Society, Vol. 19, N.º 4/5, pp. 355-380.

Dezoort, F. T., Hermanson, D. R. y Houston, R. W. (2003): "Audit committee support for auditors: The effects of materiality justification and accounting precision", Journal of Accounting and Public Policy, Vol. 22, N.º 2, pp. 175-199.

Dezoort, T., Harrison, P. y Taylor, M. (2006): "Accountability and auditors' materiality judgments: The effects of differential pressure strength on conservatism, variability, and effort", Accounting, Organizations and Society, Vol. 31, N.º 4/5, pp. 373-390.

Holstrum, G. L., and W. F. Messier, Jr. (1982). "A review and integration of empirical research on Materiality" Auditing: A Journal of Practice and Theory 2 (1): 45-63.

International Federation of Accountants (IFAC) (2006a): Proposed International Standard on Auditing 320 (revised and redrafted): Materiality in planning and performing an audit, 15 November. (http://www.ifac.org)

—. (2006b): Proposed International Standard on Auditing 450 (redrafted): Evaluation of misstatements identified during the audit, 15 November. (http://www.ifac.org)

—. (2008): International Standard on Auditing 320: Audit materiality,

Handbook of International Auditing, Assurance, and Ethics Pronouncements, March. . (http://www.ifac.org.)

Iselin, E. R., Iskandar, T. M. (2000): "Auditors' recognition and disclosure materiality thresholds: Their magnitude and the effects of industry", British Accounting Review, Vol. 32, N.º 3, pp. 289-309.

Iskandar, T. M., Iselin, E. R. (1999): "A review of materiality research", Accounting Forum, Vol. 23, N.º 3, pp. 209-239.

Jones, T.M., Ryan, L.V. (1997). The link between ethical judgement and action in organizations: A moral approbation approach. Organizational Science, 8, 663-680.

Jones T. (1991), "Ethical decision making by individuals in organizations: An issue contingent model", Academy of Management Review, vol. 16, pp. 366-395.

Levitt, A. (1998) "The 'Numbers Game' – Remarks of Chairman Arthur Levitt at the N.Y.U. Center for Law and Business" New York, N.Y., September 28, 1998.

—. May 10, 2000, Renewing the Covenant with Investors. Speech delivered at the New York University Center for Law and Business.

Libby, R. y Kinney, W. R. Jr. (2000): "Does mandated audit communication reduce opportunistic corrections to manage earnings to forecasts?", The Accounting Review, Vol. 75, N.º 4, pp. 383-404.

Martínez García, F. J., Fernández Laviada, A. y Montoya del Corte, J. (2007): "La financiera: Una revisión de la investigación empírica previa", Contaduría y Administración, UNAM, mayo-agosto, N.º 222, pp. 21-40.

McKee, T. E. and Elifsen, A. (2000), "Current materiality guidance for auditors", The CPA Journal, Vol. 70 No. 7, pp. 54-7.

Merchant, K. A. and J. Rockness: 1994, 'The Ethics of Managing Earnings: An Empirical Investigation', Journal of Accounting and Public Policy 13, 79–94.

Messier, W. F. Jr. (1983): "The effect of experience and firm type on materiality/disclosure judgments", Journal of Accounting Research, Vol. 21, N.º 2, pp. 611-618.

Messier, W. F. Jr., Martinov-Bennie, N. y Eilifsen, A. (2005): "A review and integration of empirical research on materiality: Two decades later", Auditing: A Journal of Practice & Theory, Vol. 24, N.º 2, pp. 153-187.

Montoya del Corte, J. (2008): "La vertiente cualitativa de la materialidad en auditoría: Marco teórico y estudio empírico para el caso español", Tesis doctoral (inédita), Universidad de Cantabria.

Morris, S. A. and R. A. McDonald: 1995, 'The Role of Moral Intensity in Moral Judgments: An Empirical Investigation', Journal of Business Ethics 14, 715–726.

Nelson, M. W., Smith, S. D. y Palmrose, Z.-V. (2005): "The effect of quantitative materiality approach on auditors' adjustment decisions", The Accounting Review, Vol. 80, N.º 3, pp. 897-920.

Nelson. M. W., J. A. Elliott, and R. L. Tarpley. (2005) "Evidence from auditors about managers' and auditors' earnings management decisions". The Accounting Review 77 (Supplement 2002): 175-211.

Ng, T. B.-P., Tan, H-T. (2003): "Effects of authoritative guidance availability and audit committee effectiveness on auditors' judgments in an auditor-client negotiation context", The Accounting Review, Vol. 78, N.º 3, pp. 801-818.

Ng, T. B.-P., Tan, H-T. (2007): "Effects of qualitative factor salience, expressed client concern, and qualitative materiality thresholds on auditors' audit adjustment decisions', Contemporary Accounting Review, Vol. 24, N.º 4, pp. 1171-1192.

Prat dit Hauret C. (2004), "Ethique et audit", Cahier de recherche du CRECCI, IAE de Bordeaux.

—. (2007), "Ethique et décisions d'audit", Comptabilité Contrôle Audit, Tome 13, vol 1, Juin, pp. 69-86.

Security and Exchange Commission (SEC) (1999) Materiality. SEC Staff Accounting Bulletin No. 99. (August 12). Washington, D.C.: SEC. (http://www.sec.gov.)

Shafer W., Morris R., Ketchand, A. (1999), "An analysis of the role of moral intensity in auditing judgments", Research on Accounting Ethics, vol. 5, pp. 249-270.

Shafer W., Morris R., Ketchand, A. (2001), "Effects of personal values on auditors' ethical decisions", Accounting, Auditing and Accountability Journal, vol. 14 (3), pp. 254-277.

Shafer, W. E. (2004): "Qualitative financial statement disclosures: Legal and ethical considerations", Business Ethics Quarterly, Vol. 14, N.º 3, pp. 433-451.

Stead, E., Worrell, D., & Garner Stead, J. (1990). "An integrative model for understanding and managing ethical behavior in business organizations" Journal of Business Ethics, 9, 233242.

Trevino L.K., Weaver G. (2003), Managing Ethics in Business Organizations: Social Scientific Perspectives, Stanford: Stanford Business Books.

Trevino L.K. (1986), "Ethical decision making in organizations: A person-situation integrationist model", Academy of Management Review, vol.11, n° 3, pp. 601- 617.

Trevino, L.K. & Youngblood, S.A. (1990). Bad apples in bad barrels: A causal analysis of ethical decision making behavior. Journal of Applied Psychology, 75, 378-385.

Wright, A. y Wright, S. (1997): "An examination of factors affecting the decision to waive audit adjustments", Journal of Accounting, Auditing and Finance, Vol. 12, N.º 1, pp. 15-36.

PART 5.

FINANCE

DOES CO-INTEGRATION AND CAUSAL RELATIONSHIP EXIST BETWEEN THE NON-STATIONARY VARIABLES FOR CHINESE BANKS PROFITABILITY? EMPIRICAL EVIDENCE

OMAR MASOOD[1], PRIYA DARSHINI PUN THAPA[2] AND MONDHER BELLALAH[3]

Introduction

In the last two decades economists have developed a number of tools to examine whether economic variables trend together in ways predicted by theory, most notably co-integration tests. Co-integration methods have been very popular tools in applied economic work since their introduction about twenty years ago. However, the strict unit-root assumption that these methods typically rely upon is often not easy to justify on economic or theoretical grounds. The multivariate testing procedure of Johansen (1988, 1991) has become a popular method of testing for co-integration of the I(1)/I(0) variety, where I(1) and I(0) stand for integration of orders one and zero, respectively. In the Johansen methodology, series are pre-tested for unit roots; series that appear to have unit roots are put into a vector auto regression from which one can test for the existence of one or more I(0) linear combinations.

Utilizing the co-integration and error correction models on all Chinese banks over the study period, various potential internal and external determinants are examined to identify the most important determinants of

[1] Royal Business School, University of East London, Docklands Campus, e-mail: omar@uel.ac.uk.
[2] Maritime Greenwich College, Equitable House, No 10 Woolwich New Road, e-mail: pdpthapa@gmail.com.
[3] E-mail: Mondher.bellalah@eco.u-cergy.fr.

profitability. Co-integration methodology has been extensively used as a convenient way of testing for the weak-form of asset market efficiency, which states that no asset price should be predictable from the prices of other assets The Johansen (1988) method of testing for the existence of co-integrating relationships has become standard in the econometrics literature.

Since unit-root tests have very limited power to distinguish between a unit-root and a close alternative, the pure unit-root assumption is typically based on convenience rather than on strong theoretical or empirical facts. This has led many economists and econometricians to believe near-integrated processes. Near-integrated and integrated time series have implications for estimation and inference that are similar in many respects. Co-integration, however, simply requires that co-integrating linear combinations have lower orders of integration than their parent series Granger (1986). In Granger and Joyeux (1980) and Hosking (1981), where continuous orders of integration from the real line are considered, the case where there exists an I(d − b) linear combination of two or more I(d) series has become known as fractional co-integration.

The co-integration approach is one of the recent methodologies employed to identify the determinants of profitability in banking. It enables the estimation of a relationship among non-stationary variables by revealing the long-run equilibrium relationship among the variables. This paper will help to determine the most important factors of profitability in Chinese banks, and is supposed to help banks' stakeholders, especially the managers and regulatory authorities, to improve the sector soundness by boosting the impact of positive factors and lessening the impact of the negative factors.

A good econometric practice is to always include tests on the co-integrating vectors to establish whether relevant restrictions are rejected or not. If such restrictions are not tested, a non-zero co-integrating rank might mistakenly be taken as evidence in favour of co-integration between variables. This is particularly relevant when there are strong prior opinions regarding which variables "have to" be in the co-integrating relationship. Unit root tests are performed on unvaried time series in order to test the order or integration. If individual time series are found to be integrated of the same order after the unit root tests, then these variables may be co-integrated. Co-integration deals with relationships among the group of variables where each has a unit root. Application of co-integration test in the estimation of money demand were analysed by Johansen and Juselius (1990) and Dickey, Thansen and Thornton (1991).

The purpose of this paper is to investigate the effect of deviations from the unit-root assumption on the determination of the co-integrating rank of the system using Johansen's (1988, 1991) maximum Eigen value and trace tests. The paper will contribute towards the existing literature by interrogating the determinants of profitability of Chinese banks using a co-integration approach. First we test for the stationary roots using augmented Dickey-Fuller test, then the Johansen's unit root test and granger causality test are applied to these variables.

The paper is divided into five sections. Section 1 describes about the previous existing literatures, Section 2 describes an overview of the Chinese banking system, Section 3 will give a complete description about the methodologies of the various tests performed in this paper, and Section 4 contains the empirical results. Finally, Section 5 concludes with a short summary.

1. Literature Review

Despite an extensive literature on savings behaviour, there are not many studies which focused primarily on the factors that determine the level of deposits made by various categories of depositors at the commercial banks. These studies, however, concentrated mainly on private and household savings and not on the business and government sectors. Lambert and Hoselitz (1963) were among the first researchers to compile the works of others on savings behaviour. They extended the works of researchers who studied the savings behaviour of households in Sri Lanka, Hong Kong, Malaysia, India, and the Philippines. Snyder (1974) and Browning and Lusardi (1996) also presented a similar study which reviewed micro theories and econometric models.

Masood, Akhtan & Chaudhary (2009) studied the co-integration and causal relationship between Return on Equity and Return on Assets of Saudi Arabia, and they found that there are stable long run relationships between the two variables. They also argued that unidirectional causality from ROE to ROA implies that sustainable development strategies with higher levels of ROE may be feasible and fast economic growth of Saudi Arabia may be achievable. Loayza et al. (2000b) listed papers and publications of the saving research project of a particular country and gave general reference in this area. Thereafter, lots of work has been done on this area; Cárdenas and Escobar (1998), Rosenzweig (2001), Kiiza and Pedreson (2001), Athukorala and Kunal Sen (2003), Dadzie et al. (2003), Ozcan, et al. (2003), Athukorala and Tsai (2003), Qin (2003) and Hondroyiannis (2004) have all studied the savings behaviour of a particular country. A large empirical literature was developed on the cross country comparison, which was contributed by Doshi (1994), Masson et al. (1998), Loayza et al. (2000a), Agrawal (2001), Anoruo (2001), Sarantis and Stewart (2001), Cohn and Kolluri (2003), and Ruza and Montero (2003).

The first works on co-integration methods were first studied by Wallace and Warner (1993), Malley and Moutos (1996), and co-integration-based tests of foreign exchange market efficiency were studied by Cardoso (1998), Bremnes et al. (2001), Jonsson (2001), Khamis and Leone (2001) and Bagchi et al. (2004). Studies arguing the stationarity of these variables include Song and Wu (1997, 1998), Taylor and Sarno (1998), Wu and Chen (2001) and Basher and Westerlund (2006). Sephton and Larsen (1991) showed that inference based on Johansen co-integration tests of foreign exchange market efficiency suffers from structural instability. Cheung and Lai (1993) argued that there is significant finite-sample bias in the performance of the Johansen test statistics when asymptotic critical values are used for inference in finite samples.

As unit-root tests have very limited power to distinguish between a unit-root and a close alternative, the pure unit-root assumption is typically based on convenience rather than on strong theoretical or empirical facts. Stock (1991), Cavanagh et al., (1995) and Elliott (1998) argued that near-integrated processes, which explicitly allow for a small deviation from the pure unit-root assumption, are a more appropriate way to describe many economic time series. Phillips (1988) concluded that spurious regressions are a problem when variables are near-integrated as well as integrated and presented an analytical discussion. Elliott (1998) shows that large size distortions can occur when performing inference on the co-integration vector in a system where the individual variables follow near-unit-root processes rather than pure unit-root processes.

The bank's profitability is generally classified into two broad categories: internal and external. The internals factors are in the control and framework of the bank, for instance number or employees, investments, etc., whereas the external factors are out of the control and framework of the bank, for instance market share, competition, inflation, etc.

Lots of literature has already been developed that interrogates the profitability of banks of the particular country in question. Hester and Zoellner (1966) argued that the balance sheet structure has a significant impact on profitability. Smirlock (1985) found a significant positive relationship between demand deposits and profits. Lambert and Hoselitz (1963) were among the first researchers to compile the works of others on savings behaviour. Heggested (1977) interrogated the profitability of commercial banks and reports that time and savings deposits have negative impact on profitability. Steiner and Huveneers (1994) found similar association while studying overhead expenditure. Bourke (1989), and Molyneux and Thorton (1992) found that capital and staff expenses are positively related to a bank's profitability.

Mullineaux (1978) found a positive impact of banks' size on profitability. Studies of Pelzman (1968), Vernon (1971), Emery (1971), Mullineaux (1978) and Smirlock (1985) concluded that regulation has a significant impact on banks' profitability. Emery (1971) examined the effect of competition on banks' profitability and found insignificant association between the two variables. Smirlock (1985) further examined the effect of concentration on profitability and the findings of these studies were mixed and inconclusive. Demirgüç-Kunt and Huizinga (1998) concluded that that the well-capitalized banks have higher net interest margins and are more profitable.

Keynes (1936), despite arguing the quantitative importance of the interest rate effect, believes that in the long run, substantial changes in the rate of interest could modify social habits considerably, including the subjective propensity to save. Regarding the importance of the rate of interest on consumption, many researchers using various methodologies have tried to establish the strength of relationship between these two elements. Wright (1967), Taylor (1971), Darby (1972), Heien (1972), Juster and Watchel (1972), Blinder (1975), and Juster and Taylor (1975) in their studies found an inverse relationship between interest rate and consumption. Modigliani (1977) based on his works and after seeing evidence on the effect of interest rate on consumption concludes that the rate of interest effects on demand, including the consumption component, are pervasive and substantial.

Alrashdan (2002) found that the return on asset (ROA) is positively related to liquidity and total assets, while ROA is negatively related to financial leverage and cost of interest. Naceur (2003) examined the determinants of Tunisian banks' profitability over the period 1980-2000, and found that the capital ratio, loans and stock market development have positive impact on profitability, while the bank's size has a negative impact. Hassan and Bashir (2003) stressed the importance of customer and short-term funding, non-interest earning assets, and overheads in promoting profits. They also argued that profitability measures respond positively to increases in capital ratio and negatively to loan ratios. Liu and Hung (2006) examined the relationship between service quality and long-term profitability of Taiwan's banks and found a positive link between branch number and long-term profitability and also proved that average salaries are detrimental to banks' profit.

2. An Overview of Chinese banking system

More than 85% of financial resources in China are allocated through the banking system hence the economic reforms of China are dominated by Chinese commercial banks. The measurement of profitability and competitive conditions of the banking system depicts the economic growth of China. Since 1978, the Chinese economy has experienced an impressive annual growth rate of about 10 percent. China's financial assets have grown at an annual rate of about 18 percent, or more than twice the growth rate of GDP.

Since the People's Republic of China was founded in 1949, the People's Bank of China (PBOC) was the only bank in Mainland China until 1978. During this period, the PBOC played a dual role in China's financial system: as a central bank and as a commercial bank. Upon nationalization of private banks in the 1949, bank management in China essentially followed the approach of centrally-planned economy.

During the period of 1953-1978, four of the Chinese banks had operated intermittently as separate units, or as a single entity. During the period 1978-1984, there were People's Bank of China (PBC), Agriculture Bank of China (ABC), Bank of China (BOC), and Construction Bank of China (CBC). During the period 1978-1984, the PBC retained the central banking activities, while four other banks—ABC, BOC, CBC, and ICBC, were carved out from the PBC to provide specialized services. The modern Chinese banking system comprises of four state-owned commercial banks, as well as several joint-stock commercial banks, city commercial banks, rural credit cooperatives, finance companies, and trust and investment companies, foreign banks have been allowed to be an integral part of the banking system.

As the economy started shifting toward market-orientation, profitability and liquidity—if any—of state-owned enterprises suffered due to their inability to adapt to the challenges imposed. State-owned banks have been hampered by non-paying or delinquent loans to other state-owned enterprises. Both the state-owned and private banks had to extend credit to the inefficient, monopolist, state-owned enterprises or public projects.

In 1994, three policy banks - China Development Bank (CDB), Agricultural Development Bank of China (ADBC), and the Export-Import Bank of China (China Eximbank) - were established. They undertook the most part of policy loans business from the four national specialty banks. Meanwhile, the four national specialty banks became state-owned commercial banks. In 2003, China Banking Regulatory Commission (CBRC) was established to take over most supervisory functions of PBOC, becoming a main regulator of China's banking industry. By the end of 2007, there were 3 policy banks, 5 large state-owned commercial banks, 12 joint-stock commercial banks, 124 city commercial banks, and 29 locally incorporated foreign bank subsidiaries as well as other banking institutions.

Chinese authorities have adopted a more flexible approach in seeking help from foreign banks in rescuing weak banks. Foreign banks, when they are well-capitalized and have access to external markets, and are less likely to turn off the credit when monetary authorities pursue tight monetary policies. Foreign banks' presence also provided needed competition to domestic banks unburdened of non-performing loans. Competitive pressure in turn provided incentives to local banks to improve management practices.

According to Commercial Banking Law of the People's Republic of China, which came in to effect on July 1st of 1995, one of the prerequisites to establish commercial banks is "Having directors and senior management personnel with professional knowledge for holding the post and work experiences". In June 2002, the People's Bank of China promulgated Guidance on Independent Directors and External Supervisors of Joint-Stock Commercial Banks, which aims to establish and enhance the arrangement of independent directors.

For Chinese banking, the most crucial issue is to convert the four state-owned commercial banks, with 70 percent of the nation's financial assets and loans, into share-holding companies. During system-wide crisis, state-owned banks often become safe havens because the public perceives that their funds will be fully guaranteed by the state. Chinese banks have suffered from bad loans and high operating costs for a long time. A sound banking industry is essential for development of efficient financial markets, in turn, efficient markets are crucial for ensuring effectiveness of the market-oriented economy. Excessive bad debts reflecting inefficient bank management are thus antithetical to the goal of market orientation for the Chinese economy.

They were underperforming compared to their counterparts in other countries. In recent years, the Chinese government has carried out a series of reforms aiming at making banks more market driven, more profitable, and well managed. One important reform among these is to establish a board of directors system in existing banks to improve corporate governance. In this context, how effective a role the board of directors have played in the profitability of Chinese banks is up to close examination.

3. Methodology

The estimation of the long run relationship between the variables, time series properties of the individual variables are examined by conducting Augmented Dickey Fuller (ADF) stationary tests, then the short run dynamic and long run co-integration relationship are investigated by using the multivariate Johansen's co-integration test and Granger Causality test.

3.1 Unit root tests

The Augmented Dickey-Fuller (ADF) unit root test method put forward by American scholars Dickey and Fuller is widely used in academia to examine the stationary property of the time series and determine the integration order of non-stationary time series. Unit root tests are first conducted to establish the stationary properties of the time series data sets. Stationary entails long run mean reversion, and determining a series with stationary property avoids spurious regression relations. It occurs when series having unit roots are regressed into one another.

The presence of non-stationary variables might lead to spurious regressions and non-objective policy implications. Augmented Dickey Fuller (ADF) tests are used for this purpose in conjunction with the critical values, which allows for calculation of critical values for any number of regressors and sample size. The ADF model used in the study is as follows:

$$\Delta \ln Y = \alpha + T + \omega \ln Y_{t-1} + \sum_{i-1}^{p} \delta\, \Delta \ln Y_{t-1} + \varepsilon \qquad (1)$$

Here Y is the variable used for unit root test, α is the constant, T represents the trend, ω = p-1 and ε is the white noise series. The null hypothesis is H_O: ω =0. If the ADF value of the lnY is bigger than the McKinnon value at 5% significant level, the null hypothesis is accepted, which means lnY has unit root and is non-stationary. If it is less than the McKinnon value then the H_0 is rejected and lnY is stationary. As for the non-stationary series, we should test the stationarity of its 1st difference. If the 1st difference is stationary, the series has unit root and it is first order integration I (1).

3.2 Johansen's co-integration test

According to the co-integration theory, there may be a co-integration relationship between the variables involved if they are of 1st order integration series, i.e. their 1st difference is stationary. There are two methods to examine this co-integration relationship; one is EG two-step procedure, put forward by Engle and Granger in 1987, the other is Johansen co-integration test (Johansen, 1988, and Juselius, 1990) based on Vector Auto Regression (VAR).

For the co-integration test, we will conduct the Johansen's multivariate co-integration tests. The Johansen's multivariate co-integration test involved testing the relationships between the variables following vector auto-regression (VAR) model:

$$\Delta \ln Y = \sum_{i=1}^{p} \Gamma_i\, \Delta \ln Y_{t-1} + \Pi \ln Y_{t-1} + BX_t + \varepsilon \qquad (2)$$

Here $\Gamma_i = -\sum_{j=i+1}^{p} A_j$ and $\Pi = \sum_{i=1}^{p} A_i - I_m$

Y_t represents n*1 vector of I (1) variables. Γ and Π are n*n matrix of coefficients to be tested. B denotes n*h matrix and X_t denotes h*1 vector of I(0) variables. Π denotes the rank of the matrix and interrogates the long-run relationships in the variable and is equal to the number of independent co-integrating vectors. If rank of Π is 0, the variables in are not co-integrated.

Johansen developed two test statistics: the trace test and the maximum Eigen value test. λ_{trace} statistic tests the null hypothesis that r=0 (no co-integration) against a general alternative hypothesis of r>0 (co-integration). The K_{max} statistic tests the null hypothesis that the number of co-integrating vectors is r against the specific alternative of r+1 co-integrating vectors. The test statistics obtained from λ_{trace} and K_{max} tests are compared against the asymptotic critical values of the two test statistics by Johansen and Juselius.

3.3 Granger Causality test

The pair wise Granger causality tests are used to examine whether the past value of a series X_t , will help to predict the value of another series at present Y_t taking into account the past value of the previous value of Y_t. The two series are first tested for stationarity using the ADF unit root test, followed by the Johansen co integration test, before performing the Granger causality test. If the time series of a variable is stationary or I(0) from the ADF test, or if the time series are found to be I(1) and co integrated. The Granger causality test is as follows:

$$X_i = \sum_{i=1}^{n} \alpha_{x,i} X_{t-i} + \sum_{i=1}^{n} \beta_{x,i} Y_{t-i} + \mu_{x,t} \quad (3)$$

$$Y = \sum_{i=1}^{n} \alpha_{y,i} Y_{t-i} + \sum_{i=1}^{n} \beta_{y,i} Y_{t-i} + \mu_{y,t} \quad (4)$$

Where X_t is the log of the first variable at time t, and Y_t is the log of the second variable at time t. $\mu_{x,t}$ and $\mu_{y,t}$ are the white noise error terms at time

t. $\alpha_{x,i}$ is the parameter of the past value of X, which tells us how much the past value of X explains the current value of X and $\beta_{x,i}$ the parameter of the past value of Y, which tells us how much the past value of Y explains the current value of X. Similar meanings apply to $\alpha_{y,i}$ and $\beta_{y,i}$.

3.4 Data

The data used in this paper was collected from 16 most significant banks of China, which includes: Agriculture Bank of China, Agricultural Development Bank of China, China Development Bank, China Merchant Bank, Bank of Communication, Industrial and Commercial Bank of China, China Everbright Bank, China Construction Bank, Bank of China, Hua Xia Bank, Export-Import Bank of China, Shen Zhen Ping An, Shen Zhen Development Bank, Xia Men International Bank, Min Sheng, and Shangai Pudong Development Bank. The dataset was developed by collecting the information from these banks.

The pooled data was made by combining the datasets from all the banks, and the regression analysis was performed on this pooled data to obtain the results which are discussed in the next section. The mean square and double accounting techniques were also used on the dataset, wherever required.

4. Empirical Analysis

4.1 Unit root test

We test for the presence of unit roots and identify the order of integration for each variable using the Augmented Dickey–Fuller (ADF) test. The null hypothesis is considered as non-stationary. The test on the variable total assets gave the following result.

The computed ADF test-statistic (1.331162) is greater than the critical values (-8.033476, -4.541245, -3.380555 at 1%, 5% and 10% significant level, respectively), thus we can conclude that the variable total assets have a unit root, i.e. it is a non-stationary series.

Table-1 ADF test statistics Null Hypothesis: total assets has a unit root Exogenous: Constant, Linear Trend. Lag Length: 1 (Fixed)

t-statistic			**Prob***
Augmented Dickey Fuller Test Statistic		1.331162	0.9773
Test critical values	1% level 5% level 10% level	-8.033476 -4.541245 -3.380555	

*MacKinnon (1996) or Augmented Dickey-Fuller Test Equation Dependent Variable: D(total assets). Method: Least Squares

Augmented Dickey fuller test equation
Dependent variable - D(total assets)
Method – Least Squares

Variable	Coefficient	Standard error	T-statistic	Prob.
Total assets	0.523410	0.393198	1.331162	0.4102

R-squared	0.639249
Mean dependent variable	1.29E + 08
Adjusted R-squared	0.278497
S.D. dependent variable	615510168
S.E. of regression	52281516
Akaike info Criterion	38.61691
Sum squared resid.	2.73E + 15
Schwarz Criterion	38. 01598
Log likelihood	-55.92536
Hannan Quinn Criterion	37.40897
F-statistic	1.771993
Dublin Watson stat	2.997813
Prob (F-statistic)	0.410164

In order to eliminate the heteroscedasticity of total assets and total equity, we take their natural logarithm and define them as LnTA and LnTE. Similarly, ADF tests were conducted on total equity and the logged variables of total assets and total equity differentiated by their order of integration are reported in Table 2.

Table-2 Results of ADF unit root test

Variable	ADF-statistic	Critical value (5%)	AIC	SC	Result
Total assets	1.331162	-4.541245	38.61691	38. 01598	non-stationary
Total equity	-0.831217	-4.542245	32.61347	32.01255	non-stationary
LnTA	0.646288	3.850555	-2.032422	-2.633347	stationary
LnTE	0.599704	3.380555	9.105954	8.504869	stationary

The lag is added to make the residual be white noise, AIC is Akaike Info.Criterion and SC is the Schwarz Criterion.

As shown in Table 2, for the variables of total assets and total equity, the results indicate the presence of a unit root at conventional levels of statistical significance for the variables of total assets and total equity. To see whether they are integrated of order one I(1) at the 1% level, we performed augmented Dickey–Fuller tests on their first difference. The results of the unit root test show that the first differences of both series are stationary which are found to reject the null hypothesis of unit root. Therefore we can conclude that all series involved in the estimation procedure are regarded as I(1), and it is suitable to make a co-integration test.

4.2 Johansen's Co-integration test

As proved by the previous test, the variables under analysis are integrated of order 1 (namely I(1)); now the co-integration test is performed. The proper way to test for the relationship between total assets and total equity is certainly to test for a co-integrating equation. In testing co-integration relationships, we use the Johansen and Juselius method of testing. For selecting optimal lag length for the co-integration test, we adopt the Schwartz Information Criterion (SIC) and Schwarz Criterion (SC). The co-integration test results performed on the variables gave the following result.

Table 3. Cointegration rank test Series: total_assets____total_equity Lags interval (in first differences): 1 to 1

Unrestricted Cointegration Rank Test (Trace)

Hypothesized No. of Prob*	Eigen values	Trace statistic	0.05 critical value	CE(s)
None**	0.874563	44.57638	12.64738	0.0010
At most 1**	0.598298	8.746002	4.983491	0.0194

Trace test indicates 2 cointegrating eqn(s) at the 0.05 level
** denotes rejection of the hypothesis at the 0.05 level
* MacKinnon-Haug-Michelis (1999) p-values

Unrestricted Cointegration Rank Test (Maximum Eigenvalue)

Hypothesized No. of Prob*	Eigen values	Trace statistic	0.05 critical value	CE(s)
None**	0.874563	38.98723	11.56473	0.0010
At most 1**	0.598298	8.746002	4.983491	0.0194

Trace test indicates 2 cointegrating eqn(s) at the 0.05 level
** denotes rejection of the hypothesis at the 0.05 level
* MacKinnon-Haug-Michelis (1999) p-values

Therefore, by applying Johansen test on total assets and total equity series we found the presence of two co-integration vectors. Hence our findings imply that there is a stable relationship between the two variables, i.e. total assets and total equity. The results for the Johansen test are concluded in Table 4.

Table-4 Results of Johansen's cointegration test

Eigen-value	t-statistic	Critical value	Prob.	Null-hypothesis (0.05)
0.874563	44.57638	12.64738	0.0010	$r=0$
0.598298	8.746002	4.983491	0.0194	$r\leq 1$

Trace test indicates 2 co-integrating eqn(s) at the 0.05 level.

4.3 Granger Causality Test

The Granger causality test demands that the economic variables should be stationary series. So we need to examine the stationary property of the 1st difference. Hence we test variables LnTA and LnTE so as to observe the causality between total assets and total equity. As the sample of observation for this test is small, we take the lag to be 1. The results of Granger Causality test are shown in table 5.

Table-5 Pairwise granger Causality test

Null Hypothesis	F-statistic	Prob
LN_TA does not granger cause LN_TE	3.91826	0.1632
LN_TE does not granger cause LN_TA	6.02545	0.0984

Hence, by applying the granger causality test to the variables, we can interpret that total assets is a granger cause to total equity, and total equity is also a granger cause to total assets. In other words total assets can affect total equity input; similarly total equity can also affect the total assets in the Chinese Banking sector. Therefore, there exists a bi-direction cause-effect relationship between total assets and total equity. The results of the Granger Causality are concluded in table 6.

Table-6 Results of Granger Causality Test

Lag	Ho	F-value	P-value	Result
1	LnTA	3.91826	0.1632	Accept Ho
1	LnTE	6.02545	0.0984	Accept Ho

To further illustrate the relationship between total assets and total equity in the Chinese Banking sector, we also conducted a graphical comparison of the two variables over a four year period. Figure 1 depicts that both the variables show a similar kind of trend till 2006. After 2006, the total assets observed a positive growth, while total equity experienced a small decrement.

4.4 Graphical Comparison

Figure 1. The relationship between total assets and total equity in the Chinese Banking sector

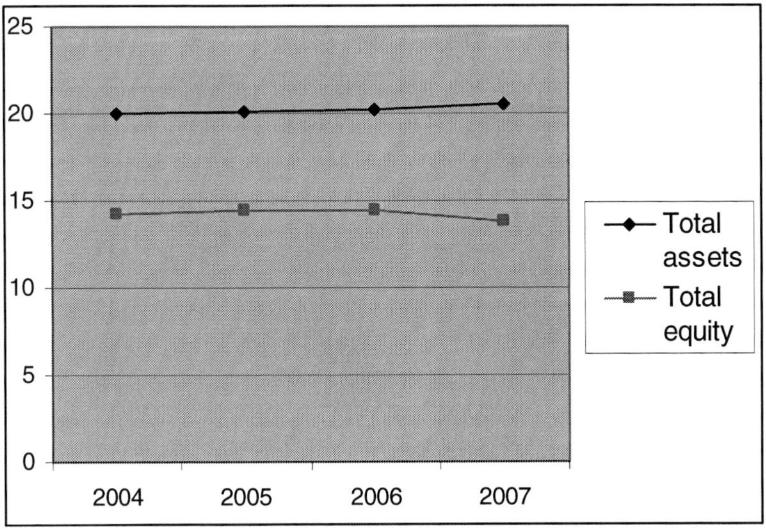

5. Conclusions

In testing the co-integration and causal relationship between total assets and total equity, the time series model of ADF unit-root test, Johansen co-integration test, Granger causality test, and graphical comparison model are employed. The empirical results have found strong evidence that the variables are co-integrated and feedback.

By applying Johansen decision rule, we found that there are two co-integration vectors for the model. Hence our findings imply that there are stable long run relationships between the two variables, i.e. total assets and total equity. Furthermore, after applying the granger causality test to the variables, we found that there exists a bi-directional cause-effect relationship between total assets and total equity in the Chinese banking sector. By applying the granger causality test to the variables we found that total assets are a granger cause to total equity, and total equity is also a granger cause to total assets. The evidences of long-run bi-directional causality from total assets to total equity implies that sustainable development may be feasible, and fast economic growth in China may be achievable. Furthermore by graphical comparison we found that both the variables were observed as having similar kinds of trends over the period of last four years.

References

Anoruo, Emmanuel (2001), 'Saving-Investment Connection: Evidence from the Asean Countries', American Economist, spring, Vol. 45, No. 1, pp. 46-53).

Athukorala, Prema-C, and Long Pang Tsai (2003), 'Determinants of Household Saving in Taiwan: Growth, Demography and Public Policy', Journal of Development Studies, Vol. 39, Issue. 5, pp. 69-88.

Agrawal, Paradep (2001), 'the Relation between Savings and Growth: Cointegration and Causality Evidence from Asia', Applied Economics, Vol. 33, pp. 499-513.

Athanasoglou, Panayiotis, S. Brissimis and M. Delis, (2008) Bank-specific, industry-specific and macroeconomic determinants of bank profitability, Journal of International Financial Markets, Institutions & Money, Vol.18,Iss.2;p.121-136.

Bashir, Abdel-Hameed (2003), Determinants of Profitability in Islamic Banks: Some Evidence from the Middle East, Islamic Economic Studies, Vol. 11, No. 1, 31-60.

Blonigen, B. A.(1997), "Firm-Specific Assets and the Link Between Exchange Rate and Foreign Direct Investment," American Economic Review, Vol. 87, No. 3, pp. 447-465.

Bourke, Philip (1989), "Concentration and Other Determinants of Bank Profitability in Europe, North America and Australia", Journal of Banking and Finance, 13, 65-67.

Boldla, B., R. Verma (2006), Determinants of profitability of banks in India: A multivariate analysis, Journal of Services Research, Vol.6, Issue .2; p.75-89.

Browning, Martin and Annamaria Lusardi (1996), 'Household Saving: Micro Theories and Micro Facts, Journal of Economic Literature, Vol XXXIV, December, pp. 1797-1855.

Cardenas, Mauricio and Andreas Escobar (1998), 'Saving Determinants in Colombia: 1925-1994', Journal of Development Economics, Vol. 57, Issue. 1. Pp.5-44.

Cesaratto, Sergio (1999), 'Savings and Economic Growth in Neoclassical Theory', Cambridge Journal of Economics, November, Vol. 23, No. 6, pp. 771-793.

Cheung, Yin-Wong, and K.S.Lai (1993), 'Finite-sample Sizes of Johansen's Likelihood Ratio Tests for Cointegration', Oxford Bulletin of Economics and Statistics, Vol. 55, pp.313-328.

Doshi, Kokila (1994), 'Determinants of Saving Rate: An International Comparison', Contemporary Economic Policy, January, Vol. 12, Issue. 1, pp. 37-45.

Demirgüç-Kunt, Asli and Huizinga, Harry (1998), Determinants of commercial bank interest margins and profitability: some international evidence, (Electronic Version), The World Bank economic Review, Oxford University Journal Vol. 13, May 2, 1999: PP. 379-408.

Darby, M.R. (1972), 'The Allocation of Transitory Income among Consumers' Assets', American Economic Review, December, pp. 928-41.

Dickey, D.A., W.A. Fuller, Distribution of the Estimates for Autoregressive Time Series with a Unit Root, Journal of the American Statistical Association 74 (1979) 427-431.

Dickey, D.A., W.A. Fuller, Likelihood Ratio Statistics for Autoregressive Time Series with a Unit Root, Econometrica, 49 (1981) 1057-1072.

El-Bdour, Radi and Cengiz Erol (1989), 'Attitudes, Behaviour and Patronage Factors of Bank Customers Towards Islamic Banks', International Journal of Bank Marketing, Vol. 7, No. 6, pp. 31-37.

Engle, R.F. And C.W.J. Granger (1987), 'Co-integration an Error Correction Representation, Estimation, and Testing, Econometrica, Vol. 55, pp. 251-276.

Erol, C., and El-Bdour, R. (1989), 'Attitudes, Behaviour and Patronage Factors of Bank Customers towards Islamic Banks', International Journal of Bank Marketing, Vol 7, No. 6, pp. 31-39.

Friedman, Milton (1957), 'A Theory of the Consumption Function.' General Series 63, National Bureau of Economic Research, Cambridge, Mass. Processed.

Fraser, Donald R. and Peter S. Rose (1972),"Bank Entry and Bank Performance." Journal of Finance, Vol. 21, No 1 (March), 65-78.

Granger, C.W.J. (1980), Testing for Causality: A Personal Viewpoint, Journal of Economic Dynamics and Control, 2, 329-352.

—. (1969), Investigating Causal Relation by Econometric Models and Cross-Spectral Methods, Econometrica, 37, 424-438.

Haron, Sudin (1996a), The Effects of Management Policy on the Performance of Islamic Banks, Asia Pacific Journal of Management, Vol. 13, No. 2, 63-76.

Heggested, Arnold A. (1977), "Market Structure, Risk, and Profitability in Commercial Banking." Journal of Finance, 32 (September), 1207-16.

Heien, D.M. (1972), 'Demographic Effects and the Multiperiod Consumption Function', Journal of Political Economy, Vol 80, no 1, pp. 125-88.

Hondroyiannis, George (2004), 'Estimating Private Savings Behaviour in Greece.' Journal of Economic Studies, Vol. 31, Iss. 5, pp.457-476.

Pesaran, H., Y. Shin, Generalized Impulse Response Analysis in Linear Multivariate Analysis, Economics Letters 58 (1998) 17-29.

Johansen, S. And K. Juselius1 (1990), 'Maximum Likelihood Estimation and Inference on Cointegration with Application to the Demand for Money', Oxford Bulletin of Economics and Statistics, Vol. 52, pp.169-210.

Johansen, S. (1988), 'Statistical Analysis of Cointegration Vectors', Journal of Economic Dynamics and Control, Vol. 12, pp. 231-254.

Juster, F.T. And Taylor, L.D. (1975), 'Towards a Theory of Saving Behaviour', American Economic Review, Papers and Proceedings, May, pp. 203-9.

Kwast, Mayron L., and John T. Rose (1982), "Pricing, Operating Efficiency, and Profitability among Large Commercial Banks." Journal of Banking and Finance, Vol. 6 No. 2 (June), 233-254.

Kahf, Monzer and Khursid Ahmad (1980), "A Contribution to the Theory of Consumer Behaviour in Islamic Society", Studies in Islamic Economics, Leicester: The Islamic Foundation.

Kiiza Barnabas and Glen Pederson (2001), 'Rural Household Savings Mobilization: Empirical Evidence from Uganda,' Journal of African Economics, Vol. 10, No. 3, pp. 390-409.

Loayza, Norman and Rashmi Shankar (2000), 'Private Savings in India', The World Bank Economic Review, Vol. 14, No. 3, pp. 571-594.

Loayza, Norman, Klaus Schmidt-Hebbel, and Luis Serven (2000a), 'What Drives Private Saving Across the World', the Review of Economics and Statistics, May, Vol. 14, No. 3, pp. 393-414.

Liu, Yong, and Jung-Hua Hung (2006) Services and the long-term profitability in Taiwan's banks, Global Finance Journal, Vol. 17, Iss.2; p. 177-191.

Li-Zhou, WU Yu-ming, LI Jian-xia, Co-integration and Causality between R&D Expenditure and Economic Growth in China: 1953—2004. 2007 International Conference on Public Administration

Molyneux, Philip and John Thornton, (1992), Determinants of European Bank Profitability: A Note, Journal of Banking and Finance, 16, 1173-1178.

Metwally, M.M. (1997), “Differences between the Financial Characteristics of Interest-Free Banks and Conventional Banks”, European Business Review, Vol 97, No 2, pp. 92-98.

Masood O., Akhtan B. and Chaudhary S., An empirical study on the banks profitability in the KSA: a co integration approach”, African journal of Business Management Vol 3(8) August 2009 pg 374-382

Mullineaux, Donald J., (1978), Economies of Scale and Organizational Efficiency in Banking: A Profit-Function Approach, Journal of Finance, 33, 259-280.

Modigliani, F. and R. Brumberg (1954), Utility Analysis and the Consumption Function: An interpolation of the Cross-Section Data, in Post-Keynesian Economics, (Ed.) K. Kurihara, Rutgers U. Press, New Brunswick, NJ, pp. 388- 436.

Ozcan, Kivilcim M., Asli Gunay, and Seda Ertac (2003), ‘Determinants of Private Savings behaviour in Turkey,’ Applied Economics, Vol. 35, Iss. 12, pp. 1405- 1416.

Ruza, Cristina and Jose, M. Montero (2003), ‘Empirical Analysis of Savings Behaviour in European Countries: New Insights’, International Advance in Economic Research, Vol. 9, No. 4, November, pp. 279-287.

Sarantis, Nicholas and Chris Stewart (2001), ‘Saving Behaviour in OECD Countries: Evidence from Panel Cointegration Tests’, The Manchester School Supplement 2001, 1463-6786, pp.22-41.

Snyder, Donald W. (1974), ’Econometric Studies of Household Saving Behaviour in Developing Countries: A Survey’, Journal of Development Studies, Vol. 10, Iss. 2, January, pp. 139-154.

Short, Brock K. (1979),”The Relation Between Commercial Bank Profit Rates and Banking Concentration in Canada, Western Europe and Japan, Journal of Banking and Finance, 3, 209- 219.

Smirlock, Michael (1985),”Evidence on the (Non) Relationship Between Concentration and Profitability in Banking.” Journal of Money, Credit and Banking, Vol. 17, No 1(February), 69-83.

Steinherr, A., and Ch. Huveneers (1994), “On the Performance of Differently Regulated Financial Institutions: Some Empirical Evidence.” Journal of Banking and Finance, Vol. 18, 271-306.

Uster, F.T. and Wachtel, P. (1972), ‘A Note on Inflation and the Saving Rate.’ Brooking Papers on Economic Activity, no. 3, pp. 765-78.

Wright, C. (1967), ‘Some Evidence on the Interest Elasticity of Consumption.’American Economic Review, September, pp. 850-4.

Yu Qiao (2005), "PPP, real exchange rate and international competitiveness—theoretical approach about calculating Chinese weighted real exchange rate index," Financial Research, No. 1, pp. 57-62.

INTERACTIONS BETWEEN FREE CASH FLOW, DEBT POLICY AND STRUCTURE OF GOVERNANCE: THREE STAGE LEAST SQUARE SIMULTANEOUS MODEL APPROACH : EVIDENCE FROM THE TUNISIAN STOCK EXCHANGE

BEN MOUSSA FATMA[1]
AND CHICHTI JAMELEDDINE[2]

1. Introduction

In the debate on the convergence-of-interest hypothesis, relief of the agency theory (Fama and Miller 1972, Jensen and Meckling 1976) as well as of the signalling theory, the main concerned actors are managers, shareholders and creditors. The basic idea of agency theory is that every agent looks for the maximization of his self-interest, from where there is the apparition of conflicts (Ross, 1977). In these conditions the idea that the financial markets are perfected is rejected. Indeed, these will be determined by asymmetries of information and conflicts of interest.

Several works attempted to estimate agency costs and to test their effect on the cost of capital and also on the firm value. Moreover, an abundant literature is interested in the possible relations between the choice of the level of leverage and the agency problem. Two main cases have been exposed. First, debt may reduce agency conflicts resulting from opportunistic behaviour of managers. We principally mention the overinvestment problem (Jensen, 1986). Secondly, the debt aggravates Shareholder-creditor agency conflicts. The most studied examples are the asset substitution problem, the problem of transferring wealth from the

[1] Ecole Supérieure de Commerce de Tunis, Université de la Manouba.
[2] Directeur de l'école doctorale ECCOFIGES, Campus Universitaire de la Manouba, 2010 Tunis, Tunisia.

firm's bondholders to the stockholders, and the under investment problem (Smith and Warner (1979), Jensen and Meckling (1976) and Myers (1977)).

In this study we are going to define the role of debt and ownership structure as a control mechanism of the manager's behaviour for the firms generating free cash flows.

The concept of free cash flow has been introduced by Jensen (1986). It is cash flow in excess of that required to fund all projects that have positive net present values. The problem is how to encourage managers to disgorge the cash rather than investing it below the cost of capital or wasting it on organization inefficiencies. Therefore, the affectation of the free cash flow is at the core of the problem of agency relations.

Indeed, the distribution of these abundant free cash flows appears not to be constrained by the use of them in profitable investments, nor in contributing them to operating expenses or to the repayment of the debt. The temptation for managers is to affect this free cash flow to non-profit investments, or to destine them to other finalities such as inefficient restructuring plans or increase of the size of the firm with the only objective being to increase their remuneration (Dorff, 2007).

In the context of the agency theory, leverage is considered as an efficient solution to conflicts of interests that can appear between shareholders and managers, contrary to the thesis of Modigliani and Miller (1958), where the capital structure is associated solely with a model of cash flows, its importance is related to the capacity of creditors to exercise control.

Thus in the case of issuing debt, the manager is obliged to face remittances of annuities (Jensen and Meckling, 1976), to stop the current operations of the firm and to opt for its liquidation (Harris and Raviv, 1990), to be more competitive (Grossman and Hart, 1982) and to limit his discretionary behaviour on free cash flow (Jensen, 1986; Stulz, 1990; and Pindado and De La Torre 2005).

Also, the development of the relative theory to corporate governance came to specify other mechanisms in order to control managers and to reduce these conflicts. Among these control mechanisms we distinguish the ownership structure. Indeed, the composition of the shareholding of a firm, as well as its degree of dispersion, influences its strategic and financial orientations. In this case, several authors (Leland and Pyle, 1977; Hermalin and Weisbach, 1991; Himmelberg and al., 1999) consider managerial ownership as an evident solution to agency conflicts that permits the alignment of interests of managers with those of shareholders.

Also, the majority of studies related to the effect of ownership concentration confirm the hypothesis of their positive role in corporate governance. Berle and Means (1932) affirm that a diffuse ownership structure decreases the relationship between the ownership and the control and minimizes, therefore, the role of value maximization. To this effect, Jensen and Meckling (1976) affirm that agency costs decrease with ownership since ownership change lead to alignment with the interests of managers and shareholders.

Furthermore, theories on corporate governance developed in parallel with the financial market development and the rise in power of the institutional investors, and numerous reforms have been taking place in many countries in order to reinforce the power of shareholders. The institutional investors play an important role in these transformations while requiring new norms favourable to shareholders and while exercising an important pressure on managers (Pound and Millar, 1999).

This research intends to test the efficiency of the ownership structure and the debt policy as a mechanism of resolution of agency conflicts between shareholders and managers due to the problem of overinvestment, in the limitation of the problem of free cash flow. So we estimate a three stage least square simultaneous model. For the financial policy we are going to test the role of the long term debt in the reduction of investments in excess, in firms that have strong agency problems. For the ownership structure we take account of the managerial ownership, the institutional ownership, and the ownership concentration.

Tests using a sample of 206 observations for 35 non-financial Tunisian listed firms from 1999 to 2008 indicate that debt policy represents the principal governance mechanism that can limit the level of free cash flow. However, ownership concentration and managerial ownership increase the risk of free cash flow. Finally, the level of free cash flow is not affected by institutional ownership.

The rest of the paper is organized as follows. Section 2 reviews the previous theoretical and empirical research. Section 3 describes the empirical framework. The empirical results are presented in Section 4; and Section 5 concludes.

2. Literature Review and hypotheses

2.1 Debt policy and agency costs of free cash flow

The role of debt monitoring in reducing the agency costs of free cash flow is well emphasized in the theoretical and empirical literature.

Jensen (1986, page 323) defines free cash flow, as the "cash flow in excess of that required to fund all projects that have positive NPV". He says that managers may use free cash flow to invest in negative NPV projects rather than return the free cash flow to the shareholders, for example as dividends. This problem is especially bad in firms who are mature and with low growth opportunities, as they have low profitable investments. However, by increasing debt with its required interest payments, managers are "bonding their promise to pay out future cash flows". Jensen indicates that firms with excess cash flows and low growth opportunities will use more debt financing for monitoring purposes. Stulz (1990) also suggested positive relation between leverage and free cash flow. But their theories find no support from the empirical research of Chaplinsky and Niehaus (1990).

Also, Hart and Moore (1995) suggest that the debt doesn't resolve the overinvestment problem by the reduction of free cash flow but rather it is its priority statute that limits the external amount can be collected by the firm.

Empirically, Lang et al. (1996) find a negative relationship between the leverage and growth opportunities in firms with low growth opportunities, in accordance with free cash flow theory, and find that changes in free cash flow lead to positive changes in leverage in the 142 American listed firms from 1970 to1989.

Gul and Jaggi (1999) develop a composite IOS measure by conducting a common factor analysis on six growth variables in order to classify firms with growth opportunities. The authors use data from 1989 to 1993 for non-regulated industrial firms. Results indicate that the debt has a positive effect on free cash flow firms with low growth opportunities in terms of the bottom quartile of IOS.

Vilasuso and Minkler (2001) develop a dynamic model that incorporates the issues of agency cost and asset specificity. Results based on an unbalanced panel of 28 publicly-held firms show that these two factors are significant determinants of the optimal capital structure of firms. Moreover, results show that agency costs increase with degree of assets specificity.

De Jong and van Dijk (2007) empirically examine the determinants of leverage and agency problems, and they test the relations between leverage and four agency problems, i.e. direct wealth transfer, asset substitution, underinvestment, and overinvestment. Based on a sample of Dutch firms from 1992 to 1997, the results prove that the trade-off between tax advantages and bankruptcy costs determines leverage. Moreover, free cash flow and corporate-governance characteristics appear to be determinants of overinvestment. Despite findings that agency problems are present, there is no evidence for any relationship between agency problems and leverage.

Li and Cui (2003) test the effect of capital structure on agency costs in 211 non-financial Chinese listed firms for the period from 1999 to 2001. Based on a system of simultaneous equations, results prove that firms with a high debt to asset ratio have a high ratio of annual sales to total assets and high ratio of return-on-equity. In this case, creditors are more concerned about the payment of interest and of principal, and will have incentives to monitor the firm. Consequently, a capital structure with high debt decreases agency costs. Results also show a positive relationship between ownership concentration and the return-on-equity ratio. This is because the blockholders have a strong interest in firm performance and therefore a high capability to monitor the manager in order to reduce agency costs.

Wu (2004), using 833 observations of listed Japanese firms for the period 1992-2000 tests the disciplinary role of ownership structure in corporate capital structure policy. Estimating OLS regression with leverage ratio as the dependent variable and several independent variables, which are ownership structure, free cash flow, and growth opportunities, the results confirm that the leverage has a positive effect on free cash flow, greater for firms with low growth opportunities than firms with high growth opportunities.

Zhang and Li (2008) employ multivariate tests and univariate tests to analyse the hypothesis, which suggests that increase of leverage may reduce agency costs. Based on a sample of 323 UK companies, the results confirm that the increase of leverage does reduce agency costs. Nevertheless, when the leverage is sufficiently high, the additional increase in leverage has a positive and non-significant effect on agency costs. Finally, no significant evidence is found when testing whether the effect of leverage on agency costs becomes stronger as the differences of leverages of firms at different leveraged stages becomes larger.

Nekhili et al. (2009) test the capacity of governance mechanisms, in the limitation of the problem of free cash flow in the case of French firms. By estimating a three stage least square simultaneous model, results prove that distribution of dividends – rather than debt level – lead to a reduction of free cash flow risk.

Recently, D'Mello and Miranda (2010) present a direct test of the overinvestment control hypothesis which states that long-term debt influences the degree to which firms overinvest. They do so by examining the pattern of overinvestment in cash and capital expenditure around new debt issues by unlevered firms. Based on a sample of 366 debt issues between the year 1968 and the year 2001 by firms that have been unlevered for at least three years, the results confirm that issuing debt leads to a reduction of overinvestment. Also, this relation is more significant for firms with poor investment opportunities, confirming that debt plays an important role in reducing excess investments in firms that have the highest agency problems.

Agostinho and Prudencio (2010) analyse the capacity of the capital structure policy, the dividend policy, the board and ownership structure, and the practices of social responsibility in the limitation of free cash flow risk. Using a sample of 298 firms of the NYSE Euronext of the year 2007, the results show that corporate governance mechanisms limit the arbitrariness of the management. In particular, the results confirm the role of leverage in reducing agency costs of free cash flow.

Based on these theoretical and empirical works, the following hypotheses apply:

Hypothesis 1: Leverage is positively related to free cash flow in the firms with low growth opportunities and generating free cash flows.

2.2 The previous empirical studies testing capital structure determinants

Harris and Raviv (1991) imply that the leverage of firms may be affected by many factors, such as investment opportunities, advertising expenditures, fixed assets, the possibility of bankruptcy, and the profitability and uniqueness of product. For our empirical purposes, we focus on size, tangibility, tax, growth opportunities, profitability, risk, and industry classification.

2.2.1 Firm size

Theoretically, the effect of size on leverage is ambiguous. On the one hand, some authors find a positive relationship between size and leverage, for example Rajan and Zingales (1995), Huang and Song (2002), Delcoure (2007) and Pao (2008). Larger firms are much more diversified than smaller ones and so have lower variance of earnings, making them able to accept high debt ratios. On the other hand, some studies report a negative relationship, for example Kim and Sorensen (1986), Titman and Wessels (1988), Fluck et al. (2000), and Chen (2004). Due to asymmetry information, small firms are more likely to be under-priced by investors than large firms, and could not get a favourable price when financing through equity (Halov and Heider, 2005). While using debt with a fixed interest rate, small firms could suffer less loss from mispricing. Thus small firms should tend to consider using more debt, compared to large firms.

Hypothesis$_2$*(a):* According to the static trade off theory (agency theory), size has a positive impact on leverage.

Hypothesis$_2$*(b):* According to the asymmetric information theory and the pecking order theory, size has a negative impact on leverage.

2.2.2 Tangibility

Booth et al. (2001) state: "The more tangible the firm's assets, the greater its ability to issue secured debt." Consequently, a positive relationship between tangibility and leverage is presumed since tangible assets can be used as collateral. Also, in the case of conflict of interest between shareholders and creditors, Jensen and Mecklings (1976) demonstrated that the problem of overinvestment is less serious with more tangible assets.

Several empirical studies confirm this suggestion (Rajan and Zingales, 1995; Kremp et al., 1999; Hovakimian et al., 2001; Chen, 2004; Drobetz and Fix, 2005; Fattouh et al., 2005; Huang and Song, 2006; Delcoure, 2007; Pao, 2008; De Jong et al., 2008). On the other hand, Booth et al. (2001) suggest that the relationship between tangible fixed assets and debt financing is related to the maturity structure of the debt. In such a situation, the level of tangible fixed assets may facilitate the firms getting more long-term debt, but the agency problems may become more severe with further tangible fixed assets, because the information revealed about future earnings is less in these firms. In this case, a negative relationship between tangible fixed assets and debt ratio is presumed.

H_3 (a): according to the agency theory, there is a positive relationship between leverage and tangibility.

H_3 (b): according to the pecking order theory, there is a negative relationship between leverage and tangibility.

2.2.3 Taxation

Numerous empirical studies have explored the impact of taxation on corporate financing decisions. According to the trade-off theory, a firm with a higher tax rate should issue more debt since it has more income to shield from taxes. However, for example Fama and French (1998) declare that debt has no net tax benefits. MacKie-Mason (1990) also stipulates: "Nearly everyone believes taxes must be important to financing decision, but little support has been found in empirical analysis."

Empirically, Graham and Tucker (2006) use a sample of 44 tax shelter cases to examine the degree of tax shelter activity and whether participating in a shelter is associated with debt policy. The results show that the firms use less debt when they engage in tax sheltering. The tax shelter firms appear underlevered if shelters are ignored but do not appear underlevered once shelters are considered.

Buettner et al. (2009) test the impact of taxes on the capital structure of German firms. The empirical analysis confirms that the local tax burden exerts important effects on an affiliate's leverage. This refers not only to external debt; the results show that a higher local tax has a positive impact on internal debt. This confirms that multinationals have access to another instrument which can be used to exploit the tax savings opportunities of debt finance.

Hypothesis $_4$: According to the trade-off theory, there is positive relationship between leverage and tax rate

2.2.4 Growth opportunities

Jensen (1986) suggests that in the case of low growth opportunities, agency costs of free cash flow augment, so, debt should be issued. In doing so, probability of overinvestment by managers is reduced, as firms commit to utilizing future free cash flows for paying out to investors. Consequently, a negative relationship between growth opportunities and debt ratios can be predicted.

Myers (1977) indicates that high leverage reduces the incentives of the managers and shareholders to invest in profitable investment opportunities, since the benefits return to the bondholders rather than to the shareholders. Thus, highly levered firms are less likely to exploit valuable growth opportunities as compared to firms with low levels of leverage. So the values of stocks diminish when there is information that the firm will issue stocks according to the asymmetric information theory. In this case, firms should not issue stocks and must use all internal resources and then financing via debt, according to the pecking order theory.

Empirically, Aivazian et al. (2005) examine the effect of leverage on investment in 1035 Canadian industrial firms for the period from 1982 to 1999. They found a negative relationship between investment and leverage and that the relationship is more significant for low growth firms rather than high growth firms. Chen and Zhao (2006) find a non-monotonic and positive relationship between growth opportunities and leverage for more than 88% of COMPUSTAT firms. Billett et al. (2007) conclude that although growth opportunities negatively affect the leverage, there is a positive relationship between leverage and growth opportunities because of covenant protection. Debt covenants may attenuate the negative effect by attenuating the agency costs of debt for firms with high growth opportunities.

H_5 (a): according to the agency theory and the asymmetric information theory, there is a negative relationship between leverage and growth opportunities.

H_5 (b): according to the pecking order theory, there is a positive relationship between leverage and growth opportunities.

2.2.5 Profitability

There are no consistent theoretical predictions on the effects of profitability on leverage. According to the trade-off theory, more profitable firms should have higher leverage because they have more income to shield from taxes. Also, the free cash-flow theory would suggest that more profitable firms should use more debt in order to discipline managers. However, from the point of view of the pecking-order theory, firms prefer internal financing to external. Thus more profitable firms have a lower need for external financing and consequently should have lower leverage.

Most empirical studies observe a negative relationship between leverage and profitability, for example (Rajan and Zingales, 1995; Huang and Song, 2002; Booth et al., 2001; De Jong et al., 2008; and Karadeniz et al., 2009)

H_6 (a): according to the agency theory, there is a positive relationship between leverage and profitability.

H_6 (a): according to the pecking order theory, there is a negative relationship between leverage and profitability.

2.2.6 Firm risk

Several authors stipulate that the level of leverage is a decreasing function of the gain variability. The negative relation is predicted by the Trade-off theory, the pecking order theory, and the agency theory. Indeed, in a hierarchical financing perspective the volatility of profits can allow the firm to form a reserve of easily mobilizable assets in order to avoid an overinvestment problem. However, there are arguments demonstrating the effect positive of risk on leverage. Indeed, firms having a higher risk can also have a strategy of overinvestment, which creditors have difficulty discerning because of the asymmetry of information between lenders and borrowers and which will reduce the costs of the agency. Huang and Song (2002) suggest, based on findings of Hsia (1981): "As the variance of the value of the firm's assets increases, the systematic risk of equity decreases. So the business risk is expected to be positively related to leverage."

Empirically, the effect of risk on leverage is ambiguous. On the one hand, some authors find an inverse relationship between risk and leverage, for example Bradley et al., 1984; Titman and Wessels, 1988; Friend and Lang, 1988; MacKie-Mason, 1990; Kale et al., 1991; Kim et al., 1998). Other studies suggest a positive relationship (Jordan et al., 1998; Michaelas et al., 1999; Wiwattanakantang, 1999; Kremp and Stöss, 2001; Esperança et al., 2003; and Pao, 2008).

H_7 (a): according to the trade-off theory and the pecking order theory, there is a negative relationship between leverage and firm risk.

H_7 (a): according to the asymmetric information theory, there is a positive relationship between leverage and firm risk.

2.2.7 Industry Classification

Some empirical studies identify a statistically significant relationship between industry classification and leverage. Titman (1984) and Titman and Wessels (1988) show that firms manufacturing machines and equipment should be financed with relatively lower debt because they incur some very important liquidation costs. They use a dummy variable equal to one if the firm belongs to the industry sector and zero otherwise. Harris and Raviv (1991) declare, based on a survey of empirical studies: "Drugs, Instruments, Electronics, and Food have consistently low leverage while Paper, Textile Mill Products, Steel, Airlines, and Cement have consistently large leverage". More recently Awan et al. (2010) examine the relationship between growth opportunities and capital structure of the firms for a sample of 110 manufacturing companies listed on Karachi Stock Exchange for 15 years (1982-1997) from 9 different sectors. They found a significant positive relationship between growth opportunities and leverage that is greatly significant for sectors such as textiles, sugar, cement, paper, and jute. The possible explanation for such leverage behaviour in these sectors could be that the owners of these firms, with a nominal foreign representation, view the available growth opportunities as unsustainable and more risky and intend to pass on a higher risk to their creditors, which would result in a high debt level. However, some empirical studies find no significant relationship between the leverage and industry classification. We especially mention the study of Drobetz and Fix (2005) for the Swiss firms and that of Kim, Heshmati and Aoun (2006) for the non-financial listed firms in Korea. For the Tunisian firms, the industrial sector grants a high importance to restructurings, requiring some enormous amounts.

H_8 : The industrial firms should be financed with relatively higher debt which will have as a consequence the reduction of their free cash flow level.

2.3 Ownership structure and agency costs of free cash flow

The literature provides mixed guidance on the role of ownership structure as a corporate governance mechanism. The ownership concentration, the managerial ownership, and institutional ownership are three attributes that characterize the ownership structure of a firm.

Theoretically, for a firm whose capital is highly dispersed, a minority shareholder will not have the incitement nor the necessary funds to exercise control over managers. While, for a shareholder, possessing an important part in the capital, he will grant more interest to the control of managers; this can be exercised by voting rights that he possesses, by resources that he can use to supervise managerial actions, or by the influence that he can exercise on the minority shareholders in order to sustain him in the case of disagreement with the managerial team.

Jensen and Meckling (1976) affirm that large shareholders are more motivated and have stronger power to guarantee shareholder value maximization, by aligning the interest of managers and shareholders and therefore reduce agency costs.

Zeckhauser and Pound (1990) test whether presence of large shareholders is related to systematic differences in expected earnings growth, dividend pay-out ratios, and leverage ratios. Based on a sample of firms from 22 industries, results show that in 11 industries with a relatively open information structure, large shareholders are associated with significantly higher expected earnings growth rates.

More recent works suggest the benefits of large shareholders in a different context.

Pindado and De La Torre (2005) examine the effect of ownership structure on debt policy on the basis of a sample of 135 Spanish companies from 1990 to 1999. Results show that ownership concentration enhances debt financing in the presence of a free cash flow problem, even though debt is less used when there is a problem of expropriation of minority shareholders by controlling owners. Furthermore, they provide some results regarding the interaction between insider ownership and ownership concentration. Results show that ownership concentration does not change the relationship between managerial ownership and debt because when entrenched managers are in control, the monitoring role of outside owners become ineffective. Even though the additional debt promoted by outside shareholders increases when managers are entrenched, the relationship between ownership concentration and debt is affected by managerial ownership.

Al-Deehani and Al-Saad (2007) test the impact of the ownership structure on the capital structure of the firms listed in the Kuwait Stock Exchange. Empirical results show a positive relationship between the amount of debt and the level of control rights relative to the level of cash flow rights. Moreover, findings point out a positive relationship between the level of debt and the existence of a manger from a controlling family. Finally, a third positive relationship between the amount of debt and the amount of controlling rights, and cash flow rights and a family concentrated ownership has also been found.

Driffield et al. (2007) empirically examine the effects of ownership structure on capital structure and firm value among listed non-financial companies in Indonesia, Korea, Malaysia and Thailand. Results obtained from 3SLS model confirm that ownership concentration has significantly positive effects on leverage and firm value. Moreover, results show that ownership concentration tends to minimize agency costs for all groups of firms.

Syriopoulos et al. (2007) tend to show how different ownership structures may influence the allocation of firms' resources and investigate the impact of debt and dividend policies on corporate performance and firm market value. Based on a sample of 166 Greek companies listed in the Athens Stock Exchange, the empirical results confirm the importance of debt and dividends in terms of firm value creation by demonstrating a negative relationship between firm value and both leverage and dividend ratios in firms with high growth opportunities. Concerning the effect of ownership structure on firm resources, results show a positive relationship between ownership concentration and market value of firm, higher in the firms having growth opportunities, which is consistent with the idea that large shareholders have power to monitor management and reduce the free rider problem of corporate control associated with dispersed ownership.

Chen and Yur-Austin (2007) examine the efficiency of blockholders in mitigating agency costs such as managerial extravagance, poor asset management, and underinvestment. Based on a sample of large publicly traded companies from 1996 to 2001, empirical results show that outside blockholders are more effective in mitigating managerial extravagance, whereas inside blockholders are more vigilant about improving the efficiency of firm asset utilization. However, only managerial blockholders significantly overcome underinvestment problems, which may be attributable to the duality of their roles.

Nevertheless, Nekhili et al. (2009) show that the ownership concentration increases agency costs of the free cash flow in the case of the French firms.

On the basis of a sample of Tunisian listed firms from 1995 to 2000, Omri (2003) shows that the ownership concentration permits the reduction of the managerial entrenchment and increases the possibility of change in the case of bad performance.

Hypothesis$_9$: free cash flow level will be lower at higher levels of ownership concentration.

Managerial ownership has been extensively mentioned in the literature as a governance mechanism assuring the alignment of interests. Jensen and Meckling's convergence of interest hypothesis suggests that managerial ownership serves to align the interests of mangers and outside shareholders. Indeed, managers take fewer decisions that will have negative effects on the firm's value because the portion of the costs that they will absorb as shareholders, increases with their part of the capital. Therefore, managerial ownership property represents a mechanism that permits reduction of the cost of control supported by shareholders because it is supposed to reduce managerial opportunism. However, according to the entrenchment theory, when the managerial ownership becomes very high, it sometimes becomes difficult to oust them even though their performance is judged dissatisfactory. Thus, they manage to dominate assemblies of shareholders, and, indirectly, all decisions taken by the firm (Daniel and Halperns, 1996), and try to reduce the possibility of takeover attempts (Stulz, 1988). The first developments of this theory are owed to

Shleifer and Vishny (1989). The entrenchment process passes by the execution of specific investment that is going to facilitate the realization of projects in direct relation with their formation or experience, even though these are not necessarily most profitable for the firm.

Morck, Shleifer, and Vishny (1988) propose a model in which increased managerial ownership leads to entrenchment, where the manager will indulge in non-value-maximizing behaviour. However, management's self-indulgence is expected to be less than if he has control but no claim on the firm's cash flows. The entrenchment hypothesis predicts that the value of the firm will decrease as management ownership increases.

Poulain-Rehm (2005) tested the role of governance mechanisms in the limitation of the free cash flow problem in managerial and patrimonial listed firms. The author suggests that the effect of the ownership structure on free cash flow is not direct. The empirical results show that the impact of managerial and domestic ownership is negative and significant on the affectation of free cash flow to the debt service for firms with low growth opportunities. This effect is rather positive in firms with high growth opportunities.

Using a survey sample of approximately 3800 Australian small and medium enterprises from 1996 to 1998, Fleming, Heaney and McCosker (2005) examine how agency costs change when ownership and control are separated. Empirical results provide a positive relationship between equity agency costs and the separation of ownership and control. Specifically, it is found that agency costs are lower in firms managed by equity holders, consistent with the argument that reducing the separation of ownership and control reduces agency costs. Finally, agency costs decrease as managerial and employee equity holdings increase.

Lee and Yeo (2007) examine the association between managerial entrenchment and capital structure of Asian firms. They find a negative association between managerial entrenchment and level of leverage in firms with higher agency costs of free cash flow. Specifically, the level of leverage decreases in firms with a CEO who is president of the board, a lower proportion of outside directors, and a higher CEO tenure. The authors also show a positive relationship between institutional ownership and level of leverage, which indicates that active monitoring by institutional investors diminishes entrenched managers' incentives to avoid debt.

Ghosh (2007) adopted the three stage least square simultaneous model approach to examine the interaction between leverage, ownership structure, and firm value. Results show that capital structure, ownership structure, and firm value are jointly determined. Specifically, the managerial ownership is a nonlinear determinant of firm leverage and also leverage is a negative determinant of managerial ownership. These findings reveal the existence of a substitution monitoring effect between debt and managerial ownership. Then, the findings indicate that firm value decreases as promoters' ownership increases. Since control of such companies can still be in the promoters' hands because of the dispersed nature of shareholding, such companies need to be subjected to more vigilant external monitors through debt and to the discipline of an active market for corporate control.

Florackis and Ozkan (2008) indicate that important governance mechanisms for the UK listed companies are managerial ownership, ownership concentration, executive compensation, short-term debt, and bank debt. The authors examine the interactions between these mechanisms and firm growth opportunities in determining agency costs. The results show that impact exerted by governance mechanisms on agency costs varies with firms' growth opportunities. Specifically, high-growth firms face more serious agency problems than low-growth firms due to information asymmetries between managers, shareholders, and debt holders. Moreover, results reveal that managerial ownership is more effective for high-growth firms.

McKnight and Weir (2009) examine the impact of ownership structure on three measures of agency costs, which are the ratio of sales-to-total assets, the interaction of free cash flows and growth prospects, and the number of acquisitions of agency costs. To do so, they employ a range of techniques to analyse the data collected for large UK listed companies: fixed-effects, instrumental variables, and Tobit regressions. Results show that the changes in board structures have not affected agency costs. This suggests a range of mechanisms is consistent with firm value maximization. Results also indicate that having a nomination committee increases agency costs, which indicates that there are costs associated with certain governance mechanisms. Increasing board ownership also helps to reduce agency costs. Finally debt reduces agency costs.

In our study we presume, in accordance with the theory of interest convergence, that as the managerial ownership increases, their behaviour comes closer of that of the shareholders. This results in a limitation of the free cash flow risk.

Hypothesis$_{10}$: free cash flow level will be lower at higher levels of managerial ownership.

The internationalization of financial markets made the institutional investors the major actors of the world economy given their large portfolio size. According to the OECD (2000), the institutional investors form four types of institutions: funds of pension, the mutual funds or investment Society, companies of insurances, and the other institutional investors are formed as foundations or Private investment partnerships. Forester (1995) stipulates that the institutional investor presence pushes enterprises to be more conformable to recommendations of the various codes of good governance and can have an effect on the corporate performance by minimizing agency costs.

In this context, Bohn (2007) indicates that the movement of governance benefitted from an important increase in 2002 following the study achieved by the management consulting McKinseys & Company concerning the institutional investors through the world. It showed that these investors would be ready to invest significant funds in the control of firms and to pay for a supplement up to 40% to make a firm have good corporate governance practices.

Several studies confirmed the positive role of the institutional investors in the corporate governance. Thus, McConnel and Servaes (1990) indicate that the implication of the institutional would result in their propensity to vote in general assembly (Brickley, Lease and Smith, 1988). Their study establishes that these investors exercise their voting rights more frequently than the individual shareholders and that they don't hesitate to oppose managers' decisions in order to defend their interests in the case of dissatisfaction.

In a seminal paper, Pound (1988) presented three hypotheses concerning the effect of institutional ownership on firm performance: efficient monitoring, conflict of interest, and strategic alignment. According to the first hypothesis, institutional investors may have a positive impact on corporate performance if they monitor the managers effectively. They held more stocks and were more professional than private investors, so they had stronger motive to inspect the listed companies. Under the second hypothesis, institutional investors are less subject to information asymmetries than are other shareholders because they have greater resources, incentives for controlling firms, and financial resources.

Finally, the third hypothesis suggests that the institutional investors and managers find that cooperation is mutually advantageous. This cooperation reduces the beneficial effects on the firm value that could result from direction by the institutional investors.

According to Solh (2000), the institutional investors can influence the long-term investment decisions and encourage the company's management to choose the optimal projects from the point of view of shareholder interest.

Henry (2010) indicates that the institutional investors have a larger experience and they are more efficient monitors than the minority shareholders on the plane cost of control. Strategies that are accepted by the institutional investors are those that will be undertaken by the firm through the accumulation of an important number of votes at the time of the board meeting, which has the tendency to privilege the strategies that are creative of value, to the detriment of those that are destructive of value to shareholders. Indeed, resources they arrange allow them to control the firm to a weaker cost than the other shareholders. This is due to the fact that they have better access to information, because of their activity and the numerous investments that they achieve; a rich information on the environment; and an excellent knowledge of the labour market. So institutional investors should help to facilitate the alignment of shareholder and managerial interests and, therefore, lower estimated agency costs. Darren (2010) identifies the mechanisms that are effective in reducing agency costs using data for the period from 1992 to 2002 for listed companies on the Australian Stock Exchange. Empirical results indicate that institutional ownership has a negative effect on agency costs and there are non-linear relationships between managerial ownership and external ownership and the level of agency costs generated by companies. However, the results provide limited evidence, in the effect of capital structure on agency costs. Finally, it is shown that internal governance and external shareholding influences are substitute mechanisms in their effect on the level of agency costs.

Several works test the interaction between corporate governance mechanisms. Agrawal and Knoeber (1996) examine the relationship between seven corporate governance mechanisms in mitigating agency problems between managers and shareholders. These mechanisms are: shareholdings of insiders, institutions, and large blockholders; use of outside directors; debt policy; the managerial labour market; and the market for corporate control. Results show that ownership concentration and institutional ownership constitute a substitute to external ownership. Moreover, the findings demonstrate a relation of complementarity between OPA, shareholdings of institutions, and large blockholders.

Kale, Ciceksever and Ryan (2006) estimate a system of three equations to analyse the interrelations among governance, debt, and activist institutional ownership as disciplining mechanisms. Using two-stage least squares, the findings of their analysis indicate that mechanisms for disciplining managers serve as both substitutes (institutional ownership and debt) and complements (governance and institutional ownership).

Al-Khouri (2006), finds for a sample of listed firms on the stock market of Amman during the period 1998-2001, a positive and significant relationship between the institutional ownership and the firm value proxied by Tobin Q whether or not institutional investors are on the board of directors. This relationship is verified provided that the part of institutional ownership exceeds 25%.

Wu (2004) shows that in the firms with low growth opportunities, institutional investors discourage managerial overspending by governance process and hence compensate for the debt monitoring. However, in the firms with high growth opportunities, institutional investors encourage higher leverage. Thus, the author finds the institutional substitutes ownership for leverage in controlling the managerial self-interest.

McKnight and Weir (2009) prove that at higher levels of institutional ownership, institutions become less effective in supervising managerial actions and may not moderate the agency cost problem.

Hypothesis$_{11}$: free cash flow level will be lower at higher levels of institutional ownership.

3. Methodology

The review of the empirical literature treating the role of debt and ownership structure as mechanisms of resolution of agency conflicts between shareholders and managers due to the overinvestment problem, brings us to note that the contradiction and the ambiguousness of empirical results do not seem to allow us to reach robust findings. It is therefore useful to expand knowledge on this topic and to see if the same factors hold in a different environment, such that of Tunisia.

3.1. Sample Selection and definition of the variables

3.1.1. Sample selection

Our sample consists of firms listed on the Tunisian stock exchange. Because banks and insurances are subject to specific rules and regulations, their leverage is severely affected by exogenous factors. So, following Rajan and Zingales (1995), we exclude all firms categorized as "Financials" and focus exclusively on non-financial firms. Moreover, we eliminated firms not having long term debts (a variable important for the model). Data used is provided by the Tunisian Stock Exchange and the Council of Capital Market through, respectively, their official bulletins and their annuals reports covering the period from 1998 to 2008. The analysis covers the period from 1999 to 2008. The year 1998 serves to calculate some parameters that are variations. Our final sample consisted of 35 firms with a total of 206 firm year observations.

3.1.2 Definition of the variables

3.1.2.1 Dependent variables

We use two dependent variables in this study: the leverage (proxied by the long term debt ratio) and the level of free cash flow.

The literature provides mixed guidance on the measures of free cash flow, which Jensen (1986) defines as cash flow left after firms have invested in all available positive NPV projects. Since the value of positive NPV projects is unobservable, free cash flow is difficult to measure in practice. The most commonly used FCF definition is the one suggested by Lehn and Poulsen (1989). Their measure of FCF is the operating income before depreciation, minus taxes, interest expenses, and preferred and common dividends. Also, some authors define it as the operational income before depreciation, capital expenditures and taxes, divided by the book value of total assets, in order to eliminate any size effect (Lang and al., 1991). Gul and Tsui (1998) argue that these measures of FCF by themselves do not provide a measure of the availability of positive NPV projects. However, in combination with low growth, they suggest the existence of cash flow in excess of that required to fund positive NPV projects.

Recently, Richardson (2006) constructs a measure of free cash flow. This measure is "the cash flow from operations, plus research and development expenditure less the 'required' maintenance, less the 'expected' level of investment". Richardson applies "the label 'free' cash flows to the resulting measure, which is cash flow less the assumed non-discretionary and mandated components of investment". He suggests "The stated goal is to create a measure of the amount of cash flows that are not encumbered by the need to maintain the existing assets of the firm".

In our study we measure cash flow as:

$$\text{CASHFLOW} = \frac{\text{OI} - \text{T} + \text{D} - \text{NI} - \Delta\text{WCR}}{\text{TA}}$$

OI : operating income
T : tax
D : depreciation
NI : Net Investment
ΔWCR : change in working capital requirements TA : total assets

To take account of growth opportunities we refer to studies of Miguel and Pindado (2001), Pindado and De la Torre (2009), and Nekhili et al. (2009), and we are going to measure the risk of free cash flow while multiplying free cash flow by the inverse of the Tobin Q. This last factor is measured as in Dennis et al. (1994), which is market value of equity divided by book value of equity.

Also, in accordance with Nekhili et al. (2009), we consider the Tobin Q at the year t-1. The authors argue that investments that are determined at the year t concern growth opportunities relative at the year t-1.

$$\text{Free Cash Flow Risk}_{\text{i,t}} = \frac{FCF_{i,t}}{\text{TobinQ}_{\text{i,t-1}}}$$

Surprisingly, there is no clear-cut definition of leverage in the academic literature. The specific choice depends on the objective of the analysis. On one hand, the total debt ratio has been used by several authors (Kremp and Stöss, 2001, and Hovakimian, 2005). Whereas Rajan and Zingales (1995) assert that a ratio that includes the total debts does not constitute a good indicator, notably to put in exergue risks of bankruptcy of the firm.

However, the short-term debt ratio has also been used by Titman and Wessels (1988). On another hand, some authors use the market value of debts, such as Taggart (1977), Titman and Wessels (1988), and Flannery and Rangan (2006). Other authors, such as Benett and Donnelly (1993), Chang, Lee and Lee (2008), and Huang and Song (2006), used both market value and book value of debt. In our study, we use the same definition of leverage as Lang et al. (1996), namely the ratio of the book value of long-term debt to the book value of total assets in order not to neutralize the impact of agency costs joined to the leverage (Myers, 1977). This measure would not reflect recent changes in the markets. This measure has been used by Mello and Miranda (2010) who investigate the role of long-term debt in influencing over-investments by analysing the pattern of abnormal investments around a new debt offering by unlevered firms. Pao (2008) précises that all studies interested in determinants of the capital structure judged that the difference between the market value of debt is very close to book value of debt.

$$Leverage = \frac{\text{Book value of long term debt}}{\text{Total Assets}}$$

3.1.2.2 Independent variables

A detailed discussion of the variable construction is presented in Table 1.

Three explanatory variables are included as control variables on the basis of prior studies that investigate the determinants of free cash flow: state ownership, firm size, and industry classification. According to the agency theory, state ownership is reputed to be inefficient due to the lack of capital market monitoring. Thus, it would incite their managers to pursue their own interests instead of those of their institutions. Managers of the private firms will have a stronger pressure from their environment and a more intense disciplinary effect from the capital market, which can considerably reduce the inefficiency of these firms (Lang and So, 2002). Indeed, through the control by goods and services market (competitive pressure of the sector), the badly managed companies should naturally disappear. However, often, public corporations are in a position of monopoly and do not have competitors. Besides, through the control by the financial market, badly managed firms constituent targets for the more effective acquirers. However, stocks detained by the state are generally non-transferable and the state imposes a strict control on partners. Also, the diffusion of information concerning the firm to the capital market is often confused (political considerations, rules of public accounting). Also, managers who are members of the board of directors have no interest in

Table 1: Definition and measurement of the variables

	Code	Proxy
		Dependent variables
Leverage	Lev	$Leverage = \frac{\text{Book value of long term debt}}{\text{Total Assets}}$
Free Cash Flow Risk	FCF	$\text{Free Cash Flow Risk}_{i,t} = \frac{FCF_{i,t}}{\text{TobinQ}_{i,t-1}}$
Independent variables		
Firm size	Size	Log total Assets
Fixed assets	Tang	$\text{Tang} = \frac{\text{Tangible Assets + Stock}}{\text{Total Assets}}$
Profitability	Profit	$Profit = \frac{\textit{Earning before}\text{ interest and taxes}}{\textit{Total}\text{ Assets}}$
Tax paid	Tax	$Tax = \frac{\textit{Tax Paid}}{\text{Earning before interest and taxes}}$
Operational risk	Risk	Risk =Variation of Return On Capital Employed= $\frac{\textit{V}\text{ariation of operating income - tax}}{\text{Fixed assts + working capital requirement}}$

Growth opportunities	Growth	Total $assets_t$-total $assets_{t-1}$ / total assets $_{t-1}$
Industry classification	Ind	Dummy variable equal to one if the firm belongs to the industry sector and zero otherwise
Managerial ownership	Man	Percentage of shared owned by directors
Ownership concentration	Conc	Percentage of share owned by the largest five shareholders in a firm.
Institutional ownership	Inst	Percentage of shared owned by institutional investors wich banks, investment society, companies of insurances and cases of social security (state excluded)
State ownership	State	Percentage of shared owned by State

contesting the president's decisions being discerned as emanating from the government. So we presume that a negative relationship between state ownership and firm size (proxy as logarithm of total assets) is used to explain the complexity of the surveillance required in the largest firms. We presume a negative relationship between the size and the risk of free cash flow in accordance with Jensen (1986), which supposes that large firms having much cash flow would prefer debt financing in order to discipline managers, which limits the risk of free cash flow. For the variable "industry" we anticipate that the sign is negative. Indeed, following restructurings of the Tunisian industrial firms, they will issue debts, which minimizes the level of free cash flow.

3.2 Descriptive Statistics

Table 2: Descriptive Statistic of the variables

	Observation	Mean	Stdv	min	max
LEV	206	0.200	0.270	0.0002	2.254
FCF	206	0.173	0.239	-0.415	1.235
Size	206	10.963	0.892	9.240	14.205
Tang	206	0.494	0.163	0.143	0.869
Tax	206	0.087	0.091	-0.159	0.361
Growth	206	0.078	0.176	-0.241	1.391
Profit	206	0.074	0.079	-0.237	0.282
Risk	206	-0.001	0.091	-0.551	0.395
Man	206	0.652	0.144	0.303	1.000
Inst	206	0.236	0.240	0.000	0.880
Conc	206	0.708	0.130	0.274	0.961

Table 2 shows the statistics descriptive of the characteristic of the endogen and exogen variables in the relationship between debt policy, free cash flow, and ownership structure of this study. It is mainly about the non-weighted averages, of standard deviation as well as of the minimal and maximal values of distributions. Mean value of the debt ratio (leverage) is 0.20 (20%). It shows that the firms in Tunisia do not use debt so much for financing their activity. Minimum value of using debt is 0.0002 (0.02%) and maximum value is 2.254 (200.254%) with a standard deviation of 0.27 (27%). Otherwise, an important stylized fact regarding Tunisian firms is the concentration of the ownership, the mean value of which is 0.708 (70.8%). Also, the mean value of the managerial ownership is 65.2% with a maximum that reaches 100%. Managers and administrators of the Tunisian firms hold a strong proportion of the capital and therefore of what sustains the joining of functions of ownership and control. Finally, we note that the institutional ownership is restrained. It is on average equal to 23.6%.

According to the free cash flow theory, the divergence of interest between shareholders and managers should be most severe in the firms with few growth opportunities and large free cash flow. Hence the relations between ownership structure, free cash flow, and leverage are most important for these firms. Following the study of Nekhili et al. (2009) and Awan at al. (2010), we decompose our sample in to two groups of firms depending on whether their level of free cash flow is low or high in order to determine variables that can characterize every group. The first decomposition (table 3) is based on the "mean criteria". The second decomposition (table 4) is based on the "median criteria".

As expected, high-fcf firms have a higher amount of debt in their capital structure than low-fcf firms. The mean leverage for high-fcf firms is 22.4 percent, compared to a mean of 18.7 percent for low-fcf firms. This is consistent with the free cash flow hypothesis in which firms with higher fcf and fewer growth opportunities have higher levels of leverage. There is also evidence that ownership structure differs between the two subsamples. Nevertheless, the mean institutional ownership for high-fcf firms is 21.3 percent compared to a mean of 25 percent for low-fcf firms. Low-fcf firms have lower managerial ownership and concentration ownership. The mean managerial ownership for low-fcf firms is 62.9 percent, compared to a mean of 69.2 percent for high-fcf firms. The mean concentration ownership for low-fcf firms is 68.5 percent, compared to a mean of 74.9 percent for high-fcf firms. It appears, therefore, that some governance mechanisms of governance intervene as soon as the level of the free cash flow increases.

Table3: Provides descriptive statistics for low-fcf and high-fcf firms.

Variables		Total sample (Nb = 206)	Group 1 : low fcf (Nb = 131)	Groupe 2 : high fcf (Nb = 75)	T statistic (p-value)
LEV	Mean	0.200	0.187	0.224	2.3229** (0.0212)
	Std deviation	0.270	0.267	0.276	
	Min	0.0002	0.0003	0.0003	
	Max	2.254	2.254	2.075	
MAN	Mean	0.652	0.629	0.692	-0.3487 (0.7277)
	Std deviation	0.144	0.138	0.144	
	Min	0.303	0.303	0.328	
	Max	1.000	1.000	0.890	
INST	Mean	0.236	0.250	0.213	2.9996*** 0.0030)
	Std deviation	0.240	0.235	0.248	
	Min	0.000	0.000	0.000	
	Max	0.880	0.880	0.880	

CONC	Mean	0.708	0.685	0.749	-0.4995 (0.6180)
	Std deviation	0.130	0.130	0.121	
	Min	0.274	0.274	0.475	
	Max	0.961	0.946	0.961	
SIZE	Mean	10.963	10.972	10.947	2.2482** (0.0256)
	Std deviation	0.892	0.874	0.928	
	Min	9.240	9.560	9.240	
	Max	14.205	14.108	14.205	
STATE	Mean	0.27421359	0 .345	0.209	3,416 (0,0008)***
	Std deviation	0.29232878			
	Min	0			
	Max	0.88			

Tableau 4: Provides descriptive statistics for low-fcf and high-fcf firms

Variables		Total sample (Nb = 206)	Group 1 : low fcf (Nb = 103)	Group 2 : high fcf (Nb = 103)	T statistic (p-value)
LEV	Moyenne	0.200	0.13818301	0.26260884	3.3884*** (0.0008)
	écart type	0.270	0.34881535	0.13122317	
	Min	0.0002	0.00036139	0.00025963	
	Max	2.254	2.25439277	0.68070775	
MAN	Moyenne	0.652	0.64263107	0.66091845	-0.9139 (0.3618)
	écart type	0.144	0.1330422	0.15342378	
	Min	0.303	0.3031	0.3031	
	Max	1.000	0.88	1	
INST	Moyenne	0.236	0.28320194	0.18957291	2.8476 (0.0049)***
	écart type	0.240	0.2676912	0.19923364	
	Min	0.000	0	0	
	Max	0.880	0.88	0.78	

CONC	Moyenne	0.708	0.6975466	0.71897233	-1.1828 (0.2382)
	écart type	0.130	0.12368388	0.13600461	
	Min	0.274	0.43	0.274	
	Max	0.961	0.926	0.9613	
SIZE	Moyenne	10.963	11.0105487	10.9161422	0.7589 (0.4488)
	écart type	0.892	0.9957781	0.77600949	
	Min	9.240	9.56018706	9.24037479	
	Max	14.205	14.1081361	14.2048321	
STATE	Moyenne	0.27421359	0.35735825	0.19106893	4.2486*** 0.0000
	écart type	0.29232878	0.30639898	0.25280049	
	Min	0	0	0	
	Max	0.88	0.88	0.761	

Table 4: the correlation matrix of the independent variables

	Leverage	**FCF**	**Size**	**Tang**	**Tax**	**Growth**	**Profit**	**Risk**	**Conc**	**Man**	**Inst**	**State**
Leverage	1											
FCF	-0.144	1										
Size	0.156	-0.086	1									
Tang	-0.043	-0.107	-0.061	1								
Tax	-0.282	0.149	-0.207	-0.139	1							
Growth	-0.185	-0.033	-0.005	-0.008	0.092	1						
Profit	-0.511	0.247	-0.121	-0.196	0.500	0.175	1					
Risk	0.005	0.001	-0.037	-0.057	0.067	-0.093	0.160	1				
Conc	0.316	0.241	0.244	-0.098	-0.086	-0.091	-0.184	-0.004	1			
Man	0.345	0.244	0.329	-0.047	-0.016	-0.138	-0.151	0.032	**0.727**	1		
Inst	0.404	-0.130	0.050	0.186	-0.095	-0.035	-0.307	0.089	0.104	0.233	1	
State	0.3387	-0.318	0.315	0.205	0.109	-0.127	-0 .37	-0.005	0.261	0.35	0.401	1

Before achieving regressions it is indispensable to study the correlation between the independent variables and to test the multicollinearity problem. The correlation matrix shows relations between all explanatory variables. This is to signal that correlations between the independent variables are weak or moderate, which reduces the multicollinearity problem. However, the correlation matrix shows that variable "MAN" and variable "CONC" are highly correlated. So, we may keep only one variable in every equation in order to examine the true relationship between the independent variables and free cash flow, and avoid the problem of correlation between variables.

3.3 Specification of the simultaneous equations model and method of estimation

3.3.1 Specification and identification of the model

A simultaneous equations approach, particularly 3SLS, is deemed to be appropriate on the basis of the interrelationships among the agency-cost-reducing mechanisms. This study uses a two-equation model with free cash flow and leverage as the dependent variables. Additional leverage appears as a regressor in the free cash flow equation and vice-versa. Thus, leverage and free cash flow are simultaneously determined.

$$FCF_{i,t} = \alpha_0 + \alpha_1\, Leverage_{i,t} + \alpha_2\, MAN_{i,t} + \alpha_3 INST_{i,t} + \alpha_4 State + \alpha_5\, Size_{i,t} + \alpha_6\, Ind_{i,t} + \varepsilon_{2i,t} \quad (1)$$

$$Leverage_{i,t} = \beta_0 + \beta_1\, Size_{i,t} + \beta_2\, Tang_{i,t} + \beta_3\, Tax_{i,t} + \beta_4\, Growth_{,t} + \beta_5\, FCFi_{,t} + \beta_6\, Profit_{i,t} + \beta_7 Risk_{i,t} + \beta_8 Ind_{i,t} + \varepsilon_{1i} \quad (2)$$

$$\begin{cases} FCF_{i,t} = \gamma_0 + \gamma_1 Leverage_{i,t} + \gamma_2 CONC_{,t} + \gamma_3 INST_{i,t} + \gamma_4 State + \gamma_5 Size_{i,t} + \gamma_6 Ind_{i,t} + \varepsilon_{2i,t} & (3) \\ Leverage_{i,t} = \delta_0 + \delta_1\, Size_{i,t} + \delta_2\, Tang_{i,t} + \delta_3\, Tax_{i,t} + \delta_4\, Growth_{,t} + \delta_5\, FCFi_{,t} + \delta_6\, Profit_{i,t} + \delta_7\, Risk_{i,t} + \delta_8 Ind_{i,t} + \varepsilon_{1i,t} & (4) \end{cases}$$

The free cash flow equation includes long term debt (Leverage), institutional ownership (INST), managerial stock ownership (MAN), concentration ownership (CONC), state ownership, size of the firm (Size), and industry (Ind). While the leverage equation includes measures of firm size (Size), tangible assets (Tang), tax paid (Tax), asset growth (GROWTH), level of free cash flow (FCF), earning (profit), variation of the economic profitability rate (Risk), and industry (Ind).

$\varepsilon_{1it} = a_{1i} + \mu_{1it}$
$\varepsilon_{2it} = a_{2i} + \mu_{2it}$
$\varepsilon_{3it} = a_{3i} + \mu_{3it}$
$\varepsilon_{4it} = a_{4i} + \mu_{4it}$
$i = 1, \ldots\ldots\ldots\ldots N$ and $t = 1, \ldots\ldots\ldots\ldots T$
N : the number of firms and T : the estimation period

ε_{1it}, ε_{2it}, ε_{3it} and ε_{4it}: Error Term corresponding respectively to the first, to the second, to the third, and the fourth equation,

a_i et μ_{it} are random non-correlated perturbations

a_{1i}, a_{2i} ,a_{3i} and a_{4i}: specific individual effects corresponding respectively to the first, to the second, to the third and the fourth equation

$\beta_1 \ldots\ldots \beta_8$ and $\delta_{11} \ldots\ldots \delta_8$ representative parameters of the relative weight of each exogenous variable on the variable to explain "leverage";

$\alpha_1 \ldots\ldots \alpha_5$ and $\gamma_1 \ldots\ldots \gamma_5$: representative parameters of the relative weight of each exogenous variable on the variable to explain "Free Cash Flow";

β_0, α_0, δ_0 and γ_0: constants corresponding respectively to the first, to the second, to the third, and the fourth equation.

3.3.2. The identification condition in the model.

Order conditions are determined equation by equation. They are verified when the number of endogenous variables excluded (k - k') plus the number of exogenous variables excluded (g - g') is superior or equal to the number of equations less 1: $(k - k') + (g - g') \geq (e - 1)$.

The equation is under - identified if $(k - k') < (g' - 1)$
The equation is exactly identified if $(k - k') = (g' - 1)$
The equation is over - identified if $(k - k') > (g' - 1)$
With:
g: number of endogenous variables of the model;
k: number of exogenous variables of the model;
g': number of endogenous variables introduced in an equation;
k': number of exogenous variables introduced in an equation;

Table 5: the identification condition in the model

Equation	**g**	**k**	**g'**	**k'**	**k-k'**	**g'-1**	**Identification**
Equation 1	2	10	2	4	5	1	k-k' > g'-1; The equation is over - identified
Equation 2	2	10	2	7	3	1	k-k' > g'-1; The equation is over - identified
Equation 3	2	10	2	4	5	1	k-k' > g'-1; The equation is over - identified
Equation 4	2	10	2	7	3	1	k-k' > g'-1; The equation is over - identified

Rank conditions assure here that the model, under its reduced form, possesses a unique solution. The rank conditions for empirical identification are relatively complicated.

A simultaneous linear equation model is identified if all the equations are identified.

3.3.3 Method of estimation

The model describes below is a simultaneous equations model of the leverage and the level of free cash flow. We can estimate parameters of the system when equations are exactly-identified or over-identified. We distinguish the limited information method and full information method. The first consists of estimating, equation by equation, the model by the two stage least square method. The second considers the model in its totality, and we use here the three stage least square method (Cadoret and al., 2004). Our model will be estimated by the three stage least square method with 206 observations for the period 1999-2008. The system of two simultaneous equations, for every firm i and every year t, can be written:

$$y = Z\delta + \varepsilon \quad (5)$$

as,

$$y = \begin{bmatrix} y_1 \\ y_2 \end{bmatrix} = \begin{bmatrix} Z_1 & 0 \\ 0 & Z_2 \end{bmatrix} \begin{bmatrix} \delta_1 \\ \delta_2 \end{bmatrix} + \begin{bmatrix} \varepsilon_1 \\ \varepsilon_2 \end{bmatrix} \quad (6)$$

Y' = (y_1, y_2) is vector of endogenous variables (long term debt and free cash flow).

Vectors of the explanatory endogenous and exogenous variables of the equation of leverage Z_1 and the level of free cash flow Z_2, are:

Z_1= Leverage,Man, Conc, Inst, State, Size

Z_2 = FCF, Size, Tang, Tax, Growth, Profit, Risk, Ind (7)

δ_s represents the vector of coefficients of all explanatory variables (endogenous and exogenous).

For error term:

$E(\varepsilon)=0$
$E(\varepsilon\varepsilon')=[\sigma_{sh}I]$ is the variance-covariance matrix.

In the case of the simultaneous equations, the interdependence of endogenous variables deal place to an interdependence of error terms, what calls at the time of the estimation on the three least square method. This method consists in estimating the system in three stages. The first two stages are those of the two least square method applied separately to every equation of the system under its reduced form. Therefore, in our case we have three equations to estimate. The reduced form of the system is achieved by the application of the following stages: while using vectors (7), we can define a matrix B of three endogenous variable coefficients and a matrix A of exogenous variable coefficients as:

$$y' = (B-I)' + X'A = \varsigma$$
$$y' = -X'A(B-I)^{t-1} + \varsigma'(B-I)^{t-1}$$
$$y' \equiv X\Pi + v$$
$$\Pi \equiv -A'(B-I)^{t-1}$$

Π_h and Π'_h the generic elements of the matrix

$$v' \equiv \varsigma(B-I)^{t-1}$$

the variance-covariance matrix of error terms $E[vv']$ is:

$$E[vv'] = (B-I)^{-1}\sum \Omega I(B-I)^{t-1}$$

Then, the reduced form of the explicit system is the following:

$$FCF_{it} = \Pi'_0 + \Pi'_1 MAN_{it} / CONC_{it} + \Pi'_2 Leverage_{it} +$$
$$\Pi'_3 INST_{it} + \Pi'_4 State + \Pi'_5 Size_{it} + \Pi'_5 Ind_{it} + v'_2$$
$$Leverage_{it} = \Pi_0 + \Pi_1 Size_0 + \Pi_2 Tang_{it} + \Pi_3 Tax_{it} +$$
$$\Pi_4 Growth_{it} + \Pi_5 \text{Pr}ofit_{it} + \Pi_6 Risk_{it} + \Pi_7 Ind + v_1$$

To this level the evaluation is done while applying the ordinary least square method, and we get $\hat{\Pi}$ the estimator of Π

$$\hat{\Pi} = (X'X)^{-1} X'y$$

This method permits us to get values $\hat{y}_1$ and $\hat{y}_2$ serving to achieve the instrumental variables in the two equations. The following procedure consists of estimating every equation of the structural system while using the achieved instruments, while applying the two least square method. So, we get an estimator $\hat{\sigma}_s$. The objective will be to construct the estimated matrix of variance-covariance matrix of error terms that is going to be used like the ponderation matrix whose generic element $\hat{\sigma}_{ij}$ is:

$$\hat{\sigma}_{ij} = \frac{(y_i - Z_i\hat{\delta}_i)(y_j - Z_j\hat{\delta}_j)}{n}$$

n : the number of years.

The third and last stage consists of estimating simultaneously the three equations with the triple least square method.

4. Empirical results and discussion

Three stage east square results

Result of the joint estimation of debt policy and free cash flow level are presented in panels A, B, C, and D of Table 1.

Table 6: Estimated Coefficients for the leverage and free cash flow Using Three-Stage Least Squares Method

Panel A: Equation 1: $FCF_{i,t} = \alpha_0 + \alpha_1 \, Leverage_{i,t} + \alpha_2 \, MAN_{i,t} + \alpha_3 \, INST_{i,t} + \alpha_4 \, State_{i,t} + \alpha_5 \, Size_{i,t} + \alpha_6 \, Ind_{i,t} + \varepsilon_{2i,t}$

Variable	Coefficient	t-Statistic	Prob.
Constant	0.105	0,55	0,585
Leverage	-0.195***	-3, 25	0,001
Man	0.734***	6,11	0,000
Inst	0.004	0,07	0,947
State	-0.316***	-5,5	0,000
Size	-0.025	-1,43	0,152
Ind	-0.042	-1,11	0,265
R-squared	0.2758		
Number of observation	206		

Panel B: Equation 2: $Leverage_{i,t} = \beta_0 + \beta_1 \, Size_{i,t} + \beta_2 \, Tang_{i,t} + \beta_3 \, Tax_{i,t} + \beta_4 \, Growth_{i,t} + \beta_5 \, FCF_{i,t} + \beta_6 \, Profit_{i,t} + \beta_7 \, Risk_{i,t} + \beta_8 \, Ind_{i,t} + \varepsilon_{1i,t}$

Variable	Coefficient	t-Statistic	Prob.
Constant	0.255	1,16	0,248
Size	0.020	1,08	0,282
Tang	-0.227	-2, 18**	0,030
Tax	-0.110	-0,54	0,588
Growth	-0.113	-1,22	0,221
FCF	-0.108	-1,56	0,118
Profit	-1.670	-6,87***	0,000
Risk	0.177	1,09	0,277
Ind	-0.019	-0.45	0,654
R-squared	0. 2988		
Number of observation	206		

Panel C: Equation 3: $FCF_{i,t} = \gamma_0 + \gamma_1\ Leverage_{i,t} + \gamma_2\ CONC_{,t} + \gamma_3\ INST_{i,t} + \gamma_4\ State_{i,t} + \gamma_5\ Size_{i,t} + \gamma_6\ Ind_{i,t} + \varepsilon_{2i,t}$

Variable	Coefficient	t-Statistic	Prob.
Constant	0.003	(0,02)	0.985
Leverage	-0.216***	(-3, 48)	0.000
Conc	0.653***	(5,20)	0.000
INST	0.065	(0,92)	0.356
State	-0.289***	(-4,96)	0.000
Size	-0.015 *	(-0,87)	0.386
Ind	-0.071 **	(-1,86)	0.063
R-squared	0.2398		
Number of observation	206		

Panel D: Equation 4: $Leverage_{i,t} = \delta_0 + \delta_1\ Size_{i,t} + \delta_2\ Tang_{i,t} + \delta_3\ Tax_{i,t} + \delta_4\ Growth_{,t} + \delta_5\ FCFi_{,t} + \delta_6\ Profit_{i,t} + \delta_7\ Risk_{i,t} + \delta_8\ Ind_{i,t} + \varepsilon_{1i,t}$

Variable	Coefficient	t-Statistic	Prob.
Constant	0. 273	(1,24)	0.217
Size	0.019	(1,02)	0.306
Tang	-0.231**	(-2,22)	0.027
Tax	-0.124	(-0, 61)	0.542
Growth	-0.107	(-1,17)	0.243
FCF	-0.129**	(-1,86)	0.063
Profit	-1.663***	(-6,86)	0.000
Risk	0.175	(1,08)	0.279
Ind	-0.021	(-0,51)	0.609
R-squared	0.2961		
Number of observation	206		

* Significant at the 0.10 level. ** Significant at the 0.05 level. *** Significant at the 0.01 level.

4.1 The impact of debt policy on free cash flow levels

The findings suggest that there is a significant impact of leverage which serves as a monitoring device to mitigate agency problems between owner and principal. The leverage variable has the negative predicted sign in the free cash flow equation and is statistically significant at the 0.01 level. Our result corroborates the hypothesis of free cash flow of Jensen (1986) and confirms the empirical study of Wu (2004) who explore the implications of the free cash flow hypothesis concerning the disciplinary role of ownership structure in corporate capital structure policy. The author finds that the sensitivity of ownership structure to leverage depends on growth opportunities and free cash flow. When firms in the sample are classified as low-growth and high-growth firms, relation between leverage and free cash flow are significantly greater for low-growth firms than for the high-growth firms. Moreover, we observe evidence that firms with a more severe overinvestment problem have higher levels of leverage, and the coefficient of free cash flow is significantly positive, consistent with the free cash flow hypothesis. Our result corroborates the previous result of D'Mello and Miranda (2010) who show that issuing debt leads to a dramatic reduction in this form of overinvestment, and within three years of the offering, the sample firms' cash ratios are similar to their industry benchmarks. Also, these relations are stronger for firms that have poor investment opportunities relative to other sample firms, implying that debt plays an especially important role in reducing excess investments in firms that have the highest agency problems.

However, our result contradicts the empirical evidence of Nekhili et al. (2009), who show that it is distribution of dividends – rather than debt level – that leads to reduction of free cash flow.

In sum, our results indicate that debt plays a critical role in reducing the agency costs of free cash flow in Tunisian firms.

4.2 Capital structure determinants

Our findings show that the coefficient associated with the weight of immobilizations in the total of assets has a negative and significant sign at the 0.05 level. Our hypothesis H3(b) concerning the relation between the leverage and the structure of assets is therefore confirmed. Our finding corroborates the empirical study of Hosono (2003) concerning the capital structure determinants of Manufacturing Firms in Japan.

Otherwise, this finding seems to confirm the pecking order theory that suggests firms with few tangible assets will be most sensitive to the information asymmetry; and so they will use the debt that is an external financing vehicle less sensitive to information asymmetry than stocks (Harris and Raviv 1991). Indeed, in Tunisia it is the major part of the firm debt banking. According to Rajan and Zingales (1995), the tangibility of assets must take less importance in countries that are bank-dominated.

Another explanation more specific to the Tunisian firms, and relative to the real value of fixed assets which is appreciated (and the appreciation has not been reflected in accounts of the firms), will be able to explain the origin of this relation.

Furthermore, profitability is strongly negatively related with leverage. This negative correlation demonstrates that the highly profitable firms have need of less external funds. This is support for the pecking order theory by Myers and Majluf (1984). It is also consistent with Huang and Song (2006) for listed firms in China, and Sheikh and Wang (2010) for firms listed on the stock market of Karachi. An explanation consists in considering that the profitable Tunisian firms are more incited to finance their activities by the financial markets and not by debt. This finding also comes in support of the hypothesis that stipulates that managers choose the internal financing resource in the first place in order to control agency costs resulting from external financing.

Finally, it is to be noted that no conclusion can be made regarding the effect of size, of variation of the risk, of the firm growth, or of the tax on the leverage from the moment the relative coefficients are non-significant in the two equations of the leverage. In the same way, the relative coefficient to the variable "industry" is always non-significant. In other words, the industrial firms do not appear more levered, nor less levered than the non-industrial firms. This finding comes in support of those found by Drobetz and Fix (2005) for the Swiss firms, and Kim et al. (2006) for the non-financial listed firms in Korea.

4.3 The impact of ownership structure on free cash flow levels

Results show that the coefficient of the variable "*MAN*" is positive and statistically significant at the 0.1 level, in accordance with the entrenchment theory. So, when managerial ownership increases, the risk of wasting the free cash flow is raised, which can amplify conflicts between shareholders and managers. Thus, managers try to spend the free cash flow that is at their service in non-profitable projects and negative NPV, with the only objective being to increase the firm size and to increase, consequently, their remuneration. Therefore, our hypothesis 10 is invalidated. Our result corroborates Lee and Yeo (2007) who suggest that firms where the principal manager is himself the president of the board of directors, and where more than half of the members are not outside directors, have a weak level of debt. In this case managers have an enormous amount of free cash flow that is going to be used in activities that serve their own interests at the expense of those of shareholders.

Also, our results show that the coefficient associated with ownership concentration has a positive and significant sign at the 0.01 level, which demonstrates that companies characterized by the presence of a large blockholder have higher risk of free cash flow. Our finding confirms the result of Nekhili et al. (2009) for the case of French firms. The authors explain these findings by 3 arguments. First, the majority shareholders undertake non-profit investments with other firms that are affiliated to them. Secondly, the majority shareholders cannot acquire all information detained by managers. Third, the limited relationship that shareholders maintain with the entrenched managers does not permit them to criticize their choices.

Otherwise, analysis showed that institutional ownership had a non-significant effect on free cash flow. The non-significant impact can be explained by the restricted part detained by the institutional investors in the capital of the Tunisian listed firms. Our findings corroborate the neutrality thesis of ownership structure developed by Demsetz (1983), Demsetz and Lehn (1985), and Demsetz and Villalonga (2001).

The coefficients of the variable "State" are significant for two regressions. We find a negative correlation between level of free cash flow and state ownership at the 0.01 level, which is in concordance with our hypothesis. As state ownership increases, there is more pressure on management to limit the wasting of free cash flow. Our results bring this accusation a quasi–evident conclusion admitted by economists, which is the primacy of the private sector. Also, they put in exergue the importance of public firms. In fact, these firms not only fill several social objectives but control also the behaviour of managers. These results are essentially owed to the context of the study: a developing country where the state plays a determining role in the economic life and where the private sector cannot assure alone the good functioning of the economy.

In reality, the presence of the state still remains predominantly in most Tunisian firms in spite of the privatization program started several years ago. The public powers constitute the authority of regimentation and thus define a set of measures of repressive character or purifying in order to discipline managers.

Finally, the coefficient of the variable “Industry” is negative and statistically significant in the equation of free cash flow, which shows that the risk of free cash flow is weak in the industrial firms.

5. Conclusion and implication

The purpose of this paper is to explore the implications of the free cash flow hypothesis concerning the disciplinary role of ownership structure and capital structure policy in an emerging stock exchange, such as that of Tunisia. We adopted the three stage least square simultaneous model approach based on a sample composed of 35 non-financial listed firms during the period from 1999 to 2008. Our results show that firms with a more severe overinvestment problem have higher levels of leverage and the impact of the leverage on the free cash flow is significantly negative, consistent with the free cash flow hypothesis. Moreover, state ownership has a positive effect on the level of free cash flow. Hence, in the Tunisian firms, the overinvestment problem can be mitigated by issuing debt and by increasing state ownership. However, the ownership concentration and the managerial ownership increase the risk of the free cash flow. However, the impact of institutional ownership on free cash flow is not significant. Finally, we should signal that the estimated model does not integrate all corporate governance mechanisms. We note the dividend policy and the board of directors that also constitute the main systems of control are omitted in our study.

References

Agrawal A. and Knoeber C.R. 1996. Firm Performance and Mechanisms to Control Agency Problems between Managers and Shareholders. *Journal of Financial and Quantitative Analysis* 31 (3). 377-397.

Al-Deehani. T.M and Al-Saad.K.M 2007. Ownership Structure and Its Relationship with Capital Structure: An Empirical Study on the Companies Listed in the Kuwait Stock Exchange. Arab Journal of Administrative Sciences Arab Journal of Administrative Sciences 14 (2)

Al-khouri. R. 2006. Corporate governance and firms value in emerging markets: the case of Jordan. Advances in Financial Economics 11, 31-50.

Andrés P. López F.J. and Rodríguez J.A. 2005. Financial Decisions and Growth Opportunities: A Spanish Firms Panel Data Analysis. *Applied Financial Economics* 15(6), 391- 407.

Aoun. D and Heshmati. A. 2006. The Causal Relationship between Capital Structure and Cost of Capital: Evidence from ICT Companies Listed at NASDAQ . The Ratio Institute Working Papers *87.*

Bennett. M. and Donnelly. R. 1993. The Determinants of Capital Structure: Some UK Evidence. *British Accounting Review*. 25 1, 43-59.

Berger P. Ofek E. and Yermach D. 1997. Managerial Entrenchment and Capital Structure Decisions. *Journal of Finance* 52. (4), 1411-1438.

Billett. M.T. et al. 2007. Growth Opportunities and the Choice of Leverage, Debt Maturity, and Covenants. *The Journal of Finance* LXII (2), 697-730.

Booth. L. Aivazian. V. Demirguc-Kunt. A. and Maksimovic. V. 2001. Capital structure in developing countries. *Journal of Finance* 56, 87-130

Brickley J.. Lease R. and Smith C. 1988; Ownership structure and voting on an takeover amendments. *Journal of financial economics* 20, 267-291.

Buettner. Overesch. Schreiber. Wamser and George. 2009. Taxation and capital structure choice: Evidence from a panel of German multinationals. *Economics Letters*. 105 (3), 309-311

Cadoret. B. Martin. H and Tanguy. 2004. Économétrie appliquée: méthodes, applications. corrigés. De Boeck Université.452 pages

Cai K. R. Fairchild. and Guney. Y. 2008. Debt maturity structure of Chinese companies. *Pacific-Basin Finance Journal 16, 268-297*

Chang. C. Lee. Alice C.and Lee. Cheng F. 2009. Determinants of capital structure choice: A structural equation modeling approach. *The Quarterly Review of Economics and Finance* 49, 197–213.

Chen. J. J. 2004. Determinants of capital structure of Chinese-listed companies. *Journal of Business Research* 57, 1341 – 1351.

Chen. X. and Yur-Austin. J. 2007. Re-measuring agency costs: The effectiveness of blockholders. *The Quarterly Review of Economics and Finance* 47(5), 588-601.

Ciceksever. B. J. Kale. and H. Ryan. 2006. Corporate governance, debt, and activist institutions. Georgia State University *working paper*.

De Jong A. and Dijk R.V. 2007. Determinants of Leverage and Agency Problems: A Regression Approach with Survey Data. *European Journal of Finance* 13(6), 565-593.

De Jong.A. Kabir.T.T and Nguyen. R. 2008. Capital structure around the world: The roles of firm- and country-specific determinants. *Journal of Banking and Finance 32(9*), 1954-1969

De Miguel. A. and Pindado J. 2001. Determinants of capital structure: new evidence from Spanish panel data. *Journal of Corporate Finance* 7, 77-99

Del Brio E.. Perote J. and Pindado J. 2003. Measuring the Impact of Corporate Investment Announcements on Share Prices: the Spanish Experience. *Journal of Business. Finance and Accounting* 30,715-747.

Delcoure N. 2007. The determinants of capital structure in transitional economies. *International Review of Economics and Finance*. 16, 400–415.

Demsetz.H. 1983. The structure of ownership and the theory of the firm. *Journal of Law and Economics 2 (June), 375-390.*

Demsetz.H. and Lehn K. 1985. The structure of corporate ownership: causes and consequences. *Journal of Political Economy 93(6), 1155-1177.*

Demsetz.H. and Vilallonga B. 2001. Ownership structure and corporate performance. *Journal of Corporate Finance 7(3), 209-233.*

D'Mello.R. and Miranda.M. 2010. Long-term debt and overinvestment agency problem. *Journal of Banking and Finance* 34, 324-335

Doukas. J.A. C. Kim. and C. Pantzalis. 2005. Security Analysis, Agency Costs and Firm Characteristics. *International Review of Financial Analysis* 14(5), 493-507

Driffield.N.L. and Pal .S. 2007. How does ownership structure affect capital structure and firm performance? Recent evidence from East Asia. *Economics of Transition* 15 (3), 535-573

Drobetz W and Fix R. 2005. What are the determinants of the capital structure? Some evidence for Switzerland . *Revue Suisse d'Economie et de statistique* 1(mars), 71-114

Duggal R. and Millar J.A.1999. Institutional ownership and firm performance: The case of bidder returns. *Journal of Corporate Finance 5.*

Eriotis. N., V. Dimitrios and V. N. Zoe. How firm characteristics affect capital structure: an empirical study. *Managerial Finance* 335, 321-331.

Ezeoha. A.E. 2008. Firm size and corporate financial leverage choice in a developing economy. *The Journal of Risk Finance*. 94. 351-364.

Faccio M. and Lasfer M.A. 2002. Institutional Shareholders and Corporate Governance: The Case of U.K. Pension Funds In: J. McCahery. P. Moerland. T. Raaijmakers. and L. Renneboog. eds. Corporate Governance Regimes: Convergence and Diversity. *Oxford University Press*

Fattouh. Scaramozzino and Harris 2005. Capital structure in South Korea: a quantile regression approach. *Journal of Development Economics* 761, 231-250.

Flannery. M.J. and K.P. Rangan. 2006. Partial adjustment toward target capital structures. *Journal of Financial Economics* 79(3) 469-506

Fluck. Z. D. Holtz-Eakin. and H.S. Rosen. 2000. Where does the money come from? The financing of small entrepreneurial enterprises, New York University Working paper.

Frank. M. and Goyal. V. 2000. Testing the pecking order theory of capital structure. *Journal of Financial Economics* 67(2), 217-248

Garvey G.T. and G. Hanka. 1999. Capital structure and corporate control: the effect of anti-takeover statutes on firm leverage. *Journal of finance* 54 (2), 519-546

Ghosh. S. 2007. Leverage, managerial monitoring and firm valuation: A simultaneous equation approach. *Research in Business 61*, 84-98.

Graham. J.R. and Tucker. A.L. 2006. Tax shelters and corporate debt policy. *Journal of Financial Economics* 81, 563-594.

Grossman. S. J. and O. D. Hart 1982. Corporate Financial Structure and Managerial Incentives. In: *The Economics of Information and Uncertainty*. Ed. Par J. J. McCall. Chicago: The University of Chicago Press, 123-155.

Gul F.A. Jaggi B. 1999. An analysis of joint effects of investment opportunity set. *free cash flow* and size on corporate debt policy. *Review of Quantitative Finance and Accounting* 12(4), 371-381.

Halov N. and Heider.F. 2005. Capital Structure, asymmetric information and risk. *EFA 2004 MAASTRİCHT*, 1-56.

Harris M. and Raviv.A. 1991. The theory of capital structure. *Journal of Finance* 46(1), 297-355

Henry. 2010. Agency costs, ownership structure and corporate governance compliance: A private contracting perspective. Pacific-Basin Finance Journal 181, 24-46.

Hosono 2003. Growth Opportunities. Collateral and Debt Structure: The Case of the Japanese Machine Manufacturing Firms. Japan and the World Economy 15(3), 275-97

Hovakimian 2006. Are Observed Capital Structures Determined by Equity Market Timing?. *Journal of Financial and Quantitative Analysis* 41 (1), 221-243

Huang. G. and F.M. Song.. 2006. The Determinants of Capital Structure: Evidence from China. *China Economic Review* 17, 14-36

Hudson M.R. Parrino R. and Starks L. 1998. International monitoring mechanisms and CEO turnover: A long term perspective. Unpublished manuscript University of Pennsylvania.

Imam. M and Malik. M 2007. Firm Performance and Corporate Governance through Ownership structure. *International Review of Business Research Papers 3(4), 88-110*

Jensen. M. and Meckling. W. 1976. Theory of the firm: Managerial behavior, agency costs and capital structure. *Journal of Financial Economics* 3, 305-360

Jensen. M. 1986. Agency costs of free cash flow, corporate finance and takeovers. *American Economic Review* 76, 323-329

Karadeniz. S. Y. Kandir. M. Balcilar and Y. B. Onal. 2009. Determinants of capital structure: evidence from Turkish lodging companies. *International Journal of Contemporary Hospitality Management* 215, 594-609

Kim. H. Heshmati. A. and Aoun. D. 2006. Dynamics of capital structure: the case of Korean listed manufacturing companies. *Asian Economic Journal 20*3, 275-302.

Kremp E. and Stoss E. 2001. L'endettement des entreprises industrielles françaises et allemandes: des élutions distinctes malgré des déterminants proches. *Economie et Statistique* n°1/2.

La Rocca. La Rocca and Cariol *2007.* Overinvestment and Underinvestment Problems: Determining Factors: Consequences and Solutions. Corporate Ownership and Control 5 (1), 79-95

Lang L.H.P.. Ofek O. and Stulz R.M. 1996. Leverage, Investment. and Firm Growth . *Journal of Financial Economics 40, 3-29.*

McKnight and Weir. 2009. Agency costs, corporate governance mechanisms and ownership structure in large UK publicly quoted companies: A panel data analysis. *The Quarterly Review of Economics and Finance 49, 139–158*

Miller. Merton H. 1977. Debt and Taxes. *Journal of Finance*, 261-275.

—. 1991. Leverage. *Journal of Finance* 46 (2), 479-488.

Modigliani F. and M. Miller 1958. The cost of capital, corporation finance and the theory of investment. *American Economic Review*, 261-297.

Modigliani F. and M. Miller 1963. Corporate Income Taxes and the cost of capital. *American Economic Review*, 433-443.

Myers. Stewart C. 1977. Determinants of Corporate Borrowing. *Journal of Financial Economics* 5(2), 147-175

Nekhili M. Wali A. and Chebbi D. 2009. Free cash flow, gouvernance et politique financière des entreprises françaises. *Finance Contrôle Stratégie* 12 (1), 5-31.

Pao. 2008. A comparison of neural network and multiple regression analysis in modeling capital structure *Expert Systems with Applications* 35, 720–727

Pindado J. and De la Torre C. 2005. A Complementary Approach to the Financial and Strategy Views of Capital Structure: Theory and Evidence from the Ownership Structure. *SSRN working paper.*

Poulain-Rehm T. 2005. L'impact de l'affectation du *free cash flow* sur la création de valeur actionnariale : le cas de la politique d'endettement et de dividendes des entreprises françaises cotées . *Revue Finance. Contrôle. Stratégie* 8 (4), 205-238.

Pound J. 1988; Proxy contests and the efficiency of shareholder oversight. *Journal of financial economics* 20, 237-266.

Rajan R.G. and Zingales. L. 1995. What do we know about capital structure? Some evidence from international data *Journal of Finance* 50(5), 1421-1460

Sheikh and Wang 2010. Financing Behavior of Textile Firms in Pakistan. *International Journal of Innovation. Management and Technology* 1 (2), 130-135.

Shyam-Sunder L. and S.C Myers 1999. Testing static tradeoff against pecking order models of capital structure. *Journal of Financial Economics* 51, 219-244

Singh M. and Davidson III W.N. 2003. Agency costs, ownership structure and corporate governance mechanism. *Journal of Banking and Finance* 27, 793-816.

Solh. M. 2000. Fonds de pension et politique d'investissement à long terme des entreprises. thèse de doctorat en sciences de gestion. Université de Paris X Nanterre

Stulz. 1990. Managerial Discretion and Optimal Financing Policies. *Journal of Financial Economics* 26, 3-27

Taggart. 1977. A model of corporate financing decisions. *Journal of Finance* 32, 1467-1484

Tang. C.H. and Jang. S.C. 2007. Revisit to the determinants of capital structure: A comparison between lodging firms and software firms. *International Journal of Hospitality Management* 261, 175-187.

Titman and Wessels 1988. The determinants of capital structure choice. *Journal of Finance* 43, 1-19.

Vilasuso. J and Minkler. A. 2001. Agency costs, asset specificity, and the capital structure of the firm. *Journal of Economic Behavior and Organization* 441, 55-69.

Wiwattanakantang and Yupana. 1999. An empirical study on the determinants of the capital structure of Thai firms . *Pacific-Basin Finance Journal* 73(4), 371-403.

Wu and Yue 2009. Corporate tax, capital structure. and the accessibility of bank loans: Evidence from China. *Journal of Banking and Finance* 33(1), 30-38

Wu L. 2004. The Impact of Ownership Structure on Debt Financing of Japanese Firms with the Agency Cost of *Free cash flow. EFMA Meetings Paper.*

Zhang. H and Li. S. 2008. The Impact of Capital Structure on Agency Costs: Evidence from UK Public Companies. *Proceedings of the 16th Annual Conference on Pacific Basin Finance Economics Accounting Management PBFEAM Conference*

Zou.H. and J. Z. Xiao. 2006. The financing behavior of listed Chinese firms. *The British Accounting Review* 38, 239-258.

Zwiebel J. 1996. Dynamic Capital Structure under Managerial Entrenchment. *American Economic Review* 86 (5), 1197-1215.

FINANCING CONSTRAINTS THEORY: A NARRATIVE APPROACH

WALID MANSOUR[1] AND JAMEL E. CHICHTI[2]

1. Introduction

The financing constraints theory (FCT) is the study of the impact of financial frictions on the firm's investment. It constitutes one of the most important cornerstones of corporate finance. The relaxation of Modigliani and Miller's (1958) conjectural framework leads to the interdependence of financing and investment decisions. Indeed, three main failures link between them, i.e., information, bankruptcy, and taxation. The FCT theory hinges on the theoretical underpinnings that encompass the information-driven problems of studying the firm's investment under the incentive restriction(s). The objective of this paper is to present the salient features characterizing this theory and its main implications. Section 2 presents the contributions of the progenitors. Section 3 explains the role of net worth, which is at the hub of FCT. Section 4 presents the split-sample approach and its "discontents". Section 5 focuses on the theoretical debate that is related to the usefulness of the investment-cash flow sensitivity as an indicator for financing constraints. Section 6 discusses the financial contractibility and Gibrat's law from the perspective of FCT. Section 7 presents the role of FCT in the explanation of the "small-shocks-large cycles" puzzle. Section 8 concludes.

2. The Progenitors' Contributions

Although the mathematical study of information asymmetries dates back to the beginning of the 1970s, its appearance dates back to the era of Hammurabi Code. Indeed, the Babylonian civilization was first organized

---

[1] Institut Supérieur de Finances et de Fiscalité de Sousse, Université de Sousse, Tunisia.
[2] Ecole Supérieure de Commerce de Tunis, Université de la Manouba,Tunisia.

by the arrangement stipulated by such a code in order to make the running of business quite formalized. Two kinds of financing instruments were explicitly allowed to be enforced, namely debt and equity. Some amount of information asymmetries did exist in both kinds of instruments. However, it is less risky to the lender to raise funds to the farmer, relative to the merchant, who raises equity funds. In compliance with Baskin and Miranti (1997), the debt financing was "more effective in protecting investors against risk than partnerships were." Indeed, debt financing (e.g., fixed-income bond) is better to the external credit claimant than the equity financing. In fact, the creditor may raise external funds to the farmer once he is certain about his capacity to pay back the raised funds plus the interests.[3] Nevertheless, the equity investments enforced in the context of partnerships raise several problems. Indeed, the merchant incurs more risks than the external credit claimant. He should have better information about the technology and the conditions of the production process such as the land's fertility and the expected weather patterns. Such kinds of information are pivotal to the merchant since crop-generated profits will condition his own return. It is therefore crucial to discover any attempt by the farmer to camouflage the true crop yield.

Debt financing is less risky to the lender since Hammurabi Code allows the utilization of various types of collaterals. Indeed, the debt contracts may include some clauses mentioning that, in case of bankruptcy, it is possible to seize the collateralized assets and get paid. Such mortgage-based debt contracts may encompass a variety of collaterals under the form of securities, such as farmlands, slaves, and even wives and children. One notices that Hammurabi Code did contain – implicitly – some arrangements to alleviate the consequences of information asymmetries reigning among contracting parties. Such asymmetries still do exist in modern times. However, the techniques to take account of them are categorically different.

In modern times, the architect of Information Economics studying the information asymmetries is Joseph E. Stiglitz[4], the 2001 Nobel prizewinner.

---

[3] Hammurabi Code included an important staple, namely forbidding the usury by fixing an upper limit to interest rates. For instance, the rate charged on all silver-based loans cannot exceed 20%. See Baskin and Miranti (1997).

[4] Joseph E. Stiglitz shared the 2001 Nobel Prize with prizewinners Michael Spence and George Akerlof; he is recognized to be the architect of Information Economics. His work on that area is of paramount importance and this goes back to his stay in Nairobi (1969-1971) during which he realized the distortion between

Many authors, however, contributed to the field in various ways. The long-standing microeconomic prejudices were at the heart of markets and transactional analyses, through the rational theorizing of individual and aggregate behaviours. Though the formal analyses built on those prejudices are theoretically acceptable, their empirical relevance is of trivial import. Indeed, the standard competitive equilibrium model was the overriding road map used by the economists who followed suit to describe the micro- and macro-economic environments, albeit not all of them believed in its explanatory power of how markets operate.[5]

Financial Economics needed a transitional alteration toward a new style. The significant milestone is the 1970 pioneering paper by George Akerlof who compared why people are reluctant to buy used (or rented) cars to other transactional situations occurring in the markets for loans and insurance.[6] Akerlof's first interest was macroeconomics, or, more precisely, the causes of Business Cycles. By the end of the 1960s, a prominent driver underlying the Business Cycle was the fluctuation of transactions in the second-hand cars market and problems of disproportional distribution of information were suspiciously thought of as being the culprit.

In essence, because the information asymmetry is quasi-omnipresent in every transaction, the market may entirely collapse — an equilibrium situation characterized with no trade at all — when its severity is extremely acute. This rationale is used to tackle the consequences of the informational imperfections in connection with insurance, labour and loan markets, in the light of various risk exposures of economic players. The

---

the standard competitive equilibrium model and economic facts. Albeit the theoretical development and empirical applications of markets with asymmetric information rests on Stiglitz (alongside with Michael Spence and George Akerlof), other authors have their own contribution (e.g., in 1996, James Mirrlees and William Vickrey were rewarded the Nobel Prize for their fundamental contributions to the theory of incentives under asymmetric information, in particular its applications to the design of optimal income taxation and resource allocation through different types of auctions.)

[5] See Stiglitz (2001) for an extensive discussion.

[6] This problem was originally analysed in the market for education (and later extended to other fields) where different levels of education, and hence qualification, or, in quantitative terms, returns to schooling, would impact the firm's productivity since the employer is not able to distinguish at first sight between high-productivity and low-productivity workers. For full coverage of the area for which the asymmetrical information setting applies, see Hillier (1997).

information-theoretic concerns arise as an intellectual revolution versus Marshall's dictum "Natura non facit saltum", positing that an economy whose information is nearly perfect could be similar to another one with information asymmetry. Things are much more difficult than Marshall's simplifying dictum. Stiglitz (2001) argues that the nature of equilibrium is prodigiously affected by even a small deviation from the full information state. Information Economics overcomes the neoclassical school that was unable to answer a host of puzzles and paradoxes (e.g., market volatility, risk sharing, equity premia.) Furthermore, the existence of shocks to the economy affecting the cyclical movements would show that something is going wrong.

The research agenda in the Finance profession, over three decades after Akerlof's (1970) paper, was highly motivated by loads of conceptual changes. The new style embedded — among others — random shocks and unexpected states into the Arrow-Debreu model, and questioned the long-standing economic laws such as those of the single price and market clearing, etc. The particular study of decentralized markets in occidental economies put into the picture the informational asymmetries as the striking facet of capital-market imperfections such that the corporate veil is hardly pierceable, unless at a cost, as in the costly state verification literature (see for example, Townsend, 1979). The overwhelming persistence of information asymmetries gave rise to major implications which are utterly at odds with the neoclassical school's predictions. The seminal works of the 2001 Nobel prizewinners transformed the way by which economics analyses the functioning of markets.

Although Akerlof's paper was rejected three times by three editors, its influence is far-reaching till today. Akerlof analyses a market for a commodity where one part has more information than the other. The then strange term he used was "lemons" (nowadays a colloquialism) to label the defective cars (or any other defective wares), which became a common term used by economists around the world. He pointed out that the logic underlying his analysis may be kindred to Thomas Gresham's law.[7]

---

[7] Sir Thomas Gresham (1519-1579) was an English financier. He was the brother of Queen Elisabeth I and the advisor of King Edward VI. His law means that bad money will drive good money out of circulation. In other terms, when there are two or more kinds of money circulating in the economy, the good money (i.e., for which there is a no significant value between its exchange value and commodity value) is driven out by bad money (for which there is a substantial difference between its exchange value and commodity value which means that its actual value

Gresahm's law claims that "bad money drives out good", which is not, according to Akerlof (1970, p. 490) himself, a perfect analogue to the lemons principle, since both sellers and buyers can presumably distinguish between "good" and "bad" money. The most leading, distinguishable "teaching" of G. Akerlof is showing that a situation with asymmetrical distribution of information can give rise to *adversely selected* markets. That is, risky borrowers may crowd out low-risk ones and take part in the same advantages. As was shown later by Hellmann and Stiglitz (2000), three effects may occur in an adversely selected debt market. First, the *price* effect is brought forth by the fact that an increase in the debt price (i.e., lending rate) will increase the lender's revenue. This effect is always positive. Second, the *positive selection* effect is brought forth if the lender loses entrepreneurs that are less profitable than the average, in terms of the risk-return couple. Third, the *adverse selection* effect is brought forth by losing entrepreneurs that are more profitable than the average.[8]

The encompassing of information-driven problems in the theory of corporate finance was at its heart. Many authors contributed to the development of this literature. For instance, Greenwald and Stiglitz (1994) develop a model[9] in which the firm's behaviour under information

---

is below its market value). That is to say, the two currencies circulating in the economy will be quickly dominated both by the bad currency since people tend to will hand over the bad currency rather than the good one. That is, they will keep the one of greater value for themselves by hoarding it. Gresham's law can sometimes be applied in other situations in which true value of a given ware is markedly different from the value most of people are thinking of, due to several factors such as information asymmetries. As for the example of lemons given by Akerlof (1970), this situation will render it "lucky" to buy a good ware at a fair price, seeing that the buyer runs the risk to pay an extra-price for a lemon. Consequently, the buyers tend to only pay a low (i.e., fair) price for the defective wares in order to elude being ripped off by the sellers. The high-quality wares tend to be driven out (i.e., pushed out of the market) by the lemons since the buyers cannot find out a good way to distinguish between both wares.

[8] See the figures in Hellmann and Stiglitz (2000) showing the consequences of rationing in credit and/or debt markets.

[9] One of the most the most important result of the model of Greenwald and Stiglitz (1994) is showing that the new firm is financially constrained relatively the neoclassical one. However, it is somewhat difficult to identify a *totally* constrained firm. We rather prefer to classify the firms in terms of their ability to access external funds. Accordingly, we can have different degrees of financial constraints. For instance, the firms that cannot even raise short-term debts may be thought of as the most constrained, those that may raise are thought of as partially constrained,

asymmetries and financing constraints is not compatible with the one predicted by the neoclassical approach. Indeed, the authors show the positive role of net worth in determining the firm's capital expenditures as a consequence of capital-market imperfections in the presence of random shocks in the economy. They argue that "Asymmetrically distributed information between a firm, as an employer, and its workers has replaced the traditional view of a firm which hires labor at fixed (or monopolistically increasing) wages in well-defined labor markets with one in which firms actively manage long-term employment relationships, on average pay wages in excess of those available, on average, in the labor market at large, control workers with carefully designed incentive mechanisms and often ration access to jobs. Similar asymmetries of information between outside investors, who provide capital, and inside managers, who control its use, have led to comparable developments in the theory of how firms acquire and deploy capital."[10] (p.2). See Mansour (2004, 2009) for a deep review of the literature.

3. The Role of Net Worth

In the previous section, we emphasized the role of the progenitors in the study of the information asymmetries and their role in the characterization of the new theory of the firm. Indeed, as is stressed by Greenwald and Stiglitz (1994), the equity and credit markets may clear on a rationing outcome in long-run equilibria due to an asymmetrical distribution of information with respect to the firm's risk-return profile and its prospects. The internally-generated funds therefore play a crucial role in driving the firm's capital expenditures. This is the major prejudice of the new theory of the firm emphasizing the role of net worth, since high borrowing costs drive a wedge between internal and external finances.[11]

---

whilst those that can issue all types of debt with different maturities, can be thought of as financially unconstrained.

[10] The authors conclude that there are two main theoretical developments. On the one hand, the first dimension is related to "the internal structure of the firm — how rewards for individual workers should be designed, what constitutes appropriate hierarchical or reporting structures [...]". On the other hand, the second dimension is related to the behaviour of the firm in front of external environmental and policy changes.

[11] Other prejudices also characterize the new behaviour of the firm in the context of Information Economics relative to the one in the neoclassical context. For instance, it acts as if it is an individual maximizing the utility of end-of-period wealth. Their utility function is supposedly characterized by *DARA* (decreasing

Basically, Myers and Majluf's (1984) paper posits that firms could be credit-constrained because external finance providers have no or have less information than management/shareholders as regards the current value of assets in place. The basic model implies that the management maximizes the current shareholders' net wealth (i.e., the present value of the streams of net profits discounted via a risk-adjusted discount rate). Swoboda (2003) distinguishes three major implications of Myers and Majluf's contribution. Firstly, when a firm suffers from financial constraints, it does not issue new securities, unless its net worth is overvalued. Frequently, the management does not issue new securities and thus foregoes some positive NPV-projects. Secondly, the informational asymmetry between management and external suppliers of funds brings on a signalling effect. Thirdly, another direct reverberation — which is widely known as the financial hierarchy or the pecking order theory — brings forth a *rough* preference for the internally generated funds. Indeed, the management — who is implied to operate in behalf of the shareholders but also in their interest — finances the investment process by retained earnings at the first step and the shortcoming funds are hierarchically financed.

Hubbard (1998) shows graphically the extent to which the situation of information asymmetries may be worsening by causing underinvestment. Figure 1 shows the supply curve which has an upward-slope, conversely to the neoclassical analysis which considers it as constant at a risk-adjusted real market interest rate. It shapes also the sloping-downward schedule of investment demand. At the intersection of the capital stock demand — which is driven by the marginal investment opportunities — and the external finance supply — which is driven by the profitability return — one breaks even at the equilibrium level at K^*, which is the *first-best* capital stock in a frictionless setting. With regard to this conventional setting, net worth does not matter since the firm could raise external funds at this equilibrium-value rate.

Let us now consider an *ex post* situation in which the distribution of information is asymmetric. For instance, the business operator observes quite well the expenditures on soft capital, whereas the external claimants do not, but observe the other outlays on capital goods. This situation of "cheat" instigates the external claimants to act so as to protect themselves from the business operator's fraud temptation. Thereby, they require an

absolute risk aversion.) That is to say, the capital-market imperfections beget noisy-effects "interfering with the proper distribution of risk" since the firm tends to act in a risk averse manner. See Greenwald and Stiglitz (1994).

agency premium to compensate the default risk for the uncollateralized borrowed debts. Hence, the upward-sloping shape of the supply curve shows the increasing informational costs. Indeed, as Hubbard posits (p.197), "the higher are the marginal informational costs, the steeper is the upward-sloping portion of the *S* curve". The new equilibrium of the capital stock is hereinafter K_0 which shows that the information-related frictions bring forth underinvestment.

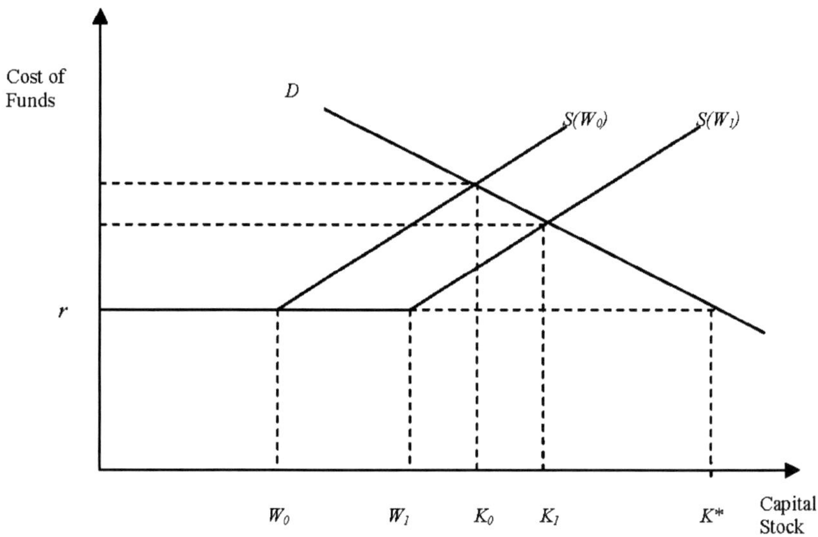

Fig. 1: Financial Reverberation of the Asymmetrical Distribution of Information
Source: Hubbard (1998, p. 196)

From this figure, some consequences arise. First, *ceteris paribus*, the shift of internal earnings from W_0 to W_1 shifts the supply curve from S (W_0) to S (W_1) and the equilibrium capital stock from K_0 to K_1. Second, the spread $\Delta K = K^* - K$ "depends inversely on the entrepreneur's net worth" (p. 196). The higher business operator's net worth is, the lower their reliance on external financing. A positive shock to the firm's net worth therefore alleviates its reliance on external funds. Third, the collateralized external financing is markedly more costly than the internal finance.

It is noticeable that market imperfections, especially the asymmetrical distribution of information, affect negatively the corporate investment and often lead firms to pass up positive NPV-projects. Thereby, the firm undergoes, under this state of affairs, the underinvestment effect. Specifically, the increase of costs of funds in the credit markets increasingly affects the user cost of capital, which is worsening the growth of capital stock. The net worth, hence, plays a crucial role in the financing of capital expenditures. Indeed, Lamont (1997) shows that net worth is the determinant for more than 75% of the capital spending by US industrial and manufacturing firms.[12]

4. The Split-Sample Approach and its "Discontents"

The first paper that focussed on the role of net worth in driving the firm's capital expenditures was Tinbergen (1939). Tinbergen's study cleared on asserting the role of profits earned in the explanation of corporate investment. Notwithstanding that Tinbergen's paper — which dealt with data for several countries and industrial sectors spanning over long period — provided empirical evidence of net worth role, it was denied since choosing the steel consumption to statistically assess the investment expenditures is not fulfilled with appropriateness, inasmuch as these two variables are driven by a positive linear relationship through time. Thus, it is obvious that a high correlation coefficient be obtained.

Fazzari, Hubbard, and Petersen (1988) (for short, FHP88) argue that, holding constant the future growth opportunities, an incremental in firm's net worth entails a positive effect on the corporate investment. Such an effect is easily assessed through the graphical analysis of Hubbard. Thereby, the corporate investment is positively correlated, especially for the short-run, with measures of net worth (e.g., cash flow, operating post-tax profit, etc.). Such a correlation arises when the firm bears the conditions of credit rationing (i.e., high quoted rates charged on loans or/and upper boundary of funds afforded by banks). Furthermore, this positive relation arises because shocks to current earnings positively affect the discounted net worth and therefore the terms of credits available to the firm, i.e., the higher the firm's net worth is, the more its collateralized assets are highly valued, and hence the easier raising pledged loans is.

The empirical approach of FHP88 is based on the three challenges enumerated by Hubbard (1998): (*i*) the choice of one or more clustering

[12] Lamont (1997) interprets this result in terms of the role of internal capital markets in the industrial economies since a high percentage of funds for financing investment is provided by net worth.

criteria that should be closely related to the informational costs; (*ii*) a cross-sectional analysis of the investment-cash flow sensitivities (ICFS)[13]. The sub-sample of firms that are more prone to be financially constrained should theoretically exhibit the highest ICFS whereas the sub-sample of firms that are financially less constrained should exhibit conversely the lowest ICFS. The direct nexus between ICFS and the degree of financing constraints is, in compliance with FHP88, *monotonic*. In fact, the latter inference constitutes the pivotal argument by FHP88 inasmuch as "the centre of our argument is that for firms having asymmetric information in capital markets, *q* can fluctuate over a substantial range in excess of unity [...] while investment can be excessively sensitive to cash flow fluctuations" (p. 8).

This is the well-known monotonicity conjecture stating that the higher ICFS is, the more severe the financial constraints. This positive nexus investment-cash flow — disclosed by an excess of sensitivity — could be seen through the direct dependence between the required agency premium and the collateralizeable assets. Such a dependence means that when the net worth picks up (i.e., improved by positive shocks), the premium charged on external finance will be scaled down (enhancement of credit terms). Consequently, the corporate investment responds positively to cash shock.

FHP88 divide up their sample of 421 U.S. manufacturing firms spanning over the period 1970-84 into sub-samples. The splitting approach they use is borrowed from the one used in the macroeconomic analysis testing for liquidity constraints on consumption for where the splitting is performed, inasmuch as sub-groups of households are high-wealth and low-wealth. Indeed, "the logic of the test implied is akin to that in test of consumption of whether consumption is excessively sensitive to current income" Hubbard (1998, p. 204).

The splitting approach clears on the utter comparison of the cross-sectional sensitivities. The first splitting criterion was the payout policy. Indeed, in the first version of FHP88, a model from public economics literature was extended. With regard to the public economics setting, the dividend

[13] Prior studies did not perform the *ex post* cross-sectional comparison of sensitivities, but the paper by Eisner (1978) [Eisner, Robert, 1978: *Factors in Business Investment*, Cambridge: Ballinger Press] who demonstrated that the investment by start-up businesses is more sensitive to profits than that by large ones.

proceeds represent an advantage-tax internal source of funds conversely to external finance insofar as dividend tax rate is higher than the tax on capital gains. Such a difference favours dividends to externally raised finance. FHP88 demonstrate via their splitting procedure that cash flow is more significant for low-payout sub-samples and computed *q* has less significance power, whereas cash flow is not significant for the high payout sub-sample — and thus less sensitive to corporate investment.

The approach by FHP88 was pursued by Hoshi, Kashyap and Scharfstein (1991) who operationalized the criterion affiliation in a Keiretsu (a Japanese moniker meaning industrial group[14]) so as to perform their splitting procedure. On the basis of whether the firm is a Keiretsu member or not[15], the authors basically show that cash flow does not have a sizeable effect on the investment by networked firms. Conversely, the fluctuations of cash flow have a positive effect on the investment by independent firms.

Although FHP88's approach gained a lot of interest from many authors, many authors do not stand for its relevance (e.g., Moyen, 2004; Cleary, Povel, and Raith, 2007; Hennessy and Whited, 2007). The major findings of FHP88's opponents cast doubt on the vicariousness of the monotonicity hypothesis. Kaplan and Zingales' (1997, 2000) (KZ for short) theoretical and empirical results fall under this heading. Their main critique is that the firms that are supposed to be financially constrained exhibit the lowest investment-cash flow sensitivity, which is at odds with FHP88's prediction. The following table summarizes the regression results of both landmark papers alongside with Moyen (2004). FHP88 identify firms according to paying out dividends. The most constrained firms are those with low dividends, whilst the least constrained firms are those with high dividends.

---

[14] The Korean equivalent of Japanese Keiretsu is known as Cheabol.

[15] The membership of a firm is considered in compliance with Keiretsu no Kenkyu — a prior Japanese publication which appeared before 1991 attempting to distinguish Keiretsu and non-Keiretsu firms — when it responds at least to one of the following conditions: one bank is the largest debt-holder during three consecutive years and the firm's stock percentage negotiated among the group's firms is at least 20%; the firm's bank debt constitutes at least 40% afforded by the largest lender; an historical membership is required.

	Cash Flow to Capital Ratio	Tobin's Q
FHP88: Most Constrained	0.461	0.001
	(0.027)	(0.000)
FHP88: Least Constrained	0.230	0.002
	(0.010)	(0.000)
KZ97: Likely Constrained	0.340	0.070
	(0.042)	(0.018)
KZ97: Never Constrained	0.702	0.009
	(0.041)	(0.006)
Moyen (2004)*: Highly Constrained	0.248	0.131
	(0.006)	(0.005)
Moyen (2004): Weakly Constrained	1.443	-0.163
	(0.030)	(0.006)

Notes on table: This table presents the investment-cash flow sensitivities and Tobin's Q estimates obtained using a linear-in-the-variables regression of the neoclassical investment model augmented by cash flow. Standard errors are in parentheses. *The estimates of Moyen (2004) are obtained from her two models (the first model is constrained whilst the second is unconstrained) and thus using simulated series that represent both theoretical models.

As shown in Table 1, the most constrained firms have investments that are the most sensitive to change in net worth, i.e., cash flow, relative to the least constrained ones. KZ97 do not stand for this empirical evidence and propose a different classification scheme[16] based on a variety of qualitative and quantitative information contained in various corporate reports.[17] In sharp contrast with FHP88, KZ97 consider that the firms that have a limited access to external funds are to be likely constrained, and those with access to more funds than are needed to finance their investment are never constrained. They argue that the firms that can pay out dividends, but do not choose to do so, are considered as constrained.

Moyen (2004) constructs two models. The first model (called the unconstrained model) allows the firm to have perfect access to external financial markets, whilst the second one (called the constrained model)

[16] Cleary (1999) propose the Z-score to be computed for each firm-year as an alternative criterion to classify the grand sample. Z-score is an index of the likelihood that the firm will increase its dividends in the future.

[17] Cleary, Povel, and Raith (2007) argue that the classification scheme proposed by KZ97 is too work-intensive for a large sample. Furthermore, it has been criticized due to its subjectivity. Indeed, their scheme is primarily based on managerial statements (e.g., letters to shareholders from the CEO and further notes).

restrains the firm's access. Moyen (2004) uses this laboratory to test for the contest between FHP88 and KZ97 in the light of their diverging findings. Her results reduce to two findings. On the one hand, the criterion dividends pay-out leads to the same results identified by FHP88, i.e. low-dividend firms' investments tend to be more responsive to cash flow relative to those paying out higher dividends. On the other hand, Moyen's (2004) constrained model stands for KZ97's findings, i.e. constrained firms' investments are less responsive to cash flow relative to those of unconstrained firms.

From the aforementioned diverging results, it turns out that the regression sensitivities hinge on the criterion chosen by the econometrician to identify whether a firm experiences financing constraints. There are three pivotal explanations of these results.

(1) Erickson and Whited (2000, 2002) consider that the grouping criterion must be exogenous (i.e., not affected by management's actions), the mis-measurement problem is the most "dangerous" problem threatening the whole investment-cash flow literature. It is for this reason that they propose a cure for this problem (a high-order moments GMM estimator taking account of the error-laden proxy problem.) In a leading paper published in the review Financial Management, Erickson and Whited (2006) notice that, inter alia, there are three major sources bringing forth the measurement error. (*i*) The difference between the manager's valuation of firm assets (average *Q*'s numerator) and their market value (Tobin's *Q* numerator). (*ii*) The market value of debt is not always equal to its book value. (*iii*) The denominator of most proxies for marginal *Q*, the replacement value of assets, is not necessarily equal to its common empirical proxy, the book value of assets.[18]

(2) The second explanation is borrowed from Moyen (2004) arguing that, in the framework of her two models, internal funds are highly correlated with investment opportunities. That is, both unconstrained and constrained firms tend to invest more when profitable investment opportunities are coming along. Particularly, the unconstrained firms issue debt to debt-claimants in order to finance their investment opportunities. Accordingly, debt issuance "inflates" the investment-cash flow sensitivity, which is at

[18] Bond et al. (2004) test whether the significance of cash flow is due to the weakness of Tobin's *Q*. This problem could be more important if "bubbles" beget a deviation of the stock market valuation from the true expected stream of future cash flows.

odds with FHP88 conventional result. An unconstrained average firm has the incentive to increase its investment and dividends payments after it has increased its debt level. By contrast, an average constrained firm is concerned by allocating its internal funds into either investment or dividends. It turns out, therefore, that the unconstrained firms exhibit a higher investment-cash flow sensitivity since the available internal funds are not fully "dumped" into investment expenditures.

(3) Cleary, Povel, and Raith (2007) study the reasons behind the diverging results among authors rather than documenting such differences. They show that the findings of FHP88 and of KZ97 and Cleary (1999) are not truly conflicting. Indeed, they are just different facets of the U-shaped, concave relationship linking internal funds and investment. Hence, the differences among authors are primarily caused by the classification criteria.

5. Is the Investment-Cash Flow Sensitivity a Reliable Metric for the Detection of Financing Constraints?

One of the central questions addressed in corporate finance is: Is the investment-cash flow sensitivity still the relevant measure of financing constraints in the light of the KZ-FHP contest? Since the primal paper of FHP88, the literature on the investment-cash flow sensitivity became very large and diverse. After controlling for future growth opportunities (either using Tobin's average *Q* or any other market-based measure like the market-to-book ratio), the single-numeral coefficient (point estimate) is taken to be a useful indicator of financing constraints. The central conjectural basis of this literature is to assume that the observed (empirical) investment-cash flow sensitivity must be larger for highly constrained firms (e.g., small-sized firms whose moral hazard problem is more pronounced) relative to the unconstrained ones. In this section, we will try to shed some light on the debate about the usefulness of the investment-cash flow sensitivity as an indicator of financing constraints.

Notwithstanding the large consensual agreement with respect to Fazzari, Hubbard, and Petersen's (1988) method, the first disparaging paper — KZ97 — hit out at their approach. KZ97's detracting critiques cast doubt profoundly on the consensual, implicit Monotonicity Conjecture stating that the investment-cash flow sensitivity the firm exhibits follows a sloping-upward scheme. More explicitly, the higher the degree of financing constraints, the higher its inherent investment-cash flow sensitivity. That is, the sensitivity increases monotonically with the increase of informational problems.

KZ97 focused on FHP88's sub-sample encompassing 49 low-dividend firms and performed an in-depth analysis with an innovative splitting procedure — they termed "direct observation" — and proposed some (mathematical) conditions for the exactness of the monotonicity hypothesis. Instigated by Jeremy Stein to get involved in this issue, KZ97 provided a theoretical framework emphasizing a new idea of what makes a firm financially constrained. Whereas the firm is deemed to be more constrained when financial afflictions increasingly drive a wedge between internal and external finances, Kaplan and Zingales (1997, p.173) consider that "unconstrained or less constrained firms are those firms with relatively large amounts of liquid assets and net worth."

Let us take the following notations: I is the firm's investment, k is a parameter proxying for the degree of financing constraints, and W is the level of internal funds. In KZ97's model, the higher the parameter k, the higher the external funds' costs. FHP88 measure the investment-cash flow sensitivity as the first derivative of the investment function with respect to W, i.e., dI/dW. Along with Fazzari, Hubbard, and Petersen (2000), it is sufficient that $d^2I/dW^2>0$ so that the investment-cash flow sensitivity increases monotonically with respect to k, i.e., with the degree of financing constraints. In a paper published in the same journal, namely *The Quarterly Journal of Economics*, Kaplan and Zingales (2000) responded to Fazzari, Hubbard, and Petersen (2000) by including the intrinsic characteristics of the firm and how the factor k is included into the variation of the sensitivity. Kaplan and Zingales (2000) reject the sufficient condition for monotonicity by Fazzari, Hubbard, and Petersen (2000). They rather argue that the so-called monotonicity hypothesis is accepted when $d^2I/dWdk>0$. Indeed, Kaplan and Zingales (2000, p.709) assert that "firms with higher k have a higher slope of external finance schedule."

In this manner, the FHP-KZ contest could be articulated around the signs of the derivatives d^2I/dW^2 and $d^2I/dWdk$. The signs of these two expressions are not always positive. Indeed, as stressed by Almeida and Campello (2007), "the most we can say is that an unconstrained firm (W very high or k equal to zero) has sensitivity equal to zero, while a constrained firm has a positive dI/dW". Mansour (2009) proposes a simple model based on moral hazard and costly state verification. He derives an equilibrium investment equation that is equal to[19]

$$I = \frac{(z_h - z_l)[W + z_h \tilde{\pi}(I,W)]}{(z_h - z_l) + z_h \varphi}, \tag{1}$$

where z_h and z_l are respectively the high and low states of shock, $\tilde{\pi}(I,W)$ is a random profit-generation function, and $\varphi \in (0,1)$ is a parameter that reflects the degree of financing constraints. A high value of φ means that the firm's degree of financing constraints is high. It is equivalent to the parameter k in Kaplan and Zingales' (2000) formulation.

The computation of the aforementioned derivatives yields the following expressions

$$\frac{d^2 I}{dW^2} = \left[\frac{(z_h - z_l) z_h}{(z_h - z_l) + z_h \varphi}\right] \frac{d^2\, \tilde{\pi}(I,W)}{dW^2} > 0, \ \forall\, \varphi \in (0,1) \tag{2}$$

$$\frac{d^2 I}{dW d\varphi} = -\left[\frac{z_h (z_h - z_l)\left(1 + z_h \frac{d\tilde{\pi}(I,W)}{dW}\right)}{((z_h - z_l) + z_h \varphi)^2}\right] < 0, \ \forall\, \varphi \in (0,1) \tag{3}$$

Similarly to Fazzari, Hubbard, and Petersen (2000), Mansour (2009) finds that the second partial derivative (2) is positive, which means that at a high level of net worth (i.e., high *W*'s) the investment-cash flow sensitivity is high too. That is, when the firm constructs a buffer of cash stock its investment is more sensitive at high levels of net worth. Accordingly, if the partial derivative (2) is positive, then the claimed monotonicity hypothesis is also true. This result hence corroborates the definition of financing constraints by Fazzari, Hubbard, and Petersen (2000). It is important to notice that (2) is positive only under the assumption that $\pi(I, W)$ is convex.

In their response to Kaplan and Zingales (2000), Fazzari, Hubbard, and Petersen (2000) argue that the second partial derivative (3) should necessarily be positive. Using his own moral hazard framework and notations, Mansour (2009) does not confirm their condition and corroborates the critique by Kaplan and Zingales (2000) who provide theoretical examples for which Eq. (3) is not positive. It is therefore quite

[19] We implicitly report the investment equation. For further details on its derivation, see Mansour (2009).

clear that the investment-cash flow sensitivity does not necessarily respond in an increasing-monotonic manner to the increase of information asymmetries' acuteness, as proxied for by φ. Such a theoretical result makes the interpretation of the investment-cash flow sensitivity an indicator for financing constraints "sceptical".

6. Financial Contractibility and Gibrat's Law

Although there are several remarkable advancements in the field, many theoretical problems are not solved yet, such as those that are related to the nature of financing constraints themselves. The current section will first give special attention to some aspects such as the approach of Albuquerque and Hopenhayn (2004) in their modelling of financing constraints. Afterwards, we will shed some light on Gibrat's law and its link with financing constraints.

6.1 Is the Financial Contract Optimal under Incentive Restrictions?

The theoretical modelling of financing constraints is mainly based on two chief incentive restrictions, namely information asymmetry and limited enforceability. Indeed, Pratap and Rendon (2003, p. 516) claim that "there is a large literature that explains the tightness of the borrowing constraint as a consequence of asymmetric information or enforceability restrictions [...] While such an approach is theoretically more complete, we cannot identify these models with our data. We therefore simplify the analysis by assuming that the tightness of the equity constraint is captured by a parameter which we estimate. The borrowing constraint arises as a consequence of the exit rule. This relatively simple model is also able to account for several of the stylized facts that other models can. Estimating models with enforceability and information restrictions is left for future research."

As for the information asymmetry restriction, it is assumed that financing constraints arise because the information between the lender and the borrower is asymmetrically distributed. That is to say, the lender cannot observe the revenue outcome, which is considered as private information to the entrepreneur. An alternative approach considers that the lender cannot monitor the ex-post use of funds, once the financial contract is enforced. Financing constraints may also arise as a result of limited enforceability. Clementi and Hopenhayn (2006) argue that "there are no informational asymmetries, but borrowers can default on their debts and take an outside option [...] The incomplete enforcement model that we describe is the natural counterpart to our moral hazard model."

Before addressing the question that is related to the existence of an optimal financial contract, it turns out to be crucial to address another question that is related to the nature of financing constraints: *Are they endogenous or exogenous*?[20] The answer to this question will motivate the research articles during the forthcoming years in corporate finance. In models with exogenous financing constraints, "the ability to raise short term capital is limited by some pre-specification function of debt", whilst in models with endogenous financing constraints, such constraints must satisfy a dynamic consistency requirement, i.e., equity restricts current access to capital, but is itself determined by future access to credit. In contrast, the endogeneity of such constraints reflects the fact that the relevant variable is not assets but equity. In fact, when studying the macroeconomic implications of limited borrowing, Kiyotaki and Moore (1997) show that some types of assets (e.g., human capital) are not perfectly appropriate, and lending cannot be fully collateralized with assets. Accordingly, as in the model of Albuquerque and Hopenhayn (2004), "more lending can be sustained with the threat of depriving the borrower from its equity."

In compliance with Albuquerque and Hopenhayn (2004), "Of all dynamically consistent lending plans, the optimal contract is the one that maximizes access to short term capital and the expected rate of decrease of long term debt. But there are others, which can be suboptimal and thus lead to tighter borrowing constraints [...] Models of exogenous borrowing constraints always leave open the question of whether there are better contracts that could imply weaker constraints." The exogeneity of financing constraints reflects the fact that "borrowing is limited by firm's assets." The authors develop a theory of financing constraints in which the lending contract specifies an initial loan size, future financing flows, and a repayment schedule. The choice of these variables determines the firm's borrowing capacity (and in turn its ability to raise external funds) as well

[20] In compliance with Whited (2006, p. 8), "It would be ideal to model external finance costs endogenously. [...] However, such an approach becomes analytically intractable. In the main, the model's tractability means that it can be easily controlled, governed, its implications may be tested empirically, and the components of its underlying mappings are observable."

as its dynamics. That is, borrowing constraints and firm dynamics are jointly determined[21] (Albuquerque and Hopenhayn, 2004).

The optimal contract in Albuquerque and Hopenhayn (2004) can be defined through a Pareto frontier between the lender's entitlements (i.e., the long-term debt) and the entrepreneur's entitlement (equity). If the entrepreneur decides to leave the match then he loses his equity but gains an outside value that is higher than the incumbency premium. In compliance with the authors, "equity grows over time as the firm pays-off the long-term debt. This weakens borrowing constraints, as the increased equity provides the bonding necessary to accumulate increasing amounts of capital." The authors show that the initial set-up cost (the initial long-term debt) is determined through the competition among lenders. The optimal lending contract maximizes the entrepreneur's entitlement for which there is a unique debt maturity structure corresponding to the highest value of the firm. "Any other debt maturity either leads to default or a lower initial firm value."

The main contribution of Albuquerque and Hopenhayn (2004) in modelling borrowing constraints is including limited enforceability in the modelling of financing constraints. In the basic, frictionless set-up (i.e., in the absence of enforcement problems), the firm and the non-residual claimant can simply commit to the contract maximizing the expected streams of the match, since such streams are discounted at the same rate. Nonetheless, when the firm has the possibility to exit the match, the authors show that the long-term contract proposes a unique debt repayment plan. In this case, the firm chooses to leave the match and it will not make any payment if it has an outside opportunity. The long-term debt contract specifies a liquidation policy, history-dependent contingent advances of capital, and a dividend policy. The authors assume that the total value of debt includes the short-term debts advanced at different dates.[22] They derive an important result regarding the negative relationship between long-term and short-term debts. In fact, a high level of long-term debt restricts the access of the firm to short-term debt. In compliance with

[21] The authors join the result of Zingales (1997) [Zingales, L., 1997, "Survival of the Fittest or the Fattest? Exit and Financing in the Trucking Industry," NBER WP no. 6273] that capital structure is an important determinant of the firm's growth and exit decisions.

[22] It is also assumed that the short-term debts are homogenous and there is only one lender which eliminates the problem of seniority claims.

the authors, this negative relationship is at the heart of financing constraints.

6.2 Does Gibrat's Law Hold under Financing Constraints?

Gibrat's law (known also as Gibrat's rule of proportionate growth) is a rule claiming that the size of the firm and its growth rate are not dependent. It establishes that the growth rate is a random pace which means that the size change's probability distribution is uniform for a set of firms within an industry.[23] Many results on firm dynamics have shown that firm growth decreases with firm size, which is inconsistent with Gibrat's legacy. For instance, Albuquerque and Hopenhayn (2004) show that when equity grows "so does the size of the firm and its probability of survival", which is consistent with the firm age and size effects documented in the literature on firm dynamics. By the same token, as surveyed by Hubbard (1998) and Stein (2003), financing constraints affect growth and survival.

Albuquerque and Hopenhayn (2004) show that the optimal lending contract has some comparative statics. Indeed, "Projects with lower sunk costs, better prospects or growth opportunities can sustain a larger initial debt and size, exhibit a higher survival probability, the repayment of long-term debt is faster and borrowing constraints are eliminated sooner. A lower value of default (e.g., better outside enforcement) implies larger firm size and leverage. Higher interest rates lead to a smaller initial sustainable debt and firm size. Though the relationship between risk and borrowing constraints is less clear, our analysis indicates that riskier projects could face tighter constraints. These and other comparative statics questions obviously cannot be addressed by existing models of firm dynamics which assume exogenous borrowing constraints." It is therefore clear that firm dynamics and financing constraints are jointly determined and Gibrat's law is not true when financing constraints do bind.

7. Can the "Small Shocks, Large Cycles" Puzzle be Explained in Terms of Financing Constraints?

The major studies of the financing constraints theory focused on the firm level. A plausible extension could start from the study of the "Small

---

[23] Indeed, if size does not depend on growth, then any (proportional) change in the firm's size will be the same for all the firms independently of growth.

Shocks, Large Cycles" Puzzle and the question that may seem to be leading is: Do financing constraints explain that puzzle? A booming literature appeared in the recent past studying the monetary policy's transmission mechanism from the perspective of capital-market imperfections. Strictly speaking, this literature links the small shocks — fluctuations of interest rates in the economy — and large cycles — fluctuations of business cycles — and explains this link through financing constraints. That is, the longstanding "Small Shocks, Large Cycles" Puzzle in business cycle analysis postulating that large fluctuations in the aggregate economic activity sometimes arise from what appear to be relatively small impulses (Bernanke, Gertler, and Gilchrist, 1996).

Though this link remained a puzzle for a long time, an answer was given more than twenty years ago. Indeed, Greenwald, Stiglitz, and Weiss (1984) were concerned with imperfections in equity (and debt) markets and the role that informational imperfections in capital markets are likely to play in business cycles. The authors studied adversely selected borrowing decisions and how they may bring forth large fluctuations in the effective cost of capital in response to relatively small demand shocks. The answer to the puzzle is explained, in this manner, in terms of borrowing/lending conditions under capital-market imperfections. That is, little changes in debt-markets conditions beget a propagation of real (or monetary) shocks to the rest of the economy. Bernanke, Gertler, and Gilchrist (1996) argue that although there are various ways of rationalizing a financial accelerator theoretically, one useful framework is the "principal-agent" view of credit markets, which has been extensively developed in recent years.

The first, innovative work related to the financial accelerator goes back to Irving Fisher's Debt-Deflation analysis of the causes of the 1929 Great Depression.[24] Through his analysis, Fisher argues that the capital-market imperfections are the origin for the transmission of cyclical shocks to the economy. In Bernanke and Gertler (1996), financial frictions do arise from the state of affairs where the costly state verification problem does hold. The idea the authors showed is that the productivity shocks may affect the firm's internal net worth, and, subsequently, impact the rest of the

[24] Indeed, Tirole (2006, p. 471) argues that "in the first issue of *Econometrica* (1933), Irving Fisher stressed the key role of credit constraints in amplifying the current recession [...]; furthermore, the reduction in the firm's cash flows and the fall in collateral values increased leverage and reduced investment, thereby exacerbating the recession."

economy through the propagation and transmission mechanisms. Carlstrom and Fuerst (1997) develop a model in which endogenous agency-driven costs are considered as the direct impulses for the modifications of business cycles. The aim of their model is to quantitatively measure the impact of agency costs on business cycles.

The rationalization of the financial accelerator is pinned down from the principal-agent approach to debt markets. In line of the net worth literature, this approach corroborates three theoretical facts. First, it considers that external funds are more costly than internal funds, unless the latter are collateralizable. In fact, a high cost of funds reflects high agency costs to take account of the information asymmetry. Second, there is a negative linkage between the agency premium and the entrepreneurial net worth. Third, a fall in the entrepreneurial net worth raises both the agency premium on external financing and the required proceeds (collateral assets), leading to a reduction in spending and production.

The prior analysis of Fisher in the beginning of the last century is known these days as the "balance-sheet channel"[25]. This device "hypothesizes that monetary policy affects loan demand through its effect on firms' net worth. Higher interest rates increase debt service, erode firm cash flow, and depress the value of collateral, exacerbating conflicts between lenders and borrowers. "This deterioration in firm credit worthiness increases the external finance premium and squeezes firm demand for credit" (Ashcraft and Campello, 2007). The "lending channel" mechanism postulates that the lending by banks is influenced by monetary policy. Indeed, "firms in the productive sector may not be hit solely by their own capital shortage (the balance-sheet channel), but also by a weakness in the balance sheets of their financial institutions that lend to them (the lending channel)" (Tirole, 2006, p. 478), i.e., when financial institutions face financial constraints.

8. Conclusion

This article developed narratively some salient insights concerning the FCT. When Modigliani and Miller's (1958) conjectural framework is violated, the firm does not behave similarly to the neoclassical one. In

---

[25] See Tirole (2006, Ch. 13) for an analysis of the impact of interest rates on economic activity through the extension of moral-hazard and adverse-selection models on the aggregate level.

compliance with Greenwald and Stiglitz (1994), its finance/investment decisions are jointly determined and constrained by its access to external finance sources. The central reason lying behind the existence of financing constraints is information asymmetries between contracting parties. The firm gets punished with an agency premium by its residual and non-residual claimants once the distribution of information is asymmetrical.

The FCT's central question is the usefulness of the investment-cash flow sensitivity as an indicator of financing constraints. KZ97 hit at FHP88 by claiming that such sensitivity and its underlying monotonicity hypothesis cannot theoretically hold true. After reviewing some theoretical results and empirical regularities, we reported the findings of Mansour (2009) advocating that the investment-cash flow sensitivity does not necessarily behave in an increasing-monotonic manner. Therefore, its interpretation as a useful indicator of financing constraints is quite "sceptical".

Modelling financing constraints mathematically will constitute one of the most important challenges to corporate finance. The models of Albuquerque and Hopenhayn (2004) and Clementi and Hopenhayn (2006) link the firm's investment and two incentive restrictions, namely information asymmetry and limited enforceability. Although they modelled financing constraints under the first and/or the second restriction, the question of endogeneity and exogeneity of the financing constraints remains an open issue.

We ultimately discussed the explanation of the "small shocks-large cycles" in terms of financing constraints. Indeed, there is a sheer link between increasing charged interest rates on debts and the propagation mechanism at the aggregate level, which leads to a reduction in the aggregate spending and production.

References

Albuquerque, R., and H. A. Hopenhayn, 2004, Optimal Lending Contracts and Firm Dynamics, *The Review of Economic Studies*: 71, pp. 285-315

Almeida, H. and M. Campello, 2007, Financial Constraints, Asset Tangibility, and Corporate Investment, *Review of Financial Studies* 20, 1429-1460

Akerlof, G.A., 1970, The Market for 'Lemons': Quality Uncertainty and the Market Mechanism, *The Quarterly Journal of Economics* 90(3), pp. 475-498

Baskin, J., and P. Miranti, 1997, A History of Corporate Finance, First Edition, Cambridge University Press

Bernanke, B., M. Gertler, and S. Gilchrist, 1996, The Financial Accelerator and the Flight to Quality, *The Review of Economics and Statistics* 78(1), pp. 1-15

Bernanke, B. and M. Gertler, 1995, Inside the Black Box: The Credit Channel of Monetary Policy Transmission, NBER Working Paper no. 5146

Carlstrom, C.T., and T.S. Fuerst, 1997, Agency Costs, Net Worth, and Business Fluctuations: A Computable General Equilibrium Analysis, *American Economic Review*, 87(5): 393-910

Cleary S., P. Povel, and M. Raith, 2007, The U-shaped Investment Curve: Theory and Evidence, *Journal of Financial and Quantitative Analysis* 42, 1-39

Clementi, G. L., and H. A. Hopenhayn, 2006, A Theory of Financing Constraints and Firm Dynamics, *The Quarterly Journal of Economics*, pp. 229-265

Erickson, T., and T. Whited, 2006, On the Accuracy of Different Measures of Q, *Financial Management* 35: 5-33 (lead article)

Erickson, T., and T. Whited, 2002, Two-Step GMM Estimation of the Errors-in-Variables Model using High-Order Moments, *Econometric Theory* 18: 776-799

Erickson, T., and T. Whited, 2000, Measurement Error and the Relationship between Investment and *q*, *Journal of Political Economy* 108(5)

Fazzari, S., G. Hubbard, and B. Petersen, 1988, Financing constraints and corporate investment, *Brookings Paper on Economic Activity* 1, 141-195

Fazzari, S., Hubbard. G., and Petersen B., 2000, Investment-Cash Flow Sensitivities are Useful: a Comment on Kaplan and Zingales, *Quarterly Journal of Economics*, pp. 695-705

Greenwald, B. C., J. E. Stiglitz, and A. Weiss, 1984, Informational Imperfections on the Capital Market and Macro-economic Fluctuations, NBER Working Paper no. 1335

Greenwald, B. C., and J. E. Stiglitz, 1994, Asymmetric Information and the New Theory of the Firm: Financial Constraints and Risk Behavior, NBER Working Paper no. 3359

Hellmann, T. K., and J.E. Stiglitz, 2000, Credit and Equity Rationing in Markets with Adverse Selection, *European Economic Review* 44(2), pp. 281-304

Hennessy, C., and T., Whited, 2007, How Costly is External Financing? Evidence from a Structural Estimation, *Journal of Finance* 62, 1705-1745

Hoshi, T., A. Kashyap, and D. Scharsftein, 1991, Corporate Structure, Liquidity and Investment: Evidence from Japanese Industrial Groups, *Quarterly Journal of Economics*, Vol.106, Issue 1, 3-60

Hillier, B., 1997, The Economics of Asymmetric Information, 1st Edition, MacMillan Press Ltd

Hubbard, R.G., 1998, Capital-markets Imperfections and Investment, *Journal of Economic Literature* 36: 193-225

Kaplan, S. and L. Zingales, 1997, Do Financing Constraints Explain why Investment is Correlated with Cash Flow?, *Quarterly Journal of Economics* 112: pp. 169-215

Kaplan, S., and L. Zingales, 2000, Investment-Cash Flow Sensitivities are not Valid Measures of Financing Constraints, *Quarterly Journal of Economics*, pp. 707-712

Lamont, O. 1997, Cash Flow and Investment: Evidence from Internal Capital Market, *Journal of Finance*, Vol. 52, no.1

Mansour, W., 2009, On the Theory of Financing Constraints, Ph.D. Thesis, University of La Manouba (Tunisia, North Africa)

Modigliani, F., and M. H. Miller, 1958, The Cost of Capital, Corporation Finance, and the Theory of Investment, *American Economic Review*: 48, 261-297

Moyen, N., 2004, Investment-Cash Flow Sensitivities: Constrained Versus Un-constrained Firms, *Journal of Finance* 59, 2061-2092

Myers, S., and N. Majluf, 1984, Corporate Financing and Investment Decisions When Firms Have Information That Investors Do Not Have?, NBER Working Paper Series no. 1396

Pratap, S., and S. Rendon, 2003, Firm Investment in Imperfect Capital Markets: A Structural Estimation, *Review of Economic Dynamics*: 6, pp. 513-545

Stein, J., 2003, Agency, Information and Corporate Investment, mimeo, Harvard University

Stiglitz, J. E., 2001, Information and the Change in the Paradigm in Economics, *Nobel Prize Lecture*

Swoboda, A. M., 2003, Cash Flow-Investment Sensitivities of European Companies in the 1990's: Evidence for Empire Building and Costly External Finance, Working Paper, University of Vienna

Tinbergen, J., 1939, A Method and its Application to Investment Activity, in: Statistical Testing of Business Cycle Theories, League of Nations, Geneva. Lamont, 1997,

Tirole, J., 2006, The Theory of Corporate Finance, Princeton University Press

Townsend, R., 1979, Optimal Contracts and Competitive Markets with Costly State Verifications, *Journal of Economic Theory* 21, pp. 265-93

THE DETERMINANTS OF THE NEW VENTURE DECISION IN TUNISIA: A GEM DATA BASED ANALYSIS

ISLEM KHEFACHA[1], LOTFI BELKACEM[2] AND FAYÇAL MANSOURI[3]

Introduction

A huge literature on entrepreneurship has been produced in the last twenty years (see among others Acs and Audretsch, 2003; Audretsch, 2002; Casson, 1982, 2003; Gartner, 1989; Glancey and McQuaid, 2000; Shane, 2003; Storey, 2000).

These approaches include situation, attribution, cognition, economic, sociologic, and public policy; and have found that for many, entrepreneurship represents a means to create wealth (Teece, 1998) or escape social bondage (Hagen, 1960). For others, entrepreneurship is the answer to job displacement (Shapero, 1975), career dissatisfaction (Storey, 1982), or an inability to submit to authority (Collins, Moore and Unwalla, 1964). Several authors consider entrepreneurship as a vehicle for self-expression (Timmons, 1999), autonomy (Hornaday & Aboud, 1971), security (Collins, Moore and Unwalla, 1964), and/or control (Rotter, 1966).

In this study, we focus on the crucial stage in the process of creating a new business: the start-up decision.

Indeed, several authors take recourse to a variety of approaches to understand the process wherein potential entrepreneurs choose to start new

[1] Assistant Professor, Research Unit: Quantitative Finance, IHEC - University of Sousse.
[2] Professor, Research Unit: Quantitative Finance, IHEC - University of Sousse.
[3] Professor, Research Unit: Quantitative Finance, IHEC - University of Sousse.

businesses and others do not. Shapero (1984) argues that in the new venture creation process there is no single variable or factor can determine exclusively the outcome of the process. These variables are necessary but not sufficient (Parker, 2004; Shepherd & DeTienne, 2005; Kolvereid & Isaksen, 2006; Shapero, 1984).

Hence, a substantial entrepreneurship research literature indicates that the socio-demographic traits, human capital resources and attitudes towards entrepreneurship identified do explain creation decision in varying degrees (Wagner & Ziltener, 2008).

These factors have been the subject of several research studies. Nonetheless, the question remains unsolved about why certain individuals tend to start and manage business.
In this framework, this research attempts to identify, among the variables included in National Tunisian Global Entrepreneurship Monitor Project (GEM) carried out in 2010, those having an impact on the process of starting a new business venture.

To do so, we develop an approach based on previous theoretical studies to provide an analysis of key determinants of business creation and their impacts. In particular, we attempt to select the traits and characteristics having most relevance to start-up decision-making in the context of the entrepreneurial personality.

The paper is structured as follows. The first section contains a literature review of factors having an impact on start-up decision based on a set of hypothesis. Section 2 presents our sample, data collection procedure, measures, and variables. Section 3 develops binary logistic regression models to test for the formulated hypotheses. Section 4 discusses the findings. Section 5 concludes and sets up and future research extensions.

Theoretical Background: The decision of a new project as a process

A central issue in the analysis of new venture creation is the identification of factors underlying this decision. Amit and Muller (1994) show that the decision to start up a new enterprise is a process that is the outcome of two decisions: some new ventures are undertaken as a result of a dissatisfaction process with his/her current situation, whereas others are undertaken as a desire to pursue an opportunity.

However, entrepreneurship research literature shows that the creation decision largely exceeds the perimeter of these two factors.

The objective is to identify the most relevant determinants of entrepreneurial intention as developed in the well-known social psychological theory of planned behaviour (Ajzen, 1991).

In fact, this parsimonious model shows that in order to predict whether an individual will engage in a given behaviour, one needs to identify whether the latter is influenced by a set of factors which could increase or decrease the likelihood to create new business.

In this context, institutional economic theory analyses, in a holistic way, the contextual factors as determinants of entrepreneurship which can be formal or informal (Veciana, Aponte and Urbano, 2005). The former are related with some political and economic rules and the latter with some codes of conduct, attitudes, values, norms of behaviour, and conventions. Based on these theoretical grounds, Krueger and Brazeal (1994) develop an entrepreneurial potential model which draws upon not only Ajzen's theory of planned behaviour but also Shapero's work on entrepreneurial event.

Shapero's model of entrepreneurial event formation focuses on how the cultural and social environment affects the choice of an entrepreneurial path. It states that the intent to start a business derives from perceptions of both, desirability and feasibility.

Krueger and Brazeal (1994) argue that although the individual perceives new venture creation desirable and feasible, and therefore credible, he/she has not the intention to realize the behaviour because the precipitating event may be lacking.

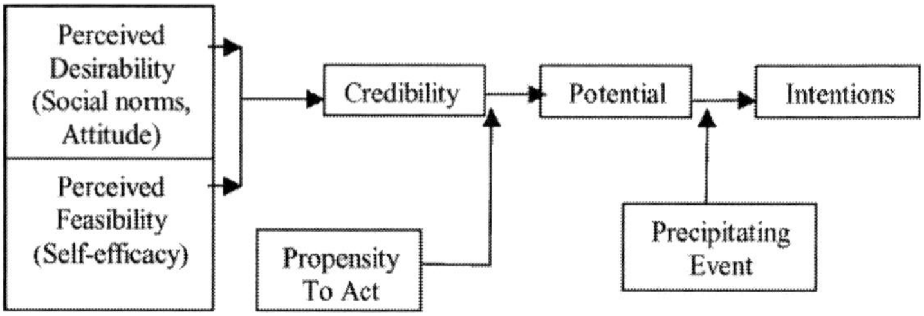

Source: Krueger and Brazeal, 1994:95

On the basis of this model, we will now present the analysis of factors which can explain the individual's main reason that "pushes" someone into deciding to start up their own company.

Perceived Venture Desirability

According to Krueger and Brazeal's model, perceived desirability is tied to our perceptions of what important people in our lives would think about our launching a venture. It embraces the two "attractiveness components" of the Theory of Planned Behaviour: *attitude* toward the act and *social norms*.

Attitude

Attitude towards behaviour is related to the anticipated utility and perceived value of future actions. According to Ajzen (1991), attitude toward a behaviour could be defined as "the degree to which a person has a favorable or unfavorable evaluation or appraisal of the behavior in question" (p. 188). As a consequence, actions with high anticipated utility are perceived as favourable.

In this setting, many previous attempts have shown that a wide range of personality traits and abilities with a distinct psychological profile strongly influence the anticipated utility (Wagner & Ziltener, 2008).

Among personality traits that may characterize entrepreneurs, we mention the need for achievement (McClelland and Winter, 1969), the greater desire for independence (De Jong, 2009), the ability to innovate (Schumpeter, 1934) and the locus of internal control (Shapero, 1982).

Persons with the last trait have the tendency to act autonomously under their own supervision and emphasize their own will, ability and actions in their professional life. This behaviour is closely related with the trait of self-efficacy - as the belief in one's own ability to perform a given task (Shane, 2003, p. 111) - where a high degree leads people to perceive more opportunities than risks in certain situations. Hence, the fact that individuals see themselves as capable of taking risk is related to the individual's perception of whether they perceive that they possess the necessary skills to initiate various tasks.

***H1**: The perception of having the necessary skills, knowledge and experience necessary to establish a new firm has a positive influence on the decision to create a new business.*

In the contrary, individuals with a less developed sense of self-efficacy will tend to be more aware of costs and risks. In fact, the general tendency to take or avoid risks defined as "aversion to take risks", is another factor related to the entrepreneurial decision that has been frequently studied in the relevant literature (Cooper and Gimeno-Gasc´on, 1992; Gartner, 1989; Gnywaly and Fogel, 1994). When assessing risk, it is necessary to analyse two important aspects: the level of perceived risk in the creation of any new firm and the perceived likelihood of failure if the business is unsuccessful (García, Cuervo, Ribeiro, 2007).

***H2**: Fear of failure would prevent an individual from starting a business.*

Subjective or social norms

The desirability of creating a new venture is particularly related to the existence of entrepreneurial models in the individual's social surroundings. According to Ajzen (1991), social norm is defined as "the perceived social pressure to perform or not to perform the behavior" (p. 188). In the entrepreneurship literature, the role of pressure in decision-making has been studied mainly for persons and groups that the entrepreneur has close, frequent and intimate contact with. These key individuals including friends, family, and close business contacts which can actively support or not an entrepreneurial venture.

Moreover, while demographic models have been criticized because they provide little insight on *how* family background and social forces shape the individual's decision process (Katz, 1992), entrepreneurship literature shows a strong relationship between the presence of role models in the family with new venture creation. Notably, empirical research realized by Collins, Moore and Unwalla (1964) has shown that the influences over a new venture idea go back to the childhood and the family circumstances of the entrepreneur.

H3: *Knowing someone personally who started a business influences the decision to start up a business.*

Related to this construct, Shapero (1982) mentioned that advice makes the act of venture creation feasible to the potential entrepreneur. In fact, individuals do not make important decisions in isolation. Decisions are often made by individuals after consulting with, and being influenced by, others (Bonaccio & Dalal, 2006).

In the context of venture creation, a new investor may likely consult his or her parents, spouse, friends and work colleagues about the consequences of his decision.

Slaugher and Highhouse (2003) argue that "choices among job alternatives are almost never made in isolation. Individuals choosing among jobs are likely to consult those with whom they have social contact, such as friends, and those individuals for whom the decision will have indirect yet important consequences, such as family members" (p. 12).

Notably, when someone decides to quit voluntarily his current job (Lee & Mitchell, 1994), he or she would presumably first discuss the issue with their spouse and perhaps other individuals whose opinion is valued and/or who may be affected by the decision.

For example, talking to his or her spouse might lead a new investor to realize that it could be difficult given the financial costs associated with the decision to create a new venture whereas advice from somebody with much business experience or a bank might make the new investor realize that it could be profitable to invest in a new project.

H4: *Advice impacts the decision to start up a new business.*

From another optic, several scholars have analysed the relationship between gender and attitudes towards new venture creation or entrepreneurial behaviour (Delmar and Davidsson, 2000; Kolvereid, 1996), and have found that males have a higher preference for entrepreneurship behaviour than females (Delmar and Davidsson, 2000; Reynolds et al. 2004). According to Hindle, Klyver and F. Jennings (2009), it has been suggested that female entrepreneurs are disadvantaged compared to men with respect to most forms of human capital and also because of a lack of suitable and effective social networks (Fielden et al., 2003; Timberlake, 2005).

H5: *There is a relationship between the individual's gender and the serious intention to create a new firm*

Perceived behavioural control or Perceived Venture Feasibility

Perceived behavioural control is the "perceived ease or difficulty of performing the behaviour of interest" (Ajzen, 1991, p. 188).

This definition can be associated with the definition proposed by Venkataraman (1997) of the Entrepreneurship which is considered as "an activity that involves the discovery, evaluation and exploitation of opportunities to introduce new goods and services, ways of organizing markets, processes, and raw materials through organizing efforts that previously had not existed" (in: Shane, 2003:p. 7).

It seems hence that resources and opportunities available to a person must to some extent dictate the odds of decision to create new venture. This concern is based on the presence of requisite resources and abilities which decrease obstacles or impediments anticipated by peoples and increase consequently the perceived control over the behaviour. If insufficient control is perceived, the individual assesses the likelihood of reducing the discrepancy between the desired and actual state by procuring resources elsewhere, such as from a superior, colleague or supplier (De Jong, 2009).

H6: *Perceived control to exploit identified opportunities is positively related to the decision to create new business.*

From another point of view, Wagner and Ziltener (2008) showed that the situational character of start-up decisions is increasingly being emphasized within some body of theory originally conceived as a sub-discipline of neoclassical economics. In this context, Shapero (1982) emphasized the availability of some resources allowing to potential entrepreneur to create a new project, such as education, level of income, and occupation.

For the first factor, there is a great deal of discussion and debate about the nature of impact of academic level in the decision to start up a new business. In fact, some research has provided contradictory evidence to the extent to which education can affect a person's decision to become an entrepreneur. Usually, a high level of education is important to be competitive in today's market and individuals are more likely to exploit opportunities if they are better educated (Casson, 1995). This concern joins the empirical study of Storey (1994) and Yusuf (1995) while for Lee and Tsang (2001), and Stuart and Abetti (1990), the level of education has a negative effect. Even though empirical studies have not conclusively shown whether having a university degree increases the prospect of success of an entrepreneurial venture (Brüderl and Preisendorfer, 1998), in our study, we consider that:

H7**:** *A higher academic level has a positive influence on the decision to start up a new business.*

For the level of income, the relation with the decision of creation has been analysed from different perspectives. Particularly, individuals with a high level of income can count on resources to implement the firm's needs, while for someone with a smaller income it would prove difficult to achieve a new venture (Singh & Lucas, 2005). According to Audretsch (2002) and Gartner (1989), we consider that the level of income may have an influence on the availability of funding for the business project, notably:

H8*: A high level of income has a positive influence on the decision to start up a new business.*

Finally, as for the academic level, there is no consensus on the extent of the influence of work status to the decision to start up a new business.

Some authors (Audrestch, 2002; Evans and Leighton, 1990) show that unemployed individuals are more likely to take entrepreneurial decisions than those having a steady job. In this framework, individuals engaged in full-time work are less convinced by the idea of starting up their own business than unemployed ones, part-time workers or students.

Nevertheless, this point of view contradicts what Reynolds et al. (2004) exposed in their study by showing that people in full or part-time work are more likely to set up their own firms than the unemployed or those employed in other categories or work. Although, the relation between occupation and the new venture decision were found to be tenuous (Davidsson, 1995). Accordingly, we consider that:

***H9**: Work status impacts the individual's decision to create a new business.*

Interaction

In the previous section, we focus on factors autonomously having a potential impact on the decision to create a new venture. However, the presence of certain conditions in isolation may not be enough. In the context of entrepreneurial decision-making, if one factor fails, the investment may in general become less likely. Consequently, it seems interesting to explore interaction effects between these factors. For example, De Jong (2009) shows that the connection between attitude and the decision to start-up may be stronger if other 'conditions' are met, i.e. if business owners perceive strong social support of their close ties, and feel that they are capable of successfully implementing the opportunity. It seems that the opportunity exploitation may be stronger if two or more other factors are satisfied simultaneously.

Venkataraman (1997) adds that the ability to make the connection between specific knowledge and a business opportunity requires a set of skills, aptitudes, insights, and circumstances that are neither uniformly nor widely distributed.

This concern reinforces the fact that the odds of creating a new business may be increased or decreased with the presence of interaction between some factors.

H 10: *The interaction between some factors increases or decreases the odds to create new venture.*

Empirical estimates of a simple model of the decision to create new business

Data set and variables

Data has been provided by the National Tunisian Global Entrepreneurship Monitor 2010 Project, based on the analysis of a sample of 339 cases.

Table 1 lists all the independent variables that we used in our study in order to test our hypotheses and presents descriptive statistics:

- *Perception of skills, knowledge and experience*: This variable indicates whether the individual sees themselves as having the ability to create a new business or not. This perception was gauged in the questionnaire by asking: "*Do you have the knowledge, skill and experience required to start a new business?*"
- *Relations with entrepreneurs*: This variable is measured using the question *"Do you know someone personally who started a business in the past 2 years?"*, and indicates whether an individual is acquainted with an entrepreneur or not. This variable is related to the perception of the viability of creating a business.
- *Perception of opportunities*: This variable, which is also a dichotomy, tells us directly whether the individual does or doesn't perceive the existence of business opportunities in the local area through the question "*In the next six months will there be good opportunities for starting a business in the area where you live?*"
- *Fear of failure:* This variable shows whether an individual is afraid of failing in the creation of a new business. It can be considered as an approximate measurement of the aversion to risk. The question related to this item is "*Would fear of failure prevent you from starting a business?*" It is important to point out that overconfidence can reduce the fear of failure to a certain extent.
- *Advice:* This variable is measured using the question *"During the last year, have you received advice from family or relatives?"*, and indicates the influence of the family members on the decision to start-up.
- *Level of income*: this variable indicates the interviewee's level of income.
- *Occupation*: this variable has the following categories: full or part-time; only part-time; retired/ disabled; homemaker; student, not working, other and self-employed.
- *Academic level*: This variable presents the following categories: pre-primary education, primary education, lower secondary, upper secondary, post-secondary, first stage of tertiary, and second stage of tertiary.

Our dependent variable was dichotomous, indicating if entrepreneurs expect to start-up in the next 3 years. In 33.6% of the cases, this appeared to be true.

Table 1: Variables and descriptive statistics (n=339)

Variables	Hypothesis	Statistics
Skills, knowledge and experience	*H1:* The perception of having skills, knowledge and experience necessary to establish a new firm has a positive influence on the decision to create a new business.	Yes =74.9% ; No =25.1%
Fear of failure	*H2*: Fear of failure would prevent an individual from starting a business.	Yes =18.6% ; No =81.4%
Knows someone	*H3*: Knows someone who started a business positively influences the decision to start up.	Yes =73.7% ; No =26.3%
Advice	*H4*: Advice impacts the decision to start up.	Yes =38.9% ; No =61.1%
Gender	*H5*: There is a relationship between the individual's gender and the serious intention to create a new firm	Male =56.9% Female =43.1%
Opportunities	*H6*: Perceived control to exploit identified opportunities is positively related to the decision to start up.	Yes =52.8% ; No =47.2%
Academic level	*H7*: A higher academic level has a positive influence on the decision to start up a new business.	Primary education=19.2% Lower secondary =9.7% Upper secondary =32.4% Post-secondary =17.7% First stage of tertiary =10.9% Second stage of tertiary =5.6%
Income	*H8*: A high level of income has a positive influence on the decision to start up a new business	Less than 2 000 =2.1% 2 000 to 3 000 =1.8% 3 000 to 5 000 =12.7% 5 000 to 7 500 =17.1% 7 500 to 11500 =25.7% 11500 to 20000 =26.8% More than 20 000=13.9%
Occupation	*H9*: Work status impacts the individual's decision to create a new business	Full or part time =34.8% Part time only =6.5% Retired. disabled =3.5% Homemaker =11.8% Student =6.5% Not working =6.2% Self-employed =30.7%
Interaction	***H10*:** The interaction between some factors increase or decrease the odds to start-up.	

Results and Discussion

Given the qualitative nature of the dependant and independent variables, we have conducted a binary logistic regression which is used for prediction of the probability of an event's occurrence (known as reference event) with regard to the complementary event. This type of regression applies maximum likelihood estimation after transforming the dependent into a logit variable (i.e. the natural log of the odds). Therefore, we estimate the relationship between series of social, demographic, cultural and socio-economic factors to create new venture. Various specifications of the model were applied by introducing the independent variables at successive steps. We will also study the impact of the two- and three-way interaction effects on the likelihood to create.

For example, on the basis of the log-linear modelling of three variables (X as dependant variable, Y and Z as independent variable), the transformation into a *logistical binary* model allows us to get the following equation (DeMaris, 1992):

$$\log O_1^X = \alpha + \tau_j^Y + \tau_k^Z + \tau_{jk}^{YZ} \tag{1}$$

With:

- $\log O_1^X$: is the logarithm of the odds to have the modality 1 of the dependant variable regarding the modality 2.
- α : intercept which represents an effect of "general average" in the sense that it doesn't depend on modalities of the independent variables.
- τ_j^Y : is the coefficient estimation of the *main effect* of the modality j of variable Y on the odds of the occurrence of modality 1 regarding the modality 2 of the dependant variable.
- τ_k^Z : is the coefficient estimation of the *main effect* of the modality k of variable Z on the odds of the occurrence of modality 1 regarding the modality 2 of the dependant variable.
- And finally τ_{jk}^{YZ} : represents the *interaction effect* between the two variables y and z on the odds of the occurrence of the modality 1 regarding the modality 2 of the dependant variable.

In other words, for each of the independent variables, we tried to express a measure of its influence on the occurrence of the corresponding event of the dependant variable. These influences are called main effects of variables while the particular combinations of modalities of independent variables correspond to the interaction effects (DeMaris 1992).

To do this, we must firstly study a possible presence of multicollinearity between the independent variables, which is a basic ingredient for the application of logistical regression.

The calculated correlations (Table 2) showed values close to zero, which suggests that there is no linear relation between the independent variables or that the degree of association between them is extremely low. As a rule-of-thumb, multicollinearity problems may be present if correlations exceed absolute values of 0.80 (Hair et al., 1998: p. 189).

On the basis of these results, we can now analyse the variations of the variable corresponding to the question *"Are you, alone or with others, expecting to start a new business, including any type of self-employment, within the next three years?"* with two modalities in the setting of a logistical model.

Table 3 presents the results. The goodness-of-fit of logistic regression models is assessed by comparing the transformed log likelihood value -*2LL* with the previous model. The difference between both values follows an X2 distribution and may be tested accordingly (Verbeek, 2004). Other fit measures include the hit rate (representing the share of correctly classified cases) and *Nagelkerke's* R^2 (indicating the strength of association in the overall model).

The first model was an empty model (estimating only the intercept) permitting to obtain baseline values for -2LL and the hit rate. It appears that 66.4% of persons who expect to start a new business within the next three years without any stimulus are correctly classified.

The second model added the control variables to the equation in order to test hypotheses *H5, H7, H8 and H9*: gender, level of education, level of income and work status.

Surprisingly, we found that the effect parameters of all factors were insignificant.

Table 2 : Correlations between independent variables. The Kendall Tau-b Coefficient.

	(1)	(2)	(3)	(4)	(5)	(6)	(7)	(8)	(9)
(1) Occupation	1								
(2) Knows someone	0.033	1							
(3) Opportunities	0.132**	0.161**	1						
(4) Skills, knowledge and experience	0.120*	0.088	0.176**	1					
(5) Fear of failure	-0.103*	-0.008	-0.034	-0.109*	1				
(6) Advice	-0.025	0.018	-0.088	-0.029	-0.054	1			
(7) Gender	0.027	-0.185**	-0.013	-0.033	0.090	-0.063	1		
(8) Income	-0.019	0.039	-0.114*	-0.160**	0.051	0.461**	-0.039	1	
(9) Academic level	-0.257**	0.000	-0.112*	-0.150**	0.064	0.154**	0.041	0.245**	1

significance
** $p < 0.01$; * $p < 0.05$; ^ $p < 0.10$

Table 3. Binary Logistic regression models of the decision to start-up (n=339)

	Models				
	I	**II**	**III**	**IV**	**V**
Effect parameters :					
Constant	-0.680**	-0.109	-0.862^	-2.275	-5.296**
Academic level		-0.092	-0.057	-0.074	-0.067
Income		-0.020	0.100	0.093	0.118
Occupation		-0.048	-0.100	-0.106*	-0.100^
Gender		0.060	0.013	-0.005	0.041
Advice (A)			-0.203	0.902	2.442^
Skills knowledge and experience (S)			1.021*	0.873	2.681
Fear of failure (F)			-0.482	-0.537	19.690
Knows someone (K)			-0.925*	0.499	2.638
Opportunities (O)			0.988**	1.934^	7.518*
A*F				-0.728	20.160
A*K				-0.918	-2.146*
A*O				-0.447	-3.735*
A*S				-0.095	-0.898
S*F				0.983	-19.476
S*K				0.162	-0.234
S*O				0.034	-0.854
F*K				0.700	2.982
F*O				-0.188	-3.621
O*K				-0.404	-6.133*
A*F*K					-0.895
A*K*O					3.461*
A*F*O					1.957
A*O*S					0.438
S*K*O					0.110
S*F*O					1.106
F*K*O					-0.930
F*A*S					19.253
Model fit:					
Hit rate	66.4%	66.4%	69.0%	70.8%	71.4%
Nagelkerke R^2		0.009	0.149	0.179	0.220
-2LL	432.930	430.803	394.283	386.193	374.252
Δ-2LL			36.520	8.090	11.941
ΔDf		4	5	10	8
significance					

** $p < 0.01$; * $p < 0.05$; ^ $p < 0.10$

In the third model, we entered the main planned behaviour constructs to test hypotheses *H1, H2, H3, H4 and H6*. Goodness-of-fit improved significantly *(Δ-2LL = 36.520 with $\Delta df = 5$, $p < 0.01$).*

Furthermore, we find that the share of correctly classified cases (hit rate) and *Nagelkerke's* R^2 increased to 69% and 14.9%, respectively. From the Wald tests, we conclude that for the control variables, advice and fear of failure are not related to the decision to start-up. Their effect parameters were non-significant and consequently hypotheses *H2* and *H4* are not confirmed. As for factors of "perception of skills, knowledge and experience", we found that the effect parameter *(b = 1.021)* was significant at the *5% level.* This implies that a one unit increase in attitude toward the act *"Perceived Venture Desirability"* increases the odds of the creation by *exp(1.021) = 2.776*. H1 is supported in our sample. For the role of pressure in decision-making related mainly to groups that the entrepreneur has close, frequent and intimate contacts with, we found a strong and negative connection with the decision to start-up a new venture *(b = -0.925, $p < 0.01$).* This implies that key individuals including friends, family, and close business contacts don't support an entrepreneurial venture - such subjective norms decrease the odds by *exp(-0.925) = 0.396*. Hypothesis 3 is supported and gives-us the sign of the relation (negative impact).

Finally, the perception of opportunities is positively related to the decision to create a new business. Its effect parameter was significant (b = 0.988, $p > 0.10$), and hypothesis H6 is confirmed.

On the other hand, following Jaccard's (2001) recommendation of hierarchically well-formulated models, the fourth model contained all two-way interactions between attitude, subjective norm and perceived behavioural control. This model served only as a baseline to test the proposed three-way interactions in the next step. One notable finding however was that none of the two-way interactions was significant.

The fifth model tests hypothesis *H10* related to the interaction between the five focal independent variables. We found that model fit improved significantly *(Δ-2LL = 11.941. $p < 0.05$).* We also found that the hit rate and *Nagelkerke's* R^2 were better compared to model IV.

Among the different three-way interactions, the interaction between consulting his or her family about the consequences of the decision, knowing someone personally who started a business in the past 2 years and presence of good opportunities for starting a business in the area where potential entrepreneur lives increases significantly the odds of start-up by exp(3.461) = 31.849.

Table 4: Results of the contrast of hypotheses

Hypothesis	Result
H1: The perception of having the necessary skills, knowledge and experience necessary to establish a new firm has a positive influence on the decision to create a new business.	***Accepted***
H2: Fear of failure would prevent an individual from starting a business.	***Rejected***
H3: Knows someone who started a business positively influences the decision to start up.	***Accepted***
H4: Advice impacts the decision to start up.	***Rejected***
H5: There is a relationship between the individual's gender and the serious intention to create a new firm	***Rejected***
H6: Perceived control to exploit identified opportunities is positively related to the decision to create new business.	***Accepted***
H7: A higher academic level has a positive influence on the decision to start up a new business.	***Rejected***
H8: A high level of income has a positive influence on the decision to start up a new business	***Rejected***
H9: Unemployment has a positive effect on the individual's decision to create a new business	***Rejected***
***H10*:** The interaction between some factors increase or decrease the odds to create new venture.	***Accepted***

Conclusion

This research focuses explicitly on various determinants influencing the entrepreneurial decision in Tunisia. Despite, the absence of consensus, a large number of researchers converge to believe that the creation of a new venture is one of the principal outcomes of entrepreneurship.

However, previous work has measured and modelled the decision to create new business by neglecting some factors having an important impact, such as advice and consultation with people whom potential entrepreneurs have social contact, notably family members.

In this context, our paper emphasizes the characterization of the entrepreneurial decision and purposes a classification of this choice's determinants based on the distinctions between perceived and feasibility perceptions. Among the most relevant aspects shaping the entrepreneurial decision, we analyse the role of "Perceived Venture Desirability" like the perception of having the necessary skills, knowledge and experience, fear of failure, advice or gender. Conversely, "Perceived Venture Feasibility" is represented by perceived control to exploit identified opportunities, occupation, academic level and income level. The interest in perceived venture recalls the idea of the importance of both perceived desirability and feasibility in entrepreneurship theory.

Our findings confirm that the decision to create new venture is not just a matter of either 'like' or 'ability'. Results suggest the decision to become an entrepreneur is best explained by a composite of some factors, notably the advice of some family members about the consequences of the decision, knowing someone personally who started a business in the past 2 years and presence of good opportunities for starting a business. Start-up is much more likely when all three precursors are satisfied simultaneously.

This could contribute to a better understanding of entrepreneurial psychology in a manner potentially valuable for efforts to structure and design entrepreneurial decision.

However, it is important to point out that these characteristics may also be found in individuals that are not entrepreneurs and it cannot thus be regarded as an exclusively entrepreneurial characteristic (Gartner, 1989).
Finally, we must pay attention that after the examination of how different strands of literature have conceptualized the entrepreneurial decision by identifying some determinants having a crucial impact on the decision to create new business, we need to focus on the constraints that might limit entrepreneurs in making their own choice. These constraints are notably related to the external and institutional environment in terms of policies, reforms, or geographical localization.

References

Acs, Z. J. and D. B. Audretsch, (2003), Handbook of Entrepreneurship Research, Dordrecht: Kluwer Academic Publishers.

Ajzen, I. (1991), The theory of planned behavior, Organizational Behavior and Human Decision Processes, 50, 179-211.

Amit, R. & Muller, E. (1994) "Push" and "pull" entrepreneurship. in W. Bygrave, et al.(eds.) Frontiers of Entrepreneurship Research, 1994. Babson College, Wellesley.

Audretsch, D. B., R. Thurik, I. Verheul and S. Wennekers, (2002). Entrepreneurship: Determinants and Policy in a European-US Comparison, Boston/Dordrecht: Kluwer Academic Publishers.

Bonaccio, S. and Dalal, R.S. (2006), "Advice taking and decision making: an integrative literature review, and implications for the organizational sciences", Organizational Behavior and Human Decision Processes, Vol. 101 No. 2, pp. 127-51.

Bruderl, J. & P. Preisendorfer (1998). Network support and the success of newly founded businesses, Small Business Economics, 10, 213-225.

Casson, M. (1982/2003). The Entrepreneur – An Economic Theory, 2nd ed., Edward Elgar: Cheltenham, UK, 2003.

—. (1995), Entrepreneurship and business culture, Aldershot, UK: Edward Elgar.

Collins, O.F., Moore, D.G., Unwalla, D.B. (1964). The Enterprising Man, East Lansing, M.I., Michigan State University Business Studies, 254 pages.

Cooper,A.C. & Gimeno-Gasc´on, J. (1992). Entrepreneurs, processes ofFounding, andNewFirmPerformance. In Donald L. Sexton & John D. Kasarda (Eds.), The state of the art of Entrepreneurship: 45–67. Boston, MA: PWS-KENT Publishing Company.

Davidsson, P. (1995). Determinants of entrepreneurial intentions. Paper presented at the RENT IXWorkshop in Entrepreneurship Research, November 23–24, Piacenza, Italy.

De Jong, P.J. (2009).The decision to innovate: Antecedents of opportunity exploitation in high tech smal l firms Working paper, Version January.

Delmar, F., Davidsson, P. (2000), Where do they come from? Prevalence and characteristics of nascent entrepreneurs. Entrepreneurship and Regional Development, 12. p. 1-23.

DeMaris, A. (1992). Logit modeling: practical applications. Sage University Papers series on Quantitative Applications in the Social Sciences, 07-086, Newbury Park, CA.

Evans, David S. and Linda Leighton, (1990). "Small Business Formation by Unemployed and Employed Workers," Small Business Economics, 2(4), 319-330.

Gartner, W. B., 1989, 'Some Suggestions for Research on Entrepreneurial Traits and Characteristics', Entrepreneurship: Theory & Practice 14, 27–37.

Glancey, K-S. and Mcquaid R-W. (2000). Entrepreneurial Economic, Basingstoke, Macmillan

Gnyawali, D.R. & Fogel, D.S. (1994). Environments for Entrepreneurship development: Key Dimensions and Research Implications, Entrepreneurship Theory and Practice, 18: 43–62.

Hagen, E. (1960). The entrepreneurs as rebel against traditional society. Human Organization, 19(4): 185-187.

Hair, J.F., R.E. Anderson, R.L. Tatham & W.C. Black (1998), Multivariate data analysis: fifth edition, Englewood Cliffs: Prentice Hall.

Hornaday, J.A. & Aboud, J. (1971). Characteristics of successful entrepreneurs, Personnel Psychology, 24: 141-153.

Jaccard, J. (2001), Interaction effects in logistic regression, Sage: Thousand Oaks, CA.

Katz, J. A. (1992), A Psychosocial Cognitive Model of Employment Status Choice. Entrepreneurship Theory and Practice, 17(1). p. 29- 37.

Kolvereid, L. (1996). Prediction of employment status choice intentions. Entrepreneurship Theory and Practice, 21(1), 47–57.

Kolvereid, L., & Isaksen, E. (2006). New business start-up and subsequent entry into self-employment. Journal of Business Venturing, 21(6), 866–885.

Krueger, N. & Brazeal, D. (1994). Entrepreneurial potential and potential entrepreneurs. Entrepreneurship, Theory and Practice, 18: 91–104.

Lee, D.Y. & Tsang, E.W. 2001. The effects of entrepreneurial personality, background and network activities on venture growth. Journal of Management Studies, 38: 583–602.

Lee, T. W., & Mitchell, T. R. (1994). An alternative approach: The unfolding model of employee turnover. Academy of Management Journal, 19(1), 51-89.

McClelland, D.C. and Winter, D.G. (1969). Motivating Economic Achievement. NY: Free Press.

Reynolds, P.D., Carter, N., Gartner, W. B. & Greence, P. (2004). The prevalence of Nascent entrepreneurs In the United States: Evidence from the Panel Study of Entrepreneurial Dynamics. Small Business Economics, 23: 263–284.

Rotter, J.B. (1966). Generalized expectancies for internal versus external control of reinforcement, Psychological Monographs, 609(80): 1-28.

Schumpeter, J.A. 1934. The theory of economic development: An inquiry into profits, capital, credit, interest and the business cycle. Oxford University Press: New York. [Printed in: 1964].

Shane, S. (2003). A General Theory of Entrepreneurship: The Individual-Opportunity Nexus. Boston, MA: Edward Elgar.

Shapero, A. (1984). The entrepreneurial event. In Calvin A. Kent (Ed.), The environment for entrepreneurship: 21–40. Toronto, MA: Lexington Books.

—. (1975). The displaced, uncomfortable entrepreneur', Psychology Today, Vol. 9, Nov, pp. 83-88.

Shapero, A., Sokol, L. (1982). "The Social Dimensions of Entrepreneurship" in C. Kent, D.L., Sexton, K.H. Vesper (eds.), Encyclopedia of Entrepreneurship, Englewood Cliffs, N.J., Prentice Hall.

Shepherd, D.A. et De Tienne, D.R. (2005). Prior knowledge, potential financial rewards, and opportunity identification. Entrepreneurship Theory and practice, 29(1), 91-112.

Singh, R P and Lucas, L M (2005). Not just domestic engineers: an exploratory study of homemaker entrepreneurs, Entrepreneurship Theory and Practice, 29, 79-90.

Storey, D-J. (2000). Six Steps to Heaven, Evaluating the Impact of Public Policies to support Small Businesses in Developed Economies", in D.L. Sexton and H. Landstrom (eds.), "Handbook of Entrepreneurship", Blackwells, Oxford, pp. 176-194

Stuart, R.W. & Abetti, P.A. (1990). Impact of entrepreneurial and management experience on early performance. Journal of Business Venturing, 5: 151–162.

Teece, D-J. (1998), " Capturing Value from Knowledge Assets : The New Economy, markets for Know-How, and Intangibles Assets", California Management Review. Vol 40, n°3, Spring 55-79

Timmons, J.A. (1999). New venture creation. Singapore: McGraw-Hill

Veciana, J.M., Aponte, M., Urbano, D. (2005). University Students' Attitudes Towards Entrepreneurship: A Two Countries Comparison. International Entrepreneurship and Management Journal, 1(2), 165-182.

Venkataraman, S. (1997). The Distinctive Domain of Entrepreneurship Research: An Editor's Perspective. Advances in Entrepreneurship. J. Katz and R. Brockhaus. Greenwich, JAI Press. 3: 119-138.

Wagner, K. & Ziltener, A. (2008). The Nascent Entrepreneur at the Crossroads: Entrepreneurial Motives as Determinants for Different Types of Entrepreneurs. Discussion Papers on Entrepreneurship and Innovation are edited by the Swiss Institute for Entrepreneurship.

Yusuf, A. (1995). Critical success factors for small business: Perceptions of South Pacific entrepreneurs. Journal of Small Business Management, 33: 68–73.

Comparability of Financial Information and Segmental Reporting: An Empirical Study of the Information Disclosed by International Hotel Groups

Frédéric Demerens[1], Pascal Delvaille[2], and Jean-Louis Paré[3]

1. Introduction and Background

The objective of this study is to analyse the accounting practices of international hotel groups reporting segment information in their annual report. Both standards, Statement of Financial Accounting Standards No. 131 (SFAS 131) and International Accounting Standard N°14 (Revised) (IAS 14(R)), deal with segment reporting and should lead to a better comparability of the financial information of the companies. Prior research on segment reporting has determined several areas of problems, such as segment identification and aggregation, geographic information, and consistency with the internal reporting system. Standards have improved, but segment information remains a major challenge for international accounting. While recent adoption of IFRS 8 opens the ways of convergence between US GAAP and IAS/IFRS, companies' practices and managerial decisions about segment information could be very different even in the same industry. Differences also subsist about segment information between national accounting standards and IAS/IFRS (Street, 2002). For these reasons, we decided to study the segment information reporting practices of international hotel groups claiming to comply with US GAAP standards or IFRS standards. As far as we know, there are no

[1] Professor, *Advancia-Négocia.*
[2] Professor, *ESCP Europe.*
[3] CFA, PhD, Professor, *Advancia-Négocia.*

papers about the hotel industry accounting practices. However this industry is very concentrated and companies have the same management and strategic constraints. This should lead to comparable segment information practices. The principal contribution of this descriptive study is to compare segment information practices under SFAS 131 and IAS 14(R) within the same industry worldwide.

Segment disclosure practices research represents a large part of segment information research. They consist mainly in analysing segment information items disclosed (Gray, 1978; Gray & Radebaugh, 1984).

Another important field is the analysis of the explanatory factors of segment disclosures. Country of domicile, firm size, and exchange listing appear to be important factors influencing segment disclosures (Herrmann & Thomas, 1996). The competitive structure of the industry can also explain segment disclosures. Tsakumis, Doupnik, & Seese, (2006) showed that firms exposed to greater competitive harm costs provide less detailed country specific revenue disclosures. The standards offer some flexibility to the managers that persist in aggregating segments in some conditions (Nichols & Street, 2007). Management approach seems to be better and should lead to consistent segments, but companies do not fully comply with this approach (Paul & Largay III, 2005).

The enforcement of the standards generated research dealing with the improvement of segment information.

SFAS 14 to SFAS 131: Some papers determine the improvement of Lines of Business (LOB) and geographic segments disclosures (Doupnik & Seese, 2001). Street, Nichols & Gray (2000), using descriptive statistics, showed that the adoption of SFAS 131 led to a greater number of LOB segments reported, and to more meaningful and transparent geographic groupings. "By increasing information disaggregation, the new standard induced firms to reveal previously hidden information about their diversification strategies" (Berger & Hann, 2003). *IAS 14 to IAS 14 Revised*: According to several authors, the adoption of the IAS 14R has improved segment information under IAS (greater number of LOB segments reported, more meaningful and transparent geographic groupings, more items of information about each LOB and/or geographic segment) but the compliance with IAS 14R is still imperfect (Street & Nichols, 2002) ; (Prather-Kinsey & Meek, 2004).

Accounting researchers and regulators of IASB and FASB agree to encourage disaggregated geographic segment disclosures (Behn, Nichols, & Street, 2002; Herrmann, 1996; Nichols, Street, & Gray, 2000). Despite the improvement due to the new standards, geographic aggregation and country-specific information are still poorly reported. Segment information is often useful for financial analysts. The increase of segment disclosures leads to better financial forecasts (Alliouallla & Laurin, 2002; Ettredge, Soo Young, Smith, & Zarowin, 2005). Seese & Doupnik (2003) showed that financial analysts' judgments are affected by the quality of geographic disclosures about the level of country risk and country operations.

Few papers deal with segment information within an industry. One paper determines ways of bank industry segment information improvement (Homölle, 2003). This paper does not assess the practices of the companies. Link (2003) evaluated the potential consistencies existing between the segment disclosures of eight US banks and concluded a poor uniformity.

Segment information is also linked to voluntary disclosures. Diversification strategy, firm size, and the level of minority interest are related to voluntary segment disclosure (Aitken, Hooper, & Pickering, 1997). Some findings confirm that proprietary costs are particularly relevant and limit the incentive for companies to provide segment information to the market (Prencipe, 2004). Voluntary segment disclosures are also related to the type of ownership (Leung & Horwitz, 2004).

The convergence of the standards is one of the main goals of international accounting regulation. The adoption of IFRS by European listed companies in 2005 is a very important stage of the international convergence of the standards (concerning the compliance with IAS and the adoption of IFRS, see Street & Gray (2002) and Larson & Street (2004)). The paper by Ampofo & Sellani (2005) gives a good summary of the main issues of the convergence between US GAAP and IFRS at a general level. Two papers compare the compliance with both US GAAP and IAS. The companies of Germany's new market must choose between US GAAP and IAS for their financial reporting. Glaum & Street (2003) determine a higher compliance for the companies reporting under US GAAP. Leuz (2003) concludes that the choice between IAS and US GAAP appears to be of little consequence for information asymmetry and market liquidity.

2. Research Questions and Sample

This paper examines the following questions concerning the comparability of segment information disclosed by the main international hotel groups: (1) What items of information are disclosed under SFAS 131 and IAS 14(R) within the hotel industry in 2006 (compared to 2004 and 2005), and do the companies comply with the reporting obligations concerning segment information? (2) What are the practices of these companies in reporting business and geographic segments? (3) Is the calculation of ratios from segment information comparable?

This research is mainly descriptive and based on the analysis of the companies' annual reports (10k reports for US Companies, annual report for IFRS Companies). We only analyse the segment information section identified within the annual reports.

In order to compare the segment information disclosed by the companies, we selected the main items required by SFAS 131 and IAS 14(R). Then, we assessed the compliance with the standards in each annual report. For a better comparison, items were classified in four categories: first level of segment information (main information under SFAS 131, primary level of segment information under IAS 14(R)); reconciliation of segment information; second level of segment information (complementary disclosures under SFAS 131 – mainly geographic segment information, secondary level of segment information under IAS 14(R)); other information. Table 1 shows the items selected for each standard.

Twenty-nine (29) items are selected to analyse segment information under SFAS 131. Our approach is closer to Herrmann & Thomas's methodology (2000). To compare, Street et al. (2000) selected twelve main items, and have analysed the main items of voluntarily segment disclosure.

Twenty-one (21) items are selected to analyse segment information under IAS 14(R). We analyse in detail several items (such as reconciliation items). Secondary level is also analysed. Street & Nichols (2002) selected eight items and assessed the major items disclosed voluntarily. Prather-Kinsey & Meek (2004) selected eleven items, analysed in detail the reconciliation items, but neither studied other segment information items nor voluntary segment disclosure.

Each item has the same weight in our study.

Table 1: Disclosure items analysed under SFAS 131 and IAS 14(R)

SFAS 131	IAS 14	SFAS 131	IAS 14
Information for each reportable segment	**Primary segment format information**		
Revenues from external customers	Sales to external customers	✓	✓
Revenues from transactions with other operating segments of the same enterprise	Inter-segment revenue	✓	✓
Interest revenue / expense		✓	
Depreciation, depletion, and amortization expense	Depreciation and amortisation charges and other significant non-cash expenses	✓	✓
Unusual items as described in paragraph 26 of APB Opinion No. 30		✓	
Equity in the net income of investees accounted for by the equity method	Aggregate share of the profit or loss of associates, joint ventures, or other investments accounted for under the equity method	✓	✓
Income tax benefit / expense		✓	
Extraordinary items		✓	
Significant non-cash items other than depreciation, depletion and amortization expense		✓	
Measure of profit or loss	Result (before interest and taxes) from continuing operations and separately the result from discontinued operations	✓	✓
Total assets	Carrying amount of segment assets	✓	✓
	Segment liabilities		✓
Amount of investment in equity method investees		✓	

Total expenditures for additions to long-lived assets other than financial instruments, long-term customer relationships of financial institution, mortgage and other servicing rights, deferred policy acquisition costs, and deferred tax assets	Cost incurred in the period to acquire property, plant and equipment, and intangibles;	✓	✓
	Information in accordance with IAS 36		✓
Reconciliation	**Reconciliation**		
Reconciliation of the total of the reportable segments' revenues to the enterprise's consolidated revenues	Reconciliation of total segment revenue	✓	✓
Reconciliation of the reportable segments' measures of profit or loss to the enterprise's consolidated income before income taxes, extraordinary items, discontinued operations, and the cumulative effect of changes in accounting principles	Reconciliation of total segment measures of profit or loss	✓	✓
Reconciliation of the reportable segments' amounts for every other significant item of information disclosed to the corresponding consolidated amount.		✓	
If an enterprise allocates items such as income taxes and extraordinary items to segments, the enterprise may choose to reconcile the total of the segments' measures of profit or loss to consolidated income after those items		✓	
Reconciliation of the reportable segments' assets to the enterprise's consolidated assets	Reconciliation of total segment assets	✓	✓
	Reconciliation of total segment liabilities		✓

SFAS 131	IAS 14	SFAS 131	IAS 14
Information about geographic areas	**Information for the secondary segment format**		
Revenues from external customers attributed to the enterprise's country of domicile and attributed to all foreign countries in total from which the enterprise derives revenues	Revenue, separately disclosing sales to external customers and inter-segment revenue	✓	✓
Long lived assets other than financial instruments (,,,) located in the enterprise's country of domicile and located in all foreign countries in total in which the enterprise holds assets	Carrying amount of segment assets	✓	✓
	Cost incurred in the period to acquire property, plant and equipment, and intangibles		✓
Explanation of the segmentation	Explanation of the segmentation	✓	✓
Other information	**Other information**		
Information about major customers		✓	
Types of products and services from which each reportable segment derives its revenues	Types of product and service included in each reported business segment	✓	✓
Basis of inter-segment pricing	Basis of inter-segment pricing	✓	✓

Factors used to identify the enterprise's reportable segments		✓	
The nature of any differences between the measurements of the reportable segments' profits or losses and the enterprise's consolidated income before income taxes, extraordinary items, discontinued operations, and the cumulative effect of changes in accounting principles		✓	
The nature of any differences between the measurements of the reportable segments' assets and the enterprise's consolidated assets		✓	
Nature and effect of any asymmetrical allocations to segments		✓	
Restatement of previously reported information	Restatement of previously reported information	✓	✓
	Composition of each reported geographical segment		✓
	TOTAL OF MAIN ITEMS	**29**	**21**

Sources: (FASB, 1997) ; (IASC, 1997) ; (Editions-Francis-Lefebvre & PWC, 2004) ; (PriceWaterhouseCoopers, 2005)

The hotel industry, as a part of the tourism industry, benefited from the global growth of tourism in 2004. The global turnover was 4 trillion euros. "The world hotel accommodation capacity worked out at close to 17 million rooms in 2004" and "Europe, the leading tourism area in the world, had 34% of total hotel accommodation capacities, coming far ahead of North America (28%) and Asia (23%)" (XERFI-IMA, 2005). The hotel industry is led by a small number of big international hotel groups, integrated and franchised groups. Small independent hotel companies are the most numerous (2 rooms out of 3) but hardly compete with international hotel groups. Independent hotels must join a network in order to survive the competition and to enjoy the benefits of such a network: advertising, reputation, booking centre, management tools, etc. (Best Western is a good example of hotel network worldwide).

The hotel industry is now concentrated in North America and Europe. International hotel groups are redeploying over areas with high growth potential. Asia presents the highest potential due to social and economic development and due to tourism growth, especially with the hosting of the Olympic Games in 2008. Another common attitude in hotel groups' management is the sale of real assets. Hotel groups benefit from the global growth of real estate prices enabling them to finance their strong development in high potential areas. The development is mainly based on franchising structures (57% of chain hotels were franchised in 2004) allowing the hotel group to concentrate on their core competence: hotel management.

We see in TABLE 2 that American hotel groups dominate the industry.

Potential sample hotel groups were identified from a cross selection of different data bases or rankings of year 2005. The InFinancials data base gave us a first potential sample (the lists were obtained from the following request: ICB Classification, -, reference HOTELS). We crossed the results from InFinancials with a Datastream request.

We wanted to have a representative sample of international hotel groups. We decided to complete the sample selection by analysing the rankings of MKG Consulting. MKG Consulting is an international consulting group specialised in hotel management. Their worldwide database is now a reference (40,000 hotels, 2.2 million rooms) and supplies different rankings. The rankings are based on the economic size, the numbers of hotels, and the number of rooms. We especially analysed the international and European rankings (MKG-Consulting, 2005a, 2005b, 2005c) in which the smallest hotel groups appear. We selected international hotel groups' financial information under US GAAP and/or IFRS. Hotel groups were deleted if they didn't comply with US GAAP or IFRS (some companies report under other GAAP), if they didn't report financial information directly (for example private companies, hotel groups linked to investment funds), or if they represent a hotel network (such as Best Western).

The final sample is made up of fourteen (14) international hotel groups. Six (6) companies comply with US GAAP and eight (8) companies comply with IFRS. The small size of the sample is mainly linked to the concentration of the hotel industry. The first six hotel groups account for more than 80% of the total number of rooms and more than 85% of the sales revenue (except TUI, a German tourism specialist, see TABLE 3).

The hotel groups selected are concentrated on hotel management competence. The average hotel income (in these companies) represents more than 75% of the total income. The most diversified companies of the sample are TUI, SAS (which in 2006 split their hotel activities – The Rezidor Hotel Group – from their travel activities) and Cendant Corporation (which split, in 2006, their hotel activities – Wyndham Worldwide – from their real estate activities).

The size of the sample leads essentially to descriptive statistics.

Table 2: Sample selection and key data

	Country	Accounting Standards	Rooms (2)	Hotels (2)	Revenue
Intercontinental Hotels Group	Great Britain	***IFRS***	532 701	3 532	1,910 £m
Cendant Corporation	United States	***US GAAP***	520 860	6 396	18,236 $m
Marriott International , Inc.	United States	***US GAAP***	469 218	2 564	11,550 $m
Accor SA	France	***IFRS***	463 427	3 973	7,622 €m
Choice Hotels International	United States	***US GAAP***	403 806	4 987	477.4 $m
Hilton Hotels Corporation	United States	***US GAAP***	354 312	2 226	4,437 $m
Best Western (1)	United States		308 131	4 097	
Starwood Hotels and resorts	United States	***US GAAP***	230 667	733	5,977 $m
Carlson Hospitality worlwide (1)	United States		147 093	890	
Global Hyatt (1)	United States		111 651	355	
Hilton International (1)	Great Britain	***IFRS***	99 257	395	
Sol Melia	Spain	***IFRS***	80 834	328	1,165 €m
TUI AG	Germany	***IFRS***	74 454	283	19,619 €m
Louvre Hôtels (1)	France		67 532	895	
La Quinta (1)	United States		65 110	582	
MGM Mirage (1)	United States		37 867	24	
US Franchise Systems (1)	United States		35 683	462	
NH Hoteles	Spain	***IFRS***	35 241	242	994 €m
Le Meridien (1)	United States		33 287	135	
Fairmont hotels and resorts (1)	Canada		32 967	81	
Interstate hotels and resorts	United States	***US GAAP***	env. 66000	env. 290	222.48 $m
Whitbread PLC	Great Britain	***IFRS***	31 000	470	1,584 £m
Millenium and Copthorne Hotels PLC	Great Britain	***IFRS***	26 270	97	595 £m
SAS Group	Sweden	***IFRS***	10 158	217	6592 €m

Table 2 continued: Sample selection and key data

Hotels revenue	*Total Equity*	*In Financials ICB : Hotels*	*Datastream*	*Auditors*
1,910 £m	1,104 £m	✓	✓	Ernst & Young LLP
1,527 $m	11,292 $m	✓	✓	Deloitte & Touche LLP
11,129 $m	3,252 $m	✓	✓	Ernst & Young LLP
5,195 €m	4,396 €m	✓	✓	Ernst & Young Deloitte et associés
477.4 $m		✓	✓	PricewaterhouseCoopers LLP
3,883 $m	2,811 $m	✓	✓	Ernst & Young LLP
4,995 $m	5,236 $m	✓	✓	Ernst & Young LLP
1,770.8 £m		✓		
911 €m	944 €m	✓	✓	Ernst & Young S.L.
14,097 €m (tourism)	4,375 €m		✓	PricewaterhouseCoopers
		✓		
910 €m	820 €m	✓	✓	Deloitte and Touche PricewaterhouseCoopers
		✓		
222.48 $m	131.33 $m	✓		KPMG LLP
408 £m	1,547 £m		✓	Ernst & Young LLP
581 £m	1,378 £m	✓	✓	KPMG Audit PLC
581 €m	1,287 €m			Deloitte AB

(1) :	Not integrated in this study
(2) :	MKG's 2005 world ranking of hotel groups, March 30th, 2005; MKG Group The 2005 ranking of hotel groups in the 25 European Union member states, January 27th 2005; MKG Group

Nine companies were not included in the final sample for different reasons:

- Best Western is a hotel network: the analysis of the annual report is not meaningful concerning segment information and economic size;
- Hilton International (Great Britain) were sold in early 2006 and appears in Ladbroke's 2005 annual report as a discontinued operation;
- Carlson Hospitality and Global Hyatt do not directly report consolidated financial statements;
- Louvre Hôtels, La Quinta and Le Méridien were sold before the year-end 2005;
- MGM Mirage has an important number of hotel rooms but reports only one business segment and does not disclose segment information.

The financial statements were obtained from the companies' websites, from the SEC website, and from the InFinancials data base. We worked from the 10k document (for American companies) and from the registration document or the annual report for European companies. All groups have a December 31 year-end except Whitbread PLC (March 2 year-end).

TABLE 3 shows only the hotel revenue of each group extracted from the financial statements.

Table 3: Sample Hotel Revenue (as at December 31 2005)

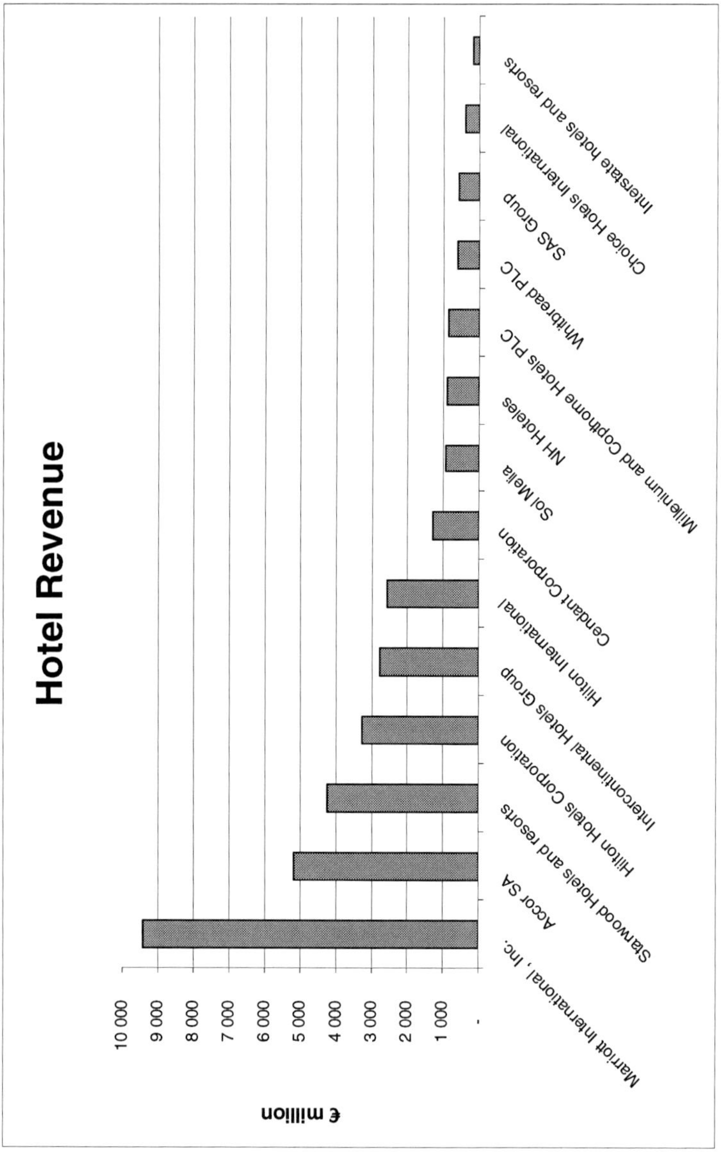

3. Findings and Discussion

The results of our study on segment information practices under SFAS 131 and IAS 14(R) are presented as below:

- first, the level of information disclosed by companies applying their respective standards (compulsory items) is discussed;
- second, the segmentation practices - especially the number of lines of business and geographic segments - are detailed;
- third, items of voluntary segment disclosure found in the financial statements are explained;
- fourth, we identify ratios and indicators that users of annual reports could compute from the segmented data.

For each of these points, we compare both sub-samples: "US companies" and "IFRS companies".

Table 4: Disclosure practices of US GAAP companies – compliance with SFAS 131 (% of companies) – 2006

	Average
	2006
Standard	Reported information
Information for each reportable segment	
Revenues from external customers	100%
Revenues from transactions with other operating segments of the same enterprise	17%
Interest revenue / expense	17%
Depreciation, depletion, and amortization expense	83%
Unusual items as described in paragrah 26 of APB Opinion No. 30	0%
Equity in the net income of investees accounted for by the equity method	50%
Income tax benefit / expense	0%
Extraordinary items	0%
Significant noncash items other than depreciation, depletion and amortization expense	17%
Measure of profit or loss	100%
Total assets	100%
Amount of investment in equity method investees	17%
Total expenditures for additions to long-lived assets	83%
Total Information for each reportable segment	***45%***

Reconciliations	
Reconciliations of the total of the reportable segments' revenues to the enterprise's consolidated revenues	100%
Reconciliation of the reportable segments'measures of profit or loss to the enterprise's consolidated income befor income taxes, extraordinary items, discontinued operations, and the cumulative effect of changes in accounting principles	100%
Reconciliation of the reportable segments' amounts for every other significant item of information disclosed to the corresponding consolidated amount	17%
If an entreprise allocates items such as income taxes and extraordinary items to segments, the enterprise may choose to reconcile the total of the segments' measures of profit or loss to consolidated income after those items	67%
Reconciliation of the reportable segments' assets to the enterprise's consolidated assets	100%
Total reconciliations	***77%***
Information about geographic areas	
Revenues from external customers attributed to the enterprise's country of domicile and attributed to all foreign cuntries in total from wich the enterprise derives revenues	83%
Long lived assets other than financial instruments (,,,) located in the enterprise's country of domicile and located in all foreign countries in total in wich the enterprise holds assets	83%
Total information about geographic areas	***83%***

Reconciliations	
Reconciliations of the total of the reportable segments' revenues to the enterprise's consolidated revenues	100%
Reconciliation of the reportable segments'measures of profit or loss to the enterprise's consolidated income befor income taxes, extraordinary items, discontinued operations, and the cumulative effect of changes in accounting principles	100%
Reconciliation of the reportable segments' amounts for every other significant item of information disclosed to the corresponding consolidated amount	17%
If an entreprise allocates items such as income taxes and extraordinary items to segments, the enterprise may choose to reconcile the total of the segments' measures of profit or loss to consolidated income after those items	67%
Reconciliation of the reportable segments' assets to the enterprise's consolidated assets	100%
Total reconciliations	***77%***
Information about geographic areas	
Revenues from external customers attributed to the enterprise's country of domicile and attributed to all foreign cuntries in total from wich the enterprise derives revenues	83%
Long lived assets other than financial instruments (,,,) located in the enterprise's country of domicile and located in all foreign countries in total in wich the enterprise holds assets	83%
Total information about geographic areas	***83%***

The compliance with SFAS 131 remains moderate: only 48% of the items are reported by the companies.

Main economic information of the "first level" is always disclosed: external revenues, measure of loss or profit, and total assets. Hilton Hotels Corporation is the only one that does not disclose information about depreciation and capital expenditures. Other items are poorly reported (if at all). Most companies disclose global information about reconciliation. Five (83%) companies disclose geographic segment information but have a small number of geographic segments. For the "other information" category, companies do not disclose a large number of items. This could be explained by the strong concentration of the companies. The findings are consistent with the findings of prior research based on larger samples (Herrmann & Thomas, 2000; Street et al., 2000).

Total average increased between 2004 and 2005 (Appendix 1), from 39% to 47%.

Table 5: Disclosure practices of IFRS companies – compliance with IAS 14 (Revised) (% of companies) – 2006

	Average
	2006
	Reported information
Primary segment format information	
Sales to external customers	100%
Inter-segment revenue	25%
Depreciation and amortisation charges and other significant non-cash expenses	100%
Aggregate share of the profit or loss of associates, joint ventures, or other investments accounted for under the equity method	88%
Result (before interest and taxes) from continuing operations and separately the result from discontinued operations	100%
Carrying amount of segment assets	100%
Segment liabilities	100%
Cost incurred in the period to acquire property, plant and equipment, and intangibles;	100%
Information in accordance with IAS 36	63%
Total primary segment format information	***86%***

Reconciliations	
Reconciliation of total segment revenue	100%
Reconciliation of total segment measures of profit or loss	100%
Reconciliation of total segment assets	100%
Reconciliation of total segment liabilities	100%
Total reconciliations	***100%***
Information for the secondary segment format	
Revenue, separately disclosing sales to external customers and inter-segment revenue	100%
Carrying amount of segment assets	88%
Cost incurred in the period to acquire property, plant and equipment, and intangibles	88%
Total information for the secondary segment	***92%***
Explanation of the segmentation	100%
Other information	
Types of product and service included in each reported business segment	75%
Basis of inter-segment pricing	25%
Restatement of previously reported information	75%
Composition of each reported geographical segment	63%
Total explanation and other information	***68%***
Total average	**85%**

The companies of the sample mostly comply with IAS 14. This good level of compliance is also better than the compliance observed by Prather-Kinsey & Meek (2004) and by Glaum & Street (2003). The adoption of IFRS by European listed companies should explain this good compliance. The international weight of those companies could also be an explanation. Almost all the primary and secondary level items are disclosed by the companies in the sample. The strong concentration and the choice of the reportable segments could explain why some companies do not report inter-segment sales. Items of Reconciliation are fully disclosed.

Only Intercontinental Hotels Group and SAS Group have chosen geographic segmentation as their primary level of segment information. Other companies disclose business segments in their primary level of segment information. This is consistent with prior research. For example, Street & Nichols (2002) found that of a 210-IAS-company sample, only 23 companies have primary segments based on geographic areas.

Between 2004 and 2005 (Appendix 2), we notice a better average of disclosed items. Few companies of the sample presented segmental information based on IAS14 in 2004. Most of the companies of the sample complied with IAS 14 in 2005.

We wanted to take into account the segmentation practices.

The number of LOB segments is comparable between US companies and European companies. Our results are consistent with prior research. Based on a sample with no industry specificity, Herrmann & Thomas (2000) found a mean of 3.8 LOB segments (the sample was made up of 100 firms reporting under SFAS 131). Street & Nichols (2002) found a mean of 4.04 LOB segments with a sample of 140 companies reporting under IAS 14R.

Only seven hotel groups disclose a specific hotel segmentation, for example Hilton Hotels Corporation identifies segments based on owned, managed, and franchised hotels, while Accor SA has a market segmentation (see Table 6). These seven groups are the largest hotel groups. We note that there is no uniformity in the hotel segmentation chosen by the leaders, which makes comparisons very difficult. This lack of uniformity in the segment definition within a same industry was also observed by Link (2003) in the US bank industry.

Table 6: Number of lines of business (LOB) segments and geographic segments reported - 2006

	2006				
	LOB	LOB (hotel)	Geog. areas	Domestic data	Country-specific Information
US GAAP Panel					
Cendant Corporation	4	3	3	Yes	Yes/No
Marriott International , Inc.	8	4	8	Yes	Yes/No
Choice Hotels International	2	1	1	No	No
Hilton Hotels Corporation	4	2	3	Yes	Yes
Starwood Hotels and Resorts	3	1	3	Yes	Yes
Interstate Hotels and Resorts	3	2	2	No	Yes
US GAAP Panel	***4,00***	***2,17***	***3,33***		
IFRS Panel					
Intercontinental Hotels Group	4	3	3	No	No
Accor SA	9	3	6	Yes	No
Sol Melia	3	1	4	No	No
TUI AG	4	-	5	Yes	No
NH Hoteles	2	1	6	Yes	Yes
Whitbread PLC	5	1	1	Yes	-
Millenium and Copthorne Hotels PLC	3	1	6	No	Yes
SAS Group	5	3	4	No	No
IFRS Panel	***4,38***	***1,63***	***4,38***		
Total	***4,21***	***1,86***	***3,93***		

An interesting but not surprising finding of our study is that IFRS companies disclose more geographic areas than the US GAAP companies. So transparency of geographic segment disclosures remains an issue at stake. Six companies do not report information separately for their country of domicile (domestic data). Nor is there uniformity in the aggregation of the geographic areas. The companies still disclose groupings of geographic areas. Only seven companies give country-specific information.

We notice that between 2004 and 2006 (Appendix 3) groups report more hotel based segmentation information. Wyndham and Rezidor (split off from Cendant and SAS) are focused on hotel activities and have decided to present real hotel segmented information.

In order to assess voluntary segment disclosure, we have counted the items provided beyond those required by SFAS 131 or IAS 14. For example:

cash flow, details on assets and liabilities, number of employees, etc. We have only taken into account the disclosures reported in the segment information section of the annual report. Some voluntary segment disclosures may be provided within other parts of the annual report but are not included in our study.

Table 7: Number of Voluntary Segment Information Items - 2006

2006	*Voluntary Segment Information*					
	LOB			Geographic areas		
	Average	Max	min	Average	Max	min
US GAAP Panel	0,67	2	-	0,17	1	-
IFRS Panel	7,71	21	-	6,33	17	-

Of the US GAAP panel, Marriott International is the only one giving two voluntary disclosures. There is no surprise about this result, which is consistent with the results of Street et al. (2000). IFRS companies disclose more voluntary segment information, especially since 2005 (Appendix 4). Voluntary segment disclosures frequently give details on assets and liabilities. For example, Intercontinental discloses non-current assets and liabilities classified as held for sale, impairment information, etc. Accor SA is the leader, providing voluntary segment information about financial complements (segment balance sheet), hotel key indicators (EBITDAR for example) and other topics (evolution of key indicators for example). Accor SA often presents this information in matrix format (interrelationship of the LOB and geographic segments). Few disclosures are provided concerning segment cash flow, expenses, financing strategy, etc. There is no uniformity of the voluntary segment information items within this industry. We can't assert that this voluntary disclosure is relevant.

In order to evaluate the comparative usefulness of the segment information disclosed by the international hotel groups, we assessed the calculation of several ratios or indicators. Four basic financial ratios were chosen representing profitability (EBIT / Revenues, EBITDA / Revenues), asset turnover (asset / revenues), and investment rate (Investment / Revenues). We expected that these four hotel ratios would be disclosed and/or calculable for most international hotel groups (see Table 8). Other indicators are commonly used within hotel management, for example: Labour performance (Revenues / number of employees), Revenue Per Available Room (RevPAR), Occupancy Rate, and EBITDAR (Earnings Before Interest, Tax, Depreciation, Amortization and RENT). EBITDAR is an operational performance indicator independent from financial and investment policy (expressed by depreciation, financial result and rent) and is usually used to compare hotels' performance.

Table 8: Ratios and indicators obtained from segment information - 2006

	2006					
	US GAAP Panel		IFRS Panel		Total	
	LOB %	Geo %	LOB %	Geo %	LOB %	Geo %
Profitability ratio : EBIT / Revenues	100%	0%	100%	38%	100%	21%
Profitability ratio : EBITDA / Revenues	100%	0%	88%	38%	93%	21%
Asset turnover : Asset / Revenues	100%	50%	88%	63%	93%	57%
Investment rate : investment / Revenues	83%	0%	88%	63%	86%	36%
Total Financial Ratios	**96%**	**13%**	**91%**	**50%**	**93%**	**34%**
Voluntary and/or hospitality disclosures						
Labor performance : Revenues / Number of employees	0%	0%	13%	13%	7%	7%
RevPAR	0%	0%	0%	0%	0%	0%
Occupancy Rate	0%	0%	0%	0%	0%	0%
EBITDAR	0%	0%	38%	13%	21%	7%
Total Voluntary and/or hospitality disclosures	**0%**	**0%**	**13%**	**6%**	**7%**	**4%**

Basic ratios are easily calculable for the LOB segments for both panels. This result is purely linked to the obligations of the two standards. Appendix 5 shows that the adoption of the IFRS in 2005 has led to a better financial approach among the IFRS panel. We notice also the weakness of geographic segment disclosure. Under SFAS 131, only possible for two companies, the calculation of asset turnover is that IFRS companies disclose more useful geographic segment disclosure. Hotel-specific ratios or indicators calculation is very difficult. For example, Accor SA, TUI AG and Sol y Melia disclose EBITDAR but labour performance ratio is only calculable for Accor SA and TUI AG. Nevertheless, we noticed that most of the hotel-specific ratios or indicators are available in other parts of the annual report but not necessarily under the same segmentation.

4. Conclusions and Future Research

The objective of this paper is to assess the comparability of segment information disclosed by the main international hotel groups using IFRS or US GAAP standards. We find that: (1) Compliance with segment information obligations is medium for US GAAP companies and higher for IFRS companies. Geographic segment disclosures remain poor, essentially for US GAAP companies. (2) There is no uniformity of LOB segment definition and geographic segment definition within the hotel industry. Despite the same management constraints and practices of international hotel groups, we cannot assert that there is a real similar hotel segmentation reporting in this industry. (3) The usefulness of segment information also remains poor concerning geographic ratios calculation and hotel-specific indicators disclosure.

Our findings show that there is still room for improvement in segment reporting information. In a competitive environment such as the hotel industry, could the future convergence of the standards, especially under IFRS 8 adopting US approach, affect compliance positively or adversely with the segment information? This research should be completed by multiple-year observations within the industry.

Explanations of segment disclosures practices also have managerial sources that should be revealed. Case studies highlighting managerial practices decisions concerning the relationship and the consistency between internal and external reporting within the same industry could be carried out. Segment information is still a good field of investigation for international accounting and management accounting research.

Appendix 1: Disclosure practices of US GAAP companies – compliance with SFAS 131 (% of companies) – 2004 & 2005

Standard	Average 2005 Reported information	Average 2004 Reported information
Information for each reportable segment		
Revenues from external customers	100%	100%
Revenues from transactions with other operating segments of the same enterprise	17%	17%
Interest revenue / expense	17%	0%
Depreciation, depletion, and amortization expense	83%	67%
Unusual items as described in paragrah 26 of APB Opinion No. 30	0%	0%
Equity in the net income of investees accounted for by the equity method	50%	33%
Income tax benefit / expense	0%	0%
Extraordinary items	0%	0%
Significant noncash items other than depreciation, depletion and amortization expense	0%	0%
Measure of profit or loss	100%	83%
Total assets	100%	100%
Amount of investment in equity method investees	17%	17%
Total expenditures for additions to long-lived assets	83%	67%
Total Information for each reportable segment	***44%***	***37%***

Reconciliations		
Reconciliations of the total of the reportable segments' revenues to the enterprise's consolidated revenues	100%	100%
Reconciliation of the reportable segments'measures of profit or loss to the enterprise's consolidated income befor income taxes, extraordinary items, discontinued operations, and the cumulative effect of changes in accounting principles	100%	83%
Reconciliation of the reportable segments' amounts for every other significant item of information disclosed to the corresponding consolidated amount	17%	17%
If an entreprise allocates items such as income taxes and extraordinary items to segments, the enterprise may choose to reconcile the total of the segments' measures of profit or loss to consolidated income after those items	83%	50%
Reconciliation of the reportable segments' assets to the enterprise's consolidated assets	100%	100%
Total reconciliations	***80%***	***70%***
Information about geographic areas		
Revenues from external customers attributed to the enterprise's country of domicile and attributed to all foreign cuntries in total from wich the enterprise derives revenues	67%	67%
Long lived assets other than financial instruments (,,,) located in the enterprise's country of domicile and located in all foreign countries in total in wich the enterprise holds assets	67%	67%
Total information about geographic areas	***67%***	***67%***

Explanation of the segmentation	100%	100%
Other Information		
Information about major customers	17%	0%
Types of products and services from which each reportable segment derives its revenues	17%	17%
Basis of inter-segment pricing	0%	0%
Factors used to identify the enterprise's reportable segments	67%	50%
The nature of any differences between the measurements of the reportable segments' profits or losses and the enterprise's consolidated income before income taxes, extraordinary items, discontinued operations, and the cumulative effect of changes in accounting principles	17%	0%
The nature of any differences between the measurements of the reportable segments' assets and the enterprise's consolidated assets	17%	0%
Nature and effect of any asymmetrical allocations to segments	17%	0%
Restatement of previously reported information	0%	0%
Total explanation and other information	***28%***	***19%***
Total Average	***47%***	***39%***

Appendix 2: Disclosure practices of IFRS companies – compliance with IAS 14 (Revised) (% of companies) – 2004 & 2005

	Average	Average
	2005	**2004**
	Reported information	Reported information
Primary segment format information		
Sales to external customers	100%	100%
Inter-segment revenue	50%	38%
Depreciation and amortisation charges and other significant non-cash expenses	100%	25%
Aggregate share of the profit or loss of associates, joint ventures, or other investments accounted for under the equity method	75%	50%
Result (before interest and taxes) from continuing operations and separately the result from discontinued operations	100%	75%
Carrying amount of segment assets	100%	63%
Segment liabilities	100%	38%
Cost incurred in the period to acquire property, plant and equipment, and intangibles;	88%	38%
Information in accordance with IAS 36	50%	13%
Total primary segment format information	***85%***	***49%***

Reconciliations		
Reconciliation of total segment revenue	100%	100%
Reconciliation of total segment measures of profit or loss	100%	75%
Reconciliation of total segment assets	100%	63%
Reconciliation of total segment liabilities	100%	38%
Total reconciliations	***100%***	***69%***
Information for the secondary segment format		
Revenue, separately disclosing sales to external customers and inter-segment revenue	100%	100%
Carrying amount of segment assets	100%	63%
Cost incurred in the period to acquire property, plant and equipment, and intangibles	38%	38%
Total information for the secondary segment	***36%***	***67%***
Explanation of the segmentation	100%	25%
Other information		
Types of product and service included in each reported business segment	63%	25%
Basis of inter-segment pricing	0%	13%
Restatement of previously reported information	13%	25%
Composition of each reported geographical segment	63%	13%
Total explanation and other information	***48%***	***20%***
Total average	**80%**	**48%**

Appendix 3: Number of lines of business (LOB) segments and geographic segments reported – 2004 & 2005

	2005					2004				
	LOB	LOB (hotel)	Geog. areas	Domestic data	Country-specific information	LOB	LOB (hotel)	Geog. areas	Domestic data	Country-specific information
US GAAP Panel										
Cendant Corporation	7	1	3	Yes	Yes / No	7	1	3	Yes	Yes/no
Marriott International , Inc.	6	2	8	Yes	No	6	2	1	Yes	No
Choice Hotels International	2	1	1	No	No	2	1	1	No	No
Hilton Hotels Corporation	4	2	-	No	No	4	2	-	No	No
Starwood Hotels and Resorts	3	1	3	Yes	Yes / No	3	1	3	Yes	Yes
Interstate Hotels and Resorts	4	3	4	No	Yes / No	3	1	4	No	Yes
US GAAP Panel	***4,33***	***1,67***	***3,17***			***4,17***	***1,33***	***2,00***		
IFRS Panel										
Intercontinental Hotels Group	4	4	4	No	No	2	1	3	Yes/No	Yes
Accor SA	9	3	6	Yes	No	9	3	6	Yes	No
Sol Melia	3	1	4	No	No	7	3	2	Yes	No
TUI AG	4	1	5	Yes	No	5	-	5	Yes	No
NH Hoteles	2	1	5	Yes	Yes / No	6	1	6	Yes	Yes
Whitbread PLC	4	1	2	Yes	No	8	2	2	Yes	No
Millenium and Copthorne Hotels PLC	2	1	6	Yes	No	2	1	6	No	Yes
SAS Group	6	1	5	Yes	Yes	6	1	5	Yes	Yes
IFRS Panel	***4,25***	***1,63***	***4,63***			***5,63***	***1,50***	***4,38***		
Total	***4,29***	***1,64***	***4,00***			***5,00***	***1,43***	***3,36***		

Appendix 4: Number of Voluntary Segment Information Items – 2004 & 2005

2005	*Voluntary Segment Information*					
	LOB			Geographic areas		
	Average	**Max**	**min**	**Average**	**Max**	**min**
US GAAP Panel	0,17	1	-	0,17	1	-
IFRS Panel	9,14	27	-	4,33	18	-

2004	*Voluntary Segment Information*					
	LOB			Geographic areas		
	Average	**Max**	**min**	**Average**	**Max**	**min**
US GAAP Panel	0,50	2	-	-	1	-
IFRS Panel	3,75	23	-	2,75	8	-

Appendix 5: Ratios and indicators obtained from segment information – 2004 & 2005

	2005						2004					
	US GAAP Panel		IFRS Panel		Total		US GAAP Panel		IFRS Panel		Total	
	LOB %	Geo %	LOB %	Geo %	LOB %	Geo %	LOB %	Geo %	LOB %	Geo %	LOB %	Geo %
Profitability ratio : EBIT / Revenues	100%	0%	100%	50%	100%	29%	83%	0%	50%	25%	64%	14%
Profitability ratio : EBITDA / Revenues	100%	0%	88%	50%	93%	29%	83%	0%	50%	25%	64%	14%
Asset turnover : Asset / Revenues	100%	33%	88%	100%	93%	71%	100%	33%	63%	50%	79%	43%
Investment rate : investment / Revenues	83%	0%	75%	88%	79%	50%	67%	0%	38%	25%	50%	14%
Total Financial Ratios	**96%**	**8%**	**88%**	**72%**	**91%**	**45%**	**83%**	**8%**	**50%**	**31%**	**64%**	**21%**
Voluntary and/or hospitality disclosures												
Labor performance : Revenues / Number of employees	0%	0%	13%	13%	7%	7%	0%	0%	25%	0%	14%	0%
RevPAR	0%	0%	0%	0%	0%	0%	0%	0%	0%	0%	0%	0%
Occupancy Rate	0%	0%	0%	0%	0%	0%	0%	0%	0%	0%	0%	0%
EBITDAR	0%	0%	50%	25%	29%	14%	0%	0%	38%	13%	21%	7%
Total Voluntary and/or hospitality disclosures	**0%**	**0%**	**16%**	**9%**	**9%**	**5%**	**0%**	**0%**	**16%**	**3%**	**9%**	**2%**

References

Aitken, M., Hooper, C., & Pickering, J. (1997). Determinants of voluntary disclosure of segment information: A re-examination of the role of diversification strategy. *Accounting & Finance, 37*(1), 89-109.

Allioualla, S., & Laurin, C. (2002). L'impact d'une nouvelle norme en matière d'information sectorielle sur les prévisions des analystes financiers. *Comptabilité – Contrôle - Audit, Tome 8 - volume 1*, 69-88.

Ampofo, A. A., & Sellani, R. J. (2005). Examining the differences between United States Generally Accepted Accounting Principles (U. S. GAAP) and International Accounting Standards (lAS): implications for the harmonization of accounting standards. *Accounting Forum (Elsevier), 29*(2), 219-231.

Behn, B. K., Nichols, N. B., & Street, D. L. (2002). The Predictive Ability of Geographic Segment Disclosures by U. S. Companies: SFAS No. 131 vs. SFAS No. 14. *Journal of International Accounting Research, 1*, 31.

Berger, P. G., & Hann, R. (2003). The Impact of SFAS No. 131 on Information and Monitoring. *Journal of Accounting Research, 41*(2), 163-223.

Doupnik, T. S., & Seese, L. P. (2001). Geographic area disclosures under SFAS 131: materiality and fineness. *Journal of International Accounting, Auditing & Taxation, 10*(2), 117.

Editions-Francis-Lefebvre, & PWC. (2004). *IFRS 2005*: Editions Francis Lefebvre.

Ettredge, M. L., Soo Young, K., Smith, D. B., & Zarowin, P. A. (2005). The Impact of SFAS No. 131 Business Segment Data on the Market's Ability to Anticipate Future Earnings. *Accounting Review, 80*(3), 773-804.

FASB. (1997). Statement of Financial Accounting Standards No. 131 (Vol. FAS 131): FASB.

Glaum, M., & Street, D. L. (2003). Compliance with the Disclosure Requirements of Germany's New Market: IAS Versus US GAAP. *Journal of International Financial Management & Accounting, 14*(1), 64-100.

Gray, S. J. (1978). Segment Reporting and the EEC Multinationals. *Journal of Accounting Research, 16*(2), 242-253.

Gray, S. J., & Radebaugh, L. H. (1984). International Segment Disclosures by U. S. and U. K. Multinational Enterprises: A Descriptive Study. *Journal of Accounting Research, 22*(1), 351-360.

Herrmann, D. (1996). The Predictive Ability of Geographic Segment Information at the Country, Continent, and Consolidated Levels. *Journal of International Financial Management & Accounting, 7*(1), 50-73.

Herrmann, D., & Thomas, W. (1996). Segment reporting in the European Union: Analyzing the effects of country, size, industry and exchange listing. *Journal of International Accounting, Auditing & Taxation, 5*(1), 1.

Herrmann, D., & Thomas, W. B. (2000). An Analysis of Segment Disclosures under SFAS No. 131 and SFAS No. 14. *Accounting Horizons, 14*(3), 287-302.

Homölle, S. (2003). From the theory of financial intermediation to segment reporting: The case of German banks. *Accounting Forum, 27*(1), 60-83.

IASC. (1997). International Accounting Standard N°14 (Revised): Segment reporting: London: IASC.

Larson, R. K., & Street, D. L. (2004). Convergence with IFRS in an expanding Europe: progress and obstacles identified by large accounting firms' survey. *Journal of International Accounting, Auditing & Taxation, 13*(2), 89-119.

Leung, S., & Horwitz, B. (2004). Director Ownership and Voluntary Segment Disclosure: Hong Kong Evidence. *Journal of International Financial Management & Accounting, 15*(3), 235-260.

Leuz, C. (2003). IAS Versus U. S. GAAP: Information Asymmetry-Based Evidence from Germany's New Market. *Journal of Accounting Research, 41*(3), 445-472.

Link, K. W. (2003). Segment Reporting: Analysis of the Impact on the Banking Industry. *Journal of Bank Cost & Management Accounting, 16*(3), 34-40.

MKG-Consulting. (2005a). The 2005 ranking of hotel groups in the 25 European Union member states

—. (2005b). *MKG's 2005 world ranking of hotel groups.*

—. (2005c). *Ranking - Top Ten Worldwide Hotel Chains Growth 1995-2005.*

Nichols, N. B., & Street, D. L. (2007). The relationship between competition and business segment reporting decisions under the management approach of IAS 14 Revised. *Journal of International Accounting, Auditing & Taxation, 16*(1), 51-68.

Nichols, N. B., Street, D. L., & Gray, S. J. (2000). Geographic Segment Disclosures in the United States: Reporting Practices Enter A New Era. *Journal of International Accounting, Auditing & Taxation, 9*(1), 59-82.

Paul, J. W., & Largay III, J. A. (2005). Does the "management approach" contribute to segment reporting transparency? *Business Horizons, 48*(4), 303-310.

Prather-Kinsey, J., & Meek, G. K. (2004). The effect of revised IAS 14 on segment reporting by IAS companies. *European Accounting Review, 13*(2), 213-234.

Prencipe, A. (2004). Proprietary costs and determinants of voluntary segment disclosure: evidence from Italian listed companies. *European Accounting Review, 13*(2), 319-340.

PriceWaterhouseCoopers. (2005). *International Financial Reporting Standards Disclosure Checklist 2005*.

Seese, L. P., & Doupnik, T. S. (2003). The materiality of country-specific geographic segment disclosures. *Journal of International Accounting, Auditing & Taxation, 12*(2), 85-103.

Street, D. L. (2002). GAAP 2001 - Benchmarking national accounting standards against IAS: summary of results. *Journal of International Accounting, Auditing & Taxation, 11*, 77-90.

Street, D. L., & Gray, S. J. (2002). Factors influencing the extent of corporate compliance with International Accounting Standards: summary of a research monograph. *Journal of International Accounting, Auditing & Taxation, 11*, 51-76.

Street, D. L., & Nichols, N. B. (2002). LOB and geographic segment disclosures: an analysis of the impact of IAS 14 revised. *Journal of International Accounting, Auditing & Taxation, 11*(2), 91.

Street, D. L., Nichols, N. B., & Gray, S. J. (2000). Segment Disclosures under SFAS No. 131: Has Business Segment Reporting Improved? *Accounting Horizons, 14*(3), 259-285.

Tsakumis, G. T., Doupnik, T. S., & Seese, L. P. (2006). Competitive harm and geographic area disclosure under SFAS 131. *Journal of International Accounting, Auditing & Taxation, 15*(1), 32-47.

XERFI-IMA. (2005). Hotel groups in the world: FXI Research.

PART 6.

MANAGEMENT AND FINANCE

THE KNOWLEDGE STRUCTURE OF FRENCH MANAGEMENT CONTROL RESEARCH: A CITATION/CO-CITATION STUDY

TAWHID CHTIOUI[1] AND MARION SOULEROT[2]

Introduction

Management Control is often considered part of the academic field of accounting. However, in France, Bouquin and Pesqueux (1999) demonstrate that in the last decade Management Control became an independent academic discipline and field of research. In the same way, Chtioui and Soulerot (2006) use bibliometric analysis to show that French management control research is developing its own knowledge base, which differs from that of financial accounting and auditing.

Therefore, assuming that management control can be considered as a scientific discipline in itself, and which has reached a certain degree of maturity, it is important to reify and codify its existing knowledge using bibliometric analysis, as according to the custom for emerging areas of academic research (Ramos-Rodriguez and Ruiz-Navarro, 2004).

Using a set of published documents on management control and their bibliographic citations, this study investigates the knowledge structure of management control research in France. More specifically, this chapter aims to examine the impact of different types of publication, the extent of use of classic and non-accounting literature, as well as the impact of foreign and French journals. The networks that have contributed to the internal construction of management control theory are also examined.

This research relies on the use of bibliometric techniques, analysing 74 articles (3049 references) published in the French review "Comptabilité,

[1] ISEG Business School, France.
[2] IRMAPE- ESC Pau, France.

Contrôle, Audit"[3] (CCA) from its first publication in 1995 through to 2003.

The chapter is divided into three main sections. After brief definitions of the concept of knowledge and bibliometric techniques, section 1 focuses on a review of similar bibliometric studies in the field of accounting. Section 2 describes the methodology employed in collecting and analysing the data. Finally, section 3 presents the results of our investigation.

1. Literature Review

Bibliometric studies rely on different techniques (1.1) and have been widely used in accounting. The extent to which these kind of studies have been conducted are presented in order to contextualise our study (1.2.).

1.1. Identifying knowledge structure using bibliometric techniques

The development of knowledge in an academic discipline relies, essentially, on sharing ideas through articles published in research journals and books, and also in school manuals and professional journals. Thus, management control research depends heavily on the distribution of information through specialized publications. Advances in technology relating to the "automatic treatment of language" have encouraged the development of bibliometric methods, or tools that extract knowledge from textual data.

Bibliometry provides quantitative analyses of scientific knowledge. It is based on the premise that the number of times a text is cited demonstrates the impact it has had on the discipline (Brown and Gardner, 1985a). Virgo (1977) shows that, according to qualitative indices, texts judged as the most important are also those cited most often. Garfield (1973) notes that all the Nobel prizes awarded in 1972 were given to the top 0.1% of most cited scientists. However, numerous authors have criticized bibliometric analysis. Woodward and Hensen (1976) consider that published review articles are inclined to be cited more frequently than other forms of research. Ewing (1966) and Garfield (1979) believe that references can be cited for other reasons than for their influence. For example, some authors tend to cite each other, or colleagues in the same department, even if the contribution they have made to their work is minimal. Brown and Gardner

[3] "Accounting, Control, Auditing"

(1985b) say that the probability of a document being cited increases with the age of the text. However, despite these limits, many scientists view bibliometry as the most objective means of measuring the influence or importance of published research. Bibliometric studies use a variety of techniques of which the most important are:

- **Citation analysis**: this technique is based on the premise that authors cite documents they consider important to the development of their research. Therefore, frequently cited documents are likely to exert a greater influence on the discipline than those cited less frequently (Culnan, 1987; Sharplin and Mabry, 1985).
- **Co-citations analysis**: Small and Griffith (1974) developed co-citations analysis. Since then, this method has been used by researchers to examine the knowledge structures of certain disciplines. It was subsequently introduced to the field of accounting by Gamble and O'Doherty (1985a, 1985b). This technique involves analysing the frequency with which two citations appear together in a text. The approach is instrumental in identifying groups of authors, topics or methods and can help understand the way in which these clusters relate to each other (Pilkington and Liston-Heyes, 1999).

Considering the contribution that bibliometric techniques have made in identifying knowledge structures, they have been widely used in various disciplines, including: medicine (McMillan and Hamilton, 2000), urbanism (Matthiessen et Al., 2001), physics (Dieks and Chang, 1976), economics (Garcia-Castrillo et al., 2002), marketing (Hoffman and Holbrook, 1993; Pasadeos, 1985), and finance (Borokhovich, Bricker, and Simkins, 1994). To our knowledge, no bibliometric study has yet been carried out specifically on the field of management control, but has been carried out on accounting research.

1.2 Bibliometric studies in accounting research

Bibliometric studies are, in fact, carried out regularly for management and accounting research. They have been used in conjunction with several journals (*The Accounting Review*, *Strategic Management Review*, *Auditing: a Journal of Practice and Theory*, among others) and have served different purposes. We have observed that this research can be classified according to two criteria (Figure 1):

- The level of analysis: bibliometric studies concern the analysis of published articles and the analysis of references cited. The first helps to characterise scientific production, whereas the second makes it possible for us to identify factors that influence knowledge.

- The type of results: bibliometric studies can measure frequency and ranking (quantitative results). They also help to produce typologies or classifications (qualitative results).

Figure 1: Typology of bibliometric studies in financial accounting, management accounting and auditing

	Quantitative results	Qualitative results
Analysis of published articles	**Bibliometry as a tool for quantifying publications' usage**	**Bibliometry as a tool for the qualitative analysis of influence**
Analysis of cited references	**Bibliometry as a tool for quantifying influence**	**Bibliometry as a tool for identifying knowledge structures**

1.2.1 Bibliometry as a tool for quantifying influence

The first aspect of bibliometric tools consists of assessing the influence an article, an author, or a review has on the field of research by establishing some rankings. This influence can be statically measured: the ranking highlights the impact of several texts on a given subject during year N. The impact can also be measured dynamically when authors try to identify how that influence has evolved over a period of time. Krogstad and Smith (2003), for example, use citation analysis on 16 leading journals in accounting research to rank the 29 most cited articles published in *Auditing: A Journal of Practice and Theory*. By doing so, they explore both the impact and the standing of a review within a specific field of knowledge. Pilkington and Liston-Heyes (1999) present the citation frequency of both articles and the 42 most cited reviews in the *International Journal of Operations and Production Management* between 1994 and 1997. In this case, the aim of the article is to assess several disciplines contribution to the knowledge of one given field. In the same way, Krogstad and Smith (1984) use citation analysis within *Auditing: A Journal of Practice and Theory*. In 1988 and 1991, these authors introduced the notion of dynamic evolution, observing changes in the variety of disciplines that influenced this journal. The aim of Brown and

Gardner (1985a) was to measure the contribution of several journals and articles on accounting research produced from 1976 to 1982. Three periods were consequently identified, taking into account the first issues of each of the four journals studied. Authors could then demonstrate how the impact of each study had changed over the period 1976 to 1982. More than just demonstrating static rankings, Brown and Gardner (1985a), contribute to understanding the dynamic of influence for the four journals studied. Using their findings, they drew up a ranking of the most influential texts during that time period. Brown *et al.* (1987) also divided their period of study into three parts: 1976-1978, 1979-1981 and 1982-1984. In this way, they managed to identify how much the impact of *Accounting, Organization and Society* on other social science journals had changed. Furthermore, Heck and Bremser (1986) found it relevant to differentiate the contributions of authors published in *The Accounting Review* during the first sixty years of the journal by defining four time periods. More recently, Ramos-Rodríguez and Ruíz-Navarro (2004) ranked the 50 papers and the 10 journals most cited in the *Strategic Management Journal* between 1980 and 2000. Then they divided the period studied into three sub-periods in order to analyse possible changes in the frequency of citations.

Comparing results from the most influential research and authors, with different levels of analysis, enables us to assess the contribution made to a specific fields of research. Chung et al. (1992), for example, drew up a ranking of the 102 most cited authors in 14 accounting journals over the period 1968-1988. By looking at the academic origin of the most prolific authors, they concluded that more than a third of these authors came from seven doctorate programs. In a research article published in *The Accounting Review*, Brown and Gardner (1985b) also used citation analysis to assess accounting education, doctorate programs and individual contributions made to accounting research. They studied references cited in articles published in four journals from 1976 to 1982. In addition, several studies have highlighted links between where individuals gained their doctorate, academic affiliation and publications in various accounting journals (Bazley and Nikolai, 1975; Gamble and O'doherty, 1985; Heck and Bremser, 1986; Jacobs et al., 1986; Snowball, 1986; Weber and Stevenson, 1981; Williams, 1985). More recently, Judge et al. (2007) found that the journal citation rate, as well as the location of an article in a journal, both had a significant influence on the impact of an article.

1.2.2. Bibliometry as a tool for assessing the concentration of publications

Another use of bibliometric methods consists of measuring the number of contributions, or concentration of contributions made within a given field (Chung *et al.*, 1992) by using Lotka's general law[4]. Chung *et al.* (1992) tried to verify Lotka's law in 14 accounting journals. They concluded that knowledge production in accounting was less concentrated than it was in other sciences. Nevertheless, *The Accounting Review*, *Abacus* and *Journal of Accounting Research* appeared to be the most concentrated journals; in other words, the same authors are more frequent in these than in the *Journal of Accounting Education*, the *Journal of Accounting Literature* or the *Journal of Accounting, Auditing and Finance.*

1.2.3 Bibliometry as a tool for the qualitative analysis of influence

Going beyond simple quantitative measurements, some authors develop their bibliometric data further by carrying out qualitative analyses of the content of cited references. These studies contribute greatly to this research. Mizruchi and Fein (1999) used citation analysis as a tool to identify the number of quotes taken from the Di Maggio and Powell article[5]. Then they introduced a qualitative dimension by studying the articles that refer to Di Maggio and Powell. More specifically, they dealt with the way in which the three forms of isomorphism identified by Di Maggio and Powell had been reused in research material. To this end, citation analysis on articles published in six leading American journals from 1984 to 1995 led them to identify 160 texts quoting Di Maggio and Powell's article. Mizruchi and Fein (1999) noted that authors referring to this research, considered by some as the founding text in neo-institutional theory, focused mainly on mimetic isomorphism in favour of coercitive and normative mechanisms.

---

[4] Lotka A.J., (1926), "The Frequency Distribution of Scientific Productivity", *Journal of the Washington Academy of Sciences*, June

[5] DiMaggio P.J., Powell W.W., (1983), "The Iron Cage Revisited : Institutional Isomorphism and Collective Rationality in Organizational Fields", *American Sociological Review*, Vol. 48, pp. 147-160

1.2.4 Bibliometric studies as a tool for identifying knowledge structures

Combining these two aspects (quantitative and qualitative analysis) with a dynamic use of bibliometric tools allows us to demonstrate how a specific field of knowledge has evolved. Lord (1989) uses citation analysis to determine the most influential behavioural research in accounting. He then reconsiders his work from a historical perspective in order to explain the growth of the behavioural approach. Snowball (1986) takes a particular interest in studies that deal with accounting experiments on human judgment. In the first part of his article the author identifies different types of text in four journals. He then uses citation analysis to establish the impact of several fields, journals, articles, authors and institutions on this given field between 1964 and 1984. However, this article relies on a "manual" counting of studies made in this specific area: the authors themselves decided whether the articles should be included in the field of study or not.

Boissin et al. (1999) used co-citation analysis to define the structure of French research in the area of Strategy. This co-citation analysis was based on 249 articles published between 1990 and 1995 in seven journals. This first step led to the identification of 34 co-citation networks. When looking at the content of studies conducted within each network, authors, first of all, determined external networks linked directly with the area of Strategy, then networks which contributed to the internal construction of the field's theoretical background and finally, networks which were connected with one of the four themes dealt with in fields of Strategy. From a historical perspective, this sequencing enables us to understand the different steps that have led to the current structure of Strategy research in France. Ramos-Rodríguez and Ruíz-Navarro (2004) also presents a "map" of the knowledge structure in the area of Strategy, which appears in the *Strategic Management Journal* over the period 1980-2000. This was followed by a set of two "maps" representing sub-periods in order to identify changes in this field of research. With regards to Pilkington and Liston-Heyes (1999), they conclude that there is no distinct research field for Production Management; on the one hand, major journals and the most influential works belong to other disciplines, while on the other hand, articles that are specific to the field tend to be spread throughout various co-citation groups.

2. Methodology

In order to achieve our objective of identifying a knowledge structure in French Management Control research, we have chosen to limit our study to a group of French Management Control studies published in *CCA* over nine years. The *CCA* journal was selected on the basis of its prominence in the field of accounting (Management Control, financial accounting, and auditing), as the best ranked French journal in this field according to the National Committee for Scientific Research.

The next step was to find an impartial analysis tool: bibliometric analysis.

2.1 The database

A long and thorough process has been undertaken to collect data for building a reliable database. Data was gathered from the analysis of 74 articles published in *CCA* from its first publication in 1995 to the last issue edited at the time this study was started (November 2003)[6]. This lengthy process was implemented in three steps:

- Creation of the database using Microsoft Access.
- Data collation from the 74 article's references: bibliometric studies of Anglo-Saxon journals often use previously constructed databases such as SSCI (Social Science Citation Index), GCI (Genetic Citation Index), SCI (Science Citation Index) or AHCI (Arts and Humanities Citation Index). As none of them register French journals, we needed to enter data manually. *CCA*'s articles have been arranged according to financial accounting, Management Control or auditing issues. When an article could be classified as belonging to more than one field, we chose the dominant one. At the end of these two steps, we obtained a folder containing 3049 citations.
- The third step consisted of verifying data captured by homogenizing the citations. We only kept the first edition for books which had several revised versions and we deleted redundant texts. This step has been crucial to guarantee the reliability of results obtained through the data analysis.

[6] This is composed of 9 volumes (18 issues) and 4 special issues

2.2 The analysis techniques

In order to research the database, we created SQL requests. These requests enabled us to manipulate the database, to show the citation analyses results and to build the co-citations matrix.

- The citation analyses were based on the average citation rate per published article. In fact, Garfield (1972), in considering the relationship between the number of articles and citation frequency, suggests discounting the effect of size by calculating relative impact. He divides the number of citations by the number of articles published during a specific period. "*The impact-factor will thus reflect an average citation rate per published article.*" (Garfield, 1972, p. 476).
- The co-citations were set out in a table of the 20 most cited references. This led to the creation of a 20 by 20 co-citations matrix (Appendix 1). The diagonal elements were computed by taking the three highest intersections for each document and dividing by two so as to reflect the importance of a particular document within the field. In doing so, we followed the procedures recommended by White and Griffith (1981) and reported by Pilkington and Liston-Heyes (1999). In the next step, the raw co-citation matrix was factor-analysed using varimax rotation. The factor analysis summarizes the correlation structure of data, by identifying inherent factors explaining a maximum part of the variability of data. The orthogonal varimax rotation attempts to refine the interpretation of factors by fitting the maximum number of documents in the minimum number of factors.

3. Results

The data analysis began by classifying citations into different types of publication (Figure 2). This was followed by dividing them into classic and recent citations (Figure 3) and by categorizing the journal citations into foreign or French and accounting or non-accounting journals (Figures 4, 5 and 6). Finally, the co-citations matrix was analysed and factors illustrating the different networks were presented (Figures 7 and 8, Appendix 2).

3.1 The impact of the different types of publications cited

Figure 2 shows the distribution of works cited by source type. The book category is interpreted rather broadly, and includes collections of books and articles. The "other documents" category includes dissertations, and reports.

Two points are appropriate here. The first relates to the strong impact of books on French Management Control research (an average of 16 book citations per article, representing 40% of the total number of citations). Moreover, the top 10 cited documents are all books, a trend which is noticeably different to that of French financial accounting or auditing research (Chtioui and Soulerot, 2006). This can be explained by the emergent character of Management Control as a distinct management discipline. Because this discipline is emerging, researchers still need to resort regularly to academic books that explain universally understood and widely accepted rules and concepts.

The second point deals with the high impact of doctoral theses (about 2 theses cited per article) despite being less accessible to scholars in electronic form. These represent 95% of French doctoral thesis on Management Control. Assuming that scholars prefer to cite published papers and books derived from doctoral research rather than actual theses (Lariviere et al., 2006), we have questioned why Management Control theses are not often used in publications. A possible explanation could be that French theses on Management Control are relatively long (more than 300 pages), and are not constructed as three articles as in the case of the Anglo-Saxon model. Extracting articles from theses, therefore, requires a lengthy process of editing and rewriting. A second possible reason is that they tend to explore more conceptual and theoretical frameworks, which is useful for other researchers, particularly if similar works don't exist elsewhere.

Figure 2: Impact Factors of the different types of publication

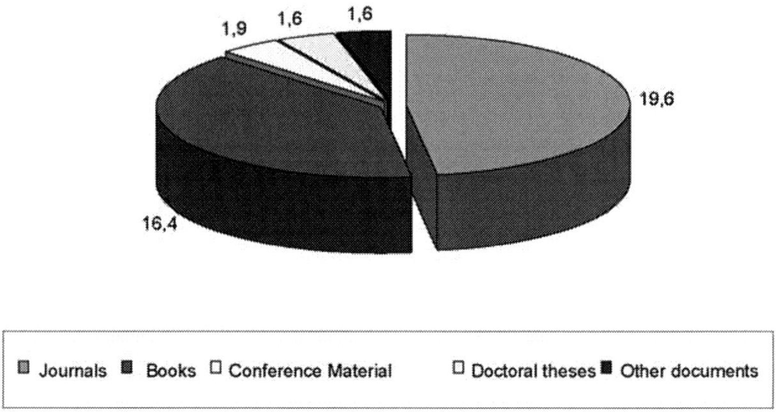

3.2 The knowledge preservation in Management Control research

Figure 3 illustrates the distribution of classic and recent citations divided according to the year the citing article was published. By classic citations, we mean those published before 1985 and by recent citations, those published from 1985 onwards. The choice of 1985 is due to the fact that this period is considered as a key phase for the history of Management Control teaching and research in France. In fact, Bouquin and Pesqueux (1999) believe that the 1980s were characterised, in France, by the assimilation of a technical model of Management Control and that it is only in the 1990s that Management Control moved beyond this instrumental approach to a more managerial one. They consider that this change was confirmed by the publication of R.N. Anthony's book, "*The Management Control Function*" in 1988.

As figure 3 shows, Management Control researchers tend to cite classic texts more and more infrequently. In fact, pre-1985 citations changed from 43% of the total citations in 1995 to 15% in 2003. If this rate of change were to continue, (see projection in Figure 3), the earliest Management Control knowledge could become forgotten in future generations. This result confirms the conclusion drawn by Bricker (1988) concerning accounting research. The first explanation is closely linked to the impact of Anthony's work and, as Bouquin and Pesqueux (1999) conclude, this book marked a change in accounting research, rendering past works inconsistent with the theoretical framework proposed. In this context, the accumulation of knowledge has become less important, and new references have to be used in order to tackle fresh issues. Secondly, the social aspects of citation networks need to be taken into account. In fact, as we have pointed out, authors often cite researchers from within their own network, which has the added effect of increasing the use of contemporary literature in favour of older literature.

Figure 3: Distribution of classic and recent citations according to year

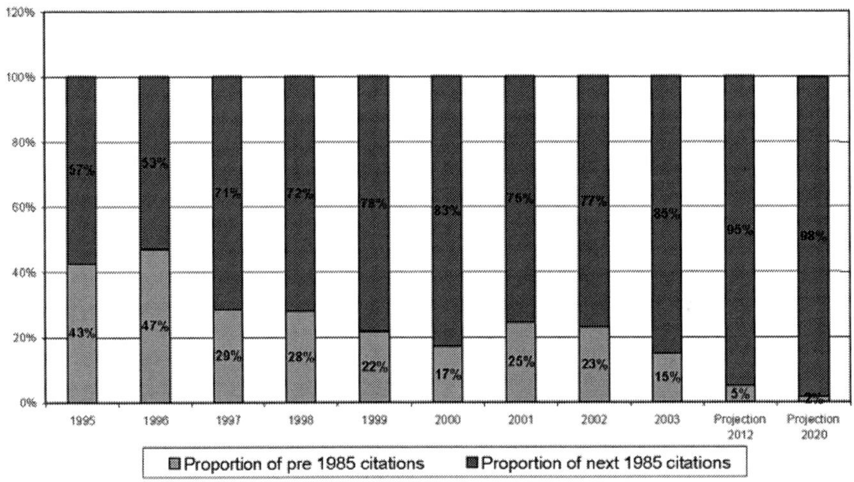

3.3 The impact of foreign and non-accounting journals on Management Control research

Further analysis of our results highlights two other interesting findings:

- For example, we noticed that foreign journals (Impact-factor equal to 14.5) have a much stronger impact on Management Control research than French journals (Impact-factor equal to 5.15). However, the analysis of the change in these factors from 1995 to 2003 (Figure 4) indicates that this difference between foreign and French literature will reduced steadily, especially for accounting journals (Figure 4).

Figure 4: Impact of Foreign and French Journals according to year

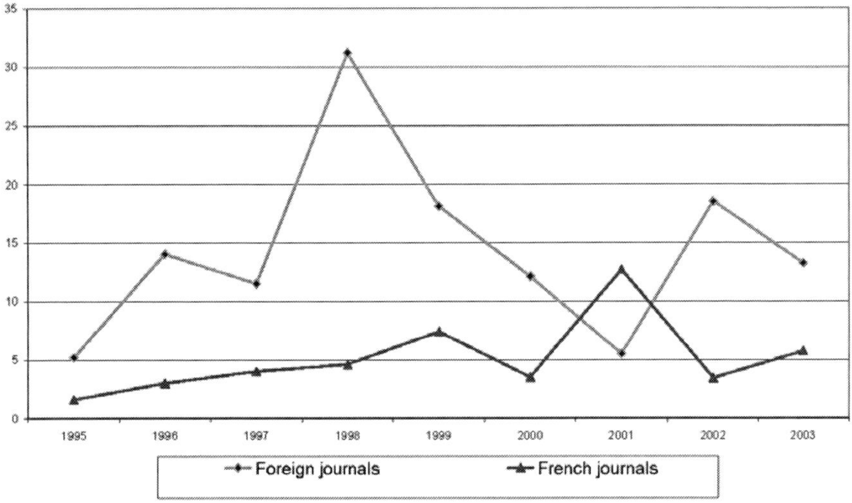

- Another example concerns the distribution of accounting and non-accounting journals cited in the 74 articles sampled. Our analysis demonstrates that these two types of journal have an exactly equal impact on Management Control research for the 9 year study period. In Figure 5, we can observe the segmentation by year of their impact-factors. This shows us that, overall, the two curves have the same tendency and that the small fluctuations are due to foreign journals (Figure 5).
- Finally, we can identify a steady amount of knowledge of Management Control coming from French and non-accounting research. The use of foreign accounting literature is less steady. This may be due to the fact that French speaking researchers find it difficult to read works in a foreign language.

Figure 5: Impact of Accounting and Non-accounting Journals segmented by year

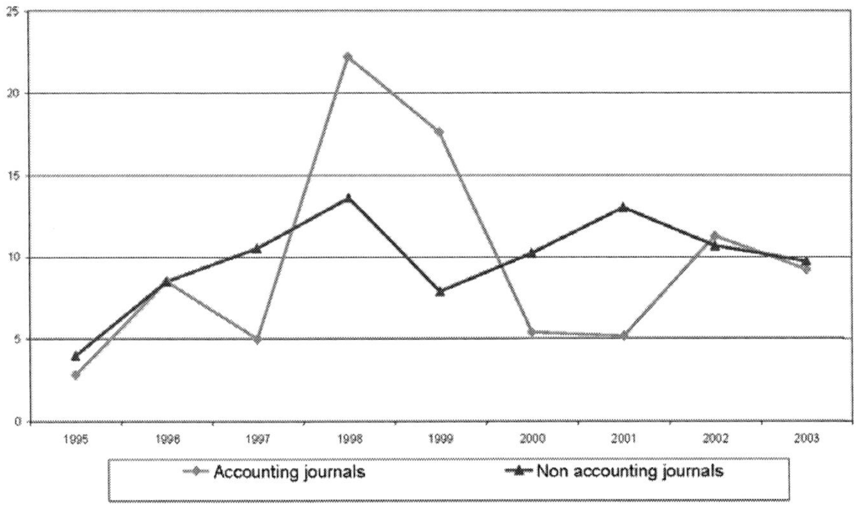

Figure 6: Impact of the different types of journal according to year

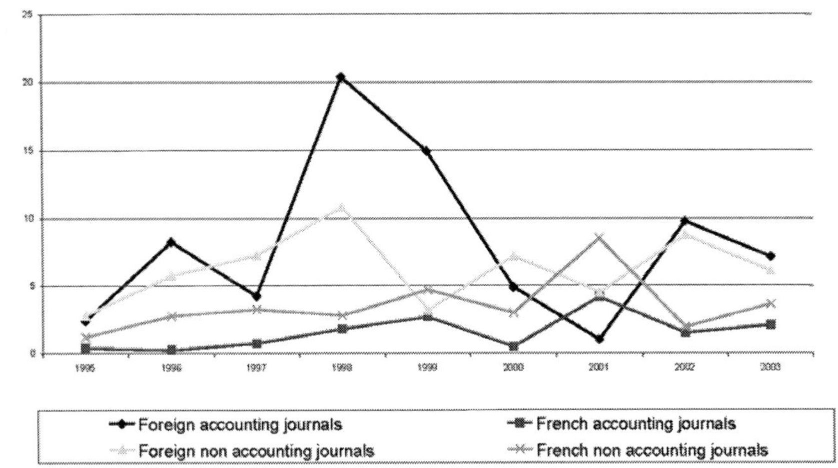

3.4 Research streams within Management Control

In this section, the focus will be on specific areas of research in the field of Management Control and on how author co-citation maps can provide a means of visualising and organising the literature in a more intuitive way. This analysis is based on the co-citation matrix.

The co-citation matrix factor analysis allows us to determine which documents can be grouped and, therefore, which ones share a common thread. The results are shown in Figures 7 and 8, and are represented by a scatter plot of variables obtained from the factor analysis. Three factors are retained and presented and together they demonstrate 69% total variance. To interpret these factors, we only use the variables whose factorial score is higher than 0.5, as is common for such analyses. Thus, variables which are located around the origin of factorial plans are not significant for the interpretation of results. All details and tables coming from this analysis are presented in Appendix 2.

Figure 7 shows the variables on the factorial plan composed by the first two factors. The first factor (component 1) is explained by two groups of citations:

- The first (the blue circle on the left) is composed of three doctoral theses in accounting history.
- The second (the green circle on the right) is composed of three books on the fundamentals of Management Control.

If we were to give this factor a definition, on the basis of our own interpretation of the documents with high associated loadings, we might say the evolution of Management Control practice within the organizations. This gives us two opposite groups: the first focuses on the technical dimensions of Management Control and the second represents the managerial dimensions.

The second factor (Component 2) is represented by the five references shown by red squares at the top of the graph (we can also see these references in Figure 8, at the right hand side of the graph). These documents discuss management accounting themes.

Figure 8 presents the variables on the factorial plan composed by factors 2 and 3. Component 3 is represented by the purple pentagon group of references at the top of the graph which are, to a certain extent, all related to organizational dimensions.

Figure 7: First Factorial Plan

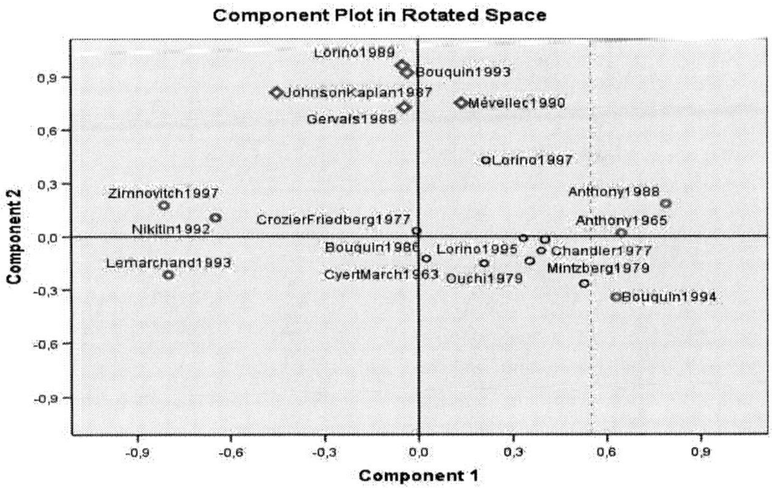

Figure 8: Second Factorial Plan

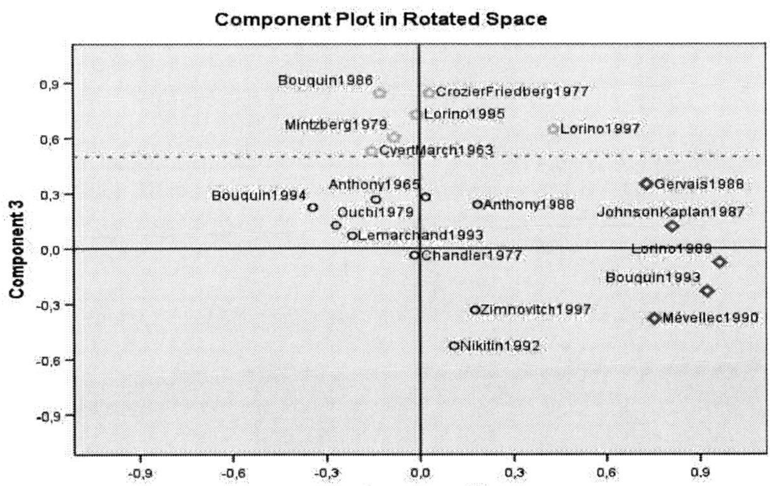

Conclusion

For a number of years, we have noticed an increasing interest in bibliometric studies. This interest responds to the concerns of researchers whose objective it is to measure scientific activity results. Using citation and co-citation analysis, we have attempted to identify and statistically validate the knowledge structure of French Management Accounting research.

The results show that Management Control has succeeded in creating its own boundaries and a well-characterized knowledge structure, even if being established as an entirely separate discipline will require a little more time.

Co-citation analyses highlight three streams of Management Control research: the first is associated with organizational structure and theories, the second is linked with the evolution of Management Control practice, and the third relates to managerial tools and management accounting. However, it is necessary to note the absence of a methodological dimension which can be considered as a sign of maturity for a discipline.

Citation analysis concerns the impact of literature on Management Control research: the results are marked by a strong impact by books, weak influence by classic and foreign texts, and equal impact between accounting and non-accounting cited journals.

However, even if the quantitative aspect of bibliometry, based on a scientific approach, are attractive because of their precision and objectivity, it is important to note that the educational characteristics of this approach attract much criticism. In fact, the use of numbers and statistical methods for the analysis of textual information can be considered insufficient.

More sophisticated analysis of citation and co-citation techniques could be used in future works and the potential of these techniques and the database used have not yet been exhausted. Finally, a wider study, which includes a significant sample of texts and reviews, could lead to a better assessment of the knowledge structure of Management Control research.

References

Anthony, R.N. (1988) *The Management Control Function*. Boston, The Harvard Business School Press.

Bazley, J.D. and Nikolai, L.A. (1975) 'A Comparison of Published Accounting Research and Qualities of Accounting Faculty and Doctoral Programs', *The Accounting Review*, 50(3), pp. 605-609.

Boissin, J.-P., Castagnos, J.-C., Guieu, G. and De Looze, M.-A. (1999) 'La structuration de la recherche francophone en stratégie: une analyse bibliographique', *Finance Contrôle Stratégie*, 2(3), pp. 63-85.

Bouquin, H. and Pesqueux, Y. (1999) 'Vingt ans de contrôle de gestion ou le passage d'une technique à une discipline', *Comptabilité Contrôle Audit*, 5(11), pp. 93-106.

Bricker, R.J. (1988) 'Knowledge Preservation in Accounting: A Citation Study', *Abacus*, 24(2), pp. 20-131.

—. (1989) 'An Empirical Investigation of the Structure of Accounting Research', *Journal of Accounting Research*, 27(2), pp. 246-262.

Brown, L.D., Gardner, J.C and Vasarhelyi, M.A. (1987) 'An Analysis of the Research Contributions of *Accounting, Organization and Society*, 1976-1984', *Accounting, Organization and Society*, 12(2), pp. 193-204.

Brown, L.D., Gardner, J.C and Vasarhelyi, M.A. (1989) 'Attributes of Articles Impacting Contemporary Accounting Literature', *Contemporary Accounting Research*, 5(2), pp. 793-815.

Brown, L.D. and Gardner, J.C. (1985a) 'Using Citation Analysis to Assess the Impact of Journals and articles on Contemporary Accounting Research', *Journal of Accounting Research*, 20(1), pp. 84-109.

Brown, L.D. and Gardner, J.C. (1985b) 'Applying Citation Analysis to Evaluate the Research Contributions of Accounting Faculty and Doctoral Programs', *The Accounting Review*, 60(2), pp. 262-277.

Chtioui, T. and Soulerot, M. (2006) 'Quelle structure des connaissances dans la recherche française en comptabilité, contrôle et audit? Une étude bibliométrique de la revue CCA sur la période 1995-2004', *Comptabilité-Contrôle-Audit*, 12(1), pp. 7-25.

Chung, K.H., Pak, H.S. and Cox, R.A.K. (1992) 'Patterns of Research Output in the Accounting Literature: A Study of the Bibliometric Distributions', *Abacus*, 28(2), pp. 168-185.

Culnan, M. (1986) 'The intellectual development of management information systems', *Management Science*, 32, pp. 156-72.

Dickman, T.R. and Zeff, S.A. (1984) 'Two Decades of the *Journal of Accounting Research'*, *Journal of Accounting Research*, 22(1), pp. 225-297.

Gamble, G.O. and O'Doherty, B. (1985a) 'How Accounting Academicians Can Use Citation Indexing and Analysis for research', *Journal of Accounting Education*, 123-44.

Gamble, G.O. and O'Doherty, B. (1985b) 'Citation Indexing and its Uses in Accounting: An Awareness Survey and Departmental Ranking', *Issues in Accounting Education,* 3, pp. 28-40.

Garfield, E. (1973) 'Citation and Distinction', *Nature*, 242, p. 485.

—. (1972) 'Citation Analysis as a Tool in Journal Evaluation', *Science,* 178, pp. 471-79.

Grundstein, M. (1994) 'Développer un système à base de connaissances: un effort de coopération pour construire en commun un objet inconnu'. Actes de la journée « *Innovation pour le travail en groupe* », Cercle pour les Projets Innovants en Informatique (CP2I), novembre 1994.

Heck, J.L. and Bremser, W.G. (1986), 'Six Decades of *The Accounting Review*: A Summary of Author and Institutional Contributors', *The Accounting Review*, 61(4), pp. 735-744.

Jacobs, F.A., Hartgraves, A.A. and Beard, L.H. (1986), 'Publication Productivity of Doctoral Alumni: A Time-Adjusted Model', *The Accounting Review*, 61(1), 179-187.

Judge, T.A., Cable, D.M., Colbert, A.E. and Rynes, S.L. (2007) 'What causes a management article to be cited – article, author, or journal?', *Academy of Management Journal*, 50(3), pp. 491-506.

Krogstad, J.L. and Smith, G. (2003) 'Assessing the Influence of *Auditing: A Journal of Practice and Theory*: 1985-2000', *Auditing: A Journal of Practice and Theory*, 22(1), pp. 195-204.

Krogstad, J.L., Smith, G. (1984) 'Impact of Sources and Authors on *Auditing: A Journal of Practice and Theory* a Citation Analysis', *Auditing: A Journal of Practice and Theory*, 4(1), pp. 107-117.

Krogstad, J.L. and Smith, G. (1988) 'A Taxonomy of Content and Citations in *Auditing: A Journal of Practice and Theory*', *Auditing: A Journal of Practice and Theory*, 8(1), pp. 108-117.

Krogstad, J.L. and Smith, G. (1991) 'Sources and Uses of *Auditing: A Journal of Practice and Theory*'s Literature: The first Decade', *Auditing: A Journal of Practice and Theory*, 10(2), pp. 84-97.

Larivière, V., Zuccala, A. and Archembault, E. (2006) 'The thesis paradox: An empirical study of the impact of doctoral research', Paper presented at the 9th International Science and Technologies Indicators Conference, 7-9 September, Leuven, Belgium.

Merchant, K.A., Van Der Stede, W.A. and Zheng, L. (2003) 'Disciplinary Constraints on the Advancement of Knowledge: The Case of Organizational Incentive Systems', *Accounting, Organization and Society*, 28(2), pp. 251-286.

Mizruchi, M.S. and Fein, L.C. (1999) 'The Social Construction of Organizational Knowledge: A Study of the Uses of Coercive, Mimetic, and Normative Isomorphism', *Administrative Science Quarterly*, 44, pp. 653-683.

Pilkington, A. and Liston-Heyes, C. (1999) 'Is Production and Operations Management a Discipline? A Citation/Co-Citation Study', *International Journal of Operations and Production Management*, 19(1), pp. 7-20.

Ramos-Rodríguez, A.-R. and Ruíz-Navarro, J. (2004) 'Changes in the intellectual structure of strategic management research: a bibliometric study of the *Strategic Management Journal*, 1980-2000', *Strategic Management Journal*, 25(10), pp. 981-1004.

Sharplin, A. and Mabry, R. (1985) 'The relative importance of journals used in management research: an alternative ranking', *Human Relations*, 38, pp. 139-49.

Small, H. and Griffith, B.C. (1974) 'The structure of Scientific Literatures: Identifying and Mapping Specialties', *Science Studies,* 4, pp. 17-40.

Snowball, D. (1986) 'Accounting Laboratory Experiments on Human Judgment: Somme Characteristics and influences', *Accounting, Organization and Society*, 11(1), pp. 47-69.

Subotnik, D. (1991) 'Knowledge Preservation in Accounting': Does It Deserve to be Preserved?', *Abacus*, 27(1), pp. 65-71.

Virgo, J.A. (1977) 'A Statistical Procedure for evaluating the importance of scientific papers', *Library Quarterly,* 47 (4), pp. 415-430.

Weber, R.P. and Stevenson, W.C. (1981) 'Evaluations of Accounting Journal and Department Quality', *The Accounting Review*, 56(3), pp. 596-612.

White, H.D. and Griffith, B.C. (1981) 'Author co-citation: a literature measure of intellectual structure', *Journal of the American Society of Information Science*, 32(3), pp. 63-71.

Williams, P.F. (1985) 'A Descriptive Analysis of Authorship in *The Accounting Review'*, *The Accounting Review*, 60(2), pp. 300-313.

Appendix 1: The co-citation matrix

Citations	Bouquin1993	Bouquin1986	Johnson&Kaplan1987	Anthony1988	Crozier&Friedberg1977	Lorino1989	Lorino1995	Gervais1988	Mintzberg1979	Ouchi1980	Zimnovitch1997	Nikitin1992	Lorino1997	Anthony1965	Ouchi1979	Lemarchand1993	Cyert&March1963	Bouquin1994	Chandler1977	Mévellec1990
Bouquin1993	12	1	9	5	3	9	3	6	3	3	4	5	3	3	3	0	2	1	2	5
Bouquin1986	1	9	5	5	6	3	5	6	6	3	2	0	6	5	6	5	3	2	2	0
JohnsonKaplan1987	9	5	11	1	2	7	4	3	1	0	4	4	3	1	1	2	1	0	2	2
Anthony1988	5	5	1	8	2	3	5	2	2	3	0	1	4	6	3	0	1	5	4	3
CrozierFriedberg1977	3	6	2	2	8	0	6	3	2	1	1	0	2	0	1	0	3	2	1	0
Lorino1989	9	3	7	3	0	10	0	4	1	0	1	1	2	1	0	0	0	0	0	4
Lorino1995	3	5	4	5	6	0	8	1	5	1	0	0	3	3	0	0	3	5	2	1
Gervais1988	6	6	3	2	3	4	1	8	1	0	1	0	3	1	0	0	2	0	1	4
Mintzberg1979	3	6	1	2	2	1	5	1	8	4	0	0	1	2	3	0	1	3	0	1
Ouchi1980	3	3	0	3	1	0	1	0	4	7	0	1	1	2	5	0	2	2	1	0
Zimnovitch1997	4	2	4	0	1	1	0	1	0	0	8	7	0	0	0	4	0	0	1	2
Nikitin1992	5	0	4	1	0	1	0	0	0	1	7	8	0	1	1	4	1	1	2	1
Lorino1997	3	6	3	4	2	2	3	3	1	1	0	0	7	3	0	0	0	1	1	1
Anthony1965	3	5	1	6	0	1	3	1	2	2	0	1	3	7	3	0	2	2	3	1
Ouchi1979	3	6	1	3	1	0	0	0	3	5	0	1	0	3	7	0	1	1	1	0
Lemarchand1993	0	5	2	0	0	0	0	0	0	0	4	4	0	0	0	7	0	0	0	0
CyertMarch1963	2	3	1	1	3	0	3	2	1	2	0	1	0	2	1	0	5	2	1	0
Bouquin1994	1	2	0	5	2	0	5	0	3	2	0	1	1	2	1	0	2	7	3	1
Chandler1977	2	2	2	4	1	0	2	1	0	1	1	2	1	3	1	0	1	3	5	1
Mévellec1990	5	0	2	3	0	4	1	4	1	0	2	1	1	1	0	0	0	1	1	7

Appendix 2: SPSS Output – Factor Analysis

Total Variance Explained

	Component	Initial Eigen-values (a)			Rotation Sums of Squared Loadings		
		Total	% of Variance	Cumulative %	Total	% of Variance	Cumulative %
Raw	1	33.731	34.140	34.140	19.850	20.091	20.091
	2	23.555	23.841	57.982	29.231	29.586	49.677
	3	10.871	11.003	68.984	19.075	19.307	68.984
	4	8.347	8.449	77.433			
	5	7.318	7.407	84.840			
	6	5.498	5.564	90.404			
	7	2.865	2.899	93.304			
	8	2.404	2.433	95.737			
	9	1.164	1.178	96.915			
	10	.775	.784	97.699			
	11	.742	.751	98.451			
	12	.588	.595	99.045			
	13	.385	.390	99.435			
	14	.225	.228	99.663			
Re-scaled	1	33.731	34.140	34.140	4.300	21.501	21.501
	2	23.555	23.841	57.982	4.099	20.495	41.996
	3	10.871	11.003	68.984	4.026	20.128	62.124
	4	8.347	8.449	77.433			
	5	7.318	7.407	84.840			
	6	5.498	5.564	90.404			
	7	2.865	2.899	93.304			
	8	2.404	2.433	95.737			
	9	1.164	1.178	96.915			
	10	.775	.784	97.699			
	11	.742	.751	98.451			
	12	.588	.595	99.045			
	13	.385	.390	99.435			
	14	.225	.228	99.663			

Extraction Method: Principal Component Analysis.

a) When analyzing a co-variance matrix, the initial eigen-values are the same across the raw and re-scaled solutions.

Rotated Component Matrix (a)

	Raw			Re-scaled		
	Component			Component		
	1	2	3	1	2	3
Bouquin1993		2.758			.922	
Bouquin1986			1.991			.843
JohnsonKaplan1987	-1.327	2.386		-.451	.811	
Anthony1988	1.664			.789		
CrozierFriedberg1977			1.827			.844
Lorino1989		2.981			.963	
Lorino1995	.793		1.728	.333		.726
Gervais1988		1.691	.812		.729	.350
Mintzberg1979	.817		1.265	.390		.603
Ouchi1980	.970			.528		
Zimnovitch1997	-1.918		-.788	-.813		-.334
Nikitin1992	-1.553		-1.272	-.646		-.529
Lorino1997		.824	1.243		.429	.647
Anthony1965	1.243			.646		
Ouchi1979	.755			.352		
Lemarchand1993	-1.699			-.799		
CyertMarch1963			.661			.528
Bouquin1994	1.165	-.635		.630	-.344	
Chandler1977	.526			.402		
Mévellec1990		1.416	-.717		.753	-.381

Extraction Method: Principal Component Analysis.
Rotation Method: Varimax with Kaiser Normalization.
a) Rotation converged in 5 iterations.

Component Transformation Matrix

Component	1	2	3
1	-.511	.755	-.412
2	.488	.649	.584
3	-.708	-.097	.700

Extraction Method: Principal Component Analysis.
Rotation Method: Varimax with Kaiser Normalization.

ANALYSIS OF MANAGERS' USE OF MANAGEMENT ACCOUNTING

WALID CHEFFI[1] AND ADEL BELDI[2]

1. Introduction

The manager[3] is supposed to undertake diverse organizational roles: informational, decisional, and relational. The success of the manager in playing these roles is vital for any organization (Mintzberg, 1989). To do so, this actor uses several tools, among them management accounting. A manager, according to Anthony (1988), is someone who must achieve results that are in general expressed by objectives in the form of figures and dates. Hence management accounting has to produce information that must be diversified and global in order to be used by different managers. The majority of researchers agree on three functions of management accounting: 1) providing information on results and past performance, 2) facilitating decision-making, and 3) orienting the behaviour of others in the expected direction (Burchell et al., 1980; Anthony, 1988; Mellemvik et al., 1988; Macintosh and Scapens, 1990; Sprinkle, 2003; ven Veen-Dirks, 2009). Nevertheless these roles are more assumed than demonstrated at the level of the individual manager (Hall, 2009). Certain authors severely criticize the inability of management accounting to aid managers in their decision-making (Sillince and Sykes, 1995; Ahrens and Dent, 1998). So far, few studies have investigated accounting practice according to managers' own perceptions, or the importance of each role of accounting for these actors (Wiersma, 2009). Several theories and paradigms have been used to understand the roles of accounting within organizations (contingence theory, strategic management). This paper adheres to a less

[1] Department of Accounting, Control and Information Management, Rouen Business School, France.
[2] Department of Finance, Auditing and Control, IESEG School of Management Lille-Paris, France.
[3]A manager is an organizational player who has responsibility for an organization, or for one of the entities within it. He has also been given formal authority.

conventional perspective. It contributes to "alternative perspectives on accounting" (Baxter and Chua, 2003), by mobilizing Giddens' structuration theory (ST). We believe that the three dimensions suggested in Giddens' structuration theory (signification, domination, and legitimation) help in understanding managers' use of management accounting information. This study aims to provide an analysis of managers' use of management accounting information in their daily business life. This paper, based on the analysis of the discourse of twenty-five managers in large French companies, provides evidence that management accounting is mainly used to legitimate decisions and to dominate others. Our results question the assumption in the literature that management accounting is used by managers to build representations of managerial situations and for decision-making.

Our paper is organized as follows. Section 2 briefly presents the theoretical framework. It shows how structuration theory provides the elements for the understanding of the management accounting use.

Section 3 sets out the methodology deployed in this study. Section 4 interprets the discourses of managers regarding the use of management accounting. The paper concludes with a discussion of the findings and a statement of the main contributions.

2. Theoretical framework

The three dimensions of structuration theory

A detailed exposition of the concepts of structuration theory has been provided by several authors (Macintosh, 1994; Macintosh and Scapens, 1991). Our aim in this paper is to explain how the main concepts of ST will be relevant to understanding the use by managers of management accounting.

According to Giddens, ST is concerned with the relationship between agents' actions and social structures in the production, reproduction, and regulation of social order. Social structures are defined as rules including codes of signification or the constitution of meaning (signification structures), normative elements (legitimation structures) and command over allocative and authorative resources that enable the exercise of power (domination structures).

Signification

Social systems have structures. Structures include codes of signification or the constitution of meaning. The construction of signification necessitates a system of interpretive schemes by which agents communicate with and understand each other. Interpretive schemes are the cognitive means by which each actor makes sense of what others say and do. The system of signification corresponds to the mutual knowledge shared by individuals and diffused via communication actions.

Domination

Giddens considers that agents have the ability at the level of interaction to exercise influence and draw on facilities or resources of power. He identifies two types of power resources: command over allocative resources and command over authoritative resources. The study of the forms of domination in the organizational context is part of the traditional field of research on control practices within organizations (Burchell et al., 1980). For instance, the determining of responsibility centres (authority resources), and their budgets (allocation resources) enters into this framework. Moreover, in the context of the delegation of responsibilities and the decentralizing of the decision-making process, the budget is still viewed by managers as a device for controlling delegation, of which they find themselves the guardians' *vis-à vis* top management (Abernethy and Brownell, 1999; Otley and Pollanen, 2000; Van Der Stede, 2001).

Legitimation

Legitimation structures consist of the normative rules and moral obligations of a social system. They constitute the shared set of values and ideals about what is important and should happen in social settings (Macintosh, 1994). Accounting is in fact a device that actors interpret using diverse representations and frames of reference. Moreover, accounting cannot be disassociated from the representations of the different actors (Dent, 1991; Boland, 1993).

The usefulness and dissemination of structuration theory in management accounting research

For more than 20 years, Giddens' theory of structuration has been proposed as a useful means of conducting alternative management accounting research (see Baxter and Chua, 2003).

ST "has created a small but distinctive contribution to alternative management accounting research" (Baxter and Chua, 2003, p.100), whilst Giddens' work has fostered some meta-theoretical debates in the AOS journal (Boland, 1996; Scapens and Macinstosh, 1996). Previous research shows that ST has not yet revealed all its usefulness for understanding and analysing accounting roles within an organization (Macintosh and Scapens, 1996; Baxter and Chua, 2003; Englund and Gerdin, 2007; Coad and Herbert, 2009). This paper extends the research employing this theory by focusing on the study of management accounting in action at a managerial level. This is particularly important because the analysis of managers' use of accounting remains critically under-represented in the literature (Hall, 2010). We believe, as do other authors (Roberts and Scapens, 1985, Ahrens and Chapman, 2002), that an explicit use of Giddens' structuration theory is useful to emphasize the production and reproduction of accounting practices through their use by managers. We believe that using some concepts of ST might provide clearer insights into the role of management accounting in everyday management. Roberts and Scapens (1985) and Macintosh and Scapens (1990) argue that management accounting represent modalities of structuration in the three dimensions of signification, legitimation, and domination.

Below, we will present a series of managers' actions drawn from our fieldwork seeking to draw on the use of management accounting information through the three dimensions of ST.

3. Research Method

The objectives of this study were addressed using in-depth interviews that facilitated obtaining managers' perceptions directly. The method adopted may be classified as a cross-sectional field study (Lillis and Mundy, 2005). Our field concerned managers operating in large French companies. This study is of an interpretive nature. We follow Ryan et al. (2002), who note that the case selection criteria should be governed by theoretical rather than statistical considerations.

Access to these organizations was acquired through the use of personal and institutional contacts. In the following paragraphs, we describe the methodology of the research undertaken, the characteristics of the people questioned, and the techniques for collecting and analysing the data.

Our sample was created to attain a certain variety in profiles. This helps to capture the richness of the interpretations and uses of management accounting. Furthermore, taking diversity into account with regard to companies meant considering them from different activity sectors (Mia and Chenhall, 1994). This allowed us to understand various managerial situations. Table 1 summarizes our sample.

We used as the basis of the study the discourse of the actors-managers. We argue that considering "the manager" as the unit of analysis, rather than "the organization" or "the accounting systems," may bring additional insights. The method of interviewing concerned the actors' discourses in relation to their personal managerial practices. To analyse the data we relied on the content analysis of managers' discourses. Content analysis was undertaken alongside data collection and coding. This coding was done by applying the principle of 'systematic comparison' supported by Glaser and Strauss (1967). We analysed the managers' discourse according to signification, domination, and legitimation.

Table 1. List of interviewed managers

N°	Group	Business sector	Function
E1	VE-ONYX	Environmental Industry	Director for Development
E2	DELPHI	Automobile Components Manufacturer, Transport industry	Director for European Operations
E3	Shiseido-Decléor	Cosmetics	Sales Director
E4	Bank CM	Bank Insurance	Ex-Human Resources Director, Director for International Relations
E5	X (anonymous)	Property Management	CEO
E6	France Télécom	Telecoms	Ex-Director « Fixed Line Phone for General Public »,
E7	Renault	Automobile Industry	Director for Communication
E8	France Télécom	Telecoms	Group Resources Director (Director Resource Management)
E9	Air Liquide	Chemical Industry	ex-Director African Operations, Communication Director
E10	Shiseido-Decléor	Cosmetics	Commercial Director
E11	Groupe W	Telecoms	Director Computing Department
E12	Kraft	Food Industry	Human Resources Director
E13	DELPHI	Automobile Components Manufacturer, Transport Industry	Director for French Operations, ex-Director for Finance-Europe
E14	Alstom	Electrical Construction and Transport	Director for Investor Relations
E15	Renault	Automobile Industry	Director for Economic Intelligence
E16	Renault	Automobile Industry	Strategic Planning Director (Marketing and Commercial)

E17	DHLWorldWide- DHLexpress	Transport and Logistics for Companies-France	CEO
E18	Renault	Automobile Industry	Factory Director
E19	Y (anonymous)	Entertainment	Commercial & Marketing Director
E20	FAURECIA	Automobile Equipment	Supply Chain Director, Asia and Mercosur
E21	HSBC	Bank	General Services Director
E22	DHL	Transport and Logistics for Companies-France	Marketing Director
E23	Air France/KLM	Cargo-Fret	Director for Lines Management
E24	Air France/KLM	Cargo-Fret	Product Director
E25	Lincoln Electric	Manufacturing of Welders	Export Consumer Service Manager

4. Research findings

We interpret the managers' discourse according to signification, domination, and legitimation. We recognize that the ST mechanisms are obviously recursive. However, hereafter the separation has been made for analytical purposes.

Accounting is not an integral part of manager's representation of the organizational reality

The strong pressure on middle managers to account for accounting indicators involves a mental emphasis on them. These actors, and especially top managers, are even implementing economic and accounting training for their co-workers, to facilitate the sharing of mental representations based on accounting indicators.

Management accounting information is made intelligible by the interpretive scheme of each individual (actor), according to his abilities and interests. The overall shared concern with regard to accounting is related to its inability to give a fair representation of organizational reality: *'a history of economic life,' 'a film which has already been shown,' 'a guarantee of reliability within the company.'* It is a reconstruction of facts.

It emerged from the analysis of the managers' quotations that several of them thought themselves unable to interpret the accounting reports: *"I am sure that I will never be an accounting person, as I cannot get the logic!"* (E25, Export consumer service manager) This seriously questions Giddens' concept of the "knowledgeable actor." Indeed we disclose the severe 'self-inefficacy' (Bush, 1997) of managers regarding accounting. Such a cognitive inability contributes to the fact that managers consider accounting as merely "*a simple parameter amongst several others."* (E8, Director of group resources). In this sense, managers have little belief in the decisional usefulness of accounting, and do not really perceive it as a positive help for action (McKinnon and Bruns, 1992, 1993; Sillince and Sykes, 1995; Ahrens and Dent, 1998).

The manager does not have the necessary self-assurance concerning his ability to understand and interpret accounting information. Thus, two types of managers who have such a passive attitude regarding the accounting system can be identified.

The first group of managers consider themselves not competent to interpret accounting. They choose to 'keep in the background' behind the technical device. In this case, the manager only agrees to carry out the directives that are translated into accounting language, without being able to understand them or to critique them.
The second category of managers consists of individuals who completely reject accounting; they rarely use it in their decision-making, as illustrated by the following:

> I know how to do everything [...] except how to enter an accounting figure into the computer. Accounting is, after all, a field for specialists... (E5, CEO).

The limited use that directors make of accounting also depends on what stems from the cognitive ineffectiveness of the accounting information (difficulty of accessibility, inadaptability to their needs, cost, and the time needed for effective production). This is mainly what influences them on the extent to which they will make use of such information.

The directors interviewed clearly think that accounting systems do not allow them to act and to represent their organizational reality, because they do not make it possible to identify the levers of action in a prospective manner. The operational directors (production and commercial) seem to agree on the failure of the management accounting system and, in particular, that it focuses on the professional vision of accountants, not the operational one. They particularly evoke the local specificities of their activities, which are directed towards operational actions and the exploration of the market.

Interestingly, we can reveal that managers criticize the accountant much more than the technology/device. In addition, we note that the managers' knowledge of accounting (such as E2, E4, E5, E8, E18) is the main determining factor in their representation of it, and the functions they attribute to it (Bush, 1997). Nevertheless, with the increase in complexity and uncertainty (cause and effect) of the decisional situation (Burchell *et al.*, 1980; Mia and Chenhall, 1994), and paradoxically, above all in the case of major financial difficulties within the company, the relationship between accounting and managers' actions changes substantially. Accounting then becomes one of the main devices in the decision-making process, both before (making the action) and after (controlling the action). The worse the financial situation, the more accounting becomes the basis on which decisions are made.

A large use of management accounting as a device for domination

Domination structures consist of the codes or templates for the relations and ordering of dependence and autonomy within a social institution. These structures are characterized by the 'dialectic of control.' Here social relations involve a systemic integration of autonomy and dependency. This is the case in which managers intend to maintain their relative autonomy vis-à-vis the board of directors and shareholders by means of information asymmetry. The latter are likely to intervene and put pressure on managers in the case of unsatisfactory performance. Such a situation can render managers more dependent, and subject to restricting/firing decisions. Therefore, accounting has close links with power relationships. It can even serve to mask an insecure economic reality to enable the CEO to remain in his position (E8, Director of Group Resources). Indeed, some interviewees openly mentioned the manipulation of accounting information by top managers. What was particularly salient is that one CEO interviewed mentioned such a manipulation by his predecessor (E5). We noted that, for some of the managers interviewed, smoothing over accounting information is a necessity, given the emotional uncertainties of the shareholders. This view was shared as much by a director for development (E1) as by a CEO (E5).

The policeman role played by accountants is perceived as fulfilled at the expense of managers' own responsibilities. The issue here is that the actors stress that the firm's value is created by operational managers, not by top directors. The former have authoritative resources as they have the required business expertise. The ambivalent relation pointed out is that the top directors will be rewarded in the case of good performance, although the value creation is achieved by the middle levels.

Therefore, management accounting information is generally the basis for negotiations with the top directors, as illustrated by the following quotations:

> I feel in a strong position when I go and see the Executive Director with some accounting figures. This isn't the case when I go to see him with a good story. (E24, Product Director)

Indeed, middle managers are more interested in accounting when the issues concern negotiating an investment contract with the top management, or requesting a budget extension (E1, E8, E22). This is also the case when it concerns explaining achievements in relation to those budgeted for. One medium of this domination that is allowed by central management control is the predetermination of standard costs/prices. This is felt by the managers to be very frustrating. For instance, a Director of Commercial Strategy expressed his irritation about this matter in the following manner:

> I do not really appreciate the devices that are used in the group, we too often compare budgets, re-forecasts and the Plan; we compare our dreams with our expectations, our hopes. A failure must obviously be in real terms, whatever the conventions of the real terms are, true or false. But there is too often a sort of worry about the accuracy of the figures that I don't see much use for. All our figures in a firm as large as ours are obviously based on conventions. The conventions should simply be known by everyone within the company. (E16, Director for strategy)

Using MA to legitimate decision-making is crucial for managers

The signification structure of any social order is intertwined with the legitimation structure that provides it with its moral underpinnings. The legitimation structures consist of legitimacy codes, normative rules, and moral obligations (Macintosh and Scapens, 1991). During actions and interactions, the agents rely on legitimation structures, which they consider through the normative rules of behaviour. By doing so, they reproduce the current morality by the sanctions used to reward or punish other agents, according to the extent to which they conform to the codes of conduct.

The legitimation structures find their basis in the signification structure. In a strongly competitive context, showing the capacity to improve financial viability and achieve good economic performance seems to be the source of the legitimation structures for managerial actions. In our study, management accounting serves as an argument by which managers make their decisions credible (Cooper, 1983; Mellemvik *et al.,* 1988). Even more so, certain managers succeed in building and developing their managerial credibility, *"thanks to showing empathy, transparency and looking for a common interest with the chief accountant."* (E25)

The majority of managers interviewed pointed out the persuasive capability of MA. A CEO can earn the trust of the board of directors by regularly taking out the MA reports:

> The first year, when I was appointed in November, I planned five meetings of the board of directors, to show them the state of the company, because

> they weren't expecting it, and they believed that it had been turned around, whereas in fact that was not at all the case! (E5)

With regard to other stakeholders, this same manager added the following:

> When the shareholders, the trade unions, ask you certain things that you consider to be unreasonable, you must use the accounting reports to show them that it isn't possible. (E5)

In the case of painful decisions, such as a personnel downsizing, MA helps to legitimize such decisions made by top management. Middle managers feel shocked, and regret that they cannot understand

> Why the CEO decides to cut off the human resources while sales increase, and the related daily work is more intensive than ever due to the sales increase (of course), but also due to the additional documentation, internal controls, SOX, etc. (E25, Export consumer service manager)

The manager needs to *"measure the achievements in relation to the objectives" (E2, E5, E10, E17, E22)*. In this case, the management accounting system is used as a device to follow up and monitor how they diverge from the original forecasts. MA *"makes it possible to keep one's feet on the ground, and then do business with the rest."* (E10). MA, by providing information about the actions accomplished, allows the organizational actors to feel responsible (Anthony, 1989). It is a device that upholds the justifications for granting rewards or sanctions with regard to the standards fixed internally (objectives) or externally (benchmarking, competition, activity sectors, etc.) (van Veen-Dirks, 2009). In this sense, the manager uses it to evaluate the performance of members of his team as well as the entity under his control (Ouchi, 1979; Merchant, 1989, 1998). MAI is 'firstly' to know where the gains and losses are, which are the teams that make money and others that don't make money (E5, CEO).

Often, managers must make a choice concerning the accounting indicators that are used to evaluate the performance of their co-workers and the entities. As one manager claims,

> I think that an indicator is quite interesting, but I would be quite careful. There are accounting indicators upon which your direct performance is evaluated. So you are made responsible for it… Yet, our brand image (non-accounting indicator) is, in a sense, more of a probing element: am I going in the right direction? This indicator (the opposite of accounting ones) helps to identify the problems. (E16, Director of Strategy)

Interestingly, managers are aware of the legitimating force of accounting indicators. Thus their choice of indicators is of great importance because it cannot easily be reversed.

Table 2 below presents the main results of our study. It explains how managers use management accounting through the three dimension of structuration theory.

Table 2. Uses of management accounting by managers

Structuration theory dimensions	Managers' perceptions and use of MA
Signification	Priority for budgeting, profitability and return on investment, MA as a language for specialists Difficulty in interpreting and using MAI MA is considered as more oriented to short-term goals Management accounting as an information driver MA fails to support decision making Paradox of using accounting in case of major financial difficulties
Legitimation	Trust in figures Persuasive force of MAI Communicate results of actions External reporting to maintain shareholders' loyalty Legitimate less accepted decisions Legitimate sanctions and rewards
Domination	MAI used to negotiate within shareholders and other stakeholders MAI used to Assess people and distribute resources within the company Reliance on management accounting performance measures Allocation of financial and human resources

Discussion

Previous studies using ST (Macintosh and Scapens 1990, Macintosh and Scapens 1991, Conrad, 2005, Gurd 2008) concentrated mainly on organizational change using company case studies (University of Wisconsin, GM, British Gas, Electricity Trust of South Australia, respectively). Each of these organizations was going through a period of organizational change, and accounting was implicated in their change of structures (Gurd,

2008). For our study, we concentrated on the use of accounting at a managerial level, and its enactment by managers who were non-specialists in accounting. Our objective was to represent the use of the management accounting information in a more general context than the specific context of organizational change alone. We recall that little research has deployed this theory to analyse the interpretation and use of accounting at the level of individual managers. Above all, this question is critically under-considered in the literature, regardless of the theoretical framework (Pierce and O'Dea, 2003; Hall, 2010).

The findings highlight the importance of the role played by the MAI as a resource for domination, and for providing legitimation, with regard to managers' responsibilities and actions. Further, our study reveals that whilst the use of MAI for decision making is limited, it becomes an important device in the case of major financial difficulties within a company.

It appears that managers perceive management accounting as a means of enhancing their power, and influencing organizational members' behaviour. Thanks to the authoritative and allocative resources offered by accounting, it is used as an important source for evaluating the performance of individuals and entities. In this way, and conforming to the works in *"Reliance on Accounting Performance Measures,"* it appears that managers consider accounting a means of influencing internal behaviour (Sprinkle, 2003). It is an instrument that makes it possible to involve a certain number of people, and to make them agree with the manager's vision. This is expected to result in the realization of 'common' objectives. This confirms that ST is particularly appropriate for examining how control systems influence behavioural rules (Macintosh and Scapens, 1991). The social relations associated with the use of MAI by managers involve a systemic integration of autonomy and dependency (Macintosh, 1995). This is related to the position of the manager as a pivot between his subordinates and the stakeholders of the entity under his control.

MA, interpreted according to Giddens' structuration theory, can be assumed to be a social structure. It is both structuring and structured through the managers' actions. MA can be used in different ways by managers belonging to a variety of companies, although they all have similar positions. This can be explained by the fact that management accounting systems are the modalities of action structuration (Macintosh and Scapens, 1990; Englund and Gerdin, 2008), and by the degree to which managers can be considered "knowledgeable actors" regarding accounting. This is consistent with the conclusion of Scapens (2006), who mentioned (1) that the management accounting techniques used in practice are often not the 'ideal' ones, as might be expected—practice is never perfect—and (2) the knowledge and backgrounds of key individuals can affect their use of management accounting in practice. MAI is used in a variable and sometimes contradictory way by managers. This can be explained by the ability of the managers (knowledgeable actors) to interpret and use MAI in a flexible manner. This fundamental concept in structuration theory is based on the idea that all human agents have the ability to affect the action. They have the knowledge to manage their actions. The study of managers who are non-specialists in accounting reveals the importance of considering the competencies of accounting users, in order to better understand its issues in use. A lack of technical skills in assimilating accounting methods and conventions, as well as a feeling of self-inefficacy with regard to accounting, favour managers' tendency to make decisions without really making use of the MAI.

Conclusion

This paper offers a structuration analysis of the use of management accounting by managers without accounting expertise. Admitting the possibilities of conflict, the paradox in using MAI and the contradictions in the managers' discourses structuration theory contributes to explaining behaviour patterns that do not seem to conform to the technical-economic and rational approach to accounting. These managers, whether operational or functional, when faced with external pressure (investors, suppliers) or internal pressure (unions, employees, and top management), tend to benefit, in one sense or another, from the potential advantage of the use of MAI. The analysis of the managers' discourses shows that MA is used to justify or interpret an action, and to enhance managers' power. Seeking coherence with regard to these three dimensions of ST, makes possible a better understanding of the reasons for managers' actions.

Our study presents an attempt to look at MA as a managerial practice. It is a response to the recommendations of Goddard (2004). Structuration theory has made it possible to discover and bring together the practices of managers, when using MA, with their own perceptions of accounting as a social structure that can be interpreted according to the three dimensions of ST. In this respect, this theory clarifies the process by which users interpret and use management accounting. How the competencies and the objectives of users are analysed in relation to MAI represents an important line of research for the development of the norms, tools, and methods originating from accounting, and that can be fully used by managers.

This paper points out that the significations that managers have, involve a gap of incomprehension and distancing vis-à-vis accountants. Our study seriously challenges the decision aid for managers that accounting is assumed to provide. Hence management accountants can increase their organizational usefulness by moving away from a mainly technical validity toward an organizational one. In addition, by showing the focus of managers on the relational roles (signification, legitimation and domination) of accounting, this study calls for better awareness and training of accountants, in order to assist managers in fully playing similar roles. Academics may wish to further integrate the relational aspects of accounting use into the discipline's curriculum.

References

Abernethy, M.A., and P. Brownell, 1999, "The role of budgets in organizations facing strategic change: an exploratory study". *Accounting, Organizations and Society*; 24, 3:189–204.

Ahrens, T., and F. Dent, 1998, "Accounting and organizations: realizing the richness of field research". *Journal of Management Accounting Research*; 10, 1–39.

Anthony RN. 1988, *The management control function*. Boston: The Harvard Business School Press.

—. 1989, "Reminiscences about management accounting", *Journal of Management Accounting Research*;1–20.

Baxter J. and W.F. Chua. 2003, "Alternative management accounting research: Whence and Whither". *Accounting, Organizations and Society*; 28:97–126.

Boland RJ, Jr. 1993, "Accounting and the Interpretative Act". *Accounting, Organizations and Society* , 18(2/3): 125–46.

Boland RJ., 1996, "Why shared meanings have no place in structuration theory: A reply to Scapens and Macintosh",. *Accounting, Organizations and Society*, 21(7/8), 691–7.

Burchell S, C., Clubb, A .Hopwood, J, Hughes and J. Nahapiet, 1980, "The roles of accounting in organizations and society", *Accounting, Organizations and Society,* 5(1):5–27.

Coad A.F., and I.P. Herbert 2009,"Back to the future: New potential for structuration theory in management accounting research? *Management Accounting Research*; 20(3):177–92.

Conrad L., 2005, "A structuration analysis of accounting systems and systems of accountability in the privatised gas industry", *Critical Perspectives on Accounting*, 16:1–26.

Dent J.F. 1991, "Accounting and Organizational Cultures: A Field Study of the Emergence of a New Organizational Reality". *Accounting, Organizations and Society,* 16(8):705–32.

Englund H., and J. Gerdin, 2008, "Structuration theory and mediating concepts: Pitfalls and implications for management accounting research". *Critical Perspectives on Accounting,* 19, 1122–34.

Giddens A. 1984, *The Constitution of Society.* Cambridge: Polity Press.

Glaser B.G., and A.L. Strauss, 1967, *The Discovery of Grounded Theory: Strategies for Qualitative Research*, New York; Aldine.

Goddard A.., 2004, "Budgetary practices and accounting habitus. A grounded theory." *Accounting, Auditing & Accountability Journal,* 17,543–577.

Gurd, B., 2008, "Structuration and middle-range theory: a case study of accounting during organizational change from different theoretical perspectives", *Critical Perspectives on Accounting,* 19:523–543.

Hall, M. 2010, "Accounting information and managerial work." *Accounting, Organization and Society,* 35(3), 301-315.

Lillis A.M., and J. Mundy, 2005, "Cross-Sectional Field Studies in Management Accounting Research - Closing the Gaps between Surveys and Case Studies." Journal of Management Accounting Research, 17,119–141.

Macintosh N.B., and RW Scapens, 1990, "Structuration theory in management accounting." *Accounting, Organizations and Society,* 15(5):455–477.

Macintosh N.B., and RW Scapens, 1991, "Management Accounting and Control Systems: A Structuration Theory Analysis". Journal of Management Accounting Research, 3:131–158.

Macintosh N.B. 1994, *Management accounting and control systems.* Chichester, England; Wiley:

—. 1995, "The Ethics of Profit Manipulation: A Dialectic of Control Analysis." *Critical Perspectives on Accounting*, 6(4):289–315.

Mellemvik F., N., Monsen and O. Olson, 1988, "Functions of accounting- a discussion." *Scandinavian Journal of Management,* 4(3/4), 101–119.

Merchant K.A., 1989, *Rewarding results, Motivating profit center manager.* Boston; Harvard Business School Press.

—. 1998. *Modern management control systems,* Upper Saddle River NJ; Prentice Hall.

Mia L.,and R. Chenhall, 1994, "The usefulness of management accounting systems, functional differentiation, and managerial effectiveness.", *Accounting, Organizations and Society* ;19(1):1–13.

Mintzberg H., 1989 *Mintzberg on Management: Inside Our Strange World of Organizations*. New York; Free Press.

Otley D. and R.M. Pollanen, 2000, "Budgetary criteria in performance evaluation: A critical appraisal using new evidence." *Accounting, Organizations and Society*, 25(4/5):483–496.

Ouchi W.G.1979, "A conceptual framework for the design of organizational control mechanisms." *Management Science,* 25(9):833–48.

Pierce B. and T. O'Dea, 2003, "Management Accounting information and the needs of managers, Perceptions of managers and accountants compared." *The British Accounting Review*; 35(3):257–290.

Roberts J, and R. Scapens, 1985, "Accounting systems and systems of accountability—understanding accounting practices in their organisational contexts." *Accounting Organizations and Society,* 10(4): 443–456.

Ryan B., R. Scapens and M. Theobald, 2002, *Research method and methodology in finance and accounting*. New York; Harcourt Brace Jovanovich:

Scapens R.W. and N.B. Macintosh, 1996, "Structure and agency in management accounting research: A response to Boland's interpretive act.". *Accounting Organizations and Society*; 21(7/8):675–690.

Scapens R.W., 2006, "Understanding management accounting practices: a personal journey." *British Accounting Review*, 38:1–30.

Sillince J.A., and G.M. Sykes, 1995, "The role of accounting in improving manufacturing technology." *Management Accounting Research,* 6(2):103–124.

Sprinkle G.B., 2003, "Perspectives on experimental research in managerial accounting". *Accounting, Organizations and Society,* 28(2/3):287–318.

van Der Stede W.A., 2001, "Measuring tight budgetary control." *Management Accounting Research,*; 12(1):119–137.

van Veen-Dirks P. 2010, "Different uses of performance measures: The evaluation versus reward of production managers.". *Accounting, Organizations and Society,* 35(2), 141-164.

Wiersma E., 2009, "For which purposes do managers use Balanced Scorecards? An empirical study". *Management Accounting Research*, 20(1), 239–251.

"THE DRAFT AMENDMENT TO STANDARD IAS 18 REGARDING THE CAPITALIZATION OF PROCEEDS FROM NORMAL ACTIVITIES" WOULD BE AN IMPEDIMENT TO THE ASSESSMENT OF THE FINANCIAL PERFORMANCE OF ENTITIES: A FIELD STUDY IN THE CELL-PHONE SECTOR

ALDO LÉVY[1] AND GEORGES PARIENTE[2]

Introduction

International Accounting Standard (IAS) 18 was first published in December 1993 by the International Accounting Standards Board (IASB). It was approved by the European Union in 2003, and subsequently amended repeatedly by other standards or by approved interpretations until 2008.

IAS 18 concerns the recording of the proceeds from activities, such as the sales of goods and the provision of services, and use by third parties of the entity's assets, leading to the payment of fees, interest, etc. IAS 18 extended the concept of sales to that of "proceeds of normal activities" (PNA).

The IASB and the Financial Accounting Standards Board (FASB) in the United States are constantly working towards a common format for financial statements; their motivation is increasingly dominated by financial considerations. The legitimacy of this endeavour continues to raise questions (Burlaud and Colasse, 2010). The accounting standards

[1] Faculty Member, Professor at CNAM and the ISC Paris School of Management.
[2] Dean of Research, ISC Paris School of Management.

used in Europe - the International Accounting Standards (IAS) - have become the International Financial Reporting Standards (IFRS).

This follows from the premise that financial information will be improved by a merging of their conceptual frameworks to enable a greater comparability of the performances of globalized entities.

Some authors consider the IAS-IFRS standards to be the quality standards for financial reporting (Ball et al. 2003; Schipper 2005; Daske 2006) but others have shown that the quality of a financial statement also derives from the manner in which the reference system is interpreted and applied (Ali and Hwang 2000; Ball et al. 2000, 2003; Soderstrom and Sun 2007). With the goal of improving these standards, the IASB and FASB issued an "Exposure Draft" of a proposal for a new IAS 18 regulation, open for discussion until October 22, 2010. This "Revenue Recognition in Contracts with Customers" is intended to enable a new approach to the classification of "Proceeds of Normal Activities", allowing the option of capitalizing them either in whole or in part. The definitive standard should be issued in mid-2011.

The changes are not merely cosmetic: they will drastically alter financial statements. Financial analysts who make use of basic indicators will no longer be able to rely on performance figures to establish their judgments, since the compositions of their numerators and denominators will have changed. This will lead to erroneous financial interpretations or even an opportunistic management of profits, owing to the increased complexity of the standard and the danger of creative accounting to support such management.

1. Sales and proceeds of normal activities (PNA)

Each time that their compositions are changed to fit international standards, the problem becomes less a matter of the desired improvement in the accounting data, than of the bias which it introduces into financial information (Lévy and Nguyen 2010).

These proceeds of normal activities must be assessed at the fair value of the contra received or to be received. Under the IAS-IFRS, Fair Value is defined as the *"price at which an asset could be exchanged, or a liability settled, between two willing and completely independent parties, with full freedom to act*" (Hoarau and Teller 2002). It is approximated by "*the* value of an exchange *between two free, willing, and independent parties*".

In the view of some authors this value is the ratio between perceived value and price which determines the behaviour of the consumer: "the customer's assessment of all the benefits obtained from a product or service in relation to the total cost represented by its purchase price or its use..." Barwise and Meehan (1999).

Fair value is the value of an asset that is exchanged, or a liability cancelled, between well-informed consenting parties acting under normal competitive conditions. This is the case in our field study with ISPs (Bouygues, Orange, SFR, Free).

1.1 The difference between sales and PNA

Sales comprise all the selling operations recorded as routine operations, while PNAs - because of the abolition of the systematic division between operating and non-operating items - cover a wider range.

If the sale remains a contract under which one of the parties, the access provider in our study, undertakes to transfer the ownership of an asset and to deliver it to the other party (the customer), the latter undertakes to pay the price. Thus the "proceeds" account is intended to record the resources acquired by the firm for the price of the goods sold, the work done, or the services rendered. This accounting approach means that, as of now, the sale of cell-phones and the monthly payments for service plans fall under the same account: sales or PNA. But under the Exposure Draft and its proposed new regulations, there would suddenly be separate treatments for the sale of the merchandise (the cell-phone sold by itself) and for the undertaking to make monthly payments for service plans designed for the needs of this same customer. On the one hand the sale clearly sets out reciprocal undertakings, which do not require immediate execution, and on the other hand the subject of the sale may not exist, or may not be individualized at the time the contract is signed. This is precisely the case in our field study on the cell-phone sector. The changes will have their major effects in the area of accounting.

1.2 Accounting issues

The sales figures represent the sales of merchandise and completed sales of goods and services valued on the basis of the sales price (excluding recoverable taxes) carried out by the entity with third parties, in the course of its normal routine activities.

However, the obligating event which will determine the date on which a sale is effective and becomes an item of accounting and financial data is going to be an issue: should it be the date of the order, of receiving the merchandise or service, of receiving the invoice, or something else?

At present, under the national and international standards, a sale becomes an item of accounting and financial data when:

- The entity has transferred to the purchaser the major risks and benefits inherent in ownership of the assets;
- The entity is not involved either in the management that normally is the responsibility of the owner, or in the effective control of the assets sold;
- The amount of the proceeds arising from the sale of the assets can be reliably assessed;
- It is probable that the economic benefits associated with the transaction will accrue to the entity;
- The costs incurred or to be incurred concerning the transaction can be reliably assessed.

These points usually coincide with the transfer of ownership in legal terms; otherwise it is the transfer of risk, benefits, and control that is decisive.

Thus phone operators record cell-phone sales and their corresponding service plans, whether packaged or not, in the proceeds from the operating account.

However, the amendment of IAS 18 will lead to a dichotomy between the tangible cell-phone, which the phone operators do not themselves manufacture, and the provision of service; one being capitalized, and the other remaining in the proceeds of normal activities. This has consequences for the accounting choices offered by IFRS 1 and remains of interest in view of the importance of the data in assessing the performance of the firm and its management (Degeorge, Patel, and Zeckhauser, 1999; Graham, Harvey, and Rajgopal, 2006).

2. Consequences of recapitalization

2.1 Reinterpretation of capitalization

The definition of "asset" poses a problem, and the IASB has recently redefined assets as part of the revision of the IFRS's conceptual framework. ANC and EFRAG have released a research study intended to guide the IASB's discussion concerning the definition of an asset. From now on they will be current economic resources over which the entity holds rights or other access that other parties do not possess. We see that the major changes will affect:

1. The word "control", which is replaced by "right or other access": an entity may thus use, limit, or prohibit the use of a resource by a third party;
2. "Anticipated future economic benefits" have been replaced by the definition of a resource, i.e., the ability to generate inputs or reduce outputs of funds. Since the concept of anticipated future economic benefits depends on a strong probability of obtaining such benefits, the word "anticipated" has been withdrawn, and any certainty of obtaining these benefits is no longer a condition for qualifying as an asset;
3. The words "as a result of past activities" have been withdrawn, in favour of having a certainty that the resource does indeed exist on the closing date;
4. The words "economic and current" have been added to "resource". “Current” shows that on the date of the financial statements the resource and the right over it did indeed exist.

All this naturally has consequences.

2.2 Consequences

- **Informational**

– Removal of the polysemous word "control" resolves the ambiguity that existed with respect to the concept of the "control" of consolidated accounts. Under IAS 18 it calls to mind the power of the holder of the asset to deal with it as it pleases;

- The economic concept of a "resource" enables a better clarification;
- Repeal of the concept "of past events" enables a clarification of the existence of the resource on the closing date.

However, once an asset is recorded, its contra must be determined.

In our field study, a cell-phone service provider includes a cell-phone in the packaged offers sold, so that customers can consume the services in the plan they have selected. But "since the customer is not a uniform reality, the value for the customer will, at the very least, be variable and unstable".

Since the sale of the cell-phone takes place at a price less than the purchase cost, the operation may be likened to a (partial) exchange of goods or services in return for services of a different nature. In this case the exchange must give rise to the recording of proceeds. Thus depending on the various offers made available, there would be an element involving a transfer of equipment with a view to providing services to the customers. Accordingly, it would consist of an exchange, even if only a partial one, because the access provider is in fact required to provide services in compensation for the partial uninvoiced cost of the equipment. Under IAS 18, this provision is the source of proceeds that must be recorded in the "Proceeds of normal activities". It follows that the connection is a stand-alone service which has a value in itself for the customer, and that the fair value (Châtelain S. and Lévy A. 2009) of this connection service can indeed be reliably determined.

Since a number of services may be identified (promotions, packages, offers, double-, triple-, or even quadruple-play bundles, etc.), the fair value of the overall payment received could be distributed over each of the services. Since the service is continuous, the proceeds are recorded over the period: 12 or 24 months.

- **On the relevance of financial statements**

- The recording of the proceeds of normal activities depends on the services that the entity obtains in return for the reduction in the price of the asset transferred. This may be connection to a network, provision of continuous access to goods or services, or both;

- By redefining the term resource, this will increase the number of items liable to be capitalized. Items that have a very low value that could only be recorded as income could be capitalized;
- The concept of an economic resource, which is essentially based on cash flows, is more restrictive than the more general term "benefits".

Thus the distinction which is made between the rules applying to capitalization and those that apply to recording in the profit and loss account inevitably impact the presentation and valuation of financial statements. In fact, the ratios for debt-equity, leverage, hedging, asset turnover, solvency, risk, profitability, and so on will be unchanged, but their contents and their dynamic comparison from one year to another, or between companies, will thereby be altered.

- **On cost differentiation**

Any new method of recording will necessarily involve costs:

- Hidden organizational costs for the detailed monitoring of the various sales operations,
- Costs of changes in the computer and information systems
- Training costs, etc.

But can the costs be increased without increasing the price to the customer (Lorino 1989, Baglin 1995)?

In the case of the cell-phone sector studied here, in view of the consequences, the Cell-phone Operators are trying to mount an opposition to changes in IAS 18, as the field study shows. "The issue is to optimize the firm's offer by adjusting the costs it incurs to the value that its product represents for the customer" (Bouquin 2004).

3. Field study

3.1 Products and services, a couple in need of separation

Cell-phone Operators offer packaged products consisting of a cut-rate generic cell-phone, and service plans tailored to the customer's needs. The package is assumed to be an integrated unit.

In our study the packaged offers are essential if the customer is to avoid paying the real price of the cell-phone. At a modest cost they include a

good, not manufactured by the service provider and thus described as merchandise that can be held as stock and capitalized, and an offer of customized services, usually covering one or two years.
Hitherto these two operations have been merged in the sales figures, on the one hand the sale of generic merchandise, essential for the provision of services, and on the other a set of intangible customized service plans.

- **Are these two concomitant obligations considered to be separable or not?**

Hitherto they could not be separated, and Cell-phone Operators recorded them both in the Proceeds of normal activities, with the customer making monthly payments for the tangible asset over the term of the contract.
Currently, IAS 18 considers that they can be separated because the good and the provision of services can be sold separately, even if the price of the equipment by itself is a deterrent. For the service provider this then requires the calculation of a different profit margin. In fact,
Cell-phone Operators:

- Provide an almost infinite variety of offers;
- Offer free software updates;
- Offer specific warranties and warranty extensions with respect to the manufacturers. But although the legal warranty is inseparable from the cell-phone, the warranty extension is separable, and depends on the customer's wishes. In fact, the exposure draft proposes that the percentage of cell-phones that are liable to be returned during the legal warranty period no longer be recorded as sales, since the rate of returns is statistically known. Thus instead of having all the sales in the PNA and a provision for the warranty, we will have the total amount of sales net of returns under warranty: this leads to changes in the financial statements.

If analysts take the sales or the added value as a criterion of growth, they are in danger of drawing ridiculous conclusions, for example: "*although Apple's sales went from nearly $12 billion to almost $16 billion for the first quarter of 2010, this is not due to the success of its products, but to changes in the US accounting regulations. Apple is actually applying them in advance; they will become obligatory in 2011.*"
This is going to turn the sector upside down.

3.2 Sectorial study

- **Income in this sector**

The fact that there are several items in the package requires that these items be clearly identified and a fair value assigned to each, according to the terms of the offer. The obligating event for the accounting entry, the accounting data item, is currently the delivery of the service. Since the components of the offer are certainly separable and identifiable, each item comprising the offer is included in the sales figure.

- **Cash-flows**

Operators record them according to the customers' real consumption of services, when they are delivered. Thus the invoiced sale is identical to the one recorded.

- **Income connected to initial connection charges for subscribers**

The accounting entry for the initial connection of subscribers may be approached in two ways:

- Either it is considered that the first connection generates an income, which is the case for operators whose connection costs are identifiable and separable, as with British Telecom;
- Or (and this is what French operators do) the connection income is spread out over the term of the contract for offers whose separable items are not considered identifiable. Accordingly, the income associated with the initial service connection is distributed over the average duration of a contract.

- **Current method of recording package sales**

According to the cell-phone operators it is a matter of providing services, not cell-phones. These phones should therefore not be viewed as merchandise but as accessories of the principal.

The operators confirm that they value their stocks at the lower end of their entry cost and their net realization value. But very few of them indicate how they arrive at the Fair Value, because these cell-phone packages are sold below their acquisition cost.

So when an operator buys a cell-phone from an equipment manufacturer it records it as stock, and withdraws it when it is sold to a customer, and this income is recorded in the proceeds of normal activities for the entire package.

- **Calculation of the differential between IAS18 and the revised IAS18**
  - **Big Telecom Study**

On 6/30/2010 Big Telecom sells a package offer which includes: an iPhone at €149 and a Service package at €55.90, covering: 24 months of 3 hr of calling + unlimited calls from 7 PM to 8 AM and WE + SMS /MMS + TV + unlimited internet.

This telephone sold alone would cost €659 according to the Apple catalogue.

The approach would be to break down the components of the packaged offer and to value each item. We know that one minute of calling time is valued at €0.36.

Breakdown of the monthly price of the calls sold separately:

Unlimited 7 PM or 8 PM + WE	€13
1hr + unlimited 9 PM to 8 AM	€15
2hr or 120 min @ €0.36	€43.20
Unlimited internet + SMS + MMS + TV	€10
Monthly payments	**€81.20**

→ The monthly costs exceed the suggested package costs by €55.90.

A non-packaged sale would come to an overall price of: Cell-phone at €659 + Service Plan (24 months) = (€81.20 x 24 months) + €659 = €1,948.80 + €659 = **€2,607.8**

While the package offer = (€55.90x 24 months) + €149 = **€1,490.60**

Comparison of separately-valued offer and package offer:

	Price breakdown	In %	**Package offer**	**Reduction** of separately-valued price
Cell-phone	€659	⇦25%⇨	€372.65	⇨ - €286.35
Service	€1,948.80	⇦75%⇨	€1,117.95	⇨ - €830.85
Total	**€2,607.80**	**⇦100%⇨**	**€1,490.60**	**⇨ - €1,117.20**

Financial accounting data:
Beginning June 2010

	Debit	Credit
Package	€1,490.60	
Contract debt – Cell-phone		€372.65
Contract debt – Service plan		€1,117.95

End June 2010

The operator has met its obligation of result to deliver a Cell-phone and recognizes the corresponding income at the original list price:

End June 2010

	Debit	Credit
Contract debt – Cell-phone	€372.65	
Proceeds of normal activities Cell-phone		€372.65

and

Bank	€149	
Contract		€149

The operator records the removal of the telephone from stock (the catalogue price is not the price paid by the operator). Here the iPhone was purchased for €500.

On June 15, 2012

24 months later, the operator has met its obligation for service, and has received an income equal to the price assigned to this obligation when the contract was signed. Monthly entries for the period in question:

June 15, 2012

	Debit	Credit
Bank	€55.90	
Contract		€55.90
Contract debt - Monthly service: **€117.95/24 mo.** =	€46.58	
Proceeds of normal activities – Service		€46.58

Comparison

	1st day	Cash-flows spread out over the period		Total
PNA under IAS 18	**€149**	€67.90 × 24 months	…	= €1490.60
PNA under Revised IAS 18	**€372.65**	€46.58 × 24 months	…	= €1490.60
Difference	= €222.35	**- €222.35**		**= €0,00**

This means that as regards risk in terms of cash-flow the move to the revised IAS 18 ➔

	2010							2011				
	PNA Package	June	July	August	September	October Nov.	December	January	February	March	April	May
IAS 18	**€149**	€68	€68	€68	€68	€68 €68	€68	€68	€68	€68	€68	€68
IAS 18 Revised	**€659**	€45	€45	€45	€45	€45 €45	€45	€45	€45	€45	€45	€45

Then

	2011						2012				
	June	July	August	September	October, November	December	January	February	March	April	May
IAS 18	€68	€68	€68	€68	€68 €68	€68	€68	€68	€68	€68	€68
IAS 18 Revised	€45	€45	€45	€45	€45 €45	€45	€45	€45	€45	€45	€45

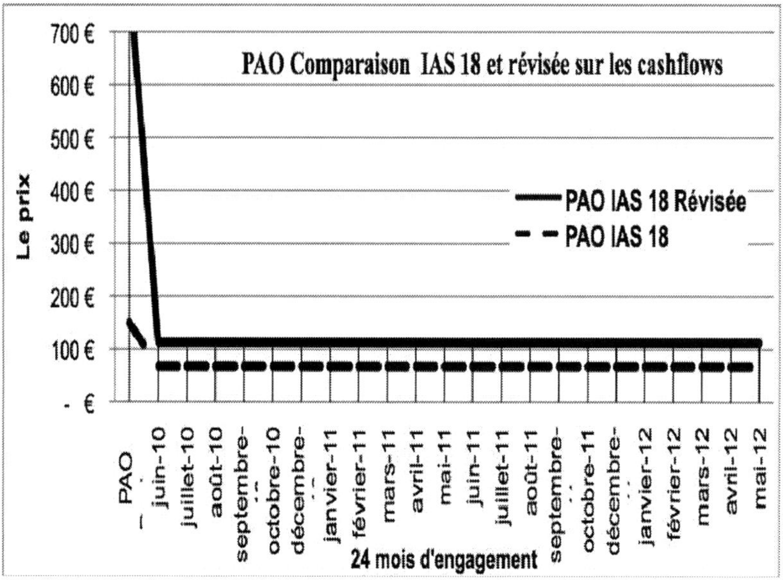

The PNA is going to be recorded upon the purchase of the cell-phone and the phone will be considered to be sold and paid for. Thus the invoicing system put in place will be dissociated from the recording of the PNA.

Conclusion

The impacts of the revised IAS 18 on operators will be substantial, and it will be difficult to implement.

- **Hard to quantify**

"The IASB and the FASB wish to improve the quality of financial information by:

- Providing a more relevant framework to base their investigations on,
- Highlighting the growing comparability between cell-phone operators,
- Providing more reliable information,
- Simplifying the accounting required by their contracts".

- **Distortions of information**
  - The firms will be responsible for their assessments, which are a major risk factor in opportunistic management;
  - This sector is characterized by a vast number of small, customized contracts, not by the long-term contracts which characterize the construction firms that are the real targets of the Discussion Paper.
  - The information used in financial reporting will no longer be connected to the economic reality.

All of the financial reporting on cell-phone operators would be similarly affected.

According to a recent study based on questionnaires submitted to industry analysts, strong trends can be identified in the telecommunications sector.

The Cash-Flow, closely linked to income, is the reference indicator because there is a significant correlation between the Free Cash-Flow and incomes in the telecommunications sector.

- **Consequences foreseen by operators within their own companies**
  - An obvious danger is the split between pricing and invoicing. As the figures have shown, the invoicing cannot change, but the internal posting for financial reporting purposes will have to be modified. Operators want to avoid the cost of an overhaul of their invoicing systems. The revision requires that the posting be carried out offer by offer, depending on the cell-phone selected by the customer. Currently, Bouygues Telecom has sold about 1,600 offers since it was established, and anticipates more than 4,000 in 2012, for more than 12 million customers.
  - The revised IAS18 over-values the impact of sales of Cell-phones, which are no more than a means of access to the system, not merchandise. This runs counter to the development of the market, which sees Cell-phone suppliers emerging from their role of manufacturers to become prescribers who can influence the prices offered, thereby reining in the operators.

But managers pay attention to published accounting data because these can have an effect on their wellbeing (Watts and Zimmerman, 1986), and on the firm's competitive position (Jones, 1991).

MANAGEMENT CONTROL THROUGH COMMUNICATION

TAWHID CHTIOUI

Introduction

Ever since it was first introduced at General Motors in 1920s, the concept of management control has continually been called into question, with a shift from a financial and scientific management approach with the focus on the task at hand, to a more interpersonal vision that takes the diversity of actors within an organisation into consideration. If management control continues to evolve in this direction today, it is no doubt because organisations have become ever more complex and operate in an increasingly uncertain environment. Consequently, more than ever before, managers need to keep a close eye on both the coherence of their goals and their activities coordination. This coherence and coordination entails the creation of a vertical and horizontal communication network that, in the final analysis, has a profound impact on the cogency of management control.

In effect, communication has become a decisive factor in business organisations. Its specialists present it as the solution to a range of problems like the management crisis, for example, (Felts, 1992); as a key aspect of new management (Cosette, 1991); as the ultimate route to excellence (Peters and Waterman, 1983); as a strategic factor and a major component in an organisation's success (Taylor and Van Every, 2000); and lastly as "*the essential modality for the constitution of organisation and, more generally, of society,*" to use Giddens' words (1984).

Consequently, communication is a major consideration for management, even though it is rarely mentioned in management control research. This could be due to one of two reasons: firstly, the apparently simple link between control and communication is often associated with a certain inability to develop a concrete understanding of the operative aspects needed to resolve the issues they generate in a firm. Secondly, the intangibility and multidimensional aspects of communication mean that, at the end of the day, it is liable to become detached from management control or else be confused with other concepts (like information and relationships).

Based on a review of the literature, this paper aims to illustrate the shifts in control practices from a more limited approach based on financial and technical aspects to a communications-based approach. We begin by looking at the extent to which communication contributes to management control objectives based on a study of the main theoretical movements regarding organisations. In the second part, we explore the different conceptions of management control by classifying them in line with a communicational approach. We conclude by presenting our own definition of management control.

1. Communication according to the main theoretical movements in organisational research: A contribution to management control objectives

Our paper explores the shifts in the way communication is considered in organisations from a review of the main theoretical movements. Our aim is not to draw an exhaustive picture of organisational schools or trends, but rather to highlight those which illustrate different concepts of communication so as to provide insights into the whole spectrum. Our conclusion is as follows: communication contributes to the realisation of control objectives. Depending on the model adopted, it acts as a control tool (2.1.), a motivational factor (2.2), an instrument of influence (2.3.), or a coordination mechanism (2.4.).

1.1 Communication as a control tool

The traditional concept of communication was marked by Shannon's mathematical theory of communication and the traditional school. Taylor (1911) and Fayol (1918) recommended a division of labour based on the specialisation of functions and the separation of power. For Fayol, authority indicates a right granted to the leader to hold power in order to make people obey. Even when he speaks of 'coordination' as one of the five elements on which administration must be based,[1] it is reserved for the hierarchy via what he calls "the weekly conference of department managers."

In this context, communication is considered as the tool of a control system. The leader is the transmitter and the worker is the recipient. The transmission of information linked to the execution of tasks is mainly descendant, passing through the formal network either verbally or in writing. Ascendant transmissions are exceptional and are mainly used to clarify the accuracy of communication.

Initially considered as stemming naturally from 'administrative' activities, communication gradually became a concern for business leaders wishing to improve their effectiveness. Their interest, however, remained instrumental, and mainly concerned information transmission systems, communication techniques and the best ways to pass on a message. For Taylor and Fayol, communication only involved formal communication from the management team who monopolized the role of transmitter and reserved the role of recipient for the workers.

1.2 Communication as a motivational factor

For the human relations school, human motivation is not exclusively economic but is also affective and social. Arguments of feelings ran alongside those of cost. In this framework, the organisation, defined as a social system, has two main functions, namely to produce goods and to satisfy its members. In the 1930s, Elton Mayo, an American psychologist and sociologist, and precursor of this school, refuted the Taylor-oriented philosophy of personal interest. He highlighted the social factor in organisations and argued that workers are motivated by spontaneous cooperation and creative relationships. Going even further, MacGregor (1960) argued that decisions would be more enlightened if they were taken by those who must execute them. Control operations are often performed better by those who take part in the work than by those who are outside the operational circuit.

Unlike the traditional one-dimensional vision, the human relations school enlarges the perception of communication. Firstly, it is no longer limited

[1] For Fayol (1918), administration meant to forecast, organise, command, coordinate and control.

to data transmission, perceptions and work-related emotions, but also involves the creation and sustenance of social relations. In addition, data transmission is no longer reserved for management alone, as, in their social and affective relationships, workers are both transmitters and recipients.

For the human relations school, there are two facets to communication: in informal terms, it is considered as a motivational factor for the organisation's members while from the production perspective, it remains a largely linear data transmission process which, in addition to the instructions linked to the task, includes information about social and affective needs. This information is supplied by the employee who in turn becomes a transmitter, although in circumstances governed by the management.

1.3 Communication as an instrument of influence

The theory of decision-making, of which Herbert Simon (1945) was one of the founding fathers, attempts to integrate the rational concepts of the traditional school and the affective concepts of the human relations school. This theory puts the focus on communication and the transmission of information. According to Simon (1945, p. 136), "*there is no organisation without communication.*" Effectively, communication is no longer considered as arising simply from social relations but is instead an organisational function that needs to be managed. "*Communication within organisations is a two-way process; it simultaneously encompasses the transmission of orders, information and advice to a decision-making centre (in other words, to an individual invested with specific responsibility), and the transmission of decisions taken from this centre to other parts of the organisation.*" (Simon, 1945, p. 136).

In this context, communication forms an integral part of control processes both in the phase of access to information and in the dissemination phase. Consequently, it is the management control function which formulates downstream information as clearly as possible and explains it at all levels of the hierarchy. It is also the control function that organises the upstream information flows that are indispensable for decision making. However, according to Simon (1945, p.97), "*no stage in the administrative processes is more generally ignored, or more poorly accomplished than the communication of decisions.*" This stage is nonetheless fundamental as it governs the implementation of decisions. As such, it not only involves transmitting information, but also influences the process designed to obtain the recipient's collaboration.

The theory of decision-making has numerous implications for communication. In this context, subordinates are no longer simply passive recipients but instead act as transmitters of the information influenced by their perceptions, while they are also able to interpret the information they receive. Although it remains instrumental and managerial in its application, this system considers communication between business leaders and subordinates as a more complex phenomenon than the preceding visions. It is bidirectional and multidimensional, and simultaneously provides a way of transmitting information, governing motivation, exercising influence, and facilitating adaptation or even learning.

1.4 Communication as a coordination mechanism

Systemic analysis is an interdisciplinary field that deals with the study of complex realities. In certain cases in particular, traditional linear causality constructs are insufficient to understand the bigger picture for an analysis of a whole. The systemic approach arose from interaction between Wiener's cybernetics and Bertalanffy's general theory of systems.

The work conducted by Wiener (1948, p. 280) during the Second World War led to a generalisation of the principle of feedback, or retroaction, that he defined as "*a process enabling the control of systems by informing them of the results of their action.*" Thus, the concept of feedback replaced the traditional linear explanation of communication which was consequently considered as a circular process (Winkin, 1981).

At the same time, Bertalanffy's research group (1950, 1968) set out a general systems theory whereby, whatever its nature, the system was defined as *"a complex of elements in interaction, these interactions being of an ordered (non-random) nature"* (Bertalanffy, 1973).

The "*one best way*" was definitively rejected in favour of a contingent vision of the organisation which was no longer articulated as a vertical hierarchy of authority, but instead as a set of interwoven sub-systems (Morgan, 1986). The actor as recipient or transmitter gives way to a more global vision that considers all the actors as a human resource system that interacts with the rest of the system. The communicational interest focuses more on the structures, processes, and technology, and the organisation's performance depends on the coordination between the structure, technologies and human capital. For Mintzberg (1982), communication and control form part of the "*coordination mechanisms*" that he argued could be considered "*as the fundamental aspects of the structure, the glue that holds together the different parts of the organisation.*" (p.19).

2. Where does communication fit into management control?

In the theories we mentioned, communication may be considered as contributing to management control objectives. Control processes are therefore strongly influenced by the communication situation, and their effectiveness will depend on the effectiveness of the said communication. And yet this communicational dimension has generally been neglected in the management control literature.

In this section, we set out a typology of the principle concepts of management control, depending on the role attached to notions of information, relationships and/or communication. Some 'models', while giving more or less importance to the human aspect of the function, fail to consider the communicational dimension of control (3.1.). However, we would argue that the control process concept must be underpinned by communication, which is why we decided to develop a definition on this basis (3.2.).

2.1 Management control defined without communication

2.1.1 The Sloan-Brown model: too financial for a management control model

According to many authors (Chandler, 1977; Johnson and Kaplan, 1987, Bouquin, 2005a), management control first appeared in the 1920s at the instigation of Alfred Sloan and Donaldson Brown, respectively president and vice-president of General Motors (GM).

Bouquin (2005a) describes the Sloan-Brown model as based on three key hypotheses. The first consists of a vertical division of the organisation into responsibility centres that are evaluated on the basis of their accounting and financial performance with the application of internal transfer prices. The second hypothesis, which is linked to the first, involves the coordination of projects by forward planning, conveyed in the accounting reports. The third hypothesis is based on an extremely hierarchical, contractual relationship between general management and the decentralised entities, resulting in objective evaluations and improved performance.

This model owes its success to three control process components, identified by Bouquin (2005a): choice or decision-making criteria (measured largely by ROI); measurement instruments (mainly accounting tools) that are used to forecast, monitor realisations and make choices; and an operational process based on anticipation (developed via plans and budgets).

Thus, we can see that the traditional management control model, as it was conceived and implemented at GM, consists of using accounting as an instrument of analysis, forecasting, coordination and motivation for operational staff. It is not so much a management control process as a financial control process, and this can lead to communication difficulties between business leaders and operational managers. In the Sloan-Brown model, the financial aspect predominates over organisational behaviour aspects, particularly those related to developing communication between the leaders and managers. Although Sloan created cross-sector committees in order to get division managers involved in the strategy design process and to create bridges (Bouquin, 2005a), organisation of these meetings remained spasmodic and, in a present-day context, fails to promote coherence for the organisation as a whole.

2.1.2 Management control for Anthony: a one-way process

Anthony's conceptual framework is a reference in management control research. Its 3-layered typology (strategic planning, management control, and operational control) together with its well-known definitions of management control are often cited in research papers and textbooks on the discipline. Management control, as defined by Anthony in 1965 and 1988, is designed to give managers the indispensable tools needed to set objectives and ensure their implementation, to plan the resources needed, taking into consideration the organisation's strategy.

In his 1965 typology, Anthony focused on economic aspects rather than cultural and behavioural factors. His work fit into a management-by-objectives model with a universal vocation, something that was questioned by Hofstede and, more generally, by the defenders of the cultural approach (Ekoka, 1999). His framework did not consider the "*processing of information*" as part of the "*planning-control system.*" In effect, data processing is seen as a parallel process that informs all three levels of the system (Figure1). The same was true for Giglioni and Bedeian (1974) who considered information processing as a system concomitant with control processes. Based on the definition by Mundel (1967, p.160), they defined control as a "*cyclical and constant activity of planning – action – comparison – correction, supported by a communication system or a flow of continuous and concomitant information.*"

Internally-oriented processes

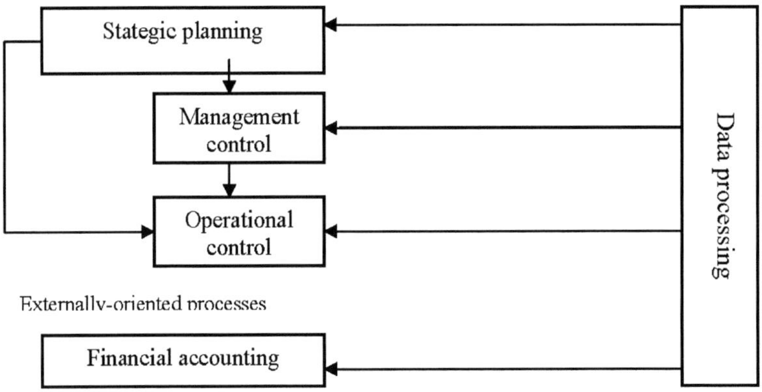

Figure 1. Anthony's conceptual framework (Source: Anthony, 1965, p. 22)

Anthony (1965, p.17) defined management control as "*the process by which managers obtain assurance that resources have been obtained and used efficiently and effectively in order to achieve the organisation's objectives.*"

In 1988, he redefined the term to give it a wider meaning: "*Management control is the process by which managers influence other members of the organisation in order to implement the organisation's strategies.*" (Anthony 1988, p. 10).

The definitions are similar insofar as both consider managers as the owners of control processes. However, they differ in that the managers' goals have changed. Initially, the aim was to "obtain assurance", in other words, not so much to check efficiency and effectiveness but rather a "*process of convergence of goals*" (Bouquin, 2005c). Secondly, the aim

was to *"influence other members of the organisation."* This involves directing others' actions (always managers according to Anthony, but certainly at other levels too) in order to achieve the organisation's goals.
In both cases, it is a one-way process: the strategy inspires managers who orient others' actions towards implementation. Bouquin (2005a) states that in this sense there is no *"inverse control loop towards strategy."* The conceptual framework drawn up by Anthony presents a control model in which managers are transmitters and the organisation's other actors are recipients (Figure 2).

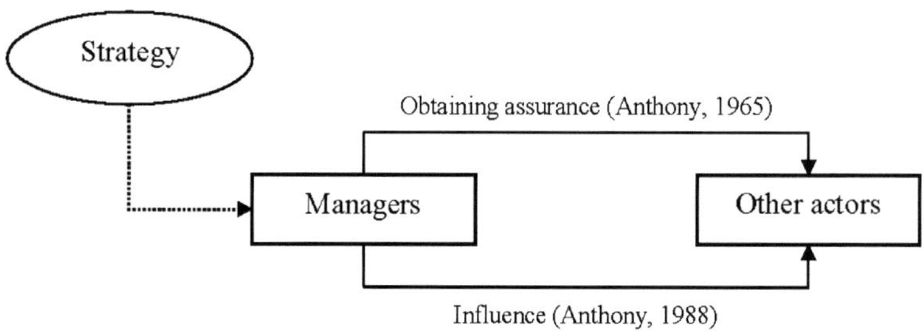

Figure 2. Management control according to Anthony

2.1.3 Management control: a process based on information

So far we have seen that neither the traditional Sloan-Brown model nor the framework drawn up by Anthony considers the informational process as an inherent part of management control. Lowe (1971) broke away from this vision by refusing to accept information processing as being separate from the decision-making process. He argued that all decision-making centres are also centres of information as, at the very least, they must provide information about the decisions taken. In comparison with Anthony's framework, Lowe also incorporated the notion of feedback. He argued that it was one of the bases of the control system and that in this context it helped provide input for the modifications required to pre-established plans.

In the same way, Mintzberg (1990) considered the information process as one of the keys to management, underpinning the decision-making process. He grouped managers' different roles into three categories: interpersonal, decisional, and information-related. Among other things, the latter include a role of active observer where the manager is looking for information from his or her contacts and subordinates, and a role of disseminator where he or she must share and disseminate much of the information obtained. Thus Mintzberg argued that managers not only transmit information but also ensure the dissemination of information coming from other members of the organisation.

In 1994, Henri Bouquin also stressed the importance of information in the framework of management control process: "*Leaders need information to help them make decisions and especially to help them to think ahead. This is one of the primary roles of management control*" (Bouquin, 2005a, p. 3) A few lines later (p. 4), he adds: "*Construction of interlinked mechanisms of external and internal coherence: the two control missions are determined by these aspects. They are based on information.*"

In turn, Simons (1995, p.5) defined management control as "*the formal, information-based routines and procedures managers use to maintain or alter patterns in organizational activities*."

The acknowledged importance of information in the context of management control process is the outcome of changes to the environment. In effect, the traditional control model is perfectly valid in a predictable and relatively simple environment. Rapid changes in the business world have now made information a key control factor. Effective decisions rely on the deciders' capacity to get the right information at the right moment, thereby enabling the organisation to adapt to a fluctuating environment (Cyert and March, 1963).

2.1.4 Management control with a relational dimension

The Taylor-oriented work organisation aimed to limit information and the exchange of information to the minimum needed for work: highly formalised task instructions demanded relatively little interaction between agents. The development of new rationalities led to a major upheaval in professional contexts (autonomy, cross-sector organisation, team projects, etc.) involving intensive and more complex coordination.

Hopwood was the first to go beyond a purely functional approach in his thinking on accounting and management control by also taking the impact of organisational and social contexts into consideration. Linking the use of budgets with management style, Hopwood (1972) conducted an empirical study on the impact of this relationship on managers' behaviour, notably in their relations with other members of the organisation.

Löning (2005) reports that Hofstede called into question instrumental and functional studies on management control as early as 1967, which he considered too remote from corporate realities. Instead, he began focusing on the social and human aspects of the function. He studied the budget-related behavioural factors, observing superior-subordinate relations. His research "*opened the door to all the literature on performance evaluation styles, (and) the use of budgets to assess performance and budgetary pressure*" (Löning, 2005, p. 352).

Even earlier, during the era of Taylorism and the division of labour, one author stood apart for his modernist thinking on management in general and management control in particular: M.P. Follett focused on developing an understanding of human and social relations on negotiation and conflict resolution, work organisation, and people management on a daily basis. She was particularly interested in interactions between individuals. She argued that control is "*a process for coordinating the responsibilities, decisions and actions of the principal actors in a firm to serve the coherence of the team that they jointly form*" (Fiol, 2005, p. 278). Managers need to develop cross-sector relationships as far as possible in order to ensure that such coordination is effective. Lateral relations thus need to be developed and maintained so as to facilitate all the control processes.[2]

Recent empirical studies in France have focused on the relational aspect of the control function. A study by Chiapello (1990) involving 138 corporate controllers illustrated the importance of interpersonal factors regarding the position. "*According to the controllers, degrees and know-how are far less important than interpersonal skills for a successful career in this field,*" (p.19). In a similar study involving 230 financial managers and/or corporate control managers, Jordan (1998) noted a shift in cooperation between controllers and deciders. "*In reality, the role of designer and that of coordinator in particular are highly developed. As for what controllers actually want, we have again seen the role of people coordinator develop to the detriment of a more technical role.*"

---

[2] Follett in his conference "the control process", Gulick and Urwick (1937), p. 161-169, cited by Fiol (2005, p. 273).

Bollecker (2000) conducted an analysis of 198 management controller job offers published in a news weekly specialised in the field, and noted the importance of interpersonal skills in the job profile. "*This aspect of the work is of considerable importance for firms, as 40.4% of them demand these skills in their job descriptions.*" In two articles related to his thesis which focused on 81 industrial firms from the key industrial area in the East of France, Bollecker looked at the coordination role played by controllers between an organisation's different units and demonstrated its importance in "*the match between decisions and organisational goals, or in other words, a convergence of goals*" (Bollecker, 2001). He also highlighted the development of cooperation between corporate controllers and operational managers and so, "*implicitly, the importance of the controller's sociological dimension*" (Bollecker, 2003).

2.2 Management control based on communication

In the conceptual literature, we have seen that what we call management control is presented in accordance with different models that vary between a financial and technical approach, a one-way approach, a set of data-based procedures, or a process with a relational and sociological dimension. Some control-focused authors have highlighted the importance of communication, although generally speaking, this is limited to just one of its aspects (verbal or oral communication, communication resources, communication skills, etc.), or is studied in relation to the corporate controller's work rather than the control process.

In 1968, Vardaman and Halterman highlighted the importance of communication in all management processes. They argued that "*good results are linked to good management control ... a good control process results from the appropriate skills for passing on decisions and information. If managers cannot manage the communication function correctly, their perceptions will be deformed, their conclusions will be inexact and subsequent decisions will be defective*" (p.14). In this study, the authors consider three key factors for the analysis and evaluation of "*managerial control*": problem definition, communication skills, and managerial competence.

More recently, a study on the image of corporate controllers by Chiapello (1990) indicated that the latter put good communication skills at the top of their list of major concerns. 58% consider them as "indispensable" in their job, 38% judge them as "very important", and the remaining 4% consider them to be “important”. Nobre (1998) investigated corporate controller job offers and noted that firms mentioned the need for communicational skills more often than attention to detail and analytical skills. In a study on corporate controllers’ oral communication practices involving 118 controllers, Fornerino *et al.* (2003) concluded that specific communication techniques are a key success factor in management control and that “*the practice of open communication*” leads managers to evaluate the control function more favourably.

Thus, communicational skills appear to be extremely important for both managers and controllers. Nonetheless, we believe that a wider perspective should be taken with regard to communication in the global control process.

In effect, the objective of management control is to provide managers with the tools and information they need to analyse situations, set goals and ensure coordination, schedule the actions to be taken and ensure their execution, measure performance and make the necessary corrective decisions. While this process concerns all managers, it cannot be limited to each entity’s sphere of action separate from all the others. Thus, by dividing the organisation into responsibility centres, each with its own goals, management control promotes local objectives to the detriment of the global objective (Ekoka, 1999). Managers must therefore ensure the coherence of their goals and synchronise their actions. This implies developing vertical and horizontal communication; a process which, at the end of the day, governs the effectiveness of control. Vertically, the purpose of control is firstly to set out and explain the organisation’s objectives at all levels of the hierarchy, and secondly to stimulate the steady flow of information that is indispensable to strategic planning, and to process the information needed to assess performance. Horizontally, cross-sector communication is organised within the control process framework to respond to the coordination needs of decentralised units.

It therefore appears useful to include the communicational dimension in a definition of control. We thus define management control as: “**the process by which managers communicate with other members of the organisation so as to guarantee the coherence of their daily activities and the convergence of these activities towards the strategy.**”

Conclusion

By incorporating disciplines such as sociology and communication, our paper offers clearer insight into the use of concepts regarding information, interpersonal relationships, and communication in management control. It also demonstrates the importance of the communicational factor in management control process: in the framework of an instrumental vision, communication contributes to the realisation of control objectives: it is a control tool, a factor of motivation, an instrument of influence and a coordination mechanism, depending on whether one follows, respectively, the traditional organisation approach, the human relations school, the decision-making theory, or systemic analysis theory.

This paper also sets out a typology of management control definitions, in accordance with a communicational approach. Thus, we identified 4 types of management control representations: a financial and technical model, a one-way approach, a set of data-based procedures, and a process with a relational and sociological dimension.

Our definition of management control explicitly incorporates communication.

However, our paper is limited insofar as it is underpinned by a theoretical construct only. It would therefore be useful to supplement it with empirical studies in order to reveal the true extent of the communicational dimension on control processes. In addition, this study does not allow us to explore the communication 'black box' and consequently to examine its impact on effective management control.

Bibliography

Anthony R.N. (1965), *Planning and control systems, A framework for analysis*, Boston, Division of Research, Harvard Business School

—. (1988), *The Management Control Fonction*, The Harvard Business School Press, Trad. Fr. (1993) *La fonction contrôle de gestion*, PubliUnion, Paris

Bertalanffy L. (1973), *Théorie générale des systèmes*, Dunod, Paris

Bollecker M. (2000), "Contrôleur de gestion: une profession à dimension relationnelle ?", *Actes du 21ème congrès de l'AFC*, Angers

—. (2001), "Les contrôleurs de gestion: des hommes de liaison ?", *Revue Direction et Gestion*, N°188-189, juillet, p.57-63

—. (2003), “La dimension sociologique du contrôle de gestion par l’analyse des relations de coopération entre contrôleur de gestion et responsables opérationnels”, *Les cahiers de recherches du GREGOR*, IAE de Paris, avril

Bouquin H. (2005a), *Les fondements du contrôle de gestion*, PUF, Paris (1ère éd., 1994)

—. (2005c), “Robert Newton Anthony: la référence”, in *Les grands auteurs en Contrôle de Gestion*, Bouquin, H. (dir.), EMS, 2005, p. 109-143

Chandler A.D. (1977), *La main visible des managers*, Economica, Paris, 1989 (trad.)

Chiapello E. (1990), “Contrôleurs de gestion, comment concevez-vous votre fonction?”, *Echanges*, N° 92, p. 7-11

Cyert R.M., March J.G. (1963), *A behavioral theory of the firm*, Prentice Hall, New Jersey

Ekoka B., (1999), *Comptabilité et contrôle et de gestion appliqués aux nouvelles méthodes de production et de commercialisation*, thèse de doctorat, Université de Toulouse I

—. (1999), *Comptabilité et contrôle et de gestion appliqués aux nouvelles méthodes de production et de commercialisation*, thèse de doctorat, Université de Toulouse I.

Fayol H. (1918), *Administration industrielle et générale*, Dunod, Paris

Felts A. A. (1992), “Organizational communication: a critical perspective”, *Administration & Society*, Vol. 23, Iss. 4, p. 495-517 Cosette M. (1991), “Penser autrement le système relationnel de l’organisation”, *Actes du troisième colloque en communication organisationnelle*, GISCOR / Département de communication, Université de Montréal

Fiol M. (2005), “Mary Parker Follett: le contrôle pour penser”, in *Les grands auteurs en Contrôle de Gestion*, Bouquin, H. (dir.), EMS, 2005, p. 253-281

Fornerino M., Godener A., Deglaine J. (2003), “L’influence des pratiques de communication orale des contrôleurs de gestion sur les attitudes et comportements des managers”, *Actes du 14ème Congrès de l’Association Francophone de Comptabilité*. Louvain-la–neuve, Belgique.

Giddens A. (1984), *The constitution of society*, Tr. Fr., L*a constitution de la société* (1987), PUF

Giglioni G. B., Bedeian A. G. (1974), “A conspectus of management control theory : 1900-1972”, *Academy of Management Journal*, Vol. 17, N° 2, p. 292-305

Hopwood A.G. (1972), “An Empirical Study of the Role of Accounting Data in Performance Evaluation”, *Journal of Accounting Research*, supplément, Vol. 10, p. 156-193

Johnson H.T., Kaplan R.S. (1987), *Relevance Lost, the Rise and Fall of Management Accounting*, Harvard Business School Press, Boston

Jordan H. (1998), “Planification et contrôle de gestion en France en 1998”, *Cahiers de recherche du Groupe HEC*, N° 644/1998

Löning H. (2005), “Geert Hofstede”, in *Les grands auteurs en Contrôle de Gestion*, Bouquin, H. (dir.), EMS, 2005, p. 347-366

Lowe E.A. (1971), “On the idea of a management control system: integrating accounting and management control”, *The Journal of Management Studies*, Vol. 8, N° 1, p. 1-12

MacGregor D. (1960), *The human side of Entreprise*, MacGrawHill.

Mintzberg H. (1982), *Structure et dynamique des organisations*, Les éditions de l’organisation, Paris (trad.)

—. (1990), *Le management : voyage au centre des organisations*, Editions d’organisations, 1999, Paris (trad.)

Morgan G. (1986), *Images of Organization*, Sage Publications, Beverly Hills

Nobre T. (1998), “L’évolution du contrôle de gestion. Analyse à partir de l’étude des offres d’emplois”, *Actes du 19ème congrès de l’AFC*, Vol. 2, p. 741-753

Peters T., Waterman R. H. (1982), In search of excellence: Lessons from America’s best-run companies, Harper & Row, New York, Tr. Fr., *Le prix de l’excellence* (1983), Interéditions, Paris

Simon H.A. (1945), *Administrative Behavior*, McMillan, New York, Tr. Fr., *Administration et processus de decision* (1983), Economica, Paris

Simons R. (1995), Levers of Control, Harvard University Press, Boston.

Taylor F.W. (1911), *The principles of scientific management*, Harper, NewYork, 1929, Tr. Fr., *La direction scientifique des entreprises* (1971), Dunod, Paris

Taylor J. R., Van Every E. J. (2000), *The Emergent Organization : Communication as its site and surface*, Lawrence Erlbaum Associates, Mahwah, New Jersey

Vardaman G. T., Halterman C. C. (1968), *Managerial Control Through Communication: Systems for Organizational Diagnosis and Design*, New York: Wiley (Trad. Fr., *La communication au service du contrôle de gestion : les systèmes de diagnostic et de conception des organisations*, Paris, collection France-Gestion, 1974)

Wiener N. (1948), *Cybernetics, or Control and Communication in the Animal and the Machine*, MIT Press, Boston, ds Willett, G., *La communication modélisée*, Renouveau Pédagogique inc., Ottawa, 1992.

Winkin Y. (1981), dir., *La nouvelle communication*, Du Seuil, Paris

Organizational Learning and Knowledge Development Peculiarities in Small and Medium Family Enterprises

Samy Basly

Abstract

The aim of this theoretical contribution is to analyse the processes of organizational learning and knowledge development within the small and medium sized family firm. Due to its founding characteristics, family SME seems to be a closed, hermetic, and rigid organization. Furthermore, the specificity of mechanisms of learning and knowledge management, in general, within this entity are justified by:

- First, the overlapping of "family" and "company" spheres: the family sphere realizes a unique contribution because it constitutes a supplementary source of knowledge inbound to the company compared to a firm without family involvement,
- Then, the frequency of the exchanges within the organization: the processes of exchange of piece of information and knowledge take place not only in the organizational context but also and especially in the family context. The family meetings constitute, for example, supplementary occasions for exchange and sharing of knowledge.

Schematically, two major characters inherent to this entity constitute obstacles to organizational learning. Indeed, conservatism and independence orientation strongly influence the processes of learning and knowledge development.

The literature suggests that the family system attempts to create and maintain a cohesiveness that supports the family "paradigm" which is described as the core assumptions, beliefs, and convictions that the family holds in relation to its environment. Information that is not consistent with this paradigm is resisted or ignored (Davis, 1983). The search for security, conformism and tradition are characteristic of conservative organizations. Particularly to the family firm, the conservative posture could be studied through three dimensions (Miller et al., 2003). First, on the governance level, the conservatism is exhibited by the plateauing and the growing rigidity of the owner-manager and by the inefficacy of the board of directors. Second, on the strategy level, conservative family SME favourites its actual markets, customers and products and globally is unwilling to change and adopt new paradigms. Then, on the organizational and cultural levels, this entity tends to be closed and introvert. These three components have an impact on knowledge development as the conservatism tends to limit the variation and the exposition to new environments. In short, within this entity the level of organizational knowledge would be weak.

The second variable influencing the processes of development of knowledge within family SME is the independence orientation. This orientation is a consequence of the family long-term commitment to the business. Paradoxically, this commitment has two contradictory effects on growth. First, it implies the pursuit of future development and continuity of the firm to make sure that the family heritage is passed on to the following generations. On the other hand, commitment implies a strategy of conservation of the heritage which passes by a strong search for independence. Aiming to guarantee its continuity, the (small and medium-sized) family firm establishes an independence orientation of three different types. First, from the financial point of view, it avoids turning to outside partners as much as possible (Hirigoyen, 1985). Then, on the human plan, it would be favourable on the appointment of family members or individuals belonging to the close relational circle to the posts of direction and would be reluctant on the recruitment of professional directors. Finally, to retain the decision-making in the hands of the family, the family firm tends to avoid the inter-organizational relations, cooperative investments, and tries to limit sharing of control of its investments. The contribution of outsiders (financiers, directors or partner organizations) can, however, be precious to the company. And the introversion would be a major obstacle to the perpetuity of the firm because it inhibits growth. As a consequence, independence orientation limits the accumulation of knowledge because, on one hand, the horizons of the company will be limited and have little variation, and on the other hand, the potential valuable knowledge contribution of outsiders is excluded.

The study of these variables raises questions about the efficacy of the organizational memory within the family firm. This organization runs particular risks because of the peculiarity of its knowledge management mechanisms. Because of its founding natural characteristics, the family firm nurtures mechanisms which reinforce the causal ambiguity (Nelson and Winter, 1982) by strengthening the voluntary effort to avoid either a too fast imitation or the loss of knowledge-based resources if the individual or the group holding it leaves the organization (Arrégle, 1995). In short, family firms show an inclination to concentrate the processes of knowledge management around its tacit dimension by encouraging its formation contrarily to the explicit component. However the weak externalization of knowledge coupled with the avoidance of sharing outside the family causes serious risks. First, an obvious risk of deterioration is present because of the weak importance of the organizational protection mechanisms and the strong reliance on individual memory. Moreover, we suggest a risk of erosion of knowledge due to the fragmentation caused by successions that do not preserve the unity of the firm. There is risk of "fragmentation" of the strategic knowledge if the company is shared between the potential successors. This risk would be less pronounced if a prior sharing of knowledge with outside directors had been engaged.

Another particularity of family firms is about the intergenerational transmission and transfer of knowledge (Cabrera-Suarez et al., 2001). Mechanisms inciting intergenerational transfer of knowledge must be set up because of the negative impact of conservatism and independence on organizational knowledge and due to the fragility of family firm organizational memory.

Keywords: Organizational knowledge, family business, conservatism, independence orientation.

A series of observations carried out by various authors leads to the observation that the crucial value-creating activities of the firm are based on knowledge. The greatest part of the activity of employees consists of processing information, and managing competences and knowledge (Wright et al., 1995). Generally, the performance of the firm depends more and more on its capacity to develop, gather, integrate, mobilize, and exploit flows of knowledge. Accordingly, knowledge-based approaches of the firm try to conjure up an integrated vision of the firm as a locus of knowledge creation (Nonaka and Takeuchi, 1998) or as an applicator of knowledge (Grant, 1996), knowledge being considered as the main valuable resource (Drucker, 1993). This new trend of conceptualization conceives of the firm as a portfolio of knowledge-based resources (Wright et al., 1995). These resources are varying in transferability and imitability and evolve along a life cycle and different phases of maturity. In an extreme vision, the elements of the value chain of the firm could be redefined in terms of knowledge-based activities or services (Wright et al., 1995). Already, for Penrose (1959), connections between tangible organizational resources and the services they provide are established through managerial knowledge, an ever-growing intangible resource. For Penrose, the firm is at the same time an administrative organization and a set of productive, human and physical resources. More importantly, the inputs of the production process are not the resources themselves but the services originating from them. It is on this level that knowledge intervenes since the services are a function of accumulated experience and knowledge that are specific to the firm. In sum, the knowledge-based view and its different components emphasizes the role of knowledge within the organizational processes and allows for a new conceptualization of this entity.

Despite the profusion of research about knowledge-based processes within the firm, rare studies tried to analyse them for the family firm[1]. The family firm can be defined as a firm controlled by one or more families involved in governance or management, or at least holding capital stakes in this organization[2]. Due to its specificities, this entity exhibits a specific behaviour as for the creation, development, sharing, protection and transmission of knowledge. Habbershon and Williams (1999) initiated the research aiming at the identification of the specific resources of the family firm. But, more than specific resources and capacities, the family firm uses a collective tacit knowledge needed to integrate, coordinate and mobilize effectively its resources (Cabrera-Suarez et al., 2002). The aim of the present contribution is to analyse the characteristics of the family firm critical to the knowledge-based processes. Due to its founding characteristics, family SME seems to be a closed, hermetic and rigid organization. Although this description can be criticized and challenged, it

[1] The study of Cabrera-Suarez et al. (2002) seems to initiate a knowledge-based approach for the family firm.

[2] The recurring problem of the family firm definition will not be addressed. On this question, cf. Astrachan et al. (2002); Litz (1995). Here we choose to adopt a general and common definition.

remains valid for many of these entities. The interaction between the family system and the firm system appears to be the essential element preventing the organization from quickly adapting to the changing conditions (Moloktos, 1991). Moloktos (1991) explains that when the life cycles of these two systems do not evolve at the same speed, the risks of crisis are significant. Thus, conservatism constitutes a first obstacle to knowledge development. Besides, small and medium family enterprise is strongly oriented towards independence which has advantages but also many drawbacks. The impact of this orientation on the system of resources and in particular on knowledge can be crucial.

This article is structured as follow: after analysing the two main variables influencing the development of knowledge within the family SME, we discuss some theoretical implications. Indeed, the study of these variables raises questions about the strength of the organizational memory within the family firm. This organization runs particular risks because of the peculiarity of its knowledge management mechanisms. Intergenerational transmission and transfer of knowledge could be the solution to protect and perpetuate valuable knowledge.

1. Idiosyncratic Characteristics of Small and Medium Family Enterprise and Development of Knowledge

Knowledge is an individual interpretation of information based on experience, abilities and personal competences (Bollinger and Smith, 2001). It is about understanding, awareness, or familiarity acquired, through time, by study, investigation, observation or experience. Generally, within organizations, two types of knowledge are encountered. The first form is the individual's or the team's knowledge. It is a specific expertise of the firm which is made up of a simple network, i.e. having few components and having easily identifiable limits (Arrégle, 1995). The second form of knowledge present within organizations is a collective one. It is organizational knowledge defined as a set of organizational routines created by a complex network of components (Arrégle, 1995). These routines do not depend on individual components, but on the whole organization, to exist. The collective aspect is emphasized by Bollinger and Smith (2001) who conceive organizational knowledge as the collective and cumulative knowledge or the "wisdom of the organization". Accumulated through time, incrementally and cumulatively, organizational knowledge constitutes the base which attracts, organizes and deploys other knowledge resources which are independent of the organization. Organizational knowledge is also essential to define the organization's operations and to found its identity. Organizational knowledge could be considered as a result of the organizational learning processes. Indeed, a large number of approaches and research in the field of organizational learning assimilate this phenomenon to a process of knowledge development. Serving to improve the performance of the organization or to enable it to explore new strategic paths, organizational learning should produce organizational knowledge.

Two variables are distinctive for the processes of knowledge development within the family SME. These are characteristics frequently emphasized by the literature as being specific to this organization. We will study the effects of conservatism and independence orientation on the development of the knowledge base of small and medium family enterprise.

1.1 Conservatism

Conservatism is the attachment to the choices of the past (Timur, 1988). The literature about cultural specificities emphasizes the willingness to maintain the *status quo* and harmonious relations not only within the group but also within the entire society. The pursuit of security, conformism and tradition are characteristic of conservative organizations. The conservatism limits the variation and accordingly the extent of knowledge developed by the firm. Indeed, the literature stresses that this variation, i.e. the diversity of environments to which the firm is exposed, is strongly correlated with the amount of accumulated knowledge. Organizations exposed to a variety of business and institutional actors are likely to develop knowledge of an important set of events and thus learn more than poorly exposed ones. They are more able to define problems, errors, and opportunities than firms whose horizons of action are more reduced. The weak variation indeed implies a limited number of customers, competitors and other institutional actors. Accordingly, conservative organizations carry out only a simple loop learning which does not reform their theories-in-uses since they accumulate little knowledge. Particularly with a family firm, Miller et al. (2003) explain that the conservative posture of this entity is reflected on its governance, strategy and organization (mainly culture). We will discuss these three components in order to be able to understand their impact on the knowledge base.

1.1.1 Conservatism and firm governance

The first sphere concerned with conservatism is the governance of the firm[3]. Conservative organizations and particularly family firms are characterized by the persistence and substantial power of old generations who exert a strong supervision on the owner-manager. Otherwise, conservatism can be due to the owner-manager himself. He plays a significant role in the processes of organizational learning and influences the strategic posture that his firm adopts. A patriarchal family controlling a paternalist organization is the extreme case of figure (Jenster and Malone, 1991): being dependent to a high degree on its founder, the organization would be unable to promote change as it is not instigated by him. However, the founder or owner-manager may be unwilling to promote change. Hambrick, Geletkanycz and Fredrickson (1993) call this tendency to slow down change "commitment to the *status quo*" (CSQ). The management believes in the permanent accuracy of current strategies or organizational behaviours (Hambrick et al., 1993). Therefore, personal paradigms, which in the past proved their efficacy, constitute inhibitors to change. Thus, in spite of the evolution of the environment and performance requirements, the owner-manager could become inflexible and rigid by promoting practices and strategies resulting from past successes and avoiding decisions which can threaten his image or his economic wealth (Ward, 1997). Consequently, he perceives a weak need for adjustment even in the case of critical changes in the external environment. In sum, conservatism of the owner-manager constitutes a significant barrier to organizational learning and knowledge development within family SME.

The efficacy of the board of directors[4] is an indicator of the struggle against conservatism and strategic inertia. According to theoretical descriptions, this corporate body constitutes a source of strategic initiative and relevant information and also a source of expertise, counsel and control since it must also correct the trajectory in case of unsatisfactory management. However, its role within family SME needs to be moderated. Mustakallio and Autio (2001) argue that the role of the board of directors, measured by its composition and by the intensity of the control it exerts, would be more significant as the implication of the family members in the

[3] In France, Gérard Hirigoyen distinguishes between government and governance, the first pertaining to direction and decision, the second dealing about mechanisms of control.
[4] For the firms which adopt one.

management decreases - suggesting on the opposite side that the more the family is involved, the less decisive the role of the board would be. In general, the traditional family firm is known to have a board of directors whose members, selected according to their status and influence within the family and not according to their knowledge of the activity or industry, occupy their positions for long periods and have insufficient or inadequate professional competences. According to this description, they constitute a barrier to any attempt of change, potentially threatening the stability of the firm. Ranft and O'Neill (2001), notice that the founders of high-performing firms are even tempted to deliberately weaken the board of directors of their firms in order to maintain the *status quo*. The inward orientation is more corroborated in some family firms who simply do not implement such a body (Melin and Nordqvist, 2000).

However, the role of the board of directors can be crucial since it should increase the amount of information available to the operational management when planning or implementing strategies. This role is accomplished by insiders as well as external administrators[5]. The insiders contribute through their thorough understanding of the firm. The outsiders would prevent the dominance of a single line of thought by challenging the assumptions underlying the firm's strategies and injecting external knowledge. The results obtained by Schwartz and Barnes (1991), based on a sample of 262 family firms, prove the relevance of the incorporation of external administrators. The authors find that they provide unbiased points of view and constitute a precious means for the establishment of networks. In brief, the role of counsel accomplished by the board would have a significant influence on the strategic orientation of the firm by improving the variety and quality of information available for the strategic processes and, consequently, the variation, selection and retention of alternative paths of development (Mustakallio and Autio, 2002). This function of counsel should thus improve the capacity of the firm to innovate and establish new strategic directions. Unfortunately, small family enterprises do not seem to rely strongly on such a body.

The study of the conservatism of the family firm governance is a first necessary step because this factor has consequences on firm's strategy selection and implementation. Indeed, an analysis of the strategic manifestations of this posture has to be outlined.

---

[5] Nevertheless, the positive role of outsiders is frequently questioned and authors criticize their lack of knowledge of the firm and his environment, their low availability, and weak authority.

1.1.2 Strategic conservatism

Secondly, the conservatism of the firm is expressed strategically. Generally, the family firm has a tendency to be strongly devoted to a strategy which becomes a source of rigidity. The literature suggests that the family system attempts to create and maintain a cohesiveness that supports the family "paradigm" which is described as the core assumptions, beliefs, and convictions that the family holds in relation to its environment (Gudmundson et al., 1999). Information which is not consistent with this paradigm is resisted or ignored (Davis, 1983). The more conservative the family is, the less it works for change. Strategic conservatism implies stagnation and risk of insularity (Miller et al., 2003). The firm carries out few changes in its objectives, business, and product lines or markets (Miller et al., 2003). Generally, family SME is known to maintain its differentiation through the same activities and policies (Gallo and Sveen, 1991) and to privilege a defensive position with protection of its niche. Accordingly, its market shares are likely to be narrowing and its market potential exhausting. Consequently, the conservative strategic attitude can inhibit knowledge development. In fact, the organizational learning remains weak since the top directors focus primarily on problem solving rather than on the search and pursuit of new opportunities. Indeed, they have a tendency to deal exclusively with internal issues pertaining to the efficiency of operations or quality of products and neglect issues pertaining to the evolution of market requirements or consumers' needs.
The third dimension where conservatism is exhibited is the culture of the firm. Instead of nurturing the will of change and development, cultural conservatism implies characteristics of preservation and rigidity.

1.1.3 Cultural conservatism

How are conservative organizations culturally characterized? According to theory, they are strongly impregnated by tradition and behave in a bureaucratic and centralized manner (Miller et al. 2003). Decision-making is exclusively in the hands of top directors and formal communication is favoured. Moreover, the organization tends to maintain the same hierarchy, the same interpretation schemes and communication modes. This description may easily be transferable to the traditional family firm. More precisely, the pursuit of the goal of culture and identity protection constitutes the last element exerting a negative influence on the learning orientation within the family SME. Many authors emphasize the central role of culture and values in shaping the competitive posture of this organization (Dyer, 1986). For instance, analysing values in the family firm, Salvato et al. (2002) show that they influence activities and routines of the organization aiming to create a competitive advantage. The family firms show an inclination to be independent from their environment and the external culture (Donckels and Fröhlich, 1991). In addition, they insist on artefacts which generally originate from the firm's local environment and are the result of the influence of certain members of the family, in particular that of the founder (Gallo and Sveen, 1991). Consequently, cultural conservatism would have detrimental effects on the knowledge as it inhibits any will of change and organizational learning.

1.2 Independence orientation

The second main variable influencing the processes of knowledge development within family SME is independence orientation. This orientation is a consequence of the family long-term commitment to the business. Paradoxically, this commitment has two contradictory effects on growth. First, it implies the pursuit of future development and continuity of the firm to make sure that the family heritage is passed on to the following generations. On the other hand, commitment implies a strategy of conservation of the heritage, which passes on through a strong search for the independence. Aiming to guarantee its continuity, family SME establishes an independence orientation on three levels (see Figure 1).

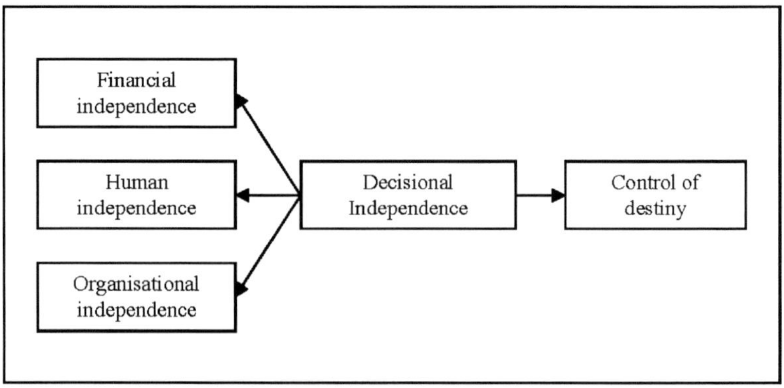

Figure 1. Dimensions of the independence orientation

First, from the financial point of view, it avoids turning to outside partners as much as possible (Hirigoyen, 1985). Then, on the human plan, it would be favourable to the appointment of family members or individuals belonging to the close relational circle to the posts of direction and would be reluctant to the recruitment of professional directors (Astrachan and Kolenko, 1996; King et al., 2001). Finally, to retain the decision-making in the hands of the family, the family firm tends to avoid inter-organizational relations, cooperative investments, and tries to limit the sharing of control of its investments (Donckels and Fröhlich, 1991). The contribution of outsiders (financiers, directors or partner organizations) can, however, be precious to the company. And the introversion would be a major obstacle to the perpetuity of the firm because it inhibits growth. Independence orientation limits the accumulation of knowledge because, on one hand, the horizons of the company will be limited and unvaried, and on the other hand, the potential valuable knowledge contribution of the outsiders is excluded.

1.2.1 Financial independence

Devoted to its goal of continuity, family SME tries to evolve in a more or less hermetic universe. Accordingly, external financial intervention is avoided because it could deteriorate the independence of the firm. The resource dependence theory provides an explanation for this attitude (Davis et al., 2000): the higher the dependence on the (resource) capital, the more the potential financier would have power and influence in the decision-making within the firm (Davis et al., 2000). Consequently, family SME seems reluctant to adopt modes of financing other than internal ones. Schematically, it appears strongly predisposed to implement or at least to adhere to the recommendations of the pecking order theory (Myers and Majluf, 1984). It favours generally internal financing by the retention of earnings and the constitution of reserves. Moreover, it avoids opening financially to external sources. First, it tends to avoid debt and relies enormously on costly internal capital. Financing through equity has other specificities that fear family SME. Quotation, for instance, could involve a major change in the ownership structure and governance of the firm due to the entry of external shareholders (Schulze et al., 2003).

Financial independence has significant consequences on the knowledge base of the firm. Initially, even if internal financing helps to avoid the diffusion of the cognitive map of management and endangering growth opportunities not perceived by competitors (Charreaux, 2002), this advantage is compensated for by the fact that, at the same time, internal financing implies an inward orientation and a weak development of the knowledge base as it prevents the penetration of a potentially relevant external cognitive contribution. In addition, debt avoidance, even if it permits limiting the risk of diffusion of information and management cognitive schemas towards bankers, implies a lot of disadvantages relative to the firm's knowledge base. Indeed, the contribution of the bank could be valuable since it can take part in the development of the knowledge base through adhering or enriching the management vision and cognitive map (Charreaux, 2002). Lastly, external shareholders can play a valuable role for the firm's knowledge base. First, they could exert their influence on the development of the vision of the firm. Then, they can play a significant role in providing proposals for investment opportunities. External ownership thus makes it possible to extend the knowledge base. Family SME seem not to recognize these valuable contributions and follow a conservative financial behaviour (Hirigoyen, 1985). As a result, financial independence is likely to limit the amount of knowledge inbound to the small and medium family firm.

1.2.2 Human independence

The pursuit of independence inhibits knowledge development from the human point of view. The family firm adhering completely to the principle of managerial independence is limited quantitatively and qualitatively by the lack of human resources. Indeed, trying to avoid loss of control, family management tends to limit external managerial implication even if it would be valuable to undertake organizational learning. To justify the customary recruitment of directors and managers from the family sphere, the literature speaks about paternalist management and nepotism which would be characteristics of the traditional family firm. Welsch (1996) observes that when the family firm makes a decision relating to its human resources, it is more influenced by family values and personality issues than by a standardized set of performance and competence indicators. The altruism characterizing the owner-manager, generally the father or head of the family, implies a feeling of natural right among members of family. The owner-manager is thus incited to make use of firm resources to provide employment and other privileges to the family members (Schulze et al., 2001). Dunn (1995) emphasizes a critical consequence of this behaviour. Indeed, the pursuit of the objective of preferential employment of family members may often signify the hiring of sub-optimal employees. Further, the analysis of Harris et al. (1994) shows that the rigidities of the family firm when it is about change of paradigm, are primarily due to the sclerosis to the human element:

- Family firms privilege internal succession, which is one of its main goals, and are devoted to the principle of loyalty, whereas new paradigms are likely to originate from outside employees or management,
- Internally-trained successors have weak external experience, whereas new paradigms are likely to emerge from the variety of personal experiences,
- Heir of the entrepreneur can suffer from a lack of self-confidence, whereas the possibility of emergence of new paradigms generally requires a great confidence in personal judgment.

Another characteristic of family firms is to be emphasized. This type of organization is known to be loyal, i.e. seeking to keep the same employees for long periods. According to Miller et al. (2003), the same policies of recruitment and promotion, for example, are implemented at the profit of the same people. The absence of recruitment implies, however, an ageing of human resources and management in particular (Jenster and Malone, 1991).

Overall, the prerequisite in external competences is explained by the contribution in knowledge resources that outsiders can offer. Therefore, human independence, implying exclusively internal recruitment and responsibility transfer, has a notable negative impact on the knowledge base of the small and medium family firm.

1.2.3 Relational independence

Gray (1995) observes that owner-managers of small firms adhere to an organizational culture impregnated by individualism and anti-participation. The potential attenuation of independence constitutes a short or long term threat explaining probably the weak co-operative orientation of family SME. Indeed, the co-operation contains a dynamics which can evolve the co-operation in to a relation of global dependence. Indeed, the attenuation of the independence, initially limited to the only field of agreement, would be extended to the entire firm (Adam-Ledunois and Le Vigoureux, 1998). Another explanation of the weak organizational networking of family SME can be induced from the explanations of the network approach. Belonging to a network implies, indeed, acceptance of external influence. The position of a firm within its network can influence, and is also influenced by, the expectations of other actors as regards the way it should behave and interact with other organizations (Johanson and Mattson,

1988). Consequently, the position occupied by a firm, even if it permits access to new and valuable resources, relations and markets, is constraining because it shapes its role and relations with the other firms. According to some authors, when they cooperate, family firms would choose similar firm to themselves, i.e. other family firms. Indeed, pursuing the same principles, in particular independence, and having a comparable size, they would not constitute a threat to independence[6]. In summary, family SME exhibits a weak co-operative orientation and a disinclination to integrate economic networks (Donckels and Fröhlich, 1991). Consequently, it is likely to develop a poor knowledge base since the role of the network can be crucial at least on three levels. First, through its implication in a network, a firm can develop a high awareness of opportunities and threats pertaining to its activities, since it is strongly exposed to environment. Second, its decisions and actions (concerning strategies to be adopted, for example) can be founded on an imitation of other more experienced actors of the network. Finally, the network may allow for a direct transfer of knowledge between participants. In sum, we can argue that the influence of relational independence orientation on the development of knowledge is negative.

2. Implications: Specificities of Learning and Knowledge Development within Family SME

The characteristics of conservatism and independence orientation strongly influence the processes of organizational learning and knowledge development within family SME. The justification of this specificity is due to the fact that this entity shows:

- First, the overlapping of "family" and "company" spheres: the family sphere realizes a unique contribution because it constitutes a supplementary source of knowledge inbound to the company compared with a firm without family involvement,
- Then, the frequency of the exchanges within the organization: the processes of exchange of pieces of information and knowledge take place not only in the organizational context but also and especially in the family context. The family meetings constitute, for example, supplementary occasions of exchange and sharing of knowledge.

[6] According to Adam-Ledunois and Le Vigoureux (1998), when they cooperate, the natural preference of SMEs is for situations which see the emerging of a mutual dependence rather than subservience for one of the parties (Adam-Ledunois and Le Vigoureux, 1998).

Two main consequences are to be analysed. In this entity, the activities of organizational learning and development of strategic knowledge are centred on the family encouraging causal ambiguity. The second phenomenon is that within the family, knowledge is preserved and perpetuated through a process of intergenerational transfer.

2.1 The family in the heart of the processes of knowledge development

The analysis of the conservatism and independence orientation raises questions about the efficacy of the organizational memory within the family firm. What are the mechanisms of preservation of knowledge within the family firm? This organization runs specific risks because of the singularity of the mechanisms of knowledge management.

The typical paternalistic management of the family firm which implies a centralization of power and decision obviously allows the flexibility of the organization. But, at the same time, it influences the processes of learning and development of knowledge which are henceforth centred on the family sphere. The family holds the monopoly of the acquisition, sharing and transfer of knowledge within the organization. Taking advantage of its rights of decision and control, the family dominates the management of knowledge. Overall, internalization of strategic knowledge would be primarily the fact of the owner-manager and his family. Then, the family firm shows a weak socialization of strategic knowledge out of the family circle. In spite of the contribution they provide to the development of the knowledge base outsiders are likely to be excluded. The essence of knowledge, i.e. its tacit component, being mainly acquired by the family members, there is a tendency to limit its diffusion. There would be, consequently, a conscious will of the top familial management of not engaging a process of externalization. Firms whose "familiness" (Habbershon and Williams, 1999) is weak would behave differently and tolerate sharing activities of strategic knowledge management with outsiders. This sharing should have a beneficial effect on the construction and development of the organization's knowledge base because of the variety and richness of externals' contributions.

Therefore, because of its founding natural characteristics, the small family firm nurtures mechanisms which reinforce the causal ambiguity (Nelson and Winter, 1982) by strengthening the voluntary effort to avoid either an overly fast imitation or the loss of knowledge-based resources if the individual or the group holding it leave the organization (Arrégle, 1995). The family firm is quite inclined to privilege mechanisms of protection of knowledge such as:

- Strengthening the tacit aspect and avoiding formalizing,
- Voluntarily maintaining the complexity.

In short, family firms show an inclination to concentrate the processes of knowledge management around its tacit dimension by encouraging its formation contrarily to the explicit element. However, the weak externalization of knowledge coupled with the avoidance of sharing outside the family causes serious risks. First, an obvious risk of deterioration is present because of the weak importance of the organizational protection mechanisms and the strong reliance on individual memory. This risk depends on the level of learning, local or organizational, and more particularly seems to be expressed when knowledge is attached to particular groups of individuals. This risk of deterioration is also correlated with the extent of diffusion of knowledge. Particularly to Chinese family firms, Tsang (1999) observes that they can be classified as "the one-man institution" within Shrivastava's (1983) typology. The owner is the man "who is knowledgeable about all aspects of the business, (and) is the key broker of organizational knowledge. He acts as a filter and controls the flow of information to and from every important manager" (Shrivastava, 1983, p. 20). In sum, even if the family firm exhibits a weak erosion of knowledge because of the weak rotation of directors, an important risk is inherent in the eventuality of a sudden loss of a key member of the family and the company. The organizational memory of the family firm is fragile. Thus, even if operational knowledge gained from the daily activities and profiting the operational management team is better protected from extinction, the strategic knowledge held primarily by the owner-manager and the members of his family is endangered. Moreover, we suggest a risk of erosion of knowledge due to the fragmentation caused by successions that do not preserve the unity of the firm. There is indeed a risk of "fragmentation" of the strategic knowledge if the company is shared between the potential successors. This risk would be less pronounced if a prior sharing of knowledge with outside directors had been engaged.

In summary, in order to protect experience and knowledge acquired from its activities, which could be lost with the departure of the person or the team holding it, the organization have to set up mechanisms of sharing and diffusion. The solving of the problems of diffusion and transfer of knowledge can, in the case of the family firm, be founded on a specific process: the intergenerational transfer of knowledge.

2.2 Intergenerational transfer of knowledge: means of knowledge preservation

Mechanisms inciting intergenerational transfer of knowledge must be set up because of the negative impact of conservatism and independence orientation on the knowledge base and due to the fragility of family firm organizational memory. The process of transfer of knowledge through generations is thus crucial to be able to maintain the competitive advantage of the firm. It is important to operate a distinction between the strategic knowledge on one hand and the operational knowledge, on the other hand. Strategic knowledge is the competence generally held by the management involved in decision-making. Operational knowledge is that which is used or acquired by employees confronted with daily operational management. In fact, the modes of appropriation of these types of knowledge are different. Ward and Aronoff (1996) make a similar distinction between the acquisition of business knowledge and the acquisition of leadership capacities. Initially, the successor has to be able to acquire and use the operational knowledge which encompasses the founding know-how of the company. But the learning of the successor is more importantly about strategic knowledge stemming from the experience of direction acquired by the predecessors. It is a question of passing on not only the content of knowledge founding the advantage of the firm but the way of operating and of running business. Indeed, the transfer concerns a managerial competence of direction.

Competence being a competence in action (Le Boterf, 1994), the successor has to show competence, i.e. that he can act with competence. Not subject to formalization, the most suitable strategy of transfer of strategic knowledge would be observation that young managers supplement by a process of action learning. The predecessor has to delegate to the potential successor increasingly significant missions. Thus, the successor has to learn from his actions, discoveries and interactions and also from his experiences and the observation of his peers (Hugron and Boiteux, 1998). The learning of the successor is grounded mainly on an intense process of socialization. Indeed, strategic knowledge is shared within the family management and communicated to potential successors. In sum, transmission is less about content of knowledge than a methodology of problem solving.

Intergenerational transfer of knowledge within family firms is nevertheless problematic. Cabrera-Suarez et al. (2001) identify four obstacles against knowledge transfer:

- Characteristics of transferred knowledge, its causal ambiguity,
- Characteristics of the source (the predecessor) and especially its lack of motivation,
- Characteristics of the target (the successor): its absence of motivation, limited absorptive and retention capacity,
- Context of the transfer: sterile organizational context or difficult relations between the predecessor and the successor.

Conclusion

This contribution tries to develop an analysis of the processes of organizational learning and knowledge development within the small and medium sized family firms by focusing mainly on their characteristics of conservatism and independence. Even if conservative behaviour can be justified in the case of extreme uncertainties or abnormal risks weighing on the economic environment, it is, nevertheless, criticisable. Conservatism establishes an attitude and a thinking hostile to renewal. Yet, the theories of organizational learning stress that the commitment of the management team is an essential condition to the trigger and success of organizational learning. A strong and committed management is necessary in order to motivate the organization and to help it overcome the difficulties. Since human capital of the family firms shows positive characteristics of strong commitment, are cordial, friendly, and have close ties, and also the potential allowing for a deep specific tacit knowledge, we can suppose that this organization could successfully implement organizational learning activities. A condition would be that family SME could draw, from its human resources, the necessary commitment to struggle against the forces of conservatism. In order to obtain human resource commitment, it is necessary to involve all levels of direction and management and to sensitize them to the importance of their implication for the success of this orientation. The presence of a strong personality (generally the founder or the owner-manager) who motivates the employees and bring them together to achieve the organizational goals is essential. In particular, the owner-manager should support and encourage the process and also could transmit the knowledge accumulated through his personal commitment to other family members (Tsang, 1999). Thus, in spite of a rigid organizational structure, the owner-manager can lead his organization towards flexibility and change. More generally, the entire organization must change its posture and adopt a positive attitude and open-mindedness.

In addition, family SME needs to tolerate an attenuation of its independence on financial, human and relational plans. Indeed, the policy of conservation of financial independence can constitute a significant barrier to organizational learning. Opening up, the family firm can facilitate its access to capital by the institutionalization of appropriate governance mechanisms. In order to ensure that the aspirations of capital suppliers, on the one hand, and those of the family, on the other hand, are taken into account simultaneously for decision-making and pursuit of organizational goals, Davis et al. (2000) recommend a dual structuring of organizational governance processes. Family SME must, in addition, overcome its human independence and seek outside for these valuable resources. This can be done through a process of "familization", i.e. the incorporation to the dominant family of certain external elements through alliances and marriages. This process is justified by the quality of the relations established with those people and by their honesty and value in the eyes of the family. "Familization" indicates a relative broadmindedness and an attenuation of the independence attitude. Also, family SME can open up through its natural tendency to networking which could allow for an intense exposure to international economic environment.

Another factor which could influence knowledge development positively is social networking. The network orientation of the owner-manager and his family is to be distinguished from organizational networking. The family firm shows a weak cooperative orientation in the sense of the pursuit of common objectives with an economic partner, but a strong orientation toward social networking. It favours social relationships to economic ones that risk alienating its decision-making independence. The role of social networking in development of knowledge is crucial. Overall, networking was defined as an organizational means aiming to strengthen entrepreneurial processes. In total, social networking positively influences the amount of knowledge of family SME.

Schematically, not only do small and medium family firms internalize and develop weak knowledge but they also externalize and share little knowledge. The risks associated with this knowledge strategy are the possible extinction of valuable knowledge. Therefore, the process of knowledge transfer through generations would be crucial to the family SME in order to be able to maintain its competitive advantage. In addition, if know-how is the core resource underlying this competitive advantage then its "transferability" will determine the period during which its holder will obtain returns (Spender, 1996). In sum, small and medium family firms have to implement a deliberate strategy of knowledge preservation through, for instance, externalization of articulable tacit knowledge and socialization of non-articulable knowledge with external managers (Nonaka and Takeuchi, 1998). This strategy is not optional, but could be vital to ensure the survival of these firms.

References

Adam-Ledunois, S. and Le Vigoureux, F. (1998), 'Entreprises moyennes: l'indépendance en question', Paper presented at the 4th SME International Francophone Congress, Metz, 1998.

Arrègle, J-L. (1995), 'Le savoir et l'approche Resource-based: une ressource et une compétence', *Revue Française de Gestion*, September-October 1995, pp. 84-94.

Astrachan, J., Klein, S. and Smyrnios, K. (2002), 'The F-PEC Scale of Family Influence: A Proposal for Solving the Family Business Definition Problem', *Family Business Review*, 15(1): 45-58.

Astrachan, J. and Kolenko, T. (1996). 'A Neglected Factor Explaining Family Business Success: Human Resource Practice', in Richard Beckhard (eds), *The Best of FBR: A Celebration*, Boston, Mass.: Family Firm Institute, pp. 119-134.

Basly, S. (2005), 'Internationalization of family firms in a knowledge-based view', paper presented at the Workshop on family firm management research, Jönköping International Business School, Jönköping, Sweden, 9-11 June, 2005.

Bollinger, A. and Smith, R. (2001), 'Managing Organizational Knowledge as a Strategic Asset', Journal of Knowledge Management, 5(1): 8-18.

Cabrera-Suarez, K., De Saa-Perez, P. and Garcia-Almeida, D. (2001), 'The Succession Process from a Resource- and Knowledge-Based View of the Family Firm', *Family Business review*, 14(1): 37-48.

Charreaux, G. (2002), 'Variations sur le thème: A la recherche de nouvelles fondations pour la finance et la gouvernance d'entreprise', working paper, Université de Bourgogne.

Davis, P. (1983), 'Realizing the potential of the family business', *Organizational Dynamics*, 12: 47–56.

Davis, P., Pett, T. and Baskin, O. (2000), 'Governance and Goal Formation Among Family Businesses: A Resource Dependency Perspective', working paper communicated by the author.

Donckels, R. and Fröhlich, E. (1991), 'Are Family Businesses Really Different?' European Experiences from STRATOS', *Family Business Review*, 4(2), summer 1991.

Drucker P. (1993), *The New Society: The Anatomy of Industrial Order*, New-Brunswick, NJ: Transaction.

Dunn, B. (1995), 'Success themes in Scottish family businesses: Philosophies and practices through the generations', *Family Business Review*, 8(1): 17-28.

Dyer, W. Jr. (1986), *Cultural change in family firms: anticipating and managing business and family transitions*, San Francisco, CA: Jossey-Bass.

Fan, Y-K. (1998), 'Families in the 21st Century: The Economic Perspective', *HKCER Letters*, Vol. 50, May 1998.

Granovetter, M. (1973), 'The Strength of Weak Ties', *American Journal of Sociology*, Vol. 78: 1360-1380.

Gray, C. (1995), 'Managing Entrepreneurial Growth: A Question of Control? ', Paper presented at the 18th conference of the Institute of Small Business Affairs (National Small Firms Conference), University of Paisley, Scotland.

Gudmundson, D., Hartman, E. and Tower, C. (1999), 'Strategic Orientation: Differences between Family and Nonfamily Firms', *Family Business Review*, 12(1), March 1999.

Habbershon, T. and Williams, M. (1999), 'A Resource-Based Framework for Assessing the Strategic Advantages of Family Firms', *Family Business Review*, 12(1), March 1999.

Hambrick, D., Geletkanycz, M. and Fredrickson, J. (1993), 'Executive Commitment to the *Status Quo*: Some Tests of its Determinants', *Strategic Management Journal* 14: 401-418.

Harris, D., Martinez, J. and Ward, J. (1994), 'Is Strategy Different for the Family-Owned Business?', *Family Business Review*, 7(2), summer 1994.

Hirigoyen, G. (1985), 'Les implications de la spécificité des comportements financiers des moyennes entreprises industrielles (M.E.I) familiales', working paper, IAE de Toulouse, n°35, september 1985.

Hugron, P. and Boiteux, S. (1998), 'La PME familiale mondiale: conséquence sur la relève', Paper presented at the 4th SME International Francophone Congress, Metz, 1998.

Jenster, P. and Malone, S. (1991), 'Resting on your Laurels: The Plateauing of the Owner-manager', in Proceedings of the FBN Conference, Barcelona, Spain, 1991.

King, S., Solomon, G. and Fernald, Jr. L. (2001), 'Issues in Growing a Family Business: A Strategic Human Resource Model', *Journal of Small Business Management*, 39(1): 3-13.

Le Boterf, G. (1994), *De la Compétence. Essai sur un attracteur étrange*, Paris: Editions d'Organisation, 1994.

Litz, R. (1995), 'The Family Business: Toward Definitional Clarity', *Family Business Review*, 8(2), summer 1995.

Melin, L. and Nordqvist, M. (2000), 'Corporate Governance in Family Firms: The Role of Influential Actors and the strategic Arena', in Proceedings of the 2000 ICSB Conference, Brisbane, June 2000.

Miller, D., Steier, L. and Le Breton-Miller, I. (2003), 'Lost in Time: Intergenerational Succession, Change, and Failure in Family Business', *Journal of Business Venturing* 18 (2003): 513–531.

Moloktos, L. (1991), 'Change and Transition and Family Businesses', in Proceedings of the FBN Conference, Barcelona, Spain, 1991.

Mustakallio, M. and Autio, E. (2001), 'Optimal Governance in Family Firms', in Babson Entrepreneurship Conference Proceedings, 2001.

Mustakallio, M. and Autio, E. (2002), 'Governance, Entrepreneurial Orientation and Growth in Family Firms', in Proceedings of the 13th FBN Conference, Helsinki, 2002.

Myers, S. and Majluf, N. (1984), 'Corporate Financing and Investment Decisions when Firms Have Information that Investors Do Not Have', *Journal of Financial Economics* 13: 187-221.

Nelson, R. and Winter, S. (1982), *An Evolutionary Theory of Economic Change*, Cambridge: Belknap Press of Harvard University Press.

Nonaka, I. and Takeuchi, H. (1998), 'A Theory of the Firm's Knowledge-Creation Dynamics', in Alfred D. Chandler, Jr., Peter Hagström and Örjan Sölvell (eds.), *The Dynamic Firm, The Role of Technology, Strategy, Organization, and Regions*, Oxford University Press, pp. 214-241.

Okoroafo, S. (1999), 'Internationalization of Family Businesses: Evidence from Northwest Ohio, USA', *Family Business Review*, 21(2), June 1999.

Penrose, E. (1959), *The Theory of the Growth of the Firm*, Oxford University Press, Third Edition (1995).

Ranft, A. and O'Neill, H. (2001), 'Board Composition and High-flying Founders: Hints of Trouble to Come?', *The Academy of Management Executive*, 15(1): 126-139.

Salvato, C., Williams, M. and Habbershon, T. (2002), 'Values and Competitive Advantage: The Cultural Determinants of Dynamic capabilities in Family Firms', in Proceedings of the 13th FBN Conference, Helsinki, 2002.

Sanders, W. and Carpenter, M. (1998), 'Internationalization and Firm Governance: The Roles of CEO Compensation, Top Team Composition and Board Structure', *Academy of Management Journal*, 41(2): 158-178.

Schulze, W., Lubatkin, M. and Dino, R. (2003), 'Exploring the Agency Consequences of Ownership Dispersion Among the Directors of Private Family Firms', *Academy of Management Journal*, 46(2): 179–194.

Schulze, W., Lubatkin, M., Dino, R. and Buchholtz, A. (2001), 'Agency Relationships in Family Firms: Theory and Evidence', *Organization Science*, 12(2): 99-116.

Shrivastava, P. (1983), 'A typology of organizational learning systems', *Journal of Management Studies*, 20(1): 7–28.

Schwartz, B. and Barnes, L. (1991), 'Outside Boards and Family Businesses: Another Look', *Family Business Review*, 4(3): 269-285.

Spender, J-C. (1996), 'Making Knowledge the Basis of a Dynamic Theory of the Firm', *Strategic Management Journal*, 17, Special issue, 1996: 45-62.

Timur, K. (1988), 'The Tenacious Past: Theories of Personal and Collective Conservatism', *Journal of Economic Behavior and Organization*, 10(2): 143-172.

Tsang, E. (1999), 'Internationalizing the Family Firm: A Case Study of a Chinese family Business', *Journal of Small Business Management*, 39(1): 88-94.

Ward, J. (1988), 'The Special Role of Planning for Family Businesses', *Family Business Review*, 1(2), summer 1988.

—. (1997), 'Growing the Family Business: Special Challenges and Best Practices', *Family Business Review*, 10(4), December 1997.

Ward, J. and Aronoff, C. (1996), 'How a Family Shapes Business Strategy', in *Family Business Sourcebook* II, Edited by Joseph H. Astrachan, John L. Ward and Craig E. Aronoff, pp. 113-114.

Welsch, J. (1996), 'The Impact of Family Ownership and Involvement on the Process of Management Succession', in *The Best of FBR: A Celebration, Boston: Family Firm Institute*. Ed. Richard Beckhard, Boston, Mass.: Family Firm Institute, pp. 96-108.

Wright, R., Van Wijk, G. and Bouty, I. (1995), 'Les principes du management des ressources fondées sur la connaissance', Revue Française de Gestion, September-October 1995: 70-75.

THE CASE AS A RESEARCH TOOL IN MANAGEMENT SCIENCES: AN EPISTEMOLOGICAL POSITIONING

ANIS BACHTA[1]

Introduction

A basic pillar in the practice of management and in the training of managers, the case study saw its role developing to become an instrument of research. The consensus is clear; sciences of management always remain grounded in the action. However, the evolution of the case study as a diagnostic tool for the professional of management consulting to an instrument of investigation to the service of the researchers requires a consequent methodological drive.

In fact, this transition which opposes to some extent the expert with the scientist, finds its epistemological origins in the traditional confrontations opposing the constructivists to the positivists. The former scan the field, proposing the qualities of experts, and the latter focus themselves rather on the scientificity of the methods borrowed.

However, can we really speak about antagonism between positivism and constructivism in management sciences? If not, what are the epistemological bases of the case study as research strategy?

Therefore, this paper will be organised around three sections. The first section traces the epistemological framework of the research in general. Such an epistemological framework is brought back in the second section to be compared with the specificities of management research. In the third section, we will show how the case study as an instrument of investigation for the managers makes it possible to answer the referred specificities.

---

[1] UMLT Tunis.

1.Epistemological bases of the research

According to Thiétart et al., (1999)[2], the aim of epistemology is to study the scientificity of sciences by analysing the methods and the approaches adopted in the production of knowledge. The utility of the epistemological perspective lies in its contribution to establishing criteria to appreciate the validity and the reliability of the research. In this direction, Thiétart et al. (1999) add that any research is judicious either to predict, or to prescribe, or to understand, or to explain reality.

1.1 The nature of the recognizable reality

Generally, this study of reality oscillates between two extreme epistemological positions: the positivist position, known as deductive, and the constructivist position, known as holistico-inductive.

For the *positivists*, knowledge is basically objective (Thiétart et al., 1999). It is thus, for Popper (1972): "*knowledge in this objective direction is completely independent of the claim of whomever with knowledge; it is also independent of the belief or the provision to the approval (or the assertion, with the action) of anyone. Knowledge with the objective direction is without expert; it is without knowing subject*"[3].

On the other side, the constructivists speak about inseparable knowledge of the knowing subject and the context in which it is located. The most radical, such as Glasersfeld (1988)[4] will even affirm the inexistence of reality; we speak rather about an invention of reality.

The moderate constructivists (Thiétart et al., 1999) do not take a categorical position on the existence of a personal reality. However, they are intransigent on the dependence between the observed reality, its context, and the conscience of the person who observes it.

---

[2] A. Thiétart, and al. (1999) : "Méthodes de recherche en management", Dunod, Paris.

[3] K. R. Popper, (1972) : "*La connaissance objective*", Paris, Aubier, 2nd edition, 1991, p185.

[4] E. Glasersfeld Von (1988) : "Introduction à un constructivisme radical", in Watzlawick P. (dir), L'invention de la réalité: contributions au constructivisme, Paris, Le Seuil.

Such interdependence comes like a refutation of the principle of objectivity strongly supported by the positivists. Thus, according to the constructivist position, reality is the consequence of interpretations that comes from the interactions between social actors compared to a specific context.

1.2 The access to reality

While referring to the objective design of reality, the positivists defend the ambition of a universal reality. Even if they are conscious that such a design of reality remains utopian (Thiétart et al., 1999), the holders of the positivist current persist in believing that the apprehension of the reality must be engaged through laws. Laws are then formulated in a deterministic way as a succession of causality bonds. Such causalities can be classified according to two attributes; simple versus multiple or linear versus circular. The point is to explain the reality while quantifying and evaluating the direction of the relations between the variables that seem likely to characterize it.

The constructivists, while privileging the interpretations which the social actors allot to reality, place themselves in a comprehension logic rather than explanatory one. Indeed, required interpretations are based on the beliefs, the motivations, the intentions, and the reasons of the social actors (Pourtois and Desmet, 1988; pp27/28)[5]. In this direction, Moigne (1995) adds that "*reality is built by the act of knowing rather than by an objective perception of the world'*[6].

The knowledge coming from reality seems then to be, at the same time, a process and a result (Piaget, 1970)[7].

[5]J.-P. Pourtois, H. Desmet, (1988) : "Épistémologies et instrumentation en sciences humaines", Liège-Bruxelles, Pierre Mardaga.
[6] J.-L. Le Moigne, (1995) : "Les épistémologies constructivistes", coll. Que sais-je ?, Paris, PUF, pp71-72.
[7] J. Piaget, (1970): "L'épistémologie génétique", Paris, collection Que sais-je ?, PUF.

2.Epistemological specificities of management research

2.1 The organizations reality

Burrel and Morgan (1979) [8] distinguish globally four types of social realities, and in particular organizational realities: functionalism, interpretativism, radical humanism, and radical structuralism. Such approaches are translated in the form of a certain number of meta-theoretical assumptions referring to the nature of the recognizable reality, the duality between objective and subjective dimensions, and the radical nature of the regulation mechanisms of the social changes.

The functionalist paradigm is based on two principles: the regulation and the pragmatism according to which social behaviours are intended to produce a state of business that is ordered and correctly controlled. The ontological assertions advanced in this paradigm are connected enough with the positivist epistemological positioning. Indeed, according to this perspective the apprehension of organizational reality is released from any system of values in which the researcher takes his distance from the studied situation.

In the opposite way, the interpretative paradigm refuses this purely objective positioning of the functionalists. In fact, this paradigm is based on a vision of reality where the ontological statute of knowledge is largely marginalized.

In fact, social reality, and by extension, the organizational one, do not have a concrete meaning well defined, but it is systematically grounded in the subjective experiments of individuals. Reality is explained from the point of view of the actors implied in the regulation process of the laws and the social resources rather than from the point of view of the independent observer.

Moreover, even if the interpretativists divide with the functionalist the vision of an organized reality, the idea of leading to an objective knowledge is completely excluded. Organizations are then perceived as a whole of practices that the expert conceptualizes in a subjective way. The scientificity of the released knowledge is thus regarded as an issue.

[8] G. Burrell, and G. Morgan, (1979) : “Sociological Paradigms and Organizational Analysis”, London: Heinemann Educational Books.

Thus, a third paradigm takes root in the analysis of the organizational reality according to which the human beings are prisoners of the reality that they create themselves. In fact, this paradigm allotted to the radical humanistic school is based on the principle of the individual's alienation in their apprehension of the reality. According to this paradigm, the human spirit can be contaminated by the psychic and the social mechanisms which characterize a company's reality.

According to the radical humanistic orientation, the principles of social regulation, defended as well by the functionalist as by the interpretativist, are considered as structures of ideological domination. From this point of view, the researchers focus on studying the various associations which the social actors allot to their practices for, precisely, transcending their alienation.

Sharing the same vision as the radical humanists, the reality defined by the radical structuralist paradigm finds its anchoring in the social domination mechanisms. However, it is the nature of the reality that changes here. In fact, according to the radical humanistic vision, reality exists as an objective demonstration. Such reality is characterized by some intrinsic contradictions and tensions leading to radical changes in the social systems. Considering these four realities, it appears to be hard to classify the organizational paradigms as exclusively positivist or constructivist.

2.2 The access to the organizational reality

The various visions of the organizational reality vehicle imply a diversity of the research methods. Such diversity often poses epistemological problems. In fact, while migrating from one organization vision to another, the method of investigation changes.

Thus, the subjective extreme encourages a constructivist epistemological positioning in favour of the comprehension of the processes in which the social actors perceive their relations in the business world. This basically phenomenologist prospect supposes that knowledge is closely related to the personality of the scientist (Husserl, 1962)[9].

On the other hand, the objective vision encourages a positivist epistemological positioning that focuses on the analysis of the causality

---

[9] E. Husserl, (1962): "Ideas", New York, Collier.

bonds between various dimensions of a given social structure. The apprehension of the reality supposes empirical analysis of some relations where the researcher positions themself in an external way from the studied phenomenon.

In this direction, Grawitz (1993) raises a fundamental question: "*is it better to find interesting elements in which we are not certain, or sure that what we find is true even though it is not interesting?"*[10]. The answer to this question can be formulated through the remarks of Miles and Huberman (1991) which note that "*the social phenomena exist not only in the spirits but also in the real world so we can discover between them some legitimate and reasonably stable relations* "[11]. Such an answer marks the need for an adjustment of the research paradigms, while putting a term to the opposition between *positivist* and *constructivist* positioning. Moreover, such opposition has been falsified since Piaget (1970) then by Latour (1991)[12].

3.The case as an access strategy to the reality in management science

In such circumstances, hybrid approaches combining induction and deduction take place in management investigations. The case study seems to be the more requested instrument in this direction.

In fact, the case studies imply that the exploitation of multiple data sources (Ellram, 1991[13]; Yin, 2003) is something that makes it difficult to conform to a single research approach. In this direction, the case studies which begin from the deductive point of view without borrowing some elements of the inductive step are rare (Stassen and Waller, 2002)[14]. The abductive approach, combining deduction and induction, becomes an interesting way

---

[10] M. Grawitz, (1996) : "Méthodes des sciences sociale s", Paris, Dalloz, 10th éd, p321.

[11] M. B. Miles, Huberman A. M., (1991) : "Analyse des données qualitatives", Recueil de nouvelles méthodes, De Boeck Université, Bruxelles, p31.

[12] B. Latour, (1991) : "*Nous n'avons jamais été modernes"*, La Découverte, Paris

[13] L. M. Ellram, (1991): "Supply chain management: the industrial organization perspective", in *International Journal of Physical Distribution & Logistics Management*, Vol. 21 No. 1, pp13-22.

[14] R. E. Stassen, and M. A. Waller, (2002): "Logistics and assortment depth in the retail supply chain: evidence from grocery categories", in *Journal of Business Logistics*, Vol. 23 No. 1, pp125-143.

of conducting investigations in management research. Certain authors even indicate that the majority of the great advances in science followed neither pure deduction nor pure induction (Kirkeby, 1990[15] ; Taylor et all, 2002[16]).

For the majority of the thinkers the term "abduction" returns to Charles Sanders (Santiago) Peirce. However, the author refers to Aristote. According to Peirce (1931)[17], the term of abduction results from a bad translation of the term "*retroduction*" as it was apprehended by Aristote. However, Peirce uses the abduction term to speak about "*retroduction*".

According to Kirkeby (1990) several types of abductive research can be identified in modern sciences, each one of them could develop its own abductive method. A first group of researchers sees abduction like a systematized creativity or a kind of intuition in research in order to develop "a new" knowledge (Andreewsky et Bourcier, 2000[18] ; Kirkeby, 1990; Taylor et all, 2002). The creativity is necessary to exceed the limits of deduction and induction, consisting in delimiting and establishing relations between constructs already defined (Kirkeby, 1990). Taylor et al. (2002) add that instead of focusing on following logical processes, the majority of the scientific projections are emergent in an intuitive way, which we could describe as abductive. Indeed, deductive research sweeps across the theory (for example in the review of the literature), draws certain logical conclusions of the latter, and forwards them in the form of assumptions *(h)* and proposals *(p)* and examines these in an empirical arrangement in order to finally report their confirmation or falsification (see for example, Kirkeby, 1990). The logical sequence of the research process can be articulated as follows: (1) Law, (2) case, (3) result.

---

[15] O. F. Kirkeby, (1990): "Abduktion", in Andersen, H. (Ed.), Vetenskapsteori och metodla¨ ra.Introduktion, (translated by Liungman, C.G.), Studentlitteratur, Lund.
[16] S. S. Taylor, D. Fisher, et R. L. Dufresne, (2002): "The aesthetics of management storytelling: a key to organizational learning", in *Management Learning*, Vol. 33 No. 3, pp313-330.
[17] C. S. Pierce, (1931) in C. Hartshorne, P. Weiss, (eds.): "collected papers of Charles Sanders Pierce", Vol. I: Principles of philosophy, Harvard University Press, Cambridge, MA.
[18] E. Andreewsky, and D. Bourcier, (2000): "Abduction in language interpretation and law making", in *Kybernetes*, Vol. 29 No. 7/8, pp836-45.

Inductive logic goes the opposite way: theoretical anchoring is not necessary (Andreewsky et Bourcier, 2000; Glaser et Strauss, 1967[19]); instead it is the observation of the field that will lead to the birth of proposals and their generalization within the theoretical framework. The logical sequence of the research process will be thus as follows: (1) case, (2) result, (3) Law.

Abductive research follows another proceeding; the research process can be schematized as follows: (1) laws, (2) results, (3) case (Danermark, 2001[20], Kirkeby, 1990).

In the abductive reasoning, the case reports are plausible but not necessarily logical, provided that the laws recommended at the beginning are correct (Danermark, 2001). In addition, abduction can also suggest general rules (Andreewsky and Bourcier, 2000; Kirkeby, 1990). Instead of focusing on the generalizations, the abductive approach relates rather to the specific situations which present some anomalies or which are omitted in the theory structure (Danermark, 2001). In this direction, the abductive approach is very useful to determine which are the generalizable aspects of a situation and which are the specific ones, for example, of the environmental or situational factors. These capacities will be used thereafter "to suggest" a new reformulation of general rules, assumptions (H), proposals (p), or theory (Andreewsky and Bourcier, 2000; Kirkeby, 1990).

The creator and intuitive aspect of abductive research (Taylor and others, 2002) makes it very suitable in the first phase of research, concerning the process of the formulation and choice of assumptions or proposals (Kirkeby, 1990). In this context, Abductive research will help to release one from the assumptions and proposals which can be examined later in a deductive phase of the research.

Abduction can also, while interpreting certain phenomena, allow us to understand something in a new way or according to a new conceptual framework (Danermark, 2001; Dubois and Gadde, 2002[21]). The abductive

---

[19] B. G., Glaser, and A. L. Strauss, (1967): "The Discovery of Grounded Theory", Aldine, Chicago, IL.

[20] B. Danermark, (2001): "Explaining Society: An Introduction to Critical Realism in the Social Sciences", Routledge, Florence, KY.

[21] A. Dubois, et L-E. Gadde, (2002): "Systematic combining: an abductive approach to case research", in *Journal of Business Research*, Vol. 55, pp553-560.

reasoning is integrated here from the point of view of searching the appropriate theories for an empirical observation, that Dubois and Gadde (2002) call "*theory matching*", or "*systematic combining*". In this process, the data-gathering is done in a simultaneous way with the theoretical construction, which implies a kind of "loop of training" (Taylor and others, 2002), or at least a movement "of comings and goings" between the theory and the empirical study (Dubois and Gadde, 2002).

This interactive aspect between the theory and the empirical study is rather similar to the case studies research design (Dubois and Gadde, 2002). In fact, according to Bell (1987)[22], the methodology of case study can be described as a federator topic for a group of research methods which allows the focusing of a survey around an example or a specific event. For this author, the philosophy behind the case study is that sometimes by looking at a specific example carefully, a full image can be obtained.

The case study allows the investigator, for this purpose, to focus on specific examples in order to identify the interactive processes which can be crucial and not easily apprehended by the great scale surveys. It is significant to consider the majority of the cases as complex aggregates of behaviours (Stake, 1994)[23]. The generalization of the released results of the case is not an essential condition for the validity of this type of research. The relevance of the case must be appreciated by report to the research questions more than its capacity to be generalized. Indeed, for the researcher, in addition to the intellectual satisfaction, the validity of a theory and its refinement will come in return from the ground. The case arises in this direction like the most adequate instrument to ensure this interaction between the theory and the practice. Indeed, by using the cases method, "*the border between what is academic research and what is management consulting becomes confused, (...), because the researcher will have the role of the consultant by investigating into the organization and the organizational behavior*" Gummesson (1991)[24]. The case studies are accepted more and more as a scientific instrument in the businesses administration.

---

[22] J. Bell, (1987): "Doing your Research Project: A Guideline for First-Time Researchers in Education and Social Science", Open University Press, Milton Keyness.
[23] Stake, R. E. (1994): "Handbook of Qualitative Research", edited by Denzin N. K. & Lincoln Y. S. (1994), Sage. London
[24] E. Gummesson, (1991): "Qualitative Methods in Management Research", Sage Publication, London, p2.

Conclusion

To conclude, we think that antagonisms between paradigms and approaches now become obsolete. The researcher has to take into account, explicitly, the epistemological questions in his research and to ponder on the nature of the reality which he intends to apprehend. Social reality, and more particularly the organizational one, is complex enough to be apprehended according to a specific paradigm and, even less, according to a single method.

Thus several researchers in social sciences stress the need for transcending the weaknesses of the traditional scientific method (external paradigm) and for connecting the universal knowledge with the particular or the contextual one.

Lewin (1931)[25], Weber (1951)[26] and (Piaget 1970) for a long time supported the need to consider a new category of science, combining the rigor and the standardization of the positivist science with relevance and pragmatism of other paradigms. This new category of sciences would be based more on the action and would be directed on praxis (Evered and Louis, 1981)[27]. It is precisely on the basis of this pragmatic vision that Charles Sanders Pierce (1839-1914) proposes his abductive method allowing the interpretation of the facts on the basis of theory: the point is the mutual enhancement between the two elements.

It appears that the mobilization of the cases method, as an instrument of research, is very useful. Indeed, the latter constitutes the concrete illustration of the research paradigms' adjustment. In this direction, the positivists' deductive method and the inductive one, considered as exclusively constructivist, work together.

---

[25] K. Lewin, (1931): "The conflict between Aristotelian and Galilean modes of thought in contemporary psychology". *Journal of General Psychology, 5,* 141-177, reprinted in: "*A dynamic theory of personality: Selected papers"* (pp. 1-42). New York: McGraw-Hill, 1935.

[26] M. Weber, (1951): "The methodology of the social sciences", (E.A. Schils & H.A. Finch, Trans. & Eds). Glencoe, III.: Free Press.

[27] R. Evered, & M. Louis, (1981): "Alternative perspectives to organizational sciences: Inquiry from the inside and Inquiry from the outside", *Academy of Management Review*, 6: pp385-395.

References

Andreewsky, E., and Bourcier, D., (2000): "Abduction in language interpretation and law making", in *Kybernetes*, Vol. 29 No. 7/8, pp836-45.

Bell, J., (1987): "Doing your Research Project: A Guideline for First-Time Researchers in Education and Social Science", Open University Press, Milton Keyness.

Brabet, J., (1988): « Faut-il encore parler d'approche qualitative et d'approche quantitative? », *Recherches et Applications en Marketing*, vol 3, n 1, pp 75-89.

Burrell, G., and Morgan, G., (1979): « Sociological Paradigms and Organizational Analysis », London: Heinemann Educational Books.

Danermark, B., (2001): "Explaining Society: An Introduction to Critical Realism in the Social Sciences", Routledge, Florence, KY.

Debie, F., Bouyeure, J-L., (1994) : « Le rapprochement Entreprise-École : écueils et dérives », pp53-75, in l'École des Managers de demain, par les professeurs du groupe HEC, Economica. Paris.

Dubois, A., et Gadde, L-E., (2002): "Systematic combining: an abductive approach to case research", in *Journal of Business Research*, Vol. 55, pp553-560.

Ellram, L., M., (1991): "Supply chain management: the industrial organization perspective", in *International Journal of Physical Distribution & Logistics Management*, Vol. 21 No. 1, pp13-22.

Evered, R., & Louis, M., (1981): "Alternative perspectives to organizational sciences: Inquiry from the inside and Inquiry from the outside", *Academy of Management Review*, 6: pp385-395.

Glaser, B., G., and Strauss, A., L., (1967): "*The discovery of grounded theory: Strategies for qualitative research"*, Aldine Publishing Company, New York, pp17-18.

Glasersfeld Von E., (1988): « Introduction à un constructivisme radical », in Watzlawick P. (dir), L'invention de la réalité: contributions au constructivisme, Paris, Le Seuil.

Grawitz, M., (1996): « Méthodes des sciences sociale s », Paris, Dalloz, 10ème éd.

Gummesson, E., (1991): "Qualitative Methods in Management Research", Sage Publication, London.

Husserl, E., (1962): "Ideas", New York, Collier.

Kirkeby, O., F., (1990): "Abduktion", in Andersen, H. (Ed.), Vetenskapsteori och metodla¨ ra.Introduktion, (translated by Liungman, C.G.), Studentlitteratur, Lund.

Latour, B., (1991) : « Nous n'avons jamais été modernes », La Découverte, Paris

Lewin, K., (1931): "The conflict between Aristotelian and Galilean modes of thought in contemporary psychology". *Journal of General Psychology, 5, pp*141-177, reprinted in: *"A dynamic theory of personality: Selected papers"* (pp1-42). New York: McGraw-Hill, 1935.

Miles, M., B., Huberman A., M., (1991) : « Analyse des données qualitatives », Recueil de nouvelles méthodes, De Boeck Université, Bruxelles.

Le Moigne, J.-L., (1995) : « Les épistémologies constructivistes », coll. Que sais-je? Paris, PUF.

Morgan, G., (1980): "Paradigms, metaphors and puzzle solving in organization theory", *Administrative Science Quarterly*, 25, pp605-622.

Perez, R., (2004): « Le choc des paradigmes en sciences de gestion », in G., GAREL, E., GODELIER, Enseigner le management, méthodes, institutions, mondialisation, HERMES-LAVOISIER.

Piaget, J., (1970): « L'épistémologie génétique », Paris, collection Que sais-je ?, PUF.

Pierce, C., S., (1931) in C., Hartshorne, P., Weiss, (eds.): "collected papers of Charles Sanders Pierce", Vol. I: Principles of philosophy, Harvard University Press, Cambridge, MA.

Popper, K., R., (1972): « La connaissance objective », Paris, Aubier, 2ème édition, 1991.

Pourtois, J.-P., Desmet, H., (1988): « Épistémologies et instrumentation en sciences humaines », Liège-Bruxelles, Pierre Mardaga.

Silverman, D., (1993): "The theory of organizations", London: Heinemann.

Stake, R., E., (1994): in Handbook of Qualitative Research, edited by Denzin N.K. & Lincoln Y.S. (1994), Sage. London

Stassen, R., E., and Waller, M., A., (2002): "Logistics and assortment depth in the retail supply chain: evidence from grocery categories", in *Journal of Business Logistics*, Vol. 23 No. 1, pp125-143.

Taylor, S., S., Fisher, D., et Dufresne, R., L., (2002): "The aesthetics of management storytelling: a key to organizational learning", in *Management Learning*, Vol. 33 No. 3, pp313-330.

Thiétart, A., et al. (1999) : « Méthodes de recherche en management », Dunod, Paris.

Wacheux, F., (1996): « Méthodes qualitatives et Recherche en Gestion », Economica. Paris

Weber, M., (1951): "The methodology of the social sciences", (E.A. Schils & H.A. Finch, Trans. & Eds). Glencoe, III.: Free Press.

Yin, R., K., (1994): "Case Study Research, Design and Methods", 2nd ed. Newbury Park, Sage Publications, London.

PART 7.

ISLAMIC BANKING AND FINANCE

SYARIAH ACCOUNTING AND COMPLIANT SCREENING PRACTICES

CATHERINE SOKE FUN HO[1], OMAR MASOOD[2], ASMA ABDUL REHMAN[3] AND MONDHER BELLALAH[4]

Introduction

Islamic finance and investments have grown at an average of over 20% per annum for the past decade, a momentum not shared by the conventional sector. Syariah-compliant assets have a current worldwide total worth of US$800 billion and the majority of it is in Islamic equity funds (Jaffer, 2009). There exists tremendous interest in Islamic finance and investments due to the growth of wealth from the majority of the oil producing Muslim countries, with their specific culture and religious beliefs. With the rise in commodity prices and income in the current global economy, the appetite for Syariah-compliant investments is expected to continue to improve in the future. Financial institutions and investment houses are therefore always in search of Islamic compliant investments, which are believed to have lower risks in light of the recent development in developed financial markets, in order to attract investments.

Many new Islamic institutions and established financial institutions take the opportunity to facilitate this new market trend with unprecedented growth of Islamic investment instruments. As a result, many international bodies that influence the development of *Syariah*-compliant equity have been set up in recent years. This development can be traced back to the

[1] Faulty of Business Management, University Teknologi Mara, Malaysia, catherine@salam.uitm.edu.my.
[2] Royal Business School, University of East London, Docklands Campus, e-mail: omar@uel.ac.uk.
[3] Superior University, Lahore, Pakistan, email: asmaabdul@hotmail.com.
[4] University of Cergy-ISC.

beginning of the century where the evolution of the Islamic capital market was accelerated by some Islamic bodies, including: Organization of Islamic Conference (OIC) Fiqh Academy, Accounting and Auditing Standards for Islamic Financial Institutions (AAOIFI), Islamic Development Bank (IDB), and Islamic Financial Services Board (IFSB). One of the most significant index providers who drives the equity investment momentum is the Dow Jones Islamic Market (DJIM) Index established in 1999 (McMillen, 2006).

In recognition of the need for expertise, independent advice and supervision on *Syariah*-related matters, the AAOIFI established a standard requiring every provider of Islamic financial services to have its own *Syariah* Supervisory board. Muslim countries such as Malaysia, Bahrain, and some Gulf states have made significant efforts to regulate Islamic finance separately from the conventional financial system. International developed financial markets have decided to include the Islamic financial system in their existing regulatory framework. The challenge for some of these countries is to accommodate Islamic finance within a legal and regulatory infrastructure designed for existing conventional finance (Archer & Karim, 2007). Malaysia, Indonesia, and Iran have regulations in place to ensure that any entity that is involved in the issuance of Islamic financial product complies with their own prescribed minimum standard of *Syariah* compliance (McMillen, 2006). The *Syariah* standards issued by AAOIFI are adopted by Bahrain, Sudan, Syria and some others in that region (Archer & Karim, 2007).

The process of Syariah-compliant screening differs not only due to different jurisdictions of different countries but also practiced by a different set of users: portfolio managers, providers of market intelligence and regulators. These parties have different objectives for the screening of Syariah-compliant products. Some researchers claimed that too much diversity adds cost and requires a larger number of screening processes and in the long run could hamper the growth of Islamic finance (Islamic Finance Asia, 2008). There is therefore a need for Islamic scholars to standardize their screening methodologies effectively in the international market.

This paper aims to review the *Syariah*-compliant screening methods practiced by 15 worldwide prominent Islamic finance users: 8 apply qualitative and 11 apply quantitative methods. In addition, the paper performs a comparative analysis to detect the differences and similarities of these methods. Data are collected from their respective user websites and an interview was conducted with the Assistant General Manager of Islamic Capital Market Department, Securities Commission in Malaysia.

Review of Existing Literature

The existence of the *Syariah* screening process in the financial market enables investors to invest in companies that operate permissible business activities in accordance with fair Islamic principles. Introduction of the *Syariah* screening process is essential to detect prohibited activities and avoid embarking onto a non-compliant investment. Nevertheless, there are few examples of research on *Syariah* investment screening methods. Derigs and Marzban (2008) provided a comparative study on the *Syariah*-compliant stocks screening practices by nine group of users. In addition, Khatkhatay and Nisar (2006) explored and compared the sets of criteria used by three organizations and derived critical assessments on each criteria. Their study proposed modification of the practices used by considering the nature of business of the companies as wholly *Syariah*-compliant, and rejecting companies with mixed activities.

Khatkhatay and Nisar (2006) pointed out that *Shariah*-compatible investment is judged according to the investment structure and the nature of the contracting parties. The *Shariah* law prohibits interest related investments (*Riba'*), monetary obligation (debt, currency, liquid assets), and future rights (uncertainty). The structure of share equity appears permissible because equities of stock do not grant fixed return and as long as the business does not involve chance events with high uncertainty similar to gambling. In addition, the existence of margin account practice, speculations, and short selling in the operational aspect of shares are also prohibited in Syariah (Iqbal and Mirakhor, 2007).

Grais and Pelligrini (2006) noted that *Syariah* compliance is achieved through *Syariah* authority, which is a highly respected and Syariah-knowledgeable individual or group of individuals to decide if an investment transaction complies with the *Syariah* principle. This *Syariah* authority, which is commonly known as *Syariah* Supervisory Board, usually consists of three or more *Syariah* scholars.

Nature of Business

While certain activities are accepted as *Shariah*-compliant, *Shariah* scholars have started to question the allowance of share trading of companies whose core activity is lawful but that occasionally get involved in unlawful transactions. These companies are in mixed activities with some non-compliant businesses are considered as joint stock companies. Yaquby (2000) studied the differences in justifications among contemporary scholars on trading with joint stock companies and suggested that arguments cited by advocates of permissibility are stronger than the conflicting view. This is mainly because the inclusion of joint stock companies plays an important role to the development of Islamic finance.

There are certain activities which are considered as non-permissible, or haram, according to the Syariah principles. There is consensus among all jurisdictions to prohibit investments which involve *Riba'* or interest. Prohibited business activities include gambling or *Maisir,* such as casinos. Companies which are engaged in the production, distribution, promotion, and sale of non-halal goods or services are prohibited in Islam.

Financial Structure

The second major screening criterion examines the financial structure of the business and benchmarks it against some collectively agreed level of tolerance. Derigs and Marzban (2008) explained the relevance of this type of screening in the prohibition of *Riba'* and trading of money according to the *Shariah.* Financial structures of companies are measured to gauge the involvement of these companies in non-permissible practices. Involvement in *Riba'* is measured by the company's interest-based income as well as their interest payment for debt, which is termed as interest screen and debt screen. It is also claimed that money in itself is not a permissible asset in accordance with the Islamic Syariah principles. The level of liquid assets, which may include cash and cash equivalents, short term investments and accounts receivables, should be kept to a minimum in Islamic finance.

Similarly, Khatkhatay and Nisar (2006) highlighted three aspects of business structures that need to be quantified in order to check its Syariah-compliance: indebtedness of the enterprise, interest and other suspicious earnings, as well as the extent of cash and receivables of the company. It is important to note that returns generated from short term near cash assets are not permissible in Islamic finance.

Threshold Values

Companies that have been long established are inclined towards the conventional banking system in financing their major activities; it is almost impossible for these companies to be totally free from interest and liquid assets. The threshold values, as explained by Derigs and Marzban (2008), provided a limit to the level of non-acceptable activities from the *Shariah* point of view and the relaxation of the puristic submission. The exact allowable proportion for the financial structure is however not specified in the *Quran*ic teachings, and it is instead mainly based on interpretation in the form of *Ijtihad*. Interpretations on the minimum acceptable ratios or threshold values from 5 to 50 percent tend to differ between different Syariah boards, resulting in differing standards acceptable by various Syariah boards all over the world.

This study separates the screening methods into two groups: qualitative and quantitative. Qualitative screening method is used to screen for non-permissible business activities according to Syariah principles.

Comparative Analysis

This study compiles data from 15 users of the *Shariah* screening methods from all over the world. Table 1 provides a list of different Syariah screening users and their background. The different ways of screening assets practiced by these users are examined by the level of geographical area at two levels: micro and macro. Macro level users screen available assets worldwide while micro level users tend to screen assets from a particular country or region.

This study has compiled information on four micro- and nine macro-screen users. The four international Islamic index providers are: (a) Dow Jones Islamic Market Index (DJIM); (b) Financial Times Stock Exchange (FTSE) Global Islamic Index; (c) Morgan Stanley Capital International (MSCI) Global Islamic Index; and (d) Standard & Poor's (S&P) *Syariah* Index; which pre-screened universal assets prior to forming their respective *Syariah* compliant indices. They are private profit-oriented companies with global target markets and hence screen all the assets at macro level for the construction of their indices.

Table 1: Shariah Screen Users

Users	Regulator	Index Provider	Syariah service provider	Fund Manager	Bank	Country of Origin	Stocks Screened	Screening Level
SC	✓					Malaysia	Malaysia	Micro
DJIM		✓				US	Global	Macro
FTSE		✓				UK	Global	Macro
MSCI		✓				UK	Global	Macro
S&P		✓				US	Global	Macro
Shariah Capital			✓			US	Global	Macro
Al Meezan				✓		Pakistan	Global	Micro
Azzad			✓	✓		US	Global	Macro
Amiri			✓	✓		UK	Global	Macro
Amanie			✓			Malaysia	Global	Macro
Alfa Bank					✓	Russia	Russia, Ukraine, Kazakhstan	Micro
Dubai Islamic Bank*					✓	Dubai	N/A	N/A
Saudi Arabia National Commercial Bank*					✓	Saudi Arabia	N/A	N/A
Unified Committee*					✓	UAE	UAE	Micro
HSBC Amanah					✓	China	Global	Macro

In addition, the four Sy*ariah* service providers include: (1) the *Shariah* Capital of United States that screens universal assets for global investments; (2) Al-Meezan, a joint venture of Meezan Bank and Pak Kuwait Investment Company (PKIC) in Pakistan; (3) Azzad, a joint venture between Amri Capital, a London based investment management company and Azzad Asset Management from the U.S.; and (4) Amanie Business Solutions, a Malaysian based company that screens assets based upon clients' choices endorsed by the respective *Syariah* Board such as DJIM, FTSE and others. These *Syariah* service providers are profit-oriented companies that provide *Syariah*-compliant consulting and related services and thus screen global asset based on the clients demand.

Similar to the other profit-motivated entities, some banks also provide their own screening standard and provide financial services by managing funds owned by them and their clients, and globally screening selected assets that provide good return, such as that practiced by HSBC Amanah. Two of these banks screen their assets at micro level: Alfa Bank of Russia, which only screens assets in Russia, Ukraine and Kazakhstan; as well as the Unified Committee, a joint venture between Islamic banks in UAE, which screens assets in Dubai Financial Market and Abu Dhabi Securities Exchange. The screening information from Saudi Arabia National Commercial bank (NCB) and Dubai Islamic Bank (DIB) are not available. Lastly, Securities Commission Malaysia (SC) is a micro-screen user, identified as the only Syariah screen user who is also a non-profit government market regulator with the objective to supervise the country's capital market.

Analysis of *Syariah* Screens

Qualitative Screen

This study categorized qualitative screens into five categories according to various businesses: *Riba* and *Gharar*, non-halal products, gambling and gaming, immoral and other impermissible activities. Only eight out of all the fifteen users have made available their qualitative criteria in a list of non-permissible businesses. Table 2 provides the list of five business classifications as non-Syariah compliant. It is crucial to note that some users provide only the activities they screen, while some list them exhaustively.

All eight users have a common set of industrial categories inspected, except for Al-Meezan, which does not specifically state gambling as one of their non-compliant criteria. For the first category of *Riba'* and *Gharar* based activities; SC, FTSE, MSCI, S&P, Al-Meezan, and Azzad used a general term to represent such activities, while DJIM and *Shariah* Capital provided a specific and exhaustive list of particular businesses that are involved in *Riba* and *Gharar* activities.

In addition, the degree of leniency of these users can be analysed through the immediate exclusion of companies deemed impermissible according to the qualitative criteria only - DJIM and Azzad. It is also found that some users including SC, FTSE, MSCI, S&P, Shariah Capital and Al–Meezan first screen companies according to their business categories and then further screen these companies with mixed activities using their quantitative screening methods. These users therefore use both the qualitative and quantitative screening methods and allow more flexibility in their screening process.

Table 2: Syariah Qualitative Screen

ACTIVITIES	SC	DJIM	FTSE	MSCI	S&P	SHARIAH CAPITAL	AL - MEEZAN	AZZAD
Riba and Gharar	Financial services based on riba Stock-broking or share trading in syariah non-compliant securities Conventional Insurance	Banks Real Estate Holding and Development Consumer Finance Specialty Finance Mortgage Finance Full line insurance Investment services Insurance brokers Property & Casualty	Banking or any other interest related activity, (excluding Islamic financial institutions) Brokers Life insurance	Convent-ional financial services	Financials	Conventional financial services Banks Mortgage companies Insurance Brokerage firms Securities firms	Conventional banks Modarabah companies Leasing companies Insurance companies	Conventional financial institutions

		Insurance Reinsurance Life Insurance						
Non halal products	Manufacture or sale of non-halal products and related products	Brewers Distillers & Vintners Food products Food retailers & wholesalers. Restaurants and bars	Alcohol, Pork and other non halal related products	Pork related products Alcohol	Pork related products Alcohol	Alcohol Pork and meat packing	Companies dealing in alcohol	Alcohol Meat products
Gambling	Gambling	Gambling	Gaming	Gambling / Casino	Gambling	Gaming, casinos		Gambling
Immoral	Entertain-ment activities that are non-permissible according to syariah	Broadcasting & Entertainment Media Agencies Hotels Recreational Products and Services	Night Club Activities Porno-graphy and adult entertain-ment Prostitution	Music Hotels Cinema Adult entertain-ment	Pornograp hy Advertis-ing and Media (news-paper are allowed, sub-industries	Hotels and motels Musical instrument Entertain-ment Advertising media	Pornography	Pornography Other unethical entertain-ment various magazines and media)

					area analyzed individ-ually) Stem-cell research	Pornography Amusement and recreation Movies, theatres and film distribution		
Other Imper-missible	Manufacture or sale of tobacco-based products or related products Other activities deemed permissible.	Tobacco Defense and Weapons	Tobacco Arms manufacturi ng	Tobacco, Defense / Weapons	Tobacco Trading of gold and silver as cash on deferred basis.	Tobacco Weapons	Tobacco etc	Tobacco Weapons of mass destruction
Use Quali-tative Criteria only	No	Yes	No	No	No	No	No	Yes

Table 3: Shariah Quantitative Screen (part 1)

DENOMINATOR	USERS					
	SC	DJIM	FTSE	MSCI	S&P	SHARIAH CAPITAL
Debt Screen						
Debt (D)		$< \frac{33\ \%}{\text{Av Mcap}}$	$< \frac{33\ \%}{\text{TA}}$	$< \frac{33.33\ \%}{\text{TA}}$	$< \frac{33\ \%}{\text{Av MV}}$	$< \frac{33\%}{\text{Av Mcap and TA}}$
Interest bearing Debt (IBD)						
Liquidity screen						
Debt (D) + liquid funds						
A.Receivables (AR)		$< \frac{33\%}{\text{Av Mcap}}$		$< \frac{70\ \%}{\text{TA}}$	$< \frac{49\ \%}{\text{Av MV}}$	$< \frac{45\%}{\text{Av Mcap and TA}}$
Receivables (AR) + Cash (C)			$< \frac{50\%}{\text{TA}}$			

Receivables (AR) + Cash (C) + other debtors						
Liquid assets (LA)						
Interest Screen						
Cash (C) + Interest bearing securities (IBS)		$< \frac{33\ \%}{Av\ Mcap}$	$< \frac{33\ \%}{TA}$		$< \frac{33\ \%}{Av\ MV}$	$< \frac{33\ \%}{Av\ MV}$
Non Permissable Income Screen						
Non Permissible Income (NPY)	clearly prohibited Y $< \frac{5\%}{TR\ or\ PBT}$ umum balwa Y $< \frac{10\%}{TR\ or\ PBT}$ Mixed rental payment Y $< \frac{20\%}{TR\ or\ PBT}$ maslahah Y $< \frac{25\%}{TR\ or\ PBT}$		$< \frac{5\%}{TR}$	$< \frac{5\%}{TR}$	(excluding IY) $< \frac{5\%}{TR}$	

Table 3: Shariah Quantitative Screen (part 2) continued.

DENOMINATOR	USERS				
	AL-MEEZAN	AZZAD	DUBAI ISLAMIC BANK	S. ARABIA NCB	ALFA BANK
Debt Screen					
Debt (D)		*D ratio < 33%*			33.33% <—— Owner's Equity
Interest bearing Debt (IBD)	40% <—— TA		30% <—— TA or Mcap	1 or 33% 3rd <—— TR or Mcap	
Liquidity screen					
Debt (D) + liquid funds				50% < —— MV	
A.Receivables (AR)		*AR ratio < 45%.*			
Receivables (AR) + Cash (C)					
Receivables (AR) + Cash (C) + other debtors			70% <—— TA or Mcap		

DENOMINATOR	USERS				
	AL - MEEZAN	AZZAD	DUBAI ISLAMIC BANK	S.ARABIA NCB	ALFA BANK
Interest screen					
Cash (C) + Interest bearing securities (IBS)					$< \frac{33\%}{\text{52week Av Mcap}}$
Interest income (IY)			$< \frac{5\%}{\text{Operating Y}}$	$< \frac{5\%}{\text{Total Y}}$	$< \frac{5\%}{\text{TR}}$
Non Permissible Income screen					
Non Permissible Income (NPY)	Investment in $NPY < \frac{33\%}{TA}$ $NPV < \frac{5\%}{TR}$		$< \frac{5\%}{\text{Operating Y}}$ 30% Lending on interest $< \frac{}{\text{TA or Mcap}}$		

Quantitative Screen

A comprehensive comparison of the eleven users' quantitative screening methods is compiled in Table 3. Each user has a list of ratios for each criterion and it plays an important role in the quantitative screening method. This compilation of all ratios and criteria used provide systematic information for comparison within the *Syariah* context. The classification of quantitative criteria set by the users is summarized into four broad categories: Debt screen, liquidity screen, interest screen, and non-permissible income screen.

Debt Screen

Debt and interest-bearing debt items fall under the category of debt screen, and since Islamic finance follows the principle of sharing of risks and profits, borrowings and repayments of interest and principle are not Syariah compliant. It is observed that the level of debt criterion is screened by all except SC because it does not consider debt a major issue in their quantitative screen. There seems to be a consensus among the users to apply the benchmark of one third as the parameter of tolerance level stipulated by understandings from the *Quran*.

It is claimed that market capital provides the real worth of the company, but since it is driven by market sentiments, the volatility of price movement affects the threshold value and creates an inconsistency problem where *Syariah*-compliant status of the listed companies tend to change over time. Some users therefore argue that the use of average market capital is more suitable in order to smooth out any uncertainty in market price movements. This may have led to DIB and NCB's preference to use either total assets or market capitalization to avoid the seasonality effect in the Syariah-complaint status. In addition, another unique criterion set by Alfa Bank is the application of owner's equity as the divisor to screen debt. In summary, it is generally acceptable to have some debt in Syariah-compliant business.

Figure 1: Debt Ratio of Islamic Financial Institutions

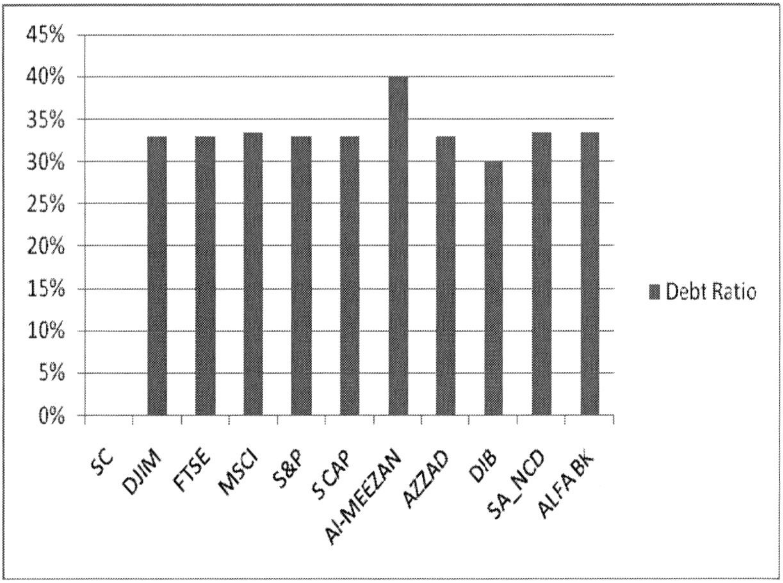

Liquidity Screen

The Syariah boards classified five sets of ratios under the liquidity screen: debt plus liquid funds, accounts receivable, accounts receivable plus cash, accounts receivable & cash plus other debt, and illiquid assets. While DJIM, FTSE, MSCI, S&P and *Shariah* Capital quantify current asset solely to measure the level of liquidity, DIB tends to include current assets and debt in its liquidity screen. This explains the term 'interest-bearing debt' used by some users for their debt screen, which imply the separation of debt and interest-bearing debt. The thresholds for liquidity screen ratios vary greatly from 33 to 80 percent, and this shows different *Shariah* jurisdictions' referral in setting the threshold level in liquidity screenings. Moreover, all users except for DJIM and MSCI tend to have higher tolerance level (45 to 80 percent) in liquidity screening compared to their debt screen, which was mostly set at one third. Similar to debt screen, the various users tend to use total asset, average and total market capital as divisor in liquidity screens and those who use total market capital will have an option to use total asset as practiced by DIB. It is interesting to note that NCB is the sole user of total market capital as the divisor in liquidity screen.

Figure 2: Liquidity Ratio of Islamic Financial Institutions

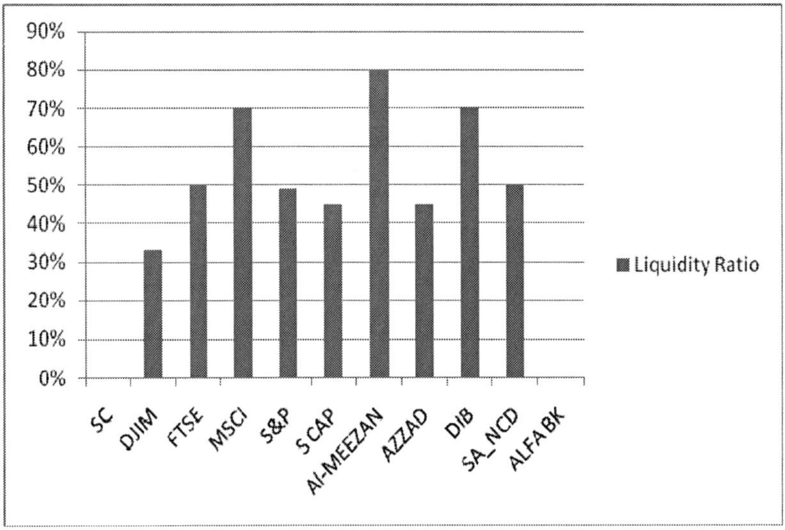

Interest Screen

Under the category of interest screen, two sets of ratios are classified: interest income and cash plus interest bearing securities. Interest income is screened by five users and the general consensus is 5 percent being the maximum threshold limit. A standard benchmark of one third is used for cash plus interest bearing securities. The difference between the users is again on the divisor, while cash plus interest bearing securities use either total assets or average market capital as the divisor, interest income ratio is divided by total revenue or income. This may be due to the existence of cash and interest bearing securities in the balance sheet instead of interest income from the income statement. The nominator and denominator are matched depending on their extraction from the respective financial statements.

Figure 3: Interest Screen of Islamic Financial Institutions

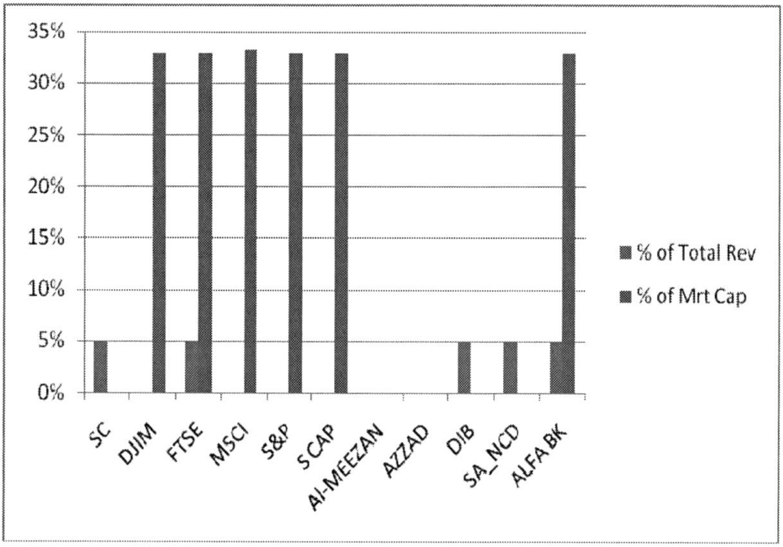

Non-Permissible Income Screen

It is important to note that non-permissible activities identified from the initial qualitative screen are further quantified to check if their level is acceptable by the respective users. From the various screens published, only SC, FTSE, MSCI, S&P, Al–Meezan and DIB further screen Syariah-compliant level of non-permissible income derived from these mixed businesses. DJIM, *Shariah* Capital, Azzad, NCB and Alfa Bank do not apply such a benchmark, and this implies that they are very strict in their quantitative screen. S&P further screen their non-compliant businesses by allowing non-permissible income excluding interest of not more than 5 percent. There seems to be a common consensus to use 5 percent as the maximum allowance for non–compliant businesses and income.

Conclusion

This paper compiled the screening methods practiced by Syariah Compliant boards around the world in terms of both qualitative and quantitative screens. Some of these users are more specific in their listing of Syariah impermissible business and activities, while some are more lenient. The majority of these users practice a two-tier method of screening: qualitative and quantitative. Under quantitative screen, the range of allowable ratios among non-permissible criteria and the measurement formula differ between boards.

Some countries including Malaysia, Russia and UAE have their respective Syariah screening boards and they set different standards depending on the roles and objectives they play in the industry. Although there are possibilities that other exchanges or countries may provide their own screening method, most fund managers, banks and industry players do not have such screening facilities and thus have to rely on market intelligence providers that screen global assets at macro level. The most prominent Syariah index providers are DJIM, FTSE, MSCI and S&P which pre-screened universal stocks to form particular *Syariah* index constituents. Their Indices are licensed for use by institutional investors around the world for portfolio management and benchmarking purposes, as well as to serve as the basis of structured products and other index-linked investment vehicles including ETFs.

In summary, we can categorize DJIM and Azzad as very stringent Syariah compliant users because they reject companies who are in one way or another involved in Syariah non-compliant businesses in the first round of qualitative screen. It is also obvious from our comparison that SC is the only user who does not practice debt and liquidity screen. Alfa Bank also does not practice liquidity screen, while Al-Meezan as well as Azzad do not apply interest screen. There exists some consensus among FTSE, MSCI, S&P, and DIB to practice all four quantitative screens. Different references of *Syariah* jurisdictions may have also contributed towards the dispersion between the screening methods. The Middle East jurisdiction, which can be represented by NCB and DIB, are very much concerned with the prohibition of *Riba'* by stringent screening for interest received and paid. SC's *Syariah* board is concerned about providing a wider range of investment instruments and only concentrates on lawful and pure returns of businesses, irrespective of how capital is generated, which can be seen from the absence of debt and liquidity screen.

Recommendation

The suggestion to set a universal standard applicable by all is thus relevant and logical to global ethical investing with efficient cost and time.

Qualitative screen

The suggestion on qualitative method is whether it should immediately exclude companies deemed impermissible or provide parameters for further screening of these companies. According to our analysis, DJIM and Azzad immediately exclude companies deemed impermissible, and this is seen as a defensive measure, as screening the real businesses of companies requires scrutinizing the company's annual report and accounts. Other information needs to be extracted directly from the company's operation and such information can only be obtained by an authorized regulator.

It is important to include a qualitative screen similar to DJIM's where an exhaustive list of industries considered as non-Syariah-compliant can be used to immediately segregate companies with impermissible businesses. In order to avoid discrepancies, there should be some consideration for questionable companies, provided all information needed to prove that they are permissible is available. More importantly, it is a preventive step to exclude industries that are involved in non-permissible activities. In summary, companies whose main business falls under the list of impermissible industries are not Syariah-compliant.

Quantitative screen

From the compiled analysis, debt screen is most frequently used, followed by liquidity and interest screens. The threshold limit for debt ratio is generally one third, while liquidity screen has a wider acceptable range, with an average of about fifty percent. As for interest screen, the allowable limit is one third for cash plus interest bearing securities and only 5 percent for interest income. The recommendation for quantitative screening method should include a debt ratio of less than 33%, plus either one of the following:

- Accounts receivables / total assets (less than 50%)
- Cash + Interest bearing securities / average market capitalization (less than 33%)
- Interest income / total revenue (less than 5%)

Other ratios may not be necessary if the debt and liquidity of firms are judged to be *Syariah*-compliant. With the standardization of Syariah screening standards by Islamic finance authorities around the globe, with clear guidelines and understanding of the issue on hand, the market for

Syariah-compliant investments would experience more growth opportunities in the future.

References

Alfa Bank (2007). http://www.btaconf.kz/files/pres/RinatGainoulline_eng.ppt

Al–Meezan (2009). Al-Meezan Investment Limited Knowledge Base Shariah Criteria http://www.almeezangroup.com/KnowledgeCentre/ShariahCriteria/tabid/124/Default.aspx

Amanie business Solution (2009). http://www.amanie.com.my/amanie/index.htm

Amiri Capital (2008). http://www.amiricapital.com/index.php

Archer, S. & Karim, R.A.A. (2007). *Islamic Finance the Regulatory Challenge*. Singapore: John Wiley & Sons (Asia).

Azzad Asset Management (2009). Ethical Investing: Social and Financial Screens. http://azzad.net/new/ethical_screens.aspx

Derigs, U. & Marzban S. (2008), Review and analysis of current *Shariah*-compliant equity screening practices. *International Journal of Islamic and Middle Eastern Finance and Management.* Vol. 1 No. 4, pp. 285-30.

Dow Jones Indexes. (2009). Guide to the Dow Jones Islamic Market Indexes. http://www.djindexes.com/mdsidx/downloads/rulebooks/imi_rulebook.pdf

Dubai Islamic Bank. (2005). http://www.financeinislam.com/article/10/1/551

Financial Times Stock Exchange (2009). Ground Rules for the Management of FTSE Global Islamic Index Series. http://www.ftse.com/japanese/Indices/FTSE_Global_Islamic_Index_Series/Downloads/islamic_indexrules.pdf

Grais, W. & Pellegrini, M. (2006). Corporate Governance and Shariah Compliance in Institutions Offering Islamic Financial Services. *World Bank Policy Research Working Paper 4054*.

HSBC Amanah (2009). *http://www.hsbcamanah.com/1/2/hsbc-amanah/*

Iqbal, Z. & Mirakhor, A. (2007). *An Introduction to Islamic Finance, Theory and practice.* Singapore: John Wiley & Sons (Asia).

Islamic Finance Asia. (2008, October/November). Are Islamic Indices the way to go? *Feature,* p. 28.

Jaffer, S. (2004). *Islamic Asset Management: Forming the Future for Shari'a-Complaint Investment Strategies.* United Kingdom: Euromoney Institutional Investor.

—. (2009). Islamic Investments Weather Most of the Storm in Asia, Islamic Finance News, Takaful Report, 6(49).

Khatkhatay, M.H & Nisar, S. (2006). Shari'a-Compliant Equity Investments: An Assessment of Current Screening Norms. *Proceedings of the Seventh Harvard University Forum on Islamic Finance,* Harvard University.

Mahmassani, S. (1987). *The Philosophy of Jurisprudence in Islam.* Malaysia: Penerbitan Hizbi.

McMillen, M.J.T. (2006). Islamic Capital Markets: Developments and Issues. *Capital Markets Law Journal*, 1 (2), pp.136-172.

Morgan Stanley Capital International (2009). MSCI Islamic Index Series Methodology. http://www.mscibarra.com/products/indices/islamic/methodology.html

National Commercial Bank, Saudi Arabia. (2005). http://www.financeinislam.com/article/10/1/551

Securities Commission. (2009). http://www.sc.com.my/main.asp?pageid=256&menuid=285&newsid=&linkid=&type=

Shariah Capital (2009). Shariah Capital: Expanding the Universe of Shariah Compliant Stocks. http://www.shariahcap.com/pubs/shariah/shariah_screening.pdf

Standard & Poor's (2009). S&P Shariah Indices Methodology. http://www2.standardandpoors.com/spf/pdf/index/SP_Shariah_Indices_Methodology_Web.pdf

Weeramantry, C.G. (1988/1996). *Islamic Jurisprudence: An International Perspective.* New York: Macmillan, London & St. Martin's Press.

Yaquby, N. (2000). Trading in Equities: A Shari'a Perspective. *Proceedings of the Fourth Harvard University Islamic Finance Forum,* Harvard University.

ISLAMIC FINANCE, ENERGY SECTOR AND FINANCIAL INNOVATIONS

MONDHER BELLALAH AND BADR ELMRABTI AND FREDERIC TEULON (IPAG)

Introduction

Islamic finance has an important additional component to conventional finance, in particular the willingness to increase the social welfare in the financing of a project. It links the investor's return to the performance of the underlying asset.

Islamic finance can be an important contributor to the financing of energy projects in the world by funding eco-friendly energy projects, such as low carbon emissions coal plants, gas power plants, wind and solar power plants.

We have seen some landmark shariah-compliant energy projects in the Middle East, like in Egypt (home to the largest wind farm in Africa and the Middle East) and in the UAE (Masdar's US$15bn project aiming to create the carbon-neutral city), with long-term plans to generate electricity from wind, oil shale, solar and nuclear energy. However, Islamic financing of power assets can be pushed to worldwide development by presenting the opportunities of different important markets (US, Europe, Australia and India).

In that purpose, we will deal in the next sections with the various issues related to the power generation industry, like the different types of power assets and their investment risks, the structure of liberalized power markets in US and Europe, and finally the Islamic financing mechanisms, which can be used to finance power assets investment deals.

This chapter is organized as follows:

- Section 1 presents some deregulated power markets by explaining the structure of these markets and the market products that can be used to sell the power output of a power generator.
- Section 2 determines the potential economic benefits that an Islamic investor can enjoy through investment in power assets.
- Section 3 presents the Islamic mechanisms that can be used to invest in power generation.
- Section 4 details the Economic and social benefits of power plants investments for Islamic investors

1. Presentation of some deregulated power markets

The construction of efficient wholesale electricity markets in different regions of the world (Europe, US, Australia) is a quite difficult task. Indeed power is a different commodity from oil for example, because it is not storable and there is a need of real-time balancing of supply and demand. That is why there is a need of various power generation technologies (nuclear, hydro, coal, oil, gas, wind and solar power plants) with different features regarding their flexibility and capacities in order to have balance of the supply and demand at every minute.

The purpose of this section is to present the main features of different power markets in Europe and US. It will not be an exhaustive overview of these markets because of the complexities of electricity markets' organization. We will mainly show what the markets are in which an owner of a power plant (independent power producer: IPP) in a particular location can sell the generated power to value its plant in the wholesale power markets.

A power producer has to be able to provide balancing and reserve resources (as required by the system operator and regulator) in order to contribute to the stability of the power system. These services are remunerated either by specific markets or by the system operator.

The supply of electricity involves three types of activities:

- Generation
- Transmission
- Distribution

European and US markets have a common structure consisting of an electric system operator (ISO, TSO), which maintains the system and a regulator.

The services can then be managed by either a highly centralized market under the control of the system operator, or through a sequence of bilateral markets, with the system operator only playing a system regulating role.

1.1 Types of markets structures

In the wholesale market, the electricity can be sold through two different types of markets: centralized pools and (decentralized) bilateral markets.

In centralized pools, all energy is sold and purchased through the pool. This is achieved by the centralized scheduling of all generation units through the pool, whereas all suppliers must purchase their entire demand from the pool. ***Electric Reliability Council of Texas*** (ERCOT) is an example of a pool.

Bilateral markets are markets where all market participants are basically free to engage in any type of contractual obligations for the delivery of energy, which then provide the basis for the self-scheduling of producers. As a consequence, the bilateral markets allow for bi-directional exchanges between any two market participants and principally allow all market participants to act as traders. Hence, whilst a producer can only sell to the pool in the first model, it may both buy and sell energy from/to any other party in the bilateral markets. Several European electricity markets are organized in this way. These bilateral markets are completed by Power exchanges, intra-day trading and balancing mechanisms in order to fulfil the requirement of real-time balancing of electricity supply and demand. It constitutes for a power plant(s) owner additional opportunities to sell the power output of his plant(s).

In the US there are several regions, which have different electricity markets (with their own transmission system operator) organization and also different power plants mix (more nuclear plants in Western regions than Texas and Eastern regions). As you can see in the below figure, the US electricity market is divided into 10 regions.

Figure 1: US electricity regions

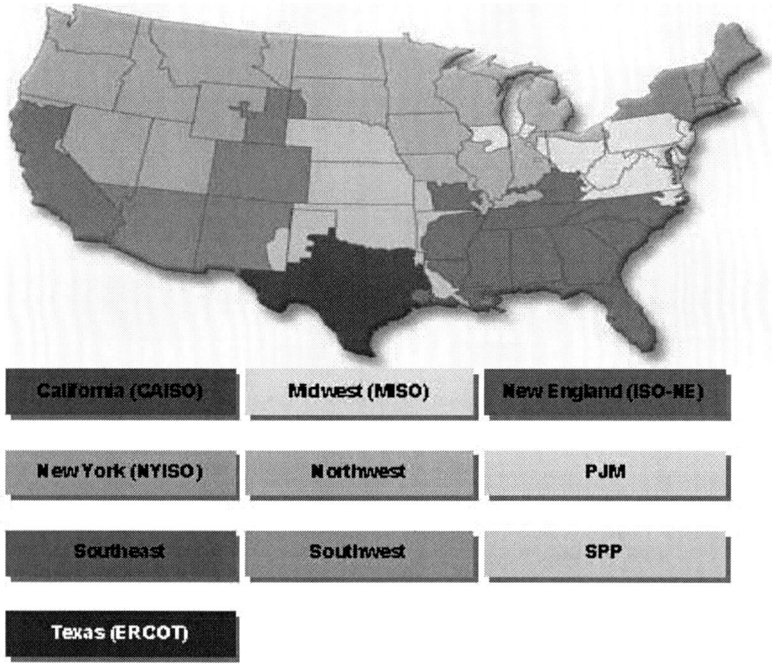

Source: FERC website

The products offered by pool markets vary widely from market to market. Several markets trade the main energy spot products as well as the ancillary services.

1.2 Type of market products

The electricity spot markets can be divided into three categories:

Day-ahead: The traders transact for production to be delivered to the network on the next day. Each hour is traded separately.

Intraday: The traders deal with generation of power for the rest of the day or the next hour.

The power is traded in USD/MWh (price in USD of a 1 Mega Watt of production for one hour) in the US markets.

The power is traded in EUR/MWh (price in EUR of a 1 Mega Watt of production for one hour) in the European markets (France, Germany for example).

1.3 Types of Traded Power

Indeed, since it cannot be stored, power sold in the morning is completely different from power sold in the same location in the evening. For this reason there are many varieties of products traded in the power markets, making the study of these markets even more difficult. Frequently encountered power products include:

On-peak Power: This corresponds to the hours of the day where the power demand (and hence the prices) is higher. It can slightly vary from 8:00–23:00 or 7:00–22:00 for five days a week (Monday–Friday) for the delivery period excluding North American Electric Reliability Council (NERC) holidays. For German or French markets, it corresponds to the period 8:00-20:00 five days a week (Monday-Friday).

Off-peak Power: This corresponds to the on-peak complementary period of the day.

A power plant owner can also sell his production in:

- 2-, 4-, 8-, or 16-hour blocks of power,
- Next day power : Base Load power,
- Balance-of-the-week power,
- Next-week power,
- Balance-of-the-month power,
- Next-month power.

1.4 Examples

Below you will find the market quotations in broker based (over-the-counter markets) day-ahead markets for on-peak and off-peak products. There are an important number of power market prices. The differences in prices are small inside a specific region (Gulf/Texas). However, we can notice that power prices show significant differences between Gulf/Texas and PJM regions. This is due to the fact that these regions can have different weather conditions (an important driver of the electricity demand and hence of the power prices).

Table 1: On-peak and Off-peak power for Gulf, Texas, Midwest and North East US regions

<HELP> for explanation. N2N265 Comdty ELWP

Page 1/1

US Power Prices

Pricing Date 06/17/10 Last Price in 10 Years Source Composite

Product	Time	Trade	Chg.	Source	Product	Time	Trade	Chg	Source
FIRM ON-PEAK					FIRM OFF-PEAK				
Gulf/Texas					Gulf/Texas				
1) ERCOT North	06/16	48.99	1.20	INCX	10) ERCOT North	06/16	29.63	0.19	INCX
2) ERCOT South	06/16	50.39	0.56	INCX	11) ERCOT South	06/16	29.50	0.16	INCX
3) ERCOT West	06/16	46.63	0.63	INCX	12) ERCOT West	06/16	20.50	[illegible]	INCX
4) ERCOT Houston	06/16	51.06	-0.41	BBSW	13) ERCOT Houston	06/16	30.25	0.19	BBSW
5) Entergy	06/16	49.00	3.00	INCX	14) Entergy	06/10	24.50	3.50	INCX
Midwest/N.East					Midwest/N.East				
6) NEPOOL	06/16	52.65	2.01	INCX	15) NEPOOL	06/14	36.38	[illegible]	INCX
7) NY Zone A	06/16	45.39	3.89	INCX					
8) PJM	06/16	56.58	4.28	INCX	16) PJM	06/15	32.27	[illegible]	INCX
9) AEP	06/01	49.00	--	INCX	17) AEP	06/01	27.60	--	INCX

91) Pacific NW, CA, Desert SW 92) Gulf/Texas, MidWest/NEast

Table 2: On-peak and Off-peak power for Pacific North West, California and desert South West US regions

<HELP> for explanation. N2N265 Comdty ELWP

Page 1/1

US Power Prices

Pricing Date 06/17/10 Last Price in 10 Years Source Composite

	Time	Trade	Chg	Source	Product	Time	Trade	Chg.	Source
FIRM ON-PEAK					FIRM OFF-PEAK				
Pacific NW					Pacific NW				
1) Mid-Columbia	06/16	12.07	[illegible]	BBSW	9) Mid-Columbia	06/14	0.89	-1.11	BBSW
2) Cal-Or Border	06/16	20.12	-1.65	INCX	10) Cal-Or Border	06/16	4.20	1.68	INCX
3) NOB	06/16	20.00	-2.14	INCX	11) NOB	06/16	6.79	0.61	INCX
California					California				
4) NP15	06/16	35.66	0.74	INCX	12) NP15	06/16	14.47	0.85	INCX
5) SP15	06/16	35.54	0.43	INCX	13) SP15	06/16	14.22	0.26	INCX
Desert SW					Desert SW				
6) Mead Substation	06/16	36.69	0.44	INCX	14) Mead Substation	06/16	16.51	[illegible]	INCX
7) Palo Verde	06/16	36.17	[illegible]	BBSW	15) Palo Verde	06/16	14.83	[illegible]	INCX
8) Four Corners	06/16	36.45	0.26	INCX	16) Four Corners	06/16	12.89	0.18	INCX

91) Pacific NW, CA, Desert SW 92) Gulf/Texas, MidWest/NEast

Tables 3 and 4 show the hourly day-ahead power market prices from the EPEX power exchange for France.

Table 3: EPEX spot French hourly day-ahead power prices

<HELP> for explanation. N265 Corp **PWNX**

Page 1/1

European Power Exchange -- EPEX Spot Market

Pricing Date 06/17/10 Last Price In 1 Month

Product	Time	Last	Chg	Vol	Product	Time	Last	Chg	Vol
Hours (€/MWh)									
1) Hour 01	11:31	44.80	8.41	5741.00	18) Hour 18	11:31	49.13	-3.91	4878.00
2) Hour 02	11:31	40.59	5.59	6193.00	19) Hour 19	11:31	48.80	-4.76	4859.00
3) Hour 03	11:31	35.50	7.45	6610.00	20) Hour 20	11:31	45.38	-7.92	5318.00
4) Hour 04	11:31	28.10	8.10	7263.00	21) Hour 21	11:31	44.71	-4.06	5694.00
5) Hour 05	11:31	28.09	8.04	7462.00	22) Hour 22	11:31	43.06	-4.50	5718.00
6) Hour 06	11:31	32.45	2.45	7317.00	23) Hour 23	11:31	48.30	-5.59	5804.00
7) Hour 07	11:31	40.11	2.33	6784.00	24) Hour 24	11:31	41.30	-6.70	5638.00
8) Hour 08	11:31	53.99	2.23	6233.00	Day Ahead				
9) Hour 09	11:31	56.19	0.25	5637.00	(€/MWh)				
10) Hour 10	11:31	58.36	0.94	4828.00	25) Baseload	11:31	47.04	-1.12	134417.00
11) Hour 11	11:31	62.24	0.24	4452.00	26) VWAP	11:31	46.83	-0.26	
12) Hour 12	11:31	66.18	1.03	4368.00					
13) Hour 13	11:31	61.10	-1.30	4701.00	27) Peakload	11:31	54.01	-3.82	57860.00
14) Hour 14	11:31	55.09	-5.31	4458.00	28) Off-Peak 1	11:31	37.95	6.00	53603.00
15) Hour 15	11:31	51.53	-7.32	4721.00	29) Off-Peak 2	11:31	44.34	[illegible]	22854.00
16) Hour 16	11:31	46.59	-7.31	5088.00					
17) Hour 17	11:31	47.47	-5.24	4552.00					

91) Auction 92) Day 93) Day Ahead 94) Futures 95) Gas 96) VWAP

Australia 61 2 9777 8600 Brazil 5511 3048 4500 Europe 44 20 7330 7500 Germany 49 69 9204 1210 Hong Kong 852 2977 6000
Japan 81 3 3201 8900 Singapore 65 6212 1000 U.S. 1 212 318 2000 Copyright 2010 Bloomberg Finance L.P.
SN 799894 G360-197-0 17-Jun-10 12:19:32

Table 4: EPEX spot French hourly and blocks intraday power prices

<HELP> for explanation. N265 Corp **PWNX**

Page 1/2

European Power Exchange -- EPEX Spot Market

Pricing Date 06/17/10 Last Price In 1 Month

Product	Time	Bid	Time	Ask	Trd Time	Last	Chg	Vol
Intraday (€/MWH)								
Blocks								
1) Block 13-16	05/27	55.00	05/27	58.00	05/27	55.00	35.00	48.00
2) Block 17-20			06/08	50.00	06/08	50.00	-3.00	50.00
3) Blocks 21-24	06/15	39.00	06/15	50.00	06/15	45.00	26.00	151.00
Hourly								
4) Hour 9-10	06/12	46.00			06/12	46.00	18.05	25.00
5) Hour 10-11	06/13	23.00	06/13	23.00	06/13	23.00	42.25	81.00
6) Hour 11-12					09:41	62.00	4.00	40.00
7) Hour 12-13	06/16	52.00	06/16	61.00	06/16	58.00	11.00	30.00
8) Hour 13-14			11:48	58.00	11:48	53.00	4.00	97.00
9) Hour 14-15			11:46	54.00	11:46	48.00	-2.00	75.00
10) Hour 15-16	11:34	44.00	11:34	48.00	11:34	48.00	6.00	50.00
11) Hour 16-17	11:20	46.00	11:20	50.00	11:20	48.00	-3.90	150.00
12) Hour 17-18	12:16	49.00	12:16	57.00	12:16	49.00	1.00	75.00
13) Hour 18-19	12:15	50.00	12:15	53.00	12:15	51.75	3.75	75.00
14) Hour 19-20	12:15	46.00	12:15	55.00	12:15	49.00	-1.00	25.00

91) Auction 92) Day 93) Day Ahead 94) Futures 95) Gas 96) VWAP

Australia 61 2 9777 8600 Brazil 5511 3048 4500 Europe 44 20 7330 7500 Germany 49 69 9204 1210 Hong Kong 852 2977 6000
Japan 81 3 3201 8900 Singapore 65 6212 1000 U.S. 1 212 318 2000 Copyright 2010 Bloomberg Finance L.P.
SN 799894 G360-197-0 17-Jun-10 12:24:59

The tables above contain the traded product (on-peak, off-peak, block hours or hourly product, e.g. in Table 3, "Hour 13" corresponds to a power contract that provides 1 MWh power from 12:01 to 13:00 for tomorrow), its price (in EUR/MWh or USD/MWh), the bid and asking prices, changes from day before closing value and volume, expressed in MWh.

There is also a real-time market that enables the system operator and power producers to balance the supply and demand due to any uncertainty that can affect one of the sides.

These uncertainties can be on the supply side:

- Outage or anticipated return (from an outage or test) of a power plant
- Outage in the power network

And on the demand side:

- Risk on power consumption fluctuations (due to always changing weather conditions)

The spot products can be sold or bought through two ways:

Bilateral or Broker-based (Over-the-Counter): the trading involves either direct contact between two parties or contact mediated by a broker (like InterContinental Exchange Trade, Prebon and Spectron).

Power Exchanges: This consists of computer-based trading systems allowing generators and suppliers to fine tune their contracted positions by buying and selling standardized blocks of electricity. Part of the electricity production can also be sold through Power Exchanges like European Power Exchange (EPEX) in France and Germany or Automated Power Exchange (APX) in the UK.

A power plant owner has access to two other markets to sell or be remunerated for the availability of his production:

- Ancillary services markets
- Installed capacity markets

The ancillary services market has been created in some regions (ERCOT region) to enable the system operator (ISO) to balance the instantaneous supply and demand balance. So, the power plant will be required to keep part of his power plant capacity in a reserve. If this reserve is called for by the system operator he will be paid the price he has requested for his reserve. There are two types of reserves: one can be mobilized in 10 minutes and the other in 30 minutes. These reserves are mainly given by peaking plants (most expensive) like hydro and oil-fired power plants. In France, there is no market for ancillary services but the system operator requires a certain amount of reserve for each power producer proportional to its power plant portfolio. However there is an agreement where the system operator pays the producer an upfront fee for this service.

The installed capacity market enables a power producer (who has several power plants) to put part of his capacity available, let us say 500 MW, to the system operator in order to balance the market if a shortage of power is observed. The power producer will be paid by the system operator for this service. However, every day he will have to keep a spare capacity of 500 MW (he will not be able to sell this capacity in the spot market) for use by the system operator in case of stress in the supply-demand equilibrium.

2. Power assets: interesting Islamic investments

In this section we will see that a sound investment in power plants can be lucrative as well as adding to social welfare of the market in which we are involved. These facts make them an ideal candidate to the Islamic asset category. A presentation of the type of power assets and the investment risks associated will then be followed by an explanation of the opportunity of investing in peaking power plants.

2.1 Type of power assets and investment risk

On the supply side, the following technologies are the main suppliers:

- Nuclear
- Coal steam
- Gas/Oil steam
- Combined cycle gas turbines (CCGT)
- Hydro
- Renewables (wind, solar, biomass)

You will find below, as an example, the energy mix in the US.

Figure 2: 2009 U.S Electricity generation by source

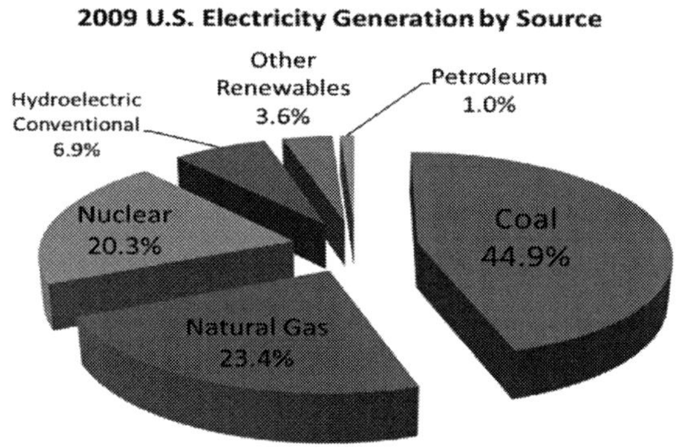

Source: Wikipedia

However, electricity generation mixes can be very different from each other across the world. Below is the electricity generation mix in France, which is dominated by nuclear technology.

Figure 3: 2009 French Electricity generation by source

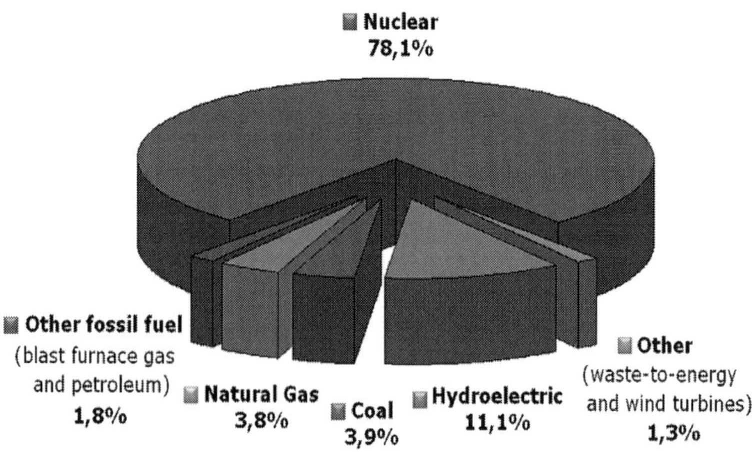

Source: Wikipedia

All these power assets have different characteristics as for investment cost, fuel cost, operating cost, and regulatory risk.

Indeed, nuclear power plants have a low fuel cost and operating cost but have very high capital cost. They also have important regulatory risk due to the security concerns over their operations. Moreover, construction times are very important and make, as a result, the investment break-even longer.

Coal fired power plants have become more capital consuming in order to benefit from economies of scale, tighter environmental constraints, and better fuel efficiency. Construction times of these types of power plants tend to be important too.

Gas-fired technologies have relatively low capital cost, good operations flexibility (which make it very valuable in stressed power markets). Its fuel cost remains between coal-fired plants and oil-fired plants costs.

Hydro power plant investments are subject to important risks in the construction phase, which can make them costly due to delays. Moreover the amortization time of hydro power plants is very important. As a result, it is difficult to find borrowing available for this type of plant. Most of the hydro capacity is used in the developed world and potential hydro projects are mainly available in the emerging markets, but there is important sovereign risk. Besides this, there is a need of a deregulated power market in order to benefit from market prices. Only developed countries have these deregulated markets. However, operations of hydro power plants are very flexible and optionality of these plants can be used at a very granular level (hourly level). It depends on exogenous factors like rainfalls, or ice melting. In deregulated markets, hydro power plants operate only a few hours in low power demand seasons (and hence store water) and produce power when power demand is high. It can be challenging to optimize these plants because of an important numbers of parameters, including water in storage, market prices forecast, assumptions on rainfalls, ice melting, etc.
On the renewables side, solar and wind power plants are also capital intensive. However, they have very short start-up and shut-off times, no fuel costs or emissions and low operations costs. However, their productions depend respectively on level of wind and nebulosity, which could not occur necessarily on periods of high market prices, making their P&L less easy to forecast.

We are going to consider peaking power plants. These plants are mainly oil-fired, coal-fired or gas-fired and produce power during hours where demand is high (and market prices are high too). They have a high flexibility, that is to say they can be started up and shut off inside a day to take advantage of price spikes and can be shut off rapidly when prices go below their marginal costs. However, these power plants have high marginal costs and can run fewer hours than a nuclear plant, which is considered as a base load production unit (run generally 24 hours a day) and has a very low marginal cost.

Flexibility clearly adds value to a power plant. This increase in value is accentuated by the lack of symmetry between high and low values for electricity prices. It also depends on the volatility of the electricity prices, and to a large extent, on the correlation between electricity and gas prices. It is interesting to note that the best strategy on average (long term versus short term arbitrage) is only possible by the interaction between the physical market and the financial one. Only the owner of a plant could carry out such a strategy. The tests on historical data confirm the pertinence of this strategy.

2.2 Investments opportunities in Peaking Plants

Estimating the profitability of peaking plants is a particularly difficult exercise in liberalized power markets. Peaking plants, by definition, depend on the high prices that appear over a relatively small number of hours to earn a return on the initial investment. The volatility of electricity and fuel prices makes prediction of the actual profits more difficult.

However, the fact that both fuel and power prices can be volatile can create not only risks, but also opportunities for the owners of peaking plants to make profits, producing electricity whenever the dark/spark spread – the difference between the electricity price and the fuel cost – is favourable.

2.2.1 Spark spread

The spark spread is measured as the price of electricity minus the price of natural gas, taking into account the efficiency of the natural gas power plant. In other words, spark spread represents the cost of generating power from a natural gas plant. Positive spark spread indicates that it is more profitable to burn natural gas to generate electricity than to purchase the electricity itself.

Clean spark spread is calculated by adjusting for the cost of carbon credit such as European Union Allowance (EUA).

Dirty spark spread = Power price - (Natural gas price / gas-fired power plant efficiency)

Clean spark spread = Dirty spark spread - (CO2 adjustment * CO2 price)
The gas-fired power plant efficiency is a factor corresponding to the number of units of natural gas needed to produce one Megawatt Hour of electricity which correspond to the for UK natural gas (i.e. NBP) is 49.131%.

The CO2 adjustment affects a percentage to the CO2 price in order to account number of metric tons of CO2 emitted when producing one Megawatt Hour of electricity by the gas-fired power plant.

It corresponds to the metric tons 42%.

For illustration purpose, historical graphs are given of the clean and dirty spark spreads for a gas-fired power plant operating in the UK.

- **Spark spread in the UK**

The formula used to display the clean spark spread data is the following:
Clean spark spread = (Power price – natural gas price / 49.13% - CO2 price * 42%)

Dirty spark spread = (Power price – natural gas price / 49.13%)

As the power price, we will consider the base load UK day-ahead power price, which is a 24-hour contract (23:00-23:00) for delivery of electricity for the next working day. This price is expressed in GBP/MWh.

The natural gas price is the day-ahead gas price for a delivery of gas for 24 hours the next working day in the National Balancing Point (NBP). This price is expressed in GBp/therm, but is converted in to GBP/MWh.

As CO2 price, we will consider the Bluenext spot EUA Phase 2 price (European Union Allowance phase 2, 2008-2012) expressed in EUR per 1000 metric tons. Bluenext is an environmental exchange formed on 21 December 2007. It is converted to get price in GBP per thousand metric tons.

The efficiency used for the gas-fired power plant is 49.13% and the CO2 adjustment is taken at 42%.

Figure 4: Clean spark spread Graph for UK (from February 2008 to January 2010

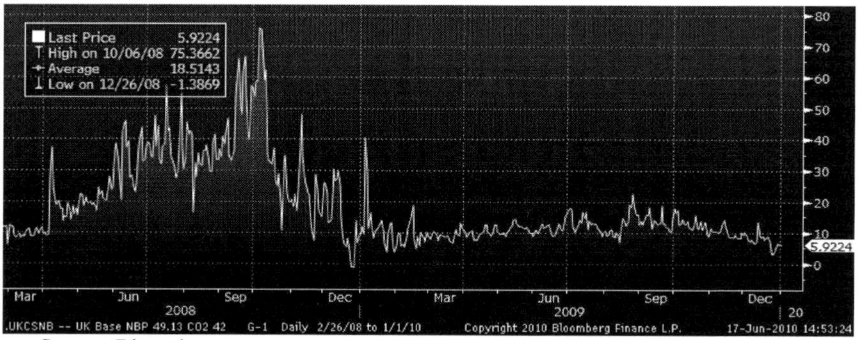

Source: Bloomberg

Figure 5: Dirty spark spread Graph for UK (from June 2006 to January 2010)

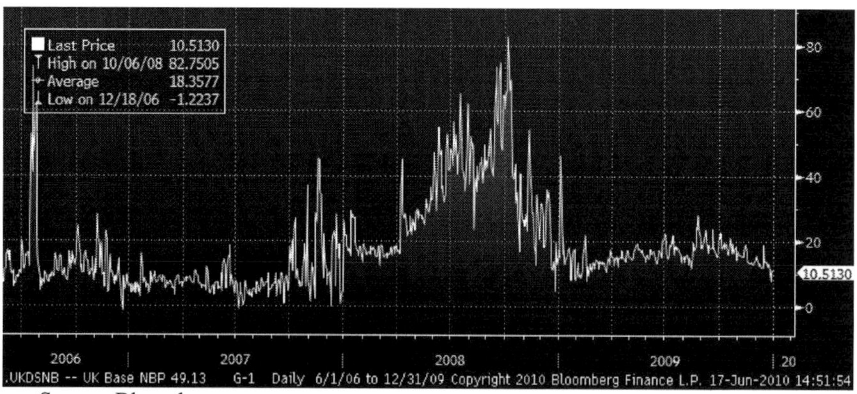

Source: Bloomberg

We can notice an important volatility of the dark spreads. The clean dark spread has been 12.5 times higher than the recent levels in a time frame of less than 2 years. This can have very good implications in the profitability of a gas-fired power plant. Logically, the dirty spark spread is higher than the clean spark spread because we do not take into account the CO2 cost of emissions in the latter. If we improve the ability of the plant to lower CO2 emissions we will increase the profitability of the power plant. However, technologies like Carbon capture and storage (CCS) are still costly.

2.2.1 Dark spread

Dark spread is measured as the price of electricity minus the price of coal, taking into account the efficiency of the coal-fired power plant. In other words, dark spread represents the cost of generating power from a coal-fired power plant. Positive dark spread indicates that it is more profitable to burn natural gas to generate electricity than to purchase the electricity itself.

Clean spark spread is calculated by adjusting for the cost of carbon credit such as European Union Allowance (EUA).

Dirty spark spread = Power price - (Natural gas price / coal-fired power plant efficiency)

Clean spark spread = Dirty spark spread - (CO2 adjustment * CO2 price)

The coal-fired power plant efficiency is a factor corresponding to the number of units of natural gas needed to produce one Megawatt Hour of electricity.

The CO2 adjustment affects a percentage to the CO2 price in order to account number of metric tons of CO2 emitted when producing one Megawatt Hour of electricity by the coal-fired power plant.

- **Dark spread in the UK**

The formula used to display the clean spark spread data is the following:

Clean spark spread = (Power price – coal price / 36% - CO2 price * 95%)

Dirty spark spread = (Power price – coal price / 36%)

As power price, we will consider the base load UK day-ahead power price, which is a 24-hour contract (23:00-23:00) for delivery of electricity for the next working day. This price is expressed in GBP/MWh.

The coal price is the North West Europe (NWE) steam coal price. The NW European considers deals that interest North West European countries like U.K., France, Netherlands, Germany, Denmark and Northern Spain and is evaluated using freight differentials between UK discharge ports and CIF Rotterdam equivalent. It is expressed in USD per metric ton and converted in to GBP/MWh.

As CO2 price, we will consider the Bluenext spot EUA Phase 2 price (European Union Allowance phase 2, 2008-2012) expressed in EUR per 1000 metric tons. Bluenext is an environmental exchange formed on 21 December 2007. It is converted to get price in GBP per thousand metric tons.

The efficiency used for the coal-fired power plant is 36% and the CO2 adjustment is taken at 95%.

Figure 6: Clean dark spread Graph for UK (from February 2008 to January 2010)

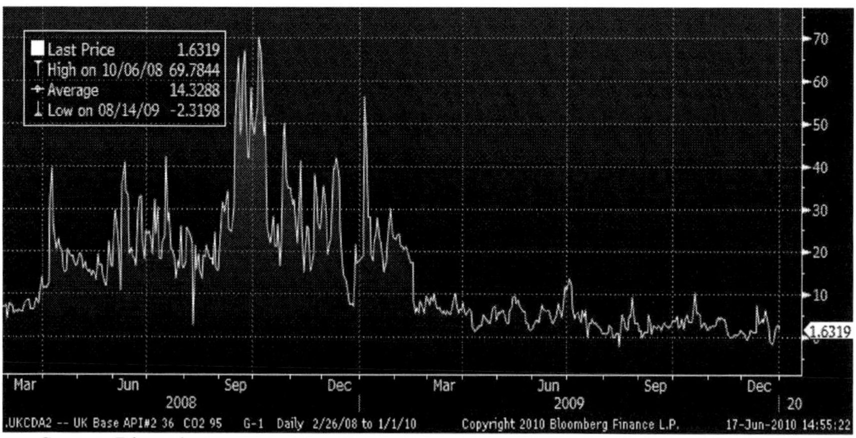

Source: Bloomberg

Figure 7: Dirty dark spread Graph for UK (from June 2006 to January 2010)

Source: Bloomberg

Dark and spark spreads can also be seen in other markets like in the US. This is an indicator of the past revenues a coal or gas-fired power plant operating in the considered US market (ERCOT Houston) during peak hours (7:00 to 22:00) every working day.

Figure 8: Clean spark spread in the ERCOT Houston market (from June 2006 to January 2010)

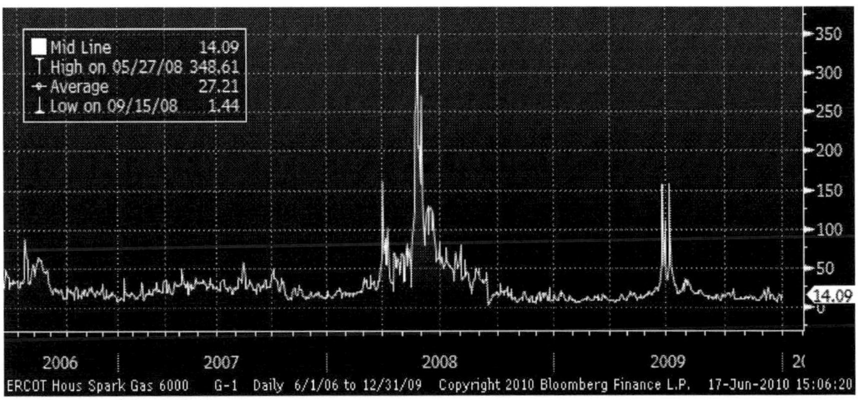

Source: Bloomberg

The dark spread displayed in the above graph corresponds to an efficiency of the gas-fired power plant of 56%.

Figure 9: Clean dark spread in the ERCOT Houston market

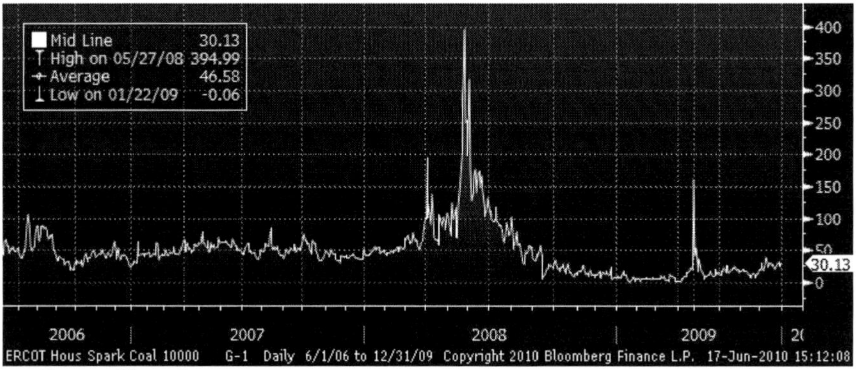

Source: Bloomberg

The dark spread displayed in the above graph corresponds to an efficiency of the coal-fired power plant of 56%.

As you can notice (in the figures x and y) the last value of clean dark spread (1.63 GBP/MWh) is very low compared to the dirty dark spread (12.01 GBP/MWh). The profitability of a coal-fired power plant is significantly lowered by the CO2 emissions costs. Indeed the 950 tons of CO2 is emitted per MWh produced for the coal plant (only 420 tons of CO2 is emitted per MWh for the gas-fired power plant). It is clear that carbon capture and storage technologies make great sense for a coal plant. Moreover the efficiency of the coal-fired power plant of 36% is also much lower than the one for the gas-fired power plant of 49% (need of less quantity of gas than coal to produce one MWh of power), which can be an added source of risk on the profitability of a coal plant compared to the gas-fired plant. Moreover the dark and spark spread do not take into account the parameters of the plant that could have a negative impact in its profitability (start-up costs, and ramping of the power output of the plant when it is started and shut off).

2.3 Valuation of power plant investment

The valuation of a power plant investment by the discounted cash flow analysis (DCF) will lead to the underestimation of the profits that can be earned by peaking plants. A more accurate method needs to estimate how likely – in any hour – the favourable spark spread will occur. Sophisticated analytical approaches applying financial options methods can provide a means to estimate how many hours such plants are expected to operate, and the profits that can be expected from their operation.

The real options method is a technique that can be used to estimate the value of a peaking plant, by valuing its ability to take advantage of volatile fuel and electricity prices. In this method, the power plant itself is treated as a financial option, except that it is a "real" physical asset – a power plant – rather than a financial security. The value of the power plant then becomes a series of call options for each hour during which the power price or the fuel price can vary. The implicit assumption is that the power plant will operate in each and every hour in which it is profitable to do so, and will not operate in those hours in which it is not.

Two important parameters have an impact on the valuation of a peaking power plant in the "real option" theory: the volatility of the power and fuel price (gas, coal, oil), and the correlation of the power prices with the fuel prices.

Figure 10: French Powernext day-ahead peak spot prices

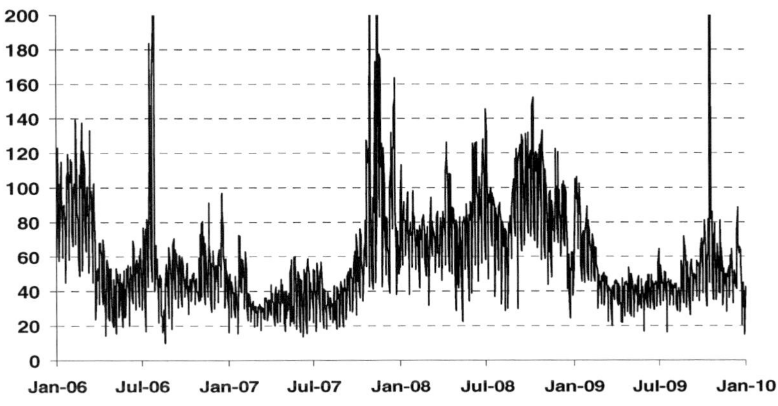

Figure 11: French Powernext day-ahead peak spot prices 30-days volatility

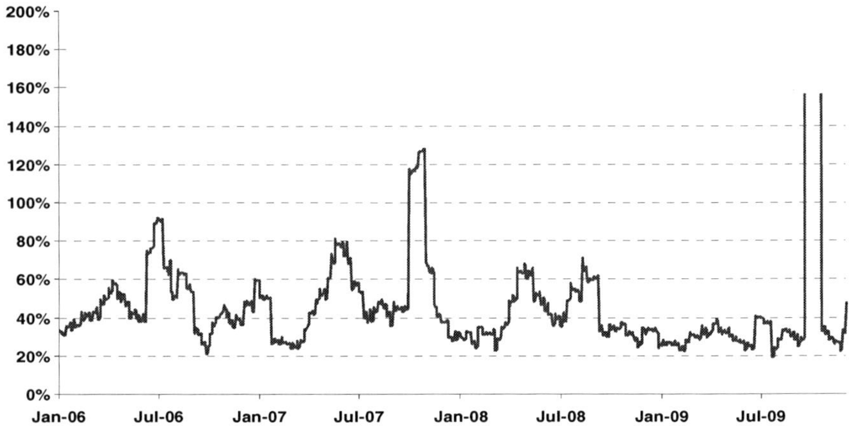

The ideal case for a peaking power plant valuation consists of a high volatility of power prices and fuel prices along with low or negative correlation between power and fuel prices. Indeed the power plant owner can benefit from potential high electricity prices and low fuel prices at the same time (because of low correlation). The dark/spark spread (margin) will be then high for the power plant owner, leading to important profitability of the plant. In reality, we can see high values of dark and spark spreads which can be due to, among others, supply demand imbalances in the short term. We have to take into account of long term supply and demand fundamentals which can depress power prices and increase fuel prices when we want to build a power plant in a specific market. The building of a power plant will require making a more thorough market study on capacity available, potential economic growth, analysis of fuel market perspectives (coal, gas or oil depending on the plant technology we want to invest in) because the lifetime of peaking plants is generally around 25 years.

The correlation between the electricity and fuel price is an important parameter in the valuation of a power plant. Indeed the ideal case for the power plant valuation is a negative correlation equal to -1 between electricity prices and the fuel price. Under this assumption, if the power prices go up, the fuel price goes down resulting in higher spread (and hence profit for the power plant). This spread (adjusted to the efficiency of the power plant) will tend to decrease as the correlation moves to the value of 1. In the below figures you will observe that in the short-term, power prices and gas prices (in UK and French power markets) have volatile correlation, making the forecast of profitability quite challenging. However the correlations remain generally below 0.4. A flexible power plant can benefit from observed correlations that are low or negative.

Figure 11: 30-days correlation between French Powernext day-ahead peak power prices and Zeebruge day-ahead gas prices

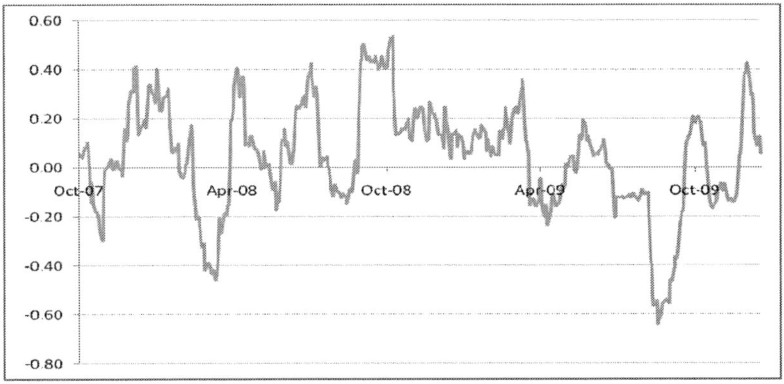

Figure 12: 30-days correlation between UK APX day-ahead peak power prices and National Balancing point (NBP) day-ahead gas prices

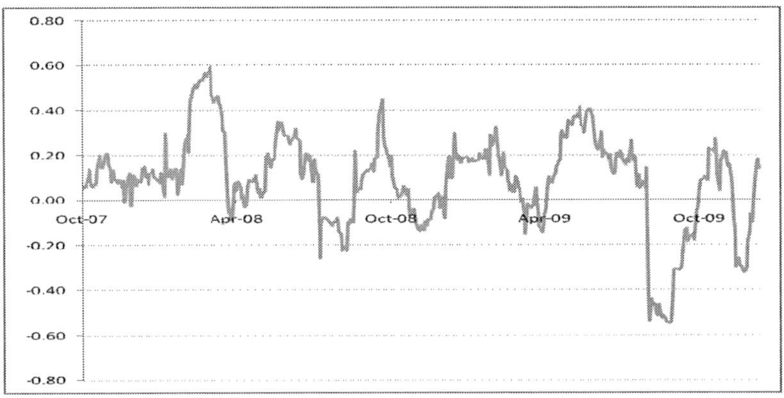

2.4 Risk reductions strategies for investing in peaking plants

Because of the numbers to take into account before investing in power plants, the investor should give himself as much flexibility as he can. For example, the building of a single large plant can be less attractive than building smaller plants with different technologies. The investor will first benefit of the diversification of his power plant portfolio and if the growth in electricity demand is less than expected he will be able to start up more frequently part of his small plant portfolio, than producing power with a larger plant with smaller margins. However the economy of scale is clearly higher for a large power plant (in terms of building cost per kW) and can be also a beneficial strategy in a less uncertain market environment.

The investor can also proceed to gradual development of new capacity and make part of his investment in a power plant and complete its initial plan when market conditions become clearer. This strategy can be implemented when building wind or solar power plants, which are quite capital intensive. If the investor has a 20 MW plan of additional wind capacity, he can only build 10 MW capacity and have the option to build the 10 MW remaining capacity within a 2 year time frame.

There are also certain types of power plants that have certain levels of flexibility in their building. For example some power plants can burn natural gas to produce power but can be converted to use gasified coal as a fuel. This type of project can be valuable in uncertain energy markets.

Opening the sector to competition has led to the internalization of risk in investment decision-making. Investors now examine power generation options according to the different financial risks posed by the different technologies.

Given the long-term nature of electricity investments, investment decisions in baseload generating capacity are being made on the basis of long-term fundamentals rather than looking at short-term behaviour in the spot or forward electricity markets. Conventional discounted cash flow methods are still most often used. Nevertheless, investors are beginning to take account of differences in risk levels in assessing the likely profitability of different investments.

3. Islamic mechanisms for the investment in power generation

As we have seen in the above sections there are different Islamic ways of financing projects. We will focus on the investment in power projects.

3.1 Islamic instruments and applicability to power investment

3.1.1 Istisna'a

Istisna'a is a contract of purchase of any object that has yet to be manufactured or constructed with the undertaking by the seller to present it manufactured with specified descriptions and at a predetermined price. The price is paid progressively in accordance with the progress of construction of the goods. This is practiced, for example, for purchases of houses to be constructed where the payments made to the developer or builders are according to the stage of work completed.

An Istisna'a structure can be used to finance the construction of a power plant. It is the most widely-used Shariah-compliant funding technique for long-term project financings in Islamic project finance.

3.1.2 Ijara

Ijara is essentially an Islamic finance lease or sale-leaseback, often used to purchase real estate, plants, or machinery. The duration of the lease and rental fees may be agreed in advance or subject to occasional review by a mutually acceptable third party. Legal ownership of the equipment remains with the lessor (the financier). Istisna'a and Ijara may be combined so that an Istisna'a is used to finance the construction of the asset and an Ijara used for the lease of the asset for the duration of the financing.

Ijara can be used with and Istisna'a contract to build a power plant and then the financing will be paid back by the borrower to the investor through leasing revenues paid by the borrower.

3.1.3 Musharakah

A Musharakah or 'partnership' transaction involves capital contributions by investors or financial institutions in a partnership arrangement with a client who is operating a business venture. Both parties share profits and losses in direct proportion to their equity participation. Management of the project may be carried out by both the parties or by just one party. This is a very flexible partnership arrangement where the sharing of the profits and management can be negotiated and pre-agreed by all parties. Losses are always shared as per capital contribution and participation.

Musharakah could be used to finance upstream activities. Investors or financial institutions would provide a portion of the capital, and a power operator (manager) would operate the properties and provide the necessary expertise. Musharakah could be used at all levels of energy finance projects.

3.1.4 Mudarabah

Mudarabah can be compared to venture capital financing in conventional finance. This is an agreement made between two parties: one an investor who provides 100 per cent of the capital for the project and another party, known as mudarib, who manages the project using his entrepreneurial skills. Profits arising from the project are distributed according to a pre-determined ratio. Any losses accruing are borne by the investor to a maximum of his capital investment. The investor has no control over the management of the project.

Mudarabah could be used to finance upstream activities. Investors or financial institutions would provide all of the capital, and a power operator (manager) would operate the properties and provide the necessary expertise. Musharakah and Mudarabah could be used at all levels of energy finance projects.

3.1.5 Murabahah

Murabahah is a contract between the bank and its client for the sale of goods at a price which includes a profit margin agreed by both parties. As a financing technique, it involves the purchase of goods by the bank as requested by its client. The goods are sold to the client at cost plus a reasonable profit. Repayment, usually in instalments, is specified in the contract.

Murabahah could possibly be used for the purchase of equipment for use in energy operations (carbon and capture storage facility for a coal-fired plant for example).

3.1.6 Sukuk

Sukuk are essentially asset-backed instruments representing a beneficial ownership interest in the underlying asset. The advantage in using Sukuk is that they open up projects to both Islamic and conventional investors, offering the required liquidity for the project. Typically, a special purpose vehicle will purchase the asset in question and lease it to the ultimate purchaser under back to back arrangements and will issue Sukuk certificates under a note issuance facility entitling the holders of the Sukuk to a pro rata ownership of the asset and a right to receive a proportion of the rental payments.

Power properties can serve as the underlying asset backing a Sukuk offering, which can be a private or a public offering. Since power projects frequently require large capital outlays with a relatively predictable stream of income stretching far into the future, Sukuk could provide a way to raise money for construction.

3.2 Examples of application of Islamic instruments in the power investment

3.2.1 Financing a power plant by a Sukuk emission

Financing Power Assets (Power plants) and getting part ownership of these assets will enable an investor to benefit from the option value of this asset by operating it regarding fuel prices depending on the technology of the plant (gas, coal, oil-fired) and the power prices when this market is deregulated (Europe, US).

With recent questioning of Sukuk's Shariah compliance, due to near behaviour with a conventional bond (benchmark to conventional rates, capital guarantee feature at maturity, unclear ownership of the underlying assets by the Sukuk holder), the sukuk emission has a significant Shariah compliance risk and care has to be taken on the sukuk structure. Power assets can overcome these types of critics.

Indeed a power asset can be financed through Sukuk issuance and the yield of this Sukuk will be the sum of the two followings components:

- **A fixed part** that come from the signature of a long term contract to sell part of the power plant output with a counterparty (electric utility) that will give a certain return. These types of contract are named power purchase agreements (PPA).

- **A variable part** that will be given by the return of the optimization of the plant output in the power markets (asset-backed trading). As we have seen in the section on investment opportunities and risks in power plants, a power plant can be used to do asset-backed trading, that is to say trading the production of the power plant owned in the electricity spot markets.

This type of Sukuk will be structured in a way that there will be no benchmark to a conventional yield, but to energy long term contract returns and optimization returns of the assets in the power markets.

This example clearly shows the asset backed by the sukuk, inherent to Islamic finance. This will contribute to a move away from purely financial and leveraged products that were one of the factor of the economic crisis.

3.2.2 Building and operating a power plant through Istisna'a and Ijara

In the case of the construction of a power plant, an Istisna'a contract can be used to build the plant. We have 3 main agents in this agreement:

- The Islamic participants represented by an Islamic agent
- The contractor (construction company)
- The operating company of the built asset (who wants to finance the construction of the assets)

The Istisna'a agreement operates during the construction of the plant (equivalent to a Turnkey contract in the power sector). The contractor will develop the power plant on behalf of a special purpose company (SPC) owned for and on behalf of the Islamic participants by the Islamic facility agent. The construction company has to follow the specifications and the completion date of the power plant. When the power plant is built, it is delivered to the operating company which transfers the ownership title to the SPC.

It consists of the following mechanism:

Figure 13: Istisna'a mechanism

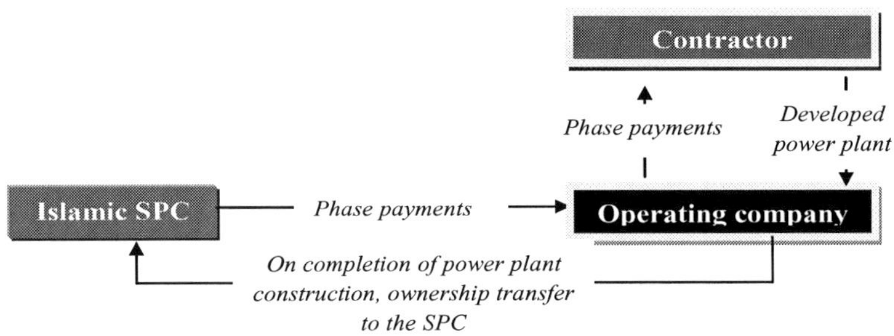

The operational phase of the power plant is secured through a lease agreement (Ijara) between the operating company and the SPC entered at the same time of the Istisna'a agreement. Under this agreement, the company leases the Islamic financed assets from the SPC in return for lease payments (including a fixed and a variable element).

Figure 14: Ijara mechanism

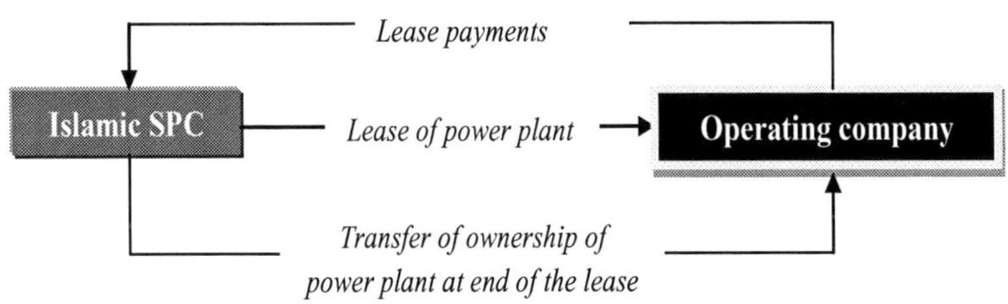

A Service agency agreement can also be contracted between the SPC and the operating company. Indeed, the SPC, in its capacity as lessor, is responsible to pay for maintenance, insurance and ownership taxes. All these responsibilities can be transferred to the operating company by a service agency agreement.

4. Economic and social benefits of power plants investments for Islamic investors

Compared to other energy or commodity assets like oil products refineries or aluminium smelters, power assets have certain advantages.

Indeed, power prices have a correlation that can change a lot with its fuel prices (coal, oil, gas) because power is not a storable commodity and there has to be a demand-offer at every time during the day. If the demand of clients of a utility company is above offer at one point of time there will be a need to start power plants or to buy power from the electricity spot markets. In this case it will lead to an increase in power prices (if the demand of clients of a utility company is increasing it will be the case for the other utilities and there will be less power available to sale). We will observe a de-correlation between power prices and fuel prices, and the power plants will have a greater value in the market as power prices increase and fuel prices which will not observe this increase because of their storability.

In the case of a refinery that produces oil products (like jet fuel or heating oil) from crude oil, these product prices have a strong correlation with the crude oil. We can see in some cases this correlation going down because of a lack of stocks of some refined products in certain periods, but these changes will be less brutal than in the case of power, as these products are storable.

The investment in a peaking power plant can be lucrative as it enables the Islamic investor to benefit from the volatility of power prices, which tend to see higher prices than lower prices in times of market stress (as compared to equity prices where the probability of prices going down is higher than going upwards). For example, an Islamic investor from the GCC (Gulf Cooperative Council) can also enjoy the low correlation between power plant revenues from the oil prices. And he can benefit from the margin taken by utility companies in US and European deregulated markets to end users. As GCC is exporting oil and gas that is used as input to power plants, he will potentially capture more revenue as power consumption is considered a downstream operation following the upstream activity of gas and oil exploration and production.

Investment in power plants adds to the development and social welfare of the society, which is an important component of Islamic Finance. Indeed, many developing countries suffer from the lack of power infrastructure, which can hinder the development of these countries. Countries like UAE, Kuwait and Saudi Arabia face an increasing power demand and limited power capacities: there were power shortages in Kuwait in summer 2010. The investment in additional power capacity is therefore critical and Islamic finance can play an important role in the financing of power throughout the world. We have shown in the preceding sections that the investment can be lucrative, although not exempt from risks; but the spirit of Islamic finance is to be rewarded for taking risks. There should be no risk-free return in Islamic finance.

Glossary

Asset-backed trading
The buying and selling of the electricity generated and fuel used by our power stations.

Availability
A measure giving the proportion of electrical energy that was actually available to be generated during the period, after taking account of both planned and unplanned outages, expressed as a percentage of the maximum potential electrical energy generation.

Capacity (installed)
Generator capacity (measured in megawatts (MW)), usually indicated on a nameplate physically attached to the generator.

Combined cycle plant
Combined cycle gas turbine (CCGT) – the combination of a gas turbine (GT) and steam turbine (ST) in a configuration that enables electricity to be generated directly from a generator driven by the GT and, by using exhaust gases from the GT to produce steam, a ST coupled to the same generator or another generator.

Cogeneration
The simultaneous generation of electricity and heat in the form of steam, typically where the need for both arises for industrial or commercial purposes and where the steam is generated by utilising the waste heat from electricity generation.

Dark spread
The difference between the cost of coal to generate electricity and the price at which electricity is sold.

Due diligence
A process undertaken before the acquisition of a business to ensure all significant risks, rewards and issues are identified and considered before any offer is made to the vendor or an acquisition takes place.

Emission certificates
Under various environmental schemes, emission certificates are required to cover the amount of relevant emissions made by a power station. Cap and trade schemes are a common type of scheme. Under a cap and trade scheme, operators are required to purchase sufficient emission certificates to cover their actual emissions,

and the operator may or may not be granted an initial volume of certificates. Examples of such schemes include the European Union Emissions Trading Scheme (EUETS) which covers emissions of CO2, based on a cap and trade system. Other examples include the Clean Air Act in the US which covers emissions of oxides of nitrogen (NOx) and oxides of sulphur (SOx).

Energy Imbalance

Resources needed for correcting supply/demand imbalances.

ERCOT

Electric Reliability Council of Texas – responsible for managing the Texas generating and transmission systems.

ETS

Emissions trading scheme – programme for the trading of emissions permits mainly relating to CO2 output.

EUETS

European Union Emissions Trading Scheme.

Feed-in tariff

Guaranteed tariff for energy produced, often provided by governments to support renewable generation.

Forced outage rate

A measure giving the proportion of electrical energy that was actually unavailable for generation during the period due to unplanned outages, expressed as a percentage of the maximum potential electrical energy generation, after taking account of planned outages.

Fossil fuel

It is generally accepted that fossil fuels are formed from the fossilised remains of dead plants and animals by exposure to heat and pressure in the Earth's crust over hundreds of millions of years. They are found within the top layer of the earth's crust and range from very volatile materials with low carbon-to-hydrogen ratios like methane, to those with high carbon-to-hydrogen ratios like liquid petroleum. They also include non-volatile materials composed of almost pure carbon, like anthracite coal. Fossil fuels are non-renewable resources because they take millions of years to form.

GSA

Gas supply agreement.

GT

Gas turbine.

GW

Gigawatt, one thousand million watts.

Gigawatt-hour (GWh)

A watt hour is the amount of energy used by a one-watt load drawing power for one hour. The gigawatt-hour (GWh) is 1,000,000 times larger than the kilowatt-hour and is used for measuring the energy output of large power plants..

IPP

Independent power producer.

kW

Kilowatt – 1,000 watts.

Kilowatt-hour (kWh)
A watt hour is the amount of energy used by a one-watt load drawing power for one hour. The kilowatt-hour (kWh) is 1,000 times larger than a watt-hour and is a useful size for measuring the energy use of households and small businesses and also for the production of energy by small power plants. A typical household uses several hundred kilowatt-hours per month.
Kyoto Protocol
A protocol to the International Framework Convention on Climate Change with the objective of reducing greenhouse gases in an effort to prevent climate change.
LNG
Liquefied natural gas.
Load factor
The proportion of electricity actually generated, compared with the maximum possible generation at maximum net capacity.
M&A
Mergers and acquisitions.
Mark to market
The act of attributing a fair or market value to a financial instrument rather than its historical cost. Marking to market is required under accounting rules for certain derivatives and financial instruments.
Merchant market
A merchant market is a deregulated market. It is a market in which electricity is bought and sold competitively by multiple market participants.
Merchant plant
Our merchant plants operate in deregulated markets selling power into the traded market without long-term power purchase agreements (PPAs).
MW
Megawatt; one MW equals 1,000 kilowatts or one million watts.
Megawatt hour (MWh)
A watt hour is the amount of energy used by a one-watt load drawing power for one hour. The megawatt-hour (MWh) is 1,000 times larger than the kilowatt-hour and is used for measuring the energy output of large power plants.
Non-spinning Reserves
Resources not synchronized to the system that are available immediately and can be brought to full capacity within ten minutes.
NOx
Oxides of nitrogen.
O&E
Operations and engineering.
O&M
Operations and maintenance, usually used in the context of operating and maintaining a power station.
OCGT
Open cycle gas turbine – turbines, typically fuelled by gas or diesel oil, are used to drive the generators to produce electricity, with no use of the waste heat for subsequent power generation.

Offtake agreement
Power purchase agreement between a company owning a power station and its customer (the offtaker) whereby the customer takes the electricity generated by a power station.

Operating Reserve
The resources that can be brought to full capacity within 30 minutes.

Operational control
Operational control includes all subsidiaries, joint ventures and associates with over 50% shareholding, and those assets where International Power always appoints the Station Manager, or Executive Managing Director, and therefore can exert significant influence over operations at the entity.

Outage
When a generating unit is removed from service to perform maintenance work. This can either be planned or unplanned.

Peak load
The maximum demand for electricity during a specified high demand period. This may require use of plant (for example pumped storage) that is kept in reserve for peak periods.

Peaking plant
Plant that runs only in times of short supply (normally during peak demand), when prices are high.

PJM
Pennsylvania, New Jersey and Maryland power pool.

Power Purchase Agreement (PPA)
See also Offtake agreement. A PPA is generally a long-term contract between an electricity generator and a purchaser of energy or capacity (power or ancillary services).

Proprietary trading
The trading of commodities for the purposes of making a profit, when the commodity is not generated by our own power stations or purchased for use by our own power stations, also known as non-asset backed trading.

Pumped storage
A method of energy generation that involves moving water between reservoirs at different elevations. When electricity prices are low, typically overnight, electricity from the grid system is used to pump water into a raised reservoir and then at times of peak demand, when electricity prices are higher, the water is released back into the lower reservoir through a turbine.

Retail
The sale of power and/or gas to end users.

Reserve margin
The amount of available plant reserve capacity above the system's peak electricity requirements.

SO2
Sulphur dioxide.

SOx
Oxides of sulphur.

Spark spread
The difference between the cost of gas to generate electricity and the price at which electricity is sold.
Spinning Reserves
Resources synchronized to the system that are available immediately and that can be brought to full capacity within ten minutes.
Spot price
Market price at a particular point in time.
Spread
The difference between the fuel costs to generate electricity and the price at which electricity is sold.
Tolling agreement
A form of long-term electricity contract where the buyer of electricity also supplies the fuel.
t/h
Tonnes per hour.
Turnkey contract
A contract where one party takes full responsibility for the construction and commissioning of a plant, delivering the plant in full working order to the owner.
Watt
Unit of power, which is the rate at which energy is delivered (i.e. work is done at a rate of one watt when one ampere flows through a potential difference of one volt).

References

Eydeland, Alexander, and Krzysztof Wolyniec, *Energy and Power Risk Management,* 2003.

International Energy Agency, *Power Generation investment in electricity markets,* Dec 2003.

SUKUKS: PRESENT AND FUTURE

MONDHER BELLALAH AND BADR ELMRABTI

Introduction

The growth of sukuk or Shariah-compliant debt securities is among the most significant developments within Islamic finance in recent years. In 2007 alone, $33bn was raised by corporate and sovereign-related sukuk issuers. Equity-linked or convertible sukuk have played a key role in this growth.

Sukuk issuance has enabled companies to finance international growth, and equity-linked sukuk represent an important mechanism for foreign institutional investors to gain exposure to issuers' equities. Global debt, convertible, and equity investors will increasingly look to sukuk to expand their opportunity set as the market continues to grow.

This chapter is organized as follows:

- Section 1 presents the principles of Islamic Finance and the importance of sukuk as an Islamic investment product.
- Section 2 develops the evolution of the sukuk market into a global market.
- Section 3 explains the main sukuk structures in the market.
- Section 4 studies the equity-linked sukuk, including vanilla convertible sukuk, pre-qualifying public offering (QPO) sukuk, and mandatory convertible sukuk.

1. An introduction to Islamic financial instruments and sukuk

The global expansion of Islamic finance coincided with the oil shocks of the 1970s, which aside from creating wealth also spurred demand for a wider range of financial products. This allowed financial practitioners to create a small industry using investment funds. In Asia, Malaysia developed a mature Islamic financial market via initiatives to integrate Malays into the country's formal financial sector. Conventional Malaysian banks offered Islamic financial products through Islamic windows and Government Investment Certificates were issued to facilitate open market and inter-bank operations.

1.1 Shariah-compliant instruments

Islamic finance is based on Shariah (Islamic law). The keystones of Islamic law include the Koran, Sunnah, Ijma, and Ijtihad. Their application to finance forms the principles of investment and Islamic scholars must approve financial instruments for Shariah-compliance. These principles include:

- The prohibition of riba. Riba is not only interest, but also connotes unjust enrichment, whether from excessive income or from unfairness in a contract. It is more than simply making money from money.
- Islamic finance is used towards real activities, e.g., trade finance, asset finance, construction finance, or leasing.
- Islamic finance cannot be provided for haram activities, i.e., those involving alcohol or pork, gambling, cigarettes, discos, or military/defence activities.
- Avoidance of gharar, or uncertainty. The structure of the financing and the contract must be clear and certain of purpose in the use of funds. There must be no speculative trading. However, interpretations of Islamic law allow for secondary market trading and derivatives trading.

An instrument is classified Shariah-compliant, or Islamic, by a Shariah board, which interprets whether the instrument meets Islamic standards. Aside from scholars in different jurisdictions, investors may, for example, question whether some instruments are Shariah-compliant. The growth of Islamic finance creates a shortage of Islamic scholars to opine upon financial instruments.

Islamic finance can resemble conventional financial instruments, meeting similar requirements for investors, companies, and financial institutions. There are forms of insurance and reinsurance (takaful and retakaful), syndicated loans (murabaha), leasing (ijara), and equity participation (musharaka). The focus is on Islamic bonds known as sukuk, or sakk in the singular form. The word ‘sukuk’ loosely translates as ‘certificates’. They are often referred to as ‘trust’ or ‘participation certificates’ due to the Islamic-compliant structure.

1.2 Sukuk as mainstream investment products

The sukuk market has been one of the more rapidly growing segments of Islamic finance. Investing in sukuk provides a medium- to long-term financing solution. Islamic banks see sukuk as a tool for managing their assets and liabilities and recycling liquidity.

- **Straight sukuk**: The straight sukuk market gained greater prominence with the international community in 2002 following a $600mn 5-year offering from the Government of Malaysia. The international Islamic bond market is divided into sovereign (and quasi-sovereign) and corporate sukuk markets.
- **Equity-linked sukuk:** As with conventional convertible bonds, these entitle holders to (irrevocably) convert the sukuk into a pre-specified number of shares during the lifetime of the security. As a ‘hybrid’ product with both equity options and debt features, performance drivers typically include the equity price, its volatility, and the presumed stock borrow cost, as well as the risk-free (swap) rate curve and the issuer’s credit quality.
- **Shariah-compliant stocks:** The availability of Shariah-compliant stocks is the most basic consideration in the development of Islamic stock markets. This led to the development of the Shariah screening of stocks based on quantitative measures (such as debt-to-asset, liquidity-to-asset, and receivables-to-asset ratios), and also based on fundamental qualitative criteria such as Shariah-compliance of the business line.
- **Shariah-compliant derivatives (interest rate swaps, cross-currency swaps, and foreign exchange forwards):** Islamic derivatives had not been approved by scholars, because they were deemed speculative. Now Shariah-compliant hedging instruments are both acceptable and necessary. Most Shariah-compliant derivatives are based around the Islamic principle of murabaha, whereby two parties

agree to the sale of goods at a price that includes a profit margin.

2. Towards a Global Market

2.1 A growth phenomenon

The total value of sukuk issued since 2007 stands at $107bn. The number of sukuk issues worldwide greater than $1bn stood at ten in 2007, declined to five in 2008 (effect of the financial crisis), before reaching 11 in 2009. These sukuk were mainly issued in the countries of Gulf Cooperation Council (GCC) and Malaysia as shown in figure 1 below.

Figure 1: Number of sukuk with issue size greater than $1bn

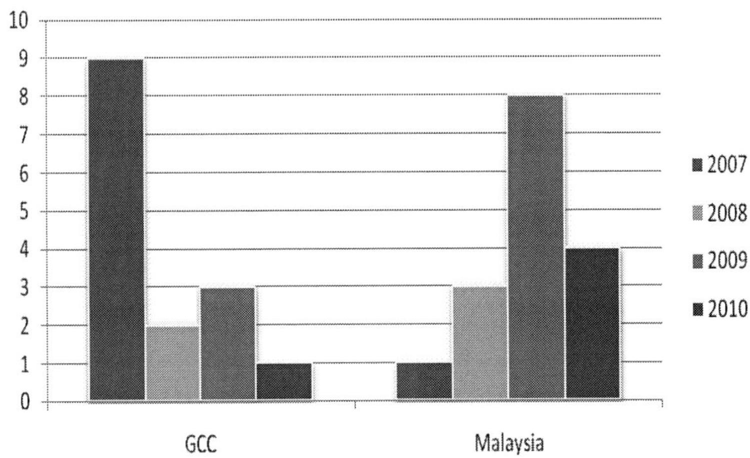

Malaysian sukuk issuance has historically dominated both in number and in total value, Gulf Cooperation Council (GCC) issuance, in absolute value, except in the year 2007, where Sukuk issuance activity in the GCC has been higher.

Figure 2: Sukuk total notional per location from 2007 (USD)

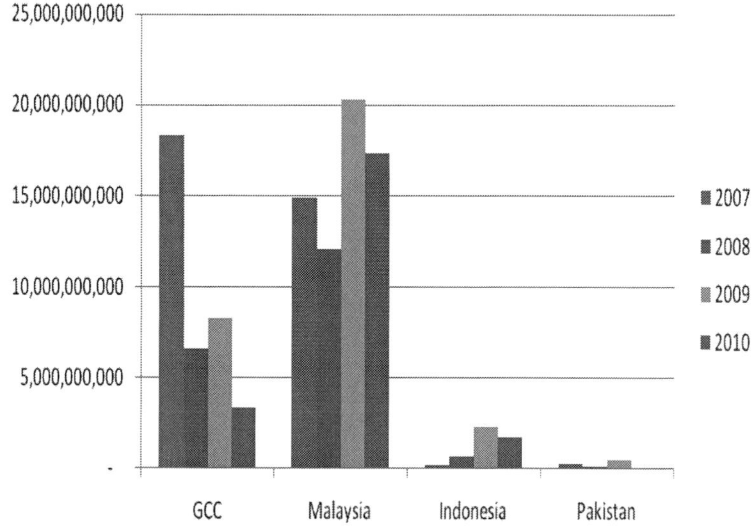

Malaysian issuance has primarily been in local currency and GCC issuance in USD. The two largest corporate sukuk are AED-denominated; Nakheel (AED3.6bn) and Aldar (AED3.75bn). None of the seven GCC sukuk issuances above $100mn equivalent value issued in Q208 were USD-denominated. Table 1 illustrates the dominance of the real estate sector issuance in the GCC, accounting for 34% by value of sukuk issues above $100mn from the region since 2006. The following sectors represented are: transportation (21%), industrial (14%), financial (13%), and oil and gas (4%).

Table 1: Global sukuk issuance above $500mn since 2007

Issue Date	Issue Name	Industry sector	Maturity Date	Issue size (currency millions)	Issue currency	Convertible
10-May-10	SAUDI ELECTRCITY	Electric-Integrated	05-Oct-30	7,000	SAR	
13-Apr-10	DANGA CAPITAL BH	Finance	13-Apr-15	2,000	MYR	
21-Oct-09	TDIC SUKUK	Tourism development	21-Oct-14	1,000	USD	
16-Sep-09	IDB TRUST SERV	Finance	16-Sep-14	850	USD	
12-Aug-09	PETRONAS SUKUK	Gas-Distribution	08-Dec-14	1,500	USD	
12-Aug-09	PETRONAS SUKUK	Gas-Distribution	08-Dec-14	1,500	USD	
06-Jul-09	SAUDI ELECTRCITY	Electric-Integrated	07-Jun-29	7,000	SAR	
17-Jun-08	ALDAR SUKUK FUND	Real Estate	17-Jun-13	3,750	AED	
16-Jun-08	DEWA FUNDING	Utility & Energy	16-Jun-13	3,200	AED	
26-May-08	SABIC	Industrial	15-May-28	5,000	SAR	
12-Mar-08	PAKA CAPITAL LTD	Special Purpose Entity	03-Dec-13	550	USD	Yes
16-Jan-08	NAKHEEL DEVELO 2	Real Estate	16-Jan-11	750	USD	
28-Dec-07	BINARIANG GSM SD	Telecommunication Equip	28-Dec-57	3,017	MYR	
28-Dec-07	BINARIANG GSM SD	Telecommunication Equip	26-Dec-14	2,000	MYR	
28-Dec-07	BINARIANG GSM SD	Telecommunication Equip	27-Dec-13	1,900	MYR	
28-Dec-07	BINARIANG GSM SD	Telecommunication Equip	28-Dec-16	1,800	MYR	
28-Dec-07	BINARIANG GSM SD	Telecommunication Equip	28-Dec-17	1,800	MYR	
27-Nov-07	JAFZ SUKUK	Industrial	27-Nov-12	7,500	AED	
31-Oct-07	DANA GAS	Oil & Gas	31-Oct-12	1,000	USD	Yes
06-Aug-07	SABIC	Industrial	15-Jul-27	8,000	SAR	
23-Jul-07	SAUDI ELEC	Electric-Integrated	15-Jul-27	5,000	SAR	
20-Jul-07	HIJRAH PERTAMA B	Diversified Operations	30-Dec-13	1,998	MYR	
16-Jul-07	DAR AL-ARKAN	Real Estate	16-Jul-12	1,000	USD	
02-Jul-07	DP WORLD SUKUK	Transportation	07-Feb-17	1,500	USD	
02-Jul-07	DP WORLD SUKUK	Transportation	07-Feb-17	1,500	USD	
13-Jun-07	DIFC SUKUK	Finance	13-Jun-12	1,250	USD	
22-Mar-07	DIB SUKUK CO LTD	Finance	22-Mar-12	750	USD	
08-Mar-07	ALDAR FUNDING	Real Estate	11-Oct-11	2,530	USD	Yes

Source: Bloomberg

2.2 Sukuk Issuance prospects

A number of factors will continue to lend support to the market:

- Investment banking resources dedicated to Islamic finance.
- More standardized products and investor familiarity.
- Corporate funding requirements.
- Issuance from new jurisdictions.

The potential for growth in sukuk issuance is not restricted to the Gulf and Malaysia: for example there are recent moves in Europe (France particularly) where there are jurisdictional changes to make issuance possible by state and corporation.

In addition to those countries, non-Islamic institutions have sought to use sukuk as an additional means of funding to appeal to a previously untapped investor base. The UK Treasury has announced plans to launch an international sukuk and the German state of Saxony-Anhalt also issued a sukuk in 2004.

2.3 Increased foreign investor participation

Investors are drawn to sukuk owing to the following factors: government backing, corporate fundamentals, and in the case of asset-backed sukuk, the quality of the underlying asset.

Many of the sukuk issues have been upsized in response to strong demand not just from local participants but also from international investors. The latter stems from several developments including the large and growing number of Islamic investable funds and the fact that, while flows embedded in the sukuk must be Shariah compliant, there is no stipulation that the investor be Shariah-compliant.

Western investors such as mutual funds, pension managers, and central banks, can employ sukuk as a means of diversification across countries and asset classes. The progression of foreign participation in some of the deals demonstrates the increasing interest in sukuk among western investors. Aside from diversification, investors with 'ethical' funds or strategies may find a rationale to invest in sukuk, as Shariah compliance prohibits some business activities of the issuer.

2.4 Examples of Sukuk performances in the Markets

Sukuk prices depend mainly on an underlying market value of the asset. The selling of a sukuk for a corporate is equivalent to the sale of a share of the asset. As a result we can see a certain relation between the share price of a company and the sukuk price. In the figures below, one can notice that the sukuk prices tend to be more volatile than the corporate bond prices because their value is linked to the company value.

Figure 2: DANA GAS 7.5% 2012 (Mudarabah sukuk)

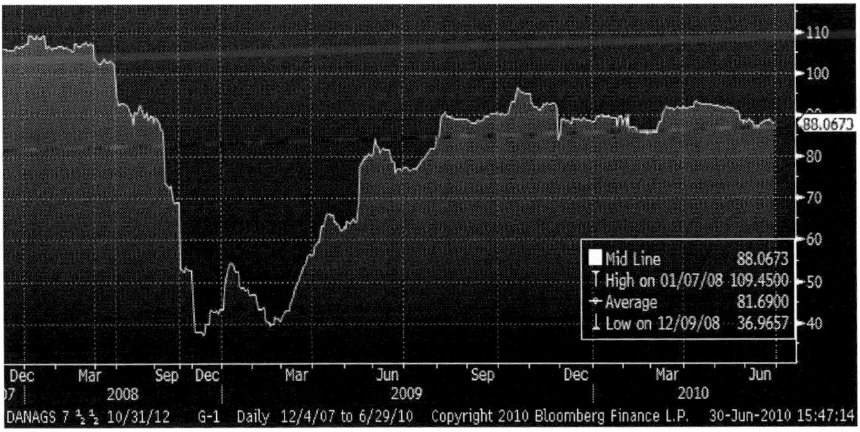

Figure 3: Abu Dhabi Islamic Bank Floating rate note (FRN) 2011 (Ijara sukuk)

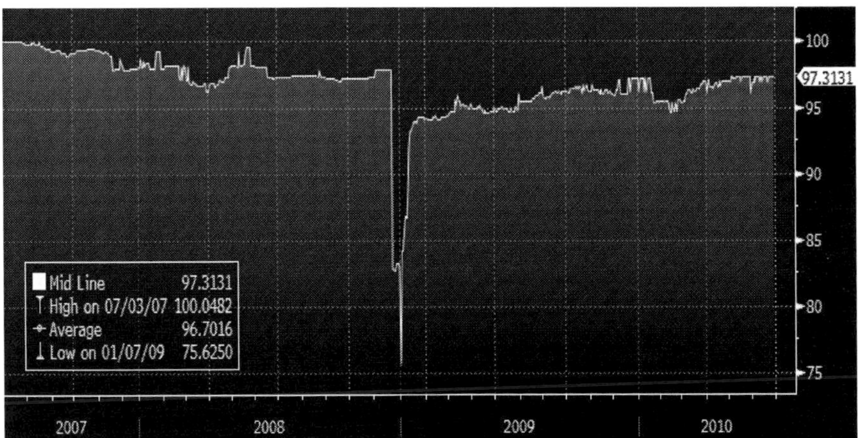

As you can see in figure 1 and 2, sukuk prices have undergone some pressure in the Sept-Dec 2008 period, corresponding to the financial crisis. Dana Gas sukuk (UAE Corporate Sukuk) have gone from above 100 to a historical low of 36.97 in September 2008. The sukuk prices have been impacted by a sharp decrease in Sovereign bond prices in Dubai (which means implicitly higher sovereign rates) leading to a decrease in the Corporate sukuk prices, as the rate of 7.5% offered by Dana Gas is below the market rate taking into account sovereign risk as well as the credit risk of the company (default risk). Once the financial crisis is over (sovereign and corporate default risk going lower), the sukuk prices go higher leading to an increase in the sukuk prices.

3. Sukuk structures

Sukuk are often issued from a special purpose vehicle (SPV), but the obligated entity (obligor) as regards satisfying redemption is normally the operating company or a subsidiary. The majority of sukuk have been issued in three basic forms, as asset-based or asset-backed structures and what the links are to those assets. They are ijara, musharaka, and mudaraba.

3.1 Ijara sukuk

Ijara sukuk are plain vanilla purchase-leaseback structures. They are the most common form of sukuk in the market. These transactions are viewed as the de facto benchmarks in the Islamic marketplace. The borrower sells the sukuk assets to an SPV. The latter finances this purchase through the issuance of sukuk. The SPV then leases the assets back to the borrower, who pays the lease rental, which is equivalent to the cost of the credit, or for example, Libor+X or information cost (IC). These lease rentals help finance the periodic distributions on the sukuk, as illustrated in the below figure.

1) An SPV issuer sells sukuk to investor
2) Proceeds of the issuance are used to purchase the beneficial title of an asset (typically real estate or leases) from the borrower.
3) The borrower leases the asset back from a term corresponding to tenor of sukuk. Lease rental is related to the cost of credit for the borrower, i.e., LIBOR + X% or Information Cost.
4) The borrower undertakes to service the asset and be responsible for maintenance/insurance, etc.
5) Purchase undertaking is exercised by the SPV upon redemption or if an event of default occurs. The asset is sold back to the borrower and the SPV becomes an unsecured creditor of the borrower.

3.2 Musharaka sukuk

Musharaka refers to equity participation or partnership. The borrower and an SPV constitute the two partners in a musharaka sukuk. The borrower contributes assets, while the SPV generates the required cash through sukuk issuance for the musharaka. Proceeds from musharaka assets are used to finance the sukuk periodic distributions. There is a more direct link between the sukuk holders and the underlying assets of the sukuk. The flowchart in the below figure underscores the equity participation or joint-venture nature of musharaka sukuk.

1) An SPV issuer sells sukuk to investors.
2) Proceeds of the issuance are invested into a musharaka with the borrower. The issuer declares a trust over its share of the assets in favour of the sukuk holders. The borrower transfers assets to the musharaka.
3) The borrower manages the assets, in order to generate a return to the musharaka.
4) Via the purchase undertaking, the borrower undertakes to purchase the issuer's rights to the assets of the musharaka upon redemption or following an event of default.

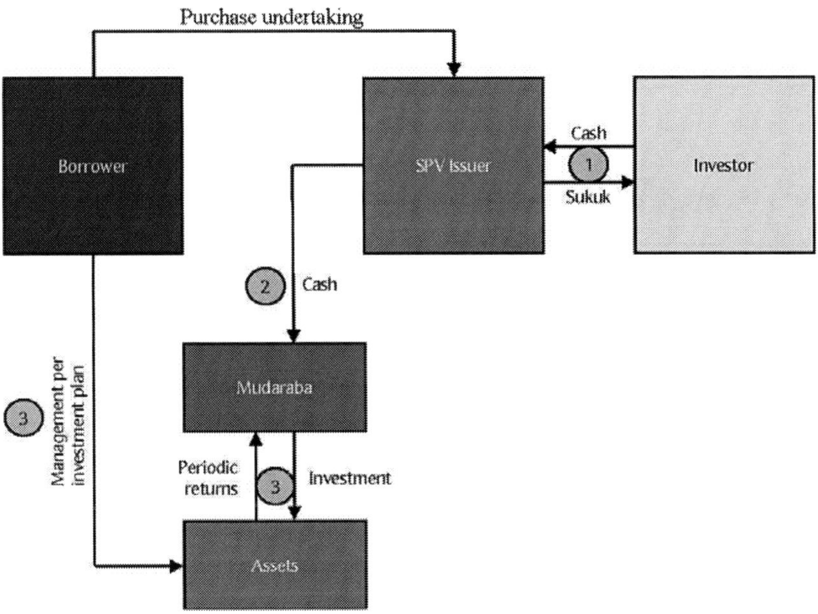

3.3 Mudaraba sukuk

Mudaraba sukuk are similar to musharaka, except the lender has no equity stake. The proceeds are passed to the mudaraba for funding development in accordance with a Shariah-approved investment plan. The investment agreement between the manager and investor allows for the issuance of sukuk by entities that do not have assets for an Ijara or musharaka sukuk: the borrower or mudarib reaches an agreement with a project owner for construction of a project and the SPV issues sukuk to finance this project. The following flowchart illustrates the transactions and flows.

1) An SPV issuer sells sukuk to investors.
2) Proceeds of the issuance enter into a mudaraba with the borrower. The issuer declares a trust over its share of the assets in favour of the sukuk holders.
3) The borrower, as mudarib, manages the assets according to a pre-specified Shariah-compliant plan, in order to generate a return to the mudaraba.
4) Via the purchase undertaking, the borrower undertakes to buy the issuer's rights to the assets of the mudaraba upon redemption or following an event of default.

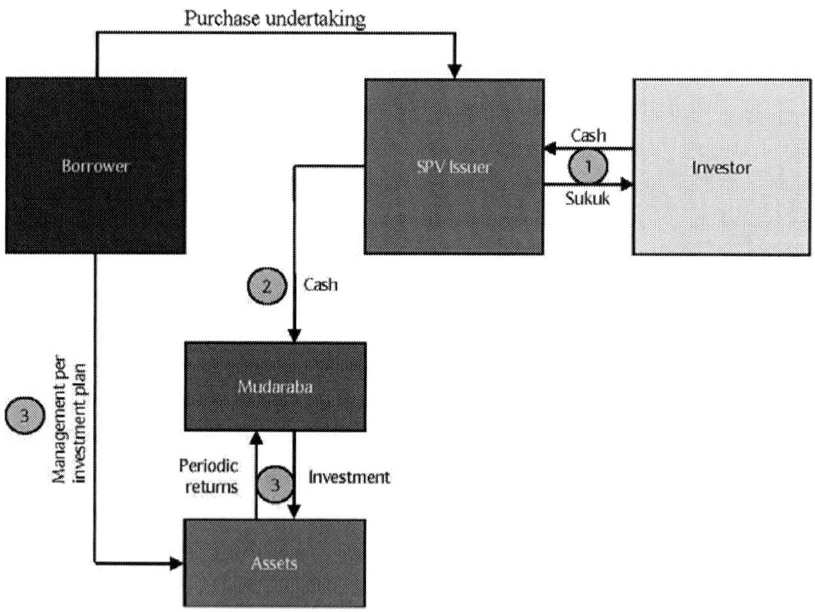

4. Equity-linked sukuk

Convertible structures can enable investors to gain access to an underlying equity investment. Equity-linked sukuk also provide the means for companies to broaden their investor base especially among institutional investors. Equity-linked sukuk issues include vanilla convertibles, pre-

QPO securities, and mandatory conversion structures.

4.1 Vanilla convertible sukuk

Vanilla convertible sukuk are issued by entities that are listed at the time of issuance. They entitle holders to irrevocably convert the sukuk into a pre-specified number of equity shares during a security's lifetime. The option to convert into shares has positive present value for holders. The initial yield to maturity offered by a convertible sukuk is generally lower than that offered on a straight, non-convertible sukuk that is identical in all other respects.

Many investors use valuation models, to estimate the theoretical value of a convertible security. It is a hybrid product with both an equity option and debt features. Performance drivers typically include the equity price, its volatility, and the presumed stock borrow cost, as well as the risk-free (swap) rate curve and the issuer's credit quality. The potential upside participation in equity movements and downside protection produces the theoretical payoff profile.

4.2 Pre-QPO convertible sukuk

Pre-QPO sukuk are debt financing instruments that are non-convertible until the occurrence of a QPO (qualified public offering) event, at which point the sukuk (or part thereof) may be redeemed in cash and/or converted into new QPO shares. During the lifetime of the sukuk, investors receive not only a fixed income return, similar to the one they would expect from a normal bond, but also a guaranteed pre-allocation in shares to be issued in any public offering (initial or secondary) that takes place during the life of the issuance.

The performance attribution can happen either through the attribution of subscription rights, or through a commitment of the company to redeem in shares part of the instrument at the time of the QPO (the terms and conditions of pre-QPO sukuk vary from deal to deal). This allows investors to benefit from the appreciation of the shares, which usually takes place immediately after the QPO. In this respect, a pre-QPO sukuk has the risk/return characteristics of a bond, but with an equity upside potential, the value of which depends on the equity performance at the time of the QPO.

An example of pre-QPO sukuk is the Nakheel Development due January 2011 ($750m, issued December 2007).

4.3 Mandatory convertible sukuk

Mandatory convertibles are hybrid securities that automatically convert into a predetermined number of shares dependent on the stock price at the time of conversion. They are closer to equity than debt because they redeem in shares instead of cash. Mandatory convertibles tend to be more volatile than equivalent convertibles as they are more closely related to the performance of the underlying stock, although they typically pay a higher annual yield.

A mandatory convertible usually offers a yield pick-up over the underlying stock. This compensates investors for reduced upside participation. As such, mandatory convertibles appeal to investors looking for high yield combined with capital appreciation. Mandatory convertibles are often treated largely as equity on the balance sheet and regarded as equity by rating agencies.

Most mandatory convertibles have maximum and minimum conversion prices, which is set at issuance. The conversion premium at issuance is the difference between the minimum conversion price and the maximum. The actual stock price at maturity determines the conversion ratio according to whether it is below, within or above this range. The conversion ratio is the number of shares per bond that investors receive at maturity. An investor that decides to convert early may receive only the minimum conversion ratio.

4.4 Equity exposure and foreign ownership limits

Equity-linked sukuk can offer investors an additional source of exposure to regional equities. In addition, this exposure may be supported by downside protection (vanilla convertibles) or yield enhancement (mandatory convertibles) while pre-QPO convertibles provide investors with subscription rights to future equity listings.

The role of the equity linked sukuk in providing equity exposure is significant given the limited access by foreign investors to the equity markets in the Gulf region. In case foreign ownership limits prohibit the attribution of shares upon conversion, investors may still participate through the cash-settlement feature, which is a common feature of convertible bonds.

Table 5: Restrictions on foreign ownership in GCC equities

Country	GCC investors	Exceptions for GCC investors	International investors
Saudi Arabia	Maximum 49%	No allowance for banks	No allowance
UAE	0-49% on request to regulators	0-40% for banks	Same as GCC investors
Kuwait	No restrictions	40% for banks	Same as GCC investors
Qatar	25%, after deduction of government stake	None	Same as GCC investors
Bahrain	No restrictions	A minority of companies have 0-25% GCC ownership limit	49%
Oman	25-70%	None	Same as GCC investors

GCC firms are increasingly loosening foreign ownership rules (to approach or meet caps set by capital market authorities). However there have been cases where sukuk holders have at times seen conversions settled in cash as opposed to shares in order to maintain the foreign ownership percentage below the limit. In order to help management of foreign ownership limits, submitted conversions notices may be recognized at discrete intervals, for example, twice a month.

References

Barclays Capital Research, *Sukuk: a Primer*, 2008

THE PERFORMANCE OF ISLAMIC CAPITAL MARKET AND MAXIMIZATION OF THE WEALTH OF SHARE HOLDERS AND VALUE OF COMPANY

OMAR MASOOD[1], ASMA ABDUL REHMAN[2] AND FATEN BEN BOUHENI[3]

1. Introduction

The concept of the Islamic financial system started fourteen hundred years ago, but according to the twentieth century principles was first introduced in Egypt in the form of Islamic saving bank and was established in 1963 based on profit sharing principles. Bank Islam Malaysia Berhad (BIMB) started working in Malaysia in 1963 as well. So, the Islamic financial system established its modern set up in 1963 in the form of banks, but it did not grow till the 80s (Salman, 2010).

The Islamic capital market developed its infrastructure, which includes all the participants, as that of a conventional market and operates parallel to its peers. It includes products, Islamic mutual funds, brokers and Islamic bonds. The identification and the introduction of Islamic financial products was a big challenge for the finance scholars and fund managers.

Islamic finance is the fastest growing industry at the moment in the field of capital markets, and is actively taken up in different parts of the world.

Even the western world, which seems to be more conservative about Islam, has shown a great interest in developing the Islamic capital market. Most of the larger organisations have already launched Islamic products in

---

[1] UEL Royal Docks Business School University of East London.
[2] Superior University, Lahore, Pakistan.
[3] University of Cergy-pontoise.

the European world to attract the Muslim community who are portion of those societies. This study is also very important for the Muslim community and the fund managers to observe the performance of the market, and also the risk and return associated with the shari'ah-compliant securities will be explained to people.

2. Literature Review

2.1 Islamic Capital Market Risk

In 2006, the Islamic capital market, which comprises of trading shari'ah-compliant equities and also the issuance of Islamic bonds called Islamic sukuk securities, showed very mixed results (Wilson, R. J. A. 2007). According to Wilson one should not assume the performance of the securities as poor or better just because of the relation of those securities with shari'ah-compliance because in 2006 there was little divergence found, but it was significantly important between the conventional market securities and shari'ah-compliant equivalents. According to Garas, 2008 the Islamic banking system has been a centre of criticism due to its risk free return and lack of understanding of the time value of money, but this argument is not acceptable in full; rather, all the modern economic theories and analysis have described Islamic banking as an equity based system that is opposite to the conventional banking system, which is a debt based system.

2.2 Malaysian Islamic Capital Market

According to Shimomoto Y. (1999), the vast majority of the Malaysian population consists of Muslims whose teachings are very straightforward with regard to interest payment. Islam is totally against the systems which are based on interest payments and discourages any type of transactions that are not ethical or contain some type of uncertainty.

Due to Islamic teachings, Muslims are reluctant to use interest-bearing Islamic financial derivatives, and keeping in mind the Muslim interest, the government established the Bank Negara Malaysia (BNM) which is the biggest unit trust company in Malaysia. BNM followed the scheme of the government while issuing the investment notes in 1983.

2.3 European Islamic Capital Market

The UK is by far the most advanced country in Europe in development of Islamic financial institutions along with conventional financial markets, and the UK is also known as a heart of trading for the world as well. London has adopted a very active and leading role in developing the Islamic finance, and France has also started taking interest in Islamic finance; not very actively, but is planning to carry out some legislative measures to introduce the Islamic finance into France, as announced in July 2008. France is the second largest non-Muslim European country, with a large Muslim community. France has a very well developed and strong banking system, and all of their Muslim community is fully engaged in their banking activities.

France has a very well diversified capital market and it has the capacity to offer many Islamic products and the assets of Islamic finance according to shari'ah-compliance (Damak et al., 2008).

2.4 Gulf Islamic Capital Market

After the establishment of the first Islamic financial institution in Egypt in 1963, this concept rapidly developed in the Gulf or the Middle East countries, which are mostly populated by Muslims. The first Islamic bank which was established in the gulf region was Dubai Islamic Bank, which started working in 1975 in Dubai, then in 1977 Kuwait established the Kuwait finance house conducting all the Islamic financial activities. Dubai has many Islamic financial products which are managed by different Islamic financial institutions, but one of the instruments which is growing with remarkable momentum is the Islamic insurance or 'takaful', which has shown a rise in the premium of about 15% in the past few years. This growth rate is rather faster than the conventional insurance.

3. Methodology

3.1 Research methods

Out of two approaches, ethnographic and scientific, this study has used bits of both. The decision been made to get a better understanding of research and its findings which involve organisations, individuals, and networks, and since the scientific approach is more like an objective approach, it is ideal for this type of study. In addition to that, scientific models are solely based on the deductive research model.

Both primary and secondary methods have been used to seek answers to research questions. The literature review has been used to analyse the secondary data. Survey questionnaires, interviews, case studies, and experiments have been performed for data gathering purpose.

3.2 Sample of study

Two sets of observations are used for this study of performance of Islamic capital market. One set consists of 20 companies selected from the KLSE randomly and their performance is analysed. The second set of companies consist of 46 Islamic funds which are also selected randomly and the dataset used to observe the performance of those funds consists of monthly net asset value returns with the time interval between 01/1997 and 08/2002.

To see the comparisons in the performance of these 46 companies which are regarded as benchmarks, all of their indices are recorded and the returns are computed arithmetically.

3.3 Data Sources

The data used in the following table to study the performance of KLSE is taken from the database of Bloomberg. Different portfolios are chosen with different characteristics which include both debt and equity investments, and the returns for these mutual funds are available for the period of two years. The period which is used to study the performance of the assets and mutual funds of Malaysia, which is the hub of the Asian Islamic market, starts from October 2005 and ends on April 2007.

4. Data Analysis and Findings

4.1 Capital Asset Pricing Model (CAPM)

The CAPM is used to analyse the data and to assess the performance of the Islamic capital market because the capital asset pricing model helps in predicting the correlation between the returns associated with an asset and the risks involved in the performance of that asset, and also the risk is assessed in terms of beta.

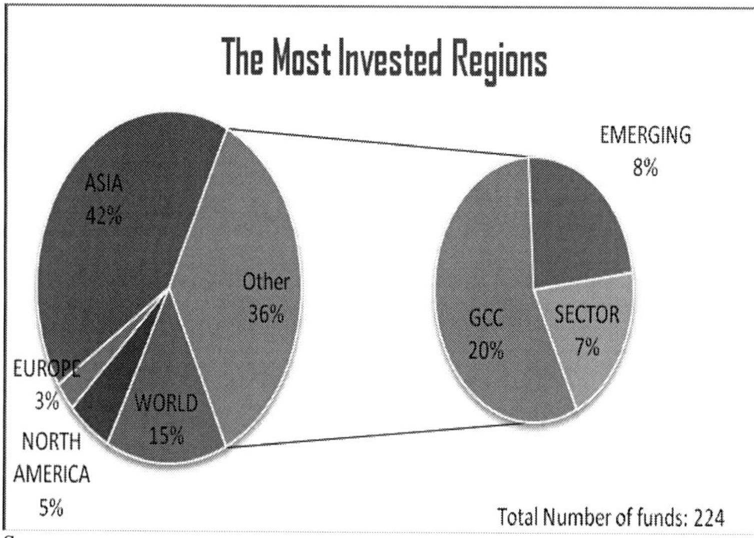

Source:
http://www.failaka.com/downloads/AbderrezakF_Perf_IslamicEquityFunds.pdf

The above plotted graph presents a picture of the distribution of the Islamic equity funds all over the world, and here we can see that gulf countries are contributing approximately one fifth of the total capital industry. It can also be seen that Asia has a major share in the market, having a contribution of 42%. If we explore the Asian countries with an Islamic capital market, we see that Malaysia and Indonesia have the biggest Islamic capital markets. If we just analyse the Malaysian market, then we can see that in 2009 Malaysia had a total of 846 securities companies which are shari'ah-compliant, the whole capital market has a worth of $171.26 billion, and the NAV estimated for the Islamic ETF is $191 million.

According to the graph, it is very clear that North America and Europe are still lacking in this industry and contribute only the 10% of the total industry. We have already discussed that all of Europe is taking an interest in making progress to develop the Islamic capital market and are working on legislations, but there are some concerns of the governments which are creating obstacles. The UK is playing a leading role for giving a very comfortable environment to develop an Islamic capital market, and also the UK has a big community of Muslims as compared to any of the other European countries.

4.2 Measure of the performance

Table 3. Performance of Malaysian MF Sort by using Treynor Ratio

No	Islamic MF	Ri	Rm	Rf	σ	B	Sharpe	Treynor	Jensen
1	AIAISTI	33.80%	36.39%	3.21%	9.88%	0.2330	3.0951	**1.3131**	0.2286
2	MAAIGIF	18.24%	36.39%	3.21%	14.44%	0.1364	1.0404	**1.1019**	0.1050
3	PRLIDAR	31.15%	36.39%	3.21%	25.82%	0.4845	1.0820	**0.5767**	0.1187
4	BHALMIZ	20.42%	36.39%	3.21%	8.38%	0.3203	2.0537	**0.5374**	0.0659
5	SBBDAIF	18.98%	36.39%	3.21%	5.24%	0.3384	3.0087	**0.4661**	0.0455
6	ALCONGP	8.88%	36.39%	3.21%	5.26%	0.1221	1.0777	**0.4641**	0.0162
7	PRUDMIK	33.38%	36.39%	3.21%	11.28%	0.6614	2.6751	**0.4562**	0.0823
8	BIMPERS	18.29%	36.39%	3.21%	11.88%	0.3657	1.2696	**0.4125**	0.0295
9	HWAFAIM	17.64%	36.39%	3.21%	10.21%	0.3511	1.4139	**0.4110**	0.0278
10	AMATEGU	27.58%	36.39%	3.21%	8.70%	0.6002	2.8015	**0.4060**	0.0445
11	PUBISBF	23.91%	36.39%	3.21%	8.74%	0.5235	2.3693	**0.3955**	0.0334
12	APXISBF	37.95%	36.39%	3.21%	14.70%	0.8985	2.3634	**0.3867**	0.0493
13	HLAITZA	25.46%	36.39%	3.21%	9.66%	0.5820	2.3022	**0.3822**	0.0294
14	TADOPTI	32.67%	36.39%	3.21%	13.16%	0.7958		**0.3702**	
15	HLGDMAR	26.78%	36.39%	3.21%	13.72%	0.7041	1.7182	**0.3348**	0.0021
16	PHEDAMA	20.88%	36.39%	3.21%	13.33%	0.6572	1.3257	**0.2689**	(0.0413)
17	RHBMDFI	18.56%	36.39%	3.21%	10.01%	0.6031	1.5333	**0.2545**	(0.0466)
18	COMDBAR	17.02%	36.39%	3.21%	12.47%	0.7538	1.1080	**0.1833**	(0.1119)
19	MCISSYA	6.84%	36.39%	3.21%	14.03%	0.2630	0.2587	**0.1380**	(0.0510)
20	MBF	8.46%	36.39%	3.21%	105.45%	1.6730	0.0498	**0.0314**	(0.5025)

Source: Ferdian I. R, 2008

The above table represents the 20 Islamic mutual funds which are listed with the Malaysian stock market known as Kuala Lumpur Syari'ah Index, and these represent the benchmark of the KLSI. Treynor, Jensen and

Sharpe methods are used to measure the behaviour and performance of the funds and then are compared with the other indices.

From the figures above it can be seen that first of all none of the Islamic mutual fund has negative value in the Treynor ratio, so all are performing well as compared to other conservative funds. Also from the figures we can list the funds according to the results.

For example AIAISTI holds first position, with the ratio 1.3131, which is higher compared to the others; and then MAAIGIF comes second, with the value of 1.1019; and PRLIDAR comes third, with the value of 0.5767.

The Sharpe ratio, which is the most popular measurement method among the three methods, is applied to measure the performance of the same Islamic mutual funds and it was found that none of the funds show negative performance. The performance of the funds is considered better if the value of the ratio is higher. But with the Sharpe calculation the results are somewhat contradictory as compared to the Treynor ratio because the companies shown by the Treynor to be on top, do not behave the same when we apply the Sharpe ratio for the same funds, except AIAISTI. AIAISTI has the highest performance according to Treynor and also has the highest Sharpe ratio, which means its performance is far better and progressive.

The Jensen measure is also used to measure the performance of the funds and we used the Jensen alpha to compute the values. According to the Jensen measure, the top three positions are attained by the AIAISTI, PRLIDAR and MAAIGIF with the values 0.2286, 0.1187 and 0.1050 respectively.

4.3 Comparative Study of Indices Performance

After analysing the KLSE, we take the data for different parts of the world. Before taking the figures for computation, we can analyse the 12 month moving average returns for the assets chosen from the different Dow Jones indices to see the performance from 1998 to 2002.

To analyse the performance of the different assets we are using the S&P500 as a benchmark for comparative study.

This can be observed from the following graph.

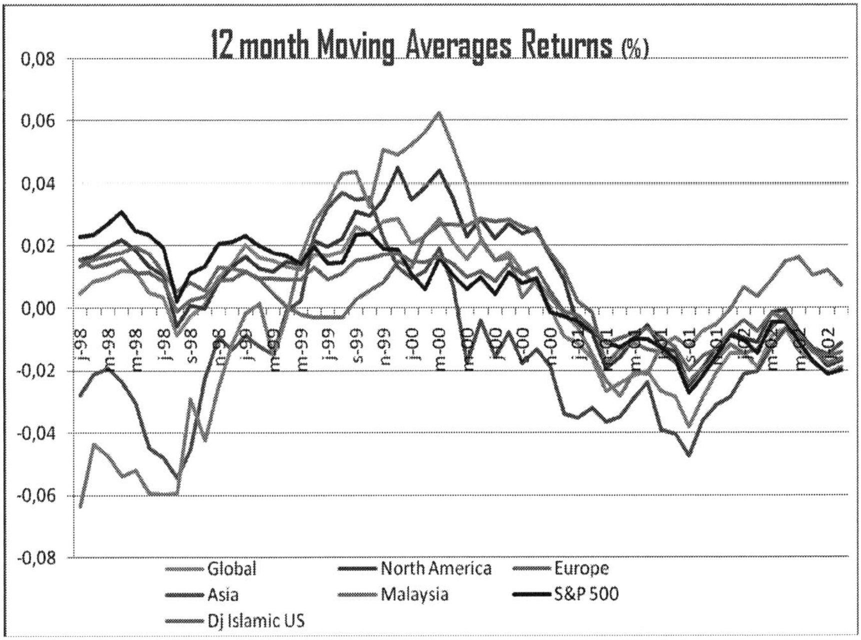

If we plot the graph showing the returns for every month then we can see that Malaysia did not perform well in 1998, but from mid 98 it starting gaining momentum and KLSI performance moved to the top in 2000 and in 2001 as all other have the same impact KLSI had the same performance and it was the time when there was an incident which crashed all the businesses in all the parts of the world. As we can see, all the parts nevertheless have the same downturn. But if we look at the performance of the Dow Jones Islamic US index there is a very consistent movement in the returns between the last quarter and the end of 2000 but they could not overcome the effects the crisis caused in 2001, and from 2001 to 2002 there is a very passive movement shown in the returns, except in the rapid momentum shown in the market of Malaysia. Malaysia has shown a greater volatility, and also with higher volatility there are more returns calculated. DJUS suffered the crisis of economic downturn, but it is not seen as much as compared to S&P500. This is why the Islamic mutual funds are considered to be safer to invest in as compared to others.

The economic down turn that can be seen in the period of 2001 is mostly due to the 9th September terrorist attacks on the USA, which affected all the markets and also the crash of the internet market and most of the technology firms.

4.4 Sharpe Ratio Measure

Sharpe ratio measure is used for the analysis of performance of different indices and also helps in a comparative study with its conventional peers.

Different Islamic indices and relative performance to their peers

1997-2002 observations

			Sharpe Ratio > Index	
Type of Index	Mean	St.Dev	Sharpe Ratio	Conventional
Dj Islamic World	0.8%	6.6%	0.07	**Yes**
Dj Islamic US	1.0%	7.3%	0.09	**No**
Dj Islamic Europe	0.7%	5.5%	0.06	**No**
Dj Islamic Asia	0.7%	7.9%	0.05	**Yes**
KLSE Syariah	0.3%	7.2%	-0.01	**Yes**
Dj Islamic Emerging markets	0.7%	10.6%	0.03	**Yes**
Dj Islamic Technology	1.3%	12.2%	-0.05	**No**
Total	0.8%	8.2%	0.05	**No**

The above table represents the data of the all the Dow Jones' operating in different parts of the world and are just concerned with the Islamic mutual funds and the shariah-compliant portfolios. After careful calculation of all the data provided by failaka, the means of the returns for the 5 years is calculated and also the standard deviation is tabulated to calculate the Sharpe ratio. If we look at the table then it is quite clear that the Sharpe ratio for all the DJ Islamic indices remains positive except two; one is KLSE Syariah, and the other is DJ Islamic technology.

In the last column the performance of the conventional index is calculated and it tells us when the conventional perform better than Islamic indices.

The first one, DJI world, underperformed compared to its conventional counterpart. DJI US and DJ Europe are the two indices that have performance better than the conventional indices.

4.5 Jensen Measure

	ISLAMIC			Proxy for Market
	Jensen α % (t-stat)	β MKT (t-stat)	R^2 adj	
Global	-0,6566 (-2,03**)	0,64 (12,97)	0,72	DJ ISLAMIC WORLD
North-America	-0,085 (0,21)	0,64 (11,6)	0,67	DJ ISLAMIC US
Europe	-0,2472 (0,84)	0,65 (12,18)	0,69	DJ ISLAMIC EUR
Asia	-1,9976 (-2,59*)	0,61 (6,21)	0,36	DJ ISLAMIC ASIA
Malaysia	1,0407 (1,56)	0,54 (5,79)	0,45	KLSE SYARIAH
Emerging[1]	-0,0206 (-0,04)	0,34 (7,1)	0,42	DJ ISLAMIC EMERGING
Technology[1]	-0,4587 (0,58)	0,70 (12,01)	0,75	DJ ISLAMIC TECHNOLOGY

In this measurement the returns from the 46 Islamic equity funds are taken and are regressed with the help of the capital asset pricing model. The monthly returns for these funds were not distributed evenly in the time period of five years from 1997 to 2002. The returns obtained from the data for some of the funds are not complete. To have a comparative study the funds are introduced into two forms including Islamic indices and conventional indices. A list of markets is used as proxy studies for the comparison in the last column of the table and which have most well-known benchmarks.

The above calculations do not clearly tell of the underperformance or over performance for any of the categories in particular. The North American Islamic equity funds have an equal tendency of fluctuation and have one to one relationship with the S&P500. The beta calculated for them is 0.92, and they also seem to be less sensitive for the Dow Jones Islamic US index, which has a beta value of 0.64. If we analyse the betas for Islamic funds in comparison to the market, we would see that Islamic funds have lower values of beta, which represent the lesser sensitivity to volatility and as a consequence there are also lower returns as compared to the other conventional peers.

The betas calculated for both the markets including the Islamic capital market is 0.53, and the beta estimated for the conventional market is 0.56.

The capital asset pricing model is not fully able to explain the behaviour of Asian equity funds, the Asian markets, and the fluctuations, and is also unable to explain why the R^2 is not able to attain the 40% level. But as explained previously by different researchers, the calculations shown in the table above are able to create an opinion that Islamic mutual funds and the Islamic capital market is a good market to invest in for the investors because the Islamic funds have far less correlation with the market volatilities and fluctuations.

5. Recommendations

After this research we can suggest the following recommendations;

- Islamic financial market should be given a chance to launch their products in the global markets to show their performance.
- The shari'ah boards should have a consensus on the set of Islamic principles about Islamic products so that opinions about Islamic products should not be confusing, and they should make clear that the products screened for Islamic market are fully shari'ah-compliant.
- With the extensive study on products, more and more research is needed, and introduction of more funds is needed for diversification for the Islamic mutual funds. Diversification would help to reduce risk and would increase the choices for the investors to pick the right fund.
- The research should be done on the conventional measures to evaluate the risk and return for the market, and also whether these measures are applicable for the Islamic capital market.
- Access should be given to the market data to analyse the performance of the Islamic financial system and it should be made public to choose them for investment.
- Individuals who are interested in the investment into the Islamic securities should be encouraged to use the models to study the performance before investment.

- Islamic financial organisations should give better services and advice to the investors as compared to their competitors to attract a big pool of investors.

6. Conclusion

This research helps in understanding the performance of the Islamic capital market and different Islamic financial institutions all over the world in comparison with their counterparts, as well as how the shari'ah-compliance affects the performance of the Islamic equity funds in different circumstances of economic life. The third point seen during this research is the selection of Islamic funds and the diversification of those funds, because Islamic shari'ah law defines very strict measures to scrutinise these funds. This study is carried out in comparison with the conventional market and observed the performance under shari'ah law.

In the first set, only the performance of the Malaysian stock market (KLSI) is analysed and three risk measures are used, including Sharpe, Treynor and Jensen measures. All three measures described that the KLSI outperforms, and none of the values are negative, but there was a slight difference in that all three measures showed different ranks for all 20 Islamic mutual funds selected for the study. The difference in performance of some of the funds is due to the two important factors which are used to determine the relation of the fund with the fluctuations in the market. The factor which determines this relation of fluctuation is called beta and the other performance factor used by the Sharpe ratio is standard deviation, which is very effective in calculating the comparative performance. Islamic mutual funds and the Islamic capital market has shown a far less sensitivity to the market volatility, and also there is seen to be a very low parallel movement of return of both the Islamic indices and the conventional market.

The second question which we studied was the effect of shari'ah-compliance on the performance of Islamic funds. Shari'ah does not allow exceeding the debt to capital ratio of 33%, and the accounts receivable should not exceed 45%. Also the businesses are not allowed to come under shari'ah law who are earning interest from their business of more than 5 to 10%. We observed the 12 months moving average for the different global indices for 5 years and found different behaviours of different markets.

The Malaysian market has shown a lot of fluctuations in the returns. It reached a peak in performance in good economic conditions, but when there was an economic downturn it also behaved in a more volatile way as compared to the market.

References

Abderrezak F., 2008,The Performance of Islamic Equity Funds, http://www.failaka.com/downloads/AbderrezakF_Perf_IslamicEquityFunds.pdf

Allderedge R. H. and John A. Prestbo, 2007, 'Constructing Risk-Based, Multi-Asset-Class Portfolio Indexes', Dow Jones Portfolio Indexes.

Bacha, Obiyathulla I, 2004,'Value Presentation through Risk Management- A Shariah Compliant Proposal for Equity Management', MPRA Paper No.12632.

Damak M., Volland E., July 17 2008, Islamic Finance in France:Paris tries to Reduce the Gap with London, Standard and Poor's Ratings Direct.

Ferdian I. R., Dewi K. M.,2007, The Performance Analysis of Islamic Mutual Funds– A Comparative Study between Indonesia and Malaysia, page 2: viewed at; http://staff.ui.ac.id/internal/060603200/publikasi/200708ThePerformanceAnalysisofIslamicMutualFunds.pdf

Farmida bi, Partner, Norton Rose, 2009, Islamic Capital Markets Respond to the Financial Crisis. http://eurekahedge.com/news/09_Oct_IFN_Islamic_Capital_Markets_Respond_to_the_Financial_Crisis.asp.

Farhat J. and M. Kabir Hassan, 2003, Dividend Signalling Hypothesis and Short term Asset Concentration of Islamic Interest Free Banking, Islamic Economic Studies, Vol. 11, No. 1.

Hussein K., Omran M., 2005, Ethical Investment Revisited: Evidence from Dow Jones Islamic Indexes, The Journal of Investing, page109.

James C. Van Horne, John M. Wachowicz, 2008, Fundamentals of Financial Management, 13th edition, pp.98-99, Pearson Education Limited.

Jobst A., 2008,Risk Management of Islamic Finance Instruments

Malaysian Islamic capital market, quarterly bulletin, 12/2009, vol.4 no.4.

Maimunah Raja 05/2010, The Malaysian Success Stories in Islamic Finance; Global Islamic Finance.

ISLAMIC FINANCE OUTSIDE THE MUSLIM WORLD: THE UNITED KINGDOM EXPERIMENT

AHMED BELOUAFI[1]
AND ABDALLAH Q. TURKISTANI[2]

Introduction

Islamic finance (IF) came into being no more than five decades ago. Its institutional development went through two phases; the first one in the sixties that witnessed the introduction of a local saving bank in the rural area of Mit-Ghamr in Egypt[3], and the second, in the mid-seventies which saw the introduction of commercial private banking and an intra-government initiative[4] at a regional level among OIC[5] countries. From then on, IF has grown steadily, spreading from one institution in one country to more than 400 institutions in more than seventy countries, with total assets slightly exceeding the threshold of 1 Trillion US Dollars[6] and it

---

[1] Researcher, Islamic Economics Research Centre, King Abdul Aziz University, Saudi Arabia.
[2] Director, Islamic Economics Research Centre, King Abdul Aziz University, Saudi Arabia.
[3] The experiment is well known by its founder; Ahmed Al-Naggar and it lasted four years from 1963 till 1967.
[4] The Islamic Development Bank (IsDB) which has been transformed into a group with many subsidiaries and affiliates.
[5] Organization of Islamic Conference.
[6] The Islamic Financial Services Board, a global standard- setting body and the Islamic Development Bank predicted that assets held by Islamic financial institutions may climb to \$1.6 trillion by 2012 from about \$1 trillion this year. Source: www.globalislamicfinancemagazine.com, accessed February 22nd, 2011 & BMB Islamic, 2011, "*Global Islamic Financial Report (GIFR 2011)*", p. 34.

grew at double digits over the last fifteen years[7]. Its operations and products have diversified as well.

As a result, IF is no longer confined to its traditional Muslim and Arab countries; rather it has spread, in various degrees, all over the globe. Among the localities that have played a "unique" role in this process is the United Kingdom. This active role has led some experts to describe this phenomenon as a "standalone" experiment in the development and promotion of IF outside the Muslim and Arab world. This papers aims at capturing the latest development of the Islamic finance industry in this country. Particular attention in this account is given to the identification of the major factors that played important roles in this evolution. The paper also aims at deriving important lessons and practical steps that can be of benefit to regulatory and supervisory authorities in other jurisdictions. In accomplishing this task the following questions have been drawn to properly address the issues relevant to exploring the aims of the paper:

1. What are the latest developments of IF industry operations in the UK? And what are the factors that stand behind the "*uniqueness*" of the role played by the UK in the spread and development of IF outside the Arab and Muslim World?
2. Is there a correlation between the development of IF in the UK and the welcoming attitude adopted by the UK authorities? In other words, does the Financial Services Authority[8] (FSA)'s approach to regulating Islamic finance provide the appropriate environment for its development in the UK?[9]
3. What lessons and practical steps can be drawn from the experiment?

In discussing and analysing the matters arising from the above questions, the paper has been divided into five sections: section **1** provides an

---

[7] According to Ibrahim Warde, "… *the rate of growth accelerated from an average of 14 percent a year in 1994-2002 to 26 percent a year in 2003-2010*". Ibrahim Warde, 2010, "*Islamic Finance and the Global Meltdown*", available at: http://www.islamica-me.com/article.asp?cntnt=633.

[8] UK single financial regulatory body. It came into being in 1997, and it operates under a single piece of legislation that applies to all financial operations and products; the Financial Services and Markets Act 2000. Financial Services Authority, 2006, "*Islamic Banking in the UK*", Briefing Note BN016/06, 9 March 2006. Available at: www.fsa.gov.uk/pages/About/Media/notes/bn016.shtml.

[9] Masood O. et al., 2009, "*Role of Islamic Mortgages in UK*", p. 377.

overview about the latest developments of the operations of IF industry in the UK. Then section **2** touches upon the factors that stand behind the development and growth of IF in the UK; while section **3** looks at the phases of the regulatory process pursued in the UK for providing a level playing field for IF products and services. Section **4,** on the other hand, explores the practical steps derived from the UK experiment and the lessons that can be learnt from the experience. Finally section **5** draws some concluding remarks and identifies some issues for future consideration as far as the accommodation of IF in conventional systems is concerned.

1. The Latest Developments of the Operations of IF industry in the UK

According to UK official sources, IF "*describes the subsection of the financial services industry that complies with the principles of Sharī'ah (Islamic Law)"*[10]. The most important principles upon which the IF framework rests are:[11]

- ✓ **Prohibition of the payment and receipt of interest**[12]: money itself is considered to have no intrinsic value – it is merely a store of wealth and medium of exchange.
- ✓ **Prohibition of uncertainty or speculation**[13]: everybody participating in a financial transaction must be adequately informed and not cheated or mislead.
- ✓ **Prohibition of financing certain economic sectors [or activities] (ethical dimension of IF):** investment is forbidden in what are considered to be socially detrimental activities. These include gambling, pornography, and alcohol.
- ✓ **Importance of profit and loss sharing:** the investor and the investee must share the risk of all financial transactions[14].

---

[10] HM Treasury, 2008, "*The Development of Islamic Finance in the UK: the Governments' perspective*", p. 5.
[11] *Ibid,* p. 7.
[12] This is the very apparent and the most important feature of *Riba* in nowadays financial dealings.
[13] This is an imprecise translation of the word *Gharar* which can be best translated as *alea* or *aleatory* contracts. Also information asymmetry and zero-sum gave can be of great benefit in exploring the wider context of *Gharar* in Islamic law.
[14] This is not the case under *Mudarabah;* a form of partnership under which one party provides capital and the other entrepreneurialship or work, the parties share-

✓ **Asset-backing principle**: financial transactions should be underpinned by an identifiable and tangible underlying asset.

Though that is how IF has been defined and framed, it has been, on the other hand, perceived as an industry that is widening financial choices by serving not Muslim customers only, but rather customers of other faiths and cultures. In this regard:

> "it is often suggested that IF products may be particularly attractive to those interested in ethical finance, due to certain characteristics … non-Muslim businesses may be attracted to IF to increase their sources of funds or liquidity." [15]

It is within this general context and perception of the nature to IF that the industry has been accommodated and promoted in the UK financial system over the last twenty years or so. Hence the presence of Islamic finance's operations and products in the London financial markets is not a new phenomenon. It can be traced back to the early 1980s through commodity *Murabaha*[16] to offer liquidity for Middle Eastern institutions and other investors. Wilson (1999) noted that:

> "Al-Baraka international bank was the only bank offering exclusively Islamic Banking Services under the 1987 Banking Act. Back in 1982 Al Baraka had taken over Hargrave Securities which was a licensed deposit taker under the previous legislation, but its business only took off in 1987 … [And] despite the absence of a United Kingdom authorized Islamic bank regulated under the Banking Act of 1987 sine the withdrawal of Al Baraka from the London Market, [in 1993], a number of conventional banks have been providing a considerable range of Islamic financing services."[17]

In addition, there are thought to be about two million Muslims in the UK, or 3 per cent of the population; 50% of these are estimated to reside in the

---

in the generated profits but losses are borne entirely by the capital provider if true and honest information and accounts are disclosed by the entrepreneur or work provider.

[15] HM Treasury, 2008, "*The Development of Islamic Finance in the UK: the Governments' perspective*", pp. 7-8.

[16] This type of transactions was carried out through the London Metal Exchange. Ainley, et al., 2007, "*Islamic Finance in the UK: Regulation and Challenges*", FSA, November 2007, p. 6.

[17] Rodney Wilson R., 1999, "*Challenges and Opportunities for Islamic Banking and Finance in the West: The United Kingdom Experience*", p. 426 & 429.

London area[18]. There are also estimated to be about half a million regular Muslim visitors to the UK and approximately 12 million Muslims living in the EU, principally in France & Germany[19]. As a result of these demographic and economic potentials, Islamic financial products are available in the UK from a number of High Street banks which offer current accounts and mortgages tailored for Muslims. But over the last few years a number of fully-fledged Islamic banks have been authorized in the UK as illustrated below.

These developments did not occur over night; rather they have evolved steadily and gradually over the years from the early days till now. However, the turning point in this respect took place in mid-1990. At that time the then head of the Bank of England, Sir Eddie George, and some other officials noticed the potential growth of the industry and its relevance to the innovation and "inclusiveness" character of the financial system in the UK. However, the rapid and significant development took place only over the last eight years[20]. Below is a brief account of some indicators of this development:

- It appears from the available sources that the UK is the 1st EU country to introduce legislative changes to provide a level playing field for IF in its tax bills.
- In the year 2000 one of its Universities[21] hosted the 4th international Conference of Islamic Economics. As a result it is the only European country that had held such an important event on the international scene. In addition, in the year 2002 one of its academics, the ex-professor of Banking at Loughborough University John Presley, was awarded the Islamic Development Bank prize in Islamic Banking and Finance.
- The year 2004 saw the establishment of the 1st Islamic retail bank; the Islamic Bank of Britain. In subsequent years four other wholesale banks[22] have been granted licenses by the financial

[18] Financial Services Authority, 2006, "*Islamic Banking in the UK*", Briefing Note BN016/06, 9 March 2006. Available at: www.fsa.gov.uk/pages/About/Media/notes/bn016.shtml.

[19] *Ibid.*

[20] HM Treasury, 2008, "*The Development of Islamic Finance in the UK: the Governments' perspective*", p. 3.

[21] The University of Loughborough.

[22] These are: European Islamic Investment Bank (incorporated in January 2005 and authorized by the FSA in March 2006), Bank of London and Middle East

services Authority (FSA); the UK single financial regulator. Furthermore, one insurance (*Takaful*) firm was also authorized by the FSA[23]. In addition to these fully-fledged banks most of the large London based conventional retail and investment banks still offer Islamic financial services to their customers[24].

- Due the well placed position of the UK financial, legal and educational establishments, many of these entities are engaged in providing IF services in one way or another. According to an IFSL report[25] there are 55 educational organizations and over 16 law firms involved in this process.
- A number of companies that engage in principal investing and fund management are operating in the UK market. Some of these are Gulf finance house, Dar Capital (UK), Fajr Capital and Al-Salam Europe[26].

From the above encounter it can be noticed that the UK has positioned itself as an international gateway for IF finance in the non-Arab and non-Muslim World[27]. The following charts provide further evidence of that:

(incorporated in August 2006 and authorized in July 2007), Qatar Islamic Bank – UK (authorized in January 2008) , and Gatehouse Bank (authorized in April 2008). Source: web site of the institutions & Mohammed Amin, 2010, "*The UK Islamic banking scene*", 1 September 2010, www.mohammedamin.com.

[23] HM Treasury and the UK Debt Management Office, 2008, "*Government Sterling Sukuk Issuance: a response to the consultation*", p. 3.

[24] The Muslim Council of Britain, 2009, "*London and Islamic Finance: Briefing Paper for the Mayor of London*", p.5.

[25] IFSL Research, 2009, "*Islamic Finance 2009*", p. 5 & 6.

[26] The Muslim Council of Britain, 2009, "*London and Islamic Finance: Briefing Paper for the Mayor of London*", p.5.

[27] The UK is even well ahead of many Muslim and Arab countries.

Chart-1- The Largest Non-Muslim & Non-Arab Country in Hosting IFIs and Islamic Windows

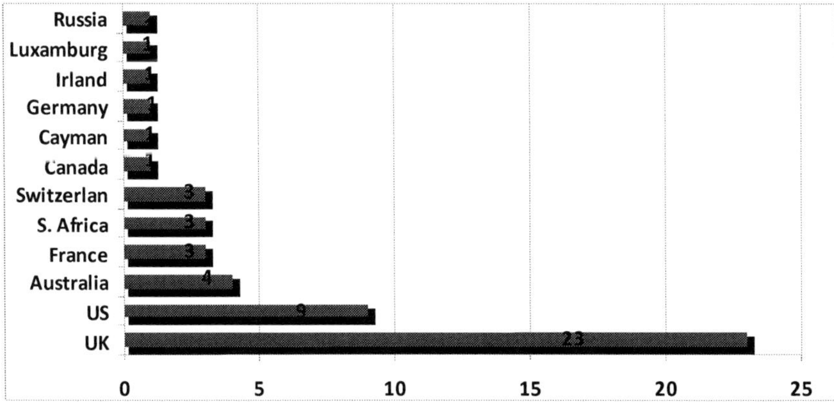

Source: IFSL Research, 2009, "Islamic Finance 2009", p. 6 & HM Treasury and the UK Debt Management Office, 2008, "Government Sterling *Sukuk* Issuance: a response to the consultation", p. 3.

Chart-2- Steady Growth of *Sharī'ah* Compliant Assets (in USD Billions)

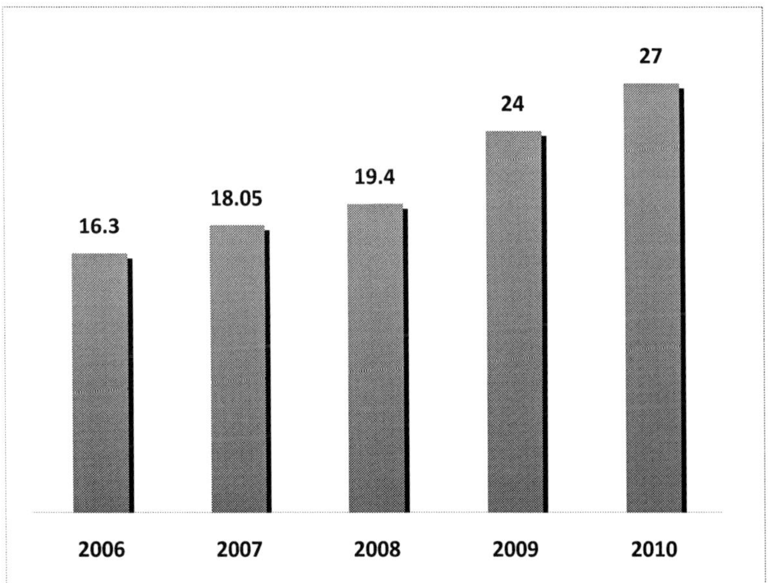

Source: IFSL Research, 2010, "Islamic Finance 2010", p. 3 & BMB Islamic, 2011, "GIFR 2011", p. 35

Chart-3- UK is the largest provider of Education & Training Programs in Islamic Finance

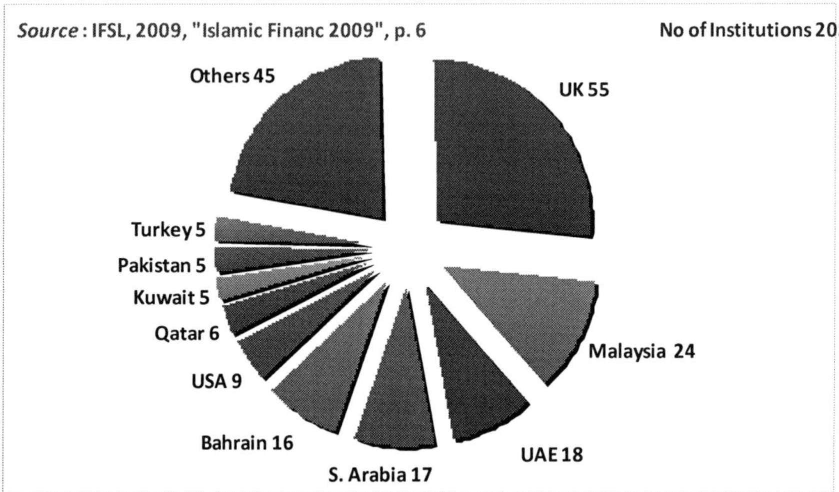

The above indicators suggest that there is a positive correlation between the welcoming attitude of the UK authorities, especially the regulatory ones, and the growth of IF in Britain. This is not a surprise since the development and promotion of any new business needs an enabling environment that sends positive signals to responsibles of that business or industry, and IF is not an exception in this regard. This fact has been acknowledged in official and other sources[28]. This fact has also been supported by the interest of other jurisdictions to learn from the British experiment. For instance in 2006 Central banking authorities in Canada and Kenya visited the FSA and met representatives of the local banks who have taken steps for starting Islamic banking operations, like the Islamic Bank of Britain, to look into the feasibility of adopting the UK model to enable investors to start Islamic banking operations in their domiciles[29]. Furthermore, the ex-governor of the Central Bank of Pakistan, Shamshad

[28] An example of that is: UK Trade and Investments assertion that the "supportive legislation boosts UK's world-leading Islamic finance industry. This success has been facilitated by important legislative changes which have created a dynamic base for *Sharī`ah*-compliant financial products". UK Trade and Investments, 2010, "*Supportive legislation boosts UK's world-leading Islamic finance industry*".

[29] Abu Umar Farooq Ahmad and M. Kabir Hassan, 2006, "*The Adoption of the UK Finance Bill Proposals on Islamic Finance into Islamic Banking in Australia*", p. 51.

Akhtar[30], in one of her keynote speeches in a conference about IF advocated that developed jurisdictions pursue the approach adopted by the UK authorities in welcoming IF in their financial systems.

2. Why was the UK able to attain this position?

Several factors contributed to the status reached by the UK in the development of IF in the British Isles. Among these are the following:

- **The nature of the political system** (pragmatism, realism, and progressiveness). In various documents and occasions the UK government and its officials spelled out the supportive and ambitious attitude relating to the development of IF in the UK. For instance, in the official document published at the end of 2008 the UK government stated that its main objectives for the development of IF in the British Isles are two-fold[31]; **First** to enhance the UK's competitiveness in financial services by establishing the UK as a gateway for international Islamic finance, and **second** to ensure that everybody, irrespective of their religious beliefs, has access to competitively priced financial products. In this regard the story of Lord Edward George, the former governor of the Bank of England, with a Muslim family has been mentioned in various sources to indicate the inclusiveness approach adopted by the British authorities to make sure that everyone in the British society, regardless of their faith and ethnicity, has access to a competitive and appropriate level of financial services and products. That incident drove the attention of Mr George to IF since the beginning of the nineties. In 2003 Mr George wrote about this: "*I became interested in it [IF] more than a decade ago when I met a very lovely, deeply, religious, Muslim couple who were living in this country with their family, and who had recently bought a house on the back of a conventional mortgage. They told me of their delight in their home, but then they explained to me –not at all in an aggressive way, in fact in sorrow rather than anger- their regret that they had had to go against their religious principles to finance it. That made a big impression on me... I thought our very inventive financial system could find ways of meeting the needs of the*

[30] Shamshad Akhtar, 2007, "*Islamic Finance- Growth, Competitiveness and Sustainability*", p.3.

[31] HM Treasury, 2008, "*The Development of Islamic Finance in the UK:* ", p. 13.

different sectors of our society in ways where this kind of problem need not arise"[32].

This concern has been iterated and carried out by other officials, like the Chairmen of the FSA. In a speech delivered at the Muslim Council of Britain "Islamic Finance and Trade" Conference, the then chairman of the FSA, Mr Callum McCarthy, stated that: "*It would have been an invidious form of social exclusion for regulation to have prevented the development of financial products which conformed with their religious beliefs [Muslims living in the UK], and therefore to have condemned them to a position where their religious beliefs prevented them from accessing financial services. We at the FSA have been concerned to avoid this*"[33].

- **The nature of the version of the capitalist model adopted**. It is a well recognized and established fact that there are varieties of capitalist models that have been adopted and implemented in various places throughout history in the localities where capitalism has been the prevailing economic model. This has led some economists to compare that to the varieties of products launched by companies to preserve their competitive edge and to meet customers' preferences. The late American economist Hyman Minsky was once asked about this phenomenon and his reply was "*At one time the slogan of the Heinz pickle and ketchup company was "57 Varieties". When I make the point about the varieties of capitalism in America, I often say that "There are as many varieties of Capitalism as Heinz has of pickles.*"[34] The implications of such a fact at the practical level centres around the emphasis on the more liberal and the less interventionist view of the state in the economic affairs *vis-à-vis* the more socially oriented version. In the nineteen-eighties, liberalism doctrine dominated the political and economic scene in the UK. As a result private ownership, liberal norms in the business domain, and deregulation of the financial system have been the main tools relied upon to attract foreign investments to the UK market. Within that context, IF saw its early entrance and development in the UK. As time passed by, other factors such as the tremendous growth rates and spread of IF influenced the

[32] Edward George, 2003, "*Towards Islamic House Financing in the UK*", p. 73.
[33] Callum McCarthy, 2006, "*Regulation and Islamic finance*", Speech delivered at the Muslim Council of Britain Islamic Finance and Trade Conference, 13 June 2006. Available at: www.fsa.gov.uk.
[34] Hyman Minsky, 1993, "*Finance and Stability: the Limits of Capitalism*", May 1993, WP #93, p.4.

approach adopted by the UK authorities to establish London as an International hub for IF.

- **London as a leading international financial centre**. Since the 17th century, London has a tradition, in the financial domain, of open attitude towards innovation and new ideas[35]. This is due to the flexibility and welcoming response of its financial system in order to maintain its competitive edge over its rivals. Several analysts, observers, politicians and academics have pointed to this factor[36]. For instance Rodney Wilson, professor of economics at Durham University, noted that "*the UK has been a gateway for IF to enter Europe, partly reflecting the role of London as the leading international financial centre, but also as a consequence of the exposure of leading British banks to the Arab and wider Islamic World and their knowledge of these markets*"[37]. Furthermore, after the introduction of the latest legislation in 2010 in relation to alternative finance investment bonds (AFIBs) or *Sukuk,* Sarah McCarthy-Fry, the Exchequer Secretary to the Treasury, stated that: "*Islamic finance is an area that has been helped by the openness to new influences and ideas that we have here in the UK. With our depth of skill, experience and connections all around the world, we have ensured that the UK has long been the leading Western centre for Islamic finance*"[38].
- **The flexibility of the legal system and the nature of regulatory approach followed**. As for the former it is noted that the existence of trust laws and equity principles under the British common law has given the UK government enough room to deal with the ownership matters that arose in the structures of most of IF instruments. As for the latter, Norton Rose, a key adviser for many significant Islamic transactions noticed this fact with regard the latest legislative initiatives taken by the UK authorities; "*for the last few years, HMRC have been very receptive to representations made for tax treatment of Islamic finance to be more onerous than conventional finance. These changes should ensure that there are now no UK tax obstacles in issuing Sukuk backed by UK land*". The

[35] Ainley, et al., 2007, "*Islamic Finance in the UK: Regulation and Challenges*", FSA, November 2007, p. 11.

[36] See also Howard Davies, 2002, "Islamic Finance and the FSA", pp. 104-105. Mr. Davies was an FSA chairman in the period 1997-2003.

[37] Rodney Wilson, (2007b), "*Islamic Finance in Europe*", p.2.

[38] UK Trade and Investments, 2010, "*Supportive legislation boosts UK's world-leading Islamic finance industry*".

firm also highlighted that "*these tax changes will give considerable boost to the UK Islamic finance initiative and ensure that in these difficult times alternative sources of finance will be available in the UK*"[39]. More importantly, the preference of English law in the development of IF products and the dispute settlements relating to IF transactions outside the UK have also played a significant role in consolidating London's position as an International hub for IF[40].

- **The establishment of a single regulator that oversees the operations of the whole financial sector**. Since the end of 2001 the FSA became the main statutory regulator for the UK financial services industry. The FSA was established by an Act of parliament in 2000[41] and thus the FSA has combined the work of 11 different regulators into a single body under a single piece of legislation[42]; the Financial Services and Markets Act (FSMA) 2000. This development may have quickened the process of the establishment of IFIs in the UK in the sense of letting a single body decide upon the licensing applications rather than the multiple entities under the old regime. In addition, the FSA has benefited from the former initiatives as there was no lack of dialogue and discussion between the previous regulators and the IF stakeholders; especially the Muslim community in the UK[43]. Furthermore, the UK's principles-based regulatory structure, which is designed to accommodate a range of financial structures to suit a multitude of clients, may have played a part in this development as well. Thus giving the City of London more flexibility than its competitors elsewhere[44].

There are, of course, other factors, such as the English language as an international financial and business language, and close trade ties between Middle-Eastern countries, especially the Gulf ones and the UK. The list is,

---

39 Gillian Walmesley, 2011, "*Another year of growth and development for the London Stock Exchange markets for Islamic finance*", pp. 1-2.

40 Aziz Tayyebi, 2008, "*Islamic Finance: An Ethical Alternative to Conventional Finance?*", p. 5.

41 www.fsa.gov.uk.

42 Ainley, et al., 2007, "*Islamic Finance in the UK: Regulation and Challenges*", FSA, November 2007, p. 11.

43 Howard Davies, 2002, "*Islamic Finance and the FSA*", p. 103.

44 The Muslim Council of Britain, 2009, "*London and Islamic Finance: Briefing Paper for the Mayor of London*", p. 6, and Gillian Walmesley, 2011, "*Another year of growth and development for the London Stock Exchange markets for Islamic finance*", p. 1.

therefore, not an exhaustive one, but, nonetheless, is illustrious in pointing out the significant factors.

3. Phases of Regulatory Process in the UK

From the date *Shari'ah*-compliant products were first introduced in to the UK markets in the early eighties till this moment, I have summarized the regulatory approach and attitude adopted by the UK financial regulation into the following three phases (see Chapter 4).

It is clear from the above account that the UK authorities have been accustomed to IF services and products for a very long period. During this period, IF industry witnessed significant developments. Those developments were captured and translated by British officials into policies that allowed IF to flourish in a gradual process in the British Isles. So despite the ambitious intention of the government, as mentioned in the previous section, with regard the development of IF in the UK, the government did not rush into hasty decisions and policies. As a result the changes came only over the last few years, as illustrated by Table 2 below.

Chart-4- Summary of the Regulatory Phases Pursued in the UK

Phase 1: Before 1995 (No action):

- **International commodity *Murabaha* operations.**
- **Al-Baraka International (1983-1993)**
- **No discussion at the regulatory level about the issue.**
- **Same regulation; neither special provision nor minimal changes for Islamic products have been introduced.**
- **Islamic modes bear higher costs (e.g. Charge of double SDLT on property transfer).**

Phase 2: 1995 –2003 (Action):

- **Sir Edward George Speech at the Islamic Foundation (September 1995).**
- **The FSA establishment (1997).**
- **Government consults Muslim community about the introduction & development of Islamic Finance (1999).**
- **Bank of England (BoE) recognition of the potential of IF growth in the UK, 1999.**
- **High-level working group to identify barriers facing IF development (2000).**
- **Sir Howard Davies, FSA chairman speeches 2002 (Markfield-UK) & 2003 (Bahrain).**
- **1st changes in the Finance Act 2003.**
- **Attendance of various activities about IF by UK officials.**

Phase 3: After 2003 (Pro-Action):

- **Other changes in Finance Acts of subsequent years. Table 2 provides some encounter.**
- **Budget speech of Gordon Brown in 2006 to promote London as the leading international financial centre.**
- **Mr. Brown pledge to support the growth of IF at "the Islamic Finance and Trade Conference", June 2006.**
- **IF summit at 11 Downing street (Islamic Finance Experts Group (IFEG) established), April 2007.**
- **FSA document about "IF Regulation and Challenges in the UK", Nov. 2007.**
- **Government document about its "Perspective of the development of IF in the UK", Dec. 2008.**

Table-2- Examples of Some of the Introduced Changes

Date	Introduced Changes
2003	Removal of the double charge of Stamp duty Land Tax (SDLT) for *Murabaha* & *Ijara* contracts that allows individuals to purchase homes. Other measures were introduced as well to offer Islamic products for Child trust fund, asset finance and ISAs.
2005	Extension of the removal to *diminishing Musharkah* (another mode of alternative finance).
2006	Extension of removal to beneficiaries (i.e. companies).
2007	Discussion of applying the same tax rules of conventional debt instruments like bonds to *Sukuk* (Islamic Bonds).
2008	Dealing with more issues relating to the issuance of *Sukuk*.
2009	Legislative measures for SDLT, Capital Gains Tax (CGT), and capital allowance rules for land transactions involved in the structuring of *Sukuk* instruments
2010	The Financial Services and Markets Act 2000 Order 2010 exempts alternative finance investment bonds (AFIBs), a class of debt-like security which includes *sukuk*, from collective investment scheme (CIS) regulations

4. Practical Steps derived and the Lessons that can be learnt from the Experiment

The practical steps derived from the UK approach in accommodating IF can be summarized in the following diagram:

Chart-5- Practical Steps of the UK Approach in Accommodating IF.

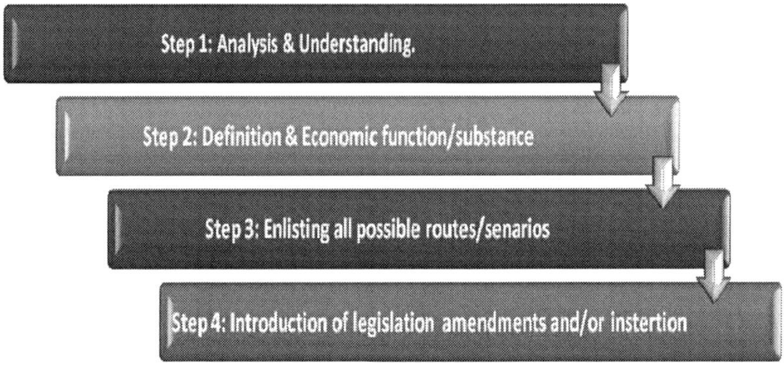

The analysis has been carried out by working groups, like the Islamic finance expert group (IFEG) and the tax technical working group (TTWG), and through the various consultation papers to make sure that an in-depth analysis has been carried out looking into the various aspects and implications of IF services and products. Furthermore, the process has been conducted through the following general guidelines[45]:

Chart-6- General Guidelines Governing the Steps Taken by the UK Authorities.

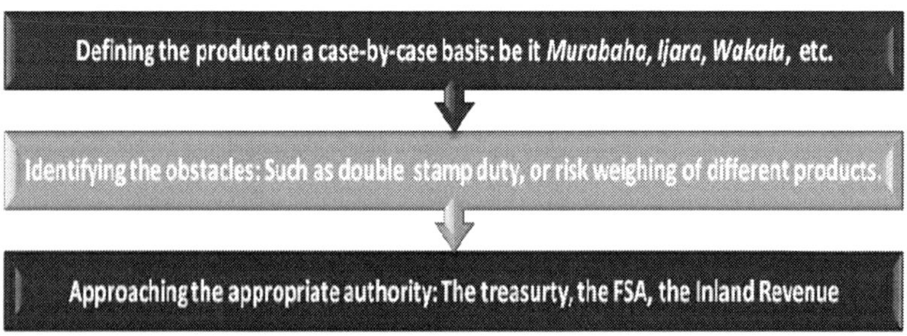

[45] Edward George, 2003, "*Towards Islamic House Financing in the UK*", p.77.

In the second step (chart 5) for example the first group that was chaired by Edward George identified four main obstacles in the area of home financing to be provided on the basis of IF products. These were[46]:

1. Treatment under Stamp Duty, where, because of the nature of the transaction, involving initial ownership by the financier, stamp duty may need to be paid twice, or it may be payable at a higher rate than on a conventional mortgage.
2. Higher regulatory capital charges where conventional mortgages – and indeed *Murābahah* mortgages - attract a capital risk of 50%, but some Islamic mortgages – *Ijārah* mortgages - attract a higher rate of 100%.
3. Disadvantages under the various public sector home ownership schemes – such as Right to Buy or Rent to mortgage - where, because of the involvement of the financier as the owner of the property, the purchaser may be unable to take advantage of the benefits offered under the schemes.
4. Disadvantages in terms of the housing cost element of Income support or income-based Jobseekers Allowances compared with that which applies in case of a conventional mortgage.

Subsequent groups have come across other obstacles as the process of accommodating IF products and services widened to include more products and more interested economic agents, as shown in the above table (2). So the process has been lengthy, as the introduction of IF products and services have wider implications that need to be taken into consideration to avoid any unintended outcome. The example of *Sukuk* given below provides a real case illustration of how the process has been carried out to reach the appropriate and suitable policy.

The Example of *Sukuk*

The UK government showed interest in *Sukuk* since 2006 after Mr Brown, the then Chancellor of the Exchequer, promised to promote the City as the international financial centre. Part of that strategy was to look into the economic potentials of *Sukuk* as an alternative and complementary instrument to conventional bonds that can be used to widen government options in diversifying the sources of its financing. The chart (7) below gives a summary of the initiatives taken between 2006 and 2010:

---

46 *Ibid*, pp. 74-75.

Chart -7- UK Initiatives with Regard *Sukuk* between 2006 & 2010.

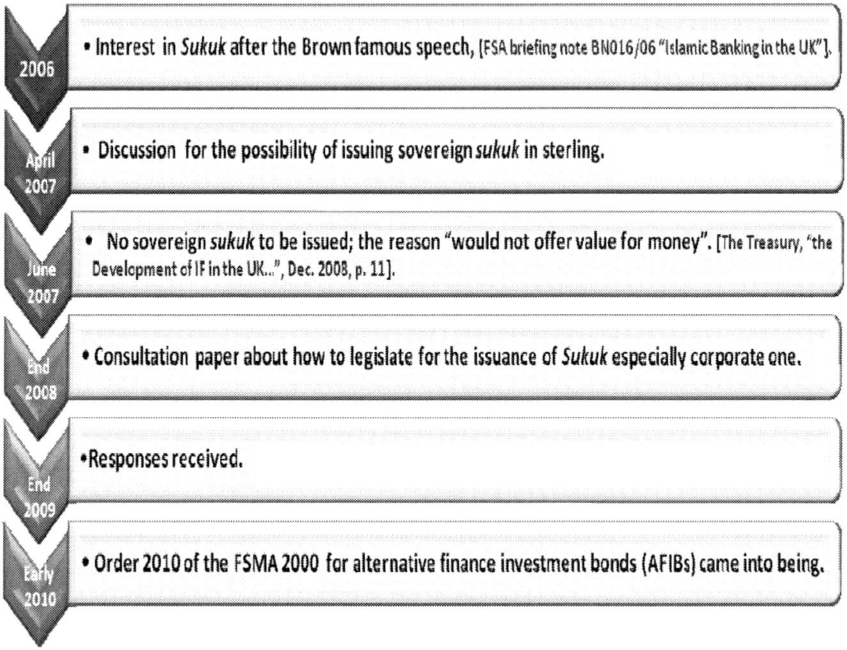

After the analysis and the consultation process, the outcome has been to enlist all possible routes/options and then select the appropriate one.

1. **The enlisted routes/options[47]:**

- Option 1: Introduction of a unique regulatory definition for AFIBs (*Sukuk*) to exempt explicitly these instruments from CIS regulations and to create a new specified investment under the regulated Activities Order (RAO).
- Option 2: Same as 1 but AFIBs will be defined by the existing tax definition.
- Option 3: Same as 1 but include AFIBs under existing specified investment of creating or acknowledging indebtedness.
- Option 4: Do nothing.

[47] HM Treasury & FSA, 2008, "*Consultation on the legislative framework for the regulation of alternative finance investment bonds (Sukuk)*", p.3 & HM Treasury & FSA, 2009, "*Legislative framework for the regulation of alternative finance investment bonds (Sukuk): summary of responses*", p. 4.

2. **Selecting the appropriate option.** The government opted for the first option as laid down in the order 2010 of the FSMA 2000 for alternative finance investment bonds as indicated above.

The aforementioned approach has led the government to conclude that while its "*objectives for IF are ambitious ... it is,[however], committed to ensuring that behind these ambitious objectives, the necessary analysis, consideration and consultation is carried out to deliver real benefits to industry and consumers in the UK*"[48].

Based upon the previous examination of some aspects of accommodating IF in the UK the following lessons that can be drawn from the experiment:

- Clear-cut objectives (i.e. city competitiveness & citizens' access to financial products) and guiding principles (commitment, fairness & collaboration). Thus, subsidence of ideological and cultural sensitivity is of prime importance to have an accommodative environment that is open to new ideas and innovations, irrespective of their origin, that are of benefit to the society or an important part of its citizens.
- Thorough analysis through high-profile groups and consultation with various concerned parties and departments.
- Gradual and progressive process.
- Passionate and steady development.
- Stakeholder approach: the UK authorities in dealing with opening the door for IF have involved several bodies and entities from their side and those of the IF industry. Above all is the fact that the Muslim community, residing in the UK, was involved in the process from the outset.
- Taxation as the main tool for legislating IF products and services. The main guiding principle of this process is look into the economic substance of the transaction rather than that of its legal structure based upon the "*no obstacles, no special favours*" policy. Hence IF products and operations have be treated as if they "were interest based" instruments. As a result, the following principles have been applied when considering tax policy on IF[49]:

  1.Treatment should follow the economic substance of the transaction.

[48] HM Treasury, 2008, "*the Development of Islamic Finance in the UK: the Government's perspective*", p. 14.
[49] *Ibid*, p. 19.

2. Treatment should be on the same basis as equivalent financial products that bear interest.
3. Ordinary tax rules should be applied where possible.
4. Rules that give undesirable or unpredictable results should be amended.

5. Concluding Remarks and Issues for Future Consideration

In the preceding sections this paper has examined and analysed various aspects relating to the growth and development of IF in the UK. Based on that, the following concluding remarks can be drawn:

- IF has grown remarkably in the UK over the last few years. Many factors contributed to this growth; political, welcoming and accommodating legal & regulatory regimes.
- Important lessons can be learnt from the British experiment. This by no means should be interpreted as a call for adopting the "*cut and paste*" mechanism, but rather it is a call to benefit from this experience in a sense of taking things further than the British have done. This is because every country has its unique characteristics and circumstances that should be exploited in the very competitive and complex environment through the "comparative advantage" notion that served the growth of trade and mutual exchanges between nations over centuries.
- There are regional and international contenders who trying to rival the UK in positioning London as a hub for IF outside the Muslim world. So who will win the race?

As for the issues for future consideration the following points can be raised:

- Does it make a great difference and impact at the practical levels to adopt the minimal changing approach as is the UK case, or the dual approach as is the case of Malaysia and Bahrain for the following:
  - Industry players.
  - *Shari'ah* boards.
  - Lawyers.

In other words are there big differences between the two approaches? Or are they almost identical in their final effects on the welcoming process of accommodating IF in conventional systems?

- What are the implications of treating IF instruments as if they "were interest based" modes of finance? Is it just a matter of convenience and "easiness" for regulatory purposes? Or are they really interest based but in "disguise"?
- If Islamic Finance is regarded as a "true" equity and asset backed industry and it has been "easily" accommodated into a conventional system, can a serious debate be initiated about providing a "level playing field" for equity modes of finance in relation to the "favours" given to debt modes of finance to put an end to the biased legislative environment that has affected the emergence of "abnormalities" in the practices of economic agents in the prevailing financial system? In other words, can a legal shift be attained to allow more equity modes of finance and the desire to play a greater role in the financial intermediation process?

References

Ahmad A. U. F., and Hassan M. K., 2006, "The Adoption of the UK Finance Bill Proposals on Islamic Finance into Islamic Banking in Australia", Review of Islamic Economics, Vol. 10, No. 1, pp. 41-57.

Ainley M., Mashayekhi, A., Hicks, R., Rahman, A., and Ravalia, A., 2007, "Islamic Finance in the UK: Regulation and Challenges", Financial Services Authority.

Akhtar S., 2007, "Islamic Finance- Growth, Competitiveness and Sustainability", Keynote speech, 14th World Islamic Banking Conference, Bahrain, 9-10 December 2007.

BMB Islamic, 2011, "Global Islamic Financial Report (GIFR 2011)", BMB Islamic publication, London, UK.

Chapra M. U., and Khan T., 2000, "Regulation and Supervision of Islamic Banks", Occasional paper 3, Islamic Development Bank and Islamic Research and Training Institute, Jeddah, Saudi Arabia.

Dar H. A., and Presley J. R., 1999, "Islamic Finance: A Western Perspective", International Journal of Islamic Financial Services, Vol.1, No.1, pp.1-9.

Davies H., 2002, "Islamic Finance and the FSA", Review of Islamic Economics, No. 12, 2002, pp. 101-108.

El – Hawary, D., Garis, W., and Iqbal, Z., 2004, "Regulating Islamic Financial Institutions: the Nature of the Regulated", World Bank Policy Research Working Paper, 3227, March.

Financial Services Authority, 2006, "Islamic Banking in the UK", Briefing Note BN016/06, 9 March. Available at: www.fsa.gov.uk

Funds@Work, 2010, "the Small World of Islamic Finance", Funds@Work & Zawya Shariah Scholers, Version 5.0, October, 5th.

George, E., 2003, "Towards Islamic House Financing in the UK", Review of Islamic Economics, No. 13, pp. 73-78.

HM Treasury & FSA, 2008, "Consultation on the legislative framework for the regulation of alternative finance investment bonds (*Sukuk)*", December 2008, the Treasury, London, UK.

—. 2009, "Legislative framework for the regulation of alternative finance investment bonds (*Sukuk*): summary of responses", the Treasury and the FSA, October 2009.

HM Treasury and the UK Debt Management Office, 2008, "Government Sterling *Sukuk* Issuance: a response to the consultation", HM Treasury, June 2008, London.

HM Treasury, 2008, "The development of Islamic finance in the UK: the Government's perspective", HM Treasury, December 2008.

—. 2009, "Banking Act 2009", the Treasury, February 2009, London, UK.

IFSL Research, 2009, "Islamic Finance 2009", IFSL in collaboration of UK Trade & Investment and City of London, January.

—. 2010, "Islamic Finance 2010", IFSL in collaboration of UK Trade & Investment and City of London, January.

Masood O., Chichti J. E., Mansour W., and Amin Q. A., 2009, "Role of Islamic Mortgages in UK", International Journal of Monetary Economics and Finance, Vol. 2, Nos. 3-4, pp. 366-383.

McCarthy C., 2006, "Regulation and Islamic finance", Speech delivered at the Muslim Council of Britain Islamic Finance and Trade Conference, 13 June 2006. Available at: www.fsa.gov.uk.

Minsky H. P., 1993, "Finance and Stability: the Limits of Capitalism", The Levy Economics Institute of Bard College, May 1993, Working Paper No. 93, available at: www.levyinstitute.org.

Tayyebi A., 2008, "Islamic Finance: An Ethical Alternative to Conventional Finance?" discussion paper, the Association of Chartered Certified Accountants, August 2008.

The Muslim Council of Britain, 2009, "London and Islamic Finance: Briefing Paper for the Mayor of London", February 2009, the MCB.

UK Trade and Investments, 2010, "Supportive legislation boosts UK's world-leading Islamic finance industry", 03/05/2010, www.ukinvest.gov.uk.

Walmesley, G., 2011, "Another year of growth and development for the London Stock Exchange markets for Islamic finance", London Stock Exchange Islamic Finance Review 2010/11, p. 2. Available at: www.londonstockexchange.com.

Warde I., 2010, "*Islamic Finance and the Global Meltdown*", available at: http://www.islamica-me.com/article.asp?cntnt=633.

Wilson R., 1999, "Challenges and Opportunities for Islamic Banking and Finance in the West: The United Kingdom Experience", Thunderbird International Business Review, Vol. 41(4/5), 421-444, (July – October 1999).

—. 2003, "Regulatory challenges posed Islamic capital market products and services", IOSCO Task force on Islamic capital market.

—. 2007a, "Islamic banking – opportunity or threat?" Common Ground News Service (CGNews), 23 January 2007, www.commongroundnews.org.

—. 2007b, "Islamic Finance in Europe", Robert Schuman Centre for Advanced Studies, European University Institute, RSCAS PP 2007/02, December 2007, Florence, Italy.

Websites

www.hm-treasury.gov.uk
www.fsa.gov.uk
www.islamicfinancecounciluk.com
www.mcb.org.uk
www.levyinstitute.org

A Comparison of Leverage and Profitability between Islamic and Conventional Banks

KAOUTHER TOUMI[1], JEAN LAURENT VIVIANI[2] AND LOTFI BELKACEM[3]

Introduction

The pioneer modern theory of capital structure was established by Modigliani and Miller (1958). The M-M proposition has shown that; provided the existence of competitive capital markets and the absence of bankruptcy costs, corporate income taxation or other market imperfections; the value of a firm is independent of its financial structure. Since, various studies have been conducted to explore the optimal capital structure and suggest restoring one or more of these excluded conditions. Under these conditions, the value of a bank is not independent of the way it is financed. Three conflicting theories of capital structure have been developed, which are the static trade off theory (Bradley et al, 1984), pecking order theory (Myers and Majluf, 1984), and agency cost theory (Jensen and Meckling, 1976). Fewer studies focus on the comparison of capital structure at Islamic and conventional banks. Conventional banks use debts and equity to finance their investments. These institutions typically engage in leverage by borrowing to acquire more assets with the aim of increasing their profitability. However, the composition of liabilities present in an Islamic bank balance sheet is different from the conventional scheme and varies depending on the Islamic bank's activity and the market orientation. The aim of our research is to determine whether Islamic and conventional banks are distinguishable from one another on the basis of financial

[1] Montpellier Research in Management (MRM-CR2M), Montpellier 1 university (France) and Unit Research in Quantitative Finance, IHEC, University of Sousse (Tunisia).
[2] IGR, University of Rennes 1, France.
[3] Unit Research in Quantitative Finance, IHEC, University of Sousse, Tunisia.

characteristics; in particular, we consider leverage and profitability ratios. All over the world, many countries currently experience a dual banking system where Islamic banks operate side by side with conventional banks. The first country which enjoyed a dual banking system is the United Arab Emirates where the Dubai Islamic Bank was established in 1973. The creation of the Dubai Islamic Bank was followed by the establishment of a large number of banks operating in various parts of the world on the same Islamic principles. In the last two decades, the number of Islamic banks significantly increased and their geographical spread has grown exponentially to cover all continents, especially in GCC countries and South Asia. According to the Global Islamic Finance Report (2010), there are now 614 registered Islamic financial institutions operating in 47 countries worldwide. Specialists often refer to Islamic finance as simply being interest free. Unlike conventional banks, Islamic banks are not allowed to offer a fixed and predetermined interest rate on deposits and are not allowed to charge interest on loans. In fact, the perception of any pre-determined fixed rate of return completely disconnected from the actual performance of the underlying asset is not permitted. The relationship between investors and financial intermediaries is based on Profit and Loss sharing principle (PLS) since the terms of financial transactions need to reflect a symmetrical risk-return distribution between counterparties. Islamic banks are expected to depend primarily upon shareholders equity and PSIA deposits. The investment deposits PSIA are profit-sharing financial instruments that are neither a financial liability nor an equity instrument in the conventional senses of these terms. PSIA depositors supply funds to an entrepreneurial party (Islamic bank) for trading and investment purposes while the Islamic bank contributes its expertise. Profits from operations funded by PSIA funds are divided between the bank and PSIA depositors according to ratios agreed in advance in the contract. Moreover, PSIA-depositors have no voting rights since they do not own any portion of the bank's equity capital. As owners of the bank, shareholders receive a proportion of the profit as a reward for the work which their agent (the management of the bank) performs in managing PSIA funds. In case the portfolio investment results in a loss from normal business causes or natural causes, PSIA holders bear all the loss pertaining to their investments to the extent of their deposits. In that case, shareholders receive no reward for work performed by the management of the bank in managing these funds. If the loss is due to misconduct or negligence of the bank, it turns into a liability of the bank.

Since the depositors are not entitled to receive a fixed interest rate but are going to share the profit with Islamic bank according to a mutually agreed ratio, depositors' funds should be considered theoretically as equity. Depositors in a conventional bank create immediate claims on the bank, whereas PSIA-depositors in Islamic banks are like partners. The Financial Accounting Standard N°6, published by AAOIFI[4] in Accounting and Auditing Standards for Islamic Financial Institutions, stated clearly that equity of unrestricted profit sharing investment account (UPSIA) holders shall be presented as an independent category in the balance sheet of the Islamic bank between liabilities and shareholders' equity. Few studies investigate this major difference and compare leverage and capital structure of the two types of banks. It is important to study the extent to which the Islamic banking sector is dependent on creditors' funding, especially as the principles governing the deposits in the liabilities side structure of Islamic banks are different. Our sample is made up of Islamic and conventional banks, resulting in a panel of 545 observations with 250 of these observations being for Islamic banks, from 18 countries over the period 2004-2008. We run t-test of equality of means, a binary logistic regression, and a discriminant analysis using leverage and profitability ratios and their determinants. Our choice is explained by the fact that the banking activity is traditionally based on high leverage and it is interesting to investigate if this similarly characterizes the Islamic banking business. Our study tests the hypothesis that differences in leverage and profitability exist between Islamic and conventional banks. The paper is organized as follows: Section 1 provides a brief review literature. Section 2 presents the methodology. Section 3 describes the data and defines the variables. Section 4 presents results. Finally, section 5 concludes our paper.

1. Literature review

In view of the rapid growth of Islamic banking, recent research has examined and compared different aspects, such as performance, efficiency, liquidity, and risk, of this new form of bank and conventional banks using financial ratios (Metwally 1997; Samad and Hassan 2000; Iqbal 2001; Hassoune 2002; Rosly and Bakar 2003; Samad 2004; Ahmad and Hassan 2007; Kader and Asarpota 2007; Olson and Zoubi 2008; Srairi 2008). The literature reviewed in table 1 draws on the results of these comparison studies across a variety of countries. The few previous studies reveal that Islamic banks hold more capital than conventional banks. In

[4] Accounting and Auditing Organization of Islamic Financial Institutions.

fact, Olson and Zoubi (2008) show that liabilities to shareholder's capital ratio are significantly smaller at Islamic banks in GCC countries. Kader and Asarpota (2007) confirm that average means of shareholder's equity to liabilities ratio is higher in Islamic banks in UAE.

Their study reveals also that the equity multiplier and the total debt to assets ratio are significantly smaller at these banks. Metwally (1997) suggests that the lower the total deposits to asset ratio, the more likely the bank is an Islamic one. He suggests also that the higher the capital to asset ratio, the higher the probability that the bank is an Islamic one. Metwally (1997) shows also that total capital to asset ratio is a good discriminator between Islamic and conventional banks. Iqbal (2001) argues that capital to asset ratio is higher for Islamic banks. Samad and Hassan (2000) reveal that Islamic banks have lower debt to asset ratio compared to conventional banks in Malaysia. The majority of empirical studies report also that Islamic banks achieve higher records of profitability compared to conventional banks. Olson and Zoubi (2008) confirm that Islamic banks in GCC countries are more profitable and reward shareholders with higher returns. Rosly and Bakar (2003), Hassoune (2002), Iqbal (2001), and Samad & Hassan (2000) report similarly that Islamic banks are doing fairly well compared to a benchmark sample of conventional banks. However, the work by Metwally (1997) finds that both Islamic banks and conventional banks offer their depositors similar returns. Ahmed and Hassan (2007) show also that both types of banks have almost the same ROE and ROA in Bangladesh. Our study tests whether there are differences between Islamic and conventional banks, with particular focus on their financial characteristics such as leverage and profitability ratios. The first hypothesis to be tested is: ***there are differences between Islamic and conventional banks with particular focus on their financial leverage characteristics and their profitability (H1).***

Table 1 : comparative studies review of Islamic banks versus conventional banks

Authors	Data	Variables	Methodology	profitability & leverage
Olson and Zoubi (2008)	2000-2005 28conv. banks 16 Isl. banks GCC region	BANK PROFITABILITY RATIOS **ROA** return on asset; **ROE** return on equity; **PM** profit margin; **ROD** return on deposits; **ROSC** return on shareholders' capital; **NOM** net operating margin. BANK EFFICIENCY RATIOS **IEE** interest income to expenses; **OEA** operating expense to asset; **OIA** operating income to assets; **OER** operating expenses to revenue; **ATO** asset turnover; **NIM** net interest margin; **NNIM** net- non interest margin. ASSET QUALITY INDICATOR **PEA** provision to earning assets; **APL** adequacy of provisions for loans; **WRL** write off ratio; **LR** loan ratio; **LTD** loans to deposits LIQUIDITY RATIOS **CTA** cash to assets; **CTD** cash to deposits RISK RATIOS **DTA** deposits to assets; **EM** equity multiplier; **ETD** equity to deposits; **TLE** total liabilities to equity; **TLSC** total liabilities to shareholder capital; **RETA** retained earnings to total assets	t-test for equality of means logistic regression neural networks model k-means nearest neighbours	Islamic banks are more profitable. ROA and ROE are higher for Islamic banks. NOM is than twice as large for Islamic banks. TLSC is smaller for Islamic banks.
Kader and Asarpota (2007)	2000-2004 5 conv. banks 3 Isl. banks UAE	PROFITABILITY RATIOS **ROA** return on assets; **ROE** return on equity; **PER** profit to total expenses. LIQUIDITY RATIOS **CTA** Cash & portfolio Inv/ deposits; **CTD** Credit to deposits RISK AND SOLVENCY RATIOS **ETD** Shareholder's equity to debt; **CA** debt to assets; **EM** Equity Multiplier EFFICIENCY RATIOS **NOM** Net operating margin; **AU** Asset utilization; **OE** Operating efficiency	t-test for equality of means.	ROE is smaller at Islamic banks. ETD is higher at Islamic banks. CA is smaller at Islamic banks. EM is smaller at Islamic banks.
Samad (2004)	1991-2001 6 Isl. banks 15conv. banks Bahrain	PROFITABILITY RATIOS **ROA** return on assets; **ROE** return on equity; **COSR** cost to income ratio. LIQUIDITY RATIOS **NetLTA** net laons / total assets; **LdSAF** liquid asset to deposit and ST funds; **LDBR** net loans/total deposit. CREDIT RISK RATIOS **EQTA** equity to asset ratio; **EQL** equity /net loan; **IMLGL** non-performing loans/gross loans.	t-test for equality of means.	-

Rosly & Bakar (2003)	1996-1999 Malaysia	**ROA** return on assets; **ROD** return on deposits; **PM** net profit to operating income; **AU** asset utilisation; **NOM** net operating margin; **OER** operating efficiency ratio	t-test for equality of means	ROA and PM are higher for Islamic banks.
Metwally (1997)	1992-1994 15conv. banks 15 Isl. banks	**LIQUIDITY RATIOS** **CD** cash /deposits **LEVERAGE RATIOS** **DA** total deposits/total assets; **EA** equity capital and reserve to asset **CREDIT RISK RATIOS** **RL** funds channelled to direct investments /loan-able funds; **DL** loans used to finance durable/total loans; **PL** personal loans /total loans **PROFITABILITY RATIOS** **YA** gross income/total assets; **PD** average return/deposits **EFFICIENCY RATIOS** **XA** operating expenses/ total assets	Logit model Probit model Discriminant analysis	**Logit and Probit model** The higher the EA, the higher the probability that the bank is an Islamic one. The lower the DA, the more likelihood that the bank is an Islamic one. **Discriminant analysis** DA is the third in importance as predictor while the EA is the fifth one.
Iqbal (2001)	1990- 1998 12conv. Banks. 12 Isl. Banks	**CAPITAL ASSET RATIO, LIQUIDITY RATIO** **CD** cash and accounts with banks to total deposits **DEPLOYMENT RATIO** total investment to total equity and total deposits **COST/INCOME RATIO, PROFITABILITY RATIO** ROA, ROE.	Comparison of the variable's means	Capital to asset ratio is higher for Islamic banks. ROE and ROA are higher for Islamic banks.
Samad and Hassan (2000)	1984-1997 1 Isl. bank 8 conv. banks	**PROFITABILITY RATIOS** **ROA** return on assets; **ROE** return on equity; **PER** profit expense ratio **LIQUIDITY RATIOS** **CDR** cash to deposits; **LDR** loan to deposits; **Current ratio** : current asset CA/current liabilities CL; **CAR** current asset/total assets **RISK AND SOLVENCY RATIOS** **DER** debt/equity capital; **DTAR** debt/total asset; **EM** total asset/share capital; **LDR** loan to deposits **COMMITMENT TO ECONOMY RATIO** **LTA** loan term loan/total loans; **GBD** deposit invested in bonds/deposits; **MML** Mudaraba-Musharaka/loans	t-test for equality of means	PER is significantly lower for Islamic banks. DTAR is significantly lower for Islamic banks.

Empirical studies have been conducted to analyse factors that influence a bank's capital structure and profitability. No empirical research has focused on the determinants of Islamic banks' capital structure. The empirical studies in the literature suggest a large set of variables that may influence the financial structure of conventional banks such as age, size, profitability, growth, risk, tax and earning volatility, etc. Caglayan and Sak (2010) found that profitability has a negative effect on leverage. However, size has a positive effect on leverage. Larger banks tend to have more leverage and the more profitable banks tend to hold significantly more capital and less leverage. Gropp and Heider (2010) reveal a negative effect of profitability and dividends and a positive effect of bank size on leverage of American and European banks. According to the pecking order theory (Myers and Majluf, 1984), firms prefer using internal sources of financing first, then debt, and finally external equity obtained by stock issues. The more profitable the firms are, the more internal financing they will have, which means lower debt levels and higher retained earnings, and therefore we should expect a negative relationship between leverage and profitability. In the trade-off theory, an opposite conclusion is expected. When firms are profitable, they should employ more debt to benefit from the tax shield. In addition, if past profitability is a good proxy for future profitability, profitable firms can borrow more as the probability of paying back the loans is greater. Hence, a positive relationship between leverage and profitability will support the trade-off theory, whereas a negative relationship will support the pecking order theory. The trade-off theory states also a positive relation between size and leverage, since larger firms have been shown to have lower bankruptcy risk and relatively lower bankruptcy cost. In addition, large firms have lower agency costs of debt; relatively smaller monitoring costs, less volatile cash flows, easier access to credit market, and require more debt to fully benefit from the tax shield. Dividend also is also recognized to have a negative effect on leverage. Financial firms which pay dividends have on average a lower level of leverage. The pecking order theory suggests that as dividends provide good signals about the firm's future prospects, the firm will issue more equity as there is less information asymmetry in the equity market. Consequently, the difference in leverage between Islamic and conventional banks may be explained by the difference in size, profitability, and dividend policy. We test the following hypotheses: ***The difference in profitability (H2), size (H3) and dividend policy (H4) between Islamic and conventional banks makes the difference in leverage between the two types of banks.***

In the same way, the determinants of a bank's profitability have also long been a major focus of banking research. Previous empirical studies examine the relationship between the performance of Islamic and conventional banks and a set of internal and external banking characteristics. Srairi (2008) investigates the determinants of Islamic and conventional commercial banks in GCC countries over the period 1999-2006. The study reveals a negative (insignificant) effect of liquid assets held by the Islamic (conventional) banks on profitability. This result is in line with results of Chong and Liu (2009) and Olson and Zoubi (2008) and confirms that Islamic banks hold more cash relative to assets or deposits, thus the liquidity surplus negatively affects the bank profitability. The study shows also that financial risk measured by total liabilities to asset affects positively (insignificantly) the Islamic (conventional) banks return on average assets. This funding reveals the importance of leverage in the practice of Islamic banks and is in line with results of Olson and Zoubi (2008) that equity multiplier (Asset/equity) is larger for Islamic banks. The author finds also that good economic conditions and larger stock market relative to the banking sector have positive effect on profitability. Finally, the study suggests a negative and insignificant effect of size on profitability of Islamic and conventional banks. Sanusi and Ismail (2005) proceed also to a panel data analysis of the determinants of 25 Malaysian Islamic bank returns between 1995 and 2004. The authors argue that high total liabilities to asset will increase bank profits, suggesting that higher leverage leads to higher profitability. Their results reveal also that growth is negatively significant in affecting the bank's profit. The negative relationship implies that a large size of total assets tends to be associated with less profitability in Islamic banks. The study shows also a negative effect of the ratio of non-interest income over total assets on bank profits. Bashir and Hassan (2003) examine also the performance indicators of Islamic banks worldwide during 1994-2001. They find that good economic conditions, leverage and loans to assets ratio are positively related to profitability. Bashir (2003) studies the factors influencing the Islamic banks' profitability in eight countries (Bahrain, Kuwait, Qatar, UAE, Jordan, Egypt, Turkey and Soudan) over 1993-1998. The author shows that profitability in Islamic banks responds positively to the increases in capital, increases in loan ratios and good economic conditions. The results revealed that larger equity to total asset ratio, larger loan to asset ratio and higher GDP lead to higher profit margins. The study indicates also the importance of consumer and short-term funding, non-interest earning assets, and overheads in promoting a bank's profits. Also, foreign ownership seems to have contributed significantly to Islamic banks' profitability. The results suggest also that the tax factors are much more important in the determination of bank performance. The negative and statistically significant effect of taxes indicates that financial repression is distorting the performance of Islamic banks. The study reports also the negative effect of the reserve ratio which reveals the opportunity cost of holding reserves. Sudin (1996) analyses also how bank characteristics and the overall financial environment affect the performance of the Islamic banks across eight Middle Eastern countries between 1993 and 1998. The study confirms that interest rate inflation and size have significant positive impact on the profits of Islamic banks. With regard to the market share, the author confirms a negative impact on profitability although conventional banking theory postulates that the bigger the market, the more the profit of banks. Empirical results of studies focusing on determinants of banks' profitability vary across countries because Islamic and conventional banks have to deal with different macroeconomic environments, legal and regulatory environments, deposits insurance regimes, financial market conditions and different tax policies (Dermirguc-Kunt and Huizinga, 1999). We test the following hypotheses: ***The difference in leverage (H5) and size (H6) between Islamic and conventional banks makes the difference in profitability between the two types of banks.***

2. Models formulation

We used binary logistic regression and the discriminant analysis to investigate whether Islamic and conventional banks can be distinguished from one another on the basis of leverage and profitability. The dependant variable for each method is the type of the bank Y where Y=1 if the bank is Islamic and Y= 0 if the bank is conventional.

The binary logistic regression model selects the n statistically significant variables that help to distinguish between the two categories of banks. The logit probabilities are represented by:

$$\ln[P_1/(1-P_1)] = \alpha + \sum_{j=1}^{n} \beta_j X_j + \varepsilon_i \qquad (1)$$

Where (P_1) is the probability that a given bank belongs to group 1; α is the constant; β_j is the coefficients of the nth predictor; X_j is the predictor variable.

The discriminant function analysis determines which variables are the best predictors to discriminate between two groups. The discriminant function is:

$$L = \alpha + \sum_{j=1}^{n} \beta_j X_j + c \quad (2)$$

Where βj is the regression coefficient for n variables; Xj is the predictor, α is the constant.

3. Data and empirical specifications

High explanatory variables were used. Data on Islamic and conventional banks were drawn from the Thomson-one database for the period 2004-2008 resulting in a panel of 545 observations. The resulting sample only considers full-fledged Islamic banks, and 18 countries are considered in our research. As shown in table 2, we collected 250 observations, or a bank year of data, for Islamic banks and 295 for conventional ones. Our sample contains 109 banks (50 Islamic and 59 conventional). The sample distribution of banks for various parts of the world under study is described in table 2 and graph 1.

Table 2: Sampled banks by region and type
Middle East: Iran, Egypt, Qatar, Turkey, UAE, Bahrain, Kingdom of Saudi Arabia, Kuwait, Jordan. ***South Asia***: Pakistan, India, Thailand, Brunei, Malaysia, Indonesia. ***Europe***: UK. ***North Africa***: Tunisia, Sudan.

	Islamic Banks	Conventional banks	Total number of Banks
Middle East	28	36	64
South Asia	14	14	28
North Africa	6	4	10
Europe	2	5	7
Total number of Banks	50	59	109
Total Obs.	**250**	**295**	**545**

Graph 1: Sample distribution of banks

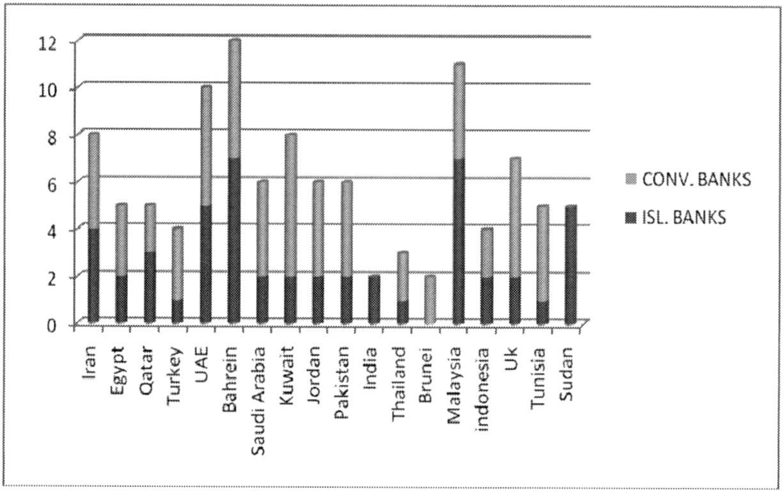

Table 3: Definitions of variables

Financial ratios
1. *ROE: return on Equity = net income/shareholder's equity*
2. *ROA: return on Asset = net income/total assets*
3. *NETMAR: net margin = net profit/revenue*
4. *DIVPAY: Dividend payout = Dividends/Net Income*
5. *DEBEQU: Total Debt to common Equity*
6. *LTDEBEQ: long term Debt to common Equity*
7. *DEBASS: total Debt to total Asset*
8. *SIZE: ln(Asset)*

4. Empirical results and interpretation

To begin the investigation of whether Islamic and conventional banks can be distinguished from one another on the basis of leverage and profitability characteristics and determinants, table 4 shows the descriptive statistics and the t-test for equality of means.

Table 4: Descriptive statistics of group, t-test of equality of means
The data are collected by the researcher from the Thomson one database. The sample contains 50 Islamic and 59 conventional for the Period 2004-2008. ROE is the return on equity defined as the net income to shareholders' equity. ROA is the return on asset defined as the net income to total asset. NETMAR is the net margin defined as the net profit to revenue. DIVPAY is the dividend payout defined as total dividend to net income. DEBEQ is defined as the total debt to total equity. LTDEBEQ is defined as the long term debt to common equity. DEBASS is defined as the total debt to total asset. SIZE is the firm size defined as the ln(assets)

	Means		**Std Deviation**		**t-test for equality of means**	
	Conv.Bk	**Isl. Bk**	**Conv. Bk**	**Isl. Bk**	**t-value**	**p-value**
ROE	15.41	15.45	22.64	34.86	.010	.992
ROA	2.01	2.26	2.54	4.31	.760	.448
NETMAR	23.05	12.83	26.20	69.36	-2.723[b]	.038
DIVPAY	24.64	15.73	47.44	23.14	-2.082[a]	.007
DEBEQ	11.48	7.83	11.11	8.92	-4.129[b]	.020
LTDEBEQ	65.27	28.35	100.29	76.26	-4.712[a]	0.000
DEBASS	88.37	82.77	9.02	16.81	-4.608[a]	0.000
SIZE	9.02	7.95	3.21	2.71	-4.037[a]	0.000

The t-test for equality of means is based on the mean for Islamic banks minus that of conventional banks for each financial ratio. The test is calculated assuming unequal sample variances. [a] denotes significance at the 1% level. [b] denotes significance at the 5% level.

The mean values for DIVPAY, LTDEBEQ, DEBASS and SIZE are significantly different at 1% level, while the mean value of NETMAR and DEBEQ is significantly different at 5% level. For the rest of ratios (ROE, ROA), the difference is not significant. Based on these descriptive statistics, results confirm that Islamic banks are slightly more profitable than conventional banks. This result is in line with results of Samad and Hassan (2000), Samad (2004) and Olson and Zoubi (2008). The results show also ROE is slightly higher for Islamic banks. This result is in line with those reported by Olson and Zoubi (2008) and Iqbla (2001). NETMAR is significantly smaller for Islamic banks. These results are not in line with those reported by Olson & Zoubi (2008) and Rosly and Bakar (2003). The DIVPAY is also significantly larger for Islamic banks. Conventional banks pay a higher percentage of earnings to shareholders in dividends. A low DIVPAY ratio for Islamic banks may indicate a fast growing bank whose shareholders willingly forego cash dividends, because the bank uses the extra money to generate higher returns. A lower DIVPAY for Islamic banks can be also a sign that they practice returns smoothing on PSIA by transferring a proportion of shareholders returns to PSIA depositors. A higher ratio for conventional banks can also point to more mature banks. With regard to DEBEQ, this ratio is significantly smaller for Islamic banks because of the greater reliance upon shareholders capital. Kader and Asporta (2007) suggest the same result. Compared to Islamic banks, assets in conventional banks are mainly financed with debt. However, the equity provides the majority of the financing in Islamic banks. A lower DEBEQ ratio reveals that Islamic banks are less risky compared to conventional ones and indicates the bank's capacity for absorbing financial shocks. This result is not in line with the finding of Olson and Zoubi (2008). The significant lower DEBASS ratio confirms the result above. Kader & Asporta (2007) and Samad and Hassan (2000) find the same result. The LTDEBEQ ratio is significantly smaller. Finally, with regard to SIZE, Islamic banks are significantly smaller.

We run also a binary logistic regression in order to explore profitability and capital structure determinants that help to distinguish between the two categories of bank. The best explanatory model was selected using a stepwise logit contained in the SPSS software. An exhaustive search was performed across all combinations of variables to select the n statistically significant ratios or variables. The dependent variable to be predicted is a categorical variable (Islamic or not) taking the value of one for an Islamic bank and zero for a conventional bank. The results of the logit model led to the following explanatory model:

$$\ln[P_1/(1-P_1)] = 5{,}869 - 0{,}008 \text{ NETMAR} - 0{,}003 \text{ LTDEBEQ} - 0{,}057 \text{ DEBASS} - 0{,}095 \text{ SIZE} + \varepsilon \qquad (3)$$

The model reveals that NETMAR, LTDEBEQ, DEBASS, and SIZE are statistically significant and carry a negative sign. These results suggest that the lower these variables are, the higher the probability that the bank is an Islamic one. The negative sign of size shows that the lower the size of the bank, the more likely that the bank is an Islamic one. Islamic banks tend to have smaller volume of assets compared with conventional banks. The size, as a determinant of leverage and profitability, may explain the difference in these between Islamic and conventional banks. Our results reveal also that the lower the debt to asset ratio, the more the probability that the bank is Islamic. Consistent with previous research, smaller banks tend to have lower leverage. We can deduce that there exists a positive relationship between debt ratio and size. Based on the capital structure theory, the trade-off theory states a positive relationship between size and leverage, since larger firms have been shown to have lower bankruptcy risk and relatively lower bankruptcy cost. Results show also that smaller Islamic banks tend to have a lower net margin ratio. Islamic banking is a new industry which partly explains their small size. Small-sized banks try naturally to grow faster, even at the expense of their profitability. We confirm the hypothesis that states that the difference in profitability between Islamic and conventional banks is explained by the difference in size. Meanwhile, Islamic banks rely heavily on activities based on trade financing contracts commonly referred to as mark-up. The mark-up price is fixed for the duration of the contracts, while the benchmark rate may change. In cases where the prevailing mark-up rate increases beyond the benchmark rate, the Islamic bank is unable to benefit from the increased rates like in conventional banks. Other reasons may explain our result. Islamic banks are known for having limited investment opportunities. Consequently, although Islamic banks are able to expand their market share, they are still unable to convert funds into earning assets. Secondly, these institutions tend to concentrate on short-term financing and this type of investment generates theoretically less income. Results show also that Islamic banks are better capitalized. They are less risky and show a better capacity to absorb financial shocks. The same results are reported by Metwally (1997), Samad & Hassan (1999), Samad (2004) and Olson & Zoubi (2008). In the event of a crisis, the lower the leverage ratio, the lower the probability that a bank will fail to pay back its debt. This result can reveal also one of the financial reporting practices of Islamic banks. The lower DEBEQ ratio for Islamic banks can be explained by the treatment of PSIAs as 'off balance sheet funds' by several Islamic banks. PSIAs may be either restricted or unrestricted. Restricted PSIAs are normally treated by Islamic banks as 'off balance sheet funds under management'. However, Unrestricted PSIAs are normally reported on the balance sheet but it is not usually the case due to a lack of PSIA's accounting standards. In fact, these special accounts do not meet the legal definition of deposits. We can explain the negative coefficient also from a regulatory view. In its pure form in which regulation constitutes the overriding departure from the Modigliani and Miller irrelevance proposition, a regulator could force riskier banks to hold more book equity. In fact, in the majority of countries where Islamic banks are implemented, the supervision authority takes the view that Islamic banks should not allow PSIA depositors to suffer a loss of their capital or a major fall in their returns, so Islamic banks have a constructive obligation to insure PSIA. Thus, instead of being voluntary, the practice becomes obligatory and PSIA is regarded as virtually certain capital (Fiennes 2007). Hence, the greater the volume of PSIA, the more equity the Islamic bank will hold to absorb the eventual losses. This result may be explained also by the greater proportion of reserves as components of the Islamic banks' capital. Since PSIA deposits are assimilated as equity and accordingly their nominal values are not guaranteed, Islamic banks hold additional reserves to cater for risks associated with the PSIA deposits. According to the asymmetric information in Mudaraba contracts, adequate reserves provide depositors with a psychological reassurance to help maintain their confidence against possible loss on the performance of banks (Makiyan 2008). The results reveal also that the lower LTDEBEQ, the more likely the bank is an Islamic one. Generally, it can be explained by the short term maturity of customer's deposits. A lower ratio may reflect also the low level of issuance of long term Islamic bonds "Sukuk" by Islamic banks. The issuance of Sukuk remains relatively insignificant. The remainder of variables is not statistically significant. No difference exists between the two types of banks with respect to ROE, ROA, DIVPAY and DEBEQ. Differences in capital structure between banks cannot be explained by the difference in dividend policy according to the logistic regression model. We find also that return on equity ROE does not discriminate between Islamic banks and conventional banks. The results do not allow us to conclude on the relationship between the return on equity and debt levels in Islamic banks.

As the binary logistic regression, Discriminant function analysis is also used to determine which variables are the best predictors to discriminate between Islamic and conventional banks.

Table 5 provides an index of the importance of each predictor like the standardized regression coefficients did in multiple regression. The larger the standardized coefficient, the greater the contribution of the respective variable is in discriminating between Islamic and conventional banks.

Debt to asset ratio DEBASS was the strongest predictor in discriminating the two types of banks, while SIZE was next in importance as a predictor. These two ratios are followed by LTDEBEQ, DEBEQ, DIVPAY and NETMAR. These results confirm furthermore the first hypothesis that there are structural differences in terms of profitability and leverage between the two types of bank. Results suggest also that Islamic and conventional banks do not seem to differ much in terms of the profitability ratios ROE and ROA.

Table 5: the standardized canonical discriminant function coefficients

	Function
	1
ROE	-.099
ROA	.015
DIVPAY	.254
NETMAR	.120
DEBEQ	.259
LTDEBEQ	.391
DEBASS	.578
SIZE	.408

5. Conclusion

This paper has attempted to find out if there are structural differences between conventional and Islamic banks using two predictive models. T-test of equality of means, binary logistic regression and discriminant analysis provide broad evidence on differences in leverage and profitability across Islamic and conventional banks. Globally, Islamic banks rely more heavily on their equity in financing assets than conventional banks. Larger equity to capital indicates a higher shock-absorbing capacity for the Islamic bank. This difference in capital structure can be explained by the difference in size and dividend policy. Profitability ratios (ROE and ROA) are not significant according to binary regression and are not good discriminators between the two types of bank. Based on these results, the difference in leverage cannot be explained by the difference in profitability if we consider ROE and ROA. Hence, the second hypothesis is not confirmed. Differences between Islamic and conventional banks can be explained on the base of capital structure theory. Moreover, the specific characteristics of Islamic banks contribute to these differences. Regardless, all of these differences must be considered to manage the risk of Islamic banks. Understanding the differences between the two types of bank is the key to building a sound regulatory framework for Islamic banks. We did not include some other determinants in our models (such as tangibility, regulation, market share, liquidity, etc.) that may affect capital structure and profitability. The inclusion of more variables permits us to better understand the differences between Islamic and conventional banks.

References

Ahmad and M. K. Hassan, 2007, "Regulation and Performance of Islamic Banking in Bangladesh," *Thunderbird International Business Review*, 49, 251–277.

Bashir, A.H.M., 2003, "Determinants of Islamic banking profitability: some evidence from the Middle East," *Islamic economic studies*, 11, 31-57.

Bashir and M., Hassan, 2003, "Determinants of Islamic banking profitability," *10th annual conference of Economic Research Forum*, Marrakech, Morocco.

Caglayan and N. Sak, 2010, "The determinants of capital structure: evidence from the Turkish banks," *Journal of Money, Investment and Banking*, 15, 57-65.

Claeys and R. Vander Vennet, 2008, "Determinants of bank interest margins in Central and Eastern Europe: A comparison with the West," *Economic Systems,* 32, 197-216.

Chong and M. H. Liu, 2009, "Islamic banking: Interest-free or interest-based?" *Pacific-Basin Finance Journal*, 17,125-144.

Gropp and F. Heider, 2010, "The determinants of bank capital structure," *Review of Finance* 14, 587-622.

Hassoune, 2002, "Islamic banks profitability in an interest rate cycle," *International journal of Islamic Financial Services,* 4, 1-13.

Iqbal, 2001, "Islamic and conventional banking in the nineties: A comparative study," *Islamic Economic Studies* 8, 1-27.

Kader and A. K. Asarpota, 2007, "Comparative Financial Performance of Islamic Banks vis-à-vis Conventional Banks in the UAE," *Proceeding on Annual Student Research Symposium and the Chancellor's Undergraduate Research Award*, http://sra.uaeu.ac.ae/CURA/Proceedings.

Makiyan, 2008, "Risk Management and Challenges in Islamic Banks," *Journal of Islamic Economics, Banking and Finance,* 4, 46-54.

Metwally, 1997, "Differences between the financial characteristics of interest-free banks and conventional banks," *European Business review*, 97, 92-98.

Myers and N.S. Majluf, 1984, "Corporate Financing and Investment Decisions when Firms have Information that Investors do not have" *Journal of Financial Economics*, 2, 187-221.

Olson and T. A. Zoubi, 2008, "Using accounting ratios to distinguish between Islamic and conventional banks in the GCC region," *The International Journal of Accounting*, 43, 45-65.

Rosly and M. A. A. Bakar, 2003, "Performance of Islamic and mainstream banks in Malaysia," *International Journal of Social Economics*, 30, 1249 - 1265.

Samad, 2004, "Performance of interest free Islamic banks vis à vis interest based conventional banks of Bahrain," *Journal of economics and management*, 12, 1-15

Samad and K. Hassan, 2000, "The performance of Malaysian Islamic Bank During 1984-1997: An Exploratory Study," *Thoughts on Economics*, 10, 7-26.

Sanusi and A. G. Ismail, 2005," A panel data analysis of the determinants of Malaysian Islamic bank returns: 1995-2004. *5th Global Finance Conference*. Trinity College Dublin, Ireland.

Saunders and L. Schumacher, 2000, "The determinants of bank interest rate margins: an international study," *Journal of International Money and Finance*, 19, 813-832.

Srairi, 2008, "A comparison of the profitability of Islamic and conventional banks: the case of GCC countries," *Bankers, Markets and Investors*, 98, 16-24.

Sudin, 1996, "Competition and other external determinants of the profitability of Islamic banks," *Islamic economics studies* 4, 49-64

Sundararajan, 2008, "Issues in Managing Profit Equalisation Reserves and Investment Risk Reserves in Islamic Banks." *Journal of Islamic Economics, Banking and Finance*, 4, 1-11.